For Joe

with

compliments,

[signature]

1. Beecham and Sibelius, 1954

FIRST PHILHARMONIC

CYRIL EHRLICH

First Philharmonic

A HISTORY OF THE ROYAL PHILHARMONIC SOCIETY

CLARENDON PRESS · OXFORD

1995

Oxford University Press, Walton Street, Oxford OX2 6DP
Oxford New York Toronto
Delhi Bombay Calcutta Madras Karachi
Kuala Lumpur Singapore Hong Kong Tokyo
Nairobi Dar es Salaam Cape Town
Melbourne Auckland Madrid
and associated companies in
Berlin Ibadan

Oxford is a trade mark of Oxford University Press

Published in the United States
by Oxford University Press Inc., New York

British Library Cataloguing in Publication Data
Data available

Library of Congress Cataloguing-in-Publication Data
Ehrlich, Cyril.
First philharmonic : a history of the Royal Philharmonic Society /
Cyril Ehrlich.
1. Royal Philharmonic Society—History. 2. Music—England—
London—History and criticism. I. Title.
ML28.L8R6244   1995   780'.6'0421—dc20   94–33585
ISBN 0–19–816232–4

1 3 5 7 9 10 8 6 4 2

Typeset by Graphicraft Typesetters Ltd., Hong Kong

Printed in Great Britain
on acid-free paper by
Biddles Ltd.,
Guildford & King's Lynn

Dedicated to the memory of
Sir Thomas Beecham, Bt., C. H.

Acknowledgements

COMMISSIONED by the Royal Philharmonic Society, this book has been made possible by a bequest from the late John Donaldson Gilmour, whose sole condition was that it should be dedicated to the memory of Sir Thomas Beecham: a pleasing duty not only for the Society but for the author who heard him conduct many times. Grateful acknowledgement is made to staff at the Bodleian Library, Oxford; London Library; and British Library Manuscript Room, where 'loan 48' resides. Arthur Searle brought unrivalled knowledge of its musical resources to his reading of my drafts, and has been a constant source of information, stimulus, and encouragement. I consulted two scholars, Leanne Langley and Simon McVeigh, about early chapters, and the immensely experienced John Denison about later ones, with much profit. As on previous occasions, Andrew Roberts was dragooned into reading the whole manuscript, and responded with characteristic scruple and tact. Richard Fisher, the Philharmonic Society's General Administrator, has been patient and indefatigable in responding to ceaseless requests for information and assistance. Barrie Iliffe read and corrected my typescript and proofs and made numerous corrections. Bruce Phillips has provided his customarily amiable and solid support. None of these friends and helpers are in any way responsible for my opinions and shortcomings, though all have tried to improve things a little.

Pictures are reproduced by kind permission of the owners as follows: Trustees of the British Museum (Fig. 3); the Royal College of Music (Figs. 4 and 9); Mrs J. L. Rosen (Fig. 6). The remaining illustrations and programmes come from the Society's archives.

C. E.

Contents

List of Abbreviations

BBCSO	BBC Symphony Orchestra
CEMA	Council for the Encouragement of Music and the Arts
DNB	*Dictionary of National Biography*
ENSA	Entertainments National Service Association
48	British Library, London, Manuscript Room, Loan 48
Grove	*Grove's Dictionary of Music and Musicians* (lst edn., 1879–89)
ILN	*Illustrated London News*
ISM	Incorporated Society of Musicians
K.6.d.3	British Library, London, Manuscript Room, K.6.d.3
LPO	London Philharmonic Orchestra
LSO	London Symphony Orchestra
MMR	*Monthly Musical Record*
MT	*Musical Times*
MW	*Musical World*
New Grove	*The New Grove Dictionary of Music and Musicians* (1980)
PRMA	*Proceedings of the Royal Musical Association*
PRS	Performing Right Society
QMMR	*Quarterly Musical Magazine and Review*
RAM	Royal Academy of Music
RCM	Royal College of Music
RMU	*Record of the Musical Union*
RPO	Royal Philharmonic Orchestra

Note: All titles listed in the notes were published in London unless otherwise stated.

1

Beginning

Their Mozart and Beethoven Sinfonias blazed like a comet in
our musical atmosphere.

(Spectator, 14 Jan. 1837)

T H E Philharmonic Society was created by professional musicians working in London who wanted a regular platform for serious, predominantly instrumental and orchestral, music. They needed 'patronage' from
people who were then described as 'amateurs'. But they had every intention of running their own show. This apparently simple description
will need reappraisal as our story unwinds, for at least two reasons.
Behind its façade of unity and determination, the Philharmonic was,
probably from its start, a loose association of diversely talented and
motivated people whose purposes, constituency, and control were bound
to change. But there would also be profound alterations in the meaning
of words we have to use to describe such changes. 'Professional musician',
and 'patronage', for example, are elusive and manipulative terms, never
particularly firm, and utterly transformed during the nineteenth century. In 1813, however, the idea of a philharmonic seemed unequivocal
and fresh—even the word was new—and launched in congenial circumstances by artists who were predominantly of acknowledged stature
and appeal.

Previous metropolitan initiatives—the Bach–Abel subscription series
of the 1760s and 1770s, the 'Professional Concert' a decade later, and
most splendidly, J. P. Salomon's ventures which brought Haydn to
London—had identified an audience for the public performance of
serious music. But such pleasures were now only sporadically on offer,
which is not to say that they were extinct. Subscribers had been allowed to disperse, and performers were unorganized. But Salomon had
revived his subscription concerts in 1801 and 1808; and in good years
there could be as many as forty benefits, some of which presented
substantial orchestral works. When the Philharmonic began, therefore,
metropolitan concert life was not the desert which has often been
depicted. It was merely exiguous, commercially unenterprising or myopic,

and rather dull. Most significantly even its brighter events lacked any
semblance of permanence. There was nothing to encourage serious
music-lovers to set aside time for a habitual commitment during the
short busy 'season' in spring and summer, when Parliament was sitting
and 'everyone' was in town. The Professional Concert was almost
moribund. The 'Antient Concert' was a tediously patrician parade of
high formality and low stimulus. Although it employed some good
instrumentalists, its gatherings were administered and publicly super-
vised by lofty non-musicians, unconcerned with live communication,
and attuned to a 'total discouragement of living genius'.[1] To qualify
for Antient readings (they were scarcely performances, and the anti-
quarian 't' was preferred), music had to be at least twenty years old,
and preferably by Handel.

After years of revolution and war, the most prosperous of cities, and
the 'spirit of the age', which Hazlitt would soon celebrate, deserved
a regular concert series, more vigorous, professional, and democratic
than anything on offer; alert to the challenge and excitements of new
music. Beethoven's First Symphony had exploded into Vienna in 1800,
and London in 1803; the *Eroica*—symbol and embodiment of revolution and modernity—detonated respectively in 1805 and, so far as we
know, 1806. The best London musicians, some of whom could claim
personal acquaintance, were alive to his genius and well placed to offer
its burgeoning harvest, in regular allocations, to a market which was
rich in purchasing power and leisure, but unstructured and barely
tapped.

Inauguration

On 24 January 1813 some friends met in the house of Henry Dance.
William, his brother, was an experienced violinist and keyboard-player
who had played at the opera and such events as the 1784 Handel
Commemoration. The others were also immersed in the practical

---

[1] On previous enterprises see two valuable studies by S. McVeigh: 'The Professional
Concert and Rival Series in London, 1783–1793', *Research Chronicle*, 22 (1989), 1–135; and
Concert Life in London from Mozart to Haydn (Cambridge, 1993). I am grateful to Dr McVeigh
for allowing me to read part of the latter before publication. It contains, for example, an
elaborate table of musical events in the 1789–90 season: *Concert Life*, 5. The remark about
the Antient Concert is in *New Grove*, xi. 194. The conventional view of a state of 'orchestral
starvation' before 1813 was expressed by M. B. Foster, *The History of the Philharmonic Society
of London 1813–1912* (1912), 4. It is effectively challenged by N. Temperley in an article
which lists considerable activity, with particular reference to performances of Beethoven:
'Beethoven in London Concert Life, 1800–1850', *Music Review* (1960), 207–14. See also A.
H. King, 'Sterland, the Harmonic Society and Beethoven's Fourth Symphony', in *Musical
Pursuits: Selected Essays* (1987).

business of music. J. B. Cramer, known in England as 'Glorious John', was familiar with most of Europe's eminent musicians, had been highly rated as a pianist by Beethoven, composed more than a hundred piano sonatas, and had recently set up in publishing. His brother Franz or François was a leading violinist at the Antient Concert and would later become Master of the King's Music. Philip Antony Corri, a modestly successful composer and singer, came from another active family of musicians. The 'easy going William Ayrton' who, contemporaries observed, 'always lagged behind in conversation', had the useful distinction of faltering in the best company; a matter of some importance when educated patronage and influence were sought. Among Ayrton's frequent companions were Hazlitt and Madame de Staël, that 'most eminent literary female of her age . . . Dr Johnson in petticoats'.[2] Although his practical musicianship was limited to teaching the piano to young ladies, and putting the odd crotchet on paper, Ayrton was beginning to make his mark with words: as a music critic, or publicist, and as an administrator of opera. In 1817 he would mount the first English performance of *Don Giovanni*. Finally there was Charles Neate, pupil and friend of John Field, who would soon go to Beethoven, returning to act as his agent and give some of the first English performances of the early concertos.

Within a fortnight a second meeting resulted in thirty signatures to a manifesto which proclaimed 'the title of the Philharmonic Society', and declared strict obedience to its laws.[3] That declaration of *title* was highly significant, because it was already well understood that for concerts, as for most marketable goods and services, 'an established name is . . . a throne in possession': or in modern language, that an 'image' can become a valuable property and should therefore be protected.[4] The signatories included some of London's most prominent musicians, with wide-ranging spheres of influence. Muzio Clementi was, of course, immensely experienced and distinguished. Thomas Attwood had been a favoured pupil of Mozart. Vincent Novello, a cultivated musician and publisher, was also fortunate in having a wife whose salon, later described by Charles Lamb, attracted the liveliest writers, artists, and musicians living in or passing through London. The ageing Salomon was another signatory, as was the young, recently knighted, socially

[2] S. Jones, *Hazlitt: A Life* (1989), 24 and 128.

[3] Foundation book with signatures of members: BL Manuscript Room, Loan 48.1 (6 Feb. 1813). The First and Second Prospectus, and the original set of 'laws' are in BL, K.6.d.3: Philharmonic Society, Programmes.

[4] There appears to have been no previous institutional usage; at least none with surviving documentation. The *Oxford English Dictionary* defines philharmonic as 'Loving harmony; fond of or devoted to music. *Philharmonic Society* name of various musical societies, *esp* that formed in London in 1813'.

adroit, George Smart.[5] Deploring recent neglect of 'the Greatest Masters', which was deemed regrettable equally 'to the real Amateur and to the well educated Professor', they asserted a need to 'rekindle' public taste for 'excellence in instrumental music'. Their objectives were stated with routine pomp and considerable attention to detail, at least as regards the kind of music they proposed to play. The Society would promote performance 'in the most perfect manner possible' of a carefully de-fined repertoire:

the best and most approved instrumental music, consisting of Full Pieces, Concertantes for not less than three principal instruments, Sestetts, Quintetts and Trios; excluding Concertos, Solos and Duets; and requiring that vocal music, when introduced, shall have full orchestral accompaniments, and shall be subjected to the same restrictions.

Such pernickety exclusiveness was intended as a promise of high seri-ousness, and a 'radical departure' from customary concert procedures.[6] The widely indulged 'pasticcio'—literally a mess or hotchpotch—whether in the form of pot-pourri concerto for virtuoso and *hoi polloi*, or vocal titbit with minimal instrumental accompaniment—would have no place.

A season of eight concerts followed this curriculum, with lengthy and heterogeneous programmes.[7] The pattern was set at the first concert on Monday 8 March 1813 'under the immediate patronage of HRH George, Prince Regent': he was apparently not there, but the Duke of Cambridge was, seated with a sprinkling of nobility in the royal box. In the first part Cherubini's *Anacréon* Overture was followed by a Mozart string quartet and wind serenade, sandwiching vocal music by Sacchini, and was topped off with a Beethoven symphony. Part two opened with a Haydn symphony and proceeded, via the great 'Placido' chorus from *Idomeneo* and a Boccherini quintet, to Haydn's 'Chaconne, Jomelle and March'. The latter was presumably a misprint for 'Chaconne' by Jommelli and 'March' by Haydn. Mr Salomon was described as the 'leader' and Mr Clementi at the pianoforte (not, as seekers of

---

[5] The complete roster is listed in R. Elkin, *Royal Philharmonic: The Annals of the Royal Philharmonic Society* (n.d. [1946]), 10. On Mary Novello's salon see Lamb's 'A Chapter on Ears', *Essays of Elia* (1823). Salomon's earlier concert activities are extensively discussed in McVeigh's *Concert Life*, and in H. C. Robbins Landon, *Haydn in England 1791–1795* (1976).

[6] First Prospectus: K.6.d.3. The 'radical departure' comment is by L. Plantinga, *Muzio Clementi: His Life and Music* (1976), 231.

[7] Their contents were sometimes listed with insufficient detail to allow precise identifi-cation of individual works. A database of all available programme information, checked against contemporary accounts and reviews, is in progress. In this book discussion of repertoire derives, in part, from preliminary work on that base. See also the extensive, but incomplete, programmes listed in Foster's *History*, and the statistics in App. 1 on the evolution of the repertoire.

6th February 1813

We the undersigned Professors of Music hereby associate ourselves under the Title of The Philharmonic Society and reciprocally engage strictly to obey all its Laws ——

× 21	1	J B Cramer *Subscription not paid in 1817*	23 Sloane St.
× 22	2	P. A. Corri *resigned dec.d 1816*	9 Portman Place
× 23	3	W Dance *bur.*	17 Manchester St.
× 24	4	Clementi *died*	29 Alfred Place Bedf. Sq.
× 25	5	Will.m Ayrton	4 James St. Buck.m Gate
26	6	Wm Shield *bur.*	31 Berners St.
27	7	J G Graeff *withdrawn 1814*	5 Southampton Place Euston Sq.
28	8	Henry R Bishop	111 Long acre
× 29	9	Benj.n Blake *withdrawn*	29 Brompton Row
× 30	10	J P Salomon *died 1815*	70 Newman St.
× 31	11	C Neate	4 Duke St. Portland Pl.
× 32	12	P. H. Potter *died*	2 Foley Place
× 33	13	George E Smart	91 Gt. Portland St.
	14	J. Cramer	39 Marg.t St. Cavend. Sq.
35	15	S. Attwood *died*	11 Lower Eaton St. Pimlico
× 36	16	J B Viotti *died*	10 Charles St. Manch. Sq.
× 37	17	Henry Hill *withdrawn*	3 Old Bond St.
× 38	18	John B Moralt *died*	8 Windm. Row
	19	G E Griffin	26 Northumberland St. Strand
40	20	F. Bartleman *withdrawn 1815*	45 Berners Street
41	21	William Sherrington *withdrawn 1815*	59 Upper Berkeley St.
× 42	22	Louis Berger *Subscr.n not paid 1815*	21 Upper Thornhaugh
× 43	23	Chas Jane Ashley *died*	Abingdon Street
44	24	Rob.t Cooke — *Dead*	1 New Palace Yard
45	25	R Yaniewicz *Subscription not paid 1817*	16 Leicester Sqr.
46	26	S. Webbe Jun.r *died*	13 Howard Street
47	27	Vincent Novello —	240 Oxford Street
48	28	Wm Horsley	24 Queen's Buildings Brompton
49	29	Wm Sherrington *died*	12 Margaret Street
50	30	Andrew Ashe	60 Poland St.

2. Foundation Book: the first thirty signatures, 6 February 1813 (48.1)

authenticity may care to note, the fortepiano). According to the *Morning Chronicle* each presentation was unsurpassed 'in this or any other country', with 'celebrated leaders playing the subordinate parts' as in 'no orchestra ever before exhibited'. The band was unique in 'power and unity . . . taste and judgement of every individual'. The writer, conveniently, was Ayrton, but even if we allow for what contemporaries described as 'puff', there can be no doubt that most of London's best instrumentalists had been assembled for the launch.

And so the first season continued, with successive concerts headed by star partnerships proudly named on each programme. The Cramer brothers appeared twice. Paolo Spagnoletti, probably the strongest orchestral violinist in town, and soon familiar enough to be caricatured by Cruikshank (see Pl. 3), shared honours with Clementi; Salomon with John Cramer, and Viotti again with Clementi. On 14 June the latter was joined by Felicks Yaniewicz, a brilliant Polish violinist who had played in the 1794 Haydn concerts and was soon to leave for the busy musical life of Liverpool. At the final concert, a week later, Glorious John again presided, this time with François Vaccari, from Modena, a pupil of Nardini. Other familiar figures were on the platform, including the Irish flautist Andrew Ashe; George Bridgetower, the Black violinist for whom Beethoven had written the 'Kreutzer' Sonata; Robert Lindley, the immensely popular cellist; Johann Wilhelm Moralt, principal viola and member of a large family of successful string-players; Neate, and the inseparable horn-playing Petrides brothers. The intention was clearly to establish a Philharmonic image of unexampled excellence.

A handful of composers dominated the programmes. Mozart was at the head with fourteen works, including three symphonies, two string quartets, music for winds, and substantial vocal excerpts, particularly from *Idomeneo*. Haydn's name appeared eleven times—reflecting, perhaps in some part, the continuing influence of Salomon—with four symphonies and three quartets. Next came Cherubini, represented by nine excerpts from operas, including three overtures: a prominence which may surprise modern readers but simply endorsed his eminence among contemporaries. Indeed, his Overture *Anacréon*, which opened the first concert and probably closed the fourth (then described as 'FINALE'), would continue to be the most frequently played piece by any composer for the next half-century. A repertoire was emerging, to become central and permanent for symphony orchestras; but it took a little time to assume eventual shape. Beethoven was already present, though not yet pre-eminent in frequency of performance or acknowledged stature. Three of his symphonies were performed; probably Nos. 1, 2, and 4.[8] The very popular Septet, a peculiarly unrepresentative

[8] Not four, as Elkin claims: *Royal Philharmonic*, 17.

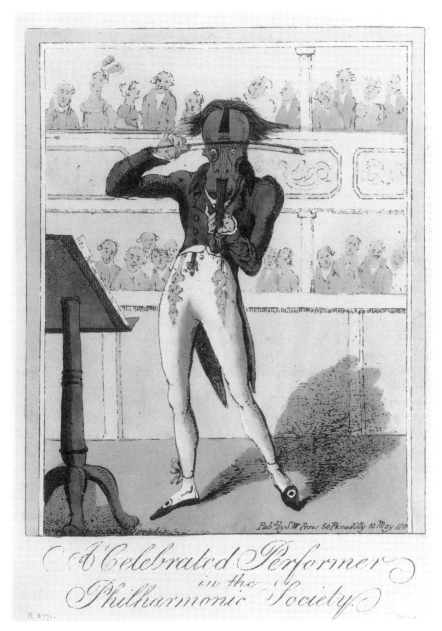

Pub.d by S.W. Fores 50 Piccadilly 10 May 1818

3. George Cruikshank, A Celebrated Performer in the Philharmonic
Society, 1818 (*Paolo Spagnoletti, 1768–1834*)

string quintet, the Piano Quartet, and two string quartets (probably from Op. 18) were not so powerful and demotic as to elbow aside all competition. 'FINALE, "Prometheus" ', which completed a ragbag sixth evening, was the overture, more representative of future exhilaration. The season also contained pieces by a minor Bach (presumably Johann Christian), Boccherini, Cimarosa, Clementi, Gluck ('FINALE, "Iphigenia in Aulide" '), Pleyel, Salieri, Viotti, and a few lesser figures. The sole English representative was W. Crotch, whose 'Lo! Star-led Chiefs' from the remunerative oratorio *Palestine* was placed in the sixth concert between a symphony by the celebrated pianist Woelfl and a Haydn string quartet.

Associates, Members, and Directors

Crotch was one of twenty-five associates eligible for promotion to full membership—the complement was not to exceed fifty—when vacancies occurred. Candidates for both categories were required to be '*bona fide* a Professor of Music', which simply meant professional musician, nominated and elected by elaborate procedures. It appears that a tight-knit organization was envisaged, with ideals of loyalty and decorum appropriate to an association of professionals, and an altruistic desire to serve 'music'. In this spirit, anyone failing to attend a general meeting, without the excuse of illness or an out-of-town engagement, could be fined half a guinea; there was even an attempt to tie down men who often needed to be highly mobile, by proposing that anyone absent from the country for more than twelve months 'without permission from the Society' should cease to be a member.[9] Unseemly behaviour risked condemnation, sometimes with a verbal intensity which belied the course of practical action. Thus, in the first of countless complaints, a member was chided for the 'irregularity of advertising the Society's name' without permission; and Smart was fierce about people whom he considered desirous of making the Society 'a footstool to fame'. In a more conventional scandal, when Corri made off with someone's wife, he was expelled 'for ever' as 'a disgrace to his profession and to Society at large' with exclamations of 'horror at having associated with such a man'. He replied 'wishing them all Health and Prosperity' and departed briefly for the United States, surfacing as Arthur Clifton of Baltimore; then shortly returned to perform again, under his own name, with the Philharmonic.[10]

[9] General Minute Book: 48.3/1 (20 Feb. 1815).
[10] 48.3/1 (14 and 22 Dec. 1813). Smart's rebuke was apropos of a controversial and widely publicized visit to inspect the Logier system of mass-producing pianists: 48.3/1 (1 Dec. 1817). See Elkin, *Royal Philharmonic*, 18–19. The Corri correspondence is also in 48.3/1 (9 and 12 Dec. 1816).

Most of the Society's original 'laws' were what might be expected to govern such an association. But there were curious exceptions, at least one of which seems to defy explanation. A rule which no gathering of lawyers or physicians, for example, would ever have countenanced, made great play with the rejection of 'pecuniary recompense' for 'assisting' at the concerts. This self-denying ordinance was sufficiently heartfelt to be reiterated in a revised set of 'laws': 'No Member or Associate who shall offer to perform and shall be accepted by the Directors, shall receive any pay for such performance.'[11] Another feature of membership which was remarkable for the times was the presence of women. The majority were teachers, but some women musicians were already accustomed to perform alongside men, as singers, of course, but also as pianists, and soon as violinists. Almost from the beginning the Society recognized and, to a limited extent, reinforced, this unusual emancipation. 'Female professors' were allowed to join, and given the same ticket concessions as other members and associates. By 1822 the lists included five in the latter group, out of a total of forty-three.[12]

In practice the alliance was probably looser, more uneasy and fragile, and less utopian, than such rules and admonitions might suggest. After two years Henry Dance could detect an advance 'to that permanence which was the earnest wish, tho' perhaps scarcely the hope of its projectors'. Doubtless the associate list was intended to be, as it soon became, probationary for junior members of the profession. But for a few years it contained the names of several firmly established musicians, which indicates that some participants regarded it as a temporary, rather than qualifying, form of membership. A few musicians, including the Dance brothers, even retained their allegiance to the moribund Professional Concert, and proposed some kind of 'union'; a suggestion which, after long and extremely polite negotiations, was quietly dropped.[13] Reading between the lines of history therefore, we discern a measure of uncertainty during these early years, about future commitments and expectations, musical and pecuniary. Nevertheless, apart from Crotch, whose various claims to elevation included an undemanding chair of music at Oxford, the associates' ranks continued to be entered by practical and eminent musicians. There was Bridgetower; Cipriani ('Little Chip') Potter, a pianist described by Beethoven as a good fellow with a talent for composition; the eccentric and highly talented organist–composer Samuel Wesley; and Nicolas Mori, another leading violinist. Soon they were joined by an even more

---

[11] Law XXIII: K.6.d.3, MS 1813–18.   [12] Subscribers' Lists: 48.8.
[13] 48.13/10 contains Henry Dance's reminiscent letter to the Directors (19 Dec. 1814); and a letter from Hill and the Dance brothers (11 Oct. 1815). More correspondence about negotiations with the Professional Society (Sept. and Oct. 1815) is in 48.3/1.

renowned colleague, the most famous instrumentalist in England, whose
name is still revered by players of his instrument.

Domenico Dragonetti was an unrivalled virtuoso of the double bass:
an endearing eccentric, with one of his large collection of dolls, and
perhaps his dog Carlo, in attendance: wonderfully attractive to audiences, and therefore commanding higher fees than practically every
other master of any instrument. A rock-solid anchor to the groups with
which he played—for the basso continuo was still fundamental to
orchestral co-ordination—he produced 'a wonderful power of sound',
as did his constant companion for fifty-two years, the cellist Robert
Lindley (see Fig. 4); 'Ven die der Lindley', said the Italian in his unique
lingo, 'suo instrument she die'.[14] Such men were the recognized leaders
of a group of musicians without whom there could have been no
Philharmonic Society. Their activities would never cease to be essential
to its survival, at least on the concert platform, even if they were not
always central to its deliberations and self-image. These were the cream
of the London freelance players. Skilled instrumentalists and sight-
readers, they customarily adopted a stance of sturdy independence,
defying society's expectation of demeanour in a calling which, intensely
competitive, ill-paid, and vulnerable to sickness and age, enjoined servility.[15] In contrast to a rapidly increasing number of dilettantes, writers,
and teachers, often without particular musical talent, whose sources of
income allowed, or whose 'profession' required, genteel postures of altruism and high art, these practical working-men were inclined to take
a down-to-earth approach to their job, and were likely to insist upon
respect for their craft, and fair pay for duties performed. Degenerating
sometimes into habitual cussedness, this could be troublesome to the
directors, and was sometimes assumed to belie true musicianship and
devotion. Since the players worked at spinning notes, rather than
words, they rarely left much record of their work, and have therefore
generally been overlooked by historians of music. The Philharmonic
archives sometimes provide opportunities to redress that neglect, beginning with a listing of forgotten names.

The new Society elected seven 'directors'—originally there were
intended to be a cumbersome twelve—to establish a system of autonomous management, with rudimentary arrangements and no resources

[14] On Dragonetti and the London freelances see Cyril Ehrlich, *The Music Profession in
Britain Since The Eighteenth Century: A Social History* (Oxford, 1985), 47–9. The reminiscence
of him and of Lindley is by their colleague John Ella in *RMU* (6 May 1851).

[15] On the vulnerability of working musicians see Ehrlich, *Music Profession*; and D. Rohr,
A Profession of Artisans, PhD thesis (Pennsylvania, 1983), 336–41. Dr Rohr estimates that more
than 25 per cent of early 19th-cent. London musicians who were successful at some time
in their career ultimately became impoverished. Between 50 per cent and 75 per cent finished
no better off than they started.

CORELLI'S SONATA, OP. 9.

4. Dragonetti and Lindley (*M. Hart after Landseer*)

except goodwill. An honorary secretary was expected to attend all
general and directors' meetings, be present at every rehearsal and
concert, and 'circulate all letters'. Such hopes of dedicated service
without pay were in line with the elaboration of other-worldly 'laws'.
Nurtured, perhaps, by previous experience of irregular concert seasons
which required neither settled routines nor an established office, these
attitudes and procedures would soon prove inadequate. The Philharmonic's administrative needs were bound to consume a great deal of
precious time at the height of the short, inflexible London season,
when professional musicians were forced to concentrate their playing
and teaching if they were to make a living. The directors had no
assistance from telephones and typewriters, of course. And, more to the
point, there was no network of agents and impresarios, appraising
repertoire and artists, booking dates, and sharing risks. A few individuals, who performed such tasks in limited fashion at this time, expected
quiet dealings, quick profits, and no long-term obligations. Successful
and active musicians among the Philharmonic's founding fathers—the
most worthy representatives of their art and calling—could not regularly undertake correspondence, and sit on committees. Similarly they
could not long be expected to play without payment, despite public
statements to the contrary, and even if that was their true original
intention. Nor, faced with the need to maintain an orchestra fit to
perform new, and increasingly demanding, music, could the directors
easily exercise sufficient authority over their colleagues and electors to
maintain high standards. The Society's initial stance, proclaimed in its
First Prospectus, was overtly democratic and pious; and not solely in
matters of remuneration. Since performances would be for their 'reciprocal gratification . . . no distinction of rank as to stations in the Orchestra are allowed to exist'. Realistic conditions of payment took some
time to settle down, and will be considered in due course. Procedures
of authority and command were similarly destined for trouble and
confusion, and their evolution must gradually be disentangled: not only
in terms of the Society's constitution and discourse, but because the
modern functions of conductor, and leader or concert-master, had not
yet been fully articulated. For the moment we may note that a second
prospectus, issued within weeks of the first, modified utopia sufficiently
to read that 'the station of every performer shall be absolutely determined by the Leader of the Night'.[16]

Despite these difficulties the first directors, including some famously
active musicians, became assiduous committee men, at least for a time.
Thus on 14 December 1813 Ayrton, Clementi, the Cramers, Dance,
Novello, Potter, and Salomon all turned up to deal with administrative

---

[16] First and Second Prospectus: K.6.d.3.

routines. A week later most of them were again present: to agree that general meetings should be held on St Cecilia's Day; and to admit Mme de Staël to four concerts. They were also willing to exert authority, admonishing a member's 'irregularity' in 'advertising the Society's name without permission', and beginning a task which would never cease to give trouble: the attempt to create and discipline an orchestra. For a start they tried to insist upon punctual attendance at rehearsals and concerts. Soon they would have to enquire whether two players had left the orchestra 'before the last overture' and, if so, 'stop their pay for the same'.[17] Such tasks of administration and communication were made heavier by the extent to which a society wedded to words did not spare them. One example must suffice to demonstrate the time wasted on circumlocution. A correspondent asks for a ticket:

It is now four years since I have heard anything in the shape of good Music (unless french Romances and quadrilles come under that denomination) and learning from several members of my family who are so fortunate as to be subscribers to the Philharmonic that all lovers of Music who are excluded from it are *real Objects of Pity* I throw Myself on your generosity to afford me the opportunity some Night of proving that Assertion by an Admission, but at the same time under a full assurance that the Gratification I shall receive will exceed the Expectation I have formed of It in my own mind. I have the honour to subscribe myself Gentlemen, Chas Knyvett.[18]

It is a tribute to the patience and energy of a few determined musicians that they were capable of maintaining the 'co-operative' without losing control to committee-men or bureaucrats, or relinquishing their essential aims. Even more remarkable is that everything was done on a shoestring. Surviving records suggest no sense of urgency in financial matters, and certainly no pressing desire to maximize receipts by increasing the 'gate'. Rather the contrary. Access to concerts was restricted, as a matter of policy, to a narrowly confined entourage. Requests for tickets were often refused. The prevailing tone of restricted access and eager application is captured in a document which, being private, is free from the manipulative possibilities of public statements in such matters. Samuel Wesley writes to Vincent Novello:

You were so good as to say . . . that you had still the privilege of a nomination for a subscriber to the Philharmonic Society this year [1814]. The lady who was so anxious to obtain one has been successful for herself through the means of Attwood, but is still desirous (if there be a possibility) of getting one for her eldest daughter. I . . . promised to use my interest with you sur le

[17] 48.3/1 (1, 14, and 22 Dec. 1813). 48.2/1 (26 May 1821).
[18] 48.13/18 (25 Mar. 1815). Knyvett was regarded as 'perhaps the best catch singer in England': Parke, quoted *New Grove*, x. 129.

sujet. If she be not too late (for I believe this is the closing day of subscription) pray favour me with the message I am to convey to her. I fear that she
ought to have applied to me sooner . . . she was sadly vexed to find that I
was disappointed.[19]

Quality and Gentry in the Argyll Rooms

In the first season 300 subscribers were admitted to the concerts 'on
the introduction of a Member' and payment of 4 guineas. Numbers
increased during the next few years, reaching a peak of 712 in 1820,
but were then deliberately reduced to 650 'because of the very
crowded state of the Room'.[20] One constraint was the seating capacity
of the Argyll Rooms, where concerts were held until the rooms were
destroyed by fire in 1830. They were a fashionable place of diverse,
sometimes raffish, entertainments, soon to be redesigned as part of
Nash's Regent Street. In the Philharmonic's inaugural year Mrs Siddons
read scenes from *Macbeth* there, and four dandies staged a memorable
ball: 'Who's your fat friend?' said Beau Brummell to a guest arriving
with the Prince Regent, and setting the general tone. What sort of
people, in addition to the musicians and their families, assembled at
such a place for serious music, and why? There have been attempts
to dissect the social class and aspirations of concert audiences, but there
is no reason to suggest that the majority of early subscribers to the Philharmonic were prompted by anything more complicated than a thirst
for music. Certainly social classification then lacked the conceptual
and statistical rigour to which we have become accustomed. In 1770
London's theatre audiences had been categorized as: '1 The Nobs. 2
The Citizens and their Ladies. 3 The Mechanics and Middling Degrees 4 The Refuse.'[21] In the ominous year 1789 a newspaper anat-
omized concert life with similarly brutal simplicity: 'The HANOVER
SQUARE (Professional Concert)—QUALITY. THE TOTTENHAM
STREET (Concert of Ancient Music)—GENTRY. The FREEMASONS'
HALL (Academy of Ancient Music)—PEOPLE. And the ANACREONTIC
(Society)—FOLKS.'[22]

After a quarter-century of political upheaval on the continent, some
traditional hierarchies were beginning to crumble, even in England,
and, as has frequently been observed, a 'rising middle class' demanded

[19] BL Add. MS 11729 (31 Jan. 1814). I thank Philip Olleson for this reference, and for
others to Wesley.
[20] Notice (28 Nov. 1820): K.6.d.3, MS 1813–18. Subscription lists: 48.8.
[21] *The Cheats of London Exposed* (c.1770), quoted in P. J. Corfield (ed.), *Language, History and
Class* (1991), 117. On the social class and aspirations of concert audiences, see W. Weber,
Music and the Middle Class (1975).
[22] *Morning Post* (21 Jan. 1789), quoted in McVeigh, 'Professional Concert', 3.

public entertainment. It would be anachronistic, however, and impute too simple a motivation, to describe the Philharmonic directors as much concerned with 'targeting' an audience. In common with their contemporaries they ignored or took steps to reject Refuse; and were not welcoming to FOLKS or even Mechanics, though ironically a growing number of their own colleagues were socially and financially no better placed than would-be listeners who were excluded. But subscribers were more firmly placed on the social ladder. Most of them can be loosely categorized as drawn from the professional, as distinct from trading, middle class, except for such musically associated businessmen as John Broadwood, and his rival Pierre Erard; the latter currently in London, avoiding Paris. Such distinctions were taken very seriously, of course. There were 'hurt feelings', for example, when one nomination was turned down, surely by mistake: 'Mr Hoffman *is* proprietor of a shop in Bishopsgate Street—but never serves there', being 'as much above such a thing as . . . the Lord Mayor'.[23] In addition there were smaller groups 'of Consequence and Distinction' who had acquired a taste for good music which they could afford to indulge at private concerts. Last and, in more than one sense, least, there was a leavening from the aristocracy and court.

This was a volatile constituency, particularly in its upper reaches for, despite what has been said about the Philharmonic's predominantly musical following, and sprinkling of radical instinct, the directors were certainly aware that attempts at social climbing by association with one's betters were already an accompaniment to public entertainment, even in London. To cater for such aspirations might soon be perceived as a tempting means of building an audience, but it had to be handled with care. Too crass an encouragement, too lax a provision of such cordons sanitaires as private boxes, could rapidly discourage participation by the best people. Upsetting so delicate a balance might even destroy the magnetic field of patronage. The essential manipulative skills were not lacking among the Philharmonic's higher echelons, if only because they were crucial to a musician's success. Sir George Smart's career was exemplary: escape from a family background in trade, and a dextrous climb, with assiduous bookkeeping and a modicum of purely musical skills.[24]

Although their presence was generally approved, even relished by some members, the court and aristocracy brought scant financial benefits. The 'Prince Regent's Immediate Patronage' graced each programme head, establishing a traditional format for his successors. Whatever its

---

[23] 48.13/6 (8 Feb. 1821). On definitions of class categories see W. Weber, 'The Muddle of the Middle Classes', *Nineteenth Century Music* (Nov. 1979), 175–85.

[24] On Smart's social, bookkeeping, and musical skills see Ehrlich, *Music Profession*, 37–42. A more heroic account can be found in P. M. Young's *Beethoven: A Victorian Tribute* (1976).

effects in attracting other subscribers, it extracted nothing directly from
the royal purse since he was not even expected to pay for his ticket.
In addition to His Royal Highness, the Dukes of Cumberland, Sussex,
and Cambridge also figured prominently, the last known to be musical.[25] The first list of 300 subscribers certainly looks imposing at first
glance, with sixty persons of title: earls, viscounts, countesses, lords and
ladies, the odd marquis and chevalier. But this assembly of notables
was modest and circumscribed in contrast to their presence and influence elsewhere in London. At the Italian opera control was exercised
by dilettante aristocrats, wooed by singers and impresarios. At the lofty
Antient Concert, as we have already noted, archbishops and dukes
'presided' over events which were not remotely democratic but were
royalty's principal outlet for public gestures towards music.[26] At the
Philharmonic, nobs were less prominent from the start and many soon
drifted away: indeed as the subscription list grew their proportion
actually fell. It was an abdication of limited significance to the Society
at first, but with serious long-term consequences.

   These social aspects of the demand for public performances of
music, and the snobbish conditions of its enjoyment, were well understood by contemporaries. In 1825 it was trite to remark that 'persons
of condition' insisted upon excluding 'all but those of their own caste
from their society and amusements'. Without boxes to 'bestow distinction' the opera would have collapsed. To sit in its pit, insisted one
observer, 'or in the body of the Argyll Rooms', was 'allied to a sense
of degradation.'[27] Did such sensitivities matter to genuinely musical
people in the age of Beethoven? Looking around and back in 1831,
the *Spectator* exclaimed,

Every year produces some instance of the growing independence of music . . . its
power to live and thrive without the incumberence of high and noble patronage. A list of titled names is sometimes appended to a concert . . . by some
very obscure and fifth rate singer or player, but nowhere else. The Philharmonic Society had the merit . . . to disown any dependence upon fashionable
control or patronage and assert the ability of musical professors to manage
the affairs of a musical society.[28]

If dependence upon persons of condition did not yet rate high at the
Philharmonic, neither was indifference ever unanimous or unequivocal.
At the start of the 1818 season, for example, there were proposals for
a dinner, inviting 'such Noblemen as may confer an honour on the
Society by their rank or talents'.[29] But nor was there much doubt that

---

[25] The Duke of Cambridge visited Moscheles 'for the express purpose of hearing Bach's
music'. I. Moscheles, *Recent Music and Musicians*, 313 (New York, 1873).
[26] Subscribers' Lists 1813–68: 48.8. Cf. Weber, *Music and the Middle Class*, 64.
[27] 'Sketch of the State of Music in London, June 1825', *QMMR* 7 (1825), 210.
[28] *Spectator* (14 Jan. 1831).   [29] 48.3/1 (12 Jan. 1818).

musical eminence and attainment among members had precedence over social rank among subscribers. The latter received courtesy, and were expected to respond in kind. It was a new and significant expectation, at a time when blue-blooded Englishmen were capable of, indeed schooled to, callous disregard for artistic sensibilities. Contemporary band-room gossip told of a 'noble Duke' who, at a private concert, tired of the music and 'closed the book' on an eminent violinist just as he was about to make his entry in a violin concerto. Serious public music-making and listening required alternative codes of behaviour.

Why then were people so eager to subscribe? The question deserves pondering, if only to prepare explanations for later desertions. The simplest answers lie in the drawing power of the music itself and, in the words of an American scholar, the fact that the Philharmonic 'was the only show in town'.[30] Very soon there would be competing shows: by the 1820 season, at its height, there were concerts in the Argyll Rooms almost nightly. And eventually the competition would become so formidable as to threaten the Society's survival. But nothing could yet truly rival the Philharmonic's 'comets', as the epigraph to this chapter suggests, and musical people found them irresistible. An observer put it simply in 1822: 'The audience at the Philharmonic are neither "the great vulgar nor the small"—they are the cognoscenti... if there be any such in the whole realm... they go to hear and to enjoy.'[31] Perhaps a decade later, as Moscheles complained, 'a certain class of subscribers' had become more numerous, preferring an 'antiquated trio' by Corelli 'year after year, played by those old campaigners F. Cramer, Lindley and Dragonetti, radiant with complacent smiles and triumphant airs'.[32] But some were drawn into listening, and even the least engrossed could enjoy the 'vanity of belonging to an audience all of whom were supposed capable of enjoying and appreciating the new wonders of the musical art'. It was a pleasure 'of the highest kind' and, as in all clubs worth joining, it was 'not opened to the public'.[33] Yet the nature of the Philharmonic's exclusiveness defies easy classification. The cost was high: 'honorary' (non-professional) subscribers to the season of eight concerts paid 4 guineas, equivalent then to at least a fortnight's wages for a skilled artisan, or fees for four appearances by a competent instrumentalist. Members and associates paid 3 guineas, and another 2 guineas for individuals in their families. The lower orders, however musical, were also completely excluded by strict dress codes, and by a time (8 p.m.) and place for concerts which made them accessible only to leisured people and to musicians and their families who were accustomed to irregular hours. Again, accessibility depended upon close residence and expensive transport. Programmes requested

[30] Rohr, *A Profession of Artisans*, 122.   [31] *QMMR* 4 (1822), 433.
[32] Moscheles, *Recent Music*, 174.   [33] *Spectator* (14 Jan. 1837).

UNDER THE IMMEDIATE PATRONAGE OF

𝕳𝖎𝖘 𝕸𝖆𝖏𝖊𝖘𝖙𝖞.

PHILHARMONIC SOCIETY.

SECOND CONCERT, MONDAY, 20TH MARCH, 1820.

ACT I.

Sinfonia, No. 5	*Haydn.*
Aria, " Arder Mai," Miss GOODALL	*Mozart.*
Concerto Piano-forte, Mr. CIPRIANI POTTER	*Mozart.*
Recit. ed Aria, MS. " Dolce pietoso Amore," Mrs. SALMON	*Garcia.*
Violino Obligato, Mr. SPAGNOLETTI	
Overture, Egmont	*Beethoven.*

[Several persons having improperly gained admission to the last Concert, the Directors are most reluctantly obliged to trouble the Subscribers to shew their Tickets at the door in future.]

ACT II.

Sinfonia in E flat, MS. (composed for this Society)	*Ries.*
Aria, " Guardami," Signor BIANCHI	*Zingarelli.*
Quartetto, two Violins, Viola, and Violoncello, Messrs. SPOHR, WATTS, COOKE, and LINDLEY	*Spohr.*
Overture, Les deux Journées	*Cherubini.*

Leader, Mr. SPAGNOLETTI—Conductor, Mr. CRAMER.

The Subscribers are most earnestly entreated to observe, that the Tickets are not transferable, and that any violation of this rule will incur a total forfeiture of the subscription.

The Coachmen are to be directed to SET DOWN AND TAKE UP *with the horses' heads towards* Oxford-street.

The Programme of each Concert will be placed in the lower Saloon of the Royal Harmonic Institution for the inspection of the Subscribers, on the morning previous to the performance.

The next Concert will be on Monday the 10th of April.

The door is now open in *Little Argyll-street* for the egress of the Company.

5. Programme, 20 March 1820

that 'coachmen be desired to set down with the horses heads towards Argyll Street (or later Oxford Street) and take up in the same direction'. (See Pl. 5.)

Applications for subscriptions were not necessarily accepted, even from the well-heeled. One detects satisfaction when the directors minute the admission of the Earl and Countess of Buckinghamshire, Viscount and Viscountess Curzon, and the Stuart ladies '(the wife and daughter of the primate of all Ireland)'.[34] But on what grounds, apart from mere excess of numbers, did they reject such applicants as General Bligh six years later?[35] Requests for visitors to be allowed into concerts were individually scrutinized by the directors. It was inevitably Ayrton who succeeded in gaining admission for two Esterházy princes; but even the good offices of Dragonetti and Bridgetower failed to get a ticket for Dr Hooker of Rotterdam.[36] On another occasion it was regretted that several 'ladies of rank . . . have been disappointed', although the Persian ambassador was invited.[37] In February 1822 Lord Bolingbroke was admitted but Lady Pocock was not, and next month a letter was addressed to Colonel Stonger asking how he had gained admission to the last concert.[38] There was great insistence in the printed programmes that 'transfers' could not be permitted, meaning that no subscriber's ticket was allowed to be be passed on to another person. Frequent admonitions about this 'unalterable law', and repeated threats of increasing penalties—from mere refusal of entry to, incredibly, 'immediate forfeiture of subscription'—indicate that the practice continued to be widespread; providing significant evidence that demand was exceeding supply: expansion of the Society's activities would have been possible.[39]

Despite elaborate defences against encroachment, there were occasional expressions of embarrassment and displeasure by subscribers. In April 1820 an 'Amateur' member complained of 'crowding and mixed company not fit for the King'.[40] In 1823 another anonymous subscriber listed social and musical solecisms which displayed a 'want of decorum and due respect to His Majesty as Patron and to the audience at large'. There had been 'repeated failures of the wind instruments', a 'considerably diminished number of leading artists in the string instruments', general unpunctuality, and, on two occasions, 'the unreasonable introduction and erection of pianofortes and the consequent exposure of the workmen, indecorously clad': all 'marks of disrespect'.[41] The mingled complaints about musical standards and mixed company were an illuminating, if premature, warning of troubles to come.

[34] 48.2/1 (19 Jan. 1821).   [35] 48.2/2 (4 Mar. 1827).
[36] 48.2/1 (13 and 18 Apr. 1816).   [37] 48.2/1 (21 Mar. and 30 May 1819).
[38] 48.2/1 (10 Feb. and 17 Mar. 1822).
[39] Notice (28 Nov. 1820): K.6.d.3, MS 1813–18.   [40] 48.13/36 (12 Apr. 1820).
[41] 48.13/36 (29 May 1823).

2

Beethoven and a Balanced Budget

I am now writing a new symphony for the Philharmonic Society, and hope to have it finished within two weeks.

(Beethoven to Archduke Rudolf, 1 July 1823)

I have now been given by the Philharmonic Society the pleasant duty of inviting you to come to England . . . 300 guineas for your visit.

(Neate to Beethoven, 20 Dec. 1824)

One Hundred Pounds . . . to some confidential friend of Beethoven, to be applied to his comforts and necessities during his illness. Carried Unanimously.

(Directors' Minute, 28 Feb. 1827)

THE most celebrated events in the history of the Royal Philharmonic Society are its dealings with Beethoven, particularly in relation to the Ninth Symphony. Every biographer discusses them, and they have been chronicled minutely and debated without cease by musicians and historians concerned that nothing about the composer and that canonic work—'a cultural symbol of enormous importance'—should escape scrutiny.[1] The relationship has also been profusely celebrated by the Society itself, taking just pride in association with genius, and in acts of enlightened benevolence. This is so familiar or accessible a story that nothing fresh can be said except, perhaps, to enquire how such generosity was made possible. For it was not via traditional sources of patronage—crown, church, aristocracy, or other rich benefactor—that the Philharmonic became a prominent and ungrudging benefactor, offering commissions, *ex gratia*, and even posthumous payments. Instead, this was a matter of working musicians paying homage and giving practical support to a revered musician. Extraordinary in itself, the sequence of events also created images, 'traditions', and a 'heritage',

---

[1] N. Cook, *Beethoven's Ninth Symphony* (1992). I am indebted to Prof. Cook for allowing me to see part of this book before publication.

all valuable properties in the late twentieth century, which still have resonance.[2] The idea of homage established a precedent for the Society which, taking various forms such as honorary membership, would eventually become definitive in its gold medal. Practical support in the form of cash was quite another matter, only feasible for a few decades, and then ceasing to have much application for more than a century. The economic circumstances which gave it temporary existence therefore deserve more than passing notice.

The Budget

For more than twenty years the Philharmonic's directors operated within strict financial limits which were, in a sense, self-imposed. Making no attempt to exploit the existing market for concerts, still less extend its potential, they evidently assumed that a restricted subscription list was sufficient to provide ample funds; seeking neither rich patrons, nor larger audiences. The size of audiences was indeed limited by the fact that London, in contrast to several provincial centres, had to wait the best part of the century for an adequate concert hall. But there was no attempt by the Society to remedy that deficiency, in an age of low building costs, and financial policy was austere and self-contained. Its accounting procedures were also rudimentary during these early years. Surviving figures are therefore too haphazard to sustain detailed analysis, but they are sufficient to provide clues, particularly when read against our knowledge of contemporary instrumental resources and performing practice. That area of scholarship has excited particular interest with the current fashion for 'authenticity', and attempts to revive the 'classical' orchestra.

When considering Philharmonic budgets during this period the essential point to bear in mind is that there were no dominating, charismatic, highly paid, conductors, in the modern sense. Nevertheless, within the orchestra, there was a marked division of competence, status, and remuneration between a few 'concertino' front-desk men, and the poorly paid 'ripieno'. The latter term, now only employed for specific purposes, continued to be used loosely for rank-and-file players almost until the end of the nineteenth century. One practical advantage of this hierarchy, as a leading authority explains, was to improve the quality of performances 'despite inadequate rehearsal time by getting the technically difficult spots accurately played and by seeing that the all important *piano forte* contrasts were automatically observed'.[3]

---

[2] See E. Hobsbawm and T. Ranger (eds.), *The Invention of Tradition* (1983), esp. D. Cannadine's chapter on the British monarchy; and R. Hewison, *The Heritage Industry* (1987).

[3] N. Zaslaw, 'Toward the Revival of the Classical Orchestra', *PRMA* 103 (1976–7), 208.

Another implication, which was crucial to the Philharmonic's finances, was the need to maintain a linchpin of concertino players who were good enough to inspire the rest of the band, and preferably also celebrated, to please subscribers. Sometimes players could be engaged who satisfied on both counts, but the process of selection was often controversial; peculiarly so, of course, in an orchestral co-operative. Above all, a good violinist leader was thought to be indispensable, almost regardless of cost. The keyboard-player who, from the wording of programmes, might appear to have shared the honours, was rarely so expensive. These were the parameters for budgeting.

It is reasonably clear that each year's expenditures on concerts amounted to a modest sum, which could easily be met out of income, without any need to pursue additional funds.[4] The opening season of 1813 was a special case, never to be repeated, because most of the immensely distinguished ripieno players, as promised, came free. The Argyll Rooms cost some £200, including payment to a couple of constables and attendants. Sheet music and fees for eight copyists amounted to another £140; and advertisements to less than £4. Exceptions to the voluntary services of leading players included Lindley, whose attendance at eight rehearsals and four concerts cost 30 guineas. The horn-playing Petrides brothers also charged: £22 for two rehearsals and performances. Other wind-players, drums, and four violinists added approximately another £230. Such costs were adequately covered in advance by income from subscriptions, which amounted to a little over £1,400. No loans were necessary and there was a balance of £760. Next season (1814) provides less detail, but it is abundantly clear that the outcome was even more satisfactory. Income from subscriptions increased substantially, while expenditure on the orchestra only rose to £566, plus £8 for refreshments. Advertising was up to £14; music-copying down to less than £68. Even choirs came cheap. As the *Harmonicon* remarked a few years later, but in similar conditions, a chorus of twenty-eight at the opera cost less for an entire season than Pasta or Sontag for a couple of weeks.[5] In 1814 the Philharmonic engaged eighteen voices to sing two performances of extracts from Beethoven's *Mount of Olives* for £27. The year's total outlays were £1,170, leaving plenty in reserve.

Subsequent seasons became more expensive because practically everyone dropped their original declaration of intent and expected remuneration. In 1816 Samuel Wesley, writing once again about admissions, reminded Vincent Novello that very few members of the band had complimentary guest tickets to spare because the great majority were

---

[4] The figures are in Account Book, 1813–66: 48.9/1. Some are also to be found in 48.3/1, e.g. 1 Nov. 1819, and 8 Dec. 1820; on the latter date it was minuted that 'a Book be prepared for the insertion of the Yearly Accounts'.   [5] *Harmonicon* (1828), 208.

now paid in cash.[6] In similar fashion the position and responsibilities of the secretary, also a practising musician, took time to settle down, and had soon to be recompensed with a part-time salary to supplement earnings from music. Henry Dance and Charles Jane Ashley both resigned after occupying the post for one season. The latter, a cellist, belonged to a prodigiously busy family of musicians with extensive provincial connections. Already secretary of the Royal Society of Musicians, he claimed he had been promised payment by the Philharmonic for similar work, and left to undertake various entrepreneurial activities.[7] Next in line was the more obscure, but doggedly loyal, W. Watts, who continued to play violin and viola, appearing at thirty-five Philharmonic concerts up to 1841, while serving as secretary until 1847, beginning with a stipend of £60.

Practically everyone taking part in the concerts received less than they could get elsewhere. Precise comparisons are difficult to pin down, through lack of sufficient comparable information, and because there were no generally agreed standards of payment. The structure of orchestral fees, which still reflected customary obligations but was also subject to market pressures, was obscure, personal, and secretive. During the 1817 season, for example, the clarinettist Willman was offered 2 guineas a night, and 1 guinea for rehearsals; Reinagle (probably Joseph, an experienced string-player living in Oxford) received the same terms, 'and his son half'; Richard Ashley, the viola-playing brother of Charles, was down a notch with 1½ guineas and, again, half-fee for rehearsal.[8] After a few years of forbearance some began to complain, or ask for better fees, with varying degrees of justification, persistence, and success. In 1819 the horn-player Puzzi insisted that 10 guineas (for how many appearances is not clear) had 'always been my public terms; ce que m'est du et justement du'.[9] In 1820 a humbler musician, John Mackintosh, pleaded that, though happy to be re-engaged, he needed more money for such arduous work: 'the bassoon is never exempt except in those pieces expressly for string instruments . . . [I am] generally so much exhausted . . . that I have a difficulty to walk home.' He might have added that he was also capable of playing the umana (a tenor oboe) in the oddly named Beethoven 'Settimetto' (Septet) on 24 May 1819. With the gentlest of hints he added that the City Harmonic paid better: £1. 11s. 6d. for rehearsals and £2. 12s. 6d. for concerts. After waiting two years for a reply, Mackintosh threatened to quit— 'not inclined to sacrifice my life for such a sum'. But years later he applied for membership, having played '15 seasons . . . never late' and,

[6] BL Add. MS 11729 (25 Feb. 1816).
[7] General Minute Book, 1813–54: 48.3/1 (Nov. 1815).
[8] Directors' Minute Book, 1816–22: 48.2/1 15 Dec. 1816 and 12 Jan. 1817.
[9] Original Letters: 48.13/27 (12 Aug. 1819).

elected in the following year, rejoiced in 'the greatest professional honour that could be conferred upon me'.[10] Even such leading singers as
John Braham gave their services free or 'for little more than nothing',
as he later complained.[11] Thus the eight concerts in 1819 included a
string of popular vocalists: Mrs Salmon, Kitty Stephens (in Zerlina's
'Batti, batti' with Lindley's obbligato), and Braham (adapting Beethoven's
soprano *scena* to 'Ah, perfid*a*'!); yet the total bill for orchestra and
vocalists (the latter claiming a mere £211) came to less than £1,600.
Subscription income that year was nearly £2,300.

First-class string-players were always a problem after the honeymoon
year of 1813, when the long-delayed return of peace in 1815 was followed
by an exodus of London's temporary resident musicians, including
several excellent French violinists. This necessitated persistent recruiting
drives and, for a few years, a willingness to pay well, even extrava-
gantly. In 1816 Ayrton, on a visit to Paris, approached two reigning
virtuosi: Pierre Baillot, who had played in Napoleon's private band;
and Charles Philippe Lafont, violinist to the Tsar and Louis XVIII,
who was about to meet Paganini in a famous and by no means humiliating contest. Both Frenchmen had recently appeared for the Philharmonic: Lafont in a sinfonia concertante of his own composition, and
Baillot as leader of two concerts. Asked 'what inducement' was required for something more permanent, neither could be persuaded to
return. The great Habeneck, who was rapidly advancing to dominate
Parisian musical life, failed to respond to offers of 50 guineas, 'terms
of the other leaders', or even 100 guineas. Similarly unsuccessful approaches were made to cellists of repute, despite, or perhaps because
of, Lindley's looming and expensive presence. One of the Duport
brothers was tempted with £200 for a 'series'. Philip Moralt, then 'in
service of the King of Bavaria' and a member of the world's first
touring string quartet, was also approached without success. His brother
Johann, who was already in London, stayed as principal violist until
1842.[12]

Some of the best and most co-operative resident musicians were
occasionally unavailable because of more attractive or peremptory engagements elsewhere, particularly at court. The latter obligation always took
precedence, whatever its effect on concerts and directors' meetings. It
is 'impossible for me to come to town' writes C. Kramer, director of
the royal band, 'His Majesty being in Brighton, having arrived at 4
o'clock this afternoon.'[13] Before the railway age slow, costly, tiring, and
unreliable transport was a major impediment to wider employment of

[10] 48.13/21 (20 Sept. 1820, 21 Nov. 1822, 1 Nov. 1833, and 5 Nov. 1834).
[11] 48.13/5 (28 Feb. 1822).
[12] 48.2/1 (31 Oct. and 24 Nov. 1816, 3, and 31 Jan. 1819).
[13] 48.13/18 (8 Feb. 1821).

the best players. In 1818 Yaniewicz, who had not played for the Society for two years, was anxious to reappear, writing from Edinburgh: 'I hear that great Beethoven is in London, is it true?'[14] But for two concerts he wanted 100 guineas, to cover the expenses of 800 miles' travel. He never played for the Society again, though in 1822 he was recompensed for previous services with plate worth £25.[15] Similarly, John Loder who presided at Bath and, unusually for an Englishman, played the violin well enough to lead, was, like Yaniewicz, prevented by distance from meeting every request, forcing the directors to select a second, or even third, alternative.[16] The desire to ensure strong leadership from a celebrated player, for at least some of the concerts, was practically the only extravagance persistently indulged in by the directors. Spohr's engagement in 1820 was, as we shall see, a special case, inflated by great and rising celebrity, and a singularly versatile offering of services, including compositions. His successor, Christoph Gottfried Kiesewetter, is now forgotten and was no composer, save for what Moscheles described as his 'inevitable Mayseder Variations in E major'.[17] But in his time Kiesewetter's reputation as a powerful violinist allowed him to appraise the market like one of England's contemporary factory masters. He initially accepted 250 guineas, but later made it known that 'as a matter of precaution (he) wished to avoid binding himself to the terms of solo playing till his arrival in town . . . when he would take an early opportunity of consulting the aspects of the approaching campaign and see whether the Talent Market was glutted or not'. Following this market research, he proposed 50 guineas for each appearance as leader, 'as often as the Directors wish', plus a further ten guineas as 'lowest terms of solo playing', excluding the first concert because he would be in Bath. Later attempts at reduction were countered—'I cannot either with justice to myself or to the profession, depart from the terms'—but for fifty guineas he was prepared both to lead '*and* perform one solo or obbligato piece without remuneration'.[18] That season Kiesewetter led only one concert, with Potter at the piano, on 26 April 1824.

Such engagements from abroad were treated by the directors as necessary luxuries, to be rationed carefully. The other concerts were shared by Franz Cramer, Spagnoletti, Mori, and Loder, all resident in England, at much lower fees. Despite silence and discretion about such arrangements, which make historical generalization difficult, they could

---

[14] 48.13/36 (23 Dec. 1818).   [15] 48.3/1 (8 July 1822).

[16] Henry Smart was the other strong English violinist. In April 1819, for example, Loder's refusal led to Smart being asked, with another in reserve: 48.3/1 (14 Apr. 1819).

[17] Moscheles, *Recent Music*, 83.

[18] 48.13/18 (24 Dec. 1820, 5 Feb. 1821, 13 Mar. and 17 Dec. 1822, 25 Jan. and 11 Dec. 1823).

rarely be kept secret for long, and were always liable to provoke antagonism, threatening either the Society's budget or its morale and unity. Thus an angry letter from Spagnoletti urged the directors to 'adhere strictly to the laws and original constitution' and 'endeavour to promote its primary objects'. They were not justified 'in bringing over foreign professors of eminence at a very considerable expense without the concurrence of the majority . . . I am not disposed to renew my engagement unless it be expressly stipulated that no larger sum shall be paid to any other Professor whomsoever than shall be paid to me.'[19] And so the directors continued to seek a precarious balance between the competing ends of economy, internal concord, and external appeal.

In these circumstances it is a remarkable fact that for the first decades of its existence the Philharmonic was consistently run on an annual budget of £2,000. Subscriptions never exceeded the peak of £2,930 in 1822, nor fell much below £2,300, and in most years, therefore, something could be put aside for investment. Preparing for the 1823 season, for example, the directors proceeded cautiously, after their upsetting encounter with Kiesewetter. They initially offered four violinists 50 guineas each to share the leadership of eight concerts, plus an extra 5 guineas 'whenever called upon to play an obbligato piece'.[20] Eventually the total orchestral budget, typical for this period, was kept down to £1,514. Most rank-and-file players were paid about £20 for ten rehearsals and eight concerts. The leaders were strong players, but not international celebrities: Nicolas Mori, son of a London Italian wig-maker, and Paolo Spagnoletti, long resident in London. They received £68 and £63 respectively for sharing most of the season. Loder (with Clementi at the piano) and Henry Smart (with brother George and Cipriani Potter) presided at the remaining three concerts. Dragonetti, who had become an associate in 1815, was the outstanding string-player and, in a sense, may sometimes have led from below. As always he drove a hard bargain, and was paid £57. 15s., probably missing several rehearsals as part of the deal. Times of attendance for prominent players were rarely specified or closely monitored.

These ingeniously low costs were the result of a unique combination of circumstances which would shortly begin to disintegrate as market forces took hold, but would never entirely cease to function for the Society, remaining open to manipulation. For a time soloists asked little or no fee, and even famous divas and virtuosi were happy, or could be prevailed upon, to accept a trinket or nominal payment to make an appearance at the Philharmonic. Their motives were typically a mixture

[19] 48.13/32 (18 Jan. 1822).
[20] Directors' Minute Book, 1822–37: 48.2/2 (1 Dec. 1822).

of goodwill, a desire for artistic recognition and prestige—which reflected and enhanced the Society's image; a cumulative and mutually enriching process—and the hope of attracting further patronage in the form of soirées, benefits, and wealthy pupils. That complex state of affairs was inevitable in a market which was not yet fully commercialized and articulated. Cash payments, particularly for leading artists, were seldom autonomous—discrete and final settlements for work completed—but would customarily be entangled in a web of obligations and expectations, financial and non-pecuniary. The system was hardly ever subjected to public scrutiny, but in 1822 a law case, *Palix* v. *Scudamore*, about a French harpist's expectations and disappointments, which did not directly concern the Philharmonic, gave it an airing. 'Connection, Sir—connection!—that is the word upon which everything in this metropolis depends' was an appropriate summing-up of this 'humiliating trial'.[21] So by 'connection' the Philharmonic directors in 1825 could get Rossini's leading young soprano, Giuditta Pasta, to sing two arias for £26. 5s. And Manuel Garcia, the renowned tenor and original Almaviva in the century's most popular opera, accepted ten guineas. There were similarly fruitful connections with creative genius. In the following year Carl Maria von Weber was in London for *Oberon*, staying in Sir George Smart's house, his last resting-place. He was honoured at a Philharmonic concert, and then 'Mr Weber' was 'engaged to preside' at the next one for 15 guineas.[22] It included the *Freischütz* and *Euryanthe* Overtures, several vocal items, Beethoven's Seventh Symphony and one by Romberg, a Haydn quartet, and a concerto, played and composed by one Schuncke.

The treatment of pianists was generally austere and *de haut en bas* in tone, demonstrating with peculiar force the workings of connection. As the quality acquired their Broadwoods, fashionable lions of the keyboard, and a few lionesses, were greatly in demand: not only for polite entertainment but, far more than was the case with singers or other instrumentalists, to give lessons. As virtuosi jostled and wheedled for a platform which gave access to these rich pickings, the directors could afford to be remote and parsimonious. In February 1823 Ferdinand Ries, pupil and eventually biographer of Beethoven, who had frequently played for the Philharmonic, was informed that 'there being no precedent for the remunerating any Member or Associate for a performance on the pianoforte', his proposal was declined.[23] A month later

[21] *QMMR* 4 (1822), 440–4. For an appraisal of this invaluable source see L. Langley, 'The English Musical Journal in the Early Nineteenth Century', Ph.d. diss., Chapel Hill, NC, 1983, 489–94.
[22] 48.2/2 (11 Mar. 1826). Weber was elected honorary member at a general meeting in April, the first musician to be so honoured. The election—curiously overlooked by historians of the Society—is recorded in 48.3/1 (6 Apr. 1826).   [23] 48.3/1 (23 Feb. 1823).

Moscheles, one of Vienna's most popular pianists, was grudgingly offered 10 guineas and reminded that 'no other resident piano player has hitherto received any remuneration for his performance'. Then yet another famous virtuoso was turned aside. Frederic Kalkbrenner, who had also performed several times for the Society, was highly esteemed in London, 'even eclipsing Cramer' according to Camille Pleyel's expert opinion, and was just beginning a great international career. But 'in consequence of a conversation Mr Smart had with Mrs Kalkbrenner' he and Moscheles were informed that 'no performance on the pianoforte shall receive any remuneration during the present season'.[24] Kalkbrenner played his concerto on 5 May, and never returned to the Philharmonic. Moscheles also declined to 'perform gratuitously', but eventually became a staunch and prominent member. Another pianist's fee is listed in a document dated 29 April 1827: 'Resolved that Mr Liszt be engaged for the 7th Concert provided his terms shall not exceed 10 gns.' He played the then popular Hummel Concerto in B minor.[25]

It will have been noticed that the initially draconian restrictions on what could be played had soon been relaxed: a move which also had implications for the budget. Vocal solos and duets were allowed in 1816. Solo concertos became frequent after 1818, and although serious works were played, with Beethoven's soon becoming pre-eminent, some trite specimens were also given a platform. Schuncke's concoction at Weber's concert, for example, consisted of a first movement lifted from Ries in C minor; a second movement extracted from Beethoven's 'Emperor'; and a final Hungarian rondo by Pixis.[26] This 'material deviation from the original plan', an 'absolute departure from the main design', was recognized at the outset as a measure of economy, arising from the 'difficulty of drawing together a sufficient number of equally great performers to sustain concerted pieces'. It might prove dangerous, the writer concluded, so 'to dilute the grand purpose of supporting instrumental music in its excellence'.[27] In other words both repertoire and performing standards were already thought to be in jeopardy. But a much deeper purse would have been required to maintain the instrumental splendours of 1813. Henceforth complaints about deterioration would become more frequent: on some occasions, no doubt, with simple justice; and on others reflecting more complex issues of taste and the rising expectations of a more experienced and discriminating audience. They generally went unheeded at this stage, without discernible effect on matters of finance.

[24] 48.3/1: Kalkbrenner resolution (29 Mar. 1823); Moscheles letters (23 Mar. and 27 Apr. 1823).
[25] 48.3/1 (29 Apr. 1827). The concerto is identified, not in the programme, but in A. Williams, *Portrait of Liszt*, 30 (Oxford, 1990).   [26] Moscheles, *Recent Music*, 81.
[27] *QMMR* 3 (1818), 344.

One method of minimizing costs without endangering standards, though it may not initially have been conceived so simply, was the extensive use of chamber music, which required few players and little or no paid time for rehearsal. Comparable advantages were enjoyed when singers came from the opera-house to perform familiar music with familiar colleagues, though the effect on performing standards was sometimes questioned. At the 1824 annual general meeting, for example, Attwood proposed, without success, that all singers should have 'previously attended a Rehearsal'.[28] For the rest of the programme there was usually only one rehearsal, which amounted to a brisk read-through: a peculiar London practice which was already subject to criticism by foreign visitors. In allocating this precious time, attention was probably devoted to works which required the full orchestra and were new or difficult. When Weber rehearsed his concert for 3 April 1826, for example, it is unlikely that he gave time to Mr Schuncke's Piano Concerto. Similarly, to take another typical marathon, one might guess that the immense proceedings on 2 June 1823, or rather part of them, were prepared, under the amiably loose direction of Potter, by making as selective an allocation of time as at a modern recording session, but with less attention to getting things right. The concert started with Beethoven's Seventh, one of the longest symphonies yet written, and by no means familiar, as yet, to every player. It proceeded, via a Rossini duet (from *La donna del lago*), a Spohr string quartet, and a Cherubini vocal canon, to Winter's Overture 'Calypso'. 'Act II' began with a Haydn symphony in D described as 'No. 7, "Grand"'. Presumably this was No. 104, which some older players and members of the audience would have known ever since Haydn's visit to London, and was therefore almost certainly not rehearsed. The eminent Mozart singer Violante Camporese, who was about to retire from the London stage, sang 'Parto' from *La clemenza di Tito* with Willman's accustomed clarinet obbligato. Then Dragonetti and the Lindleys gave one of those Corelli party pieces which irritated Moscheles. Then Ronzi de Begnis, a 'model of voluptuous beauty' and 'the best artist of *opera buffa* of her day', arrived hot-foot from Covent Garden with Rossini's greatest hit, 'Di tanti palpiti' (*Tancredi*).[29] The concert ended with the Act I Finale from *Don Giovanni*.

Favourable circumstances, a rapidly established image of quality, and frugal budgeting, allowed the directors not merely to balance their books, but to build up capital, beginning with the purchase of £1,300 of Exchequer Bills in 1814. By 1825 £3,700 was invested at 4 per cent; and by 1828 the stock stood at £4,100. This provided security against a bad season equivalent to well over an average year's subscriptions;

[28] 48.3/1 (30 June 1824).
[29] John Ebers, quoted in H. Rosenthal, *Two Centuries of Opera at Covent Garden* (1958), 61.

and it earned a dividend of £160 to add to current subscription income of some £2,700. With such healthy books, an unusual possession
for any musical society, it was probably inevitable that some of the
members should attempt to take a share of the profits, or establish a
pension scheme from the accumulated funds. An unsuccessful early
attempt, in 1820, was so hotly disputed, particularly between John
Cramer and Ayrton, that the latter was forced to resign his directorship,
under protest.[30] In 1827, after stormy disagreement and fears of dis-
solution, a general meeting passed a new 'law' which granted death
benefits to dependants: the sum on each occasion to represent a share
paid out of the Society's 'stock in the public funds' proportionate to
total membership. Moved by Kramer, the court player, and Horsley,
a founder member and glee composer, it was vehemently opposed by
Neate and Potter, who failed to get the decision reversed at the next
annual general meeting.[31] Resistance continued with a ferocious attack
in Ayrton's journal, the *Harmonicon*, which claimed to defend 'liberal
art' against 'Brokers' Alley'. If the concerts were run merely to maximize profits, ran the argument, they would 'dwindle into the commonplace trash of the day; subscriptions will fall off; and the best establishment
ever raised in this country, for raising public taste, will be converted
into the very means of vitiating it'.[32]

That sense of outrage has been endorsed by Philharmonic historians,
who all give the episode considerable attention and are unequivocal in
their condemnation. George Hogarth, then secretary, registered distaste
in 1862. Myles Birket Foster, writing as a director in the totally different circumstances of 1912, pilloried 'an entirely mistaken idea', and
piously voiced a half-truth which had by then become Holy Writ: 'the
concerts have always been carried on for artistic and not for monetary profit'.[33] In similar vein Robert Elkin, in 1946, found it 'incredible
that the members should have sanctioned such a flagrant misuse of
the Society's invested funds', and concludes with satisfaction that 'three
years later this ill considered law was rescinded'.[34] Such arguments have
obvious appeal, for both the protestors and their aspirations elicit
sympathy more easily than the narrow purposes of lesser men; though
it should also be remembered that John Cramer, a substantial musician, supported the original benefit plan and quarrelled with Ayrton.
But they do history an injustice, following the best-documented case,
ignoring the lost arguments of the inarticulate, and falling victim to a
rhetoric of altruism which later became pervasive. A historian must ask

[30] 48.3/1 (21 Jan., 17 Apr., and 1 July 1820).
[31] 48.3/1 (30 Oct. 1827). 48/13/6 (7 Nov. 1827).
[32] *Harmonicon* (1827). On Ayrton and this journal see Langley, 'English Musical Journal',
282–400.   [33] Foster, *History*, 83.
[34] Elkin, *Royal Philharmonic*, 12–13.

whether the payment of death benefits would inevitably have lowered concert standards, and thereby lost support from subscribers. And was some such scheme truly remote from the intentions of most of the original members? Their contemporary, the Professional Concert, had also tried to balance 'commercialism, patronage and professionalism' with some success, while sharing out profits to its members; and they had been so close to the Philharmonic, some people belonging to both societies, that there were initial prospects of a merger.[35] Was a measure of personal insurance unduly selfish in the riskiest of professions, or even inimical to Art? Careful funding could well have encouraged good programming and the maintenance of excellence; certainly it would have ensured closer attention to the accounts than would soon be practised. Lofty sentiments and disdain for profit were not in themselves any guarantee of high musical standards. Nor was parsimony, as had already been shown, necessarily philistine. But the real or imagined tension between money and music would find ever more frequent expression after 1830.

Commissions, Trials, and Batons

Adequate funds and a tight rein on their dispersal to performers enabled the directors to act as patrons for composers. That neat separation of function and remuneration among musicians did not yet exist, but at the Philharmonic there was an unequivocal commitment to encourage significant new work, and to court the great and famous: aspirations which did not then seem incompatible. Compositions were commissioned and money was set aside for 'trials': rehearsals open to subscribers, at which unfamiliar music was read with a view to concert performance. In January 1815 the directors voted up to £200 a year for playing through new pieces in this fashion, advertising an opportunity which 'at present does not exist'. A committee of seven was given the task of selection. In contrast to its cautious dealings with singers and instrumentalists, the Society also offered liberal commissions to established composers. The venerated Cherubini, who had visited London before as 'Composer to the King's Majesty', in Foster's resonant phrase, came over again in 1815. For £200 he 'directed' several works and provided a new symphony and overture. According to Foster, the 1816 season 'was particularly rich in works specially composed and presented to the Society'.[36] In fact most were soon forgotten. Ries contributed a symphony and the Overture 'Bardic' with six harps, one played by Pierre Erard; August Klengel submitted and played a

---

[35] McVeigh, *Concert Life.*   [36] 48.3/1 (2 Jan. 1815). Foster, *History*, 21.

piano quintet; J. F. Burrowes, organist at St James's Piccadilly and author of a long-lived pianoforte primer, contributed an overture; Potter offered yet another overture, and a septet with piano and flute. And there were commissioned pieces by Cherubini and Beethoven.

Ludwig Spohr, already an established violin virtuoso and rising composer, was eagerly courted, though his compositions were as yet hardly known in England. Initially offered, in 1817, 150 guineas (apportioned in three equal parts for performance, travelling expenses, and an approved work), he eventually turned up in 1820 for the rich fee of 250 guineas plus a benefit, initiating a long and congenial relationship with the Society. Clearly a great deal was expected from this first visit, not only in new compositions, but in general quality and range of musicianship. 'As an instrumental composer his name', says Hogarth, who was close to the spirit of those times, then 'stood lower only than the three great names which must ever be united'. His arrival was 'a great event in the annals of this country'.[37] In that first season Spohr played a violin concerto, led a quartet, and provided several works for 'trial'; at which enthusiastic applause encouraged the directors to programme the Symphony, Op. 11 for performance on 10 April. It is a date which has gained some notoriety, for the concert was recalled, much later in Spohr's memoirs, as marking 'the triumph of the baton'. And so it has been celebrated: as an 'important but bloodless revolution';[38] as the Philharmonic's 'greatest reform of all';[39] and even, in a recent seemingly authoritative survey, as a historical turning-point, the orchestra expressing 'its collective assent to the new mode of conducting'; after which 'London music was never to be the same again'.[40] It was none of these things for, in musical, as in industrial, history, innovation is usually a slow process, with several innovators, much opposition, gradual assimilation, and many a set-back. Conducting with the baton was no more a discrete, once-for-all, immediately triumphant, event than Watt's 'invention' of the steam engine, or Edison's of the phonograph; and the immediate effects of Spohr's actions were similarly muted. Indeed, the incident has even been dismissed as 'the failing memory of an aging man'; which is, perhaps, too curt a dismissal for our longer view.[41]

The actual sequence of events, and its effects upon participants and observers, deserve recapitulation, beginning with nomenclature and contemporary critics. The printed programme for 10 April 1820 introduced a new form of words. Whereas every previous concert listing indicated a 'Leader' and another musician 'At the Pianoforte', this one named

[37] 48.2/1 (14 Oct. 1817). G. Hogarth, *The Philharmonic Society of London; from its Foundation, 1813, to its Fiftieth Year, 1862* (1862), 26.   [38] Foster, *History*, 42.
[39] R. Nettel, *The Orchestra in England* (1946), 119.
[40] A. Ringer, *The Early Romantic Era*, 19–20; compare N. Lebrecht, *The Maestro Myth* (1991), 14.   [41] A. Jacobs, 'Spohr and the Baton', *Music and Letters*, 21/4 (1950), 307 ff.

Mr Spohr 'Leader' and, confusingly, Mr Attwood 'Conductor'! No one commented upon the latter's activities, and it is unlikely that they were of much account, but one critic did remark that Spohr led the orchestra in 'a novel and superior manner'. Another was far more informative. The customary practice, he explained, was for 'Cramer, Salomon, Viotti, Weichsell and others' merely to give the tempo and 'make sure that it is kept to', while playing along as leader. By contrast Spohr 'played only occasionally', otherwise tucking his violin under his arm, beating time with his bow, indicating entries, and 'shushing' for piano. These activities were unnecessary, the writer believed, 'for such an orchestra, where at least the principal of each section is a concert artist, and *certainly it was unwelcome to many*' (my italics). The latter comment, of course, is in stark contrast to Spohr's recollection of 'collective assent'. Moreover, continues this account, 'waving the bow' was an encouragement to feeble imitators without Spohr's gifts.[42] As for the baton, it is true that Spohr had used it, and a full score: but only at the trial and rehearsals, not at the concert. More important than batons and bows, however, is the fact that he insisted upon the need for sole authority, whatever its implement, instead of what he described as its 'preposterous' diffusion in London concerts and opera-houses. In a letter written only a fortnight after the concert, when memory was fresh, he denounced 'the impossibility of fifty or sixty persons ever achieving a good ensemble' when the conductor sat at the piano communing privately with a score, and the leader merely played 'his own violin part . . . allowing the orchestra to get on as best it can'.[43] Spohr's initiatives were therefore simply one stage in a long process of evolution towards authoritative conducting, with necessary skills to be learned, tested, and, not least, resisted, for old practices die hard.

Beethoven

From the viewpoint of posterity the Philharmonic's dealings with the greatest composer of the age dwarf all others; but they began badly. In June 1815 the directors allocated 75 guineas to Neate, who was visiting Vienna, for the purchase of three overtures.[44] They got two old pieces, 'The Ruins of Athens' and 'King Stephen', and one new, 'Namensfeier', all nondescript. Probably it was the latter work which was presented at the concert on 25 March 1816 as 'MS. First performance; composed for this Society'. In fact it had already been heard by the Viennese in December. The other two works may have

---

[42] *Allgemeine musikalische Zeitung*, 22 (1820), 744, cited in C. Brown, *Louis Spohr: A Critical Biography*, 132.
[43] Spohr to E. Speyer (17 Apr. 1820), cited in Brown, *Spohr*, 131–2.
[44] 48.3/1 (21 June 1815).

suffered the indignity of rejection at sight or after a trial; certainly they caused disappointment and were not allowed into a concert for another generation. Despite recriminations on both sides, the Philharmonic then made a bid—too late—for the Seventh Symphony, and Beethoven discussed with Neate, in January 1816, a possible visit to London; suggesting to Ries, in London, that 'a few commissions, as well as a concert from the Philharmonic Society would be welcome'.[45] The directors' response, in June 1817, was cordial, offering an unprecedented 300 guineas, 100 in advance, for Beethoven to come in 1818 with two symphonies specifically written for the visit. After trying to bargain by asking for an extra 100 guineas and 150 in advance, the composer accepted the original offer. He never came, of course, despite widespread rumours which, as we have seen, were picked up by Yaniewicz in Edinburgh. This is one of the great 'if only's' of English musical history, arguably a lost peripeteia, variously explained by ill health, lack of nerve, or a suitable travelling companion, or simply 'fatal indecision'.[46]

Meanwhile Beethoven continued to seek commissions for 'symphonies, an oratorio, or cantatas etc'; and in 1822 asked Ries how much he could expect for a symphony. The directors' reply was £50, which he accepted. He told Ries:

If I were not so poor that I must live by my pen, I would accept nothing from the Philharmonic Society. As matters stand, I must wait until the honorarium for the symphony has been received, but as a token of my love for and confidence in the Society, I have already given the new overture.[47]

That offering, more substantial than its predecessors, was 'The Consecration of the House'. Despite the fact that it had been written to celebrate the opening of Vienna's Josefstadt theatre, the Philharmonic gladly paid £25 and performed the overture in April 1823. It was a generous fee in comparison to the offer for a symphony, but there was increasing concern about the latter commission. At this stage Beethoven wrote the letter to Archduke Rudolf which is quoted at the head of this chapter, with its optimistic forecast of completion. Eventually, in response to urgent enquiry the composer sent a receipt for £50, for a 'symphony which I have composed for the Philharmonic Society in London'.[48] The score of the Ninth Symphony was received by the

[45] Beethoven to Ries (8 May 1816), cited in D. W. MacArdle, 'Beethoven and the Philharmonic Society of London', *Music Review*, 21 (1960), 2.

[46] 48.2/1 (19 Aug. 1817). P. J. Willetts, *Beethoven and England* (1970), 44; this book is an invaluable source for the entire sequence of events.

[47] Beethoven to Ries (5 Feb. 1823), cited in MacArdle, 'Beethoven', 3.

[48] 48.2/2 (25 Jan. 1823) authorizes payment of £25 for the overture. It also includes a quaint note that 'Mr. Clementi', then 71, should 'be written to enquiring if he has any symphonies for trial.' Beethoven's receipt is BL Add. MS 33965, fo. 174. See Willetts, *Beethoven*, 46–7. On the chronology of drafting the Ninth Symphony, with evidence from Beethoven's sketchbooks see Cook, *Beethoven's Ninth Symphony*, ch. 1.

directors in December 1824, bearing a note in Beethoven's hand repeating the statement that it was 'written for the Philharmonic Society in London': seven months after performances in Vienna, and eighteen months before publication in Germany with a dedication to the King of Prussia.

Preparations for the English première began with Cramer leading and Smart conducting a trial on 1 February. *The Times* claimed to be impressed—'In grandeur of conception, and in originality of style, it will be found, we think, to equal the greatest works of this composer'—and praised an orchestra 'of great perfection' for exemplary sight-reading.[49] Smart knew better, asking for a postponement in the hope that Beethoven would come to preside, 'for I have not the vanity to imagine that I can fully enter into the ideas of the Composer'. He was particularly flummoxed by the 'Recitative for the Bass, perhaps it should be played faster.'[50] The chance of a visit still seemed open, bargaining having started with the Philharmonic repeating its offer of 300 guineas. Beethoven replied on 19 March 1825, again undecided about coming to London: 'who knows what accident may perhaps bring me there in the autumn'.[51] Two days later the Society went ahead, with a momentous, but all too typical, concert. 'Act I' consisted of a Haydn symphony; a Mozart vocal trio, string quartet, and 'Per pietà' from *Così*; a Reicha wind quintet and Cherubini overture. 'Act II' staggered on to what the programme described as 'SYMPHONY (MS) with Vocal Finale, "Choral Symphony" Beethoven. MME CARADORI, MISS GOODALL; MESSRS. VAUGHAN, PHILLIPS and CHORUS. (First performance; composed expressly for this Society).' Dragonetti, who played the recitatives for double bass in the last movement as solos (a practice which probably continued so long as he lived), for ten guineas, complained that he would have asked twice as much if he had seen his part before accepting the fee. Critics, who had generally not shared *The Times*'s enthusiasm at the trial, were now confused, hostile, or even valedictory: 'The expence' of choir and rehearsals, said one, 'may perhaps forbid its ever being done again ... Yet it is the work of a great mind.'[52]

Two years later when he was mortally ill and desperately worried about his nephew Karl, Beethoven again sought help from the Philharmonic, 'in a state bordering on despair', asking Neate, Smart, and Moscheles about a possible benefit concert. The response, as recorded at the head of this chapter, was quick and generous. A cheque was sent to Vienna on 2 March through Rothschild's. It was acknowledged

---

[49] *The Times* (3 Feb. 1825).   [50] Willetts, *Beethoven*, 51.
[51] Beethoven to Neate (19 Mar. 1825), cited in MacArdle, 'Beethoven', 5.
[52] See A. Carse, 'The Choral Symphony in London', *Music and Letters*, 22/1 (1951), 47–58.

by Beethoven 'with pathetic relief and delight' on 18 March, offering a new symphony 'or whatever else the Society shall wish.'[53] Eight days later he died. Schindler, his amanuensis, reported the composer's desire 'to add that the Society had comforted his last days, and that even on the brink of the grave he thanked the Society and the whole English nation for the great gift. God bless them.' This was the stuff of legends, and though it later emerged that Beethoven was not destitute, and the hundred pounds lay untouched, the Society compounded its generosity by letting the matter rest.

[53] MacArdle, 'Beethoven', 6–7. M. Cooper, *Beethoven: The Last Decade 1817–1827* (1970), 64–5 and 82.

3

Mendelssohn and Hanover Square

Send Mendelssohn 30 guineas and letter apologizing inadequate
to his talent owing to the reduced state of the Society's funds.

(secretary's minute, 26 June 1842)[1]

Unless a great reduction is made in the expenses of the concerts
it will be impossible to continue them.

(Directors to the manager of Hanover Square Rooms,
10 Aug. 1842)[2]

We never heard or witnessed such unequivocal delight as was
expressed by both band and auditory.

(*ILN* on Joachim's début, 27 May 1844)

THE Argyll Rooms were destroyed by fire on 6 February 1830, three
weeks before the season's opening concert. The Philharmonic library,
which already contained precious scores and documents, was rescued,
but had to be stored in the librarian's private residence. This lack of
a permanent base weakened the Society's image and would become
increasingly burdensome as rents rose in central London. It probably
also encouraged a rather perfunctory attitude towards papers, some of
which apparently found their way profitably into the open market.[3] In
these respects painting was better served than music. The Royal Academy, which had also once been 'roofless, penniless and without equipment' was 'fostered, favoured by a partial king' and quartered in
Somerset House.[4] The Philharmonic had to shift temporarily to the
concert room in the King's Theatre, Haymarket, home of Italian

---

[1] 48.2/3 (26 June. 1842).   [2] 48.2/3 (10 Aug. 1842).
[3] 'perfect preservation of the Library from fire': 48.13/6 (6 Feb. 1830). The secretary was
accused of habitually 'making a profit of his Official Correspondence': 48.13/6 (13 Jan. 1844).
See A. Hyatt King, 'The Library of the Royal Philharmonic Society', in *Musical Pursuits:
Selected Essays*, 14.
[4] The quotations are from S. C. Hutchison, *The Homes of the Royal Academy* (1956) and
J. E. Soden, *A Rap at the R.A.* (1875), both cited in R. Wraight, *Hip! Hip! Hip! R.A.* (1968),
20–1. Cf. P. Langford, *A Polite and Commercial People* (1989), 318–19.

opera. An elegant, expensive place, it cost the Society 240 guineas for eight concerts and Saturday morning rehearsals, with the added burden of 'property boxes' and other constraints upon income.[5] It was also grimly uncomfortable. The *Harmonicon* observed that dim lighting at least had the merit of hiding the dirt, and advised that subscribers could save doctors' bills during the winter months if ladies could be persuaded to wear foot muffs and gentlemen French clogs. Fresh air was available only by opening the sash windows, a frequent source of complaint, as were more intimate deficiencies, which the directors were urged by an anonymous correspondent to remedy 'or ladies will be excluded': it was 'disgusting that the first theatre in the Metropolis shall be the scene of so flagrant a violation to decorum and decency as would disgrace the lowest entertainment in a barn'.[6] Laporte, the theatre manager, agreed to install an extra WC, and erect an 'orchestra' (platform).

After three seasons of discomfort and occasional fine music, negotiations were concluded with 'the Royal and Noble Directors of the Antient Concerts' for use of their venue, the Hanover Square Rooms, where the Philharmonic stayed until 1869. Cleaner and more comfortable, except in hot weather, they were neither cheaper nor more spacious, but these were not yet regarded as serious impediments. Costs could still be assimilated to the £2,000 budget, and those members who wanted to reach out to a larger audience never carried the day. A possible new venue was Exeter Hall, which had recently opened (where the Strand Palace Hotel now stands), with 3,000 seats and 'No Popery' placards at the entrance. In 1837 its managers declared themselves ready to scrutinize the Philharmonic's credentials and found 'nothing of an immoral tendency in the two sinfonias and a Mass of Beethoven' which were put up as a possible programme. Two years later they were even more accommodating; actively seeking engagements 'for Sacred Music to which Music the Directors at present confine themselves'. In 1842 plans were afoot for the Philharmonic to present a suitably modified Beethoven Ninth Symphony, meeting objections to Schiller's 'Ode to Joy' which 'being rather of a secular tendency shall be so altered as to render it strictly religious'.[7] Nothing came of these proposals, and with them departed any practical possibilities of expansion. In 1846 a general meeting discussed two motions. One was innocuous: that it was 'extremely desirable to increase the attractions, extend the influence, and promote the prosperity of the Philharmonic Society'. The other was more to the point: that Hanover

---

[5] Details about hiring charges and constraints are in 48.13/19 (11 and 15 Feb. 1830) and 48.13/23 (15 Sept. 1831).   [6] 48.13/36, fo. 285 (n.d.).
[7] 48.13/14 (18 June 1837, 14 May 1839); 8.2/3 (31 May 1842; 48.6/1 (16 May and 6 June 1842).

Square was 'much too limited a space to develop the resources of the Philharmonic Society in accordance with the growing wants of the musical population'.[8] No discernible action was taken. The audience would remain small and select, the directors primarily concerned with maintaining its privacy: now more difficult than ever. As Moscheles recalled, the move led to 'violent discussions about seating'. The new place had only one large box, reserved for the court, and a proposal to have stalls was 'hotly contested but not Carried'.[9]

Nor could there be any relaxation in concern for appropriate behaviour at the concerts—towards the music, the players, and one's neighbours. The latter, now more contiguous, caused mounting apprehension. Even before the move to Hanover Square it was evident that the 'restricted access and eager application' described in Chapter 1 were becoming strained. One subscriber, for example, wished to bring as guest a 'very distinguished Brahmin prince' who was 'not only passionately fond of music but possesses fine taste'. Since this royal personage had an 'aversion to be gazed at', the writer insisted that a box be provided, on which terms his daughters would keep up their subscriptions.[10] Such screening was now impossible, outside the royal box, so the said daughters, among many superior people, were possibly lost to music. An elaborate letter of remonstrance from Thomas Gladstone (William's brother), further illustrates how difficult it was to know what sort of behaviour should be expected. One Saturday morning in 1832, 'favoured with admission to the Rehearsals by Sir George Smart', he was 'occasionally reading a newspaper' when a player called out 'what's the news?'. Then 'a person calling himself a servant of the Society, came up to me and said that he was desired by the Secretary to ask me "if I should like a cup of coffee" '. Many wounded sentences later, Gladstone protests, 'if I had supposed that that which I see regularly done at the rehearsals of the Antient Music Concerts could have given the smallest offence I should have abstained from it', and adds that at those gatherings 'there was constant conversation carried on in the room, of which no notice was taken'.[11] It is an illuminating comparison for, according to a reliable observer, the Antients had by now become 'a coterie, isolated from the best musical society in London . . . the subscribers and the performers are mutually and heartily sick of one another, the former content with the distinction of being members, the latter solicitous only about their pay'.[12]

---

[8] 48.3/1 (16 Nov. 1846).

[9] Moscheles, *Recent Music*, 192. Stalls were a new means to privacy: by higher pricing and removal from the reflected glow of footlight and stage lighting. See J. A. Nicoll, *A History of English Drama*, iv. *Early 19th Century Drama 1800–1850* (1930).

[10] 48.13/6 (15 Dec. 1831).   [11] 48.13/13 (9 Apr. 1832).

[12] *Atlas* (19 June 1831). The writer was probably Edward Holmes.

The Philharmonic Society continued to seek a closer and more cultivated sense of community among musicians and 'amateurs'. One of the latter, displaying his credentials and serious intent by means of a London University address, claimed to find 'instruction and entertainment in every performance'. But at the suitably didactic *Historical Symphony* by Spohr he had been disturbed by 'marks of disapprobation' from 'a few individuals of insufficient age and experience'. The directors, he urged, with lofty disregard for economics, should display a notice saying that those 'who feel dissatisfied at the selection for the evening, or its performance, are respectfully requested not to disturb the main body of the subscribers ... but they are at liberty to retire ... a due proportion of their subscription for the remaining concerts will be refunded'.[13] Another upsetting incident was the 'violation of decorum' by 'one MacFarren ... hissing Mr Thalberg's encore ... talking loud, and flirting with his female friends'. It required immediate investigation, insisted the complainant, who threatened to 'retire from the Society rather than expose myself and my family' to further outrage.[14] But were the offenders merely boorish, or were their demonstrations a defence of sound taste, even of nationhood, by the young Turks, as Davison later remembered them, 'passing facetious and sarcastic remarks on the music and musicians at the concerts of that, to them, stupid old Philharmonic Society, whose breath froze upon young British talent, while its eyes beamed on the undeserving foreigner'.[15] Not that battle lines were always drawn between nations, for even British composers could be apprehensive. When John Barnett, prolific composer for the theatre, and no mean controversialist, was asked for some pieces, he feared 'an audience so happy to show disapprobation whenever the least opportunity is given them, and often when not'.[16]

Decorum continued to be a valid preoccupation so long as the subscription list could be maintained, which depended in turn upon at least a few good concerts each season. There was frequent endorsement of the Society's concerts throughout the King's Theatre and Hanover Square period, as central events in the London calendar. In 1851 visitors to the Great Exhibition were assured that the ' "Band" is the noblest in the world. It consists of artists of first-rate talent, not one of whom but is capable of conducting an orchestra.'[17] An equally

---

[13] 48.13/15 (10 Apr. 1840).   [14] 48.13/10 (14 June 1842).

[15] H. Davison, *From Mendelssohn to Wagner: The Memoirs of J. W. Davison compiled by his son* (1912), 41. The great pianist Thalberg was barracked in June 1842 by J. W. Davison, later music critic for *The Times*, and his friend G. A. Macfarren, later principal of the Royal Academy of Music, professor at Cambridge, and, as the *New Grove*, xi. 425 says, 'one of the most prolific composers of the 19th century'. See C. Reid, *The Music Monster: A Biography of James William Davison* (1984), 15.   [16] 48.13/2 (2 Apr. 1841).

[17] J. Wheale (ed.), *London and its Vicinity Exhibited in 1851* (1851), 62.

weighty authority, choosing words appropriate to the world's work-shop (factories were so described) recommends concerts 'which, from their excellence, have obtained a world-wide reputation and at which professionals of first-rate eminence condescend to become mere mem-bers of the orchestra, executing the sublime compositions of Mozart, Beethoven and Mendelssohn with a precision and unity unattained elsewhere'.[18] A generation later another London guidebook recalls the Philharmonic's golden age, 'the very heyday of its existence'. The best music was on offer and, in final proof of quality, the audience was 'so very critical that if any composition failed to please them they hissed it'.[19]

Breaks and Continuities

There was plenty of music which pleased during the seasons which be-gan in the King's Theatre, on 1 March 1830, introducing Mendelssohn's *Midsummer Night's Dream* Overture, and ended in Hanover Square, on 6 July 1868, with the first English performance of Bruch's Violin Concerto. Some of it, including works commissioned by the Society, proved to have sufficient staying-power to enter the 'standard' repertoire. The list of performers, several of whom became honorary members, included Mendelssohn, Spohr, Berlioz, Wagner, Sterndale Bennett, Hallé, Joachim, Piatti, Clara Schumann, and Anton Rubinstein. And, all too briefly, there was even positive and informed support from the court. Yet a period so rich in celebrated musical events can equally be described, by one of the Society's historians, as a time when man-agement 'was torpid and complacent, the orchestra was lethargic, un-disciplined and unresponsive, rehearsals were inadequate, and the programme-building was sadly lacking in enterprise and energy'.[20] How are such conflicting viewpoints to be reconciled?

It can be argued that they merely reflect the ups and downs of good and bad seasons, or even individual concerts, over a long period of time—the sort of chequered record which is familiar to many musical organizations. But that gives too easy a gloss to a period of substan-tial change. The Hanover Square years were not merely an alternation of splendid, mediocre, and miserable performances, adventurous and lethargic policies. They were also a period of upheaval, of breaks with the past, or 'discontinuities' in the historian's jargon: from old-guard directors to new; from surplus to deficit finance; from a virtual mo-nopoly of serious concert promotion to competition; from informal

[18] *London; what to see and how to see it* (1853), 131.
[19] J. G. Edwards, *Musical Haunts in London* (1895), 29.
[20] R. Elkin, *The Old Concert Rooms of London* (1955), 100.

groupings of instrumentalists on the platform to the formal discipline of a conducted orchestra (or at least attempts in that direction); from old style *primus inter pares* soloists and a few idiosyncratic stars to a steady flow of formidable artist-musicians and virtuosi. Finally, there was the question—intractable and dimly perceived—of what was to be done about conductors: as individuals, and as a new kind of specialist. The appointment of Costa for the 1846 season was, in one important sense, a new departure, because it gave unprecedented authority to one man and brought much-needed discipline to the orchestra. But it was only a temporary solution to part of the problem and, even while Costa remained, became a device for continuing old policies and avoiding new dilemmas. In so far as 1846 was a turning-point it will provide a convenient date to divide this chapter from the next. But the discontinuities were not so neatly resolved in real life, so themes and narrative must jostle for space, and there will be overlaps in chronology.

The Philharmonic's first break with its past, a change of leadership, seems to have been clear enough. Its most spectacular event was the funeral of Clementi in 1832, which filled Westminster Abbey and was conducted, 'according to family wishes', by the Society, but without 'incurring any expense' to subscribers. It cost the directors one guinea per head—the undertaker provided silk hat-bands, gloves, cloaks, a coach, and a pair of horses—and provided an opportunity to associate with greatness and display unanimity, albeit this was weakened by the secretary's failure to insert advertisements, for which he was duly admonished.[21] Most of the other founders took their leave during the following decade, including the two who had consistently exerted most influence. John Cramer and Sir George Smart lived on for many years, but left the Philharmonic platform respectively in 1840 and 1844, though Smart would still occasionally nag from the sidelines. François Cramer also retired from the concerts in 1843. Ayrton lived on until 1858, continuing to write about music with more distinction than most of his contemporaries, and taking the chair at annual general meetings. Watts remained as secretary until 1847, but William Dance died in 1840, and was succeeded as treasurer by George Frederic Anderson, a mediocre violinist turned factotum who stayed for the next twenty-eight years. His appointment as Master of the Queen's Music, succeeding François Cramer, and Christian Kramer before him, retained the palace link. According to Richard Wagner it was achieved by acquaintance with 'her Majesty's coachman'—or was it the 'Master of the Horse'?[22] In any case, Anderson's musical competence was never widely admired by musicians, and his financial prowess would soon be fully tested.

How did the newly emerging team compare with their predecessors?

[21] 48.3/1 (15 Mar. 1832).
[22] E. Newman, *The Life of Richard Wagner* (1933), ii. 458–9.

There was a rising swell of criticism. In 1839 the *Musical World* pointed to a 'growth of intolerance, exclusiveness and monopoly of patronage' and argued that 'every musical person' could 'suggest a dozen' reforms. While the directors 'are caballing for their own interests and that of their wives, the public are looking out for spirited management and entertaining and cheap concerts'.[23] After some immensely successful appearances in 1844, and close dealings with the directors, including attendance at their meetings, Mendelssohn referred to 'the radical evil which I this time amply experienced, and which must prevent the Society continuing to prosper—the canker in its constitution—musical rotten boroughs etc'. This devastating, but private and obscure, verdict from the Philharmonic's greatest benefactor, is quoted, with uncharacteristic frankness, by Foster, without a word of explanatory comment.[24] Similarly, there were accusations, at the time and later, of bias in the election of members. John Ella, the violinist organizer of a distinguished series of chamber concerts, mounted frequent public attacks upon 'the wicked factious spirit of blackballing candidates—men of genius, talent, education and character—and electing in their places such as have no claim to either of these distinctions'. In private his anger could be more strongly expressed: 'I should scarcely have believed that any seven persons in the profession residing in London could have betrayed such an utter absence of artistic feeling and shown so much disrespect to a brother Artist.'

The other alleged victims of prejudice were Costa and Moscheles. Doubtless anti-Semitism was at work, and a recent essay suggests that it 'inflicted lasting wounds on the society and contributed mightily to its later loss of public support'.[25] Yet surviving documents in the Society's archives allow no firm conclusion, indicating that in so far as there was such bias it happened earlier and was short-lived. Moscheles was indeed nominated unsuccessfully in September 1831, but elected unanimously at a second attempt in January 1832. He then appeared as composer, conductor, and pianist at many concerts for the next thirty years.[26] Costa, to an even greater degree, rose to a dominant position. Ella alone of the three remained estranged. It would be foolish to deny that there was a loss of idealism and fair mindedness as the Philharmonic stumbled through these difficult years; and, more seriously, a lack of distinguished leadership, except when it was available from abroad. But the latter was merely a reflection of the nation's cultural

---

[23] *MW* (7 Feb. 1839). The writer was again probably Edward Holmes. See Langley, 'English Musical Journal', 573–7.   [24] Foster, *History*, 182–3.
[25] Ella rejected: 48.3/1 (8 Dec. 1828). Ella accuses Watts: 48.13/11 (9 Dec. 1844). On blackballing: *RMU* (10 July 1855 and 5 May 1857). On 'lasting wounds': J. Sachs, 'London: the Professionalization of Music', in A. Ringer (ed.), *The Early Romantic Era* (1990), 216.
[26] Moscheles rejected: 48.7/1 (25 June 1828); nominations: 48.7/1 (22 Sept. and 7 Nov. 1831); 'unanimously elected': 48.7/1 (25 Jan. 1831).

impoverishment at a low ebb in its musical history; and the former should not, perhaps, be reduced to simple conspiracy or caballing. In any case the discontinuities still remain to be explored. One guide is the evolving repertoire.

The Repertoire Takes Shape

The principal works performed at Philharmonic concerts are set out in Appendix 1. These tables are intended to illustrate the evolution of the Philharmonic's repertoire in a clear and unequivocal way: as statistical facts which can be measured objectively, in so far as compositions have been identified and performances accurately listed. Comparisons with other concert series may, in due course, when the work is done, suggest a wider historical relevance.[27] A few details in the tables may require adjustment as research progresses, but the general pattern is clear. Throughout the nineteenth century a standard repertoire was assembled, sharply defined, and continuously supplemented by new music in an age when, in contrast to our own times, contemporary work was welcomed and rapidly assimilated.

A programme sequence also took shape—overture, concerto, symphony; interspersed with an aria, perhaps, or solo instrumental piece—made heavy with doubling of courses, like a gargantuan Victorian meal. Many typical menus and favoured dishes were established during this period. Most remarkable is the rapid emergence of Beethoven into a position of permanent dominance. For the Society's first decade performances of his symphonies only took third place, after those of Haydn and Mozart. Then they increased to an average of more than six a year, far greater than those of any other composer. By 1850 the Society had given 206 performances of symphonies by Beethoven; 134 from the far larger corpus by Haydn, and 128 by Mozart. Beethoven's Fifth Symphony had already become the favourite, with thirty-four performances; and the Seventh came next with thirty. A simple count of symphonies has the merit of keeping the picture clear, but it understates Beethoven's pre-eminence and the Society's commitment

---

[27] Mendelssohn's Gewandhaus series, 'a model for the nineteenth century orchestral repertory' is an obvious case for comparison: S. Dohring, 'Dresden and Leipzig: Two Bourgeois Cultures', in Ringer (ed.), *Early Romantic Era*, 153. More substantial and illuminating comparisons can be found in J. H. Mueller, *The American Symphony Orchestra: A Social History of Musical Taste* (1958) and P. Hart, *Orpheus in the New World: The Symphony Orchestra as an American Cultural Institution—Its Past, Present and Future* (New York, 1973), ch.17 'Repertory'. See also W. Öhlmann, *Das Berliner Philharmonische Orchester* (Kassel, 1974), 163–96; and H. Kraus and K. Schreinzer, *Wiener Philharmoniker 1842–1942: Statistik* (Vienna, 1942). I am indebted to Dr T. Corfield for loan of the latter scarce publication.

6. Moscheles and Smart, *c.*1830 (BL loan 102.2)

to his work. Since most of his symphonies are twice the length of their predecessors they took up a greater proportion of programmes, and probably of rehearsal time, than the count suggests, at least in early years until a sufficient number of players became familiar with the notes. This demand upon time and resources was crucial on many occasions for the Ninth Symphony: determining sometimes whether it was played at all, and always how badly; particularly because an adequate chorus became increasingly difficult and expensive to assemble and rehearse in central London. The time element was significant again with the others which were most frequently performed—the *Eroica*, Fourth, *Pastoral*, Seventh, and, easily favourite, the Fifth.

A just assessment of Beethoven's hold on the repertoire must also take account of the range and diversity of his popularity. The tables show that other composers figured large in one or two categories; Cherubini peculiarly so in that most favoured of nineteenth-century genres, the concert overture. His overtures were more frequently played, at first, than any other's; and overtaken solely by Weber, who averaged four or five performances each season after the 1830s. But Cherubini's overtures held their ground for the rest of the century, particularly that for *Anacréon*. One of the most hackneyed works of any species, often inserted 'by desire', because the instrumental parts were available, or because everyone could play it without rehearsal, this piece was rivalled among overtures only by those for *Euryanthe, Freischütz*, and *Oberon*. Their respective total number of performances by 1850 were 36, 23, 23, and 20. Cherubini's *Les Deux Journées* was almost as regular a standby, with 33 performances by 1850; and a few more of his overtures were played, but little else of this once revered composer stayed in the repertoire. Mendelssohn's overtures rapidly climbed into the favoured group, second only to Weber's by the late 1850s. Yet even in this genre Beethoven stays high, exceeded by Weber—though again the greater length of the Leonora Overtures must be taken into account—but never declining as Mozart did. Only the *Zauberflöte* Overture remained as a regular item; that for *Figaro* was given occasionally, those for *Cosi* and *Entführung* never. As the ever-vigilant Berlioz reported, the Overtures Leonora No. 3 and *Fidelio* were 'always encored at Covent Garden, so keen is the English public on Beethoven when it is well played'.[28]

Chamber music tells a similar story, until the 1840s, when it ceased to have a regular place in the Society's programmes. Beethoven's works were always prominent; the string quartets only slightly less frequently performed than those of Haydn and Mozart, with length and perceived stature again reinforcing their real status. At a more overtly popular level the Septet continued to appear: a dozen times by 1851. Some other chamber pieces were also occasionally thought big or 'public' enough to be presented. The 'Kreutzer' Sonata was performed by Liszt and the Norwegian violinist Ole Bull in 1840, and described in the original programme as 'Sonata Concertante'. The 'Waldstein' Sonata was played by Anton Rubinstein in 1876, and Von Bülow included the 'Eroica' Piano Variations, after a performance of the *Eroica Symphony*, as late as 1884.

The tables also list concertos. Here an emerging pattern of considerable significance is obscured for several decades: at first by their enforced absence for a few years, and then by the persistence of concertante and pasticcio traits from the late eighteenth century, as the virtuosi of a declining tradition peddled their idiosyncratic and usually trivial wares. Hence the listing of sixteen compositions by other composers, alongside two by Beethoven and four by Mozart in the seasons 1818–22. There were pieces by Puzzi for horn, Tulou for flute, Polledro for violin, Ries for piano 'on Swedish airs', and Steibelt 'with Bacchanalian Rondo and Chorus'. Even the 1833 season, which included Hummel performing a concerto written for the Society, and Mendelssohn playing Mozart in D minor, also boasted pieces variously

---

[28] A. W. Ganz, *Berlioz in London* (1950), 108.

titled 'concerto', 'concertante', 'concertino', and 'fantasia', by Henry Wolff, de Beriot, Maurer, Kummer, Nicholson, and Herz. But here, as everywhere else, Beethoven's advance was inexorable. In 1824 Potter proposed the 'concerto in C minor: it has never been performed in this country, and is considered in Germany the chef d'œuvre of Beethoven— I think the effect must be stupendous with the orchestra. PS. I shall arrange with Broadwood respecting a pianoforte.'[29] Potter also introduced the G major Concerto in the following year, Eliason the Violin Concerto in 1832, and Lucy Anderson, George's formidable wife, the 'Emperor' Concerto in 1835. Larger, more extrovert performances, which permanently built these works into the repertoire, awaited the arrival of stronger players, but by the late 1830s, as the tables show, Beethoven already led the field in the number of concertos regularly performed; even the Choral Fantasy and, on one occasion, the Triple Concerto, were played. The contrast with Mozart is remarkable by modern criteria. Among his many piano concertos which we now regard as exemplary, only a few were given an occasional public airing, though discriminating musicians played them privately. The repertoire works were then the Concertos in D minor (played not only by Mendelssohn but by Thalberg in 1850) and in C minor; and it is surely not by chance that these are the most Beethovenian of the series. Performances of the Mozart symphonies were similarly confined— essentially to the last three—and his violin concertos were left untouched.

There were two new challengers to Beethoven's supremacy during the 1830s and 1840s. Spohr's prominence was essentially quantitative—no single work became inescapable—and short-lived, though he appeared several times between 1820 and 1843, as violinist and conductor. The symphonies were repeated for a few years, and between the 1843 and 1847 seasons his total of nine concerto performances equalled Beethoven's. But these figures include a variety of individual compositions, none of which survived prolonged exposure. Nor did any enter the 'canon': those works which are not merely played frequently but attain an exemplary status, a standard by which others are judged. Thus for nineteenth-century lovers of music Beethoven was unequivocally canonic, Mozart not. In our own age of cultural relativism and critical abdication it may be necessary to point out that, for Victorians, the acceptance of hierarchies of taste was a way of life. The first composer to succeed Beethoven as exemplar leaps to prominence in all three tables. They measure a conquest which extended, of course, to the whole of musical England, including its monarch and her consort; on its pianos and at its oratorios. With the Philharmonic it was a victory which survived posthumously through a handful of symphonies

---

[29] 48.13/27 (n.d.; the performance took place on 8 Mar. 1824).

and overtures, and the best-loved of all violin concertos.[30] As in the case of Beethoven, but with closer intimacy, this was a relationship with the Society which started slowly, matured rapidly, and was never sundered.

Mendelssohn Mania

Mendelssohn was 20 years old when he arrived in London in May 1829, rich and well connected, highly educated and charming, with the Octet, *Midsummer Night's Dream* music, and other masterpieces already accomplished. He was on the first leg of a three-year journey, elaborately prepared by his father, to establish his musical reputation and, as George Grove tells us, 'give him a knowledge of the world, and form his character and manners', and ultimately decide where to live and work.[31] After a frosty experience in Berlin he could not have chosen a more welcoming place at a more opportune time. At his first Philharmonic appearance he was amused to be led to the piano by John Cramer, 'like a young lady', to preside over his C minor Symphony. For this occasion he orchestrated the Scherzo from his Octet and put it in place of the Minuet and Trio. It was a huge success, the orchestra overcoming initial resistance to such youthful leadership, the audience demanding that the Scherzo be repeated. Thus began a mutual infatuation. Mendelssohn presented and dedicated the Symphony to the Society, which elected him its second Honorary Member within a few months. This was his first public honour and, along with ceaseless applause, it 'lifted a stone from his heart', for which he always expressed gratitude.[32] Next year the *Midsummer Night's Dream* Overture was introduced and in 1832 'Fingal's Cave', with Mendelssohn himself returning to play the G Minor Piano Concerto twice in a single season.[33] It was during this visit that he looked in at a rehearsal to be greeted by the orchestra with prolonged applause: 'dearer to me than any medal' he wrote home. Then the Society commissioned a symphony, an overture and vocal piece for 100 guineas, copyright reverting to the author after two years.[34] It got the Trumpet Overture, a *scena* for soprano, and a canonic masterpiece. Ayrton was not alone

---

[30] In Foster's listings of performances up to 1912 the Beethoven and Mendelssohn Violin Concertos each score thirty-eight; Spohr comes next with thirteen performances of his D minor Concerto, and twelve of the 'Nello stilo drammatico'; then Bruch with six of the still popular G minor and eight of the D minor.   [31] *Grove*: 'Mendelssohn'.

[32] E. Werner, *Mendelssohn: A New Image of the Composer and his Age* (1963), 148.

[33] In payment for 'Fingal's Cave' he was presented with plate equivalent to that given to the singers Sontag and Malibran: 48.3/1 (7 June 1832).   [34] 48.3/1 (5 Nov. 1832).

1831. Philharmonic Society. 19th Season.

Violins.	R	C.	£	s.	d
F. Cramer	9	8	52	10	
Spagnoletti	8	7	52	10	
Mori	8	8	52	10	
Weichsel	9	8	52	10	
Loder	2	2	21		
Wagstaff	9	8	21	5	
Murray	9	8	13	2	6
Thomas	5	5	7	17	6
Ella	9	8	19	13	9
A. Griesbach	9	8	19	13	9
Watkins	9	8	19	13	9
Dando	8	8	12	12	
Gattie	9	8	19	13	9
Seymour	9	8	19	13	9
Watts	8	7	26	5	
Mountain	9	8	26	5	
Kearns	9	8	19	13	9
Nodarch	9	8	19	13	9
Sherrington	9	8	19	13	9
Reeve	9	8	19	13	9
Pigott	9	8	19	13	9
Hicks	9	8	19	13	9
Rawlings	9	8	19	13	9
Anderson	9	8	19	13	9
Fleischer	9	8	19	13	9
A. Mackintosh	9	8	19	13	9
Litolff	9	8	19	13	9
Rooke	9	8	19	13	9
Tenors.					
Moralt	9	8	26	5	
F. Ware	9	8	19	13	9
Daniels	9	8	19	13	9
Lyon	9	8	19	13	9
Challoner	9	8	19	13	9
Calkin	9	8	19	13	9
Dance	8	7	20	5	
Abbott	9	8	19	13	9
Violoncellos.					
Lindley	9	8	52	10	
Crouch	9	8	26	5	
Brooks	9	8	19	13	9
J. Calkin	9	8	19	13	9
Iley	9	8	19	13	9
C. Lindley	9	8	26	5	
Binfield	9	8	19	13	9
Hatton	9	8	12	12	
Basses.					
Dragonetti	9	8	53		
Hill	9	8	26	5	
Wilson	9	8	19	13	9
Anfossi	9	8	32	16	3
C. Smart	9	8	19	13	9
Howell	9	8	19	13	9
carried forward			1228	3	3

	R	C.	£	s.	d
Brought forward			1228	3	3
Oboes.					
Cooke	9	8	35		
G. Irwin	9	8	19	13	9
Flutes.					
Nicholson	8	8	35		
Card	9	8	19	13	9
Clarinets.					
Willman	9	8	35		
Powell	9	8	19	13	9
Bassoons.					
Mackintosh	9	8	35		
Tully	9	8	19	13	9
Horns.					
Platt	9	8	35		
Rae	9	8	19	13	9
C. Tully	9	8	19	13	9
Keilbach	9	8	19	13	9
Trumpets.					
Harper	9	8	29	8	
Irwin	9	8	19	13	9
Trombones.					
Mariotti	9	8	19	13	9
Schoengen	9	8	13	2	6
Smithies	9	8	13	2	6
Drums.					
Chipp	9	8	19	13	9
Flauto Piccolo.					
Price	9	8	13	2	6
Extra Performers.					
Tolbecque	4	3	13	2	6
Schulz	1		5	5	
Puzzi	1		5	5	
Bohrer	1		5	5	
Hummel	1		26	5	
Blagrove	1		5	5	
Mrs. Anderson	2		10	10	
Hubbard	1	1	1	1	
Keating	2	1	1	11	6
Beal	2	1	1	11	6
Dean	2	1	1	11	6
Vocalists.					
Mad. Stockhausen	4		60		
Mrs. Wood	1		15		
Mr. & Knyvett	1		10	10	
Miss Cramer	1		5	5	
Miss Pewire	1		5	5	
Carried forward			1839	8	9

	R	C.	£	s.	d
Brought forward			1830	8	9
Miss Inverarity	1		10	10	
Miss M. Cause	1		5	5	
Piccioni	1		10	10	
A. Phillips	2		10	10	
Lablache	3		31	10	
Bennett	1		5	5	
Vaughan	1		7	7	
E. Taylor	1		5	5	
Sapio	1		5	5	
Braham	1		15		
W. Knyvett	1		5	5	
Santini	1		10	10	
Rubini	2		30		
Horncastle	1		5	5	
Seguin	1		5	5	
Officers.					
Secretary			60		
Librarian			50		
Concert Rooms.					
King's Theatre			267	4	6
Mr Laporte for three Boxes			67	4	
Royal Society of Musicians' Room for two meetings			3	15	
Police.					
Plank & 5 Assistants			10	4	
Attendants.					
Field music porter			21	3	6
Sowell		8	4	4	
Wilding	9	8	5	1	
J. Wilding	3	8	4	5	
R. Wilding		8	4	5	
Shaw	3	8	4	5	
Williams		8	4		
Mylett	1	8	2	5	
Parsons		8	2		
Bentley		8	2		
Harris		8	2		
Bills.					
Secretary			48	6	10
Librarian			9	13	7
Bookwriter copyist			34	12	5
Maynell Printer			64	1	6
Ellis Silversmith			17	10	
Church Translating			5	5	
E. Taylor for Do			17	6	
Do correcting parts			5		
Do for chorus singers			25	4	
Boxes for Music			50	8	
Presents.					
Sowell for correcting the list of subscribers			5		
carried forward			2790	15	7

7. Accounts, 1831 (48.9/1, fo. 19ᵛ)

8. Mendelssohn's orchestration of Scherzo from the Octet (BL loan, 4.289)

in recognizing the *Italian Symphony* at its first performance on 13 May 1833, as 'a composition that will endure for ages'.[35]

And so the cordial relationship flourished between the Philharmonic and the cynosure of musical England. In December 1838 the directors ask if there will be a visit next season, and any new compositions, and for advice about singers 'having no other friend in your part of the Continent on whose judgement they could so confidently rely'. Soon there is a letter of thanks for 'valuable information' and a proposal 'you play at one and conduct another'.[36] In June 1842 he conducted the *Scotch Symphony* and played his D minor Piano Concerto. In February 1844 he is offered £180 for conducting six concerts (he did five) with 'warmest thanks for kind feelings . . . (you) will be received with a sincere and hearty welcome'.[37] During this season occurred a notorious incident. Mendelssohn's attempt to introduce Schubert's 'Great' C major Symphony was ruined in rehearsal by some of the band ridiculing the last movement's repeated triplets. The incident was 'to the Society's shame', as Foster says, but it also illustrates wider issues: about the current state of discipline and balance of authority between conductor and orchestra, and its effects upon repertoire and taste. It also touches upon Mendelssohn's personal and professional demeanour, for he bore no grudge. Two years later, on hearing that the offending players were refused engagements at the Birmingham première of *Elijah*, he insisted that they be reinstated. The incident was 'dead and buried'; it was fair to reject musicians for incompetence but not simply because 'they made themselves unpleasant'. No further explanation need be sought for his popularity with colleagues.[38] Schubert stayed out of the Philharmonic repertoire. The 'Great' C major did not enter its programmes until 1871, fifteen years after Manns brought it to the Crystal Palace, and, even more remarkably, only four years after the Society's first performance of the 'Unfinished' Symphony. Meanwhile, there were few players or listeners who doubted that Beethoven's successor was among them, giving unquestioned and unstinted artistic status and leadership.

No published review evokes the excitement of a Mendelssohn concert so well as a private letter from an ordinary listener which, a century later, found its way into the Society's archives. Replete with music-lovers' gossip, it expresses gratitude to a subscriber friend for a guest ticket to the concert on 27 May 1844. In addition to excerpts from *Fidelio*, *The Seasons*, and Spohr's *Faust*, Beethoven's Fourth Symphony

---

[35] *Harmonicon* (1833), 134.

[36] 48.6/1 (Dec. 1838 and 4 Feb. 1839). But Mendelssohn was unamused by 'the usual dictatorial style' of the Society's secretary, Watts. See J. M. Cooper, 'Aber eben dieser Zweifel: A New Look at Mendelssohn's Italian Symphony', *19th Century Music* (spring 1992).

[37] 48.6/1 (27 Feb. 1844).

[38] Mendelssohn to Moscheles (26 June 1846), in *Letters of Felix Mendelssohn to Ignaz and Charlotte Moscheles*, trans. I. Moscheles (1888), 274–5.

was conducted with 'most wonderful precision' and 'A Boy of the name Joachim, 13 years of age only, played one of Beethoven's Concertos for the violin', meeting 'with deafening applause'. The *Midsummer Night's Dream* Scherzo was 'very beautiful and was encored, but it is *awfully, fearfully* difficult, so much so that last Saturday morning Mendelssohn was *7 hours* rehearsing, 2 hours with the chorus and the remaining 5 with the band'. And with apologies for excessive zeal 'the four chords that commence and end the overture' are carefully inscribed.[39] There is no mistaking the enthusiasm and devotion of such fans, who were attached to the music of their own time with a spontaneous zest which we associate only with pop. Mendelssohn was not alone in exciting veneration: 'Spohr—the great Spohr—the composer of *The Power of Sound* and *The Last Judgement*, is in England—in London—in the midst of us all—an ideal being,' ranted J. W. Davison in 1843.[40] But Mendelssohn's flock, many of whom enjoyed the 'hands-on' intimacy of playing his *Andante and Rondo Capriccioso* and *Songs without Words* or piano duet arrangements of the overtures and symphonies, were a special congregation, utterly devoted, and capable of insisting that no one else would do:

Miss Joanna Alexander presents her compliments to Mr Watts and wishes to know if Mr Mendelssohn is to be Director of the Philharmonic Concerts the whole or any of this season as she and her sisters Lady Caroline Cavendish, Lady Howard Douglas, and Miss Douglas, are waiting for this information before subscribing.[41]

The ladies were disappointed that year, but there were more appearances right up to 1847, the year of his death at the age of 38. On 26 April he again conducted the *Midsummer Night's Dream* music, and played Beethoven's Fourth Concerto—from memory, everyone exclaimed.

These intimate associations with Spohr and Mendelssohn continued the Society's tradition of close association with the finest contemporary musicians; but there was one important difference. In October 1841 the directors wrote to both composers expressing

regret that owing to the very severe losses sustained during the late and several preceding seasons they have it not in their power to make you any pecuniary offer, but that should you have any composition likely to suit their ensuing concerts they shall have much pleasure in the performance of them to the best of their ability.[42]

Quite recently composers had been generously commissioned. In 1832 Henry Bishop, the writer of 'Home, Sweet Home' was asked for a

---

[39] Francis Deffell to Mrs Steel, 48.13/38 (1 June 1844).
[40] *Musical Examiner* (1843), 253.   [41] 48.13/1 (24 Mar. 1845).
[42] 48.6/1 (24 Oct. 1841). Cf. the letter of apology to Mendelssohn quoted at the head of this chapter.

'concerted vocal piece', and there were similar requests to Attwood, Horsley, Novello, and T. Cooke, at £35 each. A 'concerted piece for pianoforte' was required from Potter, a symphony for 25 guineas from Henry Griesbach, and instrumental compositions from Moscheles, Neukomm, and Griffin.[43] The number of English, or at least resident, beneficiaries is remarkable. Did it mark a 'new era' for the Society, as the *Spectator* was eager to suggest, a new balance of power within the membership; and how was that to be reconciled with subscribers' tastes? Previously the services of members like Bishop, Crotch, Attwood, and Horsley, which were 'only available as composers' (meaning that they lacked executant skills of the necessary standard), had been excluded. Such neglect was 'either a proof of want of judgement in the choice, or of want of taste in the exclusion', was the magazine's cryptic and temporary conclusion to a rancorous debate.[44] It would continue to fester, as has already been noted. Paid commissions had suddenly become impossible, as subsidies to English composers, or even for the foreigners whose work the subscribers were demonstrably eager to hear. It was 'a period of very low water', as Foster, temporarily abandoning a Panglossian position, confesses. The Society was 'from a financial standpoint, in a very bad way', he reports and, with masterly understatement, suggests that there were 'rumours of retrenchment'. What had gone wrong, and how did the Society survive? Foster makes no serious attempt to answer either question except with a rhetorical passage about 'high musical ideals . . . generous feelings and genuine affection'. Writing at a later time of crisis he appears more concerned to rally troops than to explain past strategies: 'Let those who speak of the Philharmonic Society as dead, and only fit for polite interment', he writes in 1912, 'take note of this piece of history, and see whether it will not repeat itself.'[45] It did on several further occasions. Since 1842—two years *before* the great Mendelssohn-Joachim concert—was merely the first of many subsequent declines and death-bed recoveries, some kind of preliminary diagnosis is required.

Money Troubles

There had been brief misgivings a decade before the Society's first acknowledged financial crisis. Committees were set up to consider the treasurer's duties, where there was 'much room for amelioration', and to find ways of reducing concert expenses so as to leave 'a *surplus* independently of the Dividends'. Apparently it was not thought desirable

---

[43] 48.3/1 (5 and 19 Nov. 1832).   [44] *Spectator* (8 Mar. 1834), 225.
[45] Foster, *History*, 136, 157–8.

to increase income. In 1835 the treasurer began to receive a £60 stipend; and was soon 'requested to vacate his situation in the Orchestra in order better to fulfil his duties as Director and Treasurer in the Room': a significant break with the original co-operative ideal of administration by fellow-players.[46] The list of duties refers to such routine tasks as checking attendance of instrumentalists, porters, and 'Police'. More fundamental questions about the budget—which was growing, and changing shape—appear to have been lost amidst vague concern about 'the state of the Society' and renewed agitation about 'transfer of tickets'.[47] An experiment with transferable tickets in 1836 excited public comment:

We hear from many quarters that the good intentions of the Directors . . . have proved anything but satisfactory to the Subscribers, for the room is crowded to a very inconvenient excess at every concert; consequently the heat is very oppressive, and will become more so, as the warm weather advances . . . we have every reason to believe that many of them will secede if the same regulation should be continued.[48]

Offenders were sought out, with scant regard for their musical standing. After a complaint from the ever-vigilant Smart, Pierre Erard, the great piano-maker, was required to report 'the name of the person you improperly introduced to the last concert', and then admonished for forcing his guest into the room. Erard in turn expressed his outrage at the behaviour of the attendants. He had provided the piano for that concert and was accustomed to 'a polite admittance . . . even at their Majesties' private concerts'.[49]

If Watts and Smart were vulnerable to criticism for a lack of tact and discrimination in their determination to restrict access to the concerts, they were also facing real dilemmas, familiar to anyone who has tried to organize a subscription series with limited accommodation. Without transfers only three-quarters of the subscribers, on average, would turn up: the rest avoided dull concerts or were committed elsewhere. With transfers there was overcrowding on popular evenings. It was decided, with scrupulous care for detail, that henceforth ladies' tickets could be transferred between mother and one unmarried daughter, or between two sisters. Gentlemen were *not* allowed transfers, but a limited number of single tickets would be available to members for 1 guinea (double the subscription price). To accommodate these changes the subscription list would be *reduced* by fifty.[50] In similarly restrictive vein no

---

[46] 48.3/1 (10 Jan. 1831 and 2 Nov. 1835); 48.2/3 (21 Feb. 1838).
[47] 48.5/1 (n.d. [1832/3]).   [48] *MW* (29 Apr. 1836), 114.
[49] 48.6/1 (21 May and 23 June 1836); 48.13/11 (28 June 1836).
[50] Smart's personal collection of programmes and notes, in the BL, meticulously lists the attempts to control transfers.

encouragement was given to journalists who were beginning to reflect and encourage a growth in public interest. Three editors who asked for tickets, were firmly advised of a resolution 'that no free admission be granted to the gentlemen of the press'.[51]

These reassertions of exclusiveness were badly timed. In 1833 there had been 600 non-member subscribers bringing in some £2,500. By 1843 the subscription list had fallen below 250, paying less than £1,000, and every recent season had ended with a loss of £400–£500. Policies were therefore suddenly reversed in an attempt to balance the books. Publicity was sought by providing journalists with tickets, and costs were cut. In preparation for the 1841 season three leaders, Cramer, Loder, and Cooke, were re-engaged at 40 guineas each, instead of the 50 guineas paid in the previous season. All principals, except Dragonetti and Lindley, who refused to accept 10-guinea cuts, were reduced to 2 guineas a concert, with the traditional half-pay for rehearsals. With customary individual increments, rank-and-file players dropped from an average of 18 guineas for the eight concerts of 1839 to 16 guineas in 1841. The violin section was reduced to 28, and free refreshments were withdrawn.[52] Soloists received similar treatment, with careless disregard for their drawing-power. The general scale of reductions was from 15 guineas to 10, 10 to 7, and 8 to 6.[53] There were few exceptions, and then only in symbolic, *amour propre* terms, rather than cash: a temporary expedient, difficult to repeat. Thus Adelaide Kemble, who had recently made a stunning début in Bellini's *Norma*, accepted 25 guineas for two arias at the opening concert of the next season, and sang excerpts from *Der Freischütz* 'gratuitously' at the fourth.[54] In that year, 1842, more severe cuts were imposed. The three leaders *shared* a total fee of £36, and most principals were paid £25. Mendelssohn received £31. 10s. for conducting one concert which included the first performance in England of the *Scotch Symphony*, and playing his D minor Concerto in another. Thalberg was paid £21 to be hissed by Macfarren. Other performers of first choice were turned away if they refused to accept low fees, and even traditional privileges in lieu of cash were sometimes cut. Thus Moscheles was offered 5 guineas to conduct a concert which included a new Spohr symphony on 18 April, and then refused six free guest tickets. Potter took his place. Dragonetti inevitably refused to make 'more sacrifices', insisted upon 60 guineas for eight concerts and took £52. 10s. for an unspecified number of

---

[51] Response to letters from editors of *Morning Post*, *Globe* and *Musical Magazine*, 48.2/2 (14 Feb. 1835).

[52] 'Two admissions for *Times*, *Herald*, *Post*, *Chronicle*, *Atlas*, *John Bull*, *Sunday Times*, *Observer*, *Athenaeum*, *Spectator*.': 48.2/3 (3 Jan. 1841); orchestra cuts: 48.9/1 and 48.9/2; accounts for 1839–41: 48.2/3 (16 July 1840).   [53] 48.2/3 (10 Jan. 1841).

[54] Rosenthal, *Two Centuries*, 53–4. 48.2/3 (17 Feb. 1842).

appearances.[55] A 'Special General Meeting' was called in June 1842 to enquire into the 'present state of the Society and its future prospects', without useful outcome. Attempts to appoint a committee of seven to consider possible improvements in performance and management failed to 'fill the list'.[56] The concert-room manager received the message which appears at the head of this chapter, and agreed to accept a reduced rent of £150.

In 1843 expenditure was finally pushed down again below the £2,000 line, with a pattern which stayed approximately in place for the next few years. Three leaders and Lindley were each paid £27; principals, including a double-bass player called Howell, £17; rank-and-file players were further reduced to £13 and, in some cases, £11. Sivori, a protégé of Paganini, was paid £21 for two consecutive appearances with his Concerto in A; Spohr £30 for the extra command concert and a concerto. Marie Louise Dulcken received five guineas for giving the first English performance of Chopin's Second Piano Concerto. The obvious risk attached to such penny-pinching was a downward spiral of demoralized bands and motley soloists, followed by reduced subscriptions, followed by more economies. There was momentary respite in 1844 with a profit of nearly £400. Many years later George Grove looked through the papers for that pivotal season, presumably in greater detail than now seems possible from the surviving archive. Was he right, he asked, to note that the later concerts had taken 'up to 120 guineas in excess of usual receipts'?[57] These were Mendelssohn's concerts, including the one with Joachim, who was paid 5 guineas for the first effective performance of Beethoven's Violin Concerto to be heard at the Philharmonic. Rare treats, they were no substitute for coherent programming; and Mendelssohn had only three more years to live.

---

[55] Leaders and principals: 48.9/2; Moscheles: 48.6/1 (6 Apr. 1842); Dragonetti: 48.13/10 (26 Jan. 1842), 48.2/3 (6 Feb. 1842), 48.6/1 (7 Feb. 1842, 9 Jan. 1843).
[56] 48.3/1 (6 June 1842).   [57] 48.13/14 (5 Nov. 1879).

4

Quest for Leadership

[Sir Henry Bishop] could not hinder Mr Loder and the band from sometimes escaping into the right tempo.

(Chorley, in *Athenaeum*, 5 Apr. 1845)

[Sir Michael Costa had] that certain influence which only a vigorous man could exercise over the disconnected folk who made up an orchestra in those days.

(Chorley, in *Grove* 406)

I am a terribly modern person . . . I prefer Bellini, Rossini, Donizetti.

(Victoria, 18 Apr. 1837)[1]

It is in our power to do a great deal by way of giving the public a good musical taste, and our immense circulation, independent of any confidence that people may have in our judgement, entails upon us a very serious responsibility.

(Mowbray Morris to J. W. Davison, *The Times*'s music critic)[2]

THE year of Disraeli's two nations, 1845, has already been identified as a turning-point in Philharmonic history. All manner of things fell apart and the directors seemed incapable of holding a plausible centre. Financial support collapsed, a mere 260 subscribers paying £1,100: less than half the comparable figures of recent years. The Society's image of excellence was badly dented, each concert bringing rancorous comment which rumbled on from criticism to diagnosis, prescription, and funeral oration. Yet by the following season subscriptions and income were revived, concerts well attended and acclaimed. Neither collapse nor turnaround could be attributed to external causes, such as those

---

[1] Quoted in M. Warner, *Queen Victoria's Sketchbook* (1979), 72. Victoria became queen two months after this entry in her journal.

[2] *History of the Times, ii. The Tradition Established, 1841–1884* (1939), 65. Morris was manager of *The Times*. Davison joined that newspaper in 1846.

periodic changes in the economic and political weather which afflict concert organizers through no fault in their offerings. This crisis was internal and severe, its resolution a reprieve from almost certain collapse. When all seemed secure one man was acknowledged to have saved the day, though he was, and has largely remained, a figure of controversy, even fun. Michael Costa's limitations as a musician have been skewered by the sharpest pens. For Berlioz he was the lover of big drum, cymbals, and 'dear ophicleide' which were 'stuck in everywhere', such as the Overtures to *Der Freischütz* and *Don Giovanni*; the conductor who did not so much beat time as 'thresh' it.[3] For George Bernard Shaw he 'had no respect for the past, no help for the present, and no aspiration towards the future'.[4] Everyone agreed that he was a tyrant, the orchestra's 'real master and despot', as Wagner reported to Liszt: in sum precisely, as Elkin remarks, 'the right man for the job'.[5] Few contemporaries would have gone so far as J. E. Cox, the Norwich minister and critic, who recalled 'The two greatest men in their profession of modern times—F. M. Bartholdy and Michael Costa.'[6] Yet in terms of Philharmonic history it is a reasonable assessment, never more so than during the mid-1840s.

Understanding these years of crisis must begin with ungrateful scepticism when confronting the sheer bulk of their documentation. If the Society's archives provide generally reliable, though incomplete, information for this period, the suddenly inflated newsprint requires careful handling. Neither bulk nor vociferousness can be taken at face value, as balanced testimony of achievement, negligence, disaster, and last-minute reprieve. Foothills (they were not yet mountains) of print stemmed from causes which, in some cases, were directly related to music, its economics and politics. Others were more broadly derived. An 'unprecedented explosion of the newspaper press' was beginning just then, and journalists jostled for a share of that market, with new opportunities to ventilate and exploit enthusiasms and prejudices, about music, as much else.[7] The *Musical Times* started in 1844. John Ella cried woe with persistence and high culture in his *Record of the Musical Union*, which began publication in 1845. The *Illustrated London News* had been launched in 1843, and was now giving regular space to musical news, gossip, and speculation. Henry Chorley, always ready with quick judgement and quip, filled more literate columns in the *Athenaeum*, with at times a semblance of objectivity. George Hogarth was about to become critic of the newly founded *Daily News*. The inescapable,

---

[3] Ganz, *Berlioz in London*, 108-9.

[4] G. B. Shaw, *London Music 1888-1889* (1937), 311.

[5] Wagner to Liszt (5 July 1855), in *Correspondence of Wagner and Liszt*, trans. F. Hueffer (New York, 1897), 101. Elkin, *Royal Philharmonic*, 43.

[6] J. E. Cox, *Musical Recollections of the Last Half Century*, (1872), i. 176.

[7] G. Best, *Mid-Victorian Britain 1851-1875* (1971), 224-5.

notoriously volatile J. W. Davison had established the *Musical Examiner* in 1842, was preparing to mount his pulpit in *The Times*, and holding forth in assorted journals, including the *Musical World*, which he edited from 1846 until the early 1880s. Understanding the shortcomings of that 'musician of no great learning' Franz Schubert, and of the 'morbidly sensitive flea' Chopin, Davison was well placed to observe the Philharmonic's shortcomings, and recommend quick correction.[8] Such print is the rawest material for history, not reasoned analysis. Yet one historian of the Society describes Davison's fulminations as a 'substantially correct diagnosis' of its troubles.[9]

The 'Music Monster' attributed blame for the crisis to three 'incubi': reliance upon foreign composers, 'effeminate yielding to the vulgarity of fashion', and 'shameful prejudice against native production . . . we have had the solo performances of Thalberg, Dohler and Vieuxtemps . . . we have *not* had the symphonies of Macfarren'. The choice of names and implication of comparable drawing power are strange conceits. The rhetoric is inflated—he surely means two incubi, for reliance upon foreigners was equivalent to neglect of natives—and too loose to carry conviction. The foreigners under attack were surely neither Mendelssohn nor Spohr, whom Davison professed to admire, the one 'imaginative and gifted' the other 'mighty and metaphysical'.[10] The Society's poor diet, to follow another of his metaphors, had been prepared by too many 'preposterously powerless cooks, who lack all the mastery of spice'. Better eating required a supreme chef, in sole charge, a 'perpetual conductor (Sterndale Bennett *is by far the best*)'.[11] Again the rodomontade of special pleading is tacked on to, and confuses, common sense. The young English composer and pianist had indeed come home with the highest credentials from Mendelssohn and Schumann, as a composer and pianist. His qualifications and experience for the position of principal conductor were negligible. Both Macfarren and Bennett would have their day, after the Society had been rescued, not by a novice cook with untried recipes, but by a vastly experienced masterchef who insisted upon a tidy kitchen. Equally fortunate for the Philharmonic, or so it seemed at the time, were new hopes of assistance from high places.

Connections, Networks, and Risks

Where could the Society turn for support in times of adversity? It might be thought that no connection was more valuable than that 'direct patronage' by the monarch which had been emblazoned at the

[8] Reid, *Music Monster*.   [9] Elkin, *Royal Philharmonic*, 41.
[10] Davison on incubi: *Musical Examiner* (Feb. 1843); on Spohr and Mendelssohn: Reid, *Music Monster*, 171.   [11] Davison, quoted in Elkin, *Royal Philharmonic*, 40–1.

head of every programme since the first concert. It was certainly esteemed by George Frederic Anderson, who began a stint of thirty-six
years as the Society's treasurer in 1840, and was soon to become, in
1848, Master of the Queen's Music. His communications from above
are sufficiently frequent and self-important to convey a sense of urgent
intimacy with great events, rather in the style of Alice's White Rabbit.
But these were times when even disinterested and unsycophantic
musicians could begin to entertain hopes of substance in royal patronage. The young Victoria had grown up with music and some opportunities to cultivate its appreciation. A concert for her sixteenth birthday
included six of the most celebrated singers in operatic history: Grisi,
Malibran, Lablache, Rubini, Tamburini, and Ivanoff. It was no passing
whim for, sketchbook in hand, she was sufficient of a fan to ponder,
on several occasions, the rival merits of the first two of these great
artists, preferring Grisi. For her eighteenth birthday King William IV
sent her a 200-guinea Broadwood, and Mrs Anderson (Lucy Philpot,
a good musician from Bath) taught her to play it. She also took singing lessons, for twenty years, from Lablache, who delighted her on
the stage in *Cenerentola*, but failed to convince her that Mozart was a
greater composer. She played piano duets, and music for two pianos,
with Prince Albert, who began to remould her taste. It was presumably due to him that, in what later generations would have regarded
as the unlikely circumstances of a palace entertainment, excerpts from
Zauberflöte were sung by a group of professional musicians, along with
court ladies and gentlemen. Soon after that 1840 event the Queen was
taken to hear the whole work at Covent Garden. And then, of course,
there was music-making with Mendelssohn.

    Attendance at concerts was more of a problem: less congenial than
the privacy of a royal box at the opera. But that did not prevent her
from accompanying a consort who was serious and active, in music as
in so much else. It began to appear that the court might be linked to
the Philharmonic in truly 'direct patronage'.[12] There was great excitement when an extra concert 'by command' was added to the Society's 1843 season.[13] It was arranged for 10 July, with the King of
the Netherlands also in attendance. The programme, under Spohr's
supervision, was a representative mixture of old and new Philharmonic favourites, probably more representative of Albert's than Victoria's

[12] Incidents related in this paragraph are drawn from S. Weintraub, *Queen Victoria* (1987),
90, 146, and M. Warner, *Sketchbook*, 66–75. On Mendelssohn's friendship see e.g., a letter
to his mother (19 July 1842), describing a visit to Buckingham Palace when Victoria and
Albert sang, and the organ was played by both men.
[13] Anderson had consulted with Prince Albert and returned to make excited arrangements. They are listed in three pages of resolutions which include an insistence that the
band wear white cravats. See 48.2/3 (18 June 1843).

taste: Mendelssohn's 'Fingal's Cave' and a chorus from his *St Paul*; a Mozart symphony and chorus from *Idomeneo*; Weber's *Freischütz* Overture; a violin concerto, aria, and overture by Spohr; and the Scherzo and Finale from Beethoven's Ninth Symphony, which had been performed in its entirety earlier in the season. For the latter Moscheles was dragooned into authenticity by the directors (one detects the unskilled, but always correct, hand of Sir George): 'there being no organ part in the score . . . which was written expressly for the Philharmonic Society they hope you will agree with them in considering it advisable to perform it in its original state'.[14] Presumably the royal visitors experienced a similarly authentic, if truncated, Ninth.

The next year's command concert, under Mendelssohn, was more balanced in content—Beethoven, Mozart, Maurer, Bellini, Sterndale Bennett, Mendelssohn, and Schubert—and probably better performed. Maurer was a particular *bête noire* of Davison's, but his concertante was requested by Prince Albert, as Mendelssohn informed the directors, to be played by Sivori, Blagrove, Ernst, and Joachim.[15] A command could hardly be more explicit; and it was obeyed, except that only the first two of the selected stars were available. Clearly royal patronage was becoming active: without direct assistance to the Society's budget, but bringing hope of more positive encouragement. Nevertheless one must avoid an anachronistic reading of great significance into these early nineteenth-century encounters with the monarch, as if they were imbued with a later generation's pomp, reverence, and hopes of profit by association. Although there was already some public interest in the young Queen, and obligatory excitement among flunkeys and those immediately concerned, the cult of adulation and elaborate ceremony was yet to be invented and developed.

The trappings of English monarchy still lacked lustre. According to the Queen, the choir of the Chapel Royal always sang 'schockingly'. Even the coronation had been something of a shambles, its music so inept, with Smart in prominent place, as to excite open derision. How could he both play the organ and give the beat to the orchestra simultaneously, it was asked, when he was incapable of doing either singly?[16] In early Victorian England, therefore, the monarch's attendance at a concert did not necessarily bring plaudits and a profitable following. In any case the Philharmonic's unwillingness to extend its audience further limited gains from any manifestations of public curiosity, or desire to be associated with royalty. Prevailing scepticism is illustrated

[14] 48.6/1 (9 Apr. 1843).   [15] 48.2/3 (1 June 1844).
[16] D. Cannadine, 'The Context, Performance and Meaning of Ritual: The British Monarchy and the "Invention of Tradition", c.1820–1977', in Hobsbawm and Ranger (eds.), *Invention of Tradition*, 113–15. The reference to 'schocking' singing is in E. Longford, *Victoria R. I.*(1964), 177; see also her account of the coronation, on pp. 99–104.

by opposition to the 'command' performance under Moscheles in July 1843. It was expressed in a generally well-disposed journal, which regularly reported the doings of the 'haut ton'. Here was an example of 'misplaced patronage', complained the *Illustrated London News*; these foreign offerings were displacing a worthier recital of native Irish song.[17] Whatever its satisfactions for Anderson and Smart, who meticulously recorded in his notebook all fourteen of Victoria's Philharmonic visits, between 1844 and 1860, royal patronage was of little practical benefit to the Society during these early years.[18]

Less conspicuous, and at times more useful, was a quieter form of influence by palace and high society: the recommendation of visiting musicians from a multiplicity of foreign establishments who arrived at court with letters of introduction from their royal and aristocratic employers. Before professional concert agents became established, and even to some extent afterwards, this network provided a regular means of recruiting soloists for the Philharmonic, and an advertisement for their alleged prowess. Thus Mr Eduard Buddeus, who played the Romance and Rondo from Chopin's First Piano Concerto on 25 March 1844 was reported to be 'Pianiste [*sic*] to His Highness the Grand Duke of Saxe Gotha'.[19] The flood of applications, personal references, and occasionally peremptory commands had to be handled with firmness and tact. A typical rebuff reads 'Your Royal Highness having honoured the Directors of the Philharmonic Society by a communication through Mr F. Cramer, I am desired to acquaint your Royal Highness that they are already pledged to several professors of distinguished talent.'[20] While such connections continued to be of use, and to exert their pressures at least until the collapse of 1914, the Philharmonic's main network of recruitment was by means of a more appropriate, less capricious, élite. The advice of fellow musicians at home and abroad, and particularly the friendship of a few acknowledged masters with broad experience and many contacts, were always essential for the acquisition of significant new repertoire and artists. Mendelssohn was the last supreme autocrat of this tradition, to be succeeded by such lesser authorities as Joachim and Clara Schumann.

Generally all of these connections had functioned reasonably well so far, along with a separate recruitment of rank-and-file orchestral players via the shadowy, undocumented, figures known as 'fixers'. But the process was slow, and increasingly subject to a wide variety of hazards. Prone to cliquishness, it inevitably excited antagonism from those who

[17] *ILN* (15 July 1843).
[18] BL Add. MS 41779, papers of Sir G. T. Smart, vol. ix.
[19] *ILN* (30 Mar. 1844).
[20] 48.6/1 (1 Apr. 1840). Cf. responses to the Duke of Cambridge's emissaries: 48.2/3 (26 Apr. 1846 and 27 Mar. 1848).

were passed over, and could result in a narrowing of musical horizons. Yet favouritism could be restrained: men who were capable of resisting a royal duke were unlikely to bend easily to lesser pressures, and there was still plenty of competition for the Philharmonic platform among solo instrumentalists. The recruitment of singers and the orchestra raised more serious problems, the latter so intransigent as to require urgent reform. With singers it was simply a matter of getting the best on offer, cheaply and without excessive sensitivity about repertoire. There had been occasions when the outcome was less than judicious, through poor judgement, special pleading, or false economy. In April 1831 a Miss Cramer performed an aria by Paisiello in a manner, it was reported, which 'should be confined to private parties'.[21] And why, complained a subscriber, had two sisters in reduced circumstances been allowed to appear in May 1840? 'You do not use us well . . . I should infinitely have preferred making them a present *not* to sing.'[22]

Such examples of absolute inadequacy were rare, but a resort to bare competence was becoming common, and short-sighted; for many subscribers who might be none too discriminating about instrumental niceties were knowledgeable about singing, or at least knew what they liked. Their expectations, nourished by exposure to great artists, in opera-house and salon, were often high. Only close contact with the theatre could ensure an affordable supply of international talent; a connection which had to be be maintained by goodwill, and meticulously flexible timetabling to avoid clashes throughout a short, intensive season. At the best of times such procedures had been hazardous when low fees were on offer; by the early 1840s they were falling apart. And there was a 'moral' dimension in a society which 'almost gave the death-blow to the English stage'.[23] As the middle-class values of Victorian England began to take shape, there were inevitably those in the Philharmonic who regarded links with theatre as subservience to a cultural institution which lacked any semblance of respectability or seriousness.

On all these counts the directors were becoming increasingly vulnerable, and the Society potentially unstable. Rivalry and factionalism were therefore inescapable. Latent hostilities were always near the surface and easily polarized: Englishmen and foreigners, composers and performers, old establishment and young pretenders, opera-lovers and the pure in heart. Again, an organization which had begun as an 'orchestral co-operative' needed to redefine its attitudes to the orchestra. Comparable relationships in the wider industrializing society of Britain were settling into factory-master and factory-hand, bourgeois and

---

[21] *Atlas* (17 Apr. 1831).   [22] 48.13/36 (18 May 1840).
[23] H. Perkin, *The Origins of Modern English Society 1780–1880* (1969), 280.

proletariat. If the emerging symphony orchestra was developing, as a social organization, into a simulacrum of the factory—certainly its working conditions and scale of payments were similar or inferior—then how could elected Philharmonic directors act as the orchestra's masters? How could they maintain discipline and standards of work, sufficiently to please subscribers, while retaining the goodwill of members, including players whose advance to seniority in the Society was frequently accompanied by deterioration in technique, earning-power, and artistic standing? And what were the conductor's emerging functions and responsibilities in this realignment of authority? Without firm, universally respected leadership by a resident musician—and no Englishman, *pace* Davison, was a plausible candidate—the elements of potential disintegration could be dispelled only temporarily by an occasional visit from Mendelssohn.

Equally serious but less understood, probably by the directors, certainly by the general membership and outside critics, were the risks attached to traditional methods of arranging concerts, which were beginning to grind to a halt. Their deficiencies were quite distinct from penny-pinching, though doubtless a little more cash would have oiled some wheels. Every important engagement was undertaken by individual negotiation: slow, often poorly informed, unpredictable, and, most significantly, without the help of professional intermediaries (agents and impresarios) to share what modern economists call 'search and information costs'.[24] Postponements and cancellations, through illness, misunderstanding, or bad faith, necessitated repetition of the whole process with another, probably less preferred, individual musician, and with reduced time to complete arrangements; all unavoidable accompaniments to an obsolescent administrative machinery. These hand-to-mouth procedures had been comparatively easy and quick in early days when 'everyone' was in London for the season. But as the home and international market for music grew in extent and prosperity, favoured artists were more widely sought and had to be booked further ahead. Even rank-and-file players might have alternative opportunities for work—further afield, and over shorter periods of time, as railways and steamships widened possibilities of employment. The postal services were also entering a short-lived golden age: in 1845 Robert Browning and Elizabeth Barrett, about to elope, could write to each other twice a day.

Like every institution tapping an international market and requiring an extensive correspondence, the Philharmonic benefited from these revolutions in transport and communications, but its administrative procedures failed to keep pace. It had grown accustomed to completing

[24] Modern 'search and information costs' are discussed extensively in R. Towse, *Singers in the Marketplace: The Economics of the Singing Profession* (Oxford, 1993).

or changing arrangements sometimes only a few days ahead, even if it was always essential to fix such irreplaceable players as Dragonetti as soon as concert dates were known. On 11 March 1826 Weber was engaged to preside at a concert on 3 April. On 29 January 1832 John Field was invited to play one of his concertos at the first concert of the season, one month later.[25] On 3 May 1837 Thalberg was offered ten guineas to play at the next concert and when he refused the directors turned to Louise Dulcken, who complained that notice was short but agreed to play Mendelssohn's G minor Concerto 'next Monday'.[26] On 10 May 1840 the directors, seemingly unprepared for a visit by the greatest virtuoso of the age, minuted 'Should Litz [sic] make a great sensation tomorrow evening he should be asked to play again at the 6th concert—and that should he not play, Lindley and Dragonetti be requested to do so.' They had to make do with Lindley. Calling on Liszt to explain that they could not exceed the 'present' given to Thalberg was insufficient courtesy to compensate for insufficient forethought. For, despite the seemingly comparable attractions of his rival, the 'thousand power digitalist', Liszt was now 'one of the wonders of the world', playing at a *concert monstre*, giving the first piano recitals and, on that desired sixth Philharmonic night, appearing at the Palace for Victoria's twenty-first birthday. This was 'great progress', he reported, 'since she never asks for instrumentalists'.[27]

The risks of last-minute arrangements were compounded by highhandedness in 1844 when Mme Dulcken's reluctance to play in a Spohr quintet was brushed aside. She wrote to the press, before and after the performance, in protest at having to play 'against my own judgement and inclination'.[28] Individual uncertainties and embarrassments were not only damaging to the Society's image and goodwill, but could have long-term implications for its repertoire. In December 1842, for example, the directors decided to write to Berlioz, asking if he would 'superintend performance of his Funeral Symphony on what terms'. Next March the secretary offered him an engagement 'for 8 or 22 May to conduct and superintend one of your compositions' and again asked terms. After a third attempt a reply was at last received on 11 June, too late for anything to be arranged. Another ten years elapsed before Berlioz made his first appearance with the

[25] Weber: 48.2/2 (11 Mar. 1826). Field: 48.2/2 (29 Jan. 1832).
[26] Thalberg: 48.2/2 (3 May 1837). Dulcken: 48.13/10 (9 May 1837). Louise Dulcken was another of Queen Victoria's teachers. Ferdinand David, dedicatee of Mendelssohn's Violin Concerto, was Dulcken's brother.
[27] Directors' Minute Book: 48.2/3 (10 and 17 May 1840). At the Palace: A. Williams, *Portrait of Liszt* (1990), 130–1. Liszt was reporting to Marie d'Agoult, who was about to join him in London. On his season and subsequent tours see also D. I. Allsobrook, *Liszt: My Travelling Circus Life* (1991). Thalberg's digits were counted in *ILN* (22 Feb. 1845).
[28] 48.2/3 (24 Apr. and 5 May 1844); *ILN* (4 May 1844).

Philharmonic.[29] Such haphazard arrangements were intrinsically unreliable, not merely prey to emergency or recalcitrance. In 1845 they went
badly wrong. Just before the season began, Ella reminded his readers
of the Society's rickety foundations and mounting crisis:

> out of fashion with the aristocracy, out of favour with the best parts of the
> profession . . . oppressed by the envy, jealousy and jobbery of its members . . .
> nothing short of a total regeneration can prevent it from becoming utterly
> contemptible . . . we fear its days are numbered.[30]

Looking for a Conductor

The 1845 season opened with the 'room very fully attended', but immediately fell victim to critical assault, with Sir Henry Bishop as the
target. Commentators, and probably most of the subscribers, agreed
that it was one thing to have him preside at an occasional concert
which could be written off as 'the most stagnant evening'; quite another to put him in charge of an entire season. A flood of vituperation
was released. Sir Henry was 'not quickened by his promotion', quipped
Chorley: 'Lenient to torpidity' at rehearsals, 'incorrect in almost every
tempo', responsible for countless miserable Antient concerts, this was
the conductor as spoiler. Almost overnight the amiable 'English Mozart',
who had often attracted criticism, became a necessary whipping-boy,
symbol of collapsed standards at the Philharmonic, betrayer of art
and high promise, in the selection and feeble presentation of a faded
repertoire. Every piece of music in the first concert, it was said, had
been 'done to death these twenty years'. They included Haydn's last
symphony and Beethoven's Fifth; the 'Emperor' Concerto played by
Mme Belleville-Oury, a pupil of Czerny, overtures by Cherubini and
Méhul, and a Spohr violin concerto. The singers Lablache and Miss
Rainforth, a popular English exponent of *Figaro*'s Susanna and Countess, were alone in escaping criticism. Instrumental standards were deemed
unacceptable: 'never has there been a more tame or ineffective performance . . . never did we hear the symphonies and overtures go more
languidly'. Not that everyone held the entire orchestra to blame.
Chorley's sarcasm is quoted at the head of this chapter, and another
commentator openly sympathized with the leader, 'poor Loder . . . for
the conductor hung upon his energies like a dead weight'.[31]

When Victoria and Albert attended the second concert, the audience

---

[29] To Berlioz: 48.2/3 (11 Dec. 1842); 48.6/1 (14 Mar. 1843). From Berlioz: 48.2/3 (11
June 1843).   [30] *RMU* (11 Mar. 1845), 7.
[31] *ILN* (5 Apr. 1845). Other critics were similarly hostile. See *RMU* (15 Apr. 1845), where
Ella cites *The Times*, the *Herald*, the *Chronicle*, and the *Morning Post*.

had shrunk, 'notwithstanding such interesting patronage', and barracking continued. This time Chorley claimed that the band was 'astonished' when Sir Henry 'took every tempo but the right one', and the indictment widened. The Philharmonic, it was said, 'not content with being the worst, is the *dearest* concert in the world'. The price of a 'single admission to its ill conducted performances' could secure admission to eight concerts at the Paris Conservatoire. To imply that those concerts were open to casual visitors was far from the truth; but again the image of a *sui generis* Philharmonic, *sans reproche*, if it had ever been more than a parochial myth, was now being publicly mocked.[32] At the third concert on 28 April Bishop, having appeared with the Antients that morning, finally bowed to the inevitable and withdrew without completing the evening's programme. It was taken over by Charles Lucas: second cello in the orchestra, pupil of Lindley, conductor and eventually principal of the Royal Academy of Music. For Bishop this was the end of an association, not a career: a month later he was again presiding at the Antients, and soon succeeded Crotch as Oxford's professor of music. Moscheles took over the rest of the Society's season: had he refused, the directors proposed to ask Julius Benedict.[33] It was a temporary and unsatisfactory arrangement. As a pianist Moscheles was still thought capable of providing 'a delicious treat to all mental musicians'. But the same journal described him as a 'disastrous' conductor, 'fidgety . . . a cypher' who 'never anticipates', so that 'performers did as they liked'.[34]

Were the directors simply inept to have placed Bishop and the Society in such an ignominious position? Our response to this question has far-reaching implications which call in question a significant, but rather pat, retrospective verdict. It was inexplicable that they should prefer Bishop to Sterndale Bennett, 'so immeasurably his superior', Moscheles later declared, claiming that 'such anomalies' hastened his own decision to end a long stay in England and settle in Leipzig.[35] Was it not at least irresponsible to expect the opera-house despoiler of Mozart and Rossini, and composer of 'Home, Sweet Home' and 'Lo Hear the gentle lark', to exert strategic authority among serious musicians? But the realities were more complex, even for Sir Henry, who accepted the position at a very late stage, and with some reluctance. For several years he had declared that he would 'conduct no more Philharmonic concerts', complaining of being 'cavilled at by Editors and those who for so long have opposed all my efforts at the Philharmonic'.[36] Moreover, despite such criticisms, Bishop's reputation at large was not then as it may appear today, 'altered more than that of almost

[32] *Athenaeum, Connoisseur, ILN* (all on 19 Apr. 1845).   [33] 48.2/3 (4 May 1845).
[34] Moscheles: as pianist, *ILN* (20 Apr. 1844); as conductor, *ILN* (9 Aug. 1845).
[35] Moscheles, *Recent Music*, 311.   [36] 48.13/4 (23 May 1841; 31 May 1843).

any other composer', as the *New Grove*[37] states unequivocally. In 1845 he was still taken seriously by many a worthy, if undiscriminating, music-lover, including the Prince Consort who was said to have been largely responsible for his recent knighthood.

The fact which throws most light upon the whole tangled affair is that Bishop was approached only after prolonged attempts to get someone better. It was common knowledge that the Society's first choice would have been a musician 'whose European reputation would insure respect from all parties'. Both Mendelssohn and Spohr were approached, and neither were available.[38] There was then a determined attempt to engage Michael Costa, by far the most experienced and admired conductor resident in London. Since 1832 he had lifted the opera orchestra at Her Majesty's Theatre out of a trough of lax incompetence, establishing unprecedented standards of discipline and ensemble. The reform had entailed more than one brush with a racket by which experienced players, particularly violinists, placed their pupils and 'made money by such engagements in addition to their own salaries'.[39] A variant of the remunerative practice, familiar among such professors as Smart, of putting out work to apprentice teaching assistants, it was a prototype for the deputy system, and was driven out of Costa's domain. This intransigence, and the unyielding baton with which he imposed unilateral authority, earned him equal measures of dislike and respect within 'the profession'. By November 1844 the Philharmonic directors took the courageous step of offending some members by offering him 80 guineas to conduct *all* of the 1845 concerts. They then had to wait until the end of January, before he admitted failure to get permission from Lumley, owner of the King's Theatre.[40] So two months before the season began the Society was still without a conductor. The veteran Habeneck, still presiding at Paris in the old manner, with bow in hand and a first violin part before him, was offered £100 for two concerts and urged to reply immediately: on receipt of his letter the directors would meet 'the same evening'. It arrived on 13 February, refusing the dates proposed. Only then was Bishop engaged, while fruitless negotiations were continued with Habeneck, Mendelssohn, and Spohr.[41] Thus Sir Henry took over belatedly and *faute de mieux*, not through the directors' disregard for high musicianship, or a premeditated plot. At the last moment he was saddled with several concerts and prospect of the whole season, rather than envisaged from the outset as the Philharmonic's first permanent conductor. It is noteworthy,

---

[37] *New Grove*, ii, 742.

[38] 48.2/3 (9 Mar. 1845); 48.13/32 (7 Mar. 1843 *et seq*). Despite a long and cordial correspondence Spohr never returned to the Philharmonic after 1843. See also *ILN* (9 Aug. 1845).   [39] Cox, *Musical Recollections*, 180–1.

[40] 48.13/7 (4 and 23 Nov. 1844; 31 Jan. 1845). 48.2/3 (26 Jan. 1845). Costa's disagreement with Lumley would soon lead to a complete break, of great importance to the Philharmonic.   [41] 48.2/3 (26 Jan.; 2, 13, and 25 Feb. 1845).

perhaps, that 1845 was the first year in which the accounts list 'Conductors' as a separate category, but the status of available candidates is suggested by scales of payment: 10 guineas for Bishop, 5 for Lucas, and 25 for Moscheles.[42] The latter insisted on a say in remaining programmes but all that can be discerned in the outcome is an incongruous series of attempts to balance irreconcilable tastes.

The great baritone Pischek made several appearances and was largely responsible, it was said, for recovering the audience which had fled from Bishop.[43] There were many other attractions. The celebrated violinist Camillo Sivori arrived with his own trumpery E flat Concerto, its first and second movements widely separated by songs, by Mme Dulcken in the Mendelssohn D minor Concerto, and by Beethoven's Second Symphony. On 26 May Sterndale Bennett gave a rare performance of Mozart's Piano Concerto in C minor, taking pains to arrange a 'preparatory rehearsal' with the wind-players.[44] As counterbalance there was Mr D. J. G. F. Godefroid's *Fantasia for Harp on Airs from Meyerbeer's 'Robert le Diable'*. The next concert began with Macfarren's Symphony in C sharp minor, a capitulation to Davison's 'Young England agitation'. It was roundly hissed.[45] Stalwarts, and latecomers, were then regaled with a Beethoven symphony, a Weber overture, several songs, and Leopold de Meyer—'the great Lion Pianist . . . When he is first heard attentively, you feel a sort of thankfulness he has concluded'. The Lion rampaged through a fantasia, possibly on themes by Rossini or Donizetti.[46] Then the Milanollo sisters performed *Concertante on Airs from 'Lucia'*, and shared the movements of a Vieuxtemps concerto. Theresa began and Maria took over for the Adagio and Rondo, but the real attraction was that ladies did not then play the violin. Foster's supposition that ingrained prejudice was 'quite dispelled by the delightful playing of two charming sisters' is unprovable, and surely premature, but a nice precedent had been set. On 23 June the directors, stepping further down-market, took a leaf, and artists, from the book of their greatest contemporary showman and democratizer of music, Louis Jullien, by giving a platform to the Distin family and their famous new saxhorns. On this occasion five of them appropriated Meyerbeer's devil, Robert, from Mr D. J. G. F. Godefroid, in yet another fantasia.[47] It was all a far cry from the Society's pious resolutions

---

[42] Accounts for 1845: 48.9/1.   [43] *ILN* (17 May 1845).

[44] The wind-players Ribas, Cooke, Walsch, Williams, Lazarus, Beauman and Godfrey were asked to rehearse at Mr Bennett's apartments: 48.2/3 (18 May 1845).

[45] *ILN* (9 Aug. 1845).

[46] The Lion's encomium appeared in *MW*. On Meyer as archetypal charlatan–virtuoso see C. Ehrlich, *The Piano: A History* (1990), 21 and 49.

[47] On the Milanollo sisters: Foster, *History*, 189. On the acceptance of women violinists: Ehrlich, *Music Profession*, 157–61. On the Distin family, its Sax instruments, and their audiences: T. Herbert (ed.), *Bands: The Brass Band Movement in the 19th and 20th Centuries* (1991).

of 1813. The season ended more conventionally, but even Mendelssohn's Calm Sea and Prosperous Voyage could not dispel a mood of desperation.

Meanwhile negotiations had been continuing with Costa for 1846. This time he was in a position to accept, but insisted upon a set of conditions, designed 'solely for the welfare of the Society', and set out in a remarkable and illuminating document. 'Long experience in the Direction of the Opera' it begins, 'has convinced me that to ensure the perfect performance of any composition the entire command of the Band is necessary.' Therefore his requirements were draconian:

'1st. The arrangement of the Orchestra to be entirely under my control and the name and title of leader to be done away with. 2ly. No performer to absent himself or to leave his place in the orchestra during the rehearsal or performance without my permission. 3ly. The Directors to pledge themselves to support me in the strict discipline of the orchestra. 4ly. The Rehearsal to commence at Eleven instead of Twelve o'clock. 5ly. The programming to be made out with my concurrence and the score of any new Sinfonia to be sent to me a fortnight before the rehearsal.

Other regulations required that, if summoned to the Palace, he should appoint his deputy; and that the entire set of rules should remain 'strictly private' until agreed.[48]

The directors responded point by point, claiming to accept most of them, including the abolition of the leader's title—a surprising concession at this early stage of bargaining. They wanted to keep a hold on players' permissions, (i.e. orchestral discipline) and were similarly reluctant to lose any control over repertoire: it was their custom, as was publicly remarked, to exert 'entire executive power . . . making up all the schemes' and treating a conductor as 'an animated metronome'. They 'would be happy to see Mr Costa at meetings when programmes were discussed'.[49] This amicable exchange and seemingly easy agreement stepped nimbly across a minefield which Costa would make tolerably safe for nearly a decade. He was quickly, and unanimously, elected as associate, and then member, 'a compliment the more marked as some years since, through sheer malevolence, he had been blackballed'. 'Flattered at the handsome manner' of his election, the Philharmonic's first permanent conductor took command for an entire season.[50]

Orchestral Reform

It was a commonplace that 'the Philharmonic orchestra' had deteriorated, but opinions differed as to causes, extent, manifestations, and cures. The angriest insisted upon extensive 'weeding out' of ineffective,

---

[48] 48.13/7 (11 and 13 Aug. 1845).
[49] 48.13/7 (14, 16, and 20 Aug. 1845). The 'animated metronome' remark is in *ILN* (9 Aug. 1845).   [50] 48.13/7 (6 Nov. and 16 Dec. 1845). *ILN* (15 Nov. 1845).

old-established, players who could be 'safely calculated at nearly one third', ensuring that 'work is consequently "slubbered" '. It was said to be a 'standing joke' that some wind-players were utterly 'blown out'.[51] Davison confirmed that wind-playing was generally poor, with 'desperately *bad*' horns; and reported that many of the strings were 'anything but what they should be'. There was also widespread agreement about the inadequacy of rehearsals, resulting, for example, in accompaniments which were 'often disgracefully performed'. Another reason for good and bad concerts, which critics failed to notice, was the increasing employment of deputies. To speak of 'the Philharmonic orchestra' is to imply a permanence or stability of personnel which, if it had ever existed, was already beginning to disintegrate by the 1840s. The standard of playing on the night depended, among other factors, upon the number and quality of substitutes. They had always been allowed but were originally subject to permission in advance by the directors. Thus a minute of 1817 allows Mr Binfield to send a deputy on 20 April 'provided he be approved by the directors'.[52]

Immediate responsibility for such precautionary scrutiny had long been abandoned, and was not consistently delegated; so a practice developed which became endemic to London's orchestral life. Established players would send deputies, not simply at times of indisposition, but if better jobs turned up: an increasing prospect as the market grew and transport improved. A great occasion, such as performances under Mendelssohn, was doubtless sufficient inducement for the finest players to turn out; and an excellent concert was almost guaranteed before a note had been heard. At other times the system could go into reverse. Faced by the negligible authority of a bishop at the Antients, or Bishop at the Philharmonic, good players might send deputies or turn up for routine sight-reading. Such contrasting levels of attainment by what is named as the same orchestra, are familiar to modern London audiences, but were then new. This is not to argue that specialist interpretative conductors were already on the scene. They only began to appear, as an acknowledged group, half a century later; but the inspiration of a great composer could lift, by his mere presence, an individual concert to a new plateau of experience.

Meanwhile the essential requirement was for someone who could provide continuous, if less spectacular, direction of a large orchestra which, though transitional, was beginning to develop significantly modern characteristics. Its labour costs were already high and inflexible, because of size rather than the level of individual fees. This simple economic fact was becoming a crucial deterrent to rehearsals, and therefore to high standards of performance. The orchestra's chain of command remained diffuse, in the traditional manner, but usually

---

[51] See various numbers of *ILN* esp. 9 Aug. 1845; Davison and *Morning Post*, quoted in Elkin, *Royal Philharmonic*, 41–2.   [52] 48.2/1 (16 Mar. 1817).

without those strong players whose function had traditionally been to
act as centres of impetus. Yet, under the new system, any attempt to
centralize direction was vulnerable to inertia, or outright challenge,
from established players. If recruitment, training, and control all demanded appraisal, whatever the precise dynamics of orchestral performance at this stage in the Philharmonic's development, there can
be no doubt that the directors were now forced to seek a conductor
as keenly as their predecessors had sought a violinist leader. Most critics who debated such an appointment were limited, or merely preju-
diced, in their perceptions of the requirements for this new sort of job.
We have already noted that Davison wanted Sterndale Bennett, a
pianist; and W. H. Glover of the *Morning Post*, who apparently played
the violin, opined that 'if we are to have a *chef*, he must at all events
be a violinist and not a pianist'. Some of the directors were ahead of
their contemporaries in that they were at least aware that a conductor
required a peculiarly new combination of skills, and they soon grew
to accept that he must also be allowed wide-ranging authority. Although in retrospect Costa appears to have been the only qualified
candidate, he did not appear so at the time. In 1846, as the *Dictionary
of National Biography* remarks, he 'astonished everyone by his unexpected
ability in the rendering of classical compositions', and became the 'first
master of the art who had appeared in England'. His Philharmonic
appointment was a precondition for its survival, and a major step in
the history of London's concert life.

Costa's unique contribution was to bring a discipline which he had
already established in the opera-house into the concert-room, but it
could not be done overnight. Far from dismissing an 'ineffective third'
of the players, he faced the first season with few strategic changes in
personnel. Considerations of humanity, cost, and expediency all played
their part, for the directors could not have afforded, in every sense, too
great an upheaval. There was, in any case, a shortage of good London
players in relation to the demand for their services, most particularly
of wind instruments. Easily exposed by the prominence of their contributions to the music, peculiarly liable to deterioration in technique
as old (or middle) age affected teeth and lip, such men lived hazardous
lives, but were still protected by lack of competition in a country
without institutional provision for training in their skills.[53] First moves
were therefore cautious and diplomatic. The orchestra's scales of payment were rationalized; rank-and-file engagements first offered at £13
and £11, which several players declined. Dragonetti was asked to play
for £32 but never appeared again, dying in April 1846. Eventually fees

---

[53] On the shortage of wind-players, and its eventual eradication by Kneller Hall and,
belatedly, the Royal College of Music, see Ehrlich, *Music Profession*, 96–8 and 111–13.

for principals were agreed at £20; and for the rest £15 and £13. Both Lindley and Cooke, the unnamed leader, were paid £30.[54] A more radical departure, clearly vital to Costa, for it was discussed at his first visit to a directors' meeting, was the orchestra's 'disposition', meaning location rather than temper.[55] The new arrangement (see Pl. 10) was sufficiently unusual and effective to excite unprecedented comment: hitherto the critics appeared not to have considered the acoustical effects of positioning, and did not even tell readers whether players sat or stood. Now they rejoiced that double basses were 'no longer in front to stifle the violin melodies'. The 'perpendicular rise' had been abandoned, with its 'drums and trombones near the roof to drown the strings'.[56] There were 15 first and 14 second violins; 10 violas; 9 cellos; 9 double basses; 2 flutes, oboes, clarinets, bassoons, and trumpets; 4 horns; 3 trombones; an ophicleide (keyed serpent); and a drummer. The sound was evidently warmer, more homogeneous and controlled than ever before. A curious relic of the past was the placing of principal cello and double bass, alone and prominent, just by the conductor, and far from their sections. Was it still considered functional, as in past continuo work, or a necessary recognition of the Society's two most honoured instrumentalists? Lindley was nearing the end of his career, and the great bass, though absent, departed in appropriately quixotic style. At the third concert on 20 April 'a little man with a glass in his eye' called out for the 'Dead March' in *Saul* in his memory. The necessary parts were not at hand, but it was promised next time.[57]

Critical reaction to Costa's first season was highly favourable. Chorley, who had opposed his appointment, said of the opening concert, which featured the *Eroica Symphony*: 'we have heard no Philharmonic performance to compare', and discerned a 'continental style of finish' approaching 'Mendelssohn at Leipsic and Habeneck at Paris'.[58] The second concert was attended by Victoria, Albert, the Duchess of Kent, and thirty-five representatives of the *haut ton*. The *Pastoral Symphony* 'excited the auditory beyond measure'; but there was 'no stoppage by the Queen's command' after the *Magic Flute* Overture, and even *Oberon* was not repeated, 'to avoid the Queen fatigue'.[59] Pent-up enthusiasm had to be unleashed on the next occasion with an unprecedented three encores: the scherzo of a Spohr symphony, Beethoven's *Fidelio* Overture, and the Allegretto of the Eighth Symphony. The fourth concert was an extraordinary demonstration of stamina and high purpose. Beginning with Mozart's fortieth Symphony, a Rossini vocal quintet, and

[54] Offers of engagement and refusals are in 48.2/3 (28 Dec. 1845, 18 Jan. 1846). List of 'candidates for orchestra' at end of this file. Some fees are listed in the 1846 season accounts: 48.9/2.   [55] 48.2/3 (6 Nov. 1845).

[56] *ILN* (21 Mar. 1846).   [57] *Connoisseur* (1 May 1846).

[58] *Athenaeum* (21 Mar. 1846).   [59] *ILN* (4 Apr. 1846).

9. Michael Costa in 1840 (*lithograph after François Bouchot (1800–42)*)

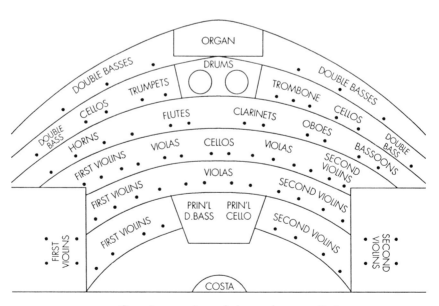

10. Costa's reseating of the orchestra, 1846

Piatti caprice (played by the great cellist), it proceeded, via Beethoven's Choral Fantasy and an interval, to the *Missa Solemnis*. For musicians who cherished the Ninth Symphony without having yet achieved a satisfactory performance, such homage was ambitious, if not foolhardy. As a London newspaper reported, the Mass had never been heard complete in England, and was regarded as 'incomprehensible', but interest had just been reawakened by its revival at a festival in Bonn, stimulating Costa to action. 'We know of no one more capable of a comprehensive appreciation of an author's score or more able to convey its meanings to the performers,' said the *Musical Times*; 'our London friends hail the news with joy' shared by 'country friends . . . in these railroad times, whereby the facility of being present is so much increased'.[60] At the 'trial' singers and instrumentalists rose to their feet at Costa's entrance and cheered him for several minutes, then he 'faced his troops instead of fronting the audience' and the great work was 'executed at sight'.[61] For the concert 'hundreds were disappointed in gaining admission' and a mixed critical response might be summarized thus: a 'band far better than at Bonn', and choir with 'not enough voices' performed 'the most sublime musical work in existence' to the bewilderment of 'a pensive public'.[62]

The rest of the season continued triumphantly with few disappointments. When Bennett played his Caprice, Op. 22 it was noticed that 'he marks nothing, there is no declamation'.[63] When the Overture to Charles Lucas's opera *The Regicide* was given an airing it was deemed suitable only for the theatre and inadequate for 'an audience accustomed to Beethoven and Weber'. But every night the room was 'crowded to excess', there were frequent encores, and outbursts of enthusiasm, such as when the magnificent Marie Pleyel, De Quincey's 'celestial pianist', stormed through Weber's *Konzertstück* and 'all cheered lustily'. Among the pages of commendation perhaps the most significant remark is that concerto players were 'in seventh heaven' because Costa had 'established that a real *piano* was to be obtained from an English band'.[64] Even Davison's *Musical World* was forced to admit that 'Costa has decidedly benefited the Society in a profitable as well as an honourable sense', while insisting that Sterndale Bennett should have been appointed, and that the maestro's success was attributable solely to a 'despotic

---

[60] *MT* (Mar. 1846).   [61] *ILN* (14 Mar. 1846).

[62] *Spectator* (9 May 1846); *ILN* (9 May 1846); *MT* (June 1846).

[63] *Connoisseur* (1 May 1846). An illuminating, and probably accurate account. Bennett was no crowd-pleaser, and now began to settle into routine teaching, declining creativity, and loss of nerve. See N. Temperley's sympathetic, but ultimately devastating, entry in the *New Grove*, ii. 499–504.

[64] *ILN* (4 July 1846). Other quotations in this paragraph are taken from the same source, at various dates during the season, but they are broadly representative of critical opinion elsewhere.

sway not enjoyed by his predecessors'.[65] Next year there was another attempt at Beethoven's Ninth Symphony. Berlioz described it as 'murder', but a realistic reporter, acknowledging 'mishaps' among the brass, concluded that no one could have achieved so much with a single rehearsal.[66] A more splendid occasion was the concert on 26 April 1847, when Costa was joined by Mendelssohn to conduct his *Scotch Symphony* and *Midsummer Night's Dream* music; and play Beethoven's Fourth Concerto, 'entirely from memory', in a manner which acted as a touchstone for all subsequent performances, as Chorley later recalled. Present were 'The Royal amateurs', the Duchess of Kent, and 'numerous attendance of rank and fashion'. Restricted seating prevented anything like an adequate supply of tickets, so many people lost a last chance of hearing their idol.

[65] *MW* (23 May and 4 July 1846).
[66] Ganz, *Berlioz in London*, 121; *ILN* (Apr. 1847).

5

Conductors

There is a fine position waiting for me here now that poor Mendelssohn is dead. Everybody keeps telling me so from morning till night.

> (Berlioz, 14 Jan. 1848, quoted in *H. Berlioz: A. Selection from his Letters*, ed. H. Searle (New York, 1973), 101)

confronted by the stupidly affable, in short, English countenance of Mr Anderson, (I) agreed to the proposition.

> (Wagner, *My Life*, trans. A. Gray (1983), 513)

It is truly ludicrous to observe how a professedly conservative society can throw itself into the arms of a desperate musical democrat like Herr Wagner.

> (*Morning Post*, 1854, quoted in Newman, *Life of Wagner*, ii. 475)

COSTA's innovations were fortunate in their timing because they were assisted by revolutions in the disparate but equally volatile worlds of London opera and continental politics. The theatrical revolt, which had been threatening to break out for several years, reached a suitably flamboyant climax in 1846. The manager of Her Majesty's Theatre, Benjamin Lumley, claimed in an open letter that he had offered Costa an increased fee to retain his exclusive services, and that it was impossible for a conductor to serve two masters. Costa responded with an uncompromising declaration of independence which reinforced his authority. Transferring to the rival establishment at Covent Garden, he took most of the best players and singers with him, and there rapidly established standards of performance which were widely regarded as 'unapproached in any other opera house in Europe'. His orchestra in particular was described by those best placed to judge as 'the finest ever assembled within the walls of any lyric theatre'.[1]

---

[1] Rosenthal, *Two Centuries of Opera*, 75, summarizing the opinions of Spohr, Mendelssohn, and Verdi; cf. J. Budden, *The Operas of Verdi*, i. *From Oberto to Rigoletto* (1973), 316–18.

Revolutions, Benefits, and Discontents

The Philharmonic Society drew immediate benefits from this move. In addition to acquiring the best available conductor, it secured privileged access to most of the resources at his command. Clashes in the time-tables of singers and instrumentalists, which were becoming more difficult to avoid as musical events increased in London, could now be handled by the individual best placed to adjudicate such arrangements. Financial costs were kept to a minimum, both as a direct result of his negotiating strength in arranging fees and, more subtly, through 'external economies' accruing to the Society. Many improvements in its concerts resulted from work done, and paid for, in the opera-house. Prevailing standards should not be exaggerated. The Philharmonic orchestra never became identical to the opera's unique band, and its lesser status was commonly acknowledged. Nor, of course, were programmes identical. But there were considerable overlaps in personnel, and sometimes in repertoire. Most significant, and commented upon by such visitors as Berlioz and Wagner, was the fact that almost every concert performance shared a discipline which was reinforced by the conductor's looming presence at both institutions. Another large, if temporary, advantage to the Society was its revived access to great singers, including several who were closely associated with the most popular and reputable composers of the age. Renewed splendours were on display in 1848 when almost every Philharmonic concert featured such stars as the new contralto Marietta Alboni, Rossini's 'elephant that swallowed a nightingale'; Fanny Persiani, Donizetti's original Lucia; Giulia Grisi, his first Norina for *Don Pasquale*; and the great dramatic artist Pauline Viardot, sister of Malibran.

   Small wonder that the directors expressed unanimous gratitude to Costa for gathering so rich a harvest, though its luxuriance owed at least as much to the temporary climate of continental politics, for which even his detractors did not hold him responsible, as to his personal *coup d'état*.[2] 1848 was the great 'year of revolution' throughout Europe, bringing an influx of refugee musicians to London, reminiscent of the heady Napoleonic days when the Philharmonic had been born. Charles Hallé wrote to his parents about 'Thalberg, Chopin, Kalkbrenner, Pixis, Osborne, Prudent, Pillet, and a lot of other pianists besides myself who have all, through necessity, been driven to England, and we shall probably end by devouring one another'.[3] In the city of refuge political revolution took the form of a 'Monster Meeting' and presentation

---

[2] 48.2/4 (13 Feb. 1848).
[3] C. Hallé, *Life and Letters*, ed. C. E. Hallé and M. Hallé (1896), 27 Apr. 1848.

of the Peoples' Charter, a key event in radical history. It was neatly, though not deliberately, timed to coincide with the Society's third concert on 10 April. 'In a few hours', wrote Berlioz that morning, 'perhaps England will be convulsed like the rest of Europe, and even this asylum will no longer be left me.' At 8 that evening, just when, in another part of London, the orchestra was beginning a Haydn symphony, he added a postscript: 'the Chartists are muffs at revolution. Everything passed off well.' Meanwhile at the Society's concert an excited audience sang the national anthem 'amidst loyal cheering'.[4]

Throughout that season singers of the first rank were engaged at fees ranging from 5 to 15 guineas, which bore no relation to what they could command elsewhere and in normal times. The Society's total expenditure was kept below £2,000, some £300 less than its income for the year, and another £250 was added to capital. The following season glittered with similar brightness and profit. There was the tenor Mario, incomparable in masculine sweetness of tone and prodigious earning-power, singing arias by Mercadante and Mozart's 'Il mio tesoro'. Sims Reeves was beginning his career, and Fanny Tacchinardi-Persiani ending hers: the clamour at her Covent Garden farewell was so great as to require three extra performances. The Philharmonic audience heard her in excerpts from the *Barber of Seville* (including 'Una voce poco fa', an aria which figures large in the Society's history) and from Bellini's *La Sonnambula*; Pischeck also returned to sing on that memorable evening. Concert music was not neglected, although there were difficulties in finding acceptable new material. Spohr's *Historical Symphony* was tried again, with no more success than at its first appearance, one listener declaring the work 'dull, pedantic, pretentious'.[5] The same critic also reported 'complete failure' from an unlikely source. Mendelssohn's music for Racine's *Athalie*, which occupied the greater part of two consecutive concerts, was 'heard with an apathy rarely witnessed at a Philharmonic concert'.[6] A more equivocal revival was the Society's revered but troublesome legacy, Beethoven's Ninth Symphony. It 'always draws a crowd', ran a typical complaint, but without an adequate chorus or sufficient time for rehearsal this masterpiece could 'never be heard to advantage at the Philharmonic'. In such circumstances adequate performance was deemed 'practically impossible . . . only Costa's authority could achieve so much'. He did wonders 'with the materials at his command . . . and scanty preparation'.[7]

Such was common agreement, about an improved reading of 'the most wonderful specimen of Beethoven's genius', and more generally about concerts under the new regime. But satisfaction brought no

[4] Berlioz, quoted in Ganz, *Berlioz in London*, 59. Concert notice in *ILN* (15 Apr. 1848).
[5] *ILN* (19 May 1849).   [6] *ILN* (17 and 31 Mar. 1849).
[7] *MW* (16 June 1849); *ILN* (16 June 1849).

peace to the Society, for the pretender to the throne was not disposed
to collaborate, and his allies were happy to keep wounds open. They
were rewarded by a famous squabble, celebrated for years even in
places which seldom showed much concern for music. Its trivial be-
ginnings later found apt expression in *Punch*:

> Sterndale Bennett was indignant with Costa
> For not playing Bennett's composition faster

The aggrieved composer did not actually hear his Overture Parisina
being played too slowly in rehearsal. Mere report was sufficient for
him to write to Lucas who, instead of having a tactful word with the
conductor, showed him a note presumably not intended for his eyes.
Costa, already irritated at not having time to study an unfamiliar score
(which, it will be remembered, had been one of his stipulations before
taking over), misunderstood and took umbrage at the phrase 'you have
often done it'. He stormed out and left Lucas to 'do it again', that is
to conduct the piece. Failing to get support from the board, Bennett
resigned his directorship. When he was re-elected in 1851 Costa in
turn offered to leave, but agreed to stay on condition that he could
refuse to conduct any piece, which was taken to mean any composition by Bennett. And there the matter festered for a few years despite
the board's appeal to 'bury everything in oblivion', and its assurance
of 'every endeavour to arrange amiably between you and Costa . . .
who will meet you on friendly terms'.[8]

Meanwhile most of the concerts continued to please most of the subscribers. Weakness among the wind instruments was still occasionally
noted, and any improvement, such as Nicholson's appearance as first
oboe, marked out for celebration.[9] There were brief periods, or special
occasions, when the orchestra was strengthened by individual players
of particular distinction. Between 1851 and 1853, for example, the most
celebrated cellist and double-bass player of the age sometimes played,
not just as visiting soloists, but in the band. Alfredo Piatti, whose
playing in a Philharmonic concert under Mendelssohn had inspired the
composer to begin work on a cello concerto; and Giovanni Bottesini,
who inherited Dragonetti's crown, must have together provided a
superb foundation to the sound whenever they led their respective sections.[10] One such occasion was a programme shared with Berlioz on
30 May 1853 which exemplified the strengths and weaknesses of 'Costa's
Philharmonic' (Pl. 12). It was a term in regular use by opponents of
Costa, who claimed that he had become dictator, a 'Director of dir-

---

[8] 48.6/3 (10 Mar. 1851). *MW* continued to reopen old wounds for more than another
decade. See e.g. letters from 'An English Musician' and 'A Lover of Truth': *MW* (10 and
17 May 1862).   [9] *MW* (9 Mar. 1850).
[10] See instrumentalists' fees for 1851 and 1852: 48.9/2.

ectors'. In fact he was neither obsessive, absolute, nor exclusive. As a working musician he was usually too busy to attend meetings, which limited his influence upon policy, including the selection of artists and repertoire. Even his dedicated enemy Davison admitted, on one unguarded occasion, that Costa 'had no authority to make the programmes or engage the band'.[11]

Nor could he loosen purse-strings, in so far as he had any desire to do so. Even for the special Berlioz concert there was no question of providing sufficient rehearsals to prepare the *Symphonie fantastique*, as the composer first proposed. The suggestion was dismissed as '*impracticable*' and there was a request for 'other pieces which may be performed with less difficulty'. It was 'absolument impossible' to have more than the single rehearsal which was 'l'usage invariable de la Société' because in London 'a special rehearsal would be an enormous expense'. The symphony was abandoned with regret, but Berlioz was assured that 'des morceaux' would be 'better executed' and 'better understood'. In this manner tight budgeting robbed London of a seminal work for a generation.[12] On the other hand, Costa was prepared to share his platform with a worthy colleague, inviting formidable and immediate comparison, despite the two men's cordial disregard for each other's music. His original intention had been simply to play the Carnaval Romain Overture, but when it was heard that Berlioz would be in London negotiations began for something more elaborate, with his immediate approval. He was 'most happy to give up the "baton" to M. Hector Berlioz not only for one or two of his pieces ... but for so many as he likes.'[13] Similarly at Covent Garden, after originally opposing the mounting of *Benvenuto Cellini*, he was acknowledged to be 'friendly and courteous', encouraging the singers to give 'their utmost co-operation'.[14] Final proof of Costa's disinterested professionalism is that he had trained an orchestra capable, on that May evening, of playing in a manner 'so admirable as to draw from the composer expressions of unbounded surprise'.[15] It was a prodigious achievement to sustain an hour and a half of music which, in content and idiom, was unfamiliar to most of the audience—it could not be studied at the piano—and *terra incognita* for many of the players. There was also a

[11] *MW* (20 Mar. 1852). In his unpublished 1937 sketch of a history, which is wholly unsympathetic to Costa's achievement, these absences from committee meetings are described (fo. 22) by H. C. Colles as a mark of 'autocracy': 48.15/8.

[12] Letters to Berlioz: asking for 'Carnaval Romain' parts, 48.6/3 (21 Feb. 1853); rejecting the *Fantastic Symphony*, 48.6/3 (9 May 1853). Berlioz's letter to Hogarth, setting out alternative programmes, appears in Ganz, *Berlioz in London*, 161–2. Further correspondence is in 48.2/4 (7 and 14 May 1853), ending with payment of 10 guineas on 19 June. The Symphony got its first London performance in July 1881, and Philharmonic début in May 1895.   [13] 48.13/7 (24 Apr. 1853).

[14] Rosenthal, *Two Centuries of Opera*, 102.   [15] Ganz, *Berlioz in London*, 162.

last-minute hazard in that Sainton had to replace the indisposed and experienced Henry Hill as solo viola in *Harold*. After that triumph the band needed to summon enough energy and composure to struggle through Beethoven's Fifth Symphony and the rest of a very long evening.

Thrift

Thrift, as Samuel Smiles would soon proclaim in an essential, best-selling, Victorian book, was becoming firmly embedded in society as a cardinal virtue. Its application to Philharmonic economics now took two predominant forms, one temporarily successful, the other potentially disastrous. The most practical way of exercising thrift in the allocation of scarce resources was demonstrated at Costa's rehearsals. His imposition of what another pundit of the age extolled as 'the discipline of the clock', was not in itself new.[16] Time for rehearsals had always been constrained by insufficient cash, and we have already noted earlier procedures for using it well. But as conducted by such men as Potter they had generally been easygoing and relaxed exercises, in amiable company and without much explication or admonition. In 1851 Costa instituted the most fundamental of reforms by insisting that rehearsals be conducted in private. This exclusion of members, associates, and directors' friends, who had been accustomed to dropping in and providing an audience, was immediately recognized as 'a stringent edict'. Under the old system it had become increasingly difficult for anyone to insist upon changes when 'fifty out of seventy' of the players might have pupils in the audience: 'no conductor could have ventured to enforce, and no English orchestra would have endured' correction.[17] Recalling Mr Thomas Gladstone's embarrassment at his club, the reader will appreciate the *Athenaeum*'s summing up of the new situation: 'A pleasant musical lounge is thereby destroyed', but 'the gain to Art is unquestionable' because, 'as we heard Mendelssohn insist a hundred times . . . no profitable or thoroughly sufficient and searching rehearsal' was possible when the room was crowded with visitors.[18]

If thrift was efficacious in the organization of rehearsals, its application to the selection of soloists was more suspect. Why, dissenters complained, were the finest artists so frequently overlooked, even when close at hand? A notorious case was Charles Hallé, who had settled in England and was acclaimed as a pianist, yet had to wait until 1852 for a Philharmonic appearance. Similarly Thalberg, Bottesini, Joachim, and other regular visitors of distinction were frequently to be heard elsewhere, at events ranging from Ella's austere chamber music gatherings

---

[16] A. Ure, *The Philosophy of Manufactures* (1833).
[17] *MW* (15 Mar. 1851); *Athenaeum* (13 Jan. 1855).   [18] *Athenaeum* (25 Jan. 1851).

to Jullien's extravagant *concerts monstres*, yet remained uninvited, or not reinvited, by the Society. Meanwhile worthy but unexciting instrumentalists were given excessive exposure. In 1850, for example, it was noticed that the violinists Blagrove and Sainton each made three Philharmonic appearances, when the far more celebrated Molique and Ernst were in town.[19] Characteristically, the *Musical World* worked up such discontents into a frenzy of indictment, printing a long 'catalogue of eminent pianists who have not played at the Philharmonic Society'. Its first list consisted of twenty-six, and a second of thirty-eight, names, including some who *had* in fact played and some who were dead, and ranging from provincial nonentities to Chopin and Marie Pleyel: 'six years younger, six times a better pianist than before (which was impossible since she was then better than the best) and sixty times more disdainfully beautiful'.[20] In their place subscribers had to make do with such players as Charles K. Salaman, whose attempt at the familiar Beethoven Third Piano Concerto was dismissed by more than one critic as 'above his capacity', his 'accent too flippant and too loose'.[21] And during the same season Lindsay Sloper, who would eventually make an English reputation as author of an elementary piano tutor, was allotted Mozart's C minor Concerto.

Another complaint was that rare appearances by leading performers could be spoiled by inappropriate choice of music. Thus Thalberg in 1850, after an absence of eight years, embarked upon Mozart's D minor Concerto, no vehicle for a virtuoso, before plunging into his own variations on themes from *L'elisir d'amore*. Nevertheless his drawing-power was powerfully demonstrated, with more than one hundred extra tickets sold and many even failing to find standing space, when more than half the audience left after he, but not the concert, had finished.[22] With similar ignorance or disregard of 'horses for courses' Heinrich Wilhelm Ernst, whose musicianship was widely respected, and whom Joachim would later describe as 'the greatest violinist I ever heard', was engaged to play only his own show-pieces at Philharmonic concerts in 1849 and 1850. On the second occasion he performed *Fantasy on Halévy's 'Ludovic'*, perhaps because the opera composer was in the audience. In the same concert Julius Benedict's trumpery *Konzertstück* for piano had no such excuse. 'It would appear', declared a thoroughly disgruntled spectator, 'that, as regards pianoforte concertos, nothing new can be created.'[23] Deficiencies in both soloists

[19] *MW* (11 May 1850).

[20] *MW*: 'Pleyel' (8 May 1852); 'catalogue' (23 Apr. and 7 May 1853). Marie Moke was taught by Moscheles and Kalkbrenner, briefly engaged to Berlioz, but married Camille Pleyel, the piano-maker, and was widely acclaimed by the 1840s as 'the greatest pianist of Europe'. Chopin dedicated Nocturnes and Liszt the superb *Norma* Fantasy to her.

[21] *MW* and *ILN* (both 23 Mar. 1850).   [22] *MW* (25 May 1850).

[23] *ILN* (22 June 1850).

11. Charles Hallé awaits the call, 1851 (*see p. 82*)

and repertoire were thus widely noticed and inextricably linked, without agreement as to their cause. Was there a real scarcity of good 'new'
concertos? Accustomed to the late twentieth-century canon, we may be
surprised by the Victorians' neglect of many works in this genre which
were available; by Bach and Mozart, for example. But a substantial
body of mid-nineteenth-century taste, in stark contrast to our own,
eagerly desired regular new additions to the repertoire. It sought
worthy successors to Mendelssohn, and suspected that the Philharmonic directors were merely incapable of seeking them out. Some critics
attributed the famine to 'antique bigotry still rampant', and a 'close
borough system'. Indeed, that cap of conjecture fitted close enough
for 'a subscriber and lover of fair play' to write in defence of Lucy
Anderson, denying that she had undue influence upon the directors.[24]

Yet lacklustre engagements probably stemmed as much, at this stage,
from thrift as from parochialism or conspiracy. When Marie Pleyel was
offered 5 guineas on 18 June 1852, which she refused on the 26th, there
appears to have been no subsequent attempt to negotiate.[25] Such crass

---

[24] *MW* (20 Mar. 1852 and 23 Apr. 1853).   [25] 48.2/4 (18 and 26 June 1852).

disregard for so great an artist may have been an oversight, or even a calculated insult, but it also suggests that the directors were still living in the past. They were not yet prepared to come to terms with the rising market price of unique talent, despite its demonstrable ability to earn a higher fee, as in the case of Thalberg, by attracting a capacity audience. If in this respect they were not capable of a form of leadership which would have benefited the Society's image and bank balance, they were only reflecting conventional attitudes. The role of instrumentalists, as distinct from the notoriously greedy opera-singers, was still not clearly articulated in the market-place. Poised uneasily between salon and concert platform, between a world of patrons obsessed with the class of their fellow auditors and one of ticket-buyers who might simply want to hear good music-making, the new professional soloists were also surrounded by modest practitioners—particularly pianists—who offered a virtually free and allegedly comparable service. The virtuoso's claims upon a concert promoter's budget remained uncertain, particularly when appraised by Anderson and his spouse at court. In their eyes, no doubt, both Mrs Anderson and Marie Pleyel were on a par: pianists, piano-teachers, and suppliants. Nor was there yet a network of agents to establish a hierarchy of performers, on a clearly delineated ladder of talent, with specific repertoire and appropriately negotiated fees. Finally, since the Philharmonic was still not continuously engaged in the business of attracting the larger audience, its directors were presumably disinclined to give close scrutiny to an instrumentalist's drawing-power.

Such attitudes towards artists and repertoire were a strait-jacket for the Society, but they could be sustained without too much damage while the potentially growing market outside was ignored, and so long as Costa remained in place within. After the exceptional operatic attractions of the 1848 and 1849 seasons, which could not be cheaply repeated once revolution had subsided, only his skills and enterprise remained to retain the loyalty of subscribers. If the 1853 Berlioz evening represents, paradoxically, a peak of Costa's achievement, a concert on 3 May 1852 was more typical of his work, in its orthodoxy, economy, and breadth of appeal.[26] The famous bass Karl Formes came from the opera-house with one of Sarastro's arias and an excerpt from Weber's *Euryanthe*. The English soprano Louisa Pyne, a pupil of Sir George Smart, who sang a Weber *scena* and an air and variations by Auber, was beginning a successful career. Other soloists were cheap but acceptable, their performance of Spohr's Double Quartet scoring triple points by pleasing the *amour propre* of several players, by avoiding rehearsal costs in time-honoured fashion, and finally by providing a

---

[26] Fees and costs for the 1852 season: 48.9/2.

sufficient body of sound to deter criticism of chamber music at the Philharmonic, which had long been aired and would soon triumph. Even Macfarren was given an airing, with his *Don Quixote* Overture, earning praise from the patriots for 'striving zealously to render justice' to one of their idols.[27] But the evening's greatest attractions were simply the best performances available in London of Beethoven's Fourth and Mendelssohn's *Italian* Symphonies. Neither had yet become hackneyed experiences, even for the keenest of concert-goers. Indeed, the latter work had been curiously neglected since its commission. Now 'dusted off by Costa', it received the 'best performance yet' and had become an annual 'universal favourite' with an audience which included many whose familiarity was nurtured by Ewer's recent publication of an arrangement for piano duet.[28] This was essentially a 'conductor's concert', half a century before such events became common. Such dependence upon one man was cheap, convenient, and an Achilles' heel.

In November 1854 Costa tendered his resignation, on grounds of 'health and other circumstances' and refused the directors' appeals to reconsider.[29] The first excuse was unconvincing, for he continued to undertake heavier tasks, including the composition and performance of an oratorio at the Birmingham festival. Among 'other circumstances' it is just possible that he was affected, as Elkin suggests, by the losses on recent seasons, but these were too small to cause much alarm. Far more irksome was the continuing threat to the quality of his orchestra which stemmed, in part, from parsimony but also from the shifting politics of the co-operative: disgruntled players could become directors and vent their resentments. Enfeebling economies were commented upon during his final season. Why, for example, were Bottesini, Piatti, and the excellent violinist Willy missing, and why was there no 'octave flute' (piccolo)?[30] Only the first of these omissions could be explained by absence from the country; Bottesini was visiting America. Other strong instrumentalists had simply not been offered high-enough fees, while some feeble players were being retained to keep the peace.[31] Finally, constant rancour from the press may at last have had some effect on a seemingly thick skin. In 1853 the excuse for an effective campaign was disagreement about a novice pianist's choice of concerto. Arabella Goddard, who later became famous, was then at the beginning of her career: a stage when it is customary to accept practically any terms of engagement. But Davison took more than a passing interest, devoting more space and acclaim than even Marie Pleyel could inspire. Eventually, as *Punch* nudged and winked, her G was changed

[27] *MW* (8 May 1852).   [28] Ibid.   [29] 48.2/4 (16 and 26 Nov. 1854).
[30] *MW* (11 Mar. 1854).   [31] Elkin, *Royal Philharmonic*, 48–9; *MW* (27 Jan. 1855).

to D, but meanwhile she was pronounced 'the best pianist in England, if not in Europe'. When, therefore, the Philharmonic gave her a choice of concertos by Beethoven, Mendelssohn, or Weber, she insisted upon Bennett in C minor, and was refused, although Costa did not stand in its way if Bennett was prepared to conduct; a concession acknowledged even by Davison. The directors, however, insisted upon something from the 'great masters'. Goddard persisted; a Mozart wind serenade replaced the piano concerto; and the hunt was up. 'Our greatest English classical composer', championed by a brave defenceless girl, had again been martyred. Compromise was forgotten and the *Musical World* returned to its usual style with a mock official notice: 'NB: No music can be performed which is not approved of by Mr Costa. Although Mr Sterndale Bennett is a Director, his concerto cannot be played until further orders. Signed the seven Directors. Viva Costa.' The cause was taken up by Mr Punch whose scansion was quite overcome by the incident:

> Likewise excluding the young and gifted Miss Goddard
> Whom with Admiration all the Critical Squad heard:
> All to be Deplored, and without more Amalgamation
> The Philharmonic will Tarnish its Hitherto Deservedly High
> Reputation.[32]

Costa departed, never to return, and the board, failing to take care of its Achilles' heel, proceeded to shoot itself in the foot.

A Damned Soul in Hell

The appointment of Costa's successor suggests diverse interpretations. Was it a courageous initiative, seeking much-needed stimulus from a genius of the avant-garde, in a manner appropriate to a society which had started life with Beethoven? Or was it a shambling and botched undertaking, reminiscent of the Bishop episode: naïve, well-meaning, and disastrous? Certainly there are resemblances to that earlier fiasco—except that an eminent foreigner was always in mind—beginning with failure to secure preferred candidates, and ending with financial losses and a volte-face. But from the outset accounts and interpretations, by contemporaries and later commentators, are thoroughly confused. There are misunderstandings about the order of selection, with Ernest Newman,

---

[32] Doggerel from *Punch*, repr. in Elkin, *Royal Philharmonic*, 46. Correspondence between the directors and Arabella Goddard: 48.2/4 (10 and 17 Apr. 1853); 48.6/3 (11 Apr. 1853); and 48.13/13 (4 and 11 Apr. 1853). For Davison's campaign of vilification see, *inter alia*, *MW* (16 and 30 Apr. 1853, and 27 Jan. 1855). Charles Reid's version of the story unaccountably attributes the disputed concerto to Macfarren, instead of Bennett! Reid, *Music Monster*, 49.

for example, claiming that Lindpaintner (in Stuttgart) was the directors' first choice.[33] There is also radically conflicting testimony about the events of the ensuing season. According to the archive it was Spohr, long established as Generalmusikdirektor at Kassel, who was first to be asked, in November 1854, and refused a month later.[34] There followed a more radical initiative; an approach to Berlioz, with stipulations for an exclusive contract which he would have liked to accept, but eventually had to refuse.[35] Meanwhile a letter was sent to 'Mons. Richard Wagner, artiste à Zurich' asking if he was interested and free between March and June. At this stage, since offers were sent on the same day, it seems likely that the directors were hoping to get both men to share the season.[36] Wagner named two conditions of acceptance. First, a subordinate must be appointed to direct vocal and concerted instrumental items, leaving Wagner the 'grandes pièces d'orchestre et d'ensemble vocale'. Secondly, he insisted upon as many rehearsals as might be necessary.[37] Anderson was asked to set out for Zurich and, if he failed, go on to Liszt and then, if necessary, Lachner. He was empowered to offer a salary up to 200 guineas, approximately double Costa's fee, but specifically not to concede either of Wagner's provisos.[38] And so it was agreed: apart from allowing two rehearsals for Beethoven's Ninth Symphony, there was never any question of Anderson's accepting Wagner's preconditions. Later accusations that he had been 'lured by unkept promises of ample rehearsal time and a deputy to conduct minor works' therefore lack substance.[39] Even if allowance be made for linguistic or diplomatic misunderstandings between the two men in Zurich, any promise of unlimited rehearsals would have been so much at variance with Philharmonic budgeting and procedures as to be inconceivable. Similarly tales of Sainton's role in the undertaking—according to Wagner, he 'swore blind that he had seen me conduct in Dresden' and thus persuaded the directors—are, as with so much else in *Mein Leben*, entertaining myths which have been written into the record.[40]

[33] Newman, *Life of Richard Wagner*, ii. 449.

[34] 48.2/4 (26 Nov. and 17 Dec. 1854).

[35] 48.2/4 (24 and 31 Dec. 1854; 7 Jan. 1855). 48.6/3 (24 Dec. 1854; 1 Jan. 1855). Ganz discusses Berlioz's reasons for refusing and is anxious to establish, correctly, that the offer was made, tilting at Wagnerians who objected to '*lèse-majesté*' to The Master': *Berlioz in London*, 182. Such controversy about the incident is an indication of how much kudos was attached to the appointment.   [36] 48.2/4 (24 Dec. 1854); 48.6/3 (24 Dec. 1854).

[37] 48.2/4 (7 Jan. 1855).

[38] 48.2/4 (7 and 21 Jan. 1855). 48.6/3 (8 and 22 Jan. 1855).

[39] B. Millington (ed.), *The Wagner Companion* (1992), 100.

[40] Wagner, *My Life*, trans. A. Gray (1983), 515. Wagner's description of Anderson in Zurich, at the head of this chapter, is taken from the same source, 513. There is an accurate account of Sainton's role in Millington's *The Master Musicians: Wagner* (1984), 57–8.

Wagner spent four months in London in 1855, orchestrating *Die Walküre*, hoping for quick money and some future arrangements for opera performances; searching for a top hat to fit his enormous head; failing miserably to cope with local customs, in dress and appropriate etiquette. Surviving like 'a damned soul in Hell' as he read Dante and wrote to Liszt, he loathed the fog, philistinism, prolix concerts which sapped his energy, and exorbitant living costs which ate away his fee. Worst of tribulations was 'the worthlessness, insolence, venality and vulgarity of the local press'.[41] For him there could be no question of following the recommended civilities of calling to offer bribes, or at least obeisance, to such creatures. They may not all have been 'rogues and fools', as a recent biographer suggests, but they lost no time in exacting retribution.[42] It was Davison, of course, who led the pack, concentrating upon the master's vulnerable prose rather than his compositions or conducting. Two years earlier the Music Monster had referred, in contemptuous parentheses, to an '(uncle of the famous Joanna Wagner) representative of what is styled the "aesthetic" school in Germany'.[43] Now, with Sterndale Bennett approaching 40 and still passed over, it was time for a lampoon of Anderson's Zurich mission in quest of one who has 'little respect for any music but his own'. And there was an additional poisonous barb: 'Where Wagner is, Liszt is sure to come.'[44] English readers would understand that not only 'classical art' but morality, which mattered far more to many of them, were endangered. Chorley was less venomous and better informed, after hearing *Lohengrin* in Weimar and *Tannhäuser* in Dresden. But he too was 'astonished' by the appointment and regarded it as 'nothing short of a wholesale offence to the native and foreign conductors resident in England'.[45] Only the *Spectator* (probably Edward Holmes) had the grace to admit that 'of his music we share the general ignorance in England; but it is evident from Wagner's career—which seems not unlike that of Berlioz—that he is no ordinary man'.[46]

For most English listeners Wagner was neither yet an icon to be revered nor a monster to be caged. Critical response to his concerts, in so far as it can be separated from the hunger pangs of Bennett-deprivation, was reacting not so much to his choice of music as to its interpretation; and even here undisguised malice was less common than bewilderment. In fact, the chosen repertoire was conventional enough,

[41] Wagner, letter to Otto Wesendonck (5 Apr. 1855), in *Selected Letters*, trans. S. Spencer and B. Millington (1987).

[42] C. von Westernhagen, *Wagner: A Biography*, trans. M. Whittal (1978), 206–7.

[43] *MW* (2 Apr. 1853).

[44] *MW* (20 Jan. 1855). On Wagner's guilt by association with Liszt, see Newman, *Life of Richard Wagner*, ii. 465–6.   [45] *Athenaeum* (27 Jan. 1855).

[46] *Spectator* (27 Jan. 1855).

with no Liszt, and little Wagner; only a selection from *Lohengrin*, at the
directors' request, and the *Tannhäuser* Overture, which was repeated at
a royal command concert. To be sure, the latter indulgence may have
been engineered by Wagner's writing a personal note to Prince Albert;
and that initiative offended Philharmonic protocol sufficiently to prompt
a special meeting of the directors.[47] But the Queen invited him to her
box and pointedly applauded his 'wonderful composition'.[48] There was
special relish in this publicly expressed regal welcome to a proscribed
revolutionary: 'the German police might let me pass in peace now', he
wrote to his wife.[49] So much for protocol; what of the conducting?
There were unprecedented opportunities, apparently missed by the critics, to make immediate comparisons. Anyone attending Wagner's command concert on Monday 11 June, for example, could have heard
Berlioz, the other great articulator of modern conducting, preside at
Exeter Hall on the following Wednesday.[50] It was remarked that the
German proceeded 'without score'; but did this imply familiarity with
every note, bringing a rich harvest: 'eyes never diverted from watchful
observation of the performers', gestures 'well understood by the band',
'light and shade', a 'true and delicate piano' not heard for years, and
'bursts of applause from all parts of the room'?[51] Or was it just vain-
glory, implicitly inferior to Mendelssohn's celebrated feats of keyboard
memory, and conducive to 'so many quickenings and slackenings of
tempo we never heard before', the audience veiling its puzzlement with
polite applause?[52] Such were the widest contrasts of reporting on Wagner's
first concert. The more sober *Athenaeum* dourly registered slow tempos,
'fits and starts', and a room thinly attended. Later it railed against
'coarse and overstrained enthusiasm', 'discreditable scrambling through
well-known music', 'loose, careless . . . rude and slack' accompaniments
to Beethoven's Second Piano Concerto, and a Mozart Thirty-Ninth
Symphony 'worse than we ever heard it go'.[53] Yet by the end of the
season the *Spectator* concluded that 'notwithstanding the hostile criticism
. . . he has acquitted himself of his arduous and responsible duties to
the general satisfaction of the public' as was demonstrated by the
'cordial greeting he received from every part of the room'.[54]

Disagreement among critics is common enough, but few Philharmonic seasons have elicited such provocative conflicts of statement and
opinion. It is abundantly clear that Wagner was attempting to make
accustomed music sound different. Gone was the regular beat and

[47] 48.2/4 (8 June 1855).

[48] B. Coules, 'An Extract from Queen Victoria's Journal', in *Wagner* (the periodical of
the Wagner Society, ed. S. Spencer) (1976).

[49] Newman, *Life of Richard Wagner*, ii. 476.   [50] *Spectator* (17 Mar. 1855).

[51] The programme, which included Mozart's Symphony No. 40 and Beethoven's Fifth
Piano Concerto, is printed in full by Ganz, *Berlioz in London*, 187. Berlioz published his *Le
Chef d'orchestre: Théorie de son art* in the following year.   [52] *MW* (17 Mar. 1855).

[53] *Athenaeum* (17 Mar., 21 Apr., and 19 May 1855).   [54] *Spectator* (30 June 1855).

UNDER THE IMMEDIATE PATRONAGE OF

𝕳𝖊𝖗 𝕸𝖆𝖏𝖊𝖘𝖙𝖞,

HIS ROYAL HIGHNESS PRINCE ALBERT.
HER ROYAL HIGHNESS THE DUCHESS OF KENT.

PHILHARMONIC SOCIETY.

SIXTH CONCERT, MONDAY, MAY 30th, 1853.

PART I.

Selection from the Works of M. HECTOR BERLIOZ; performed under his direction ;—
HAROLD IN ITALY ; Symphony in Four Parts (with Viola principale M. SAINTON).
Part 1. Harold in the Mountains: Scenes of Melancholy, Happiness and Joy.
Part 2. March of Pilgrims, singing the Evening Hymn.
Part 3. Serenade of a Mountaineer of the Abruzzi to his Mistress.
Part 4. Souvenirs of the preceding Scenes. ; Orgie of Brigands.
THE REPOSE OF THE HOLY FAMILY. A Descriptive Air, sung by Signor GARDONI.
    From an Oratorio in the ancient style, entitled the "Flight into Egypt," the words and
    music by M. BERLIOZ.
Overture, "Le Carnaval Romain," being the Introduction to Act II of the Opera, "Benve-
    nuto Cellini."

PART II.

Sinfonia in C minor, No. 5	-	-	-	Beethoven.
Recit. ("Der Hölle selbst" } Herr PISCHEK (Faust)				Spohr.
Aria. {"Liebe ist die Zarte"}				
Concertino, Contrabasso, Signor BOTTESINI	-	-	Bottesini.
Aria, "Ange si pur," Signor GARDONI (La Favorite)	-	Donizetti.
Overture, "Ruler of the Spirits"	-	-	-	Weber.

Conductor, Mr COSTA.

To commence at Eight o'clock precisely.   The doors will be opened at Half-past Seven.

THE SEVENTH CONCERT WILL BE ON THE 13TH OF JUNE.

UNDER THE IMMEDIATE PATRONAGE OF

𝕳𝖊𝖗 𝕸𝖆𝖏𝖊𝖘𝖙𝖞,

HIS ROYAL HIGHNESS PRINCE ALBERT.
HER ROYAL HIGHNESS THE DUCHESS OF KENT.

PHILHARMONIC SOCIETY.

SECOND CONCERT, MONDAY, MARCH 26th, 1855.

PART I.

Overture, Der Frieschütz	-	-	Weber.
Aria, "O salutaris Hostia," Mrs LOCKEY	-	-	Cherubini.
Concerto, Violin, Mr BLAGROVE	-	-	Mendelssohn.
Selection from "Lohengrin": Introduction, instrumental ; Bridal Proces-			
sion'; Wedding Music and Epithalamium	-	-	Wagner.

PART II.

Choral Symphony, No. 9	-	-	-	Beethoven.

Conductor, HERR RICHARD WAGNER.

₊ To commence at Eight o'clock precisely.

THE THIRD CONCERT WILL TAKE PLACE ON MONDAY, APRIL 16TH.

12. Programmes,
    30 May 1853 and
    26 March 1855

comfortably fast jog trot which had been openly advocated for London, and presumably put into effect, by Mendelssohn. That style was
calculated to provide useful camouflage for mistakes, and generally
compensate for insufficient rehearsals. Similar reasons of expedience
will have served to reinforce genuine convictions among critics and
audiences that nothing in music, particularly away from the opera-
house, should be too inflected, expressive, or, above all, extreme:
'enthusiasm' was a distinctly pejorative word; 'chaste' an accolade. We
can be sure that Wagner had every intention of breaking with these
routines, for he later expounded their opposite in irrevocable print.[55]
How far his intended revolution was achieved with the Philharmonic
orchestra can only be guessed. Witnesses remarked that brakes were
applied to cantabile passages, points of significance were underlined by
dramatic ritardandos, and excitement frequently worked up by bursts
of speed. But how much of the new style could be assimilated by the
orchestra in a single rehearsal, even by London's quick and adaptable
readers, if they were now expected to break with every ingrained
habit? Verbal communication must have been difficult, with the conductor possessing only one phrase of English—'Once more, please'—
and some French, to pass mainly through the friendly, and presumably
loyal, Sainton. But the latter's influence as leader had surely been
reduced in the course of Costa's recent reforms, his name removed
from programmes. Could much be achieved through the sole authority of a baton, no matter how formidable? Wagner's communication
with players and audience may have been intermittent, at best. At
worst, the performances could have fallen clumsily between two stools,
as Ernest Newman suggests, exhibiting the virtues 'neither of the old
straightforward kind, such as they were, nor of the new Wagnerian
kind'.[56] If the fault, as he concludes, was not Wagner's, neither was it,
as perfect Wagnerites sometimes imply, simply London's, or the Philharmonic Society's. When different worlds meet, and most particularly
when extravagant genius is let loose upon measured society, accultura-
tion can have no simple resolution. We cannot even be certain about
Wagner's working relationship with the players. There is evidence that
he earned their respect, as he later claimed, but there may be truth
in Newman's wry comment that they were reluctant to offend Costa
by demonstrating too warm a regard for the visitor. What matters most
for this history is that, thanks to the Philharmonic directors, London
was allowed a premature glimpse of the music, or at least the conducting, of the future. It may not have succeeded, but the fact that it was
tried earned the Society, once again, a place at the helm of concert life.
There would be no more such excitements for many years to come.

[55] Wagner, *Über das Dirigieren* (1869).   [56] Newman, *Life of Richard Wagner*, ii. 470.

6

Plateau and Descent

I very much regret that school teaching keeps me away from
the Philharmonic meeting this afternoon.

> (Professor Sterndale Bennett, 14 Mar. 1857)[1]

Will the day ever come when the production of a great work
shall be a matter of loving care, and not a mere question of
how to make it pass muster?

> (*Athenaeum*, 30 Apr. 1870, reviewing a Philharmonic perform-
> ance of Beethoven's Seventh Symphony)

Mr Cusins, with a host of excellent qualities, is an extraordinarily bad conductor.

> (G. B. Shaw)[2]

O N 23 June 1855 the directors sent Wagner 'cordial thanks for his
attention, zeal and ability, as Conductor of the Concerts, in carrying
out their views'.[3] There was no question of inviting him to return; nor,
of course, would he have wished to do so. Davison later recalled the
situation with unconcealed relish: 'the Music of the Future' did not suit
'our great conservative institution'; but then, thanks to the Society's
'vigorous constitution', the greatest of English musicians 'courageously
grasped the baton' and a golden age began.[4] Later commentators have
sung along with this hymn of thanksgiving after the storm. Elkin, for
example, endorses the contribution of constitutional reform to the coming of a new age, and goes on to celebrate a conductorship which was
held 'to everybody's satisfaction, for eleven years'.[5] Bennett is admitted
to have been 'neither powerful nor inspiring' on the rostrum; but he
is said to have possessed 'the more important virtues of impeccable

---

[1] 48.13/3 (14 Mar. 1857).
[2] *Music in London 1890–1894* (1932), 207. Shaw was reviewing on 10 June 1891 a concert
in which Sarasate played and Cusins conducted. This late review has been chosen, from
a very large number of adverse opinions, because conductors are generally expected to
improve with experience, and clearly Cusins never did.   [3] 48.2/4 (23 June 1855).
[4] *MW* (19 July 1862).   [5] Elkin, *Royal Philharmonic*, 58.

musicianship, sound judgement, and imaginative insight', qualities from which, by implication, the Society drew immense benefits.[6]

Bennett Ascendant

There is little evidence to support these pious beliefs. Discordant voices could be heard even during the early years of approbation, not least among the erstwhile devout. *The Times* and *Musical World* led off with celebrations of Bennett's inaugural concerts, but soon resorted to whistling in the dark, and then abandoned all pretence of harmony. Choristers of lesser devotion differed only in the timing of their desertion. Every-one knew that the 'Old Society', as it was now called—sometimes with affection—was beginning to lose too many illustrious old friends, not only through natural wastage, and was making some rather dubious new ones. There was a sense of drift and decline; and the allegedly 'vigorous constitution', far from protecting the idealism of 1813, was seen to be vulnerable to meaner aspirations. A new breed of 'profes-sional musician' began to rise so rapidly, in the country and within Philharmonic ranks, that the Society's constituency, rather than its constitution, emerged as the fundamental point of issue. It was resolved in a manner which ensured that residual excellence, still abundant in 1856, was dissipated within a decade, lowering the Society's status and beginning to eat into its capital.

The process of deterioration was concealed for some time; initially by the position of Bennett himself, as a musician of undoubted integrity, and by the unprecedented and devious manner of his appointment; later by the extent to which he allowed his prestige to be manipulated by lesser men. Sympathizers were inclined to see a respected artist who stood apart from and above mundane events, and sometimes even to mistake the Society's image and professed aspirations for continuing achievement: if Professor (later Sir) William Sterndale Bennett was at the helm, then all *must* be well and respected without question. Yet even the seemingly innocent routine of his appointment was not, as most assumed, just a matter of giving English genius its belated due. Less still did it result from the directors following an established tradi-tion of working through a carefully selected list of eminent musicians who might be persuaded to accept the conductorship. Instead, after 'much deliberation', but no approach to outsiders, so far as can be judged from the archives, they decided that 'a matter of this delicacy and importance ought to be discussed at a full meeting'.[7] This was a curious break with traditional practice, an apparent abdication of

---

[6] Ibid. 64.   [7] 48.2/4 (28 Sept. 1855).

responsibility for its prime task by a committee previously accustomed to go its own way. Was the underlying purpose democratic, as the directors claimed; or conspiratorial, as was alleged; or merely tactical: a show of consultation to ease necessary adjustments? Whatever the intention, the outcome had long-term implications. A precedent had been established for ignoring international claims to a position of allegedly international status, and for clothing decisions with a pretence of consultation and merit. When Bennett's successor was appointed in 1867 that relegation to a lower division would become all too clear. Men who were capable of switching artistic leadership within a generation from Costa, Berlioz, and Wagner to Cusins may have been subject to uncommon pressures; they were certainly adept card-shufflers in a game which continued for a few more years of professedly high aspiration.

Although he was widely respected at home, Sterndale Bennett's status among musicians abroad was on the wane. At 40, he was younger than Costa and Wagner, yet already, after a period of youthful achievement and acclaim which had been unprecedented for an Englishman, he seemed to have few aspirations beyond the schoolroom. Refusing the honour of conducting the Leipzig Gewandhaus concerts in 1853, with its opportunities for artistic development, he had settled for lacklustre routines at home which provided scant promise of income, leisure, or enough stimulus to revive flagging genius. His subsequent career, both apex and caricature of the Victorian music profession, was consolidated by positions of dignity within the narrow circle of the Philharmonic, Cambridge University, and the Royal Academy of Music. Outside he still commanded respect as a pianist, and for his earlier compositions and associations, not least with Schumann. The niceties of such a tragic career may interest a future biographer, but their general implications for the Society are clear enough. Even the most favourable gloss upon Bennett's status and surviving prowess in 1856 could hardly challenge an impression that he was capable of exerting only waning authority among professionals who worked in the vigorous, creative world of opera and symphonic music. The conservatism of his selected repertoire, as a conductor, and of his own compositions, reinforces this belief. Moreover, as we have already argued, the *manner* of his appointment in that year further diminished his authority by changing the entire balance of power within the Philharmonic. Finally, his apathetic, thin-skinned, and irresolute temperament, so cruelly demonstrated by the Leipzig abdication and the Costa and Goddard fracas, made it unlikely that he would do much to reassert that balance. A group of directors whose status was diminishing by the hour was thus left without a leader who might have challenged their parochialism and inspired them to higher purpose.

It had recently been remarked that the directors were becoming unrepresentative of 'the profession', and quite incapable of that 'energetic, enlightened, and discriminating research' essential to hold the Society's former place.[8] That indictment proved untimely since it was immediately followed by negotiations with Berlioz and Wagner. But it was soon to be amply confirmed, as if the Society's endowment of enterprise had finally been exhausted by that last attempt to stay ahead with contemporary music. Returning to its attack, the *Athenaeum* subsequently made several further attempts to play Cassandra, using the question of Wagner's successor, not unreasonably, as a touchstone for future prospects. Chorley ridiculed directors who 'engage themselves as players' and 'elect themselves and one another', and insisted that 'wholesale favouritism and wholesale antipathies . . . must come to an end, and speedily, or the Philharmonic Society will cease to exist'. The inescapable conclusion was that, unreformed, it could not 'live through many seasons more'; and to survive 'it must be a European—not an English—institution'.[9]

All was resolved at a spate of meetings. In July, after Ayrton, Calkin, Costa, Griffin, Holmes, Horsley, Potter, Sainton, and Smart refused to serve as directors, Anderson, Bennett, Blagrove, Chatterton, Griesbach, Lucas, and Murdie were elected. Anderson continued as treasurer, 'assured that the anonymous, unjust and dastardly attacks which have been made on his character . . . only raised him in the estimation of this Society'. Reform, survival, and a very thorough Englishing were rapidly accomplished, amidst much talk of selectivity and exclusiveness. A special general meeting in August recognized that 'the greater the facility of admission into our body, the less valued will be the distinction'. The assembly therefore decided upon a series of draconian remedies. Associate members would be limited in total to forty, on the perverse grounds that 'vacancies had exceeded candidates'. There would be more stringent regulations upon election to full membership, though necessary qualifications were not spelled out: diplomas and degrees had not yet taken that central place in the English music profession which would later ease such discernment. Since concerts before Easter were thought to be unprofitable, the season would be reduced from eight to six. As conductors were henceforth to be appointed by the members, a director should no longer be allowed to play in the orchestra 'so that he cannot instruct the conductor'. The latter rule, an isolated gesture towards musicianship, was approved by only ten votes to eight, and then rescinded a few days later. In November the ordinary annual general meeting, thinly attended as was now customary, elected Sterndale Bennett conductor for the next season, by nine votes to three. It was

---

[8] *Athenaeum* (22 July 1854).   [9] Ibid. (19 May, 23 and 30 June, and 21 July 1855).

agreed to pay him 15 guineas for each rehearsal and concert, less than half his predecessor's fee.[10]

As 'reform' proceeded, everything except the conductor's appointment began to alienate people outside the cabal. Even the *Musical World* shed its recently acquired equanimity and denounced a series of elections by which 'an anti-musical clique' proved itself capable of grasping such 'professors' as Harold Thomas to its bosom, and refusing Charles Hallé.[11] The *Athenaeum* reacted similarly, noticing particularly the rejection of William Thomas Best, organist at St George's Hall, Liverpool, and a virtuoso of international stature. Such actions were seen to 'stultify the purposes and provisions under which the Philharmonic Society was originally founded', reducing it to 'A Mutual Admiration Society for the use and comfort of the smaller members of the English Musical Profession'. Of what use and significance was such an institution, raged Chorley, without Molique, Pauer, Piatti, Manuel Garcia, Hullah, and others 'whose intellectual and practical worth to music in this country is . . . ascertained fact'?[12] *Punch* ran a spoof advertisement for candidates: 'No testimonials required as the qualification now recognised is the member's being known to nobody, and having done nothing. To save trouble no person who has had the bad taste to obtrude himself upon public attention as composer or executant need apply, as rejection will certainly ensue.' Teachers of music in ladies' schools were particularly urged to make application.[13]

To retain a place in the larger world of music, the Society needed leadership capable of counterbalancing the parochial interests of 'small members' by closer attention to the larger concerns of subscribers, and to a potential audience outside. It could have been an exciting prospect, for musicians abroad were embarking upon a new golden age, and consumers' expenditure on music was growing apace. Verdi was in Milan, Wagner in Dresden, Meyerbeer and Gounod in Paris, Brahms in Vienna, and Liszt in Weimar. London had the richest of audiences, and was offered Sterndale Bennett.

New Circumstances

After half a century of easy dominance the Philharmonic was no longer 'the only show in town'. A particularly irksome rival was the New Philharmonic Society. It had been launched in spectacular fashion by Dr Henry Wylde, at the Exeter Hall in 1852, appealing to the general

---

[10] All three meetings are minuted in 48.3/2 (9 July; 6 Aug.; and 19 Nov. 1855).
[11] *MW* (14 Mar. 1857).   [12] *Athenaeum* (14 Mar. 1857).
[13] *Punch*, quoted in *MW* (11 Apr. 1857).

public with more than 3,000 seats at prices from 2*s*. 6*d*. to 10*s*. 6*d*. and a fine large orchestra under Berlioz. Sixteen first violins (sometimes twenty-four) were led initially by Camille Sivori, reputedly Paganini's sole pupil, and certainly his protégé. Leading sixteen second violins was Leopold Jansa, a distinguished Czech quartet leader, and teacher of the composer Goldmark and Wilma Neruda (later Lady Hallé). At the front of the viola, cello, and double-bass sections, a dozen apiece, were Goffrié, Piatti, and Bottesini. Other masters of their instruments were Rémusat (flute), Henry Lazarus (clarinet), Jarrett and Charles Harper (horn), Thomas Harper (trumpet), Arban and Koenig (cornet), Cioffi and Winterbottom (trombone), Prospère (ophicleide), and T. R. Chipp (timpani).

At its best, therefore, the NPO could field a team of unmatched strength, which demonstrated what riches could be procured in London, given sufficient managerial expertise and financial backing. Frederick Beale, of Cramer and Beale the music publishers, was manager. Cash was provided by Wylde and three great railway engineers, Thomas Brassey, Sir Morton Peto, and Sir Charles Fox, who also built Paxton's Crystal Palace. With men of such boundless energy, wealth, and distinction among its supporters the New Philharmonic was a potent threat. We know very little about its history, but it is clear that wounds were inflicted upon the old Society by the mere act of poaching a cherished name—the first of many such 'infringements' which incurred a great deal of resentment—and by blocking access to Berlioz, as was noted in the last chapter. If he had been allowed to conduct the old Philharmonic in 1855, then Wagner would probably not have come to London: an intriguing conjecture. Even without resorting to surmise, there can be no doubting the strength of the New Philharmonic's challenge. It openly refuted 'the opinion acted upon by an elder institution, that no schools but those which may be called classical are to be considered as capable of affording pleasure and that the works of such schools can only be enjoyed by a select few amateurs and artistes'.[14] But the challenge was short-lived. After a few seasons under such visitors as Spohr and Lindpaintner, and what Berlioz described as Wylde's 'nonsensical' baton, the New Philharmonic retreated to a semblance of the old, seeking smaller audiences at higher prices. It remained until 1879 as an upstart presence, but only rarely as an effective competitor. It was not, however, the only rival show.

By the second half of the nineteenth century the long-term trend in London's concert life was one of continuous expansion, despite occasional setbacks. A jumble of events, in styles and formats old and new,

---

[14] New Philharmonic Society prospectus, quoted in P. M. Young, *The Concert Tradition* (1965), 208. Also see entry in *Grove*, ii. 452–3.

fed upon the public's clamour for music, and its insistent desire for
social reassurance and advancement. 'Benefits', 'matinées d'invitation',
and 'soirées d'invitation' (the obligatory French either *très distinguée* or
what a later generation would call 'Pooterish'), quartet and symphony
concerts, *concerts monstres* (French again, but Jullien, so often described
as a charlatan, was at least the real thing), 'recitals' (a useful new word
which was customarily parenthesized)—everything from footling displays of drawing-room accomplishments, reassuring parents that money
on lessons and instruments was well spent (on girls, never boys), to
Hallé's magisterial surveys of Beethoven, and even some Schubert
piano sonatas—all had to be squeezed into the traditional short season.[15] Yet economic growth and social change were already beginning
to make nonsense of this constraint. London's population had doubled
since the Philharmonic's early days and was still growing apace;
metropolitan life, even by the narrowest of social indicators, was no
longer confined to half the year, and trains could now bring thousands
of visitors cheaply, regularly, and peacefully to town (and musicians to
their place of work). Ten years earlier visitors to the Italian opera had
remarked upon 'a curious effect of railway conveyance that numerous
parties occupied the boxes, who came all the way from Manchester,
Liverpool and other distant places'.[16] More recently, the Great Exhibition had amply demonstrated how to widen the market for entertainment, at all levels of society, with Thomas Cook organizing fleets of
trains, and the invention of a useful tradition in place of Haymarket
'outrage': public lavatories to 'prevent an uncontrollable flood of inde-
cent exposures'.[17] An 'Orchestral Society', got up by players to organize
a winter season of eight concerts between November and February,
failed within its first year, but such extensions of the calendar would
soon be tried again.[18]

This expanding market confronted the Society with competitive pressures in two forms, for audiences and for players. It was still possible
to ignore the first by remaining in Hanover Square and keeping prices
high, although there may have been occasional twinges of anxiety
about retaining loyalty from those who were not inextricably bound by
habit or inertia. The 1856 decision to stop giving concerts in March
was more characteristic behaviour; bucking the market's trend in the
name of thrift, and with confidence in continuing loyalty from subscribers.
Competition for instrumentalists was similarly assumed to be lacking in
urgency: doubtless on first principles—who would refuse a Philharmonic engagement?—and because an orchestra of sorts could be easily

---

[15] Hallé played a large number of the Schubert sonatas in London. It is a common belief
that they waited for Schnabel, seventy years later.   [16] *Musical Herald* (30 May 1846).
[17] F. M. L. Thompson, *The Rise of Respectable Society* (1988), 261.
[18] *Athenaeum* (6 Aug., 8 and 17 Nov. 1851).

recruited, without having to bid up fees. The supply of cheap labour was a recent, and very significant, development: twenty-five years ago, wrote Ella in 1852, it had been difficult to furnish a second orchestra; but now one could find enough for six.[19] Yet, despite what amounted to a transformation of the labour-market, it was still hard to recruit first-class instrumentalists; and good wind-players were always in particularly short supply. Ella, who insisted upon high standards for his chamber concerts, reported a typical example when an 1853 performance of a Spohr quintet had to be cancelled because the flautist was in Glasgow, the clarinettist in Liverpool, the horn-player in Dublin, and the bassoonist ill. A responsible government, he argued, would do something about such scarcities by encouraging the teaching of appropriate instruments.[20]

Although there was no longer a shortage of string-players, the gap between front-desk men—who had usually acquired a first-class technique from a master in childhood, and general musicianship from wide experience as they progressed—and the rank-and-file, remained unbridgeable. The latter were already abundant, mainly Englishmen, like the Castells, who had picked up enough familiarity with an instrument to seek pit and platform employment in London. Most of them took pupils as soon as possible, in order to supplement meagre earnings, and thus contributed to a grimly Malthusian pattern of growth. Supply would soon be further swollen by the products of a peculiarly British indiscriminate and unregulated proliferation of inadequate teaching institutions.[21] The rank-and-file strings who formed the bulk of London's nineteenth-century symphony and theatre orchestras therefore came very cheap; but anyone fit to occupy a front desk continued to command, or at least demand, appropriate fees and status. And it was upon such men that the Society remained dependent for the quality of its band. Wagner's praise had been carefully placed in this context: 'A magnificent orchestra, as far as the principal members go. Superb tone—the leaders had the finest instruments I have ever listened to— strong esprit de corps—but no distinct style.'[22]

As competition increased it thus became essential to secure, and pre-

[19] Ella draws attention to the many fine instrumentalists who were among the wave of immigrants after 1848, esp. Adolf Pollitzer, a Hungarian violinist who was capable of leading the Beethoven late quartets: *RMU* (1 June 1852). Pollitzer settled in London, led the New Philharmonic orchestra on occasion, and later taught, among others, Edward Elgar.   [20] *RMU* (3 Mar. 1853).

[21] See Ehrlich, *Music Profession*, esp. ch. 5. The grim story of the Castell family is narrated in A. V. Beedell, *The Decline of the English Musician 1788–1888* (1992).

[22] Wagner, quoted in Nettel, *Orchestra in England*, 185. Acquiring good instruments was a practical form of investment among London players, their knowledge and experience of the market offering opportunities to provide a nest-egg. Dragonetti generously left his valuable collection to colleagues.

ferably monopolize, the services of first-class men, cosseting established players and identifying newcomers, dangling incentives in a continuous process of bargaining. In the absence of contractual arrangements for a permanent orchestra, which would have given players continuous incentives to loyalty, recruitment was necessarily a matter of eternal vigilance: no task was more crucial to the Society's well-being. Under Costa it had been performed with skill and dedication, delicately balancing inducements and loyalties, negotiating from the strength of personal authority and bargaining-power. Sometimes velvet gloves were removed, with a threat, for example, to engage 'substitutes at the expense of performers absent'; on one occasion twelve musicians, including principals, were sent such notices. Usually firmness was sufficient, with clearly understood priorities and sensible concern for goodwill.[23] It was probably inevitable that Costa's departure would damage that network of professional relationships, but continuing care for the priorities, and some extra cash, might have preserved the essential structure. Instead, it was demolished by parsimony, with the excuse of losses from Wagner's season: £600 deficit on the customary budget of some £2,000. Rigid thrift and inept labour relations wrought havoc within a season; not simply through familiar economies with soloists and rehearsals but, more dangerously, by sacrificing the half-dozen or so strong players who might have continued to underpin an ensemble. And old loyalties contributed to a general inconsistency in treatment of individuals. Against a background of seeming indifference to the general quality of recruitment it was possible to exercise a nicely old-fashioned solicitude towards an ageing second flautist. A letter drafted out of 'consideration and respect due to so old and valuable a member of the Society and of the Orchestra' informs William Card that 'the lapse of years had had its inevitable effect of impairing in some degree your powers of execution in the very difficult music of the most modern school', and suggests retirement 'in favour of your son Mr Edward Card'.[24]

The orchestra began to fall apart from the moment of Bennett's arrival. Chorley reported a poorly directed band 'worse than in any former year', an 'enfeebled and inferior body of executants' which had lost most of the best players and retained several who were 'never up to the mark'.[25] At Bennett's second concert the conductor was thought to be in somewhat better control, but his forces were still pronounced inadequate, particularly in senior positions, and poorly led. A reversion was noticed, for example, to the bad old system which had previously

[23] 48.6/3 (24 Jan. 1853). Other letters in the same file pursue Sivori to Glasgow and Belfast, question Hill and Mellon about clashes with Dando's Quartet Concerts, and so forth. [24] 48.2/4 (12 Jan. 1857); 48.6/3 (12 Jan. 1857).

[25] *Athenaeum* (19 Apr. 1856).

been 'wisely abolished', of sharing the *chef d'attaque* among several oc-
cupants of the front desk as the season progressed. Destroying this
Costa reform might have wrought less damage if his successor could
have exerted enough authority to secure agreement among the various
leaders. Instead, a ludicrous dogfight was allowed to take place in public between rival violinists, unsubdued by a ceaseless round of correspondence and consultation behind the scenes. It demonstrated a new
failure to keep the balance between orchestral discipline and individual
amour propre, unfairly blamed on the leading players who, quite apart
from personal vanity, depended for their livelihood upon visible status.

Battle began with offers to Henry Cooper as 'joint principal violin,
same terms as Sainton and Blagrove'.[26] The latter two declined, were
asked to reconsider, and again refused. The directors protested to
Blagrove their surprise that a violinist who in 1848 had been 'elevated
in a similar manner' should 'take offence' at one of 'distinguished talent
and high professional rank' who has 'similarly sustained the honour of
the English school'.[27] Then Dando was asked to share a desk with
Cooper as principal for the whole season, and his refusal led Bennett
to make three personal calls: asking Sainton and Blagrove to play
together for 'four concerts taking alternatively first place at first desk',
and Dando to reconsider his decision.[28] The former reported engagements with the New Philharmonic 'binding them not to perform for
this Society' and Dando continued to refuse. A letter was dispatched
to Sivori in Paris, reporting the desertions and begging him to come
as 'violon principal ou chef d'attaque conjointement avec Mr Cooper'.
A director (first Anderson, then Calkin) was deputed to set off to Paris
in his pursuit, offering three concerts for up to £60 including a concerto. Should Sivori refuse, they would offer £40 to Delphin Alard,
professor at the Conservatoire, who had just acquired Sarasate as a
pupil; but Sivori was booked for £55 with a 'promise not to perform
for the New Philharmonic Society'.[29] Meanwhile Cooper was moved
to public protest, in what was described as a 'four page pamphlet',
justifying his occupancy of the position and earning further rebuke for
indiscreet revelation of 'unaccountable secessions' from the orchestra.[30]
The fourth concert offered further proof of deterioration, and even
Bennett's most vociferous supporters were dismayed. At his first concert
they had acclaimed a return to jogtrotting as the 'difference between
good and bad conducting'. At the second they welcomed signs that
'matters began to look up'; and pronounced the third 'of more than
average excellence', with things again looking up. But by the fourth
concert 'great vigour' was found unmatched by 'great delicacy' and

[26] 48.2/4 (9 Feb. 1856).   [27] 48.6/3 (25 Feb. 1856).
[28] 48.2/4 (19 Mar. 1856).   [29] 48.2/4 (24 and 29 Mar., and 4 Apr. 1856).
[30] *Athenaeum* (17 May 1856).

even attempts upon two hackneyed overtures were pronounced unacceptable: *Fidelio* 'rattled over' and *Midsummer Night's Dream* 'scrambled through with unpardonable negligence'.[31]

New Friends

Three celebrated ladies joined the painful trudge through 1856, accompanied in flesh or spirit by diversely gifted husbands. The Goddards were easily recruited: Arabella performed Bennett's C minor Concerto; her husband declared it a masterpiece, recalled past wounds, and declared a famous victory.[32] The pattern continued until 1878, with twenty appearances of which half were devoted to piano works by the English master, all written before 1840. More exciting was the prospect of intimacy with the most venerated voice in England. A deputation to the Lind Goldschmidts inaugurated elaborate rituals of wheedling and coaxing, for though she expressed, with suitable humility, 'her inclination to comply with the views of the Directors', no one doubted that Jenny's favours would be won only by ceaseless dedication and sacrifice which included, in the first instance, an engagement for her husband. He was duly booked to perform Beethoven's Fourth Piano Concerto, after grovelling insistence that the directors would have been 'happy with any other'.[33] Thus a miserable fourth concert was further reduced, as Chorley remarked, by 'a compliment to a great singer at the expense of the subscribers'.[34] Throughout their negotiations the directors were outclassed by a veteran businesswoman: smug, sanctimonious, and rich. The Swedish Nightingale's prodigious exploitation of voice and saintly demeanour had culminated six years earlier in path-breaking American tours with the mighty Barnum; and even that prince of entrepreneurs had been forced to swallow his dose of Goldschmidt's 'plodding pianism', as part of the deal, despite protests from rowdy audiences.[35] The Philharmonic's subscribers were more docile, at least on this occasion, for Jenny, who had not so much lost as severed her connection with the opera-house, embodied all the bourgeois virtues of glamorous, but chaste, artistry, and husbands could do no wrong.

Correctly anticipating feverish applications for subscriptions—411 as against the 283 of Wagner's season—the directors overreached themselves with an uncommon display of handbills and advertisements. It

---

[31] *MW* (19 Apr., and 3, 17, and 31 May 1856).   [32] *MW* (14 June 1856).
[33] 48.2/4 (2 Feb. 1856); 48.6/3 (20 May 1856).   [34] *MW* (31 May 1856).
[35] On Jenny's mien see H. Pleasants, *The Great Singers* (1981), 197–204; on her dealings with Barnum see A. H. Saxon, *P. T. Barnum, The Legend And The Man* (New York, 1989), 162–83; on her position in mid-Victorian society see R. Christiansen, *Prima Donna: A History* (1984), 94–110.

brought prompt rebuke by special messenger for giving the impression
that diva and consort (jokey comparisons with Victoria and Albert were
commonplace among the vulgar) would appear at *all* of the Society's
concerts. In face of such a threat the New Philharmonic had complained so vehemently to the Goldschmidts as to force them to consider
that they might have 'to bestow the same favour' upon the rival group.
'Much conversation' ensued and the directors, while expressing gratitude
for a courteous slap, prayed that favours would not be extended to 'a
Society which had been set on foot in opposition to them and had
always been . . . in most hostile spirit'.[36] Bennett, who appears to have
been responsible for the original initiative, was now moved to express
wide-ranging, and typically backward-looking, apprehensions: 'Mme.
Goldschmidt's patronage of the new society may allow the public to
consider the two Societies equal in merit' and even 'to think that
concerts can be given at a cheap rate, which is a grand error.'[37]

As parleys continued there was little time to spare for anything else,
even to 'settle upon the engagements of the orchestra', which was
thought inexpedient until Jenny had been fixed.[38] Nor was there any
special attention to another wife-and-husband team, despite Bennett's
earlier acquaintance. Hard-pressed for cash in this year of Robert
Schumann's final madness and death, Clara had written, in her own
hand, to say that she had found herself lodgings and a companion, and
accepted two engagements for £21.[39] At her first appearance in England on 14 April, which 'exceeded highest expectations', she played
Beethoven's Fifth Concerto and the Mendelssohn *Variations sérieuses*,
bringing a touch of class to Bennett's opening concert with 'masterly
and intellectual' performances.[40] Her concerto at the next concert was
Mendelssohn's in D minor, and it was for the New Philharmonic that
she played the Schumann Concerto. Published ten years earlier, it still
received only a sniff of approval from Davison for the 'praiseworthy
efforts of the gifted lady to make her husband's curious rhapsody pass
for music with an uninitiated audience'.[41] Perhaps the directors decided
to cater only for the initiated, since they waited another ten years
before taking the 'curious rhapsody' into Philharmonic programmes,
after which it became the most frequently played of all piano concertos, with twenty-eight Society performances by 1910. So much delay
in filling an gap in repertoire acknowledged to be grievous—no concerto had yet 'caught on' since Mendelssohn—is truly remarkable. Was
it a lack of confidence in contemporary music, or competence in its
appraisal; or was the piece too difficult for the orchestra? The last
movement's syncopations can still defeat unwary players.

[36] 48.2/4 (19 Jan. and 2 and 23 Feb. 1856).   [37] 48.13/3 (25 Feb. 1856).
[38] 48.2/4 (2 Feb. 1856).
[39] 48.13/31 (16 Feb. 1856). N. B. Reich, *Clara Schumann* (1989), 150–1.
[40] *Spectator* and *MW* (both 19 Apr. 1856).   [41] *MW* (17 May 1856).

Ignoring one of Schumann's most ingratiating works, the directors dedicated every resource, including their meagre ration of Jenny, to a 'secular oratorio', for reasons which are not at all clear: perhaps Bennett, Prince Albert, Clara, and the Goldschmidts were all keen on the work. On the hot night of 23 June 1856, as if in centenary memory of Calcutta's Black Hole, three hours of *Paradise and the Peri* were undergone, in a small room without ventilation, made smaller by large musical forces and numerous royal visitors whose space required a cordon sanitaire. Fortunate members of an overcapacity audience were able to get some sleep, while others witnessed grotesque proceedings which Clara apparently tried to direct at strategic moments from a place within the orchestra. Professor Bennett (the title was now obligatory) 'must have been more puzzled than complimented' by such unsolicited assistance, commented the *Athenaeum* which blamed this 'want of taste' upon directors who were 'unmanly to have put her thus in front of the battle'. Critical comment was, for once, unanimous, and arguably the worst in Philharmonic history. A 'more dreary concert was never listened to', an entire evening of 'by far the least satisfactory composition of pretension which has been presented . . . in our remembrance'. Years later Cox's pen quivered in recollection of Lind's voice 'worn and strained', Clara's interference 'devoid of taste', and listeners so estranged that there would have been 'vehement demonstrations of derision had not the audience been restrained by the presence of Royalty'.[42] There were immediate gains to the exchequer: in return for their boost to subscriptions the Goldschmidts got 'an elegant tea kettle', and Mme Schumann's directorial services came free.[43] Longer-term costs of a never-to-be-forgotten evening would soon become apparent.

In 1857 the subscription list fell from 411 to 340, perhaps through surfeit of paradise and the Goldschmidts, or even disappointment at their failure to reappear. Having barely managed to balance the year's books, despite so much initial support and misplaced effort, the directors now resorted to a quieter life and cut expenditure to the bone. The orchestra was savagely reduced in quality and quantity, bringing unintended irony to Davison's remark that the players were 'being rapidly disWagnerised'.[44] They were also sometimes exhausted

---

[42] Cox, *Musical Recollections*, 304–5. *Athenaeum* and *MW* (28 June 1856); the *Spectator*, on the same date, tried to be kinder.

[43] 48.2/4 (28 June 1856). Clara Schumann's fee for playing the piano was 10 guineas for each concert, an 'amount usually paid by the Society to artists of the highest class': 48.6/3 (11 Feb. 1856).

[44] *MW* (23 May 1857). Total expenditure was reduced, mainly on strings, from £1,980 in 1856 to £1,550 and £1,533 in the next two years. In 1856 Sivori was paid £55 and Cooper £22. In 1857 Sivori received £26.5s. for appearances which included the Mendelssohn Concerto and one of his own pieces which Davison wanted 'confined to the flames'. The warring trio of Sainton, Blagrove, and Cooper got £7 apiece: could the latter payment have included his fee for playing the Beethoven concerto? Figures are in 48.9/2.

by overwork in mid-season, as was noticed at a concert which followed a morning Handel Festival.[45] Flagging interest among subscribers was stimulated by Anton Rubinstein, procured for 10 guineas on his second visit to England. Already becoming recognized as the greatest pianist since Liszt, he introduced a style of playing which was larger, not merely noisier, than had ever been heard at the Philharmonic. In the intimate Hanover Square Rooms it must have been overwhelming, earning him 'very discordant opinions among the cognoscenti'. Many preferred the earnestness and quiet authority of Hallé and Clara Schumann, as sufficient additions to customary styles of 'chaste elegance' at the keyboard for one generation to assimilate. Some were forthright in their rejection of so much bravura, finding Rubinstein 'far more wonderful than pleasing', and his Concerto in G 'bad—scarcely music at all'. Others were overwhelmed by new worlds of eloquence and virtuosity, and would demand more.[46]

But Philharmonic programmes cared little for such novelties, preferring to settle into old ways. Even Clara Schumann was allotted only a brief appearance, again for 10 guineas; not to play a concerto, but to repeat the Mendelssohn Variations; perhaps to save on rehearsal time, for her insistence upon high standards already posed difficulties which would later lead to open confrontation. The solo piece was her sole contribution to an end-of-season hotchpotch of a concert, like many a predecessor, but without lustre. Cooper, the disgruntled pamphleteer, was allowed to perform Beethoven's Violin Concerto; one critic detecting 'wonderful skill' and lamenting the soloist's migration to America, another reporting an audience 'too critical and discriminating to be what is called enthusiastic'.[47] Back from the United States with 'a considerable quantity of dollars', and arias by Rossini, Verdi, and Meyerbeer, sailed Louisa Pyne, whose waning star would now be attached to her own opera-in-English company. To fill the perceived gaps in a long evening there were symphonies by Mozart and Spohr, and the Overtures Leonora No. 3 and *Oberon*. The season ended with books just balanced, which was presumably not Davison's meaning when he used *The Times*, with a repeat in the *Musical World*, to announce that the Philharmonic was 'back on its legs again'.[48] For the *Athenaeum*, however, elections in December provided further evidence of a decline 'deeper into imitation of that luckless assemblage of mediocrities the Society of British Musicians'. A members' list which had once included Clementi was now observed to welcome Brinley Richards, composer of 'Warblings at Eve'.[49]

---

[45] *MW* (6 June 1857).   [46] *Spectator* and *MW* (both 23 May 1857).
[47] *MW* and *Spectator* (both 4 July 1857).
[48] *The Times*, quoted in *MW* (4 July 1857).   [49] *Athenaeum* (19 Dec. 1857).

An Orchestra Destroyed

Thus a complacent ship continued its seemingly prosperous voyage in calm, if restricted, seas—Mendelssohn's Overture was a great favourite. Then in 1861, with no look-out posted, it was holed and almost sunk by a hazard which was plain to see. The incident was inevitably described in the *Musical World* as a 'conspiracy against the Philharmonic' plotted in Floral Street by its ancient enemies Gye and Costa, and was, of course, nothing of the kind, for who stood to gain from destroying an institution which seemed bent upon self-destruction? Covent Garden's new initiative was simply another exercise, familiar in every opera-house, in the difficult art of fitting highly mobile performers into a tight season. Davison's diatribe was his way of saying—with touches of inspired historical revisionism ('but for the Philharmonic there would have been no Italian Opera'), and a display of erudition which called upon Bacon, Alexander the Great, Homer, and Richelieu—that opera was now available on Mondays.[50] The Society's directors shared his sense of outrage, fearing competition, not for audiences—probably few remaining subscribers were now regular opera-goers—but for orchestral players. To be sure, there were other days in the week which could have been allocated to concerts, which are always easier to organize than opera. But 'a Philharmonic concert not on a Monday would be no Philharmonic concert at all'; and, although no soloists had been fixed, the possibility of changing '*even one*' date was not to be entertained.[51]

It must be acknowledged that such inflexibility was not merely sentimental, for an audience's loyalty is maintained by a regular calendar. Yet concerts were supposed to be the Society's principal activity, and since their quality, even their existence, was now threatened, common sense might have suggested some give and take. By losing Costa and distancing their activities from the opera-house, the directors had sacrificed a comfortably profitable special relationship and taken on irksome responsibilities, particularly for the orchestra. The opera-house initiative was no sudden and unpredictable *fait accompli*, without time for negotiation and adjustments. Timetable clashes were increasing along with musical activity. The 'English Sunday' added another constraint—in Paris Sunday was concert day. This latest crisis took at least a year to develop. Early in 1860 the Philharmonic was intransigent when two of its most valuable players, Sainton and the clarinetist Lazarus, asked permission for absence and, by implication, the appointment of deputies, *if* there should be a clash with the opera on

[50] *MW* (27 Oct. 1860).   [51] *MW* (5 Jan. 1861).

certain evenings. They were refused 'in justice to' others who were also members of both bands.[52] On 13 May there was an emergency meeting of directors because Costa had told his players to be in the pit on the night of the next Philharmonic concert, eight days later. Anderson confidently assured his colleagues that many players would opt for the Philharmonic, so it was decided to write to them expressing determination to 'resist' and, if necessary, take legal action.[53] And the opera-house did indeed back down, but Monday closing could not long be enforced. Nor could players who were vulnerable, no matter how gifted, be expected to sacrifice Costa's goodwill and a considerable and comparatively regular part of their income, in return for six evenings of poorly paid work a year, with commendation from Anderson and Davison.

When the problem returned next season (1862) there is scant evidence of directors' reactions. But we are fortunate in having one document which serves both as a link with the past and a clue to subsequent action. Forty years after his retirement the octogenarian Sir George Smart was inspired to renewed and characteristically adamantine admonition, with much underlining: 'We should continue at Hanover Square rooms on Mondays—*all* performers should be required to attend Rehearsals Saturdays and Concerts Monday evenings (a change to *any* other evening would be fatal to the Concerts)...If *any* decline offer no inducements...but engage *other Artists*.' Performances could be 'rendered efficient' by '*extra rehearsals*: no right-minded member would object to the extra cost'. And he added an illuminating afterthought: 'in former years the works of the great composers were unknown to many of the *Philharmonic Band* but at present these works can be heard in *many places* from which efficient performers may be selected'.[54] Apart from foolish assumptions about extra rehearsals it was a sensible appraisal, so long as aspirations did not go beyond routine performances of hackneyed repertoire. And so the directors proceeded, losing about half of the Philharmonic orchestra, including its principal players. They were replaced from such diverse places as Her Majesty's Private Band, Her Majesty's Theatre, the Crystal Palace, and Southampton.[55] A list

[52] 48.6/4 (14 and 27 Feb. and 16 Mar. 1860).   [53] 48.2/5 (13 May 1860).

[54] 48.13/32 (16 Nov. 1860). Smart was increasingly concerned at the Society's likely demise, and its style of dying. A year earlier the abandonment of another Costa reform, allowing public access to rehearsals, had inspired him to write: 'If the Philharmonic is to fall, let its end be respected by the Public and the worthy part of the Profession.' 48.13/32 (26 Mar. 1859).

[55] Some arrangements with individual players are in 48.2/5 (5 Jan. 1861). Appointing a principal double bass was particularly difficult, for Dragonetti had never been replaced, and even competent players were very scarce. Thanks to the railway Alex Rowland could be brought in from Southampton, for a fee of £28 'and £16 compensation for expenses'; but also at the cost of frequent disturbance to rehearsal schedules. See 48.6/4 (16 Jan. 1861); 48.2/5 (21 Jan. 1861; 4 and 11 Jan. 1862; 16 Jan. 1864).

was given to 'the keeper of the Back door in order that he may point to the performers, as they enter, the places they are to occupy'.[56]

Finding one's place in an ensemble was rather more difficult, and the new team brought few pleasures as it trudged through eight concerts; the number reinstated as if to compensate for inferior goods. Davison emblazoned the orchestra list 'dedicated to Michael Costa', and jeered at 'the desertion of the forty', or was it nearer fifty, who would 'regret their want of esprit de corps'. Then withdrawing a slur upon defenceless musicians, and simply blaming Costa for forcing them into servitude, he worked up a sufficient head of steam by the end of the season to describe Philharmonic performances as 'imbued with new life and vigour'.[57] Chorley was more sensible about the causes of disintegration, but welcomed it with uncharacteristic optimism on the grounds that 'London needs two first class orchestras'. He avoided reviewing most of the 'poor old Philharmonic concerts' at first, in what was becoming a general tendency to pay less attention to the Society's activities, but later declared an 'easy Haydn symphony' ('La Reine') to be 'so badly played . . . as to be nothing short of discreditable'. Moscheles made a final appearance at that last concert of that season.[58]

The Society's fiftieth anniversary fell in 1862, but there was little to celebrate, and the year is therefore poorly documented. Verdi and Meyerbeer were invited to the fourth concert, possibly because Tietjens was singing an aria from the latter's *Robert le Diable*.[59] They were unlikely to have been tempted by a Hummel piano concerto, or Cooper's reading of the Mendelssohn Violin Concerto. An extra 'Jubilee Concert' on 14 July was intended to display every remaining resource. Mrs Anderson returned from retirement to play through Beethoven's Choral Fantasy. Tietjens was back with Gluck and Mendelssohn. Charles Santley arrived from the Pyne-Harrison company to sing Hummel and Haydn. Piatti played variations by Piatti. Joachim lent dignity to the proceedings with a Spohr concerto. Bennett contributed the Leonora and *Euryanthe* Overtures, 'Jupiter' Symphony, and an overture 'composed expressly for this occasion'. It was entitled, masochistically, 'Paradise and the Peri'. Top of the bill was Mme Lind Goldschmidt, with Chorus and Mr E. J. Hopkins at the organ, in Mendelssohn's 'HYMN, "Hear my prayer"'. Ticket prices were raised, a decision which had been specifically linked to her 'appearance or non appearance'.[60] Against Bennett's wishes the mammoth event was held in St James's Hall, Piccadilly, a 'suitable locality for giving the works of the great masters on a grand scale', but without a large choir which

---

[56] 48.2/5 (14 Feb. 1861).   [57] *MW* (5 Jan., 23 Feb., and 23 Mar. 1861).
[58] *Athenaeum* (9 Mar., 1 and 29 June 1861).
[59] 48.2/5 (3 May 1862). In 1912 Foster remarked that '*not one letter* of the Jubilee year' survived, and suspected on this, and possibly other, occasions, 'an auction or a veritable holocaust'. Foster, *History*, 276.   [60] 48.2/5 (21 June 1862).

would 'ruin the general effect' and entail 'pecuniary sacrifice'.[61] Even
the *Musical World* was lost for words, eschewing criticism because the
principal artists had given their services free.[62]

Bennett soldiered on with mounting reluctance for another five years,
contributing a new symphony in 1865, which had been composed after
a thirty-year gap, 'expressly for the Society', but was also performed
at Leipzig. During the following spring he made another futile attempt
at Schumann's *Paradise*, without the assistance of Jenny or Clara and
in an emptier, presumably cooler, hall. Since the 'unquestionable failure'
of its première, Schumann was declared to have made 'decided progress'
in England, but no amount of further time, it was thought, would
make this work more than a 'complex piece of clever dullness' and,
despite some applause, it was 'received somewhat frigidly'.[63] Little else
excited interest, and the directors settled into cosy quiescence. Anderson
still guarded the purse-strings, but George Hogarth's successor as secretary
in 1864 lasted only two years, to be followed by Stanley Lucas, son
of Charles, a cellist who had become Principal of the Royal Academy
of Music. Meetings were uneventful and infrequent. In July 1865, for
example, the only minute records that an attendant was to be stationed
in order 'to prevent seats reserved for the Directors from being appropriated by any others'. They adjourned until November, then
adjourned again because only two turned up.[64] At the end of that
season Chorley was savagely dismissive: 'a more coarse performance
could not be dreamed of', ending 'one more fruitless season' and adding
'another year of discredit' to the Philharmonic's history. Its absurdities,
he concluded, were never felt more strongly than when he heard the
Eroica Symphony described by a member of the audience as 'a pretty
piece'.[65] A year later the directors renewed their offer to Bennett for
another season in customary fashion, but this time there were additional plans. If the work should encroach too much upon his valuable
time, or be too fatiguing, they proposed to appoint Mr Cusins as his
assistant. It was also decided that only the professor's name would
appear on the prospectus and programmes, but in the event of his
refusal then Cusins must be made conductor. Lucas expressed his
conviction that they had every 'confidence in his talent and tact in an
orchestra', which 'ought to be conducted by an Englishman'. The
arrangement was formally proposed at the next directors' meeting and
carried unanimously.[66] On 24 November Bennett withdrew, assuring
them that his heart would 'always be with the grand old Society'. The
response was a suitably grandiloquent letter of gratitude for 'giving to
the musical world many of the noblest compositions both of European

[61] 48.6/4 (17 Feb. 1862).   [62] *MW* (19 July 1862).
[63] *MW* (10 and 17 Mar. 1866).   [64] 48.2/5 (1 and 8 July, and 8 Nov. 1865).
[65] *Athenaeum* (30 June 1865).   [66] 48.2/5 (3 and 17 Nov. 1866).

celebrity and those of which Englishmen are most proud, viz. your own'. Cusins was appointed, for the whole season, without any mention of terms.[67] A Mr Fish, in a letter to the *Musical World*, endorsed the valediction: Sir William Sterndale Bennett had 'sustained the fortunes and the reputation of the Society against formidable rivalry and studied hostility'.[68]

It would be uncharitable to suggest that no one had ever heard of Mr (later Sir) William Cusins. At the time of his appointment to a post which had once been canvassed throughout the world of music he was known, to Philharmonic audiences, as a modestly competent pianist in his early thirties who had played concertos by Mendelssohn and Bennett and, most notably perhaps, Beethoven's Triple Concerto with Joachim and Piatti. Beginning as a chorister at the Chapel Royal, he had gone to the Brussels Conservatoire, where there might have been opportunities for professional training, but was back at the Royal Academy by the age of 14, and appointed organist at the Queen's private chapel two years later. A couple of years playing violin in the opera-house, some deputy work in Her Majesty's undemanding band, and an 'assistant professorship' at the Academy, were the sum total of a fairly representative mid-Victorian London career. There is no evidence that he had ever conducted a professional orchestra in public before beginning the first of seventeen complete seasons with the Philharmonic in 1867. His appointment ignored the presence of several experienced men in England at the time, to look no further. Among them were Benedict, Mellon, Hallé, and, most notoriously, August Manns. The latter, in league with George Grove, was performing miracles of innovative music-making and audience-building with scarce resources at the Crystal Palace, appealing equally to the cognoscenti, who went there in search of fresh repertoire, and the general public who dropped in to hear the band. At the time of his appointment Cusins was claimed to have earned a degree of 'personal respect and esteem', but it was none the less widely recognized as 'a notorious exercise of coterie influence'.[69] He succeeded Anderson as Master of the Queen's Music three years later.

In 1869 the Society bowed to the inevitable and moved to St James's Hall in search of larger audiences, beginning, after all the fuss, on a Wednesday. Capacity was some 2,000 in comparison with Hanover Square's 800 but the move could scarcely have been worse timed. A meagre orchestra and novice conductor rarely offered much which was not done better elsewhere. Royal patronage, which in happier days could be relied upon to attract a surfeit of visitors into cramped space, was now sadly diminished, just as more seats became

[67] 48.2/5 (17 and 27 Nov. 1866).   [68] *MW* (28 July 1866).
[69] *Athenaeum* (9 and 16 Mar. 1867).

available. The death of Prince Albert in 1861 had ended serious concern for music at court; and the Queen's notoriously prolonged withdrawal from public life damaged all fashionable entertainment. Worst of all, the directors were driven by necessity rather than by any proselytizing desire to seek out a new audience. Their approach was therefore very much *de haut en bas*, despite vigorous competition in the same hall from the Monday Popular and Saturday Concerts, and at the Crystal Palace. Because of the increased love for good music 'among all classes', Lucas explained in a statement to the press, the directors were proposing to extend those 'great privileges accorded to their patrons' by making subscriptions available from 1 to 3 guineas. Single tickets would range from 10s. 6d. to 2s. 6d.[70]

Behind the façade of self-esteem and hauteur the Society's finances were falling apart. It proceeded to live on capital.

---

[70] Communication from 'SL' to *MW* (26 Nov. 1868). Cf. proof notice for the 57th season in 48.13/10 (Jan. 1869).

7

Collapse

I regret I must refuse your proposal to play the concerto of Beethoven without rehearsal. I mean that would not be respectful to the composition, nor for the old Institution of the Philharmonic Society, nor for myself as an artiste. Therefore I must beg you to arrange a rehearsal ... If you are not able to arrange it I much fear that I must decline playing.

(Clara Schumann to Stanley Lucas, Mar. 1871)[1]

I should strongly advise Bülow not playing anywhere until he has made his debut at the Philharmonic Society ... the first season in London of any artist, however great, is uphill work, and a successful appearance at the Philharmonic makes every after engagement easier.

(Lucas to von Bülow's agent, Feb. 1873)[2]

I would like to advise you not to premiere your work with the Philharmonic Society. Cusins is a mediocre conductor, who unfortunately has neither the authority (as Bennett had) nor the necessary working skills regarding the orchestra. A very great pity that not one qualified fellow stands at the head of this once laudable organization.

(Joachim to Brahms, 13 Feb. 1877)[3]

I T had always been Philharmonic policy to build up and protect a capital fund, which the directors usually described as 'stock'. The procedure was so well understood that it was hardly ever discussed, occasional transactions being merely recorded without comment. By the late 1820s a sum exceeding £4,000 was thus invested in Government securities which provided a useful supplementary income and a

---

[1] 48.13/31 (n.d. [probably Mar. 1871]). Clara Schumann played Beethoven's Third Piano Concerto on 22 Mar.

[2] This quotation is drawn from two letters: 48.6/5 (n.d. [prob. Jan. 1873] and 17 Feb. 1873).

[3] Brahms–Joachim letters. I owe this reference to Styra Avins who is preparing a new edn. of Brahms's correspondence.

precious hedge against risks: equivalent to the total budget for two
average seasons. It will be recalled from Chapter 2 that in 1827, on
the sole occasion when the Society's stock appeared to be under threat,
there was an angry dispute about establishing a pension scheme for the
members. Although at least some supporters of that idea were sensible
and scrupulous men, it was defeated on the equally reasonable grounds
of defending the invested funds. From then on there was no question
of putting them at risk. Certainly there were times when fluctuations
in the annual balance of expenditure and income were followed by
modest sales or purchases of stock; but the general level of investment
was maintained. This is not to say that the Society's financial affairs
never faltered. The structure of payments and income was subject to
many changes: in the allocation of funds to orchestra and soloists, and
in the balance of receipts between subscribers and ticket purchasers.
But despite occasional upsets the essential totals remained stable: a seasonal budget of approximately £2,000, backed by investments of £4,000.

    The directors had also taken pride in amassing capital of another
kind, equivalent, for an artistic institution, to the hallmark and goodwill
of a great business undertaking. Both forms of asset now proved to be
perishable.

Living on Capital

During the 1860s, and accelerating through the 1870s, the Society's
traditional structure of finance fell apart. There was a persistent failure to balance annual income and expenditure. Even more grievous
was the selling of stock, which removed essential underpinning. With
remarkable speed, and few expressions of concern, this capital was
allowed to crumble and disappear. The chronology is significant for,
despite first impressions, disintegration did not begin with Wagner. His
departure, and the arrival of Sterndale Bennett in 1856, were indeed
accompanied by the sale of £600-worth of stock; but no further sales
were undertaken for several years; and there were even modest purchases of securities in 1861. Nor can disinvestment simply be related
to a few extravagant events. In contrast to the excitements of 1855,
financial collapse began amidst the apparent calm of 1866, a season
which offered scant attractions of repertoire or performance, and continued through one of the most dismal periods of Philharmonic history.
Invested funds fell by 1868 to exactly half the level which had been
maintained until mid-century; then continued to slide to £1,700 in 1869
and £1,000 by 1877. In the next two years stock fell again by half;
and by 1880 there was precisely £100 left, which was finally sold off
in 1881.

This liquidation of the Society's investments is displayed in Plate 13, which shows that the collapse took place over a period of fifteen years, rather than as the outcome of a few disastrous seasons. There was, of course, an underlying drain on capital because of frequent failure to balance the books; yet the budget rarely departed far from its customary level of £2,000: only in 1877 did outlays exceed £2,500. Indeed, it could be argued that bolder initiatives at an earlier stage, involving higher expenditure, might have been more successful; but that would imply that the men in power were capable of such enterprise. Surviving financial records provide scant details, which itself suggests lazy routines and insensitivity to changes in the market. Seemingly content with casual administration and waning support, the directors appear to have been unconcerned about the relative drawing-power of different artists and works, in marked contrast to the behaviour of their predecessors, and now their competitors. Another significantly changing relationship, between income from subscriptions and from tickets, similarly escaped notice. It was no great achievement to attract larger audiences after the shift to St James's Hall in 1869, for capacity had doubled. What mattered was that takings never increased sufficiently to compensate for declining subscriptions. The ratio of ticket to subscription income was about 22 per cent in 1868, and 68 per cent a decade later, but total receipts still failed to meet expenditure, with increasingly dire effects. There is no evidence that the directors gave thought to such calculations.[4]

If subscribers and the general public alike were deterred by a long run of mediocre Philharmonic seasons, and wooed by competing attractions elsewhere, there was a strategic difference between the two groups of listeners. Buyers of individual tickets were able to pick and choose between events, whereas subscribers were saddled with a season's commitment. The effective demand for concert music, like that for literature, was continuing to grow apace.[5] But people were learning to discriminate among competing performances; sometimes in search of noisier excitements, or so thought some of the old hands, who were quick to denounce loud and showy instrumentalists. Supercilious disapproval was unsuitable for concert promoters, degenerating too easily into smug self-satisfaction and, in a contemporary phrase, a 'Rip Van Winkle' attitude to concert life.[6] The public reacted by keeping away

---

[4] This account of the finances, and the related Plate 13, are based on figures to be found in two series of Account Books: 48.9/1–6 and 48.9/11–13; and the Balance Sheets for 1866–88: 48.9/7.

[5] On the demand for concerts see Ehrlich, 'Economic History and Music', *PRMA* 103 (1976–7), 194–5. On the contemporaneous market for fiction see P. Ackroyd, *Dickens* (1990), 556–7; and C. Peters, *The King of Inventors: A Life of Wilkie Collins* (1991), 234–7.

[6] *Athenaeum* (14 Mar. 1874). The remark was singularly apt: Washington Irving's Rip Van Winkle slept for twenty years.

from concerts with tired programmes and pedestrian players. Eager to
hear celebrated performers, both in familiar repertoire and new music
of promise or repute, it was already hard to please in its choice of
pianists and violinists, and was slowly learning to expect interpretation,
rather than time-beating, from conductors. And there were many new
opportunities to compare and contrast. On all counts the Philharmonic
directors, faced by these rising expectations, failed to compete with
sufficient consistency to build and retain a loyal audience. Their programmes were generally unadventurous, drab, or just second-rate; and
when a potentially attractive 'new' work or exciting performer was
allowed to make an appearance, it was almost invariably with poor
support from conductor and orchestra. Nevertheless, an illustrious
newcomer could always attract a crowd. Thus 'a vast audience' assembled on 28 April 1873 to hear Hans von Bülow play Beethoven's
'Emperor' Concerto and Bach's *Chromatic Fantasy and Fugue*, responding
with 'prolonged cheering rarely heard within the walls of St James's
Hall'.[7] Francis Planté was another pianist, from a different tradition,
whom many wanted to hear. He was described as 'the draw' at a
concert of 'hackneyed works' on May Day 1878, when he performed
Mendelssohn's D minor Concerto and some salon pieces.[8] In the same
concert the Spanish violinist Pablo Sarasate made a second Philharmonic appearance that season—at the first he played the Mendelssohn
Concerto. Already enjoying a world-wide reputation, he was beginning
to challenge the reigning champion Joachim, in piquantly contrasting
style. A year later his performance of the Bruch Concerto earned three
recalls and an encore.[9]

But such celebrations were rare glimpses of the sun in a bleak climate, and their relief to the Society's coffers and reputation always
proved temporary. Neither repertoire nor standards of performance
were consolidated or developed in consistent and cumulative fashion.
Since concerts continued to be *ad hoc*, and seasons the outcome of
perfunctory arrangements by an untalented triumvirate, it was inevitable that audiences would come and go. There is no evidence that
Cusins became more competent with experience, nor that his presence
was ever regarded as an attraction to ticket-buyers; yet there was no
attempt to replace him for a single concert, throughout seventeen seasons. Anderson was even more deeply entrenched as treasurer, and
remained so until his death in 1877. His wife (1790–1878) had retired
from public life in 1862, 'after amassing a considerable fortune', but
the Andersons continued to exert a stultifying influence in matters
of repertoire and the engagement of artists, their network extending
from a court which, after Albert's death, allowed few intrusions upon

[7] Ibid. (3 May 1873).   [8] Ibid. (4 May 1878).   [9] *MMR* (1 June 1879).

prevailing philistinism.[10] Only the triumvirate's final member, Stanley Lucas, was a newcomer, and his appointment as secretary in 1866 coincided neatly with the Society's final slide into ruin. Whatever the balance of individual responsibility among these men, the outcome of their administration was destruction of capital until in 1881 no alternatives remained except to change course or perish. In these circumstances it was extraordinary that Cusins, ready to go down with his ship, stayed on for three more years.

The collapse was not merely financial; it had also entailed consumption of capital in a non-pecuniary and less easily redeemable sense. Great damage was inflicted by trading upon the Society's artistic reputation and professional goodwill, without doing much to maintain and replenish those precious assets. It would require more resourceful efforts of repair than could be achieved just by attracting new funds, a difficult enough task after such decline. In the past the Philharmonic's musical status, once unique in England, had been well earned by enterprise and intimate association with the 'Great Masters'. Establishing their works in London, it had continued, despite occasional setbacks, to give that repertoire a platform while promoting substantial new additions: commissioning new compositions and mounting performances which were often exemplary. The finest composers and performers had been persuaded to continue in this tradition, not simply for money and a London platform, but because they were offered propitious links with musical England, a hallmark of excellence, and mutually esteemed collaboration with fellow professionals. In its best days the Philharmonic could expect special consideration from musicians to whom it provided attractions which compensated for low fees and were difficult to resist. Under the triumvirate all was laid waste: the canonic but exploratory repertoire, the tradition of excellence and pacemaking, and the professional expectations of mutual benefits.

Meagre Seasons

A simple listing of programmes, and even to some extent of performers, for the period may convey a more favourable impression. As summarized in Appendix I, the repertoire between 1867 and 1882 shows no quantitative decline in familiar Philharmonic 'classics'. Nor does closer scrutiny of the works performed conflict with an image of continuing the great tradition. In 1870, for example, Cusins celebrated the centenary of Beethoven's birth by playing through all nine

---

[10] Reference to Lucy Anderson's fortune is in the *DNB*. The entry acknowledges 'private information' from Cusins.

symphonies, as well as the Fourth Piano Concerto, with Clara Schumann, the Overtures *Fidelio* and Leonora No. 3, and so forth. There were also extensions to the established bill of fare. Beethoven, Cherubini, Haydn, Mozart, Mendelssohn, and Weber were joined, either for the first time or with additional works and increasing frequency, by Schubert, Berlioz, Schumann, Brahms, and, of course, Bennett. But these apparent continuities mask significant departures which amounted to a twofold abdication. The Philharmonic lost its reputation for pioneering and excellence, and its entitlement to special consideration as a non-commercial association of musicians. It was no longer making the pace with important new works. This was a peculiarly demeaning change in an age when superb music was being written which people were eager to hear; and responsibility for the English première of a work, for example, by Brahms, was held in high esteem. Inadequate performances were similarly conspicuous and harmful. Philharmonic concerts had ceased to be exemplary, and were rarely even competent. Hackneyed pieces were given lackadaisical readings, except for an occasional infusion of life from a visiting soloist. 'New' works were usually botched despite the advantages of 'following on'; for a second performance carried unearned benefits of prior approval, or at least interest, and therefore a likely audience, and familiarity with the music among some of the players.

Contemporaries were left in no doubt of these shortcomings. The protracted delay in programming Schumann's Piano Concerto has already been described. Similarly Schubert's 'Unfinished', which rapidly became one of the most popular of all symphonies, was not played at a Philharmonic concert until 1867, after it had 'met with such favour' at the Crystal Palace.[11] The 'Great' C major Symphony finally turned up in 1871, fifteen years after its inauguration by Manns.[12] Repeated by him in 1868, and then many times, it was now acknowledged as the work of 'a rough, ungracious, half educated man' who nevertheless ranked 'next to Beethoven among the later Germans'.[13] But several more years elapsed before the directors began to catch up with public taste, and make amends for the disgraceful episode with Mendelssohn. Their attention to Wagner was, of course, late and perfunctory, with an occasional song or overture: *Tannhäuser*, *Flying Dutchman*, and eventually (1876) the *Mastersingers*. More surprising was their dithering with Brahms, despite frequent protests of adherence, and privileged access to the composer and his work through Joachim and Clara Schumann. Perhaps this was because the music was difficult and needed guidance from a competent conductor. Cusins began in 1872 with the Serenade in D. Never a work of immediate appeal, it

---

[11] *MW* (25 May 1867).   [12] Grove's article on Schubert in *Grove*, iii. 358.
[13] *Athenaeum* (21 Mar. 1868).

did no more, on this occasion, than raise expectations of improvement if rehearsed, or when 'players become more acquainted with their parts'.[14] In the following year a 'coarse and rough band' was observed ploughing through the First Piano Concerto in pursuit of Alfred Jaell.[15] It appears to have gained little benefit from a 'run thro', not with Jaell, but with a Miss Baylhole who had been asked to play the piano part in rehearsal with the orchestra.[16] At the next concert a rising star was ineptly clouded in orbit. The young Venezuelan pianist Teresa Carreno, beginning a tempestuous career of startling versatility and acclaim, with the blessing of Gottschalk and Rubinstein, was asked to 'select any concerto which would not give you trouble or the necessity of a rehearsal', and allowed to settle for the *Rondo brillant* by Mendelssohn.[17]

Hopes of diversity were aroused by the prospectus for 1874. Even the *Athenaeum*, from which the antagonistic Chorley had retired in 1868, thought that Rip Van Winkle might be about to awaken. There was promise of fresh music by Wagner, Raff, Brahms, and Sullivan. But the latter only turned out to be represented by his Marmion Overture, which had been composed for the Society and unsuccessfully premièred in 1867; no Wagner materialized, and of Brahms there was just the Serenade in A.[18] In 1875 the journal abandoned its truce and mounted a sustained attack on Philharmonic standards of repertoire and performance, condemning them for 'marked inferiority' to what was available in 'Paris, Brussels, Leipzig, Cologne, Berlin, etc'; and, more to the point, at the Crystal Palace. There George Grove and August Manns were demonstrating several times a week how much could be accomplished with intelligence, enthusiasm, and limited resources. There were daily rehearsals and frequent cheap concerts with a small regular band, and extra players were recruited for enterprising Saturday concerts.[19]

The opening Philharmonic concert that season was 'in Memoriam Sir William Sterndale Bennett', including the Prelude and Funeral March from *Ajax*, and his sacred cantata *The Woman of Samaria*, with a chorus mainly drawn from the Royal Academy of Music 'in tribute to the memory of their late Principal'. Cusins contributed an air from his own cantata *Gideon*, and the always co-operative Joachim played the Mendelssohn Concerto.[20] No happier were the events of 26 April when Rubinstein's Violin Concerto had to be cut to two movements, a Wagner overture was replaced by Mendelssohn's *Athalie* March, and the soprano in Elisabeth's prayer from *Tannhäuser* was hissed for being 'so awfully out of tune'.[21] Next year there was praise for the band's

[14] Ibid. (13 July 1872). [15] Ibid. (28 June 1873). [16] 48.6/5 (21 Apr. 1873).
[17] 48.6/5 (24 Feb. 1873). [18] *Athenaeum* (14 Mar. 1874).
[19] Ibid. (27 Mar. 1875).
[20] Ibid. A devastating review concludes that it was a 'wearisome' evening.
[21] Ibid. (1 May 1875).

demonstration of a skill which was becoming a mainstay of London orchestral playing: 'promptitude in reading novelties at first sight', in this case a Rubinstein symphony. It was a dubious Philharmonic legacy. Two extra morning concerts, making a total of ten that season, did nothing to improve the Society's financial or artistic health.[22] Critical disdain was further provoked by the 'great eyesore' of the high 'conductor pulpit' on which Cusins 'perched aloft', instead of standing, as did Deldevez, Pasdeloup, and Colonne before the Conservatoire, Cirque d'Hiver, and Châtelet orchestras, all deemed superior in ensemble to the Philharmonic. When conducting concertos Cusins was urged to follow continental practice: 'stand behind and not sit before the grand pianoforte'. The strings were said to need more elbow-room because the orchestra was too closely packed on an insufficiently raked platform, and was therefore 'as invisible as Herr Wagner's Bayreuth band'. The double-bass section needed strengthening, particularly because few of the instruments had four strings, as in France and Germany. It was possible, concluded this withering appraisal, that better seating and more care in selecting players might improve the 'tone and general effect'; but in comparison with the standards set by Manns it was 'manifestly absurd' to suggest that the Philharmonic orchestra was remotely as good as it should be.[23]

Such wounding comparisons were now commonplace among keen concert-goers, who voted with their feet, and among critics who continued to attend and scoff, if they were not overawed by the offer of a free seat.[24] Adverse reports were not confined to those journals whose sarcasms were thought by some Philharmonic stalwarts merely to reflect the negative stance of the 'amateur' bystander. No one could thus dismiss the *Monthly Musical Record*. It had been launched as recently as 1871 by the music-publisher Augener, under austere and initially well-disposed editorship: Ebenezer Prout was already prominent among London's schoolmen musicians.[25] Yet by 1877 the new journal was moved to protest against an extended but meagre diet, sauced by pointless innovation which disregarded the public's needs, yet failed to provide genuine initiatives and tolerable standards of performance. The concert which began that season, it complained, started at 8.30 p.m., had no interval for 'tea, coffee, ices, chat'; and presumed to court approval for introducing the Grieg Piano Concerto to Philharmonic audiences with a pianist (Dannreuther) who had already played it twice at the Crystal

---

[22] Ibid. (3 and 24 June 1875).   [23] Ibid. (3 and 24 June 1876; 3 Mar. 1877).

[24] At this time admissions were granted to reporters from twenty-six papers and journals: 48.2/7 (28 Mar. 1874).

[25] Ebenezer Prout (1835–1909) was the most redoubtable of Victorian pedant-musicians. He began teaching at the National Training School for Music in 1876 and at the RAM in 1879.

Palace. The audience was described as 'neither numerous nor demonstrative' and the band lacking in that 'elasticity of spirit and refinement to which Mr Manns has accustomed us'. The violinist, Henry Holmes, had broken down in a familiar Spohr concerto.[26] And so the dismal parade continued; a report on a later concert noting that only the solo violinist and pianist, Mlles Neruda and Mehlig, 'succeeded in rousing an apathetic conductor and evoking . . . some show of satisfaction and enthusiasm' from the audience. The pianist was known to be playing Weber's *Konzertstück* 'much against her will' since she had previously performed it both for the Philharmonic and at a Manns benefit.[27] Prout concluded that season with a simple and blunt assessment. The Society could 'no longer be said to represent musical progress in England, as it once did . . . by diffusing a knowledge of unfamiliar works'. The band's 'standards of execution' were pronounced inferior to what was 'found elsewhere both in and near the metropolis'; and, almost as an afterthought, readers were reminded that Mr Cusins had now been in charge for eleven seasons.[28] Even more damning, perhaps, was the gentler acquiescence of a subsequent note: the Society was 'principally supported by its subscribers, the public only being invited to assist', so there was no point in criticizing its lack of enterprise.[29]

If Philharmonic audiences were kept on short commons for entertainment in listening, they could, on payment of an extra sixpence, receive prodigious compensations in print. The appointment of G. A. Macfarren as 'analytical essayist' at a fee of 40 guineas was a guarantee of high seriousness, and an indication of the directors' priorities, since no performer was paid such a fee. The new tone of discourse cannot be justly sampled in brief, for the essayist's style was not terse, but it may be indicated by comparing the notes provided to accompany Beethoven's Sixth Symphony. In former days the listener to a performance under, say, Costa, would turn to his programme and find appropriate pastoral verses by James Thomson attached to each movement: 'See the country far diffus'd . . .', 'And pensive listen to the various voice . . .', 'To notes of native music the respondent dance . . .', ' . . . The tempest growls', and finally ' . . . 'Tis beauty all and grateful song around'.[30] Under the triumvirate it became necessary for the same music to be addressed with more weight. Beginning with opus number, dedication, keys of each movement and directions of mood in the original German, the reader was led to polylinguistic and multisyllabic

[26] *MMR* (1 Mar. 1877). Holmes apologized to the directors, and was assured that he had 'not lost in public estimation' and the contretemps had 'awakend an admission from those present of his great talent.' 48.2/7 (19 Feb. 1877). On the eventful careers of the brother violinists Alfred and Henry Holmes, see *New Grove*.   [27] *MMR* (1 July 1877).
[28] *MMR* (1 Aug. 1877).   [29] *MMR* (1 Mar. 1879).
[30] James Thomson the Elder (1700–48).

consideration of history and precedent, context and aesthetic, in great
wedges of pedantry:

> To proceed but one step further, let it be believed that the exception, rather
> than the rule, is for a musician to forethink in facts what he expresses in notes;
> it cannot be otherwise than that these very notes are the unacknowledged
> representation of his own feelings at the time of writing, and that he produces
> thus a piece of objective, if not subjective, portraiture.[31]

A few concert-goers may have found such enlightenment sufficient compensation for 'shortcomings' and 'most imperfect preparation' in the
performance of Beethoven symphonies that season, but others might
have agreed that 'if the Philharmonic Society would keep its place,
what is done must be better done'.[32]

   As we leaf back and forth through the Cusins programmes the
lasting impression is of amiably indiscriminate spatchcocking, a piling
of bad upon good. Even Brahms, by far the most favoured new composer, received scant justice. Since his music was widely acknowledged
to be difficult to play, it is all the more surprising that quality was
always sacrificed to quantity. In April 1876 Cusins *began* a concert—
which also included Beethoven's Second Symphony, Mendelssohn's
Ruy Blas Overture, Joachim playing a Spohr concerto and some
Brahms *Hungarian Dances*, and a 'sacred song' appropriately pleading
'Save me, O God'—with the *German Requiem*! It was an indulgent reporter
who described the 'execution as good as can be expected from the
little rehearsal a production of such complexity and magnitude ob-
tains here'.[33] There was probably a similar failure to match intention
with execution when Brahms's First Symphony was proudly announced
as given 'first time at these concerts' in April 1877, after performances
at Cambridge and the Crystal Palace, but received with 'no very great
sensation'.[34] Audiences were by no means indifferent. When Joachim
introduced the Violin Concerto to Philharmonic audiences on 6 March
1879 he 'filled the hall and greatly augmented funds by extra sale of
tickets' and then repeated the performance at the next concert on 20
March.[35] But even today the work requires strong orchestral direction
and adequate rehearsal. In prevailing circumstances it was fortunate
that, although the Society's programme boasted 'MS., new', its performances were preceded by one under Manns at Sydenham, so at
least some of the Philharmonic players would have gained useful experience. In the same concert a reading of Schumann's 'Rhenish' Symphony

[31] Thomson's verses were regularly used in programmes; e.g. 8 May 1843 and 30 Mar.
1846. Macfarren's 'Analytical and Historical Programme' is for the concert on 9 May 1870.
His engagement and fee appear in 48.2/6 (13 Feb. 1869).
[32] *Athenaeum* (28 May 1870).   [33] Ibid. (15 Apr. 1876).
[34] Ibid. (21 Apr. 1877).   [35] *MMR* (1 Apr. 1879).

was described as giving the 'music no chance' because of the 'coarseness and slovenliness of the orchestra'.[36]

Competition and New Economics

London concert-goers no longer expected initiative and excellence from the Philharmonic. Its habit of following Manns was again noticed when Rubinstein's 'Ocean' Symphony was given a hearing after appearing 'long ago . . . at the Crystal Palace and elsewhere'. Such shadowing was, at best, taken as an indication of 'amends for past omissions'.[37] Similarly an overture by Walter Macfarren, brother of the analytical essayist, had been first done by Kuhe at Brighton; and Goetz's Overture *Frühlings* was again an import from the 'Crystal Palace and elsewhere'.[38] In practice the loss of a reputation for pioneering was probably less damaging to the Society's image than persistently feeble performances; such as when Brahms's Second Symphony was introduced, and 'received very coldly' after being previously heard to better effect 'in another place'.[39] Nor were wounding comparisons confined to familiar and nearby competitors, for occasional visitors of distinction brought further reminders which by 1881 were mounting to a crescendo of nagging insistence, that mediocrity was no longer acceptable in London. In that year, Hallé followed Berlioz's *La Damnation de Faust* with *L'Enfance du Christ*. Charles Lamoureux, whose conducting was described as establishing new standards of 'precision, firmness and expressiveness' in Paris, gave two concerts after 'as many rehearsals as necessary' with more than a hundred of London's 'best instrumentalists' led by Sainton. Programmes ranged from the familiar 'Carnaval Romain' to music by Lalo, Massenet, and Saint-Saëns's 'strange and by no means lovely *Danse Macabre*', all played with unprecedented discipline and verve.[40]

A final blow was delivered by Hans Richter whose exhaustive apprenticeship under Wagner and von Bülow, ability to play most orchestral instruments, and profound experience of conducting opera in Budapest and Vienna, had culminated in responsibility for the *Ring* première at Bayreuth in 1876. Richter's first English appearances were at an Albert Hall Wagner Festival in May 1877, where he shared the platform with the composer, and did most of the conducting. An orchestra of 170 players, mostly English residents with a few from Bayreuth, including a group of tubas, was led by Wilhelmj. An experienced critic

---

[36] *Daily Telegraph*, quoted in *MW* (29 Mar. 1879).
[37] *MW* (14 June 1879). Anton Rubinstein, the model for Klesmer in George Eliot's *Daniel Deronda* was still being widely acclaimed as a significant composer.
[38] *MW* (7 Feb. 1880). [39] *MMR* (1 Apr. 1880). [40] *MT* (1 Apr. 1881).

whose standards had been set in Manchester, where concerts were generally better rehearsed than in the metropolis, later insisted that 'modern orchestral conducting' arrived in England on that occasion. 'It was
then brought home to everyone that conducting was a great art worthy
of independent cultivation. The public began to take an interest in the
style of different conductors, and to show some sensitiveness as regards
interpretations of the great masters.'[41] The assertion that 'first class
orchestral playing in England' *began* with these concerts, is surely wrong,
but they certainly won devotion, from players and audiences alike, to
wholly new standards of consistent professionalism, which Richter
practised in England for the next thirty years.[42] His reputation was
consolidated by an annual series of concerts beginning in May 1879.
In 1880 he included Beethoven's Ninth Symphony with two hundred
voices, and a performance of the *Tristan* 'Prelude and Liebestod' which
raised temperatures, one critic exclaiming 'morbid . . . it cries for itself
"unclean, unclean, unclean" '.[43] By their third season the Richter concerts
were acclaimed as 'so suddenly, but far from unaccountably, sprung
into a position of first class importance'. They were eclectic and
marvellously played, mostly, in Grove's phrase, 'without book'. They
ranged from Beethoven's Ninth Symphony and the Brahms Tragic and
Academic Festival Overtures, via Liszt's *Mephisto Waltz* and Wagner's
Siegfried Idyll (Richter had played trumpet at its celebrated first performance), to the less characteristic Berlioz *Nuits d'été*.[44]

   This efflorescence of concert life had manifold implications for the
Society. Increased competition for audiences and performers may have
appeared similar to past experience with the New Philharmonic, but
it represented far more of a threat. The season was longer—some of
Richter's concerts were in the winter—much busier, and altogether
more professional. Agents and impresarios were moving in, with expertise, international networks, business acumen, and a degree of awareness which offered both a challenge to the Society and some possibilities
of benefit. They could provide those intermediary services which are
commonly misunderstood in naïve denunciations of 'parasitic middle-
men', wherever primitive and modern economics meet. Far from bat-
tening upon music, inflating costs and taking their percentage, the
majority of agents were crucial to the functioning and growth of a
worldwide, volatile, high-risk industry. They articulated markets, providing information about repertoire and artists, and matching one to
the other; signalling relative fees and drawing-power; offering alternatives to buyer and seller, with wider perspectives and far more flexibility

---

[41] Arthur Johnstone, writing in the *Manchester Guardian* (20 Oct. 1897), quoted in C. Fifield,
True Artist and True Friend: A Biography of Hans Richter (1993), 337–8.
[42] Nettel, *Orchestra in England*, 220–3.   [43] *MMR* (1 July 1880).
[44] 'Richter' in *Grove*; *MT* (1 June and 1 Nov. 1881).

than ever in the past. They shared administrative burdens, risks, and time-scales; providing audiences with wider choice and assisting the careers of musicians by increasing their freedom to work at music. In so far as they attempted to cope with this new world the Philharmonic's directors were particularly beset by two problems: new orchestral economics, and the bidding up of soloists' fees.

The first was a matter of size and rigidity, rather than high wages. Larger concert halls and prevailing tastes dictated as big an orchestra as possible—seventy or eighty men was normal at this time (there were still no women)—regardless of the style, or original instrumentation of the music to be performed. Although players' payments were kept low by the mounting flood of applicants, the total wage bill therefore remained high and inflexible, despite occasional trimming. The structure of payments was, as always, too diversified to allow easy summary; but the general trend is fairly clear. Before the 1868 season opened, for example, there were wage cuts 'to lower expenses'; three players resigned immediately, and others doubtless followed.[45] In 1873 terms were increased for some of the men 'according to position', presumably in an attempt to retain good players; but the disastrously extended season of 1877 necessitated a total stoppage of payments for the tenth concert.[46] Yet the budget was still dominated by orchestral costs. Constituent items were approximately £320 for soloists, £274 for advertisements, £193 for hire of the hall, £112 for the conductor, £40 Macfarren's essays, £59 for deputies (several of whom received only one guinea per concert), and £939 for the listed orchestra. Returning to eight concerts next season, the directors tried to impose further cuts and a rationalization of new engagements 'on the same scale as for concerts of a similar character in London . . . Principals 2 guineas, Ripieno 1 guinea as a minimum, 2nd wind £1..11..6d.'.[47] These were much the same individual payments as during the the early 1840s, but to a considerably larger band. It cost £854 plus £51 for deputies. The general impression is that total orchestral budgets for the season, including £100 for the conductor, were always kept below £1,000, at considerable sacrifice to players' incomes and levels of recruitment.[48]

Since orchestras had become 'labour-intensive', management was resistant to improvement in wages and working conditions, except in so far as it could pass increased costs on to the consumer. As in coal-mining, 'industrial relations' tended to be unaccommodating, if superficially more cordial than in industries below ground. It is no accident that musicians' unions, when they finally emerged, were tough, even

---

[45] 48.2/6 (6 Dec. 1867).   [46] 48.2/7 (20 Dec. 1873 and 14 July 1877).
[47] 48.2/7 (28 Oct. 1877).
[48] Figures are in 48.5/1(a); 48.9/4–7; and 48.9/11–13.

among highly skilled players.[49] As the symphony orchestra became large
and unwieldy it was also subject to new pressures. The men were expected to work more intensively on 'standard repertoire' and with difficult new material, often in unfamiliar styles, with no diminution in
the length of concerts. They were also beginning to encounter conductors who wanted to impose concepts of interpretation which required
considerable time in rehearsal, and application in performance, if the
outcome were to be effective: performing the *Tristan* 'Prelude', or even
a Beethoven symphony, under Hans Richter, was more demanding
work, and needed more careful preparation, than a saunter through
'Fingal's Cave' with William Cusins. What had been outrageously experimental, and easily rejected, under Wagner in 1855, was now becoming an irresistible norm for concerts at a level of accomplishment
which the Philharmonic ostensibly desired to emulate, if not to lead.
Resulting pressures on costs were greatly increased by the changing
design of concerts: items that could be done without rehearsal were
reduced in number, and soon practically disappeared. Admittedly, it
was still common for soloists to perform one or two extra pieces, alone
or with piano accompaniment, as listed on the programme, or as
encores; but chamber music was now rarely played at symphony
concerts. The bulk of the concert required the whole orchestra, and
therefore more time for rehearsal, if there was to be any attempt at
interpretation. Even concertos, including the familiar canon, which had
hardly ever entailed preparation by the orchestra, began to demand
reappraisal; some new additions, like those of Brahms, threatening
cruel exposure if unrehearsed. A final pressure upon orchestral costs
arose, paradoxically, from the oversupply of players in London which,
although it kept wages down, also encouraged further competition.
There began a proliferation of 'orchestras', more reckless than in any
other city.

   An unstable and relentlessly competitive working environment encouraged appropriately footloose attitudes among players who were
all freelance. Therefore, although it was customary to speak of 'the
Philharmonic orchestra', the label meant little. Turnover within its
ranks, both short and long term, was becoming so commonplace that
continuity of ensemble, and a collective 'learning curve' of familiarity
with the literature, let alone of style, would have been difficult to
promote, even under a capable and respected conductor. A comparison
of orchestral lists provides one measure of these fluctuations.[50] Out of
sixty-six players listed in 1860 there were fifteen in the 1870 orchestra,

---

[49] See Ehrlich, *Music Profession*, esp. ch. 8.
[50] See App. 3, below. Although orchestral work was unhealthy the changes in personnel,
over periods discussed, generally indicate mobility, not retirement or mortality. Indeed
several names can be observed not only to leave but also, on occasion, to return.

and two in 1880.[51] From eighty-four instrumentalists named in the 1870 orchestra, twenty-four were still playing in 1880 and only four in 1890. Moreover the figures greatly understate the realities of turnover, because published lists do not include the names of extra players and 'deputies', or replacements, who were engaged for practically every concert. In 1877, for example, twenty-two such men were employed at various times during the season.[52] It is common knowledge in every workplace that high turnover decreases efficiency and raises costs, weaknesses which are compounded if mobility is highest among the most skilled. In the Philharmonic orchestra during this period, apart from the principal viola, R. Blagrove, who remained solidly in place, most survivors occupied back desks. It was the front-desk men who were more frequently tempted by alternative jobs, and tended to move most frequently. The effects upon performing standards were self-evident. Among the directors concern was expressed at the 'growing practice' of breaking agreements. Fines were suggested—the orchestra manager advised a rate of £10—and at least one player was dismissed, in an attempt 'to maintain the engagements of the Society to the strict letter'.[53] But these were ineffective gestures towards discipline and stability, reflecting past clashes with the opera. By the late 1870s Monday nights were being abandoned, which gave belated, but only occasional, access to leading players from the two Italian opera-houses.[54] Such limited and overdue measures of rationality were insufficient to deal with the fundamental need to give the orchestra a firm foundation. It was an ironic failure in a Society which had begun as an orchestral co-operative.

For more than a decade August Manns had been attempting to bring some common sense to London's orchestral anarchy. His long correspondence begins in 1869 with workaday discussion about co-operation in the provision of performers, scores, and instrumental parts. Communication between concert-givers was eased by a letter service which could deliver several times a day, taking three hours between Sydenham and central London, and by the affable knowledgeability and enthusiasm of Manns and Grove.[55] It was made difficult by the lofty indifference of Philharmonic directors who were

[51] One was the double-bass player William Castell, who died eight years later at the age of 75. See various references and photograph (p. 301) in A. V. Beedell, *Decline of the English Musician* (Oxford, 1992). [52] 48.9/11–13.
[53] 48.6/5 (24 Apr. and 18 May 1875); 48.2/7 (8 and 22 May 1875).
[54] Sacrosanct Monday was steadily abandoned. After 1869 first, and sometimes second, concerts were presented on Wednesday nights. In 1875 the opening concert, in 1876 first two, and in 1877 first three concerts were on Thursday. The next few seasons were shared between Thursdays and Wednesdays.
[55] The lengthy correspondence begins in 48.13/22 on 2 Apr. 1869. A typically negative response by the directors is in 48.2/7 (26 July 1875).

apparently unwilling to rationalize orchestras, rehearsals, and concerts. In 1874 Manns complained that 'your Philharmonic Band includes 18 members of the Crystal Palace band' who cannot be spared when times clash; and suggested a few routine adjustments. Matters came to a head two years later: 'It is a great pity that your Society did not follow my suggestion and settle an arrangement with our directors for our entire band.' Such a plan would have been 'of mutual advantage', continued the indefatigable professional: the Crystal Palace could have offered its players '6 or 8 good engagements a year' while the Philharmonic would have a 'nucleus . . . always intact and at your disposal for a cheap extra rehearsal in case of new and difficult works'. Now Manns confessed to having 'not the slightest idea how matters can be arranged'. In the past he 'could accommodate your wants as long as you had only about 5 or 6 of our people but (now) you have nearly all my wind and brass and all my double basses and some other strings'. Some of his men were breaking contracts, and he feared having to 'discharge them and thus break up a band which it has taken many years to form and train'.[56] Nothing came, therefore, of these suggestions which could have benefited players, audiences, and music. The two organizations soldiered on with varying but diminished effectiveness, and the anarchic disarrangements of London's orchestras were further entrenched. The Society's response to exigent pressures was to stay aloof and *sauve qui peut*, mainly by skimping rehearsals. Sightreading traditions were thus reinforced by functionaries who were inured to obsolete practices, and by a conductor who made few demands: a capable musician might have reacted to the changing spirit of the age by insisting upon time for orchestral training and interpretative refinement. Meanwhile competition from better concerts made such makeshifts increasingly unacceptable.

If the directors were unable to cope with the new orchestral economics, they did know how to keep soloists' fees in check by avoiding expensive performers and trading upon old loyalties. Paying below the going rate was, of course, traditional practice; no theme is more persistent in the Society's correspondence than complaints about fees. The great baritone Julius Stockhausen was moved to complain in 1856, the year he gave the first public performance of Schubert's *Die schöne Müllerin* in Vienna, 'I have never heard of an artist singer, pianist or violin player being *called to London* . . . and paid at the terms of ten guineas per concert.'[57] Nevertheless he came, and other celebrities similarly lowered their fees for the Philharmonic. By 1870 Stockhausen was immensely distinguished and very closely associated with Brahms, but still had to write

---

[56] 48.2/7 (14 Mar. 1874; 8 and 13 Mar. 1876).   [57] 48.13/33 (21 May 1856).

I hope the old relationship existing between Mr Anderson and myself will not become a cool one for the sake of professional terms. I have long time enough been singing for the cause of art, but allow me to say that when a singer now 43 years of age leaves his home to cross the channel he is not supposed to deprive himself of comfort and repose for the cause of art.

His terms were 20 guineas, or 40 if there was to be a public rehearsal.[58] In the same year Sivori refused to play for less than 20 guineas, so it was decided to ask Joachim and, failing him, Wilhelmina Neruda.[59]

The tribulations of surviving loyalties are best illustrated by the Society's dealings, over a long period, with its two favourite performing musicians. For her first engagement in 1856, when she had been playing in public for twenty-five years and was widely celebrated, Clara Schumann received 10 guineas. Five subsequent appearances were similarly recompensed, until 1868, when she refused an engagement because she was now being represented by an agent: 'Mr Chappell heightened my terms this year to 25 guineas. I promised to him not to play in other concerts for less.'[60] The directors were adamant and Clara climbed down after receiving a 'kind note' from Lucas 'telling me about the object of the Philharmonic Society ... Mr Chappell has given full liberty in respect of your concerts.'[61] Meanwhile Joachim's £10 fee had been raised in 1866 to £15.[62] Clara continued to receive 10 guineas but reminded the directors in 1870 that 'at the same time you will realise that it is an exception which I make for the old institution'.[63] Her willingness to make sacrifices in the cause of art may have been weakened by the conditions and attitudes which prompted her letter of complaint quoted at the head of this chapter. Presumably such experiences were also discussed with her intimate friend Brahms, who, as an adjacent letter shows, was well briefed by Joachim about current Philharmonic activities. In 1876 Chappell asked 25 guineas each for Clara and Joachim, and the directors adopted the usual tactic of trying to dodge the agent and 'apply direct to those artists'.[64] But this time Clara refused to budge and the directors agreed to pay her 25 guineas after voting four to one, Anderson 'entering his protest'.[65] A decade later her terms would be 80 guineas, as paid by Chappell, and Joachim's 40 guineas.[66]

It is difficult to exaggerate the plight to which the Society was being reduced. Among the copious evidence of shortcomings, Joachim's

---

[58] 48.13/33 (21 Apr. 1870).   [59] 48.2/6 (4 Feb. 1871).
[60] 48.13/31 (17 Jan. 1868).
[61] 48.2/6 (8 and 15 Feb. 1868); 48.13/31 (9 Feb. 1868).
[62] 48.2/5 (3 Mar. 1865).   [63] 48.13/31 (28 Feb. 1870).
[64] 48.2/7 (15 Jan. 1876).   [65] 48.2/7 (19 Feb. 1876).
[66] 48.13/31 (13 Feb. 1887); 48.2/9 (25 Oct. 1884).

considered opinion, quoted at the head of this chapter, is surely con-
clusive. He goes on to recommend that Brahms should preferably
get in touch with Manns at the Crystal Palace. It was a private communication from the Philharmonic's oldest, most loyal and distinguished friend, to the composer whom it was so anxious to court,
constantly requesting compositions and visits.[67] Written when Cusins
had been allowed ten years in front of the orchestra, Joachim's letter
must be regarded as utterly damning. By the end of the decade
nothing had been done to get out of this rut, although the orchestra
was increasingly described as capable of better playing. Its access to
good instrumentalists was improving, but without competent conducting no improvement could be expected.[68] Since the regime was im-
pregnable, only financial collapse could enforce change. It came in
1880, assisted, perhaps, by an intense bout of patriotism in the season's
programmes.

In November 1879 Walter Macfarren persuaded the directors to
agree that *every concert* 'should include at least one work of a resident
musician in this country'. At the next meeting, which also reduced the
orchestra's size and fees, a number of predominantly obscure British
composers were named as suitable for a Philharmonic platform. It was
suggested that works by current directors should perhaps be avoided,
and that it might be 'inadvisable to propose a new work without seeing
the score', but parochialism was generally allowed full rein without concern for public taste.[69] During the ensuing season there were pieces by
Harold Thomas, J. F. Barnett, Alberto Randegger, Charles E. Stephens,
George Henschel, Benedict, Sullivan (Symphony in E minor), Cusins
and Parry (some songs), and the Macfarrens. There was also a piano
concerto by Arthur H. Jackson, a young student at the Royal Academy
of Music, where it had previously been performed in 1878.[70] Not that
there was much unanimity in this distribution of favour among resident
musicians, as a vigorously young and untypically articulate representative
pointed out. In response to a foolish reference by Lucas to 'outsiders',
which Stanford assumed was a reference to 'Mackenzie, Parry and
myself', the latter, then in his late twenties and building a reputation
at Cambridge university, demanded explication. Were 'outsiders' simply
those who lived outside London, or were neither members or associates
of the Philharmonic, nor 'past or present pupils or members of the

---

[67] Approaches to Brahms are minuted in 48.2/7 (5 July 1873; 1 Apr. 1876; 19 Feb. 1877;
3 Mar. 1877; 28 Sept. 1877 (ask to conduct his Requiem); 23 Nov. 1878); 48.2/8 (25 and
27 July and 25 Oct. 1879 (invite to conduct; terms not more than 150 guineas)).
[68] See e.g. *MMR* (1 Mar. 1878), and *Athenaeum* (16 Mar. 1878).
[69] 48.2/8 (1 and 15 Nov. 1879).
[70] *Daily Telegraph*, quoted in *MW*, (10 July 1880).

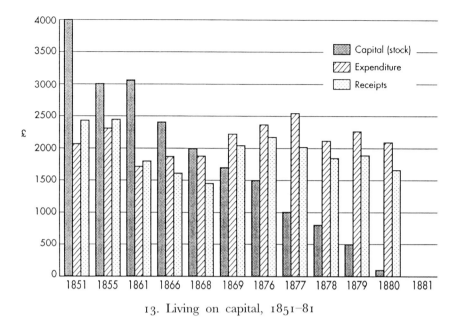

13. Living on capital, 1851–81

Academy of Music'?[71] With such divisions among English musicians, and the prospect of more seasons like 1880, the Philharmonic's mere survival through the decade into the 1880s would have been a triumph of resilience. Its collapse, recovery, and rapid entry into a golden age was something of a miracle.

[71] 48.13/32, letter 209 (n.d. [1880]). Stanford had previously written to Cummings for private advice on submitting a symphony: 48.13/32, letter 207 (7 Oct. 1879).

8

Francesco Berger and Recovery

If Sterndale Bennett ... was a tired, listless conductor ... Sir Arthur Sullivan is a veritable nightcap.

> (Eduard Hanslick, reviewing a Philharmonic concert,
> June 1886)

Novelty appears to be the order of the season.

> (*MT*, commenting on Cowen's first prospectus, Apr. 1888)

We do not suppose that the Concerto will often be performed in this country, but given a pianist competent to the task, connoisseurs cannot but receive it with interest.

> (*Daily Telegraph*, reporting a performance of the B flat minor
> Concerto, conducted by Tchaikovsky on 11 Apr. 1889)

B y the summer of 1880 the Philharmonic Society was known to be a wreck, about to go down with the few who cared to remain on board. Yet salvage and refitting were undertaken with such speed and efficiency that within a decade it was being described as a flagship for the nation. 'Foreigners', declared the *Musical Times* in April 1890, 'will largely judge our musical condition by the state of the Society which, in their eyes, represents it'. The choice of representative institution was provocative, ignoring a common belief that musical England lay 'further North' and, with more justice, denying prime place to conservatory, university, professional association, or court. But whatever its implications for music and musicians in the culture of late Victorian England, this was a realistic account of foreign perceptions, and an extraordinary tribute to the Philharmonic.

The Society's historians have not attempted to explain so remarkable a swing in fortune and status. Foster provides a useful roll-call: in 1880 'Mr. Charles Edward Stephens succeeded Mr. Walter Macfarren as Hon. Treasurer and Director; Mr. Henry Hersee succeeded Mr. Stanley Lucas as Secretary, and Dr. Francis Hueffer took G. A. Macfarren's place as Writer of the Analytical Programmes.' We note the importance attached to programme notes; and failure to mention, through adherence to rigid chronology and job-specification, the man who saved the Philharmonic, and the scale of his achievement.[1] In similar vein, Elkin addresses the crisis by glancing momentarily at financial ruin, and then passing easily to salvation, via an arbitrary mingling of people and events:

Unhappily, the crisis in the Society's affairs seems to have coincided with an outbreak of dissension among its officers, resulting in a large crop of resig-nations, including that of Walter Macfarren, the Hon. Treasurer; matters were further complicated when two of the gentlemen elected to fill the vacancies refused to serve; and, to crown it all, the Secretary (Stanley Lucas) chose this inconvenient moment to retire. However these hurdles were in due course surmounted; and rejuvenated by the new blood in its direction, and, fortified by the ample guarantee against loss, the Society embarked upon one of the most brilliant periods in its career.[2]

Any improvement upon Pangloss must acknowledge that dissension was no mere question of personalities; and that new blood, in both mem-bership and direction came, not by means of amicable succession, but through haemorrhage and transfusion. Financial reform and its admin-istrative underpinning were extraordinary achievements, which ensured that a moribund institution was revivified by 'ample guarantee', as Elkin puts it. But they were not sufficient to keep it functioning into the twentieth century. Only the Society's cultural transformation could do that: an escape from parochial senescence to a new vitality which was identified, and sometimes abused, in a vogue word of the time, as 'cosmopolitanism'.

The Return to Life

It may be objected that 1880 was neither the first, nor the last, year in which the Philharmonic Society hovered on the brink of collapse; and sceptical readers who have persevered so far may well recall the story of the boy who cried wolf. This time the threat was sufficiently real and close to encourage a few of the members and associates to attend four, rather than the usual two, general meetings in July and November. Less than twenty were present at any of the gatherings which decided the Society's future; but their procedures could no longer be confined to routine acquiescence in mediocre events and unexplained financial accounts; and the prospect of winding up may have offered glimpses of reality. Yet, to judge by the written record, nobody indulged in plain speaking. It may have been that the discourse of London's respectable musicians was already set into patterns of

[1] Foster, *History*, 377–8.   [2] Elkin, *Royal Philharmonic*, 74–5.

euphemism and gentility which fogged most issues; and innate caution was probably encouraged by desire for a semblance of unity. There was some response to the immediate need for emergency funding; but this too leaves an impression of amiable colleagues coping equably with problems which amounted to little more than a temporary setback. In fact the divisions were acute, with alternative views of any possible future diametrically opposed. The outcome was a complete change of direction.

At the first meetings in July a brief financial statement led to 'the question of how the Society was to be continued', and there was an adjournment for a week while the directors belatedly prepared a printed letter of explanation to all members.[3] Seeking compromise, its tone was alternately ominous, complacent, and valedictory, while clinging to possibilities of future life in a better world. A 'serious deficit', was admitted to be cause for 'great concern', but it could only be attributed to rival concerts which, 'doubtless in many cases merely on account of novelty', had diverted 'public support from established institutions'. Hopes of immediate improvement could be dismissed, and since the reserve fund was practically exhausted, it was now 'the very serious duty of the Society to determine in what way, *if at all*, it is to continue to fulfil the purposes for which it was sixty-eight years ago instituted' (my italics).[4] Subscription fees might be adjusted, and the Royal Family, as patrons, asked for 'substantial support'. More practically, a guarantee fund of some £1,500 might be raised, as an essential precondition for a season of six concerts, in place of the customary eight. Guarantors would be expected to bear losses, 'if any, pro rata', and £506 had already been promised. In the ensuing discussion an alternative proposition for five concerts without 'extraneous aid' lacked support, and there were no further recipes for salvation. Cusins promised to approach the Queen, and it was also suggested that she 'be asked to command a morning concert'.[5]

Fund-raising was the immediate task, poorly timed because out of season. On the eve of the next general meeting less than £1,200 had been guaranteed, and the treasurer, W. Macfarren, proposed that concerts be suspended 'for one or more seasons'. At this point Charles Hallé, who had just been invited to join the directors and, benefiting

---

[3] 48.3/2 (14 July 1880).

[4] 48.2/8 (10 July 1880). This document was read at the second general meeting, on 21 July. See n. 5, below.

[5] 48.3/2 (21 July 1880). The response was to purchase four stalls tickets for 12 guineas, which earned gratitude for 'so signal and valuable a mark of the Royal favour', but could not be advertised: 48.2/8 (19 Mar. and 7 May 1881). Further appeals for 'substantial support' were not pursued for the time being. Requesting a 'command' concert had already been deemed inadvisable: 48.2/8 (15 May 1880; 18 July 1881).

from the healthier orchestral climate of Manchester, had no personal
interest at stake, offered to make a final appeal to members.[6] He did
so in the wake of the gloomiest report in the Society's history. The
season had resulted in a loss of £382; the last one hundred pounds
of stock had been sold; and no one was prepared to undertake future
concerts unless the Fund could be raised to £1,500. It was now pushed
up to £1,442. 2s., and on this knife-edge Hallé saved the Philharmonic
by carrying a motion to proceed with next season 'on the days already
fixed'.[7] It was only a temporary respite, for though many of the
guarantors were musicians, continuing the Society's central tradition of
musicians supporting music, its allegiances were shifting by the day.[8]
Radical changes were set in motion at the very meeting which agreed
to go ahead with the season. Francesco Berger, who had briefly been
a director in 1876, the year of Anderson's death, but was only now
coming into prominence, proposed to amend the 'laws' so as to allow
an increase in the number of members from forty to sixty.[9] This was
done one week later at a meeting which recruited twenty new members
with hitherto neglected talents and connections.[10] The bustle of activity continued with yet another general meeting in December, this time
to elect directors. Three resigned, including W. Macfarren, who was
replaced as treasurer by C. E. Stephens, with Benedict, Stainer, and
Cummings also joining Berger.[11]

There were no grounds for equanimity, except that the fund now
exceeded £1,700. Bold proposals for expenditure included an undertaking to raise the orchestra's fees, increase its string sections substantially, and allow two rehearsals, the first private, the second open to
subscribers, members, and associates. These arrangements were linked
to vainglorious hopes that Brahms would conduct three of the concerts.[12] When Lucas resigned as secretary, Berger pleaded for yet
another general meeting, refusing 'the present responsibility' unless
sufficient directors could be found.[13] The placid notes of these make-
or-break discussions are supplemented by 'rough minutes' which someimes

[6] 48.2/8 (13 Nov. 1880). Hallé accepted an invitation to join the directors on 15 July
1880: 48.13/15.   [7] 48.3/2 (15 Nov. 1880).
[8] A preliminary list includes the following musicians among larger guarantors: W.
Macfarren and Cusins (£150 each), Hallé (£105), Benedict (£100), Sullivan and John Thomas
(£50 each). 48.3/2 (15 Nov. 1880).   [9] Ibid.
[10] Among those immediately elected were Walter Bache, pupil and ardent advocate of
Liszt, and therefore a controversial figure; Alberto Randegger, composer and conductor
from Trieste; George Henschel, about to inaugurate the Boston Symphony Orchestra, Carl
Rosa, and Frederic Cowen: 48.3/2 (22 Nov. 1880). Bache was invited to become a director,
and Liszt to 'assist': 48.2/8 (23 Dec. 1880).   [11] 48.3/2 (4 Dec. 1880).
[12] 48.2/8 (20 Nov. 1880). The allocation of string instruments was sixteen first violins;
fourteen seconds; and ten apiece of violas, cellos, and double basses.
[13] 48.2/8 (12 Dec. 1880).

give momentary glimpses of turbulence. It is feared that Lucas's resignation will be 'fatal'; and Cusins remarks on the ability of 'the former
clique' to 'make it pay, however': a curiously disassociating recollection
which must have raised some eyebrows. Similarly untrustworthy is his
prediction that this will be his last season. Berger's chief concern is to
'force new members' to make clear their intentions.[14] Meanwhile Henry
Hersee, the *Observer*'s critic, agreed to become secretary, at a fee of
£50, on condition that he be allowed to continue with his journalism.
When the inevitable refusal to conduct three concerts came from
Brahms it was left to Cusins to preside over all six expensive evenings,
each with its unprecedented pair of rehearsals.[15] A week later the
Macfarren brothers tried to withdraw their guarantees, finally breaking
the old alliance. After getting legal advice, the remaining directors
insisted that guarantors could not be allowed to renege on current
undertakings, for how then would the fund have any substance?[16]

Apart from witnessing an unlikely survival and temporary financial
security, 1881 was notable only for two performances of Berlioz's
Roméo et Juliette. They were intended to be spectacular events, with the
programme listing soloists, an 'orchestra of 100 players, 150 members
of the South London Choral Association, and a semichorus of 12
professional vocalists (First time in England)'. Giving a platform to a
major work was acknowledged as 'a notable event in the history of
the Society', but the conductor was not equal to the occasion, nor to
the resources placed at his disposal for the whole season: an orchestra
which contained 'the elite of the profession', and was allowed time for
unaccustomed rehearsals. Comparing what Richter could do with a 'far
inferior orchestra', and recent performances under Hallé and Cowen,
the *Athenaeum* pointed the 'difference between a conductor and a time
beater' and called for the latter's resignation.[17] But this pilot was not
easily dropped and, as in the previous year, the directors took no
further steps than to insist again upon a guarantee fund of £1,500, if
concerts were to be given. It was raised by Herculean efforts—not by
Hersee, who was seldom present.[18] The intention was clearly to signal
a new beginning; inevitably with Beethoven's Ninth Symphony, and
also with the rarer, but apt, symbolism of Berlioz's *Lélio, ou Le Retour
à la vie*.[19] In the event, only the traditional celebratory work was attempted, with customary shortcomings, and complaints more damning
because expensive resources had been wasted. An orchestra so 'exceedingly fine in quality, the tone of the strings being superb', could 'under
a competent conductor ... accomplish magnificent results', thundered

---

[14] 48.4/2 (12 Dec. 1880).   [15] 48.2/8 (12 and 18 Dec. 1880).
[16] 48.2/8 (18 and 23 Dec. 1880).   [17] *Athenaeum* (5 and 19 Mar. 1881).
[18] The treasurer wrote many personal letters to such dignitaries as Baroness Burdett-
Coutts and the Earl of Dunmore. The list is in 48.2/8 (16 July 1881).   [19] Ibid.

the *Athenaeum*. In present hands its reading of Wagner's *Mastersingers* Overture was 'almost inconceivably bad'. Such facts, concluded the writer, 'must be obvious to the least intelligent among those who attend the concerts'.[20] Yet Cusins was indulged for two more seasons, esteeming himself, a friend later recollected, 'as an underestimated genius'.[21] Meanwhile the Society's new administrators were preparing for better days.

Organizers, Guarantors, and Fellows

In a book of reminiscences, published just before the First World War, Francesco Berger paid generous tribute to Charles Edward Stephens and George Mount for sharing his task in 'reorganizing the Society' and saving it from 'wrecking'.[22] They achieved a complete restructuring of membership, finance, and administration, in which most initiatives came from Berger, and everything depended upon his unflagging energy. The new men were unlikely revolutionaries: more resourceful and in-dustrious than their predecessors—they could hardly have been less—but already middle-aged, and firmly rooted in the genteel world of London music. Mount had been a double-bass player—he is listed in the 1860 orchestra (Appendix 3). Like Cusins, but with fewer oppor-tunities, he aspired to conduct, having experimented with an 'ill-starred British Orchestral Society' and an Albert Hall Amateur Orchestral Society.[23] Stephens could claim higher connections, going back to raffish days in the Argyll Rooms. He was very much the nephew of Kitty Stephens (1794–1882), Countess of Essex, as she is billed in Foster's listing of sixteen Philharmonic appearances between 1814 and 1827. Once a prominent soprano, she had married the octogenarian Earl in 1838, who promptly died in 1839, events which occasioned scholarly questioning in *Grove*.[24] After displaying, as his entry in *Grove* precisely records, 'early tokens of musical organization', nephew Charles had studied piano with Cipriani Potter, played the organ at various churches, engaged with George Macfarren in furious dispute about a harmonic theory of crazily rigid aridity, written dots on pages and, of course, taken pupils: 'The tuition of the Piano-Forte is his principal occupation', reads his listing by the Royal Society of Musicians.[25]

---

[20] *Athenaeum* (18 Feb. 1882).

[21] H. Klein, *Thirty Years of Musical Life in London 1870–1900* (1903), 114–15.

[22] F. Berger, *Reminiscences, Impressions and Anecdotes* (n.d. [prob. 1913]), 67–8.

[23] *Athenaeum* (1 Mar. 1884).

[24] Alterations in the Hanover Square parish register were the subject of a fiercely pedantic footnote to the 'Catherine Stephens' entry in early editions of *Grove*.

[25] B. Matthews, *The Royal Society of Musicians of Great Britain: List of Members 1738–1984* (1985), 138. The controversy between Stephens and Macfarren about Day's *Treatise on Harmony* is described in P. Scholes, *The Mirror of Music 1844–1944* (1947), 709.

When Berger replaced Hersee as secretary in 1884, it was a formal acknowledgement of already well-established leadership. His credentials for redesigning the Society were entirely appropriate for, despite superficial resemblances in lifestyle and demeanour to the conventional London music professor, his background, education, and circles of acquaintance were less narrow. His father was a merchant from Trieste who married a Bavarian in London, where Francesco was born in 1834. He acquired languages (the essential prerequisite for an impresario, excluding most Englishmen), a sophisticated education, and considerable musical training in Munich, Trieste, and Vienna, with piano lessons from the celebrated Louis Plaidy. Back in London he began to piece a living together in response to market opportunities, playing piano accompaniments (sometimes for first-class instrumentalists and singers), writing drawing-room songs and simple piano pieces (*The Band Passes* was particularly successful), organizing fashionable concerts, and teaching young ladies. Most celebrated among the intimate friends of his youth were Wilkie Collins and Charles Dickens. In the house of the latter's 'invisible woman', Nelly Ternan, there would be singing to Francesco's accompaniment. For Collins he wrote and conducted incidental music to the plays *The Frozen Deep* (visited by Queen Victoria) and *The Light House*, which were famously acted by Dickens and his party of friends.[26]

Berger became an associate in 1859, proposed by Sterndale Bennett and seconded by Charles Lucas; and married the contralto Annie Lascelles, a pupil of Garcia, who then relinquished, as was customary in their circle, a career which had included five Society concerts. Elected as a member in 1871, Berger was approaching 50 when he took over in 1884, established, but neither prominent nor particularly 'distinguished'. Having emerged from this relative obscurity in 1880 to success and recognition, he would return there thirty years later, living on to the age of 98, in poverty which provoked requests on his behalf for a civil list pension. Today he is quite forgotten; his achievements as musician, teacher, or functionary, earning no place in reference books, the pages of his two books uncut in at least one major library. Yet such were his talents as organizer and enabler that he was one of a handful of men who transformed London's music for a generation; and without his rare combination of skills and unique energy, the Philharmonic would not have survived into the twentieth century.

Berger's genius lay in seeking out new possibilities and exploiting them on behalf of the Society, with minute attention to detail, at a time when the map of concert life was being redrawn and to do noth-

---

[26] Berger, *Reminiscences, passim*; C. Peters, *King of Inventors* (1991), 169–70; C. Tomalin, *The Invisible Woman* (1991), 96, 128–9, 296. A Manchester playbill for *The Frozen Deep*, featuring Berger as composer and conductor, is reproduced in Tomalin, *Invisible Woman*, 101.

ing was to invite oblivion. Audiences and other sources of income; artists, their categories, representation, and fees; orchestras, their leadership and discipline; repertoire, its scope and development: all required constant scrutiny, wise counsel, and an open mind. Routine came first. An assistant secretary was engaged, and the directors now met frequently, and worked harder than ever before. Subcommittees were set up with specific tasks and clear responsibilities, Berger agreeing to join Mount and Stephens in the vital one which dealt with the orchestra, only 'on condition that its decisions be considered final'.[27] Some reforms were simple and quickly effective, but others required patience, experiment, and a long-term view. The extension and consolidation of the guarantors' list, for example, was a sustained campaign, unexampled in the Society's recent history. At first, letters of appeal were sent to such worthies as Baroness Burdett-Coutts; the Earls of Rosebery, Dudley, and Dunsmore; and Thomas Brassey.[28] Only modest support was forthcoming—there was nothing comparable to the American munificence which funded the New York Philharmonic and Henschel's Boston Symphony—but there was sufficient response to provide a quick and essential safety net.[29] Constant supplication, and a record of only modest calls upon the fund in its early years, helped to settle it down, so that by 1890 it exceeded £2,500, with 169 guarantors contributing sums which ranged from 2 guineas to £100.[30]

The search for guarantors was only a preliminary to much wider and sustained activity which transformed the Society's objectives and membership, and therefore its approach to music, musicians, and the general public. The Philharmonic's 'primary object'—implying that there were others—had long been defined in its 'laws' as 'the encouragement of the highest branches of Music, by means of Concerts, with a full and complete orchestra, combining therewith the best talent that can be procured'.[31] In 1885 this was replaced by a 'Declaratory Resolution', which simply declared that 'The object of the PHILHARMONIC SOCIETY is to give public Orchestral Concerts of the highest class.' Regulation of membership was also modified, in line with the profession's evolving and highly sensitive vocabulary. If candidates for the

[27] 48.2/9 (16 Nov. 1883).

[28] The first list of addressees is in 48.2/8 (16 July 1881).

[29] Hart, *Orpheus in the New World*, 28–9, 54–6.

[30] £109 was called after the 1882 season, equivalent to 8 per cent of the fund; in 1885 there was no call. 48.2/8 (7 Oct. 1882); 48.2/9 (13 June 1885). The £100 subscribers in 1890 were John Broadwood and Sons, F. H. Cowen, 'A Friend (per Francesco Berger)', Edward Matthey, and Sir Arthur Sullivan. The complete list was printed in the programmes.

[31] *Laws of the Philharmonic Society, printed by order of Special General Meeting, January 1877*: 48.5/3. 'Of the object of the Society. I.' The 1859 version had read 'superior branches of Music by the establishment of Concerts . . . the highest talents that can be procured.'

associateship were no longer described as 'bona fide professors', there was still rigid insistence upon a never-to-be-defined professionalism: an applicant in 1882 was curtly informed that 'none but professional musicians are eligible'.[32] Reference to the candidate's necessary 'character and professional ability' in 1877 was also changed to 'professional abilities and *social position*' (my italics) in 1885. But 'professional' demarcations, however understood, require the exclusion of non-professionals if they are to have any meaning. How then could the allegiance of musical 'amateurs' to the Philharmonic be secured, excluding them from membership, but welcoming them to an honourable participation which went beyond mere attendance at concerts, or even acting as guarantors? Subscriptions had lost the charms of exclusiveness and privilege, and alternative concerts never ceased to attract. The solution was appropriate to a new model musical society in late Victorian London.

At a busy meeting of directors in October 1882 there had been no serious opposition to the idea of admitting a 'limited number of amateurs of note', with some such title as 'Honorary Associate', who might pay 5 guineas for the 'life privilege' of attending second rehearsals.[33] Several meetings and one month later, Mount proposed the creation of a 'class of supporters to be called "Fellows of the Society" '.[34] After passing through the necessary two general meetings without much opposition, new laws in 1885 introduced 'FELLOWS (F. P. S.), consisting of Amateur Ladies and Gentlemen', who were to pay a life fee of 5 guineas 'funded for the benefit of the Society', which meant that it was separate from the guarantee fund. They would be entitled to a ticket for 'the Rehearsal immediately preceding each Concert'—it was a wise precaution to omit specific reference to two rehearsals—and to purchase an extra similar ticket. Candidates needed recommendations from three members, and support by a majority of directors. One hundred fellows were to be chosen, with scrupulous attention to the design of a seal for stamping their certificate of election.[35] They were a diverse assembly, ranging from the statesman A. J. Balfour (1848–1930), on the brink of great eminence, to the Revd. H. G. Bonavia Hunt, Mus. B. (Oxon), Mus. B. and Mus. D. (Dublin), FRSE, FRAS, FLS, LTCL, etc. An unrivalled collector and international disseminator of paper qualifications, Hunt was the high priest of a peculiarly Victorian conception of the professional musician, as songless man of 'letters'. Conferring the title of 'Fellow' upon amateurs, worthy or vainglorious, was an eccentric exercise—particularly in a country which was obsessed with the minutiae of professional and social hierarchies—because it

---

[32] 48.2/8 (21 May 1882).   [33] 48.2/8 (21 Oct. 1882).
[34] 48.2/8 (11 Nov. 1882).
[35] Meetings: 48.3/2 (27 Nov. and 20 Dec. 1882). Laws: X, XI, and XV of 1885: 48.5/3. Design of Seal: 48.2/8 (10 Feb. 1883).

usually denotes high achievement in a specific skill. But whatever its incongruities, the fellowship scheme clearly met a need, and became a venerable repository of allegiance.[36]

The wider audience required similarly close attention. Seeking it out was already a peculiarly metropolitan problem, different in many respects from concert promotion in provincial towns. There may have been a huge potential audience in sprawling London, but it had to be articulated, coaxed, and held against rival attractions. Berger's approach to this fundamental challenge was cautious at first. No change in venue was yet contemplated, despite present discomforts: disreputable external and bewildering internal geography, uncomfortable seats, cooking-smells, and tambourine noises-off from Christy minstrels. St James's Hall, Piccadilly, was reinvestigated by a subcommittee which concluded that capacity was sufficient for the present.[37] Attempts to fill the worn-out benches began with distribution of 6,000 copies of the prospectus for 1883: one thousand among members, associates, and subscribers, and five thousand by post to 'the public'.[38] But how was the latter to be identified? By 1885 use was being made of a list of addresses in streets 'selected by Geo. Smith of Gresham House'.[39] Ticket prices were revised and—best indication of the new administrative competence, and promise for the future—figures of attendance were collected, and presumably scrutinized.[40]

Many of Berger's minor reforms would today be regarded as ordinary routines of concert organization; but for the Philharmonic of the 1880s, as he rightly claims, they were 'important innovations'.[41] Hersee understood the newspaper world, and when he handed over as secretary insisted that they 'talk Press matters', linking 'success to publicity'; and later approved that 'you're advertising with great spirit—*essential*'. The monthly cost of 'frequently inserted' advertisements was carefully noted. To launch the 1883 season there were '50 large posters, twice the size of the largest already issued'; eight large boards were exhibited at eight railway stations, for 1 shilling each a week, and one was kept at the concert-hall. Next year the traditional 'small shop bills' were replaced by 'Three sheet' and 'Double Crown Bills'. New 'heavy working expenses' caused disquiet, and since competition made

[36] H. C. Colles, 'The Royal Philharmonic Society' (unpub. typescript, 1937): 48.15/8, fos. 30–1. Bonavia Hunt's fellowship: 48.2/9 (27 Oct. 1883). For his career, professionalism, and 'letters', see Ehrlich, *Music Profession*, 116–20. A more pious biography is in C. S. Nicholls (ed.), *The Dictionary of National Biography: Missing Persons* (1993), 338.

[37] 48.2/9 (27 Oct. 1883).   [38] 48.2/8 (30 Dec. 1882).

[39] 48.2/9 (12 Jan. 1884).

[40] 48.2/9 (25 Oct. 1884). For the 1885 season subscriptions ranged from 3 guineas to 25*s*.; single tickets from 15*s*. to 1*s*. Takings for most concerts over this period can be found in the Directors' Minute Book: e.g. 48.2/9 (31 May 1884) and 48.2/10 (7 May 1887).

[41] Berger, *Reminiscences*, 69.

it 'impossible or impolitic to reduce them', they could be more sensibly targeted away from 'purely musical papers thought to be of no benefits to the funds of the Society'.[42]

Despite these indications of changing times, progress was slow in some directions. There was still reluctance to accept advertisements in the programmes: only a few for 'high class music'. Yet such caution was an advance on the conservatism which had previously rejected, out of hand, request for mention in the programme by 'Mr Beckstein's [sic] representative'.[43] Quite soon it would be possible to exploit a formidably appropriate source of funding and sponsorship in a society which bought pianos, and could spell the firms' names. Meanwhile programme books could also function as house magazines, printing, as Berger fondly remembered, 'lists of Members, Associates, Fellows and Guarantors, officers, orchestra members, and an alphabetical list of Soloists since 1813'.[44] But what of their musical content?

Repertoire, Soloists, and Conductors

No amount of financial, administrative, and social acumen would have amounted to anything without substantially improved concerts. Since there was no shortage of marketable new music and artists it was not an impossible task, given energetic funding, administration, and recruitment, to put on a better show, and attract support. Zealous casting-around for composers and performers, seeking 'artists of eminence', generated public interest which had long been dormant. The *Observer*'s comment that 'the directors of this rejuvenated society are actively engaged', though doubtless 'placed' by Hersee, was none the less true, and representative of a new image.[45] Changes in repertoire can be seen in Appendix 1. There was less Beethoven, Mozart, and Haydn; and fewer overtures by Cherubini, Weber, and Mendelssohn. Established concertos remained, but were increasingly given revitalized, more extrovert, performances. Wagner's new prominence is understated because the tables exclude the vocal excerpts and 'bleeding chunks' from the operas which continued to occupy concert programmes for more

[42] Hersee's advice: 48.13/16 (28 July 1884). Reporting costs: 48.2/8 (23 Dec. 1880). Advertisements: 48.2/8 (13 Jan. and 24 Feb. 1883); 48.2/9 (8 Dec. 1883). Heavy expenses: 48.2/9 (9 Jan. 1886). Targeting: 48.2/9 (6 Feb. 1886).
[43] 48.2/9 (26 July 1884); 48.2/8 (15 May 1880).   [44] Berger, *Reminiscences*, 68.
[45] *Observer* (9 Nov. 1884). Within the next few months there were communications with the following musicians: Moszkowski, Franz Rummell, Hallé, Piatti, Neruda, Ondříček, Sullivan, Annette Essipoff, Sophie Menter, Gounod, Delibes, Rubinstein, Cowen, von Bülow, Auer, Clara Schumann, Saint-Saëns, and Pachmann. Mackenzie was invited to compose a symphony, Brahms to compose anything; Liszt, who was reported to be coming to London, was 'borne in mind': 48.2/9 (22 Nov. 1884; 21 Feb., 11 Apr., and 18 July 1885).

than half a century. There was a memorial concert after his death in 1883, though he would not have enjoyed sharing it with Bruch, Sarasate, and Mendelssohn. It opened with the *Mastersingers* Overture, which was played five times between 1882 and 1890, and has never long been absent ever since. The modern repertoire was taking shape, with new popular classics emerging very rapidly, led by Bruch, Dvořák, Saint-Saëns, Grieg, and, late but overwhelmingly, Tchaikovsky.

British composers were no more ignored than they had been in the past. It had been possible for Foster to calculate the national origins of music performed during the Society's seventh decade (1873–82), in such a manner that works from the British Empire exceeded all other categories: sixty-six, as against thirty-one from France, the nearest contender; the German Empire scored twenty-nine.[46] Continuing this tradition the new regime hoped to stimulate new talent by competitions. A prize of £10 was offered in 1882, plus the costs of copying orchestral parts, for a home-grown overture, to be judged by Benedict, Costa, and Sullivan. After examining twenty-three out of sixty entries, Costa selected the three 'least bad', recommended none, and disapproved of those chosen by Benedict. He then pleaded illness, and was replaced by Otto Goldschmidt. The prize was awarded to 'Rex', who turned out to be Oliver A. King, 'pianist to H.R.H. the Princess Louise, Government House, Ottawa'; and his 'Prize Overture "Among the Pines" ' was dutifully performed in April 1883.[47] A similarly time-consuming exercise was undertaken in the following year, when eighty-eight overtures were examined by Stephens, Mount, and Cummings, who unanimously awarded the prize to Gustav Ernest, described by the *Musical Times* as 'a Prussian living in London'.[48] The *Athenaeum*, in a notice which also reviewed the first performance of *The Mikado*, deplored 'failure to recognise the claims of English music', and when Ernest conducted his overture, pronounced it 'feeble and amateurish', its themes 'almost identical with the tremendous argument of Wagner's *Der Ring des Nibelungen*'.[49]

Better concerts needed better conductors; a problem which had not been considered for many years, apart from several gestures towards Brahms, and one to Wagner.[50] The new directors were capable of

---

[46] Foster, *History*, 389.

[47] 48.2/8 (7 Oct. and 4 Nov. 1882; 24 Feb., 3 Mar., and 14 Apr. 1883).

[48] 48.2/9 (14 Feb. 1885). *MT* (1 Mar. 1884).

[49] *Athenaeum* (7 and 21 Mar. 1885).

[50] When Wagner visited London in 1877, it was suggested at a meeting of directors that steps be taken 'to secure his appointment as conductor or otherwise during his stay', without proposals of payment: 48.2/7 (17 Mar. 1877). In the real world of remuneration and risk, he had been promised £1,500, for six concerts in fourteen days, by the concert agents Hodge and Essex, and is said to have received £700: Newman, *Life of Wagner*, iv. 555–60. Cf. the account in Fifield, *Hans Richter*, 127–8.

more realism, but they may not yet have been ready to compete with the standards set by Richter, even if someone of such rare accomplishment, possibly Richter himself, should become available. Could they have coped with such a musician's expectations, and what was their understanding of a conductor's function in these years of transition? At this stage they appear to have been most influenced by considerations of economy, patriotism, and diplomacy. Appropriate responsibilities, they decided, could be shared out: composers presiding over their own works in traditional fashion, and a resident conductor, none too demanding, but suitably eminent, acting as figurehead. The recently knighted Sir Arthur Sullivan declared himself, after necessary cajoling, honoured to accept such a position, but not until 1885. Meanwhile he agreed to make at least one interim appearance, and Mount, now acting as 'Orchestral Director', or manager, but with higher ambitions, was allowed to conduct two concerts. The remaining work was shared among several honorary conductors.[51] If there was hesitation about this risky compromise, so much at variance with aspirations towards improvement elsewhere, the archives are quiet. Decisions may have been influenced by the outcry over Richter's appointment, that year, to succeed Costa at the Birmingham Festival. Sullivan was particularly vociferous, writing to Davison about encouraging 'blooming Germans', to another critic about foreigners being 'thrust in everywhere', and to yet another about 'the bitter humiliation for all us English'.[52]

Thus it came about that George Mount was allowed to preside at the opening concert on 21 February 1884. He contributed a 'steady beat', said one critic, but no 'poetical reading' to lift the music above the levels of mediocrity 'so long passively endured'. Since Mount had not been announced as permanent conductor, declared another, with mock forbearance, he would refrain from detailed comment: 'suffice to say that it was difficult at times to realize that the orchestra was composed of skilled professional players, and to repress a feeling of regret at the loss of Mr Cusins'.[53] Critical disdain for incompetent direction of familiar old works may also have been exacerbated by a penny-plain reading of Beethoven's Violin Concerto by the orchestra's leader, John Tiplady Carrodus, a long-standing favourite of the provincial oratorio circuit, but never a soloist of international rank. There was some improvement when Stanford, who had offered his services a year before, conducted the second concert; and Mount's shortcomings at his next stint were offset by Dvořák's first Philharmonic appearance. He conducted three works with modest success, including his D major Symphony, which had already been heard both at the Crystal Palace,

---

[51] 48.2/9 (20 June; 7, 14, and 21 July; 6 and 18 Oct. 1883).
[52] Fifield, *True Artist*, 210–12. Stanford alone among the likely contenders for that post appears to have been generous in recognizing Richter's superiority and internationalism.
[53] *MT* (1 Mar. 1884); *Athenaeum* (1 Mar. 1884).

and under Richter.[54] The fourth concert was dull, with Sullivan conducting only his In Memoriam Overture, and John Francis Barnett securing 'correct but colourless' playing.[55] So far the first season without Cusins was dampening every expectation of a brave new start, until it was saved by the youngest of the new team with two attractive concerts. In the first, dedicated to Costa, who had died a week earlier, von Bülow's 'masterly' playing of a virtuoso concerto by Raff, and of Beethoven's 'Eroica' Variations, added a measure of excitement. The second was described as a 'genuine and well-earned success' for Cowen, as conductor and composer. Ticket sales confirmed these critical judgements.[56]

The emergence of Frederic Hymen Cowen as the Society's first credible conductor in many years should not have come as a surprise. His gifts were long-proven, though his background was exotic even by the standards of London musicians. Jewish, and Jamaican-born, he had been known to the Philharmonic since 1860, when his father, secretary to the Earl of Dudley, who acted as patron, wrote about the precocious 8-year-old composer and pianist, but received no encouragement on this or several later occasions, except for one brief appearance as a pianist in 1870.[57] His progress had included a Mendelssohn scholarship, study with the best teachers in Leipzig and Berlin, experience in opera with Mapleson's company and under Costa, conducting promenade concerts at Covent Garden, and a string of publicly performed compositions, culminating in 1880 with the 'Scandinavian' Symphony, which was widely acclaimed in Europe and America. All this entitled him, when asked to conduct, to bargain with the directors, less regally than Sullivan, but in contrast to the other supplicants. He accepted on condition that one of his symphonies be played, and, after demonstrating that this self-confidence had been amply justified, stood aside once more, to make way for Sir Arthur.[58]

Opinions differed about Sullivan's prowess as a conductor. There was no doubt of his 'good understanding' with a much improved orchestra which, he would have assumed, required no goading with a baton.[59] Mutual accord was indeed a pleasant aspect of their relationship, with acts of comradeship and generosity by a bandmaster's son.[60]

---

[54] Stanford's application for conducting post: 48.13/32 (16 Jan. 1883). Review of Dvořák concert: *Athenaeum* (29 Mar. 1884).   [55] *Athenaeum* (26 Apr. 1884).

[56] Ibid. (10 and 31 May 1884). Concert takings: 48.2/9 (24 May 1884).

[57] 48.13/8 (20 Mar. 1860; 12 Mar. 1869; 20 Apr. 1870 (offering a symphony which had been performed at the Crystal Palace); 22 May 1870; 27 Feb. 1871 (offering an overture played at Brighton and Crystal Palace); 29 Dec. 1871 (repeating previous offers)).

[58] 48.2/9 (1 Dec. 1883).   [59] *Athenaeum* (7 Mar. 1885).

[60] After losses on the season of 1887, the orchestra was asked to accept a 10 per cent cut in fees. Sullivan attended a meeting with the band and made up the sum 'out of his own pocket.' His generosity was 'thankfully accepted' by the directors: 48.2/10 (4 and 9 July 1887).

Nor need one question his ability to effect improvements. Excerpts from Berlioz's *Roméo et Juliette* were now played in a style which was 'refined and finished', in contrast to Cusins's recent 'coarse and spirit-less reading'; and a performance of Schumann's Second Symphony was even described as 'absolutely perfect'. It is also pleasurable to read an enthusiastic account of this honourable Schubertian's 'performance of . . . one of the most melodious and (in spite of its enormous length) one of the most enjoyable symphonies ever written'.[61] But we also have Hanslick's withering review of the concert on 2 June 1886, and his direct comparison with the results Richter was getting from 'essentially the same group of musicians'. After beginning as we quote him at the head of this chapter, the leading music critic of his day described 'a phlegmatism probably unique. Sullivan presides on the podium from the comfortable recesses of a commodious arm-chair, his left arm lazily extended on the arm-rest, his right giving the beat in a mechanical way, his eyes fastened to the score.' The 'heavenly' Mozart symphony 'plodded along, for better or worse, listlessly, insensibly'. And when the audience applauded 'long and loudly' he 'sat stolid and immovable in his arm-chair, awaiting the second number'. By contrast, there was Richter's 'astonishing memory' and 'ever alert enthusiasm', guiding the orchestra 'with his hand and his eye'.[62] Sullivan's best defence comes from an unlikely source, inimitably vituperative, and affectionately discerning. Nobody, wrote Shaw, 'thrilled with more savage and venge-ful glee when the old heartless, brainless, purposeless, vapid, conceited, jack-in-office, kid-glove, St James's-street, finicking Philharmonic fastidi-ousness was blown into space' by Richter.

But, contemptible and inadequate as this genteel fastidiousness was in the mass, it had its good points in detail; and Sir Arthur Sullivan's delicate taste, individuality, and abhorrence of exaggeration and slovenliness raised it to a point at which, if it still did nothing, it at least did it with exquisite refinement.[63]

Phlegmatism, refinement, and expectations of drawing power, were bought at high cost over three seasons, even if Sir Arthur's Philhar-monic fee was trifling in relation to his remuneration elsewhere. Ab-sence from rehearsals, postponements, or cancellations, only sometimes justified by illness or pressing alternative engagements, required extra-ordinary forbearance by colleagues and audiences. Things came to a

---

[61] *Athenaeum* (4 Apr. and 9 May 1885; 10 Apr. 1886).

[62] E. Hanslick, *Musical Criticisms 1846–1899*, trans. and ed. H. Pleasants (1950), 263–4. The programme is listed in app. 30. The directors discussed 'Dr Hanslick's letters in the German papers': 48.2/9 (10 Aug. 1886).

[63] G. B. Shaw, *London Music in 1888–1889* (1937), 92. This review originally appeared on 5 Apr. 1889.

head in 1887 when the opening concert of the season had to be rehearsed and conducted at short notice by Mount. It included Brahms's Fourth Symphony (then regarded as extremely difficult), and the Schumann Concerto played by Clara, for the first time in a decade. Only four days earlier Sullivan, still in Naples, had pleaded indisposition, disappointing a 'crowded and brilliant audience', who paid an unprecedented £209 for admission. Nine days before the next concert Sullivan was in Paris, and again called off, with the excuse of a Berlin performance a fortnight later. Cowen was willing to take over, and asked for an immediate announcement, only to be told that 'it would not be in the interest of the Society to draw attention so long before to Sir Arthur's absence'; it would oppose his 'express wish', and, by giving longer notice, be impolite to Mount.[64] Cowen acquiesced in this subterfuge, and conducted an original and highly praised concert, which included a Mozart wind concertante, one of the Queen of the Night's arias and Handel's 'Let the Bright Seraphim', sung by the renowned American soprano Nordica, Leopold Auer in the Mendelssohn Concerto, and Cowen's own 'Scandinavian' Symphony, each movement of which was 'vigorously applauded'.[65] Berger, whose ingenuity and tact were being sorely tried, was characteristically effusive in expressing the directors' gratitude for rescue, and appreciation of 'a work which they feel sure will take its place by the side of the masterpieces which it has been their pride and their privilege to introduce in the past'. Mount and Cowen were each paid a 'small fee' of 15 guineas.[66]

The rest of the season fared badly after Sullivan's return, attendance falling from under half to barely a quarter of the opening concert. Repertoire may have lacked appeal. There were works by Corder and Randegger, composed for the Society. A concerto for pedal-piano by Gounod was deemed 'trivial, commonplace, not to say vulgar', the instrument 'fit only for organ students', its tone 'painfully harsh and wiry'.[67] More neglected Mozart—Charles Santley singing 'Per questa bello mano' to Bottesini's double bass, and Saint-Saëns in the E flat Concerto K.271—failed to attract attention. And then a 10-year-old boy appeared at the last concert, on a Saturday morning. Many were 'contented to stand' and more were 'turned away at the doors' when he played Beethoven's First Concerto. One critic recognized a 'true artist' who was undoubtedly the chief attraction; another the

---

[64] 48.2/10 (19 Mar. 1887).

[65] *MT* (1 Mar. 1887). Leopold Auer, who did not impress the critics, later taught Zimbalist, Elman, and Heifetz. For this remarkable concert the indefatigable Berger had also telegraphed Verdi's publishers to ask permission for Nordica to sing an 'air' from Verdi's *Otello*, which had been premièred at La Scala a month earlier: 48.2/10 (19 Mar. 1887).   [66] 48.2/10 (2 Apr. 1887).

[67] *Athenaeum* (21 Apr. 1887).

'interpretation of a great artist', with barely perceptible modifications in the score to accommodate tiny hands. Although, as Foster primly remarks, Josef Hofmann (1876–1957) was investigated that year by the Society for the Prevention of Cruelty to Children, he also proved the critics right by proceeding to a very long career as a very great pianist.[68] The orchestra was 'splendid throughout', ending the most profitable concert in the Society's history so far, with Sullivan's charming Overture Di Ballo.

It turned out to be a nice farewell, for Sullivan refused to accept the director's offer to conduct next season, despite a letter expressing 'deep regret and some surprise' at a sudden decision, and a deputation which begged him to reconsider. Other plans were one excuse, and unconcealed tetchiness towards 'the Press' another. He also wrote more openly to George Grove, admitting how irksome it was to be tied down in London for several months, and to be subject to 'faint praise' and the 'god Richter'. But there can surely be no doubt that the directors had done their best to keep him. His biographer's conjecture about criticism by 'fellow-musicians on the Philharmonic committee' cannot be documented from the archives, and their demeanour through-out his three seasons suggests nothing but servile acquiescence to the great man's needs. The prose of Berger's tribute was suitably purple, thankful for 'time, and trouble, and talent . . . in preparation of some of the most perfect performances which have ever been accomplished in this or any other country'.[69]

There followed a sustained attempt to appoint a distinguished conductor, without regard to nationality: the first such search since Bennett. It could have been a turning-point in the history, not only of the Philharmonic Society, but of the provision of orchestras in London.

Cowen Comes and Goes

Richter was the inevitable first choice, though Brahms, as always, was mentioned.[70] A direct approach in Salzburg came to nothing: Richter was 'surprised and flattered', asked for a fortnight to consider, and then punctiliously declined because of commitments to Vert, his London agent. The latter was consulted by Berger and Mount, to 'propose some scheme of amalgamation between the Philharmonic Society Concerts and the Richter Concerts, the title of Richter Concerts being dropped'. As 'sole proprietor' of the latter, Vert admitted to making a loss over the previous season, but intended to try one more; after

---

[68] MT (1 July 1887); Athenaeum (2 July 1887); Foster, History, 407.
[69] A. Jacobs, Arthur Sullivan: A Victorian Musician (1986), 260–1. 48.2/10 (23 and 30 July, 1 Aug. 1887).   [70] 48.2/10 (1 Aug. 1887).

that he might come to some agreement.[71] By now it was mid-October, and times had changed since the easygoing days of last-minute booking. Von Bülow was approached, with three telegrams and a letter; Rubinstein, and finally Joachim, were asked, to no avail.[72] Only then did the job go to the best qualified local candidate. Mount immediately resigned as orchestra manager, and Cowen settled to his tasks, with a zest, commitment, and professional thoroughness unknown since Costa's regime but, as would soon be seen, without the old martinet's power. Some of his concerns were necessarily similar, such as the difficulty of getting work done at public rehearsals. But he was also keen to extend the repertoire, after 'much time reading through scores'. It should include 'hitherto unperformed symphonies by Haydn'; unfamiliar Mozart and Schubert; the *Fantastic Symphony* and *Siegfried Idyll*; works by Bizet, Goetz, Svendsen, Dvořák, Raff, Mackenzie; and, in unconscious echo of Macfarren, 'one work from an English pen' in every concert.[73]

The next five seasons amply justified Cowen's appointment. Breadth of repertoire and 'excellence of performance' were immediately pronounced 'fully worthy of the traditions of the Society', and from then on poor notices were rare. Soloists were usually good, and sometimes magnificent, and it was commonly said of the orchestra that there was 'no finer body of instruments in Europe'.[74] The opening concert of 1888, which brought in £235, included Clara playing Chopin's F minor Concerto and accompanying Liza Lehmann in Schumann songs; and music by Weber, Wagner, Rameau (arr. Gevaert), and Stanford (the composer conducting). Cowen's prestige was then enhanced by a 'very lucrative engagement' as musical director of the Melbourne Centennial Exhibition, which necessitated his missing the last two concerts.[75] The directors made another attempt to get Von Bülow, then asked several other conductors, including Manns. Ultimately Johan Svendsen agreed to come, bringing the orchestral parts for his Symphony in D, and receiving a fee of £90 for three rehearsals and two concerts.[76] Meanwhile another Norwegian newcomer had arrived; already 'a household word . . . though personally a stranger'. In one respect Grieg's appeal was similar to a previous generation's love of Mendelssohn; his 'exquisite little pieces for the piano' nestling against the *Songs without Words* in domestic piano-stools. Any guilt about simple pleasures could be assuaged by reading that the music was harmonically of 'great interest from a theoretical point of view', its charm never 'vulgar or commonplace'.[77] The Piano Concerto had already been frequently heard—at the Crystal Palace, for instance, since 1874—but in Grieg's hands it

---

[71] 48.13/28 (20 Sept. 1887); 48.2/10 (24 Sept. and 8 Oct. 1887).
[72] 48.2/10 (24 Sept., and 8 and 29 Oct. 1887).   [73] 48.2/10 (2 and 19 Nov. 1887).
[74] *Athenaeum* (24 Mar. 1883).   [75] 48.2/10 (11 Feb. 1888).
[76] 48.2/10 (28 Apr. and 5 May 1888).   [77] *Athenaeum* (12 May); *MT* (1 June 1888).

caused 'delight rather than astonishment'. At the Philharmonic concert on 3 May 1888 there were also two songs, and he conducted *Two
Elegaic Melodies*. Cowen contributed Mozart's 'Linz' Symphony and the
first English performance of Bizet's *Jeux d'enfants* to another typically
unconventional and popular (£204) programme.

Innovation was not always welcome: 'in deference to the wish of a
large proportion of subscribers' it was resolved to substitute Beethoven's
C minor Symphony for the Berlioz *Fantastic Symphony* at the next concert,
and to finish with Weber's Overture *Oberon*.[78] Contrasting responses to
Grieg and Berlioz may have reflected old prejudices and limited experience of orchestral virtuosity; it also suggests that music which related
to the keyboard was easier for a piano-playing audience to assimilate. At the previous concert another exotic master, soon to dominate
repertoire and audience, had earned only a guarded welcome on his
first Philharmonic appearance. Tchaikovsky was 'on the wander in
Western Europe', and was contacted, with typical enterprise, by Berger
before his arrival in England.[79] This music was far less familiar than
Grieg's, but *Romeo and Juliet* and the First Piano Concerto had been
done at the Crystal Palace and now, a decade later, there was sufficient
interest to attract a 'large audience of musicians' to the first English
performances of the String Serenade and 'Theme and Variations' from
the Third Suite. The Russian and Austrian Ambassadors were invited;
the orchestra's 'magnificent strings' were heard to advantage; but need
was felt for music 'of greater pretence'.[80] It would soon be forthcoming.

Grieg returned for the opening of the next season, accompanying his
wife in some of his songs, and conducting something called *Peer Gynt*—
the writer of programme notes enquired anxiously about 'plot and
characters . . . our readers will expect information'. Score and parts for
the Piano Concerto were also bought for the library.[81] Cowen, having
given fair warning and returned his fee, was still travelling back from
Australia; and since Grieg would conduct only Grieg, an extra conductor was needed. Alexander Mackenzie, who had just succeeded Macfarren
at the Royal Academy of Music, took over the rest of the programme
in a quiet, but auspicious, début, which included his own Scotch rhapsody, *Burns*. The hectic pace continued, with Tchaikovsky back again,
at the third concert; his Concerto played by Wassily Sapellnikoff, and
the Suite in D, new to England (see Pl. 15). He had been asked for
a symphony and the second concerto, but anything Russian was welcome. The directors had 'from staunch Conservatives obviously turned
Communists', enthused one reviewer, 'and in respect of art matters so
much the better'.[82]

[78] 48.2/10 (12 May 1888).   [79] *MT* (1 Apr. 1879). 48.2/10 (14 Jan. 1888).
[80] *Athenaeum* (31 Mar. 1888); *MT* (1 Apr. 1888); *MMR* (1 May 1888). 48.2/10 (17 Mar.
1888).   [81] 48.13/3 (9 Mar. 1889). 48.2/10 (1 and 8 Apr. 1889).
[82] 48.2/10 (28 Apr. and 12 May 1888; 1 and 11 Feb. 1889). *MMR* (1 May 1889).

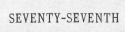

SEVENTY-SEVENTH SEASON, 1889.

PHILHARMONIC SOCIETY

UNDER THE IMMEDIATE PATRONAGE OF

Her Most Gracious Majesty the Queen,

THEIR ROYAL HIGHNESSES THE PRINCE AND PRINCESS OF WALES,
THEIR ROYAL HIGHNESSES THE DUKE AND DUCHESS OF EDINBURGH,
THEIR ROYAL HIGHNESSES THE DUKE AND DUCHESS OF CONNAUGHT,
THEIR ROYAL HIGHNESSES THE PRINCE AND PRINCESS CHRISTIAN,
HER ROYAL HIGHNESS THE PRINCESS LOUISE (MARCHIONESS OF LORNE),
HER ROYAL HIGHNESS PRINCESS MARY ADELAIDE (DUCHESS OF TECK),
HIS ROYAL HIGHNESS THE DUKE OF CAMBRIDGE,
HIS ROYAL HIGHNESS THE DUKE OF TECK.

THIRD CONCERT, THURSDAY, APRIL 11, 1889.

ST. JAMES'S HALL.

Doors open at Half-past Seven o'clock.   To commence at Eight o'clock precisely.

✦ *Programme.* ✦

PART I.

SYMPHONY in E flat ... ... Mozart.

AIR, "Divinités du Styx" (*Alceste*) ... ... *Gluck.*
Miss MARGUERITE HALL.
(Her first appearance at these Concerts.)

CONCERTO in B flat, for Pianoforte and Orchestra (No. 1, Op. 23) ... *Tschaikowsky.*
M. SAPELLNIKOFF.
(His first appearance in England. Conducted by the COMPOSER.)

PART II.

ORCHESTRAL SUITE in D (Op. 43) ... ... *Tschaikowsky.*
1. Introduction and Fugue; 2. Divertimento; 3. Andante; 4. Marche Militaire; 5. Gavotte.
(First time in England. Conducted by the COMPOSER.)

SONGS ... { *a.* "Shall I in Mamre's fertile plain" (*Joshua*) ... ... *Handel.*
{ *b.* "Arise, ye subterranean winds" (Music to "The Tempest") ... *Purcell.*
MR. W. H. BRERETON.
(His first appearance at these Concerts.)

OVERTURE "Lurline" ... ... *Wallace.*

CONDUCTOR ·· ·· ·· ·· ·· MR. FREDERIC H. COWEN.

14. Programme, 11 April 1889

Another indication of changing times was attention to new makes of piano which could stand up to athletic playing; essential to the new repertoire. An Erard was noticed to be 'by no means first rate', in contrast to 'a fine Steinway grand'.[83] New violinists similarly attacked old repertoire with fresh vigour: Ysaÿe, the 'father of 20th century violin playing', was first heard at the Philharmonic in the Beethoven and Mendelssohn Concertos. The decade ended agreeably with Cowen

[83] *MMR* (1 May 1889 and 1 July 1890). Individual pianists were increasingly linked to competing makers. On the Steinway revolution, see Ehrlich, *Piano*, ch. 3.

presiding at a Saturday morning concert which 'filled St James's Hall to its utmost capacity'. Terusina Tua (1867–1955), who would later tour with Rachmaninov, marry a few times, and eventually become Sister Maria di Gesù, was twice recalled after playing the Bruch Concerto. Vladimir de Pachmann (1848–1933), later a great eccentric, contributed some apparently blameless Chopin. There were songs, to Berger's accompaniment, some Handel, Wagner, and Sullivan; and the *Eroica Symphony*.[84]

By the 1890s the Philharmonic's good health had become a commonplace—there was no more 'flourishing institution at the present time'—and, despite odd brickbats from 'ultra fervid patriots', vitality was widely seen to depend upon 'open minded' policies, even if the 'eclectic spirit' sometimes got out of hand.[85] After one outbreak a reviewer confessed that it was 'difficult to write calmly' about Flemish works by Huberti and Benoit, and warned that a 'Society once so ultra conservative in its policy that it seemed likely to perish from inanition, must be careful not to err in the opposite direction'. But he soon became convinced that 'cosmopolitan' excess had been curbed and that 'renewed vitality' at the Philharmonic continued to be 'one of the most gratifying features of London's musical life'.[86] Dvořák arrived with 'a rich treasure', the Symphony in G, and was recalled three times to the platform.[87] There was also the novel prospect of an Englishman as virtuoso: Leonard Borwick, favoured pupil of Clara, and pronounced 'very able', began a quietly successful career with the Schumann Concerto.[88] Such was the general euphoria that Cowen even attempted to breathe life into a programme consisting of Macfarren's Overture Chevy Chase, a vocal quartet by Costa, a Spohr concerto (electricity supplied by Ysaÿe), and the Choral Symphony: 'well executed, so far as the instrumental music was concerned'; and since the last movement 'must always be more or less painful hearing', most of the audience could be excused for leaving before it began.[89] More approachable classics were equally subjected to rethinking and careful preparation; but this required time, and began to incur resentment from the players.

The 1891 season opened with works by Mackenzie, Goring Thomas, and Benedict, but also contained an outstanding interpretation of Beethoven's Fifth Symphony, conducted 'without book'. At the third concert Cowen conducted the Schubert Ninth, and Paderewski made his Philharmonic début with a Saint-Saëns concerto, giving an 'extraordinary display of mastery over the keyboard', like Rubinstein, but

[84] *Athenaeum* (29 June 1889).   [85] Ibid.
[86] *MMR* (1 July 1890); *Athenaeum* (22 Mar. 1890 and 14 Mar. 1891).
[87] *MT* (1 May 1890); *Athenaeum* (3 May 1890).
[88] *MT* (1 June 1890). Clara's recommendation of Borwick, and the subsequent invitation, are in 48.2/10 (22 and 29 Nov. 1889).   [89] *Globe* (30 June 1890); *MT* (1 Aug. 1890).

'more correct' and with less power.[90] His next appearance, with a Rubinstein concerto and such solos as the Liszt 'Erl King' transcription and *Hungarian Rhapsody* No. 2, was pronounced 'exceptionally superb'. But that concert also contained a centenary performance of Haydn's 'Oxford' Symphony which was said to be 'exquisitely played *because there had been no interruption of rehearsal*' (my italics).[91]

A time-bomb was attached to this obscure comment. It had been primed at the time of the 'Flemish' concert, when Cowen complained to the directors about Huberti's listing as a conductor. Prepared to share honours with 'foreigners of distinction', he wanted at least to be consulted before replacement by 'any Tom, Dick or Harry'; the 'position of conductor should not lapse into figurehead'. A second letter continued the remonstrance: too many foreigners were conducting their own works, and monopolizing scarce rehearsals, though Grieg was an endearing exception. As a result, Cowen was being denied sufficient time to prepare anything but 'indifferent performances'.[92] Berger's response was characteristically soothing, admitting a 'grave mistake' with Huberti, and denying any intention to hurt by 'demoting you to "interpreter"' (the phrasing is peculiar, its meaning clear). Nevertheless he insisted upon a continuing tradition that composers conduct their own first performances.[93] In this manner he evaded the essential issues, perhaps deliberately: a modern conductor, aspiring to compete with Richter, needed time and authority to rehearse concerts which were overlong, and expected to exhibit both novelty and reassessment of the classics. Next year there was another, more public, incident when Cowen countered a visitor's hogging of rehearsal time for his symphony by completely rearranging the programme, which also included the Scottish pianist Lamond's début in Brahms's demanding Second Concerto.[94] So the orchestra retired for a Goltermann cello concerto, which was done with piano accompaniment, and the well-worn *Oberon* and Prometheus Overtures replaced the promised Berlioz orchestration of Weber's *Invitation to the Dance*, and a new piece by Grieg. The *Athenaeum* argued that Cowen had behaved 'most properly' and urged the directors to learn from an experience which might have proved disastrous if the conductor had not imposed such drastic remedies.[95]

Cowen was also having difficulties with the orchestra and, even more seriously, with its leader, of a kind which would soon become endemic among London players. Initially he was supported by the directors who, 'anxious for efficiency . . . and to strengthen your hand in the

[90] *Athenaeum* (25 Apr. 1891).   [91] *Globe* (29 May 1891); *Athenaeum* (6 June 1891).
[92] 48.13/8 (23 and 25 Mar. 1890).   [93] 48.13/8 (4 Apr. 1890).
[94] The offending visitor was the Roman pianist Sgambati, whose painstaking rehearsal was rewarded by having his piece described as a 'so-called symphony': *Athenaeum* (23 May 1891).   [95] Ibid. (23 May and 6 June 1891).

matter of the band have resolved that in future you are authorised to *refuse in their name* to allow any member of the orchestra to absent himself' from rehearsals. A copy of this assurance was sent to the or-chestra manager requesting him to attend the next rehearsal 'even for a few minutes' and to keep Cowen informed about leave of absence.[96] The deeply entrenched Carrodus, who had also been admonished for absence in the recent past, was further disgruntled at the removal of his name from advertisements—a directors' decision which reopened old wounds to self-esteem at the first desk, and was soon reversed.[97] For a time peace was restored, with Cowen continuing to earn plaudits for polishing the standard repertoire: Beethoven's Seventh Symphony, for example, was praised for an 'intelligent reading . . . not merely me-chanical reproduction'.[98] But more was at stake than the approval of critics and audiences. The crunch came at the season's final marathon concert, on Wednesday morning, 15 June 1892. Following the *Siegfried Idyll*—it was foolish to compete so closely with Richter, opined the *Mu-sical Times*—Bruch's Second Violin Concerto, Sapellnikoff in a Rubinstein concerto, and two songs with orchestra, Cowen returned to conduct Beethoven's *Pastoral Symphony*. He paused to address the audience: the programme was too long, and underrehearsed, he explained, so he craved their indulgence. Press reports were heated, and not unprejudiced. Some declared that the performance 'went, on the whole, exceedingly well', or was 'very fine'. One announced that it was 'exquisitely played by the matchless orchestra led by J. T. Carrodus' and that Cowen's complaint, which might have been relevant to a new unfamiliar work, should not have been made against directors who knew that their or-chestra could play the *Pastoral* 'without any conductor or rehearsal'.[99]

Having lost Mount, and Stephens, who died that week, Berger was probably left to handle this crisis alone. One assumes that it was in response to an apology from him that Carrodus articulated the distress and bewilderment of, at least, the older players. Many of them, he wrote 'felt deeply humiliated' by Cowen's speech,

and some even expressed themselves as insulted; the work performed is so well known that rehearsal is almost unnecessary and soon becomes irritating. I told Mr Cowen that we had been rehearsing and playing it more or less all our lives under the most eminent conductors and therefore there was no need for anxiety . . . I felt extremely pained at the public apology which proved so unnecessary.

Since reconciliation seemed impossible, the directors backed the play-ers, in a decision which marks a significant stage in the evolution of

---

[96] 48.2/10 (16 May 1890). Stephens had replaced Mount as orchestral manager.
[97] 48.2/10 (15 May 1888; 24 Mar. and 27 Apr. 1891).
[98] *Athenaeum* (2 Apr. 1892).
[99] *MT* (1 July 1892); *Globe* (16 and 17 June 1892); *Daily Telegraph* (17 June 1892).

London's orchestras. Cowen was sent a long letter, evasive and irrevocable, which regretted 'the unwarrantable slight not only on the Directors but also on the distinguished and experienced artists who form
the Philharmonic orchestra'. Had Cowen requested 'extended time
or a second rehearsal if necessary it would have been granted'. His
appointment was not renewed, and he was thanked for five years'
service. Cowen's response was to say that he had already intended to
resign, with more important composing work to do, and in protest at
the 'exceedingly undignified manner' of the directors in 'treating a
purely conscientious and artistic reaction of the Musical Head of their
Society'.[100]

If the prospects for a 'Musical Head' were now dimmer than they
had ever been since the days of Costa, it was nevertheless remarkably
easy for the Society to recruit an acceptable conductor, and to regain
its composure, within a few months. Mackenzie was immediately appointed. Already familiar to audiences from brief appearances, he was
eased into a full season by the good timing of Cambridge University,
which was proposing to award a number of honorary doctorates
in 1893. Among the original possibilities neither Verdi, nor Brahms
of course, were coming, but Boito, Bruch, Grieg, Saint-Saëns, and
Tchaikovsky could all be expected to pass through London, at no expense to the Society. As always, Berger was alert to an opportunity:
they would be invited to appear at Philharmonic concerts.[101] Mackenzie
therefore began his season with quiet assurance, mixing conventional
fare with large helpings of British music—including Sullivan, Somervell,
Edward German (*Henry VIII*), symphonies by Stanford and Cliffe—
some conducted by the composer, some by himself. Parry insisted on
directing his own *Hypatia* music, which had just been written for, and
savaged by, Beerbohm Tree at the Haymarket Theatre. At the Philharmonic it got a proper hearing, in contrast to its customary reception
by a theatre audience which 'talks and drowns . . . in a sea of voices'.
An inevitably small concert audience may have shared the reviewer's
optimism: 'never mind', such good music 'can afford to wait'.[102] There
were also headier attractions, such as the experience, hitherto inconceivable, of hearing a woman—Gabriella Wietrowitz, one of Joachim's
pupils—tackle the Brahms Violin Concerto. Then temperatures began
to rise with the arrival of the Cambridge doctors, and finally reached
boiling-point with promise of a spectacle unprecedented since 1848.

At the penultimate concert there was 'a very full attendance', with

[100] To Cowen: 48.2/10 (20 June and 15 July 1892); from Carrodus: 48.2/10 (17 June
1892); from Cowen: 48.13/8 (16 July 1892). Cowen also wrote, in defence of his action,
to the *Globe* on 17 June 1892.   [101] 48.2/10 (15 July 1892 and 7 Jan. 1893).
[102] *MT* (1 Apr. 1893). On Parry's experiences with *Hypatia*, see J. Dibble, *C. Hubert H.
Parry: His Life and Music* (1993), 305–8.

ticket sales of £165 exceeding most previous peaks. Saint-Saëns was recalled four times after playing his Fourth Concerto, and Tchaikovsky, 'not so well known' but 'far more appreciated than on his last visit' conducted his Fourth Symphony: a first London performance of music which was 'strangely neglected here . . . though composed long ago'. It displayed the 'half melancholy, half bizarre, features of Eastern art' and 'unquestionably made a great impression'. A Bennett overture began that evening of excess, and a Miss Macintyre attempted both the *Semiramide* 'Bel raggio' aria and Isolde's 'Liebestod'.[103] Preparations for the last concert were necessarily frenzied because it was intended to engage two great stars. Even Berger had regarded any chance of getting Melba as 'hopelessly closed' because her terms were 'prohibitive'—they had recently been quoted at 150 to 200 guineas. Now suddenly it appeared, through Mackenzie's good offices, that she might sing for a nominal fee of £100, of which £50 would be returned. Correspondence was prolonged and ultimately fruitless because, two days before the concert, and long after expectations had reached fever pitch, a change in the opera schedules forced her to cancel.[104] Everything depended upon the other star who, for the last time in his dealings with the Society, made modest demands. He would play his own concerto without fee, provided it was advertised as 'by desire', and also on condition that a friend, Gorski, be allowed to play a violin concerto.[105]

The programme for the last Philharmonic concert in St James's Hall, on 15 June 1893, looks unexciting on paper. The newly honoured Dr Bruch, more esteemed in provincial oratorio than London concert room, was there to conduct the unknown Gorski in his familiar G minor Concerto, and three pieces from a 'secular oratorio' entitled *Achilleus*; a Miss Palliser sang Gluck and Gretry in place of Melba. Mackenzie contributed a Sullivan march and Haydn's 'Drum Roll' Symphony. Yet the concert triumphed through one event; enthusiasm undampened, said one critic, by sitting 'in a Turkish bath all evening'. Paderewski's 'ovation', remarked another, relishing a new word, was of a kind 'to which he is now accustomed . . . and at which, if he have any sense of humour, he must often be amused'.[106] Ticket sales were £231, close to the record of Master Hofmann's Saturday morning. For the whole season there was a substantial net profit of £325, the first in many years. Berger was presented with a cheque for 150 guineas and an illuminated testimonial, with one hundred signatures headed by

[103] *MMR* (1 June 1893); *Athenaeum* (10 June 1893); *MT* (1 July 1893).
[104] Correspondence about Melba visit: 48.2/10 (7 Jan. 1893); 48.13/16 (7 Jan., 2 Feb., 24 Mar., and 12, 13, and 14 June 1893); 48.13/2 (13 June 1893); 48.13/23, doc. 96 (8 Dec. 1892 (about fees)), doc. 176 (n.d. (from Savoy Hotel, sending *Lucia* score)).
[105] 48.2/10 (26 Jan. 1893).   [106] *MMR* (1 July 1893); *MT* (1 July 1893).

15. A letter from Tchaikovsky, 16 January 1893 (48.13/34, fo. 164)

Sir John Coleridge, Lord Chief Justice, to his 'indefatigable and self-denying zeal'.[107] The Society was noticed to be two years younger than Mr Gladstone, but 'far older, judged of course, by the average term over which the career of musical enterprises extends'.[108] Yet it had never been in better health, or more actively at the centre of things. It was ready to move into Langham Place.

[107] 48.3/3 (1 July and 18 Nov. 1893). Berger, *Reminiscences*, 69.
[108] *MT* (1 Apr. 1893).

9

Queen's Hall

I would hardly have believed that the less known (Mozart) symphonies are so out of date.

(Alexander Mackenzie, planning programmes in 1894)

Recreations: 'no time for any'.

(Francesco Berger's entry in *Who's Who*)

[An] attempt to establish continuity with a suitable historic past ... [that continuity] largely factitious.

(Eric Hobsbawm on 'The Invention of Tradition')

FRANCESCO BERGER began a second decade as secretary with undiminished energy. His extensive innovations in concert planning and management could not always satisfy everyone's expectations, but they kept the Society afloat, without diminishing its status. Stability, if fragile, was most opportune, because the 1890s boom in London's concert life lasted only a few years. A proliferation of orchestras and events competed for audiences which failed to materialize in sufficient numbers, and with enough regularity, to support music and musicians. Robert Newman's Queen's Hall Orchestra was founded in 1895; the London Symphony Orchestra in 1904, as a players' co-operative in defiance of Henry Wood's attempt to reform the deputy system; the New Symphony Orchestra followed; then the Beecham Symphony Orchestra, and so forth. Although these bands had access to an overflowing pool of players, none offered enough employment and security to command full-time commitment, and a chance to build ensemble and a particular style, as with the best European and American orchestras. It was a culture, as described by the young Havergal Brian in 1909, which condemned serious music to exist in a state of permanent crisis, with superfluity emanating from 'the enthusiasm of musicians rather than the craving of the people'. And even this diagnosis was naïve in speaking of 'the people': as if audiences could be recruited by some pure distillation from a craving for music. Concert life, like most activities in England at this time of crass social divide, was riven by class. In practical terms, the loyal audience, able to pay and committed to music itself, rather than to fashion or spectacle, was pitifully small. It is still not clear why long-run effective demand—as distinct from briefly profitable enthusiasm—fell so far short of perpetual supply. The growth of suburban living may have discouraged commuters from staying in town, or returning for an evening's music. This was already an acknowledged cause of decline in metropolitan choirs, and may also have affected concert audiences before, as it certainly did after, the 1914–18 War.[1] Yet retreat to the suburbs did not dampen enthusiasm for music halls, musical comedy, restaurants, and shopping. The simplest explanation is indifference: few Londoners, or those with enough cash and leisure, and the right clothes, had much taste for good music. Perhaps, as some believed, they needed training in its 'appreciation'.[2]

This was the environment in which the Philharmonic was expected not merely to survive, but to accept wide artistic and national responsibilities, or be found wanting by those prepared to sit in judgement. Since professional music-making, without public subsidy, continued to depend upon the box-office, which could only be relied upon to respond to a few very expensive stars, Berger was constantly engaged in a struggle to balance market requirements against less worldly expectations, often self-seeking and usually supercilious.

A New Venue

The opening of Queen's Hall in December 1893 provided London with its first satisfactory place for big concerts. After a slow start, with lettings for civic and private functions, it became a focal point for music, until annihilation in a 1941 air raid. The Promenade concerts, of course, were central to this process, creating a public for music more intensely and democratically than had ever been tried before. Philharmonic seasons were not comparable in their ability to reach out to a wider public, but they too enjoyed a mutually beneficial relationship with the new hall. It was centrally located and reasonably sized, with some 2,500 seats available for the renter to market at will, uncommitted to previous lessees. This contrasted agreeably with the remotely situated, elephantine Albert Hall; many of its 10,000 seats pre-empted,

---

[1] The 'regrettable decline' of choral singing in central London was a commonplace: 'So many good local choral societies now exist that amateur singers prefer as a rule to support the society in their own neighbourhood, rather than incur the trouble, expense, and fatigue of a journey to town' *Annual Register* (1900), 91–2.

[2] On the glut of music, see A. Peacock and R. Weir, *The Composer in the Market Place* (1975), 38–40. Ehrlich, *Music Profession*, 161–3.

and therefore crippling to big events—as the organizers of Wagner's
1877 concerts had discovered to their cost. The new place was also
better than St James's, which shared its advantages of sensible location,
useful size, and trustworthy acoustics, but lacked all other attractions.
Queen's Hall was cleaner, better ventilated, and decent; pleasingly decorated in red and the deliberately matched grey of a London mouse,
and quietly comfortable: no tattered benches, suffocation, cooking smells,
and minstrel noises here. Its acoustic, unmatched by later science, was
universally acclaimed. Its staff were trained to administer public concerts
and provide a congenial environment, responding in some measure to
the public's rising expectations in places of entertainment. We list these
qualities because they were peculiar to an economy and society which
excelled at housing the arts. If late Victorian and Edwardian capitalism
failed to provide a healthy market for good music, it did at least create
an infrastructure. The great new concert hall was a product of private
enterprise, competent architecture, and cheap building skills, like Frank
Matcham's contemporary theatres.[3]

Services were also on offer, as Robert Newman explained when he
urged Berger to 'place your staff under my direction'. They were not
specified, beyond making the audience 'as comfortable as possible' and
saving 'the society a considerable sum', implying that previous arrangements had been deficient in both respects. Even the door attendants,
as Mackenzie complained when the pre-Newman men locked him out,
could 'take delight in making matters as difficult as possible', when
unsupervised. Such things needed attention as concerts became more
public: fire precautions, ticket-scrutiny, and orderly admissions, even
the 'prevention and detection of Theft, PocketPicking and other of-
fences', for which a private detective had recently offered his services.[4]
Correct behaviour required rules and scrutiny. Berger later claimed
that he had been determined to abolish 'the antiquated regulation of
compulsory evening dress', but the evidence conflicts. Meticulous placing of appropriately clothed bottoms upon correct categories of seat
was always a preoccupation, and may even have been easier in the
new hall, as in the new theatres, with separate entrances for different
layers of society: '5 shilling tickets numbered and reserved, but not
evening dress—the words "evening dress" to be printed on all 10/6d
and 7/6d tickets.' The 'class uniform', as Shaw described it, was

---

[3] Including the London Coliseum. See C. Ehrlich and B. Walker, 'Enterprise and
Entertainment: The Economic and Social Background', in B. Walker (ed.), *Frank Matcham:
Theatre Architect* (Belfast, 1980), 21–35.

[4] Mackenzie's complaint: 48.13/21 (7 Nov. 1894). Private detective: 48.13/27 (11 Feb.
1890). Several years before J. Praunsmandel, 'Telegraph Inquisitor', offered such services,
which he claimed to be 'constantly engaged', the directors had enquired about the presence
of 'a female pickpocket' at a concert: 48.2/10 (19 Mar. 1887).

'considered compulsory' in certain areas. Designated rows and blocks were communicated to Newman 'with the view to their being rigidly adhered to', and were so advertised in newspapers and programmes.[5]

Behaviour affecting the enjoyment of music was also given attention. Doors were now closed for the duration of most works, in order to discourage intrusive arrivals and departures, a necessary correction to conduct which had been seen to deteriorate in recent years. Since visitations from court and aristocracy were both rarer, and less concerned to set standards of punctuality and decorum, than in the times of Victoria and Albert—*noblesse oblige* no longer applied to the arts— any impetus for improvement had perforce to be bourgeois.[6] It was rare for behaviour to degenerate so far as to provoke complaint, but hackles could still be raised, as when 'a very old subscriber' reported another's guests 'talking, laughing, singing, and occasionally whistling . . . and putting their feet up'. The matter was given 'serious attention', only to elicit counter-protests from the accused against being addressed, by Berger, like 'a gang of roughs'.[7] Coping with such troubles was no longer solely a matter of private club management, but also, in some measure, of dealing with a new public. What sort of people were to be encouraged and how could they be expected to behave? Student tickets, which had long been available, were allocated with an eye to social priorities. By the 1890s even 'non-professional' pupils from the RAM and RCM could qualify for concessions, but an application for cheap tickets from the highly professional military school of music at Kneller Hall was refused. In 1902 students at the Guildhall School of Music were offered a 'SPECIAL PRIVILEGE' of ½–guinea tickets for

[5] Berger on evening dress: *Reminiscences*, 69. Ticket regulations: 48.2/11 (10 Jan. and 14 Nov. 1895; 5 Mar. 1896). Shaw's remark concerned Benson's Hamlet in April 1890; but he returned to the subject repeatedly at the theatre—where he preferred to 'pay two shillings and go into the pit, where I can wear what I like'—in opera-houses and concert-halls, taking 'a distinct pleasure in the fact that my evening suit is by far the seediest article of clothing I possess'. *London Music*, 350. See also his letter to *The Times* on 'Sumptuary Regulations at the Opera', 3 July 1905, repr. in D. H. Laurence, *Shaw's Music* (1981), 3, 585–8.

[6] Such regulations were given considerable attention: variously described as 'Berger's plan', and responses to 'a request from subscribers and visitors' in 1888: 48.2/10 (7 and 23 Apr. 1888). Notices were inserted in programme books, the rules reiterated, and more easily imposed, in Queen's Hall. During the triumvirate the disturbance of court comings and goings at Cusins's concerts, with 'superfluous' performances of the National Anthem, had received pointed comment in the press. See e.g. *Athenaeum* (4 Apr. 1868); *MW* (11 July 1868); *Saturday Review* (15 Aug. 1868). Compare Foster's emollient comment on the Prince of Wales's 'thoughtfulness for the convenience of others', that year, in arriving 'between two of the pieces': *History*, 305.

[7] The original letter of complaint was described as 'important' and led to considerable correspondence: 48.2/11 (28 Nov. and 12 Dec. 1895); 48.13/3 (5 and 12 Dec. 1895); 48.13/1 (9 Dec. 1895).

seven concerts, and Special Chaperone Tickets for ladies at 1 guinea.[8] Compare an enthusiastic critic's advice to Prom-goers that attending 'a Mozart symphony or Bach suite with a briar pipe in our mouth' was 'surely the right way to listen to the great music'.[9]

In all these matters the Queen's Hall staff took first responsibility, and relinquishing authority to Newman signalled another break with the Society's past, in matters ranging from front-of-house management to ticket sales. Those displaced were not best pleased, including Stanley Lucas, whose protests mounted from hurt denial of any 'wish to inter-fere with Mr Newman's position', to outrage at losing to Chappell's the business of ticket distribution: 'a labour of love' since 1856, and 'in my opinion indifferently paid'.[10]

New Music, Stars, and the Box-Office

Mackenzie began the first Queen's Hall season with a concert which included a new overture by Goldmark, and Borwick playing the 'Em-peror' Concerto and Grieg Ballade. But its centrepiece was the first performance in England of a work which was immediately recognized as 'a masterpiece for the orchestra, and one that will endure'. It was uncommonly well prepared, having been previously rehearsed by Manns, so that repetition at a second Philharmonic concert, 'by special desire', enabled the orchestra to be heard to stunning effect. Perceived as a great, neglected, artist's premonition of death—'no composer ever uttered a final lay more powerful and thrilling'—Tchaikovsky's *Pathetic Symphony* was played throughout Britain within a few months, under Stanford, Manns, Hallé, and Richter, moving audiences almost beyond endur-ance.[11] It is scarcely possible for us—with every kind of music on tap—to imagine the pent-up excitement of such first encounters with the anguish of romantic genius.[12] As a Philharmonic initiative it was a

---

[8] 48.2/10 (1 Apr. 1889; 17 Dec. 1891). Printed notice to GSM students: 48.13/9 (Jan. 1902). Berger appeared to take pride in these wayward concessions, even quoting them in reply to complaints about the abolition of 1s. tickets in 1904: 48.30/11 (25 Jan. 1904). A 'poor City Clerk . . . very fond of music', but now denied access, protested that the guar-antor fund and low artists' fees should enable the Philharmonic, which 'poses as the national representative orchestral society of the country and is not run for the purposes of profit' to give him encouragement: *Daily News* (19, 20, and 30 Jan. 1904).

[9] Runciman, in *Saturday Review* (13 Aug. 1910).

[10] Newman: 48.13/28 (4 Sep. and 13 Dec. 1894); 48.2/11 (13 Dec. 1894). Lucas: 48.2/12 (25 Nov. 1898); 48.13/20 (29 Nov. 1898).

[11] 'masterpiece . . . that will endure': *MMR* (1 Apr. 1894); 'final lay': *Athenaeum* (17 Mar. 1894).

[12] On Tchaikovsky's belated triumph in Britain, and Berger's significant contribution to it, see G. Norris, *Stanford, the Cambridge Jubilee and Tchaikovsky* (1980), 475–92. A directors' minute of 27 Nov. 1893 reports a second letter sent to St Petersburg, requesting that the first performance in England of the Sixth Symphony should be reserved for the Society's concert on 28 Feb., and offering to purchase score and parts: 48.2/11.

spectacular example of leadership in the formation of public taste, but it brought no financial benefit. The two *Pathetic* concerts netted £122 and £112, the latter earning further merit, but probably losing cash, by introducing another English protégée of Clara Schumann, Fanny Davies, in Beethoven's Fourth Concerto. The next concert was also mildly enterprising: experimentally short, it consisted of Berlioz's King Lear Overture, Sapellnikoff in the Schumann Concerto, an aria from *Figaro*, an overture by Parry, and Beethoven's Fourth Symphony, with ticket sales of £110. Then an 'overflowing attendance' parted with no less than £336 to attend Paderewski's *Polish Fantasia*, on a cunningly devised evening. The piece was done after the interval and, as the programme had to state, 'by special request of the Directors'. It provoked, apparently by the process which later became known as 'milking the audience', a 'tedious number of recalls' and a Mendelssohn encore. The fans were not required to sit through a symphony by Edward German, which was safely placed in the first half of the programme.[13] Grieg was also loyally supported, returning after a five-year absence to introduce his *Sigurd Jorsalfar* music; and he was assisted by another pianist whose undoubted drawing-power fell short of fanaticism: Sophie Menter, pupil of Taussig and Liszt, who played the Tchaikovsky *Fantaisie de concert* and her own Fantasia, orchestrated by Tchaikovsky. Ticket sales that evening amounted to £216. The 'most successful season in many years' ended with a concert which introduced another new work—included because 'many American musicians' were expected in town, and it was thought appropriate to perform something by one of them, or Dvořák's 'American Symphony'. The audience was reported to be 'deeply interested', but only £136 worth of tickets were sold.[14]

The annual report for that extraordinary year of 1894 listed receipts £3,562, outlay £3,064, profit £499, and balance at the bank £788.[15] They were impressive figures, but the underlying pattern was far more significant. It meant that the presence of a major star, almost without regard to what was performed, could attract two or three times as much cash as other concerts, even those featuring new works which were destined soon to become popular classics. Both profit and pattern were repeated in the following season. Takings at seven bread-and-butter concerts descended from the opening concert's customary, and therefore misleadingly high, returns of £171, to £65, when Frederick Dawson played the Tchaikovsky Concerto and some Chopin, and £78, when the *Fantastic Symphony*, as always, kept audiences away—despite an unprecedented allowance of three rehearsals.[16] But on 3 April the soprano Adelina Patti—after dedicated cajoling which will shortly be

[13] *Athenaeum* (5 May 1894); *MT* (1 June 1894).
[14] 48.2/11 (25 Oct. 1894). *MMR* (1 July 1895).   [15] 48.3/3 (2 Feb. 1895).
[16] 48.2/11 (13 Dec. 1894).

described—sang for a few minutes and netted £373, the highest earnings of any concert so far in the Society's history. Now that the box-
office was being efficiently monitored, its message was clear enough,
but how was it to be acted upon, and with what effect? How many
supporters of the Society would acquiesce in an implicit policy of cross-
subsidy: circuses funding art? For so it was widely perceived at a time
when hierarchies of taste were strict, and critical bystanders, unerring
in their separation of the worthwhile from the meretricious, could articulate disquiet with sufficient vehemence, and disregard for practical
economics, to harm a Philharmonic image which had been sedulously
rebuilt.

   Even if Berger decided to press ahead, the practical difficulties of
procurement would be almost insurmountable. Major stars were now
extremely expensive, spoiled by Eldorado with booty beyond the dreams
of Jenny Lind and Anton Rubinstein. When 'Ruby' toured America for
Steinway in 1872/3 he was paid $200, literally in gold, for each of 215
concerts. Twenty years later Paderewski crossed the Atlantic for the
first time, just after his first Philharmonic appearance, and worked
a tour of sixty-three concerts which netted $160,000 (equivalent to
£40,000). His next American trip, in 1895–6 earned $280,000.[17] Res-
ponsible concert societies, with long-term seasonal commitments, could
not be expected to compete with these 'one off' events. In 1890 the
directors had refused to pay Paderewski 50 guineas. Such a fee was
regarded as unfair to other artists; an agent was suspected of being 'at
work', and half was thought sufficient.[18] Three years later he asked 150
guineas, and from then on his expectations, in cash and deference, as
the Philharmonic directors would soon discover, were without limit.
Another potentially blessed provider was Patti, probably the highest
paid singer in history, who had been earning an average of more than
$4,500 per performance in America. Even in Italy she commanded fees
ten times higher than those paid to Malibran in the 1830s. And there
were other needs: in the Texas desert a personal railway coach, its
'saloon furnished in monogrammed blue plush, a satinwood bedroom,
a bath, a piano, her own chef . . .'; in Russia six generals hauling a
'flower chair', with orchestral accompaniment.[19] The Society's resources,
in cash, rolling-stock, and army officers, fell short of such requirements,
but Berger's command of the indispensable language of flattery and
submission was second to none; and there were bargaining counters
available which had fallen into disuse.

   [17] Ehrlich, *Piano*, 54. A. Zamoyski, *Paderewski* (1982), 76.
   [18] Alberto Randegger to Berger, (2 Dec. 1890): 48.13/28. This is a good example of the
common tendency to attribute market realities to parasitic intermediaries.
   [19] J. Rosselli, *Singers of Italian Opera: The History of a Profession* (1992), 116, 135, 189. J.
Wechsberg, *Red Plush and Velvet* (1962), 119.

Honours and Awards

For nearly 170 years the Philharmonic has been concerned with the bestowal of honours and awards, as a profession's tributes to its peers. Honorary membership was the first such honour, and ever since a general meeting, on 6 April 1826, elected Carl Maria Von Weber, the list has been, with few exceptions, a roll-call of the illustrious, practically continuous in its recognition of exceptional talent or genius (Appendix 4). The gold medal (Appendix 5) came later, and eventually acquired similar distinction, but its origins require some explanation, and for this purpose 'the invention of tradition' is a useful concept. It implies today's scepticism, because we tend to hypostatize the past, and are prey to a 'heritage' industry which markets nostalgic images, real or fake. But scepticism does not necessarily entail disdain; for many once-respected traditions, with genuine roots, have gone through a stage of distortion or disuse, requiring an inventor's touch to bring new life. Such was the case with the medal, and its reinstatement by Berger.[20]

It was invented in 1870 to celebrate both the centenary of Beethoven's birth, and an institutional self-esteem nurtured by past involvement with genius, which had once been a genuine source of pride. Thus inauguration happened at a low ebb in the Society's fortune and status; a time when, as we have seen, such associations had dimmed, and claims to distinction were vainglorious. The Society's own centenary had prompted the directors to consider acquiring a bust and medal; the former 'to place in front of the orchestra', the latter for 'presentation to artists of eminence who have assisted or might assist the Society'; its first recipients to be Nilsson, Goddard, Joachim, Santley, and Cusins.[21] But before anything was done a letter arrived from an Austrian lady, Fanny Linzbauer, offering the Society a bust of Beethoven, sculpted by Professor J. Schaller of Vienna, 'in recognition' of the Society's 'spontaneous acts of esteem and generosity' towards the composer in times of need. Responding eagerly, the directors pledged themselves to protect the bust 'with jealous care, and to allow it only to be exhibited at the Concerts of the Society'. Cusins went to collect it from Frau Linzbauer in Budapest, with all possible pomp, and triumphantly conveyed it back to London, where it was exhibited at the first concert of 1871: the Fifth Symphony was played, as requested by the donor.

[20] On the 'invention of tradition', see Ch. 2 n. 2.
[21] 48.2/6 (18 June, 16 July, 8 Nov. 1870). At the latter meeting, recording the offer of the bust, 'the question of having two rehearsals for each concert was considered and decided impossible.' The medal was further discussed on 7 and 14 Jan., and 4 Feb. 1871.

16. Directors and bust, 1871 (48.15/4)

Many pages were subsequently devoted to descriptions of Cusins's trip and its attendant ceremonies, seeking association, perhaps, with earlier journeys and parleys of significance between the original directors and the living composer. If such accounts now evoke images, not so much of Siegfried's journey to the Rhine, or Danube, as of Monty Python's quest for the Holy Grail, it is necessary to remember that statues and busts were once regarded as significant and desirable objects, in public places and at home. They were, as Lord Briggs reminds us, 'among the most characteristic of Victorian things', sculpted at every opportunity, and mass-produced in Parian Ware. It was therefore an appropriate gesture for the Society to present copies of the bust to Cambridge University, the RAM, RCM, Crystal Palace, and Broadwood's, and a small replica to the Queen. Similar Parian replicas were manufactured for sale at 1 guinea, and a celebratory pamphlet was published. A medal was designed from the bust, and Frau Linzbauer added to the first list of recipients.[22] Intended as an alternative to a fee or gift for distinguished musicians, it was burnished by the award to Brahms in 1877.

[22] 48.3/2 (17 July 1870). 48.2/6 (10 June 1871). Exhaustive accounts of the bust, medal, and Cusins's journey are in Foster, *History*, 314–27; and Elkin, *Royal Philharmonic* (with illustrations), 68–72. On busts and Parian ware: A. Briggs, *Victorian Things* (1988), 150 ff.

Yet a medal was also collected by Lucas in 1880, which may explain the subsequent cessation of nominations for fifteen years. Berger began its reinstatement, not with a self-award which, it might have been argued, would have been well-earned, but with a great star.[23] Hobsbawm's thesis, quoted at the head of this chapter, is therefore entirely apt. At its moment of invention the medal's continuity with a distinguished past was, indeed, 'factitious', or broken; but by the 1890s it was ready for revival, in appropriate company. Thanks to the early Philharmonic directors the 'sinfonias' of Beethoven had 'blazed like a comet', the genius of Mendelssohn and the boy Joachim had delighted 'band and auditory', and established the Society's reputation for artistic judgement and leadership. Thanks now to Berger, there were new masterpieces and great performers to reinstate that reputation and, in due time, assert the medal's status, as bargaining counter and emblem.

The wooing of Patti, which began in 1885, was frostily received. Her secretary wrote from her Welsh castle that engagements permitted of charity being dispensed only to 'the poor and suffering in her own neighbourhood'. Berger's reproof was dignified, but kept his suit open: since the Philharmonic's support was improving and contrasted 'very favourably with other musical institutions', no charity was asked, but 'a graceful act from a great artiste to a great national institution'.[24] Ten years later he tried again, and a letter from her agent at a Birmingham 'Pianoforte, Harmonium and Music Warehouse' spelt out the terms of acceptance. It was the diva's 'understanding that you will on that occasion present her with the Medal of the Society (not to any other singer since Grisi) and she will only be asked to sing once during the proceedings'; and 'when announcing the affair' her appearance is 'by the consent (or courtesy, or any other word you prefer) of my firm'.[25] The directors accepted these robust conditions, which included a 'nominal fee' of £100, and made their arrangements with similar precision: the honorary treasurer and secretary would conduct her on to the platform 'and then, in the name of the Philharmonic Society, present her with the Society's Gold Medal and affix it to her dress'. Great care was taken with the medal's inscription and an 'elegant case bearing a like description'.[26]

---

[23] Elkin notes that the Society's archives contained no reference to the award of a medal to Lucas: *Royal Philharmonic*, 135 n. 1. Its existence has since been confirmed by recent correspondence.   [24] 48.13/27 (6 and 7 Aug. 1885).

[25] 48.13/15 (16 Jan. 1895). He was wrong about Grisi, who had never received a medal, but had sung for the Society in 1834 and 1835.

[26] 48.2/11 (14 Feb. 1895). The 'nominal' fee continues to be an essential part of the musician's armoury. A recent study points out that 'many singers would rather sing for nothing, say for a charity performance, than reduce their fee, because doing so would give the wrong signal to the market'. R. Towse, *Singers in the Market Place*, 135.

Although the concert was a huge success with the public, critical response was uniformly hostile. One reviewer praised 'great beauty of tone and phrasing', in Rossini's 'Una voce poco fa' and Mozart's 'Voi che sapete', but regretted the 'subsequent scene enacted upon the platform by Berger and Cummings' as 'pandering to personal sensationalism'. Only 'a widely esteemed and acknowledged composer' was considered to deserve such attention, and it was 'unkind before such an audience to dwell upon Md. Patti's "distinguished services" to the art of music'.[27] Another journalist would have preferred something 'of higher import' than Rossini and the 'mawkish ditty' 'Home, Sweet Home', while marvelling at 'florid execution'. A third found the ditty 'a curious item for such a Society' but acknowledged that Patti was singing without fee and had attracted 'the largest audience ever seen at a Philharmonic concert'.[28] Exceeding all in vituperation was the splenetic J. F. Runciman, Shaw's successor at the *Saturday Review*, who found the whole show a 'screamingly funny farce' and concluded, in a later outburst, that 'nothing whatever can be done with the Philharmonic Circus' except, perhaps, to instal a tightrope and 'have Cummings and Berger, in spangled tights, run up and down that'. The *Saturday Review* lost its press ticket, but Runciman's rancour merely overstated routine prejudices among serious arbiters of English good taste. The Rossini aria, which had been sung at seven previous Philharmonic concerts back to 1823, and has never ceased to enchant, was somehow found unworthy. A singer who had inspired poetry by Gautier and been described by Verdi as a great artist, could be traduced by a minor journalist as 'a deluded lady, well past middle age' rewarded with 'the Beethoven medal' for 'a life spent in singing "Home Sweet Home"'.[29] Patti returned her fee, as promised.[30] The next medallist was more demanding.

No one could have been in any doubt, by now, that it would require paroxysms of diligence and servility to get a free performance out of Paderewski. Whatever his musical talent—and surviving gramophone records suggest nothing remarkable—his drawing-power was, at this peak, unique in the world among instrumentalists. An English lawyer once described him as 'a cheery little chap', but everyone else, including Burne-Jones and legions of women, found him 'glorious', the quintessentially romantic pianist in the golden age of the piano.[31] In

---

[27] *MT* (1 May 1895).

[28] *Athenaeum* (6 Apr. 1895); *MMR* (1 May 1895). Note the confusion about what was sung. Probably two encores were given—Mozart and ditty—and a supercilious critic left before the second.

[29] *Saturday Review* (6 Apr. and 30 Nov. 1895). Exclusion: 48.2/11 (12 Dec. 1895). On Patti as singer and artist, see J. B. Steane, *The Grand Tradition* (1974), 14–17.

[30] 48.2/11 (6 May 1895).   [31] Zamoyski, *Paderewski*, 60.

those days fans did not scream, but they wrote notes, and two survive in the Philharmonic archive, on delicate pink paper, pleading for a private session at the Langham Hotel. The lady already has M. Paderewski's autograph and a ticket for his next concert; she is 'not rich but would be happy to give half a guinea' if he might play 'his own Menuet'.[32] A player with such a public required special blandishments, and Berger succeeded in booking two more appearances, in 1897 and 1900, after prolonged negotiations. On both occasions there was careful avoidance of display, in repertoire or demeanour, as if to appease sensitive critics. At the first, Mackenzie's 'Scottish' Concerto was performed, and it was arranged that the gold medal, which had secured the pianist's services, would be presented to him at a private ceremony. For this dignified avoidance of circus tricks the directors were rewarded by scant notice from the critics, and a masterly display of petulance from the star. First, their intention of 'waiting upon him' was rejected; then Berger attempted to deliver the medal and letter in person, only to have it returned, eventually, as unsuitably engraved (on the rim, like all others). A new medal was prepared and a 'deputation of three Directors', in frockcoats, stood attendance. Finally Berger was summoned alone: only then was honour satisfied.[33] Meanwhile Albani, who had recently sung Isolde to Jean de Reszke's wonderful Tristan at Covent Garden, accepted her award with quieter dignity. 'This medal is very rarely bestowed, and only on the greatest of artists,' reported the *Morning Post.* And a decade later Albani spoke for most recipients: 'I am always very proud of my medal and often wear it here and abroad.'[34]

Troublesome, but profitable, dealings with Paderewski were not yet at an end. Having agreed to play a Concert Piece by Cowen in June 1899, he withdrew a few days before the concert, called to Poland by 'important affairs': Mackenzie could find 'no words to express' his disgust at this behaviour. Such was the pianist's irreplaceable drawing-power that cancellation threatened untold damage, in a season already made gloomy by the Boer War; but Joachim came to the rescue with the Beethoven Concerto, fifty-five years after his first Philharmonic performance of it under Mendelssohn. In gratitude the directors wanted to award the medal, in addition to his 60-guinea fee, but found that

[32] 48.13/12 (17 and 27 June 1900).

[33] 48.2/11 (26 Mar., 2 Apr., 7 May, 4 and 18 June, 2 July 1897). 48.13/23 (2 and 26 Apr. 1897).

[34] *Morning Post* (6 July 1897). 48.13/1 (6 Oct. 1908). By then, with medals awarded to such artists as Ysaÿe, Kubelik, and Kreisler, the tradition required no further invention. Silver medals were also awarded, e.g. in 1895 to Richard Blagrove 'for long valued services as principal viola', and in 1898 to W. B. Wotton, 'first fagotto for many years': 48.2/11 (21 Mar. 1895; 11 and 25 Mar. 1898). The procedure appears to have been similar to those official decorations which distinguish between crosses for officers and medals for 'other ranks'.

he had already received one in 1871; so they presented him with a
gold wreath instead.[35] Paderewski played the Cowen piece in 1900,
collecting his 150 guineas and again breaking records with ticket sales
of £364. Earlier concerts that season included three of the most celebrated pianists of the twentieth century: Busoni in Liszt's Second
Concerto, Dohnányi in Beethoven's Fourth, and Rosenthal in Mozart
K.488 and the Liszt *Don Giovanni* fantasy. At less than one-fifth of
Paderewski's fee—25 or 30 guineas—none of them could attract one-
third of his audience.[36] It was his last Philharmonic appearance, and
further attempts at personal communication were brushed away: he
'really hasn't time to answer the numerous letters he receives about
engagements from persons who forget that he has an agent representative who transacts all his business'.[37]

Agents and Piano-Makers

Agents could no longer be avoided, even if their intervention was still
occasionally resented. Sometimes they were needed to tap new networks, as when attempts to contact Rimsky-Korsakov in 1899 were
returned by the dead letter office. But direct communication with
international musicians was bound to decline, as seasons and tours
were extended, and the market became more impersonal. If a few
major artists continued to conduct their own business, or at least some
correspondence—Saint-Saëns, for example, and Carreno, who wrote
from Pittsburgh, Havana, Chicago, and Berlin—the definitive statement of modern practice came from von Bülow. A direct approach was
rebuffed, and all negotiations referred to his Berlin agent Hermann
Wolff. 'Everyone in everywhere knows it', he protested, and letter-
writing is a 'burden, especially in a foreign tongue . . . I have to mind
my artistical business.'[38] It was also understood that Wolff represented such artists as d'Albert, Auer, Essipoff, Rubinstein, Sauer, and
Tchaikovsky; and that representation carried sufficient assurance for
the agent to report: 'Tschaikovsky accepts; you can count upon him.'[39]
By dealing with first-class agents the directors no longer needed to
approach three pianists before finally engaging a fourth, or to judge
a performer's skill simply by hearsay.[40]

---

[35] Called to Poland: 48.13/1 (20 May 1899); 48.2/12 (26 May 1899). Mackenzie's reaction: 48.13/21 (20 May 1899). Gratitude to Joachim: 48.2/12 (16 June 1899).

[36] 48.2/12 (18 May, 8 and 29 June 1900).   [37] 48.13/1 (7 Oct. 1905).

[38] Rimsky: 48.2/12 (27 Oct 1899). Saint-Saëns: 48.13/29 (various letters in 1898). Carreno:
48.13/6 (various letters in 1901). Von Bülow: 48.13/5 (13 Mar. 1888).

[39] 48.2/10/99 (*c*.1887). 48.13/36/109 (1888).

[40] In 1885 Oscar Beringer was engaged to play the Schumann Concerto after Rummell,
Hallé, and Essipoff had separately been approached: 48.2/9 (21 Feb. 1885).

Agents, who emerged in response to the market, and contributed
to its growth, were diverse in their origins, resources, and expertise.
Publishers and distributors of music were a traditional group. Chappell,
as we have seen, became Clara Schumann's London representative.
Ewer had introduced Rubinstein in 1857; and Augener, Moszkowski
in 1884.[41] Lawyers, businessmen, musician-fixers, (such as Jarrett, a
horn-player who represented the violinist Sivori in the 1860s), even
journalists, like Henry Hersee, all dabbled in the work, with a few
musicians on their books; but the major firms were now operating on
a worldwide scale.[42] Hard-selling became the norm. The notepaper
heading for Karl Junkermann, of London, Paris, Berlin, Vienna, and
New York, proclaimed 'Kubelik—Paganini Redevivus', 'Koussewitzky—
Marvellous contra-bass virtuoso (for America only)', and 'Zimbalist—
Incomparable Russian violinist'.[43] Görlitz, advising Berger on the ways
of modern commerce 'out of friendship', explained that advertising
artists in alphabetical order was 'fifty years behind the times': 'Kubelik
is a "star" and must precede all other violinists. He will draw more
money for you than all other artists put together.'[44] And this was no
more than the truth. Kubelik's Philharmonic début and subsequent
concerts in 1902 and 1903 'drew' £197 (for the Beethoven Concerto),
£241 (for a new concerto by Alberto Randegger Jun., but also with
the enormously and inexplicably popular Clara Butt on the programme),
and £195 (for Mozart's Concerto in D, probably K.218). None of the
eleven other concerts approached these figures, not even Kreisler's
début (fee 25 guineas) in March 1903: playing a nondescript concerto
by Baron d'Erlanger, subsidized by the composer, which paid for an
extra rehearsal, but also with the attractive Saint-Saëns *Rondo Capriccioso*.
'Surely if you offered Kubelik the same fees as you offer me, 20
guineas,' complained Lady Hallé in response to pleas of poverty, 'you
would have a good profit.'[45] But although she had her devotees among
the older patrons, and her Mendelssohn Concerto had probably shared
credit with Sapellnikoff's Tchaikovsky for the most remunerative concert of the 1901 season (£159), Lady Hallé's drawing-power could not

[41] Ewer: 48.13/11 (14 Apr. 1857). Augener: 48.2/9 (22 Nov. 1885).
[42] Some examples: Hugo Görlitz, representing Paderewski, Kubelik, and Lhévinne; D.
Mayer, allied with Wolff, whose artists included Stavenhagen, Ysaÿe, Borwick, Katherine
Goodson, Plunket Greene, and Albert Coates; Alfred Schulz-Curtius, who represented
d'Albert, Richard Strauss, Mottl, Weingartner, Melba, and Backhaus; N. Vert, agent for
many musicians, including Grieg, Rosenthal, and Sarasate. At least two members of the
leading 20th-cent. English firm Ibbs and Tillett—John. H. and Pedro S. Tillett—started
with Vert. The Philharmonic Archive contains much information about these firms and
their artists, best approached initially via the appropriate agency names in the series of
general correspondence: 48.13.   [43] 48.13/18 (7 Aug. 1907).
[44] 48.13/13 (10 Jan. 1903).
[45] 48.13/15 (26 Nov. 1906). Fees and gates are recorded at appropriate times in 48.2/12.

compare to that of her young compatriot, which earned him a £50 fee and gold medal.

The great piano-makers had always supported leading pianists—Erard and Broadwood supplying pianos and hospitality for such visitors as Chopin and Clara Schumann—but by the late nineteenth century they had become a major, highly enterprising, force in the agency business. When Clara's pupil Fanny Davies played for the Philharmonic in 1886, Broadwood was characteristically restrained: 'we don't put public showboards on our concert pianos' (on the side, facing the audience), but could 'piano by Broadwood' appear in the programmes?[46] Even by 1902, when they were all but overwhelmed by German and American competition, a request for their 'Steel Barless Grand' to be included in a concert advertisement, ended 'but don't insist'.[47] The new firms *did* insist, offering information, advice, pianos, pianists, advertising revenue, and direct subsidies. A few examples will illustrate the scope of their contribution to concert economics before the First World War. In 1895 Blüthner refused a fee of £50 for Moriz Rosenthal, asking 75 guineas because of the pianist's recent acclaim, and accepting 65. Next season they offered Siloti (Rachmaninov's teacher) for 25 guineas, and took up half of the fee in tickets.[48] In 1903 Bechstein reduced the joint cost of Busoni and Pachmann to 80 guineas 'by adding a solatium to each artist on the firm's account', and advised immediate acceptance because 'drawing power at the booking offices are in excess of their fees'.[49] Ibach, with Sauer and Kubelik on their books—piano firms did not only represent pianists—and various fee inducements, were more aggressive in their marketing, expecting, for instance, more prominence to be given to their name in the Society's programmes. They also requested gold medals for both artists, after 'enormous success and modest fee', but were assured that its presentation was 'always a spontaneous act'.[50]

Of the two leading French makers, Erard, who had closed their London factory in 1890, were ceasing to be fashionable—though Paderewski still sometimes played their instruments, in spite of his Steinway-organized American tours—but Pleyel were still attempting to compete. So when Raoul Pugno made his first Philharmonic appearance in 1903, with a rare performance of Mozart's E flat Concerto K.271, and bringing his own orchestral parts, his 'honorarium' was fully paid by the Paris firm. A year later he refused 30 and asked 40 guineas, at which Pleyel complained about 'the same old story—the piano house

---

[46] 48.13/16 (7 Apr. 1886).   [47] 48.13/5 (20 May 1902).

[48] 48.13/4 (2 and 17 July 1895; 30 Dec. 1896).   [49] 48.13/2 (23 Oct. 1903).

[50] 48.13/17 (23 Nov. 1900; 1 Mar. 1901; 21 Feb. and 2 Apr. 1902; 30 Mar. 1903). It will be noticed that some prominent artists, such as Kubelik, were represented by several different agents and piano firms.

must come to the rescue and match up the difference'.[51] And they promised delivery: the pianist's desire to change dates, in order to play for the Queen of Spain, was met by the assurance, 'I will see that he plays for you then even if I have to go over to France myself to bring him.' But limits were set to interference. An attempt to change a Mendelssohn programme in February 1909, celebrating the composer's centenary birthday, was set aside: 'It is not the custom of the Philharmonic Society for soloists and conductors to settle matters between them . . . play the solos as arranged.' Doubtless this assertion of authority was influenced by concern that the proposed change would have required more rehearsal time, but it was a useful reminder that the directors were able to benefit from commercial patronage without abdicating control. Nor did it harm the relationship. The Philharmonic début of France's greatest twentieth-century pianist, in 1911, with the Saint-Saëns Fourth Concerto and some Chopin and Liszt, cost the Society only 25 guineas, Pleyel paying the 'other moiety' of Alfred Cortot's fee.[52] Steinway soon came to dominate the English market for concert pianos and pianists, although studios—and stately homes, as Noel Coward reminds us—usually preferred a Bechstein grand. From the start the American firm negotiated with refreshing directness: for Sapellnikoff 'we'll subscribe 20 guineas so you can make fee 50 guineas. Send 20 guineas tickets.' Similarly Menter carried a 20-guinea subsidy, and when the modestly English Borwick raised his terms to 30 guineas, Steinway promised to contribute ten. They even claimed that 'present-day' pianists 'look to pianoforte-makers to obtain their appearance at the Philharmonic', and complained that too many of their protégés were turned down, despite 'liberal arrangements'. The sensational Olga Samaroff (née Lucy Hickenlooper from Texas; later Mrs Stokowski, and a great teacher) was offered for no fee, and not accepted. But the Society's 'old friend Sapellnikoff', when available through Steinway, was 'fitted in', entirely at the firm's expense. As with Pleyel, however, there was never any question of abdicating policy decisions. Thus Steinway's offer to pay Rachmaninov's fee, provided he was allowed to appear elsewhere in England before making his Philharmonic début, was not accepted.[53]

The importance of these connections can hardly be exaggerated, for pianos and pianists were central to the musical commerce and music-making of the day. Few people outside Haslemere were interested in

[51] 48.13/27 (5 Aug. 1902; 21 Nov. 1904).   [52] 48.2/13 (1 June 1911).

[53] 48.13/33 (16 May 1892; 6 May 1893; 6 July 1898; 28 Jan. 1902; 27 May and 11 June 1909). Rachmaninov's first appearance for the Society was beset with difficulties, including his failure to produce the second concerto in time. See 48.2/12 (16 Dec. 1898; 13 Jan., and 3 and 24 Feb. 1899). Also G. Norris, 'Rachmaninov's London Debut', *MT* (Apr. 1993).

harpsichords, less still in old pianos—the term 'fortepiano' was quite unknown—preferring the latest and best to the 'authentic'. Mutually beneficial connections between makers, players, and the Society there-fore gave free access to superb instruments in immaculate condition—manufacture, maintenance, and tuning were then at a zenith of com-petitive achievement—and to privileged, usually subsidized, choice among the world's leading virtuosi, with up-to-date information about new-comers, their availability, repertoire, and drawing-power. Leading firms also had their own recital rooms in London, notably the Bechstein (later Wigmore) Hall, which acted as show places and testing-grounds of talent: all at no cost to the Society. Possibilities of undue influence by individual firms or players were countered by intense competition for the Philharmonic platform, and by a generally well-informed audi-ence, most of whom owned instruments.

Composers, Conductors, and Rehearsals

If agents and piano manufacturers contributed to a vastly extended and improved network of recruitment and information, the Society still needed to transcend market relationships by appealing to the community of musicians. It could be difficult, as with Richard Strauss. Overtures began in 1898 when the directors, cautious after three unprofitable sea-sons, tried to get him to conduct a performance of *Don Quixote* at 'nominal terms, say £30 for expenses'.[54] A personal letter to the composer led to Berger receiving a visit from the agent Alfred Schultz-Curtius, and a formal statement 'so that there may be no misunderstanding when you report our interview to your Directors'. It insisted upon Strauss's usual terms of £75, the agent denying any intention of 'blocking the way' or narrowing competition 'as you were inclined to suppose last night'.[55] Berger pulled out some stops:

Honoured Master, the Directors of the Society had no idea that you would treat their invitation as a matter of business, requiring the advice or counsel of ... any concert agent. The Directors are all musical artists themselves and addressed their invitation to you as a confrère, wishing merely to mark this appreciation of your distinguished talent and reputation, and hoping it might be agreeable for you to come among them, quite apart from any consideration of monetary profit, just as Weber, Mendelssohn, Spohr, and other Masters have done in the past. This Society is not an association for speculation, but devotes itself solely to the furtherance of musical Art in England, and com-posers have hitherto always felt it an honour to be invited to conduct their compositions, and this is the reason why no Honorarium was offered to you, merely such a sum as you might consider would cover your expenses.[56]

[54] 48.2/11 (14 Oct. 1898).   [55] 48.13/30 (19 Oct. 1898).
[56] 48.13/33 (23 Oct. 1898).

Strauss's reply was brief and to the point: 'Your separation of a business transaction from a purely honorary one is not so practical as you might think.' It would be disloyal for a professional composer—continued the message from this most professional of composers to a country where the species was unknown—to ignore his London agent, who handled business for which he could not spare the time.[57] Differing conceptions of professionalism also entailed conflicting views about rehearsals. Strauss insisted upon three for *Don Quixote*—five had been barely sufficient in Berlin—and the employment of a 'cellist of solo calibre'. Mackenzie was asked to look at the score and, replying from the land of the sight-readers, reported that there was no time for 'odd rehearsals during season'; why not ask for *Tod und Verklärung*? The directors did so, offering two two-hour rehearsals. Strauss replied, through his agent, that all of his late works were too difficult for only two rehearsals. But, always practical, he suggested that since several works had already been done in London, at least some of the players might be familiar with either *Don Juan*, or *Till Eulenspiegel*, or *Tod und Verklärung*; unless the Philharmonic might prefer an older, simpler piece 'in the classical style'. In the event the composer conducted *Tod* and was paid £50. Mackenzie presided over the rest of the concert and, next day, resigned.[58]

His efforts on behalf of the Philharmonic had been prodigious and unceasing. He read a wide range of scores, and reported on them with zest. Despite his position at the RAM, he was no organ-loft pedant, but was capable of lecturing at the Royal Institution on Verdi's *Falstaff* a few months after its first performance in 1893, and of making liberal changes in the Society's programmes. His own compositions, many of which were performed at the Philharmonic, included concert pieces for Paderewski and Joachim (*Pibroch*), and he was aware of those around him, 'What a time we are having,' he wrote to Berger: 'Being now the only English Society, natives naturally turn to us and keep us lively.'[59] But liveliness was not enough. Disinclined 'to sit in judgement upon others', Mackenzie nevertheless did so 'as a duty to the Directors and the Society', and was capable of dismissing outright a piece by Tobias Matthay as 'cranky, long, . . . more difficult of execution than the result would justify'.[60] Some decisions were less simple, such as the response to a letter from Malvern: 'You may have heard my name as a composer during the last two years', said the writer, who was 'naturally anxious to obtain a hearing in London at the Philharmonic'. Berger

[57] 48.13/33 (27 Oct. 1898).
[58] 48.13/30 (18 Mar., 28 Oct., 12 Nov., and 13 Dec. 1898). 48.2/12 (25 Nov. and 16 Dec. 1898; 16 June 1899). [59] 48.13/21 (28 Nov. 1894).
[60] 48.13/21 (1 Dec. 1896). Matthay later resigned from the Society, protesting against its neglect of 'British Art' and 'a deliberate *boycott* of the British Instrumentalist'. See his letter to Berger, 28 Jan. 1907, reprod. in L. Foreman, *From Parry to Britten: British Music in Letters 1900–1945* (1987), 32–3.

wrote back, promising that any work submitted would get careful attention; and the composer replied, 'I, of course, do not intend to "submit" any composition of music to the judgement of your "Directors".' Thus ended Edward Elgar's first encounter with the Society.[61]

The episode touches upon important questions of repertoire, its arbitration and progress. What music got played had never been a systematically ordered process, even when the Society was controlled by leading musicians of the day. It could be limited by the printed music available, by the arbitrary offerings of visiting performers and their teachers, or by the likes, and particularly the dislikes, of the band, not least its unruly members. There might be attempts to please audiences, but how were tastes to be ascertained, and how could anything new be appraised until heard? If taste was to be given an intelligent lead—surely a prime Philharmonic task—it required better information and procedures of selection. The former was achieved by Berger's connecting up to the new networks. All traces of parochialism were removed and ignorance ceased to be an everyday state of mind. When, a decade later, Debussy had to respond to an amiable invitation to conduct his short work by pointing out that 'Pelleas and Melisande is a musical drama in five acts', it was a rare, if comic, example of the directors being caught out.[62] In former years such obtuseness would hardly have been noticed among the insular. But abundance and open minds made selection far more difficult, particularly when choosing among native compositions at the time of a so-called English Musical Renaissance. As one of its more effective champions later recalled: 'All our geese were swans, no longer need we suffer from any complex of inferiority . . . Brahms and Parry were coupled together in a a fashion that suggested an equality of achievement.'[63] The Philharmonic had grown accustomed to functioning without a native commanding genius, though one had been sought. It should cause no surprise that the Society was slow in coming to terms with Elgar.

Mackenzie's adjudications rarely carried such a burden; they were generally enlightened and stimulating. His advocacy of new music was often accompanied by a scepticism towards past masters which, as in the remark at the head of this chapter, is remote from our sensibilities— though he finished his last concert as resident conductor with Mozart's Thirty-Eighth Symphony.[64] In 1895, now Sir Alexander, he writes about

<hr />

[61] 48.13/11 (27 Oct. and 24 Nov. 1897). 48.2/11 (26 Nov. 1897).

[62] 48.13/10 (24 Sept. 1906).   [63] Sir Thomas Beecham, A Mingled Chime (1944), 42.

[64] The comment on Mozart's early symphonies is in 48.13/21 (10 Nov. 1894). The composer's centenary was not celebrated until 1892; with a concert presided over by a bust of Mozart, instead of Beethoven, and an ode by Joseph Bennett, 'declaimed with great spirit.' MMR (1 Apr. 1892). The Purcell Bicentenary concert, 22 Nov. 1895, was similarly remote from our ideas of homage and authenticity, including an arrangement of the 'Golden' Sonata for two pianos and orchestra.

the French-Irish composer Augusta Holmes: 'Schotts have nothing—
send to Paris—good idea to do something of hers.' Nothing came of
that, but in the same month he is searching out 'new Russians',
recommending Borodin as a 'striking novelty' and sending for two
symphonies and the *Prince Igor* Overture.[65] He could be fierce about
the behaviour of stars but his ideas about improving the concerts, after
a few years of conducting, were moderate and sensible. He wanted
them shorter, to prevent 'fruitless labour for me and the orchestra'; and
welcomed 'steps taken', all too temporarily, along this route.[66] With more
control over singers and their choice of songs, and of encores, he
believed the Society could match 'similar enterprises in London' and
even 'the best orchestral concerts in Europe'. His concern extended to
the social dimension, recommending 'a strong move to get the Prince
and Princess of Wales to come some nights . . . a little fashionable support would not do any harm'.[67] His cast of mind could not be expected
to attach high value to virtuoso conductors; but, unlike many of his
contemporaries, he was not oblivious to the species and its strengths.
Monitoring its behaviour, he simply preferred to keep clear and avoid
direct comparisons: with, for example, 'the great Lamoureux! We have
had enough comparison with him. God knows.' So the *Flying Dutchman*
Overture, he thought, was best replaced by *Oberon* or something else
'requiring no rehearsal'; and similarly with Saint-Saëns's *Le Rouet
d'Omphale*, another of the 'show pieces performed . . . with an execution
born of 1,000 rehearsals'.[68] And apparently the directors shared this
reluctance to compete from the podium, for they refused to take the
opportunity of getting a star conductor when Mackenzie first attempted
to resign in 1898.[69]

Breaking-point came in the following season. When he conducted a
concert in May which included 200 members of the Leeds Festival
Choir in Parry's *Blest Pair of Sirens* and Beethoven's Ninth Symphony,
the choir's goodwill in travelling down to give London a singing lesson,
and back in the same day, was matched by Mackenzie's willingness
to avoid an expensive London rehearsal and 'run down to Leeds to
hold one there'.[70] He was rewarded by reviews which, acknowledging
superb choral singing, insisted, no doubt with truth, that the instrumental movements 'lacked breadth, brilliancy, point and precision' and
were clearly 'not properly rehearsed'. In sum, the performance of the

[65] 48.13/21 (10 and 30 Aug. 1895).
[66] 'Oh! These Singers!'—on a soprano's proposal to transpose the 'Abscheulicher' from
Fidelio, with no thought for its instrumental consequences: 48.13/21 (15 Nov. 1897). 'I have
no words to express my disgust at Paderewski's behaviour': 48.13/21 (20 May 1899). On
concert reform: 48.13/21 (7 July 1896).   [67] 48.13/21 (12 Mar. 1898).
[68] 48.13/21 (1 May 1896), and doc. 118 (n.d. [prob. same month]).
[69] Letter repr. in Elkin, *Royal Philharmonic*, 95.
[70] 48.2/11 (4 Nov. 1898). 48.2/12 (21 Apr. 1899).

Society's exemplary millstone was found 'not worthy'.[71] Mackenzie's resignation prompted a tangle of gossip and confusion, exacerbated by Stanford, quarrelsome as always, who was eager to elucidate questions about the conductor's status and authority which others preferred to fudge. Rumours that the job had been offered to Henry Wood were denied, but among a list of undistinguished applications there was one from Cowen, who had 'always regretted' his 'hasty action', and now expected to be replaced from his current position in Manchester by 'our formidable rival' (Richter). He was reappointed in time for the 1900 season, despite some anonymous complaints, and the effect upon orchestral standards was immediately noticed.[72] One tribute, which threw light upon a section of the Society's regular audience, stressed the importance of improvement for 'numerous professional musicians busily engaged in forming the tastes of our musical youth, whose only idea of an orchestra is the Philharmonic. They hardly know of and never hear another . . . and their standards of excellence rise and fall with the Philharmonic.'[73] More sophisticated opinion also welcomed Cowen back as a 'chef d'orchestre of the first rank', but was concerned about his influence upon a 'band not all anxious and eager to do their best for the music': getting the attention of some players required 'exaggerated efforts'.[74] What remained of Cowen's authority was exerted without any repetition of former confrontations or, one suspects, too much renewed insistence upon intensive rehearsal. Another retreat from reform was the result of continuing concern for the box-office. Some recent concerts, Berger reasoned, had been too short, so in future, 'when any one great star could not be secured' general attractiveness should be maintained by having two soloists, 'so as to give the public a little more for their money and to meet all tastes'.[75]

Renewed attempts to catch an elusive star in 1906 were touched with anxiety, after a season of 'exceptional disaster to all musical enterprises', which had ended with a £500 deficit, and a call of 17 per cent upon the guarantors. Its causes were never in doubt: increased orchestral costs, now that everyone expected at least 100 players; intense competition for a volatile audience; and financial depression. Only the latter could be expected to abate.[76] Berger reached for his pen: 'the greatest of all living musical artists, the incomparable Melba,

---

[71] *Athenaeum* (27 May 1899).

[72] 48.13/8 (26 June 1900). Despite controversy at the time, it was generally understood that Cowen, although recognized as a good conductor in his three seasons with the Hallé orchestra, was only a 'stopgap' appointment, awaiting Richter. See M. Kennedy, *The Hallé 1858–1983: A History of the Orchestra* (Manchester, 1982), 8; Fifield, *True Artist*, 305–8. Anonymous complaints: 48.13/36 (16 Sept. and 6 Oct. 1899).

[73] *MW* (1 Aug. 1900).   [74] *Athenaeum* (17 and 24 Mar. 1900).

[75] 48.2/12 (22 July 1899).   [76] 48.3/3 (8 July and 18 Nov. 1905).

has not, up to the present, graced the Philharmonic platform. Is it too much to ask you to do so next year?' For the Society it would be 'the highest honour and brightest day in our long life', and to the diva, 'accustomed to the roaring applause of the general public' was promised 'an audience largely made up of musicians, fellow workers in that field where you are the universally acknowledged Queen and Mistress'.[77] The ensuing campaign involved talk of medals and, at one stage, almost hourly 'Strictly Private' despatches from the front, at the Ritz Hotel.[78] Nothing came of these endeavours, and perhaps it was this débâcle which forced Berger to come to terms, at last, with the only *kind* of star still neglected in his strategy: the newest to churn excitement, and possibly the most likely to revive ticket sales. At the next general meeting, which was attended by a number of wary guarantors, he was asked whether the 'possibly passing fashion of hearing and seeing foreign conductors' might not be 'a financial necessity'. It was a sensible year to take soundings, not one of grievous mishap or unusual hardship. A 'magnificent band' had cost £1,187; a 'splendid array of soloists' had been secured for the comparatively small sum of £300; takings had actually increased by more than £200; yet, like practically every season in the past decade, there was an overall loss, and there would have to be a call of 15 per cent on the guarantors.[79]

A new era of concert planning began gently with the decision to engage 'a distinguished foreign conductor' for a single concert, in response to 'what appears to be a demand by the public'. The directors denied any intention of replacing Cowen and, at the same meeting, expressed a revealing desire to interest 'what is known as fashionable society' in the Philharmonic. That the distinguished conductor need not be foreign, and that he might also link the Society to 'Society', was not yet in the reckoning.[80] Cowen acquiesced, refused a fee, and made a face-saving visit to Scotland, while Edouard Colonne took charge of the opening concert of 1907 and drew a large audience (£165).[81] But this was merely a beginning as the directors moved on to give 'serious attention to plurality of conductors' for 1908.[82] Berger's next 'Dear and honoured Master' letter was therefore addressed to the most celebrated exponent of the new cult of 'conductor as hero'. It explained that the directors 'spend all their funds upon securing the finest orchestra in

[77] 48.13/23 (26 May 1906). The ensuing correspondence, including a note from Melba (n.d.), is in 48.13/23, docs. 179–182 (28 July and 26 Aug. 1906).
[78] Landon Ronald, accompanist, conductor, and friend, led the attack, and reported from the front: 48.13/29, docs. 59, 60, 62 (n.d. [prob. summer 1906]). In 1923 he was again consulted about a Melba performance and presentation, to no avail: 48.2/14 (3 Mar. 1923).
[79] 48.3/3 (30 June 1906).   [80] 48.2/12 (12 July 1906).
[81] 48.13/8 (24 and 25 July 1906).   [82] 48.2/12 (3 May 1907).

England, perhaps in the world, so that they are not in a position to make the financial part of the question attractive to you. But to such an artist as yourself they feel sure that money is not a primary consideration.' Arthur Nikisch was presumably aware of these matters, having conducted, on several occasions, the LSO, half of whom also played for the Philharmonic.[83] For a fee of £50, on 14 May 1908, he accompanied Zimbalist in the Tchaikovsky Violin Concerto, and played the piano for Elena Gerhardt in songs by Liszt, Wolf, and Richard Strauss. A Schumann symphony, an excerpt from *Siegfried*, and Liszt's *Les Préludes*, completed a programme which attracted by far the biggest audience (£176) of this first 'plurality' season. Henry Wood took charge of five concerts, Landon Ronald and Cowen two apiece, the latter selling less than £60-worth of tickets.

The success of a single concert was obviously not just a matter of the individual conductor's drawing-power. It could be affected by programmes, soloists, weather, alternative attractions, even the news of the day. But one lesson was already clear, and would be reinforced in subsequent seasons: a star conductor could now rival celebrated soloists in his unaided capacity to treble the normal returns, as Nikisch's concert on 13 May 1909 appeared to demonstrate. Apart from John Coates, who sang Siegfried's two 'Forge Songs', there was no soloist, and the programme was short. The *Mastersingers* Overture was followed by Elgar's First Symphony, and Tchaikovsky's *Francesca de Rimini*, yet returns (£180) were three times the level of most other concerts that season. The nearest rival was Elgar's following concert, longer and more varied, which netted £127: *In the South*, *Sea Pictures*, the Enigma Variations, *The Wand of Youth*, and Sapellnikoff in Tchaikovsky's Concerto and solos by Liszt. How significant for both concerts was Elgar's drawing-power? Was the first audience primarily drawn to hear Nikisch's first performance of the Symphony in England; and the second to hear the Variations and a new work, rather than the familiar Piano Concerto? And how does one explain the mere £70 or £80 earned by Bruno Walter's three concerts, despite soloists like Sauer and Bauer, and works like the *Eroica* and the *Pathétique*? Perhaps brief excerpts from the music of Ethel Smyth were a sufficient deterrent, or Walter's newness to London, though he had been working with Mahler for a decade. On balance there seems little doubt that Nikisch's drawing-power, at the Philharmonic, as elsewhere, was a new and highly significant phenomenon. The extent to which his charisma might be

[83] 48.2/12; (7 June 1907). In 1907 forty-three members of the Philharmonic orchestra were playing in the LSO, whose intention of visiting America next season forced the Society's directors into 'lengthy and exhaustive discussion' about the possibility of securing 'these gentlemen by engaging the L.S.O. *en bloc*'. Cancellation of the trip ended yet another attempt to rationalize the London orchestras: 48.2/12 (3 May 1907).

possessed by others was not yet tested, for attempts to get Mahler, Koussevitzky, Toscanini, and Weingartner, particularly for the cente- nary year, 1912, all came to nothing. Stokowski would have come, but was refused, just before his Philadelphia appointment, despite an offer by 'a wealthy friend in America' to take up £100 worth of tickets.[84]

A second feature of the new economics was more worrying. Even if superstars could still be relied upon to treble normal box-office returns, that norm was falling fast. In the mid-1890s few Philharmonic concerts had taken much less than £100, but now most were below that level, and some, irrespective of their intrinsic quality, failed to net £50. With this ever-widening income gap between regular concerts and celebrity events, the latter carried even heavier risks and respons- ibilities for the season's budget. In so far as attention was shifting to a star conductor the implications were grim, for his engagement dif- fered from booking a celebrated singer or instrumentalist in a number of costly ways. Expenditure did not end with the individual's fee and non-pecuniary blandishments. Since many of the qualities expected from a masterfully idiosyncratic baton could only be secured by lengthy preparation with a very large orchestra, possibly in such difficult new music as the Strauss tone-poems, rehearsals were more prohibitive than ever before. Any attempt to skimp would revive, or exacerbate, the century-old incompatibilities of culture between sight-reading, cost- cutting London, and an 'honoured master' from more stable centres of western music. They could affect a visiting soloist, as Clara Schumann had once explained, and for a conductor they were likely to be crucial. They could be avoided by staying away; or endured, in cynical dis- regard for artistic standards; or fought, usually with grudging admira- tion for the orchestra's skill. On rare occasions the clash of cultures was articulated. Vincent D'Indy, for example, acknowledged the 'Eng- lish custom' of only one rehearsal, and turned aside with disdainful talk of riders and thoroughbred horses.[85] Another patrician spelt things out with a clumsier integrity. 'I told [Bruno] Walter', scribbled Ethel Smyth,

that you are not a 'commercial' but an 'artistic' society—well of course the miserable state of things as to rehearsal is . . . a question of money—and about that I feel very strongly. Rehearsing seems to me to be the basis of artistic morality—and there it is. Walter is a very conscientious musician—incapable, as many in England *become*, how do they start, of pretending things 'go very well' when they just didn't break down.[86]

[84] 48.2/13 (12 Jan., 11 and 25 Feb., and 23 Mar. 1911). 48.13/33 (13 and 17 Sept. 1910). Weingartner wanted 100 guineas and was offered 60. The directors were prepared to 'go as high' as 70 guineas for Mahler, and 50 for Mengelberg, who eventually came.
[85] 48.13/17 (22 Oct. and 2 Dec. 1909).   [86] 48.13/32 (19 Nov. 1908).

The End of an Era

Francesco Berger's retirement in 1911 ended three decades of sustained effort, with masterly deployment of every available resource for the continuation and improvement of the Society. It was a record of sustained entrepreneurship which would have earned him fortune and fame in practically any other line of business. As with most innovators, his financial procedures were *ad hoc*, but they worked, and were incomparably sounder than the shattered inheritance with which he began. The 'bottom line' had changed surprisingly little, despite substantial increases in costs: soloists and orchestra, advertising, and rent of concert hall and office.[87] Total expenditure was usually kept down to some £2,500, and income rarely fell short by more than £500. The gap was kept narrow by ingenious manipulation of a rapidly changing market, tapping available supplies of cash, time, and goodwill from the music business and profession.

It was a precarious equilibrium. Except for a few years of prosperity in the mid-1890s, there was never a chance of rebuilding the autonomous fund of capital which had been frittered away before he took over. Any season's losses could therefore be met only from the guarantee fund. But heavy 'calls' were likely to deter guarantors, or leave only those whose continued support would be conditional on having a say in artistic policy. Cautious budgeting, which reflected the need to avoid such calls, was frequently criticized—particularly by non-contributors with nothing to lose. Two relevant complaints by guarantors are more deserving of notice. The directors, wrote Steinway's London manager in 1905, 'ought to rely more upon their guarantors, and less upon trying to make the concerts self-supporting'. Since there were was no shortage of 'commercial concerts', the Philharmonic should concentrate upon 'bringing out new works and new artists of merit'. In contrasting mood, a few years later, Walford Davies, organist and choirmaster at the Temple church, and soon to become director of music to the RAF, was 'rather appalled to be asked to guarantee so large an amount'. He was 'not rich, and the risk this season seems unusually great'.[88] The 1906 and 1911 seasons which these guarantors had contemplated with varying degrees of confidence and apprehension finished with losses of, respectively, £393 and £300. If such sums were

---

[87] 48.13/28, fos. 16–17 is a Queen's Hall agreement for the 1908/9 season. It includes seating details, and a minimum fee of £36 per concert, plus 1 guinea for police and firemen.

[88] Steinway: 48.13/33 (30 Nov. 1905). Davies: 48.13/10 (28 Oct. 1910). Davies's attitude to some of Berger's policies may be deduced from the fact that, like Parry, he despised opera, believing that it was 'completely dead and that the only future lay with oratorio': E. J. Dent, *Selected Essays* (1979), 236.

paltry in an age of gross wealth and ostentatious expenditure by an untaxed upper class, they were not so for the Philharmonic. Expectations of largesse from the majority of guarantors, like the pleas of city clerks for cheap concerts, and of Renaissance prophets for English music, were counsels of perfection in the most imperfect of worlds.

Berger's administration can therefore be regarded as exemplary, if only within narrowly defined limits. It was an effective way of organizing concerts and leading a venerable institution so as to ensure its survival in the market-place. His Philharmonic was no longer remotely concerned with the idea of an orchestral co-operative; a conception which was being newly pursued, with different artistic constraints, by the self-governing London Symphony Orchestra. Even as an employer, the Society had proved incapable of giving permanence or stability to an orchestra, whose wages were still the main cost: inflexible and inflated by the band's ever-increasing size. Yet individual fees, in an absurdly overcrowded occupation, were miserably low, despite the fact that general levels of skill—instrumental technique, familiarity with a wider repertoire, and, of course, sight-reading—had steadily improved. From a player's point of view, the advantage of being in 'the Philharmonic' was a matter of prestige: a mutual benefit regained by Berger, and only to be maintained by constant vigilance and adjustment. The overall achievement was less than ideal, perhaps; but anything better would have required a continuously buoyant market and dedicated patronage. Neither were available, despite Berger's ceaseless monitoring and solicitation.[89] The Society's bargaining counters were status, experience, and goodwill, all perishable, as in the past. Since the 1880s they had been well preserved; as measured, certainly, by a 'cosmopolitan', and arguably by a patriotic, yardstick.

Although persons with special interests never ceased to complain, considerable support had been given to British performers: criticism could be met by reference to programmes and a moment's thought about box-office returns. No solo violinist of standing had yet emerged, and if such pianists as Borwick, Davies, and Lamond failed to establish drawing- and earning-power comparable to foreign celebrities, it was not because Philharmonic platforms were barred to them. The treatment of British composers could never escape dispute. Policy was weighed down by the public's indifference, except to Elgar, by deficiencies in legislative copyright protection and institutional arrangements for paying performing right and, perhaps most grievously, by a pervasive, and dominating, tradition of the gentleman-amateur. All this

---

[89] Esp. to Court, where Berger's attentions were unceasing, elaborately phrased, and generally fruitless: see e.g. 48.2/10 (12 Nov. 1891; 21 Jan. 1892); 48.2/11 (27 and 28 May, and 5 June 1893; 21 May 1897); 48.2/12 (21 Sept. 1900; 18 Apr. and 16 July 1904). See also 48.13/37, ROYAL letters.

was far beyond the Society's powers of transformation.[90] Its initial failure
to reach out to genius—provincial, self-educated, professional—was
soon remedied. Yet even that worthy and mutually enhancing collaboration was characteristically limited: a matter of skilful marketing,
rather than risk-taking and patronage. Doubtless Elgar's First Symphony was magnificently played at the Philharmonic, under Nikisch in
April 1909, but this was one of eighty-two performances in 1908–9,
most of them in Britain. As *The Times* recalled in 1934, such was 'the
rage' for the work with 'the ordinary British public' that 'enterprising
commercialists even engaged orchestras to play it in their lounges and
palm courts as an attraction to their winter sales of underwear'.[91]
Similarly the public's taste was followed, not led, when the Society
eventually took up such earlier works as the Enigma Variations, under Wood in 1908 and the composer in 1909. Nevertheless the first
performance of the Violin Concerto, by Kreisler and Elgar on 10 November 1910, was indeed a splendid Philharmonic event, instantly acclaimed as 'one of the most memorable in its history'. And brilliant
concert promotion followed up the success, along the lines of the great
Tchaikovsky *Pathétique* première, with another performance at the next
concert. Three orchestras—Queen's Hall, New Symphony, and London Symphony—had all been *'fighting hard'* for that première, as Lady
Elgar noted in her diary. Berger secured it with the extra bait of a
£200 performing fee for the work, and consolidated his gains with
maximum effect and at minimum cost, in rehearsal and publicity for
two concerts.

Artistic success was matched by the box-office, for the Elgar concerts earned £389 and £391, outdoing the best returns on Patti and
Paderewski, twice.[92] Berger's last winter season thus began with brilliant demonstrations of the promotional skills which he had established.
It then gave a glimpse of things to come. The concert on 7 December
earned less than £47 with an 'unusually interesting programme . . .
skilfully conducted'. It began with Mozart's unknown Thirty-Fourth
Symphony, and proceeded via Delius's *Paris* to D'Indy's *Sinfonie
montagnarde*. After W. H. Bell, who favoured fanciful titles and later
migrated to South Africa, had intervened with his *Phantasy-Prelude, 'The
Shepherd'*, the conductor returned with an overture by Boccherini and
the *Flying Dutchman* Overture. He resembled Nikisch in beard and
demeanour, surely by intention, and was praised in the *Musical Times*

[90] On copyright reform and the administration of composers' performing right, see C.
Ehrlich, *Harmonious Alliance: A History of the Performing Right Society* (1989), ch. 1.

[91] J. Crump, 'The Identity of English Music: The reception of Elgar 1898–1935', in R.
Colls and P. Dodd (eds.), *Englishness: Politics and Culture 1880–1920* (1986). See also D.
Cannadine's essay on Elgar, in *The Pleasures of the Past* (1989), 121–130.

[92] 48.2/13 (11 July 29 Oct., and 24 Nov. 1910). J. Northrop Moore, *Elgar and His Publishers:
Letters of a Creative Life* (Oxford, 1987), 732–7. *Athenaeum* (19 Nov. 1910).

NINETY-NINTH
SEASON.

WINTER, 1910,
AND
SPRING, 1911.

PHILHARMONIC SOCIETY

UNDER THE IMMEDIATE PATRONAGE OF

His Most Gracious Majesty the King
AND
Her Most Gracious Majesty the Queen,

Her Most Gracious Majesty Queen Alexandra,

HER ROYAL HIGHNESS THE DUCHESS OF SAXE-COBURG AND GOTHA,
THEIR ROYAL HIGHNESSES THE DUKE AND DUCHESS OF CONNAUGHT
AND STRATHEARN,
THEIR ROYAL HIGHNESSES THE PRINCE AND PRINCESS CHRISTIAN OF
SCHLESWIG-HOLSTEIN,
HER ROYAL HIGHNESS THE DUCHESS OF ARGYLL.

FIRST CONCERT, THURSDAY, NOVEMBER 10, 1910,

AT

THE QUEEN'S HALL.

SOLE LESSEES ⸱ ⸱ ⸱ ⸱ ⸱ ⸱ ⸱ ⸱ MESSRS. CHAPPELL & CO., LTD.

To commence at 8 o'clock precisely.

❖ *Programme.* ❖

PART I.

NATIONAL ANTHEM ... ... *Scored by Elgar.*

OVERTURE "Naiades" ... ... *Sterndale Bennett.*

VIOLIN CONCERTO ... ... *Elgar.*
(First performance.)
FRITZ KREISLER.

PART II.

SYMPHONY No. 1. ... ... *Elgar.*

CONDUCTOR ... ... SIR EDWARD ELGAR.

17. Programme, 10 November 1910

for 'alert style, rhythmic decision, and power to interpret'.[93] Thomas
Beecham was potential heir to a substantial fortune, and had access
to that 'fashionable society' which had generally eluded the directors.
He had dropped in upon one of their meetings, confidently chopped
and changed artists and programme, mostly through necessity, paid for
an extra rehearsal out of his father's pocket, and simultaneously rushed

[93] *Athenaeum* (10 Dec. 1910); *MT* (1 Jan. 1911).

back and forth to Richard Strauss at Covent Garden. The same number of the *Musical Times* tried to depict his 'perilously ludicrous' and
brilliant adventures there, in prose which would later be outclassed by
the conductor's own account. They involved Salome, the Government's
censor, a rechristened John the Baptist, 'a large platter completely
covered with a cloth'—without John's head—and a bewildered, rich
audience.[94]

There were other excitements in 1911, for it was coronation year,
and promised something for music. The RAM moved from Hanover
Square to new quarters in the Marylebone Road; Landon Ronald
began to upgrade the Guildhall School of Music; Oscar Hammerstein
opened an ambitious new opera-house in Kingsway, seating 2,700
people and 'representing about £2,000'. Cowen was knighted, and Elgar
appointed to the Order of Merit, recognized by experts as 'the only
honour seriously worth having'.[95] Yet the ceremonies, and a fine summer, were generally agreed to have been 'disastrous' for concerts.[96] In
the following season, the year of the *Titanic*, the Society had its centenary celebrations, which culminated with acquisition of the 'Royal'
prefix.[97] A series of concerts featured new works by Ronald, Stanford,
Hervey, Mackenzie, Davies, Dunhill, Macpherson, and Parry: intended,
as the *Annual Register* sourly remarked, 'to mark the epoch . . . but nothing has been heard of them in London since'. Two concerts provided recompense. In one, Nikisch broke the tradition of failure with
Beethoven's Ninth Symphony in a performance which was 'a blaze of
triumph'.[98] At the other, which featured Parry's B minor Symphony,
Tetrazzini earned her medal and drew a gate of £344 with a couple
of songs. But the series had begun with Elgar conducting the Enigma
Variations, and Cortot as soloist in the 'Emperor' Concerto: an evening
which netted only £60.

If celebrities were still seen as the only foolproof means of cross-
subsidy, they were now in short supply. It proved impossible, for
example, to woo Chaliapin. Nor did occasional use of such ploys
amount to a continuation of Berger's policies; less still their sustained

---

[94] 48.2/13 (22 July 1909; 12 Dec. 1910). *MT* (1 Jan. 1911). Beecham, *Mingled Chime*,
102–5.
[95] The remark was made by G. M. Trevelyan, an expert in such matters, to his daughter.
Vaughan Williams was appointed in 1935; Britten in 1965. See D. Cannadine, *G. M. Trevelyan*
(1992), 18, 22.   [96] 48.3/3 (3 June 1911). *Annual Register* (1911).
[97] The Home Secretary's notification is minuted in 48.2/13 (9 Dec. 1912). There was
later some disagreement about who had made the application. At his death, Cummings was
credited with the arrangement: 48.2/13 (23 July 1915). But this was later challenged by
Wallace, who claimed to have approached the Home Secretary, McKenna, through a
relative, presented a dexterous financial statement, and saved the Society a 100-guinea fee.
Parry was then consulted by the Home Office: 48.17, fo. 65078.
[98] *Annual Register* (1912).

application. Neither of his immediate successors as secretary—William Wallace, who left after two years, and Stanley Hawley, who died in 1915—were endowed with comparable staying-power, resourcefulness, or tact. The Society, as Mackenzie wryly remarked—and no one knew better—could not afford the right man: he was not to be got for £100 a year.[99] Wallace, ophthalmologist and composer of tone-poems, was immediately plunged into a tremendous public row with Bantock over fees for, and eventual non-performance of, the latter's *Fifine at the Fair*. The composer may well have been in the wrong, particularly in the peremptory timing of his demands, and Wallace justified in his protests at damaging press attacks. But it is hard to believe that his predecessor would have allowed matters to get so out of hand for, as Landon Ronald had recently said to Berger, and as everyone knew, 'if ever a man was born to pour oil on troubled waters with infinite success, that man is your good self'.[100] Wallace's preference for vitriol had been demonstrated, recently and all too relevantly, in an acrimonious dispute with the RCM about the allocation of an endowment fund.[101]

Without Berger's persistent drive and common sense, the system began to fall apart, despite much rhetoric about expansion and economies. Some more associates were recruited, mainly through the energies of Arthur Hinton, a composer and husband of the pianist Katherine Goodson; and the number of fellows was increased from 250 to 300.[102] Various 'reforms' were instituted, and reported to have 'given offence', and there were reassurances about the Society 'starting afresh'. Typically grandiloquent was a scheme to encourage 'eminent financiers, members of the aristocracy, and lovers of music generally' to establish an endowment fund. It changed into a foundation fund which reached the grand total of £228 in its first year, and £794 by the time of the last general meeting to assemble before the First World War. On that occasion the chairman, W. H. Cummings, now in his eighties, expressed a continuing desire to promote 'mainly English music . . . with English artists'.[103] Another chapter was added to the sad history of failure to rationalize London orchestras, when Landon Ronald offered to abandon his 'New Symphony Concerts' if the Philharmonic would engage his band 'en bloc', without necessarily appointing him as permanent conductor. After a vote, the directors refused, on grounds that

---

[99] Chaliapin was sent a copy of Foster's *History*, 'as tribute to genius displayed in recent opera season': 48.2/13 (22 July 1913). Mackenzie's remark was made openly at a general meeting: 48.3/3 (22 June 1912).   [100] 48.13/29 (4 Nov. 1909).
[101] In a letter to *The Times* (30 May 1904), Wallace accused the RCM of being 'academically antagonistic, if not openly inimical, to every modern tendency.' A long excerpt is reproduced in Foreman, *Parry to Britten*, 26–8.
[102] 48.2/13 (28 Oct. 1912). *Laws of the Philharmonic Society* (1912), law 1: 48.5/3.
[103] 48.3/3 (21 Oct. 1911; 22 June 1912; 5 Apr. and 27 Sept. 1913).

IGNAZ MOSCHELES JOHANN BAPTIST CRAMER SIGISMOND THALBERG

ARABELLA GODDARD CHARLES HALLÉ ANTON RUBENSTEIN

CLARA SCHUMANN IGNAZ JAN PADEREWSKI VLADIMIR DE PACHMANN

18. Philharmonic pianists

the scheme might entail dismissing 'players who had served the Society well'.[104] Yet a comparison of orchestra lists for 1910/11 and 1913/14, which were not yet affected by the war, reveals a turnover of no less than sixty-one players (see Appendix 3). Several of the newcomers would soon become familiar names: Albert Sammons, Waldo Warner, Eric Coates, Warwick-Evans, Claude Hobday, Eugene Cruft, Robert Murchie, Aubrey Brain. Doubtless the quality of recruitment was influenced by the requirements of such conductors as Mengelberg and Safonoff, with significant effects on performance standards. But these were temporary benefits, arising from competition in an overflowing market, not a result of consistent policy.

It was no secret that the Society needed fresh blood: infusions of cash, musical distinction and awareness, administrative competence and drive. On 10 March 1914, Sir Joseph Beecham was elected fellow; and four months later his son was elected member, without having to pass through the preliminary stage of associate.[105]

---

[104] 48.2/13 (25 June 1912).

[105] Ibid. (10 Mar. and 21 July 1914). Curiously, Adrian Boult was elected fellow, not member, on 16 Dec. 1913. The categories of affiliation were confusing.

10

Between Wars

I am informed that the Royal Philharmonic Society . . . is on its last legs.

(W. J. Turner, in the *New Statesman*, 7 Apr. 1923)

Rich Americans pay for orchestras; rich Englishmen don't.

(Henry Wood, 1926)[1]

You, of course, are the élite of London musical society. Don't feel too encouraged—it is not much to be proud of.

(Thomas Beecham, addressing the audience at an LPO concert. 14 Jan. 1940)[2]

IN 1914 London's musical life was torn apart by war; a surfeit of events followed by dearth. In the early months Mengelberg conducted four Philharmonic concerts which 'obtained a fresh glory', even if they could not match, for innovation, the 'great sensation' of Schoenberg's *Five Orchestral Pieces*, played by the Queen's Hall Orchestra, and drawing 'an immense audience'; or the intense enjoyment and artistic achievement of diverse entertainments offered by Joseph and Thomas Beecham: Russian opera and ballet in 'a veritable riot of gorgeous performances'; masterly readings of *Die Zauberflöte*, and *Der Rosenkavalier*; and even an English opera, Holbrooke's *Dylan*.[3] Then the lights went out. Opera was abandoned—the silver rose waiting ten years for its next presentation—and the Society could scarcely contemplate its next season, as the list of guarantors fell by half, and subscriptions collapsed. But members of the orchestra, with bleak prospects of employment, agreed to accept half-fees; and after Mengelberg had suggested that an Englishman should conduct at least the first few concerts, Thomas Beecham was allowed to take over. His first wartime season set a pattern of activity which continued for the duration.[4] He conducted

---

[1] *MMR* (Apr. 1926).
[2] Quoted in B. Geissmar, *The Baton and the Jackboot: Recollections of a Musical Life* (1944), 366. [3] *MT* (Feb. 1914); *Annual Register* (1914).
[4] 48.2/13 (8 Oct. 1914).

five out of seven concerts, contributed £500 towards the adequate payment of the orchestra, and financed a visit by the Hallé choir to perform Berlioz's Te Deum.[5] He also coaxed the orchestra into playing such unfamiliar and difficult works as Debussy's *Three Nocturnes*, and broke a long tradition of neglect and incompetence with an 'electrifying interpretation' of the *Symphonie fantastique*. It would be 'a permanent memory' for those who stayed the concert out, declared one critic, adding essential information that the accomplished young violinist Isolde Menges, who had played Bach's E major Concerto to emptying seats, was not a German.[6]

The Society's concessions to xenophobia were mild by the standards of the day, as befitted its long history of international connection and goodwill. The roll of honorary members was temporarily purged of 'alien enemies', and there was some fuss about advertisements in concert programmes: the publisher Augener was asked to insert 'British owned' into its entries. But even these shamefaced gestures were short-lived, and not to be compared with the rabble-rousing jingoism of hitherto obscure piano-makers and muckraking journalists who sought carnage and profit in concert-room and shop.[7] If the Philharmonic played no contemporary German music—Strauss disappeared for the duration—earlier masters, including Schumann and Wagner, were allowed to hold their place. The absence of *anything* by Beethoven, until Beecham got round to the *Eroica Symphony* in March 1918, was certainly a peculiar episode in the Society's history; but it was more a reflection of the conductor's personal taste than a gesture of patriotism. Nor was the continuing drift from the Viennese classics a product of war for, as we have seen, it had begun with Cowen and Mackenzie. Nor, again, was much time set aside for the routine trappings of a militant nation. The opening concert, on 3 November 1914, began with Stanford's 'Flourish of Trumpets (written for the Delhi Durbar)', by the Musicians of the First Life Guards, conductor George Miller, followed by 'God Save the King'. But it proceeded to Debussy, Saint-Saëns, Liszt, and two passacaglias by Cyril Scott. English music was more piously represented in a March 1915 concert directed by Elgar, Parry, and Percy Pitt: Vaughan Williams's *The Wasps*, Elgar's *Carillon* and Second Symphony, Stanford's *Songs of the Sea*, and Parry's tone-poem *From Death to Life*, but flag-waving stopped there.[8]

---

[5] 48.2/13 (20 Oct. 1914). 48.3/3 (22 May 1915). [6] *MT* (1 Mar. 1915).

[7] Among the deleted names of honorary members were Bruch, Kubelik, Menter, Nikisch, Ondricek, Richter, and Strauss: 48.3/3 (9 Oct. 1915). Confusion about the status of Czechs was brushed aside, on grounds that it was 'impossible to make distinctions': 48.2/13 (11 Feb. 1916); 48.3/3 (27 May 1916). All were quietly reinstated after the war. On Hun-baiting and the English piano trade, see Ehrlich, *Piano*, ch. 9. The preservation of Bechstein Hall as the Wigmore Hall was the sole benefit of a shabby episode.

[8] The tone-poem is exhaustively discussed in J. Dibble, *C. Hubert Parry* (1992), 470–4.

Paying Pipers and Playing Tunes

Beecham's wartime seasons were eclectic and provocative. Disdain for
the commonplace was already a characteristic trait; and a positive delight in upsetting traditionalists could not have been better timed for
maximum irritation. Much of the repertoire was new and disturbing
to players and audiences, yet a high proportion soon became accepted
as standard. Individual concerts were also original, on paper and in
performance: something more, like all well-planned programmes, than
the sum of their parts. London audiences had become accustomed to
skilful, or wilful, conductors, but here the selection and juxtaposition
of pieces was idiosyncratic, and they were played with a unique light-
ness, colour, and *joie de vivre*—everything which would be conjured
henceforth by the name Beecham. Despite wartime afflictions, including the simple necessity of competing with the trenches for capable
musicians, his money enabled the Society to survive, and his genius to
assert a fresh distinction, adding new gaiety and theatrical brilliance to
the Philharmonic's reputation.

Those who were not outraged acclaimed a 'bold . . . ruthless breaking of staid Philharmonic tradition . . . justified by results'. The 104th
season began with Balakirev's *Thamar*, Tatiana's 'Letter-Song' from *Eugene
Onegin*, Borodin's *Polovtsian Dances* and Stravinsky's *Petrouchka*: 'enough to
make such hairs as old habitués of these concerts possess stand on end'
and 'all wonderfully done'. Another concert included the first London
performance of Debussy's *Iberia*, along with the Overture to *The Barber
of Seville*, which even a staid *Musical Times* critic, surprised at the novelty
of such music played by 'a first rate orchestra'—so far had priorities
changed since the days of Costa—confessed to have 'thoroughly enjoyed'. *Iberia* was then given an extra polish and repeated, its performance now 'remarkable to the point of virtuosity'.[9] Stravinsky's *Firebird*,
similarly improved by repetition, became a showpiece for the orchestra; along with *Scheherazade*, *Daphnis and Chloë*, and the definitive 'lolli-
pop' (though not yet so designated), Chabrier's *España*. César Franck's
Symphony entered the lists, and there were selections from Glinka's *A
Life for the Tsar*, and large helpings of Delius, including a whole scene
from *A Village Romeo and Juliet*. Against all odds an orchestra was held
together and placed firmly in central position, with occasional appearances by soloists as no more than equal partners. Necessity played its
part, for international virtuosi had become scarce and, even among
patriots, no British soloist exerted continuous drawing-power. But a few

[9] *MT* (Dec. 1915; Mar., Apr., and Dec. 1916). Compare the assertion that 'the typical
Beecham style of programme' emerged 'only late in his career': H. Procter-Gregg, *Beecham
Remembered* (1976), 129.

names were earning respect. Myra Hess was slowly becoming recognizable as a home-grown successor to Clara Schumann; and Albert Sammons, a self-taught violinist whom Beecham had discovered playing tea-shop music at the Waldorf, could survive comparison with his great contemporaries. Freshness and resourcefulness in the design of programmes were not confined to new music. Works which dated back to the Society's origins, but had been previously neglected, forgotten, or routinely performed, were given new life; particularly Mozart: the Symphonies, Nos. 34, 36, and 38; the unknown G major Piano Concerto K.453; and the Sinfonia concertante, with Lionel Tertis.

There was a price to be paid for such largesse in hard times. The Philharmonic's leaders relinquished authority as its benefactor's role shifted, from guarantor of funds, selector of artists and repertoire, and conductor, to boss. By 1916, with inflation taking its toll, and 'few families ... untouched by personal grief', the Society faced its worst-ever deficit. Only three-quarters of the orchestra's bill could be met, despite an additional donation from the conductor who, as always, took no fee for himself; entertainment tax imposed a crippling new burden; and prospects of carrying on were dim.[10] When Busoni approached the directors about a forthcoming visit, he was told that it was 'very doubtful whether any concerts would be held', a prognosis confirmed by Beecham's announcement that he was too busy to continue next year, being simultaneously involved, musically and financially, with the London Symphony Orchestra. But then Sir Thomas, as he was dubbed that year, changed tack, with a plan for the 'reconstruction' (deleted in the directors' minutes) or 'modification' of the Society 'under which he would be willing to consider the possibility of continuing the concerts'. The new rules were simple. In the event of his attending a meeting of directors, he would take the chair. Donald Baylis, his factotum, would be 'elected' honorary secretary, for Hawley had recently died, and not been replaced. Sir Thomas would control programmes, orchestra, and 'concert arrangements generally'.[11]

After the directors had agreed to these 'substantial points' for next season, Beecham and Baylis turned up at their next meeting, and a

[10] 48.5/1 (15 Mar. 1916). 48.2/13 (12 May and 23 June 1916). This was the first time in the Society's history that inflation, and subsequent deflation, became significant. The Sauerbeck–Statist price index, which stood at 85 in 1914, reached 136 in 1916, 192 in 1918, and 251 in 1920, falling again to 97 by 1930. Such index numbers give a misleading impression of precision, particularly when used over long periods, and can reasonably be ignored when dealing with times of relative stability; but they do illustrate the extreme fluctuations of wartime and the 1920s. See also A. Marwick, *The Deluge: British Society and the First World War* (1965), esp. 139–59.

[11] 48.2/13 (23 June, 10 July, and 18 Sept. 1916). On Beecham's activities with the LSO see P. Kildea, 'World War I and the British Music Industry', M. Mus. thesis, University of Melbourne, 1991, 69–72.

few details were confirmed. The orchestra would 'not in any sense be a partner', but would be engaged 'at rates appropriate to the times'. This was scarcely a change in policy, for the Society had long ceased to assume any relationship to orchestral players except that of an employer, but the position was now clearly defined, against a background of increasing union militancy.[12] Since the international network of artists and agents had disintegrated, it was necessary to say something about booking procedures: soloists were not expected to appear free, but might be paid a minimum of, say, 20 guineas. And Beecham and Baylis were 'finally responsible for the financial outcome of the season', though members of the Society and outsiders would be 'permitted' to act as guarantors, with a minimum contribution of £50, in expectation of no more than a 10 per cent call.[13] A month later the factotum extended horizons by announcing his master's willingness to conduct for another five or ten years, and raise a special fund of £10,000. At a time when few men aspired to do more than live from day to day, some such scheme was 'gratefully accepted', for a period of five years, with the conductor's option of a further five. It was also agreed to invite blinded officers from St Dunstan's to rehearsals and, in another sign of the times, to ask the newly formed Performing Right Society to estimate an 'inclusive fee' for use of its members' music.[14] The *Annual Register*, having reported 'considerable difficulty . . . in keeping the Royal (and somewhat ancient) Philharmonic Society on its legs', now envisaged its 'developing into an extremely useful modern affair with renewed vigour'.[15] A few directors continued to meet, without much to do except table a resolution to 'interest musicians in the country in the work of the Society and extend to them its privileges'. Then even these gatherings were abandoned for more than eight months after October 1917: a gap later recorded in the minutes, with pointed retrospect.[16]

Peace and Democracy

In July 1918, John Mewburn Levien, a singing-teacher who had been treasurer since 1915, succeeded, at a second attempt, in rallying sufficient directors for a quorum. A letter was drafted which extracted

[12] Elkin describes one such confrontation, quoting O'Neill's smug report to the directors, who were 'tired of working gratuitously for musicians who would do nothing to help them in such difficult times'. Beecham, who was at least footing the bill, is said to have spoken 'very pointed words to the Orchestra'. The tone of officers dealing with 'other ranks' is inescapable, though Beecham always peppered such occasions with jokes. See Elkin, *Royal Philharmonic*, 106–7, and 48.2/13 (15 Oct. 1915).   [13] 48.2/13 (28 Sept. 1916).
[14] 48.2/13 (10 and 28 Oct., 8 Nov. 1916). On the first attempts of the PRS to protect British composers' intellectual property, see Ehrlich, *Harmonious Alliance*, 22–31.
[15] *Annual Register* (1916).   [16] 48.2/13 (20 Sept. 1917 and 8 July 1918).

resignations from Baylis and Beecham, and thus, as Elkin records, with disarming simplicity, 'democratic control was re-established in time for the first post-war season'. Misgivings about ingratitude, and the victorious faction's claim to be representative, were only quietly voiced, and there was a lot of financial confusion.[17]

The men who ousted Beecham came from a group which has been described as the 'professional ring of academics who dominated English music after the war'.[18] T. F. Dunhill taught composition at Eton and the RCM. J. B. McEwen would soon become principal of the RAM. J. Ivimey was an expert on public school music, and therefore had useful links with moneyed people. William Waddington Cooke, a piano-teacher, had apparently once studied piano with Leschetizky. Norman O'Neill, a composer of theatre music, became treasurer, and Levien shifted chairs to become secretary. In addition to dispensing with the services of England's most celebrated performer and patron, they parted company with two other musicians of weight. Edwin Evans, widely read in contemporary Russian, French, and English music, ceased to enlighten Philharmonic programming for a time. Percy Pitt, another cultivated musician outside the 'professional' ring, and an experienced conductor of opera, resigned his directorship, and became the BBC's first Music Adviser.[19] If the new committee lacked names to quicken the artistic pulse, it was not devoid of support. The Lord Mayor of London was a trustee, though he could not attend concerts 'in state' nor, on further enquiry, at all.[20] The Viscountess Cowdray was enlisted by Ivimey with a promise, as guarantor, not investor, of £2,000, though her subsequent desire that a niece be allowed to perform, 'as a personal favour' had to be refused, since it 'might cause questions to be asked' and damage the protégée 'professionally'.[21] Among subscribers, even the monarch's four tickets, which had recently been cancelled in the cause of national austerity, were now renewed. Hopes were entertained of substantial financial support from the Carnegie Trust, an

[17] Elkin, *Royal Philharmonic*, 108. 48.2/13 (8 July 1918 (no quorum); 22 July 1918). Meeting Pitt, McEwen, and Dunhill at the Aldwych Theatre, Baylis, who was still honorary secretary, read the letter, which was signed by Dunhill, and concluded that the directors were 'dissatisfied with Thomas Beecham's conduct of the concerts'. The report of this meeting is untidy, with some crossing-out: 48.2/13 (30 July 1918).

[18] N. Kenyon, *The BBC Symphony Orchestra: The First Fifty Years 1930–1980* (1981), 4.

[19] Evans frequently advised the Society about repertoire. See e.g., 48.13/11 (9 Oct. 1911 (Rimsky); 15 Oct. 1904 (Bruckner)); fo. 206, n.d. (Debussy); 4 Aug. 1908 (D'Indy). A drawing of him by Picasso later became one of the Society's most precious possessions. His departure is noted in 48.2/13 (8 Nov. 1919). Pitt's resignation: 48.2/13 (21 Feb. 1920). The latter's early BBC ventures included a broadcast of a symphony concert on 21 June 1923. See A. Briggs, *The History of Broadcasting in the United Kingdom*, i. *The Birth Of Broadcasting* (1961), 277.

[20] 48.2/13 (11 Oct. 1919; 17 Jan. and 6 Mar. 1920).

[21] 48.2/13 (12 Oct. 1918; 4 Sept. 1920).

appeal which would be repeated with mounting desperation in later
years.[22]

Practical assistance was enlisted from a gentleman-composer who
had some things in common with Beecham—Oxford, wealth, and patronage of music—but exhibited no desire, nor much respect, for the
baton. Balfour Gardiner claimed to be 'neither surprised nor grieved'
by Beecham's 'deserting the cause of music'. He was prepared to sub-
sidize 'fairly interesting programmes', and 'an old fashioned policy',
which might enable the Society to 'regain its reputation' with 'performances of the highest possible standard': an ideal which was clearly
assumed to have been recently forsaken, for the directors were reminded that it had once been an 'explicit object as set out in its
prospectus'. A 'really good conductor' would be difficult to find because none were 'reliable without being dull—except people like Geoff'
(Toye), who were 'no attraction to the public'. On these whimsical
terms Gardiner began with a guarantee of £1,200, but eventually
stumped up £675 for the 1918–19 season, and £750 in the following
year—insufficient to give the Society any solid foundation for forward
planning, but far more than the 10 or 15 per cent which had previously been regarded as a guarantor's maximum risk. Initially 'not wishing to meddle much', he later suggested that an outlay of more than
£500 should allow selection of 'conductors and soloists . . . the number
of concerts . . . and the works'. That kind of expenditure entitled one
to be a 'special' guarantor who, in return for taking the first burden
of a season's loss might have a say in policy.

Despite such ruminations, Gardiner's direct interference rarely
amounted to more than occasional amiable suggestions. In 1920, for
example, he recommended the Vaughan Williams *Pastoral Symphony*, which
received its first performance two years later, and opportunities for
Lamond, Jelly d'Aranyi, and Beatrice Harrison to perform.[23] For their
first season of peace the democrats chose homespun conductors. Landon
Ronald and two novices—the patron's favourite, Geoffrey Toye, and
Adrian Boult—were conveniently eager to serve without fee. Boult was
even a guarantor for £200, and proved capable of building 'a secure
reputation' with concerts which included such unfamiliar pieces as
Vaughan Williams's *The Wasps*, Bach's Third 'Brandenburg' Concerto,
Mozart's Serenade for Winds K.375, and two premières: the Delius

[22] Carnegie: 48.2/13 (20 Sept. 1918); 48.2/14 (16 Sept. 1921; 1 Oct. 1921 (requesting
£500 for five years, after which it was hoped to be 'able to make ends meet'; alternatively
expressing doubts about being able to continue)). Royal tickets: cancelled, 48.2/13 (1 Oct.
1918); reinstated, 48.2/13 (23 Nov. 1918).

[23] 48.17/1 (15 Sept. and 7 Oct. 1918; 7 and 24 June, 26 and 27 Sept. 1919; 5 Apr.,
and 10 and 17 July 1920; 12 Jan. and 18 Mar. 1921).

Violin Concerto almost foundering because Private Sammons was refused leave to perform—and Holst's *Planets*. The latter made 'an exciting impression', despite the omission of 'Venus' and 'Neptune': not, as might be assumed, on grounds of economy, but because Boult thought half an hour was all the audience could take.[24] The season resulted in losses exceeding £800, and a call of 10 per cent on the guarantors.

Then an English conductor of international reputation became available when Albert Coates was driven by revolution from St Petersburg's great Marinsky Theatre, where he had presided with distinction after long experience in German opera-houses. He wanted a modest (postwar inflated) 300 guineas for the season, an option of handing one concert over to Beecham—which was instantly refused—and a say in the booking of soloists, which was referred to a subcommittee.[25] Adapting to skimped rehearsals, Coates took the newly formed Philharmonic Choir through a plausible Beethoven Ninth Symphony, earning the singers praise for tackling it 'with especial bravery' at the second performance.[26] He introduced Skriabin with the *Divine Poem,* and reinstated Strauss with *Till Eulenspiegel* on 25 November 1920, when Heifetz also played the Elgar Concerto. And he could attract an audience: £401 receipts for the first Beethoven Choral evening, against £55 for Toye's concert; or if that comparison be thought unfair (because choirs customarily bring family and friends), £277 when Coates conducted a difficult evening of Skriabin, Holbrooke, and the first English performance of Debussy's *Fantaisie*.[27]

But there was never any question of appointing a permanent conductor. It was easier to pick and mix from the parade of maestros— magnificent, as never before or since—who passed through London when frontiers reopened. Most could be procured, briefly willing to cope with unsatisfactory conditions for modest fees: the idea of pricing conductors higher than the total cost of their orchestras had not yet been conceived.[28] Goossens, Harty, Ronald, Wood (collecting a gold medal in 1921), Ansermet, and Monteux all made an appearance. Bruno Walter was prepared to do Elgar's *Falstaff* if allowed sufficient rehearsal time, but had to settle for the First Symphony and two rehearsals: three would have involved 'a large proportion of deputies'.[29]

---

[24] *MMR* (1 Apr. 1919). M. Kennedy, *Adrian Boult* (1987), 68.

[25] 48.2/13 (13 Dec. 1919; 5 and 24 Jan., and 6 Mar. 1920).

[26] *MMR* (1 Apr. 1920 and 1 May 1922). The choir was trained by Kennedy Scott and financed by Balfour Gardiner, until 1920: 48.2/13 (23 July 1920).

[27] 48.2/13 (29 May 1920).

[28] Two books have attempted to explain this curious phenomenon by means of conspiracy theories of history: J. Horowitz, *Understanding Toscanini* (1987); and N. Lebrecht, *The Maestro Myth* (1991).   [29] 48.2/14 (13 Nov. 1924).

Stokowski, then working in Philadelphia with an ensemble beyond anything possible in London, was considered, and again rejected, but there were attempts to get Knappertsbusch (who wanted 75 guineas and refused 50), and even Toscanini—the ensuing battle over rehearsals would have been stimulating. Beecham, *persona grata* again, but not yet available, was second choice after the Italian maestro; then Weingartner, who eventually delivered the Choral Symphony and excerpts from *Götterdämmerung* for 100 guineas.[30] Furtwängler appeared in the same season; his first concert including Vaughan Williams's *On Wenlock Edge*, in its orchestral version. But he was steered away from a Mahler symphony which 'it was thought might not be attractive', and there were consultations with his formidable secretary Berta Geissmar, soon to be snapped up by Sir Thomas.[31] Her attendance was unusual, both because of her unparalleled knowledge of the European concert world, and because she was a woman. Various attempts by the Society of Women Musicians and Ethel Smyth to consolidate wartime advances by gaining 'equal privileges with men' at the Philharmonic were coming to very little: remarkable since the Society had allowed female membership since its inception.[32]

Levien stayed in office until 1928, and O'Neill until 1934; but parochialism was abandoned soon after the 'nadir' of 1923, when W. J. Turner, the *New Statesman*'s critic, urged the musicians of London to 'hang, draw and quarter' the Society's leaders, whom he named, for their incompetence in music and business.[33] Percy Pitt returned with renewed vigour, opening vital communication with the BBC, where he was creating a music policy. Foreign artists reappeared, establishing new professional links and renewing old friendships; and, at various times, in the next few years, the Committee was joined by such diverse and knowledgeable musicians as Arthur Bliss, Ernest Irving, and Edward Dent. Thus an intermittent balance was struck between the international world of live music and the organ-lofts, schoolrooms, diplomas, and gentlemanly pastoralism of South Kensington and York Gate. In 1924, for example, there were strenuous attempts to arrange a visit by Stravinsky. Would he play his new piano concerto at a concert to be conducted by Ansermet, or make it available to, say, Rubinstein? He would not, and the conductor, when asked for an alternative, arranged for Szigeti to give the English première of Prokofiev's First Violin Concerto, on 26 February 1925. At one meeting that year, Bartók, and even Gershwin, were 'favourably considered'; the former to be

---

[30] 48.2/14 (21 July 1922). The Weingartner concert was on 20 Mar. 1924.
[31] 48.2/14 (8 and 29 May 1924).
[32] 48.2/14 (14 May 1921; 20 Dec. 1921; 5 Feb. and 15 Mar. (1922). See also Smyth's letter about women players in London orchestras: 48.2/15 (11 Oct. 1928). No action was taken.   [33] *New Statesman* (7 Apr. 1923).

performed (*Dance Suite* on 25 February 1926) the latter not.[34] Equally strenuous was a prolonged attempt to organize a performance of Stravinsky's *Oedipus Rex*, under Klemperer, with three rehearsals, a specially recruited choir, and a prominent actor—Herbert Marshall or Henry Ainley—as narrator. The Committee did far more to meet the conductor's meticulous needs than his biographer implies, and his ultimate failure to accept an alternative Beethoven programme was not an outright refusal, but a disagreement about precise content.[35]

If there were occasional rumblings in the backwoods about 'the great preponderance of foreigners', particularly among conductors, it could hardly be claimed that English composers were neglected.[36] Elgar belatedly received his gold medal from Henry Wood at a concert conducted by the composer on 19 November 1925. The programme consisted of his arrangement of Bach's *Fantasy and Fugue* in C, the Enigma Variations, the Cello Concerto (with Beatrice Harrison as soloist), *Falstaff*, and *In the South*. Prodigious efforts were necessary to get a performance of Vaughan Williams's *The Lark Ascending*, when the Committee had to cope with two reluctant violinists in two consecutive seasons. The great artist Erica Morini simply dropped it, without consultation, from her concert on 25 February 1926, when she played the Beethoven concerto, precipitating a special meeting to deal with agent, publisher, composer, two ticket-purchasers asking for their money back, and the Society's solicitor. Then Sammons refused the *Lark* when accepting Delius's concerto, and only relented after the honorary secretary had been 'instructed to *beg*... as the Committee was pledged to its performance'.[37] Both works were played under Frank Bridge on 24 February 1927.

Patriotism was raising new difficulties for programme selectors in a period of cultural upheaval, and rather more sophistication, than in the heady 'Renaissance' days. A sympathetic chronicler of the period describes a concert conducted by Malcolm Sargent on 27 April 1925, as 'representative stylistically of what was then new'.[38] It consisted of Bax's *The Garden of Fand*, Howells's Second Piano Concerto (first performance), Ireland's *Mai-Dun*, the *Pastoral Symphony* of Vaughan Williams,

---

[34] Stravinsky: 48.2/14 (27 June, and 9 and 16 Oct. 1924). Bartók and Gershwin: 48.2/14 (19 June 1925).

[35] The *Oedipus* project was discussed on at least eight occasions: 48.2/14 (7 and 28 July; 4 and 11 Aug.; 13, 23, and 27 Sept.; 20 Oct. 1927). Compare P. Heyworth, *Otto Klemperer: His Life and Times*. i. *1885–1933* (1983), 319.

[36] Complaint about foreign conductors: 48.3/4 (30 May 1924). Sometimes even foreign instrumentalists who could get labour permits would be refused explicitly because 'British artists had to be considered': on this occasion rejecting Friedman, Elman, and, perhaps understandably after the *Lark* fiasco, Morini: 48.2/14 (9 Apr. 1926).

[37] 48.2/14 (1 and 4 Mar. 1926; 14 May 1926).

[38] Foreman, *From Parry to Britten*, 103.

and the *Fantaisie espagnole* by Lord Berners. We do not know whether
the evening was profitable, though Sir Gerald Hugh Tyrwhitt-Wilson
Berners, an eccentric dilettante who was said to be doing 'more to
civilize the wealthy than anyone in England', to little discernible effect,
always paid his dues. At least one subscriber was moved to complain
that the 'pledge' of a classical symphony in every concert was being
broken, and another shouted, after the Howells piece, 'And I say,
thank God it's over', earning a rebuke for 'ill mannered' behaviour
from *The Times*, and tut-tutting about 'barbarism'.[39] More substantial
criticism could be levelled against standards of orchestral playing, for
few celebrated batons, except Beecham's, and possibly Wood's, were
a regular match for prevailing conditions in the orchestra. When
Furtwängler, successor to Nikisch in Leipzig and Berlin, first appeared
for the Philharmonic, an uncommonly frank and conscientious journalist remarked that while two rehearsals had clearly been 'insufficient for
a conductor whose conceptions are so entirely unorthodox', even that
allocation was unusually generous. It had become a commonplace that
'not one in twenty concerts' was 'properly prepared', so critics and
audiences were accustomed to making 'allowances'. And this was 'a
bore—or a demoralization'. When Furtwängler returned with his Berlin
Philharmonic Orchestra in 1927, there was no need to make allowances, as delighted audiences, and most of the critics, made abundantly
clear.[40] Sometimes distinguished visitors could whip up a temporary
display of energy. Schnabel's performance of the Second Brahms Concerto, with a 'curiously assertive' conductor, was such an occasion: 'a
strange and unimpressed orchestra and a notoriously "troublesome"
soloist spurred Fried to extraordinary efforts. The effect was electric
... the entire house rose and shouted—a most un-English demonstration.'[41]

The 'deputy system', which has frequently crept into these pages,
always functioned as whipping-boy for this boredom and demoralization, its wickedness incessantly denounced. Few men knew it better
than Mewburn Levien: 'A, whom you want, signs; he sends B (whom
you don't mind) to the first rehearsal; B, without your knowledge or
consent, sends C to the second rehearsal, who, not being able to play
at the concert, sends D, whom you would have paid five shillings to
stay away.' By the 1920s, as Kenyon points out, 'A' would probably
not have signed in the first place, and two rehearsals were rare, but

[39] Subscriber's complaint: 48.2/14 (28 Aug. 1925). The civilizing influence of Berners was
reported by Osbert Sitwell. The 'barbarism' incident is discussed in the *New Statesman* (2
May 1925).
[40] *MMR* (Feb. and Mar. 1924). Comment on the Berlin Philharmonic's visit is in the
Music Trades Review (Dec. 1927) (quoting the *Morning Post*) and *MMR* (Jan. 1928).
[41] C. Saerchinger, *Artur Schnabel* (1957), 185.

there was now an additional reason for deputizing.[42] The system was gaining renewed strength from a form of popular entertainment which threatened to engulf all competitors, as 'silent' cinemas offered jobs to instrumentalists throughout the country, accounting for some 80 per cent of vastly expanded employment, not least in greater London. Philharmonic players were among those tempted to accompany show-ings of the *Rosenkavalier* film, and other less ambitious calls upon their skills in the large and prosperous cinemas which opened in every city. So a sudden increase in demand for musicians of all kinds, at a time when immigration controls kept most foreigners out, raised orchestral wages, strengthened the Union, and generally made life more difficult for concert organizers. Its numerous venues and performances rendered the cinema, as Edwin Evans tried to explain, 'the most important musi-cal institution in the country', affecting listeners as well as musicians. In this early phase of music for films, performers usually played what was familiar, available, and preferably out of copyright, including many old staples of the Philharmonic's repertoire which were now far more widely heard than ever in the past. It was a potent influence upon the nation's musical education, and therefore, perhaps, upon the size of future audiences, but without immediate benefit to the concert world.[43]

Incorporation and Fund-Raising

In administration, as in music, the 1920s were years of incoherence, punctuated by episodes of stability. The Society appeared to be per-manent because it was old and venerable, but its finances were thread-bare, and its legal status remained uncertain. The latter weakness could be remedied. The Philharmonic, as a solicitor had commented in 1902, was 'an ancient institution, but not registered, nor chartered', and therefore could not prevent others from using its name without proving 'injury by the user'. Twenty years later, incorporation was achieved un-der recent legislation which allowed non-profit-making societies to register as limited companies without having to append 'Ltd' to their names. The process protected members' liability, of course, and it helped to consolidate a name and image which had always been guarded with

---

[42] Kenyon, *BBCSO*, 8. Among many archive references, see Frank Bridge's complaint about deputies for his concert on 24 Feb. 1927; a note that 'contracts had been broken markedly by deputy system'; and meeting with union representatives about the 'system and the crisis of the Society in regard to its orchestral arrangements, and its duties to its members and the public'.: 48.2/14 (8 and 24 Mar., 8 Nov. 1927).

[43] E. Evans, 'Music and the Cinema', *Music and Letters* (Jan. 1929); Ehrlich, *Music Profession*, 194–200; and id., *Harmonious Alliance*, 35–8.

zeal, and was now a uniquely marketable asset. Incorporation might also serve to deter, or at least signal, future attempts to take over the Society; and long-term business could be undertaken with more confidence, including some tentative negotiations with brash newcomers in wireless and the gramophone industry.[44]

Legal underpinning did not alter the fact that funding was never more than temporary, and the Society was hard put to it to keep afloat. Every season except one was run at a loss, ranging from a few hundred to more than a thousand pounds, with heavy calls on the guarantors, and consequential damage to morale. Relief from further responsibility was promised in 1923, when the concert agents Powell and Holt offered to run the Society for ten years. They would provide conductors and soloists, taking profits or losses, and 'probably allow the Committee to arrange programmes'.[45] It was sufficiently tempting for the following season's plans to be abandoned while legal opinion was sought. When the scheme was said to conflict with the terms of incorporation, new proposals from Beecham for a 'partnership' were, in turn, dismissed only after consulting the solicitor.[46] Associates, members, and fellows were then urged to attend a general meeting 'to consider the critical position' and debate 'whether the concerts can be resumed'.[47] Yet another last-minute rescue was staged after several more gatherings, though canvassing for support was becoming ever more difficult: in further retreat from the Society's origins among professional musicians, the number of fellows had already been raised to 350 at a meeting attended by only a dozen members.[48] But a little cash was found or promised, some old ploys revived, and new stratagems devised, without much understanding of a changing market. Even Paderewski was approached yet again, and similarly Melba, as a desperate bid for Berger-like cross subsidies, after failure to enlist the Irish-American opera and recording star McCormack, who could indeed have filled the Albert Hall with immaculate diction and eager ticket-buyers, but found the moment 'not opportune'.[49]

A 'Propaganda Committee' was set up—the term not yet sullied by Nazi associations, but pleasingly modern and business-like in tone, if not effect—with the chair taken by Eugene Goossens, or Alfred Kalisch;

[44] 48.2/13 (20 Sept.; 1, 12, and 20 Oct.; 2 Nov.; and 7 Dec. 1918). Memorandum and Articles of Association, 1922: 48.5/3. The solicitor's quoted opinion is in 48.13/9 (4 June 1902), advising about infringement by a 'Quartet Party'. It was always policy to challenge use of the title 'Philharmonic'. Some representative examples: 48.2/8 (14 Apr. 1883), opposing use by Sarasate and Mrs Lambourne; 48.2/11 (21 Mar. 1895), rejecting 'Sunday Philharmonic Union', 'Highbury Philharmonic', and 'Philharmonic edition of piano pieces'; 48.13/13 (13 Feb. 1902), refusing permission to 61 members of the orchestra and Cowen; 48.2/15 (10 Oct. 1929), opposing Ernest Reed's use of 'Junior Philharmonic Orchestra'.
[45] 48.2/14 (17 Feb. 1923).   [46] 48.2/14 (3 Mar. 1923).
[47] Printed Notice to Members etc.: 48.3/4 (30 June 1923).
[48] 48.3/4 (21 May 1921).   [49] 48.2/14 (6 and 10 Jan., and 3 Apr. 1923).

the latter a barrister turned music critic, and ardent Straussian. Lady
Maud Warrender convened 'a representative gathering as large as her
music room, at Holland Park, would hold to obtain fresh support'; and
Theodore Holland, a cultivated musician who had studied with Joachim,
joined the cause. Percy Scholes, the profuse high priest of a burgeoning
cult of 'musical appreciation', pleaded that he had no time for committees, but was asked to put in a 'mention when broadcasting'.[50] In
the following year Powell returned, this time with a proposal to run
concerts on Sundays, and in the provinces, which might entail, by
some unspecified means, the glorious possibility of stepping 'towards a
permanent orchestra and abolition of deputies'.[51] No more practical
were expectations of active royal patronage; the connection now so
distant that, on one prompting, in 1924, a palace functionary tele-
phoned to enquire if their majesties, or King Edward, 'had been to
one of the Society's concerts at anytime'.[52] Further invitations were
refused, and elaborate arrangements for a series of concerts at the
British Empire Exhibition that year came to nothing.[53] A royal concert
was at last arranged on 22 March 1928, when Beecham conducted his
own version of Handel's *Solomon*. It was a splendid reconciliation, after
which he was presented with the gold medal, but of no help to the
funds: explaining that season's deficit of £1,141, the committee later
drew special attention to the cost of the royal visit. In the same year
Elgar, now Master of the King's Music, gave up after several attempts
to get royal support for a solid structure of funding.[54]

Generous support came, as always, from musicians, led by some of
the Society's most distinguished old friends. Cortot returned half of his
150-guinea fee in 1923.[55] Kreisler gave a special out-of-season concert
in 1927, raising £763 for the foundation fund, though repeated lob-
bying, including a direct approach to the Chancellor of the Exchequer,
failed to get this gift exempted from entertainment tax.[56] Harold Bauer
sent £100, on behalf of the Beethoven Association of New York.
Casals, long after earning his gold medal, was unsparing in the Society's cause. Far from exploiting the bargaining power which reflected
his unique position as an unchallenged master, he was unfailingly
generous; returning his 100-guinea fee in 1926, and immediately accepting another engagement, free, to play the Dvořák Concerto more
persuasively than anyone had done before.[56]

---

[50] 48.2/14 (4 Jul., 29 Aug., and 22 Sept. 1923). 48.3/4 (3 Oct. 1923).
[51] 48.2/14 (22 May 1924).   [52] 48.2/14 (6 Nov. 1924).
[53] 48.2/14 (24 Mar. 1924).
[54] 48.2/14 (6 and 13 Nov. 1924; 7 May 1925; 12 Jan., 9 Feb., 21 June ('Elgar will do
everything in his power'), 12 July, and 2 and 23 Aug. 1928).
[55] 48.2/14 (10 July 1923).
[56] 48.2/14 (6 and 31 Dec. 1926; 9 June 28 July, and 13 Sept. 1927). See also *The Times*
(21 May 1927) for an account of the Kreisler, Casals, and Bauer initiatives.

Nevertheless there was a broad consensus of opinion that sustained promotion of orchestral concerts had become practically impossible in the metropolis. The population of inner London was continuing to fall, as suburbs grew enormously, providing their own venues of entertainment. Costs of concert-giving had doubled, but audiences, or so it was said, were not prepared to spend more on tickets. Even Queen's Hall was threatened with extinction when Robert Newman died in 1926. 'The concert world was stirred almost to its depths' at William Boosey's announcement that the heartland of London's music might be 'converted into a picture house', and the committee devoted several meetings to discussing 'the present crisis'. Still lacking a permanent office, after more than a century's existence, it contemplated purchasing the Hall 'to preserve it for music', by means of public subscription. Deliberations which were rather at odds with available resources were given momentary credence when Casals offered to lead the appeal. Then William Boosey, representing the owners and old-style music-publishing, who dreaded the BBC's incursions, confirmed his preference to do business with 'a musical concern', and mentioned the sum of £250,000.[57] The Hall's salvation was left to other hands: Queen's Hall and, incidentally, the Proms, were saved by the BBC.

Next year was the centenary of Beethoven's death, celebrated, rather in the style of Anderson and Cusins but at less cost, by publication of a 'brochure', compiled by Levien; visits to Vienna by two delegates to attend a festival and lay a wreath; and a concert at the Albert Hall, with the Choral Fantasy and *Missa Solemnis*, conducted by Sir Hugh Allen, not in the style of a Beecham or Furtwängler, but economically. With a season's profit of £100 and over £3,000 in a new foundation fund, there was some mild euphoria, reflected in a project to revive the silver medal for long-serving members of the orchestra, which was later dropped in favour of occasional presentations of bust and brochure.[58] Within a year financial constraints were again lowering standards, and W. J. Turner was probably not alone in regarding the Society as a 'moribund, useless institution'. Early in 1930 there was an incident reminiscent of Clara Schumann's refusal to play a Beethoven concerto in 1871. Schnabel performed Mozart's A major Concerto K.488, with Basil Cameron, and wrote to *The Times* to explain that it had been inadequately rehearsed. The orchestra, commented Turner, were 'tired and apathetic', and Schnabel's offer to pay for an extra thirty minutes' rehearsal had to be refused because the extensive use

---

[57] *Annual Register* (1926); 48.2/14 (5, 9, and 26 Nov. and 6 Dec. 1926; 22 and 25 Mar. 1927).

[58] Silver medal proposal: 48.3/4 (27 May 1927). Geissmar, whose standards were high, makes specific mention of Beecham's 'magnificent' performance of the Mass, with the Leeds choir, in Leeds: *Baton and Jackboot*, 317.

of deputies reduced it to a meaningless gesture. With the onset of the
Great Depression, there was talk of giving chamber concerts 'rather
than giving up altogether', and concern was expressed about the
position of Trustees 'in the event of the Society being wound up'.[59]
This time resuscitation was achieved by the very forces which were
thought to have driven the patient into intensive care.

Surviving the 1930s

For everyone connected with music the early 1930s were, at best,
bewildering, at worst catastrophic. Upwards of 12,000 cinema musicians lost their jobs for ever, practically overnight, with the coming of
talkies. The plight of many more music-teachers—the two categories
of occupation overlapped, particularly among cinema pianists—is not
so easily rendered into statistics, nor attributable to a single cause. But
their numbers fell precipitously, while survivors clung to a form of
poverty in 'underemployment', rather than the dole queue, none the
less painful for its shabby gentility. Many of them were members of
the Incorporated Society of Musicians, whose voice was understandably
much heard, though less heeded, in subsequent talk about the 'crisis'
in music. The bulk of their work had stemmed from a piano culture,
at every level of society, which was giving way to new forms of leisure,
musicality, and social emulation: changes in public behaviour and taste
which removed the mainspring of livelihood for the old-style music
'profession'. It was this piano culture which had also underpinned so
many Philharmonic ventures in the past: the subscribers whose hours
at the piano had prepared them for diverse enlightenments and
satisfactions from Mendelssohn, Grieg, or Paderewski, and the old network of manufacturers, agents, composers, and virtuosi, which had
been tapped so expertly by Berger, on behalf of the Society, for pianos,
pianists, advertisements, and subsidies. His successors, though they
were often slow to recognize, or at least acknowledge the fact, had to
deal with a new world. Pianos continued to be made and played,
though by fewer amateurs. Steinways still acted as guarantors, and
virtuosi still attracted audiences, but the main thrust of musical activity
had shifted, providing new opportunities and risks for suppliers of
music, according to their response.[60]

 Recording and, more significantly at this stage, broadcasting, were

[59] 48.3/4 (17 July and 8 Oct. 1931). The Schnabel incident: *The Times* (18 Jan. 1930);
New Statesman (25 Jan. 1930). Turner's low opinion of the 1920s Philharmonic was frequently
expressed, and elaborated in *Music and Life* (1921), ch. 11. See also W. McKenna, *W. J.
Turner, Poet and Music Critic* (1990), 130–5.
[60] On the decline of piano culture, see Ehrlich, *Piano*, ch. 10.

at the centre of the revolution, both embodying an economics which
transformed the productivity of musicians, and therefore the relative
profitability of live and 'canned' music. Wireless licences had increased
from two million in 1926 to five million in 1932, and by 1935 virtually
every home in Britain was paying to receive programmes. The Corporation therefore rapidly became the country's largest employer of
musicians and distributor of music; and thanks to its powerfully administered, public-spirited, monopoly, and unexampled spending-power
drawn from licence revenue and therefore immune to commercial
pressures, it could offer effective patronage for the first time in modern
history and, under Reith, proceeded to do so.[61] The gramophone
companies were not to be compared to the BBC in scale, influence,
or unequivocal commitment to cultural improvement; but they were
similarly rooted in new uses of music and patterns of leisure. And they
too were capably led, by such men as Louis Sterling and Fred Gaisberg,
determined to exploit and develop a vast potential market, with adequate funding, despite the economic slump, and a technology which,
for the first time since Edison's invention, could do justice to orchestral
music. Just as 'pre-electric' 78 r.p.m. records had captured the human
voice for posterity, now the microphone was ready for orchestras; and
nowhere more skilfully employed than in London. Nothing could have
been more opportune for the Philharmonic, or mutually beneficial,
than to deal with these great new forces for music. In return for much-
needed finance, it could offer an image which was uniquely marketable, recognized and coveted by all contenders.

Less welcome, on occasion, was an inclination to offer advice and
services: partly, as the Society's representatives saw it, to keep the
image unblemished; partly in the belief that their musical expertise,
taste, experience, and connections, were uniformly scarce and valuable.
From the outset there was a tendency to wag an avuncular finger
which could be irritating. In 1924, for example, a proposal to broadcast two concerts met the demand that conductors and programmes
'must be submitted to the Committee before announcements are made',
which the BBC thought 'rather strong'.[62] Such gestures of authority
from established, but impoverished, representatives of ancient institutions to new, but substantial, institutions, rapidly became unacceptable
as the real balance of power toppled irretrievably. Negotiations with
the gramophone companies were comparatively simple at first, generating a useful but small trickle of income, by outright payments rather
than shares in royalties. They also sometimes raised intractable questions about the orchestra, when record-makers wanted to discriminate

---

[61] For a less appreciative account of the BBC's music policy, see P. Scannell and D.
Cardiff, *A Social History of British Broadcasting* (1991), ch. 9.
[62] 48.2/14 (17 and 23 Jan. 1924).

between players.[63] But this explorative stage of development was rapidly overtaken by the 1931 economic crisis and, more fundamental in its long-term effects, by Beecham's latest campaign, which transformed the world of orchestral recording, along with everything else in concert life.

In its protracted dealings with the BBC, the Society joined a diverse band of insurgents. Choice of associates was therefore important, and it would have been best to depend mostly upon those whose international reputation, or rare musicianship, and loyalty to Philharmonic ideals, assisted bargaining from strength. It did not necessitate subservience. Some of the finest musicians were initially sceptical about new technology and institutions. Schnabel, for example, who had famously declined the blandishments of pianola manufacturers when they claimed to able to reproduce his playing, refused to broadcast at first 'on artistic grounds', so that his performance of the 'Emperor' Concerto on 31 January 1929 could not be offered to the BBC, from a concert which left only Cameron's reading of Brahms's Third Symphony.[64] But even the most sensitive artists were soon won over by demonstrable technical advance and cultural benefit. Some other dissidents, like Hamilton Harty, trying to defend his Hallé orchestra, had worthy, if shortsighted, reasons—such as 'unfair' competition for players and audiences —to oppose the 'amiable bandits of Savoy Hill'.[65] Much animosity towards the BBC, which continued throughout the 1930s, was either blinkered against the steady accumulation of experience, or rooted in needs and frustrations far removed from the Philharmonic's best interests. Particularly damaging were attitudes based upon the false assumption of a fixed 'lump of musical activity which had to be fairly shared out between a number of existing interests'.[66] In reality the BBC was creating and educating a new market for music, which few of its critics had done much to develop.

There are several published accounts of these controversies over music policy, from which the BBC generally emerges more creditably than its opponents.[67] The details need not detain us here, since much of the talk soon proved sterile, and only a few matters were truly relevant to the Society. Attacks upon the Corporation for its

[63] Dealings with gramophone companies: 48.2/13 (25 Sept. and 15 Oct. 1920); 48.2/14 (7, 8, and 19 Nov.; and 13 Dec. 1923; 26 Nov. and 10 Dec. 1926; 14 July 1927); 48.2/15 (13 Sept. 1928 (Columbia wants to 'promote a permanent orchestra'); 8 Nov. 1928; 7 Feb., and 7 and 27 Mar. 1929 (attempts to select players); 9 Apr. and 15 May 1930 (Columbia offer); 12 June 1930 (Decca offer)).
[64] 48.2/14 (6 Oct. 1927). 48.2/15 (5 July 1928).
[65] D. Greer (ed.), *Hamilton Harty: His Life and Music* (Belfast, 1979), 43.
[66] Briggs, *History of Broadcasting*, ii. *The Golden Age of Wireless* (1965), 492.
[67] Scannell and Cardiff, *Social History*, chs. 1, 9, and 10. Briggs, *Golden Age*, 169–184; Kenyon, *BBCSO*, chs. 1 and 2.

'monopolistic' activities may have reflected genuine apprehensions, at
first, about its ventures into public concerts. Accusations that it would
force music to 'become practically a Department of State', allowing the
system of 'private initiative and enterprise' to be 'stifled or even crip-
pled', were mere rhetoric.[68] Without pausing to consider its unique
experience of that system's manifest deficiencies, which were yet again
threatening the Philharmonic with extinction, its representatives could
still 'firmly resolve that the good name of the Royal Philharmonic
should not be bartered for any financial consideration, however attractive'.[69] Fortunately good sense occasionally got the better of rhetoric,
as when Reith assured Dent and Holland that he 'would do anything
in his power to prevent the Royal Philharmonic Society being brought
to an end'. When the BBC offered £800 for six broadcasts in 1932,
it was 'accepted with thanks'.[70]

The war of the air had one significant outcome, from the viewpoint
of this history: the creation of two stable orchestras, with properly
contracted players, and no deputies. One has been justly and substantially chronicled. The other awaits its historian, for so prolonged and
tortuous was Beecham's campaign, and so elaborate the structure of
finance, management, and commitment imposed by his victory, that
the London Philharmonic Orchestra's genesis defies brief summary. Its
very title was peculiar, as the critic Ernest Newman complained, for
it 'set up confusions with the old Royal Philharmonic', without using
the full name, which Beecham had so openly coveted.[71] And though
it played for every Society concert henceforth, save for a visit by the
Dresden State Opera Orchestra in 1936, the London Philharmonic
also appeared for other organizations, notably the Courtauld–Sargent
Concerts, and outside London. Even its wonderful début, after twelve
rehearsals—'Carnaval Romain', the 'Prague' Symphony, *Brigg Fair*, and
Ein Heldenleben—on 7 October 1932, is inaccurately recalled.[72] Far from
being a 'sell-out', it was played to many empty seats. But audiences
soon rallied to a predominantly young band whose Berlioz overture
seemed to declare, recalled Newman, who was never easily impressed:
'You Londoners want to know what an orchestra ought to be like?

[68] 48.2/15, sheet 3.   [69] Ibid., sheet 4.

[70] 48.2/15 (29 Oct. 1931; 28 Jan. 1932). According to one participant, the Philharmonic
'very nearly got control of broadcast music', and it was 'a very good thing both for music
and the Society that they did not.' E. Irving, *Cue for Music* (1959), 180.

[71] Newman is quoted at length in T. Russell, *Philharmonic Decade* (1944), 18–19. Kenyon
confirms Beecham's interest in the name, which would '*bring lustre*': BBCSO, 30. The LPO's
'stability' was only in comparison with the past. App. 3 indicates that the orchestra of 1935
had lost over fifty players since 1932.

[72] 'empty seats': *MT* (1 Nov. 1932), which added that it was an 'event of first class
importance . . . a success beyond question.' Compare A. Jefferson, *Sir Thomas Beecham: A
Centenary Tribute* (1979), 88. On rehearsals, see the reminiscences of Paul Beard, who was
leading, in Procter-Gregg, *Beecham Remembered*, 39; and Russell, *Philharmonic Decade*, 18.

THE ROYAL PHILHARMONIC SOCIETY
INSTITUTED 1813
Patrons—THEIR MAJESTIES THE KING AND QUEEN

ONE HUNDRED AND TWENTY-FIRST SEASON   -   -   -   1932—1933

QUEEN'S HALL
SOLE LESSEES   MESSRS. CHAPPELL & CO., LTD.

FIRST CONCERT
Friday, October 7th, 1932, at 8.15 p.m.

Overture: "Le Carnaval Romain"   -   -   -   *Berlioz*

Symphony No. 38, in D ("Prague")   -   -   -   *Mozart*

An English Rhapsody: "Brigg Fair"   -   -   -   *Delius*

INTERVAL

Symphonic Poem: "Ein Heldenleben"   -   -   -   *Strauss*

Conductor   -   -   SIR THOMAS BEECHAM

FIRST PUBLIC APPEARANCE
OF

THE LONDON PHILHARMONIC ORCHESTRA

Page Nine

19. Programme, 7 October 1932

Well just listen to this.' Anyone who has heard the Beecham recording, or better, witnessed any of his performances, can imagine the excitement of that occasion. There were many others, and London concerts were at last comparable to the best in any city. The fact requires no further verbal evidence for the 1930s are easily documented in sound. Beecham's London Philharmonic recordings became the standard, in a large repertoire, by which others were judged: incomparable in Haydn, Berlioz, Delius, Sibelius, and much French music; to be compared with the Vienna Philharmonic in Mozart, Schubert, and some Beethoven (Beecham was an 'even numbers' man); with Toscanini's New York Philharmonic in Rossini. And in recent years we have gained access to examples of the orchestra's work in the opera house, under Beecham, Reiner, and other masters, in live recordings which confirm its brilliance and versatility: the *Tristan* recordings, with Flagstad and Melchior, are astonishing examples. When Sackville-West and Shawe-Taylor published their definitive mid-century *Record Guide*, they could still recommend Beecham's 1932 reading of the 'Jupiter' Symphony as displaying 'both orchestra and conductor at the height of their powers'.

The Society's use of the LPO, not always conducted by Sir Thomas, is summarized in Appendix I, where the 'Beecham repertoire' dominates the 1930s listings. Most notable, perhaps, is the emergence of Sibelius, with many exemplary performances, and the gold medal in 1935. Recordings of several symphonies, tone-poems, and the Violin Concerto with Heifetz, were again, *hors concours*. Since Sibelius was widely regarded at the time as the greatest symphonist since Beethoven, not excluding Brahms, the Royal Philharmonic could, once again, claim to be at the centre of informed taste—without, of course, meeting everyone's requirements. A meeting of fellows in September 1936, seven present, made a 'general request that the Society should not include so much modern music in the programmes.[73] They may have been upset that season by Vaughan Williams's Fourth Symphony, under Boult, or Primrose's performance of Walton's Viola Concerto, with Beecham. Later in the year they could see Richard Strauss receive the gold medal, at a concert where *Zarathustra* was played, and Bliss's Music for Strings. What did they make of Nadia Boulanger's concert in November 1937: Rameau, Monteverdi, Haydn (Harpsichord Concerto) and the Fauré Requiem?

Yet the great musical achievements of the 1930s were gained by musicians' toil, and within budgets almost as exiguous, and just as insecure, as in the past. When Lionel Tertis addressed the Musicians' Club in 1938 he described a typical working day for an LPO player: three hours' morning rehearsal; three hours' afternoon recording session; two and a half hours' evening concert.[74] And when the next crisis came, in 1939, it was necessary to call 85 per cent of the guarantee fund. The future again seemed imperilled.

[73] 48.3/4 (9 June 1936).   [74] *New Statesman* (9 Apr. 1938).

11

Interlude for War

What is needed is a subsidy from the State ... any Government would deserve well of its country that undertook to subsidise a *national* Opera House, a *national* Theatre, and a *national* Orchestral Society such as the Philharmonic.

(Francesco Berger, 1913)[1]

There is a very definite trend towards more serious music, and it is obvious that in times like these much frivolity in any art cannot be endured.

(Arthur Bliss, 1941)[2]

the astonishing increase in the appetite for good music cannot be denied.

(J. A. Westrup, 1943)[3]

in a single decade, during and after the Second World War, the British Government did more to commit itself to supporting the arts than it had in the previous century and a half.

(Janet Minihan, 1977)[4]

ON 3 September 1939 all public entertainment was officially cancelled until further notice. In the spring the plenitude of London's musical life had been celebrated in a festival organized by Owen Mase, a BBC executive, connected with the Philharmonic, who had managed, for that limited purpose, to 'unite the whole musical establishment on his council', with the King and Queen as patrons, and a culmination of six magnificent concerts by the BBC Symphony Orchestra under Toscanini.[5] Yet by September the rapidity and thoroughness of cultural

---

[1] *Reminiscences*, 79.

[2] Broadcasting on the Overseas Service of the BBC on 3 Oct. 1941. See *Bliss on Music: Selected Writings of Arthur Bliss 1920–1975*, ed. G. Roscow (1991), 178.

[3] *British Music* (1943), 35. This booklet, by the professor of music at Oxford, was one of a series entitled British Life and Thought, intended to present 'the life and work, the ideas and ideals, of Britain today.'   [4] *The Nationalization of Culture* (1977), 215.

[5] Kenyon, *BBCSO*, 150–1.

disintegration was depressingly similar to that of 1914, the *Annual Register* recording it, without attempting to make the obvious comparison.[6] Covent Garden closed and was later switched from opera to ballroom dancing. Concert schedules were abandoned, and the BBC stopped broadcasting serious music. Even the Proms, which had maintained continuity in 1914, started on 12 August, only to be abruptly terminated on 1 September because the BBC Symphony Orchestra had been evacuated to Bristol. It was generally understood that Broadcasting House, and therefore Queen's Hall, would be prime targets for Hitler's bombs, which failed to arrive until the fall of France in the spring of 1940.

Emergency Measures

Musicians remaining in London therefore lost practically all prospects of a job, just when their savings were low and the season should have begun. The LPO's controlling company went into voluntary liquidation, Beecham addressing a difficult meeting of trade creditors with studied eloquence and practised ease. As always he was generous, and offhand in matters of finance, *vide* a much-quoted remark, on the occasion of a previous crisis, postprandial at Lady Cunard's: 'I have to see my solicitor to discuss matters in which the Official Receiver is interested and, on my behalf, very much concerned. And for what he is about to receive, may the Lord make him truly thankful.'[7] This time around, members of the orchestra, who were also creditors, loyally kept their silence. It was neither the first nor last demonstration of a unique relationship among musicians who were professionals in every sense that mattered. Built upon mutual understanding and respect, its foundations were elucidated by Thomas Russell, than whom no one was better placed, or more entitled, to comment: he had played viola in the LPO since 1935, and was about to take the main responsibility for its continued existence. 'There was, indeed, no reason why Sir Thomas should have defended himself or the Company he represented', wrote Russell soon after these events; 'once the pre-war outlook on musical life in this country was accepted, no single man or small organization could have hoped to keep a permanent orchestra solvent except in very prosperous times'.[8] The LPO formed a new company, with a committee of players, along similar lines to the long-established LSO, and began to tour the provinces. Even this stop-gap arrangement only became possible after Beecham had found the cash for registration, rail-fares, and hire of music; for no English bank would give credit to an English orchestra, however distinguished its recent past.[9]

[6] *Annual Register* (1939).   [7] Cardus, *Sir Thomas Beecham: A Memoir* (1961), 21.
[8] Russell, *Philharmonic Decade*, 64.   [9] Ibid. 68–9.

While London's music fell apart in those early months of 'phoney war', feeble government, and cultural impoverishment, representatives of the Royal Philharmonic Society, left very much to their own devices, tried to contrive means of survival, expressing their determination to continue work 'which has been unbroken for 127 years'.[10] The precious archive was evacuated to a safe place in Yorkshire, and six concerts were organized, on Thursday afternoons, beginning 16 November 1939. The time excluded working people, of course, and was even opposed by a majority of those able to attend. Beecham presided over the first two concerts, economically without soloists, before leaving for America on an extensive tour which, despite a few patriotically raised eyebrows, had been long planned, and considerably delayed.[11] The third concert, conducted by Hamilton Harty, included a first public performance of his *John Field Suite*, soon to become very popular.[12] The fourth, under Sir Henry Wood, in much-needed aid of the Incorporated Society of Musicians' benevolent fund, featured Vaughan Williams's *Serenade to Music*, and Sammons and Tertis, returning from retirement, in Mozart's Sinfonia concertante: a famous assembly of native singers and instrumentalists, all performing without fee. Malcolm Sargent and Myra Hess gave the fifth concert, and for the last a conventional programme was conducted, with particular distinction, by Weingartner, still available because he was living in Switzerland. The orchestra, though individually hard-pressed for cash, gave its services free 'in recognition of the Society's work for music'.[13] The BBC paid £150 in broadcasting fees—most of which was absorbed by a steep increase in charges for the hall—and donated a further £100, which enabled the season's accounts to be settled, but only by calling on guarantors for 75 per cent of their pledges.[14]

Two Philharmonic functionaries were active in these holding operations, and continued to dominate the Society's affairs for the rest of the war. Keith Douglas, who had succeeded Gerald Cooper as honorary secretary in 1932, is pictured by Elkin as 'a young man of forceful character and dynamic energy' from Bradford where, we are told, he had previously established a local reputation as conductor and

---

[10] 48.2/16 (26 Sept. 1939).

[11] Concerts were confined to the afternoons by official decree, and against the wishes even of most of those who continued to attend: 48.2/16 (4 Dec. 1939). Beecham's travel plans: Russell, *Philharmonic Decade*, 72.

[12] See letter from Ernest Chapman to Erwin Stein, both of Boosey and Hawkes, Harty's publisher (30 May 1940), in Foreman, *From Parry to Britten*, 230.

[13] The compliment was returned when the Society presented a concert for the LPO's pension fund on 23 Mar. 1941, with Myra Hess, and conducted by Basil Cameron, as gratefully acknowledged by Russell in *Philharmonic* (1942), 75. £200 was paid out of the concert takings, and a donation of £100 from Mrs Courtauld was also halved with the orchestra. It was the last Philharmonic concert to be given at Queen's Hall, which was bombed on the night of May 10/11: 48.2/16 (2 Apr. and 2 May 1941).

[14] 48.2/16 (20 Jan. 1940).

concert-promoter. In the latter general capacity—not solely with the Philharmonic series—he now came to some prominence. A historian of the Proms describes Douglas as 'a clever but somewhat unreliable individual with inherited wealth which he was prepared to spend on music'.[15] George Baker (1885–1976) was also well established, and settling in for an even longer stay. He had sung with the British National and Carl Rosa Opera Companies, and was currently acting overseas music director for the BBC. A Savage Club habitué, he became its honorary secretary, and secretary to the Orchestral Employers' Association. Honorary treasurer to the Philharmonic since 1934, he represented, according to Elkin, a 'happy blend of musician and man-of-affairs so desirable in any holder of that post'.[16] Less desirable was a fondness for public expression of blunt opinions about sensitive issues, which appeared to represent Society policy, as in a notorious communication to *The Times* in the summer of 1941. It was a time of high patriotism, a year after Dunkirk, with the siege economy taking hold, and Baker decided to carry the battle into music. His letter was part of a correspondence which had been initiated by Ernest Newman as an attempt to establish the artistic standing of a young English composer whose versatile brilliance was already widely perceived. A Philharmonic representative might be expected to have views on such a subject; not necessarily enlightened at that stage in the composer's development, and the nation's history; but best confined to judgements of music, particularly when publicly expressed. Baker preferred to address 'the Battle of Britain; a programme in which Mr Britten has no part'. The letter has subsequently been described, accurately, and in full recognition of wider issues, as 'an unsavoury tailpiece' to an otherwise fruitful debate.[17] Although Douglas kept out of the newspapers, we know that he shared Baker's views, having rejected Britten's Violin Concerto—the work which prompted Newman's enthusiasm—on the grounds that the composer was 'unpopular because of his stay abroad'.[18] Bartók's Divertimento, submitted by the same publisher, was also turned down, presumably on artistic grounds.[19]

In league with Owen Mase, and in addition to the Society's concerts,

[15] Elkin, *Royal Philharmonic*, 121. D. Cox, *The Henry Wood Proms* (1980), 115.

[16] Elkin *Royal Philharmonic*, 122. Baker's position had also been entrenched by a long stint as acting Secretary when Douglas was ill.

[17] The debate ran in the *Sunday Times* and *MT*. Baker's letter was published in *The Times* (15 June 1941). The context is explained in D. Mitchell and P. Reed, *Letters From A Life: Selected Letters and Diaries of Benjamin Britten* (1991), ii. 956–9. Compare E. J. Moeran's generous and perceptive letter to the *MT* (Oct. 1941), repr. in Foreman's *Parry to Britten*, 242. See also H. Carpenter's account of the affair in *Benjamin Britten: A Biography* (1992), 151–2. Britten returned to Britain, and a conscientious objectors' tribunal, in April 1942.

[18] Chapman to Stein (6 Sept. 1940), repr. in Foreman, *Parry to Britten*, 234.

[19] Chapman to Stein (18 Sept. 1940), repr. ibid. 236.

Douglas undertook a number of other promotions, which were loosely described as taking place under Philharmonic 'auspices'. They organized a series of chamber and orchestral concerts at Sadler's Wells and, in the BBC's absence, even took on the Proms for 1940 and 1941.[20] The irreplaceable Sir Henry Wood continued to preside, despite migivings about the concert arrangements, which tended to be haphazard, and about hard bargaining with musicians who were in no position to stand out for more reasonable terms. One advantage gleaned from association with the Society, which had earned exemption in recent years after a long struggle, was the avoidance of entertainment tax. When the destruction of Queen's Hall and of players' instruments forced an orchestral migration to South Kensington, in a celebrated demonstration of 'Britain can take it' morale, Douglas moved the Philharmonic concerts in their wake. The Society's annual general meeting in June 1941 expressed thanks for this initiative, and for his 'actions in getting experts to make the acoustics of the Albert Hall reasonable': an architect, Hope Bagenal, and conductor, Basil Cameron, had been consulted.[21]

The Philharmonic series was kept going in similar fashion, with rudimentary administration and mostly routine concerts, crudely designed for the easy requirements of wartime entertainment. When Boult proposed Stravinsky's *Firebird*, which Beecham had been capable of doing in 1915, it was pronounced unsuitable for performance in 1941, and replaced by the *Eroica Symphony*.[22] Next year Myra Hess was asked to perform the Grieg Concerto, and there were plans to approach Solomon, or alternatively Clifford Curzon, or Cyril Smith, to play the Tchaikovsky Concerto: slightly less hackneyed pieces were eventually fixed as substitutes.[23] Since there was little competition, it was hardly cause for surprise that the 1942 season ended in profit and, for the first time in many years, there was no need to call upon guarantors. The committee noted that 'door sales' were responsible, rather than support from members, and resolved to call their attention to this trend.[24] At a later meeting Theodore Holland, supported by Baker, tried to spell out some implications of current behaviour. The Society was failing to

[20] 48.2/16 (12 Apr. 1940): 'Mase will probably run the Proms', and 'the Society can assume full control'.

[21] 48.3/4 (5 June 1941). Cox refers to Wood's 'exasperation' with 'amateurish handling', and to the ploy of avoiding entertainment tax: *The Henry Wood Proms* (1980), 115–20. Russell notes that Douglas had established a 'monopoly' of the Albert Hall, which still existed in April 1944: *Philharmonic Decade*, 98. The wartime acoustic 'improvements' are not to be confused with the miraculous 'flying saucer' innovations of a much later period.

[22] 48.2/16 (18 Dec. 1940).

[23] 48.2/16 (19 Mar. 1942). The general trend of programming can be seen in App. 1. Full programmes for this period are listed in Elkin, *Royal Philharmonic*, 180–4.

[24] 48.2/16 (12 June 1942).

'fulfil its function as a leader in the musical world' because the box-office had become dominant: leading to the same programmes, conductors, and soloists as could be heard anywhere else. Could the British Council help to arrange a visit from John Barbirolli—he had brought a letter of 'goodwill and friendship' from the New York Philharmonic—or Stokowski? Could the Ministry of Information procure a Russian conductor?[25] Barbirolli did come to open the season on 9 October 1943, including the *Firebird* and Vaughan Williams's *Five Variants of 'Dives and Lazarus'* in his programme. But there were further complaints at the next annual general meeting about 'easy on the ear programmes', which 'cheapened concert-going', and removed the 'unique distinction for which the Society was famous'.[26]

How much was done to reassert such 'unique distinction' as could reasonably be expected within the reduced circumstances of war? There were events in which the Society could take pride. Walton's Violin Concerto had its English première on 1 November 1941, and Medtner's Third Concerto, by the composer and Boult, on 19 February 1944; the exquisite and grossly neglected Maggie Teyte could be heard in Ravel's *Shéhérazade* on 9 December 1944, again under Boult. It must also be allowed that curtailment of resources, and disruption of the Philharmonic's communications and international networks of artists, would have made it extraordinarily difficult for any committee to have promoted concerts of consistently high quality. Too many of the best orchestral players were unavailable, some, like Harry Blech, Leonard Hirsch, and the unique young horn virtuoso, Dennis Brain, recruited into the RAF Symphony Orchestra to provide entertainments which culminated before Churchill, Roosevelt, and Stalin at the Yalta Conference.[27] A few major British artists—Solomon, Curzon, Hess, and Sammons, who had hitherto been neglected, or absurdly categorized by the record companies as minor, 'cheap label' performers, came into new and deserved prominence, even if they might sometimes have been employed with more discrimination.

Hardly any foreign stars were able to visit Britain, and even residual links with the world of music could prove to be less fruitful than might have been hoped. One source of disappointment was Sibelius, to whom Beecham, on a personal visit, had presented the gold medal in 1935 (see Frontispiece) and whose reputation continued to arouse high expectations in England and America. He had promised the Society the first European performance of an eighth symphony in 1938, and wrote in 1940 to acknowledge its offer to donate proceeds to the Finnish

---

[25] 48.2/16 (2 Nov. 1942).   [26] 48.3/4 (11 June 1943).

[27] The Yalta incident, and much else about uniformed music, is recounted by Denis Matthews, who played Beethoven's Third Concerto, with the Hallé Orchestra under Barbirolli, for the Society on 26 May 1945: *In Pursuit of Music* (1966).

Red Cross, but regretted that the work could still not be delivered.[28] Limitations of a different kind dampened benefits to be gained from association with Prokofiev. He was awarded the gold medal in 1942, and his Third Piano Concerto was played by Kendall Taylor, with the Hallé Orchestra conducted by John Barbirolli, at a concert on 26 May 1944 'in honour of the second anniversary of the signing of the Anglo-Soviet Treaty': the rest of the concert consisted of Liadov's *The Enchanted Lake*, Tchaikovsky's sixth Symphony, and a festival overture by the then politically correct composer Budashkin. But Prokofiev had to wait for the presentation of his award until 1945, at the British Embassy in Moscow, a few weeks after VE Day. The ceremony was then reported in *Moscow News* and *Red Star*, and the *British Ally* gave it a whole page.[29]

Even at home, tributes to artistic excellence, though beyond criticism in themselves, tended to leave the Society at the periphery, rather than the centre, of their celebration. Myra Hess received the gold medal in 1942, a few months after she had become Dame Myra, and was already a legend. But her charisma was identified with the National Gallery Concerts—the most potent symbol of music in Britain's finest hour—which she had inaugurated on 10 October 1939, and continued daily with a distinction, coherence (as in the Mozart piano concerto series), and benevolence (£10,000 to the Musicians' Benevolent Fund) which the Society was quite incapable of matching. In different fashion but with similar reservations, Boult's gold medal, in 1944, was accepted by him as 'a token of appreciation to the BBC Symphony Orchestra for its wartime work rather than as an award to him personally'. It was a typically modest gesture, as Kenyon remarks, but it also marked a new phase in the relationship between two institutions now utterly changed in comparative status and claims to musical leadership.[30]

Some historians of the period would give more weight to the preliminary trumpetings of a development hitherto regarded as inconceivable: government assistance to the arts. Not that the early activities of the Council for the Encouragement of Music were generously funded or helpful to professional music. In its first year the Arts Council's predecessor, according to an editorial in *The Times*, was more inclined to scratch 'an itch to discover a hitherto dormant musicality among the people', than to support 'existing institutions', leaving the 'art of the musicians ... to languish and die'.[31] It was a patrician rebuke, too easily dismissive of devoted work done, against all odds, in areas

[28] 48.13/31 (28 Nov. 1938 and 14 Feb. 1940). The Symphony was again requested for the 1951 Festival of Britain, when Sibelius was 'honoured', but regretted that it was 'not possible to promise anything definite in this matter'. 48.13/31 (13 Oct. 1949).

[29] 48.17/1 (9 July 1945).   [30] Kenyon, *BBCSO*, 190.

[31] *The Times* (15 June 1940).

of cultural impoverishment. But the absence of life-support for professional music was also beyond question.

Planning Utopia

The pre-history of the Arts Council, like much of its history, is littered with the debris of mostly good intentions. Meagerly financed, and confused in purpose and function from the outset, CEMA never grew capable of facing up to conflicting needs and expectations: amateur versus professional, metropolitan against provincial, élite and demotic.[32] While Keynes was alive (he died in 1946) government policy towards the arts was occasionally subjected to rigorous intelligence. For him, it was 'standards' which mattered, 'and the preservation of serious professional enterprise, not obscure concerts in village halls', but always with an eye to social reality: Glyndebourne, 'however glorious, was a rich man's pleasure, with no claim upon the tax-payer'.[33] Fully employed elsewhere, the great economist could spare little time for such thinking, and less for the committee manoeuvring which would have been necessary for its continuous application. Nor was he much interested in serious music. But his command of detail, disdain for bureaucracy, and refusal to mince words, were missed after his departure. No one was better placed to understand the dilemmas of arts policy, where any interference with the logic of choice imposed by market economics, of the kind which had always ruled professional music in England, required alternative logics in the allocation of public funds.[34]

Instead, policy tended to emerge from special pleading by interested groups, and was obscured by a miasma of cultural euphoria, very much of its time: a desire, wedded to Beveridge's 1942 'call to arms to a better world', for tunes to go with 'social citizenship', for 'full enjoyment . . . with full employment'.[35] Although the wartime publications of CEMA were necessarily much less glossy than their lavish Arts Council successors, they were communicative enough. Several utopian

[32] A more sympathetic account, the most scholarly of its kind, is F. M. Leventhal's, 'The Best for the Most: CEMA and State Sponsorship of the Arts in Wartime, 1939–1945', *Twentieth Century British History*, 3 (1990), 289–317.

[33] M. Glasgow, 'The Concept of the Arts Council', in M. Keynes (ed.), *Essays on John Maynard Keynes* (1975), 262, 267. Miss Glasgow was secretary of CEMA, and became first secretary-general of the Arts Council.

[34] Criticisms of Arts Council policies have been almost as voluminous as its own apologias. For an economist's view, see M. Blaug (ed.), *The Economics of the Performing Arts* (1976).

[35] P. Hennessy, *Never Again: Britain 1945–1951* (1992), 73, 310–11. K. O. Morgan, *The People's Peace: British History 1945–1990*, (Oxford, 1990), 4.

manifestos came from the pen of Dr Reginald Jacques, a tireless string orchestra enthusiast, CEMA activist—its first chairman—and member of the Philharmonic Society's Committee of Management. In one address he argued that 'no state aid (for orchestras) can be regarded as complete unless the players are assured of regular, well-paid work, with concerts a good deal less tightly packed than at present, adequate time for rehearsal, and a pension scheme'.[36] By April 1944 CEMA was claiming to support 'the whole work' of four orchestras, including the LPO and LSO, with 'clear objects' which included the 'best possible working conditions', a 'limited number' of concerts, 'sufficient time' for rehearsals and rest, opportunities for new conductors, soloists, and works, and high standards of performance. Thomas Russell, who never concealed his collectivist enthusiasm, added a footnote, for the sake of completeness, to the effect that 'a symphony orchestra must be no longer regarded as a luxury, but as a social service'.[37]

It was common knowledge that CEMA's purse was as shallow as its rhetoric. The Philharmonic approached slowly. In 1941 a 'financial crisis' prompted an appeal to the Carnegie Trust, reminiscent of the early 1930s, but muted by a proud reluctance to ask for charity: too heart-felt a plea might lead to 'an unwelcome attitude towards the position and dignity of the RPS'.[38] When one of CEMA's officials attended the Committee of Management in December 1942, it was to talk of granting perhaps £20 for each concert, and £50 in case of loss.[39] In April 1945, with costs rising fast, a £420 guarantee was on offer, possibly increasing to £500 next season. The figure, plucked from the air, was not lacking in historical irony. When Berger contemplated the ideal of a grant which would liberalise the Philharmonic, and free it from 'inartistic' constraints, he fixed upon precisely that sum; but it was reckoned in 1913 pounds of immense purchasing power.[40] By 1945 double that sum could easily be lost with three modest concerts, and the resulting financial situation was minuted as 'grim'.[41]

It has been remarked that most national institutions laid their post-war plans 'well before VE day'.[42] Without an adequately staffed office, a large and active constituency, or widely acknowledged leadership, the Society was in no state to attempt such an exercise. One could imag-ine an earlier generation of Philharmonic directors making more of available resources and opportunities in preparation for better times:

[36] *CEMA Bulletin*, 34 (Feb. 1943). [37] Ibid. 48 (Apr. 1944).
[38] 48.2/16 (2 Apr. 1941). On the complex relationships between CEMA in its early stages, the Pilgrim Trust, and Carnegie United Kingdom Trust, see Leventhal, 'The Best for the Most'. [39] 48.2/16 (18 and 31 Dec. 1942).
[40] Berger, *Reminiscences*, 78–9. [41] 48.2/16 (20 Apr. 1945; 11 Dec. 1946).
[42] Hennessy, *Never Again*, 176–7.

Mackenzie recognizing new musical genius, and associating the Philharmonic with its emergence; Berger exercising tact and diplomacy, earning goodwill from the Proms initiative, perhaps even conjuring some closer association with the National Gallery Concerts. Their successors of the 1940s lacked any such skill, but the conjuring of survival can be seen as an achievement of sorts, and peace held promise, even for institutions without blueprints, as the musicians returned.

12

Ending and Beginning

We took pride that we found Britain a country of philistines and left it respecting the arts. The open contempt for painting and music . . . at the Court and in the upper classes dissolved. Attendance at concerts, theatres, museums and galleries rose year by year.

(Lord Annan, 1990)[1]

No dinners with cabinet ministers and powerful ladies, no spending of money just for the fun of it. Nothing but work and quietude, and gathering his whole career together.

(Virgil Thomson on plans, in 1945, for Beecham's last years)[2]

Orchestral politics in London occupied a good deal of attention during the year.

(*Annual Register*, 1964)

IN the immediate post-war years, when the contemporary history of Britain and of the Philharmonic, began, the nation's thirst for 'classical' music was pronounced, and sometimes thought to be unquenchable. Orchestral concerts were preferred, consisting chiefly of a handful of romantic symphonies and piano concertos, the latter genuine or pastiche—Grieg, Tchaikovsky, Rachmaninov, 'Warsaw'—given fresh endorsement by recently popular films. 'The demand for orchestral music', wrote the reviewer of a comprehensive report in 1949, 'is the outstanding feature of our recent musical life,' though he went on to warn of 'a financial crisis facing those whose business it is to supply it'.[3] With demobilization there was no shortage of English instrumentalists to meet this demand: foreigners were restricted by labour permits and union pressures. London's orchestras were assembled in the traditional

---

[1] N. Annan, *Our Age* (1990), 395–6.   [2] *An Autobiography* (1966), 360.
[3] *Times Literary Supplement* (28 Oct. 1949), review (anon.) of PEP, *Music: A Report on Musical Life in England* (1949). In 1945 a BBC survey had found that 'only' 11 per cent of all listeners were 'enthusiastic' about symphony concerts: Briggs, *Sound and Vision* (1979), 724.

manner, more numerous even than in the past, each carrying a flag
of identity, which could be old, new, or reinvented.[4]

The creation of two superb new orchestras was a singular event,
while others continuing to function included the LSO, LPO, BBCSO,
and New Symphony Orchestra. Smaller orchestras emerged only
slowly, despite their lower cost and greater appropriateness for classical and baroque music. The latter was not yet at all popular—even
the Brandenburg Concertos were rarely played, hardly ever outside
London—'authenticity' was no part of a musician's vocabulary, and
'period' instruments were still confined to museums. Nevertheless leaner
music-making had been pioneered by Boyd Neel in the 1930s, and it
was now taken up by such groups as the London Chamber Orchestra,
The Jacques String Orchestra, Alec Sherman's New London Orchestra
(also to be found at the opera), and, most successfully, Harry Blech's
London Mozart Players. The symphony orchestras' separation from
the opera-house was probably more complete than it had been since
Sterndale Bennett's day. Covent Garden was back to its proper business
which, with state funding and prospects of longer seasons than before
the war, required a house orchestra for ballet and opera, instead of
the pre-war arrangement with the LPO. The pit at Sadlers Wells opera
was also more extensive, independent, and discriminating than hitherto.
Capable, in its primitive early days, of dismembering *Tristan* among
eighteen players, the refurbished orchestra was now required to cope,
on occasion, with *Peter Grimes*.[5] Finally a census of London's post-war
orchestras would have to take account of 'pick-up' bands, grandly titled
for routine evenings which, as Lionel Tertis complained, authoritatively
but to no avail, were a wasteful 'mushroom growth', destructive of
musicians' talents, and damaging to public taste.[6]

Although there were often as many as seven orchestral concerts a
week in London, all were sporadic, and few better than second-rate.
Some rise in standards could be expected as good conductors, who
were still in plentiful supply, returned to London, but there was a
pressing need for responsible concert planning. It was not provided by
the Society, which could no longer be regarded, even by its officers,
as a flagship for the nation; nor by the Arts Council, where opera was,

[4] On reinventing an orchestra's name, see a correspondence about recordings made by
the post-war 'New Symphony Orchestra', said, in all seriousness, to be continuing a
tradition dating back to 1905, in the *Gramophone* (Dec. 1952).

[5] In 1932 Lady Cunard had pronounced the orchestra 'shocking', and Dent feared
Beecham's intervention at Sadlers Wells, 'to the point of unreason': H. Carey, *Duet for Two
Voices* (1979), 134–5. For the 1945 orchestra's reaction to the 'Sea Interludes' in *Peter Grimes*,
see Carpenter, *Benjamin Britten*, (218).

[6] The Lynford–Joel contribution to these concert enterprises with e.g. 'full-scale' concerts
by the 'London International Orchestra', is described, with philistine candour, in J. Joel,
I Paid The Piper (1970). The Tertis letter appeared in the *Daily Telegraph* (29 Jan. 1947).

with some justification, a priority, and 'arms length' subsidies the general rule; nor even by the BBC, whose Symphony Orchestra, despite Boult's protests, was allowed to decline to 'a level of routine competence'.[7] Improvement was hindered by the Musicians Union's insistence upon wage increases and payment for rehearsals: desirable in themselves, such reforms increased costs and discouraged artistic programming. In the prevailing climate of busy mediocrity, initiatives for drastic change came from two experienced and determined men, with separate plans for an orchestra of uncompromising quality and high marketability.

A Glorious Confusion

Walter Legge was a familiar, and unlikely, figure in London music: a ruthless perfectionist, whose unique legacy of recordings is testimony to the level of his taste and achievement.[8] In 1945, released from the job of organizing concerts for ENSA, which had kept him in touch with the country's best instrumentalists, he assembled a prodigious orchestra, administered according to relentless principles.[9] The Philharmonia's sparkling first concert, all Mozart, at the Kingsway Hall on 25 October, was conducted by Beecham, who asked Legge for 'a decent cigar' as fee, and then tried to hijack the orchestra. Since its name was 'ridiculous anyway: no one will remember it', he proposed to rename it 'The Royal Philharmonic', and reimburse 'that august body with a certain participation in the royalties' from recordings.[10] The two men were well matched, so Beecham was sent packing in search of another orchestra to bear the name, to which he attached so much importance, and which he was so confident of acquiring. Both Legge and Beecham had gained sufficient experience of recording studios during the 1930s to place them high in their reckoning of profit, though neither man could have imagined the scale of future prospects. Nor, ironically, given their ultimate domination of the catalogues, did they stand to gain from the first 'long playing' discs, since they were attached to recording companies which clung to obsolete 78 r.p.m. and obsolescent 45 r.p.m. formats. But by the mid-1950s their orchestras were preeminent in a golden age of classical recording, when repertoire, the quality of performance and production, the reputations and earning

---

[7] Kenyon, *BBCSO*, 208,

[8] As a creative record-'producer' Legge had few, if any, rivals. A discography, selected from some 3,500 recordings made between 1932 and 1979, many of which are still being reissued, appears in E. Schwarzkopf, *On and Off the Record: A Memoir of Walter Legge* (1982), 243–88.

[9] They excluded 'passengers', a permanent conductor, and contracts for players. See ibid. 92–3.

[10] Ibid.

power of musicians, and the financial resources of the music industry, were developed internationally, as never before. Even in 1946 the prospects must have been pleasing to anyone with market sense, and an eye to the future.

When Sir Thomas opened formal negotiations with the Society his offer of 'record royalties' was ill-defined, and on a far smaller scale than would later become the norm. And there were other reasons for the Society's representatives to hesitate before entering into fresh association. We know, in retrospect, that he was entering a golden autumn, and would earn even wider renown than in the past. But to some of his contemporaries recollections of past mischief were still fresh, a mercurial public image had not been improved in wartime, and it was a fair guess that the great man, now approaching his seventies, was too old to change his ways.[11] Some members of the committee were therefore likely to have been sceptical, even if they were tempted by the prospect of a return to former glories. Certainly there was cause for confusion, and no commitment to a single orchestra. Five concerts had been 'pencilled' for the LPO, which Beecham had conducted three times in the previous season, and there were additional plans to invite several other orchestras, including some from abroad.[12] Now he had cut loose from his old orchestra, proposed to form yet another one, and was expecting to be granted the name which had been 'openly coveted' but never secured in 1932, despite huge success in mid depression.

On 24 May 1946 he came to put his case, expressing a 'strong desire to create a new orchestra . . . particularly for recordings, for which he had a contract'. He 'sincerely trusted that the Society would lend its old and valued name to the orchestra which he guaranteed would put no financial responsibility upon the Society', apart from the costs of its own concerts. He was 'prepared to give management rights' to the Society, without embroiling it 'in financial obligations'. The committee reacted cautiously at first, with Theodore Holland, still chairman but near the end of long service to the Philharmonic, expressing proper concern about future procedures if or when Beecham could not take charge. There was also some disconnected talk about 'interchange' with the USA and a Delius festival—which took place— and alleged BBC support. But whatever their reservations, the Society's representatives are reported to have reached unanimous agreement after he had left them, and Beecham got the title. In August he turned up again, guaranteeing that each concert would cost no more than £320, and it was decided that a formal agreement should be 'compiled

---

[11] For another sceptical view of Beecham's reputation at this time, see C. Reid, *Thomas Beecham: An Independent Biography* (1961), 229–30.   [12] 48.2/16 (17 Apr. 1946).

by lawyers'. Without further ado the Royal Philharmonic Orchestra was born.[13]

So much for the record of formal meetings. Meanwhile Sir Thomas had been corresponding privately with Keith Douglas. In a handwritten response to what was presumably a lawyer's draft, prepared *before* the decisive committee meeting in August, Beecham shrugged off all restraints, and rejected as 'too prohibitive' any attempt to describe him as 'the only person permitted to conduct the new orchestra'. In order to revive 'the splendour of pre-war days', he proposed to redraft the agreement and 'protect the Society without strangling the orchestra at birth'.[14] Douglas was jocular and reassuring: there was 'actually very little to bother about ... once the band becomes the "RPO" it remains the "RPO" wherever it plays ... under the misdirection of Mr Turtle Dove ... for films or anything else you like'. It was all straightforward and obvious, though 'not maybe to lawyers', declared the Philharmonic's secretary and, dismissing his chairman's reservations—any quibble 'stinks to me a little bit of "Sauce Hollandaise" '—he urged his accomplice to send 'suggestions' for loosening the ties, and thus to complete the *fait accompli*: 'now that we are agreed in principle there is no harm in the name of the band being announced to the public'. Of course there would be

a *glorious* confusion between the RPO and the LPO. I could not care less, nor could I be more amused by what I believe to be a highly entertaining (and satisfactory) outcome of the whole situation. It will probably cost me the hell of a bother, but I am used to this sort of thing, though, 'it may be a good thing that this is my last year as Hon. Secretary to the RPS'.[15]

In this manner the committee was led to apply its rubber stamp on 2 August, and although a later meeting rumbled on about 'absolute right' over use of the name 'in recording, films etc', there was never elucidation, still less formal agreement, about the rights which had been promised. This break with a long tradition of obsessive guardianship was remarkable, and particularly so in the light of past experiences with Beecham. Not that anyone was likely to have consulted the files, where they would have found many examples of sensitivity to intrusion, consultations with lawyers, and subsequent warnings, whenever trespass had been threatened to the Philharmonic's name and image: the archives were still 'evacuated' to Yorkshire, and rationed petrol was not yet available for a journey to recover them. But memories of past dealings, or care for administrative tidiness, might have prompted anxiety to put more 'on paper' about working procedures.

[13] 48.2/16 (24 May and 2 Aug. 1946).   [14] 48.13/38 (15 July 1946).
[15] 48.13/38 (17 July 1946).

That said, both parties stood to gain from the linking of names. The Society could expect to gain from association with an orchestra of brilliance and renown, if only so long as Sir Thomas, much given to travel, stayed alive and close at hand. The committee could acquire similar benefits, without much effort or expenditure, in times of austerity, when the public needed cheering up: a task at which Beecham excelled. In return the new orchestra acquired the prestige of a famous name overnight, just when an instantly recognizable identity was valuable as never before: it may now seem facetious to scoff at 'Philharmonia', but the jibe made sense when Legge needed to build his orchestra's reputation from scratch.

If the Royal Philharmonic alliance held promise, its hazards were conspicuous. Choice of repertoire and artists had always been troublesome when dealing with conductors of spirit, and the committee's ideas, in so far as they could be articulated and agreed, had to survive alongside Beecham's wayward genius: a recipe for incoherence and uncertain identity. The 'glorious confusion', which was Douglas's legacy to the Society, along with £10,000 left in his will, turned out to be neither glorious nor a simple matter of orchestra names. From now on the public would always be confused between a new orchestra and an old society, attributing praise or blame indiscriminately; and its conspiratorial origins was bound to make the alliance uneasy. Although Sir Thomas could never be curbed, an efficient and determined chairman or secretary might have limited damage and maximized benefits by means of promotional and diplomatic skills. 'Public relations' was not yet a profession, and the Philharmonic Society was not alone among contemporary institutions in its innocence of such skills. But it had once boasted a propaganda committee, and several of its past officials had practised the art, which Berger perfected, of making friends and influencing people. How much things had changed was soon demonstrated in the tone of an otherwise trite correspondence. When the office received a complaint from Sheffield about a clash in concert dates, it emphasized that the Society had '*absolutely nothing whatsoever to do*' with the booking; and added a censorious footnote: 'It is perhaps unfortunate that Beecham's new orchestra bears our name . . . but we have no control (as yet) over its outside engagements.'[16]

Unconcernedly Sir Thomas set about building his third and last great orchestra; changing leaders—John Pennington, Oscar Lampe, David McCallum, Arthur Leavins, Raymond Cohen—and recruiting a team of wind-players who were unrivalled anywhere in the world: Gerald Jackson, Terence MacDonagh, Jack Brymer, Gwydion Brooke, and, most famously, Dennis Brain. Again a rich legacy of recordings,

[16] 48.17/1 (8 and 9 Apr. 1947).

including Sir Thomas in rehearsal, documents better than any verbal opinion what was done, and by what means of joking blandishment, acknowledged authority, and limitless vitality, these miracles were achieved.[17]

Methuselah's Plans

Beecham conducted five concerts of the 1946–7 Philharmonic season, on Saturday afternoons at the Albert Hall, beginning with a Delius programme. The RPO also appeared under Nikolai Malko and Clarence Raybould, leaving one concert to the BBCSO, when Boult gave a performance of Tippett's *Concerto for Double String Orchestra*. Finances were described as 'grim' after nearly £1,000 had been lost on the first three concerts, and old habits of skimping were reimposed—deterring concert goers, who in times of austerity might have relished something out of the ordinary. When Malko, a renowned conductor of Shostakovich, requested an additional rehearsal for that composer's Ninth Symphony, he was made to substitute the most hard-ridden of war-horses, Tchaikovsky's Fifth, along with an unremarkable pianist in the Grieg Concerto.[18] Such forlorn decisions did not prevent the Society from requesting support on the grounds of 'adequate rehearsals which cannot be given by the commercial concert promoter'.[19]

Having given its name to a great orchestra, what was there left for the Society to do, if it was to reassert its distinction from other givers of concerts, and attract a constituency and audience as well as public funds? Could it still provide leadership, and if so of what kind? Where could it find new members, and by what forms of allegiance? Giving new life to the constituency would require both numbers and fresh definition, for the old paper credentials of 'professionalism' no longer bore any relation to modern realities in Britain, where a genuine musical renaissance was taking place, with many native performers, and a few composers, capable of winning international recognition.[20] Records of membership, as with most institutions after war's dislocations, were now all but useless, and had to be reassembled. A start was made in December 1947 by striking off eighty-one fellows and six associates, from whom nothing had been heard for more than ten years, but they could not be replaced without much effort.[21] Nor would it be easy to build a stable audience from the enlarged, but

[17] A compact disc issued in 1992 includes rehearsals of Handel–Beecham, Haydn, Mozart, Beethoven, and Liszt between 1951 and 1958.   [18] 48.2/16 (11 Dec. 1946).
[19] 48.17/2 (21 Feb. 1949).
[20] On the extraordinary revolution by which Britain's international trade in performing musicians ceased to be a one-way movement, see Ehrlich, *Music Profession*, 219–32.
[21] 48.2/16 (5 Dec. 1947).

heterogeneous, mass of new music lovers, for Beecham's RPO could be heard elsewhere, without any commitment to the Society. Even more urgent was the necessity of devising financial procedures which were more appropriate than the current reliance on a bank overdraft, paid off by small grants and donations. Losses of £2,500 were anticipated in 1949, with guarantees of £1,000 from the Arts Council, and £600 from private sources. It was also uncomfortable, in the brave new world of State support, to continue asking special favours of esteemed artists: just as in the bad old days, Arrau's agent was beseeched to reduce his fee 'for this honourable and ancient Society, which is passing through a very difficult crisis in its history'.[22]

The circumstances were made brutally clear, with characteristic aplomb and disregard for other people's dignity, by Beecham in a 1949 manifesto.[23] The scope of the Society's activities had become 'unworthy of its high reputation. Eight concerts annually are little more than a minor incident in the swollen and disordered musical life of modern London.' Philharmonic concerts had once been 'the most important of the year', and there was 'no reason why they should not regain that pre-eminence', except that funds were absurdly 'meagre'. Therefore he proposed 'a scheme under which the sum of not less than £100,000 be collected in modest contributions from all those throughout the country who have regard for the maintenance of our oldest musical institution.' Dividends from this investment, plus record royalties, would allow an increase in 1950 to sixteen, and in 1951 to twenty four concerts where 'the greatest works, old and new, will be given under the best possible conditions of performance'. If anyone should ask why such support was still required in an age of state subsidies, the answer was that policy could change at any time, and funds disappear (which happened approximately half a century later). Therefore, Sir Thomas concluded with proprietorial confidence, 'an organization so ancient and honourable as the Royal Philharmonic Society prefers to take the view that it is wiser to address itself to the minority interested in great music than to the majority which is not'.

Means of addressing that interested minority were set out by Sir Ronald Storrs, a retired proconsul and expert on T. E. Lawrence and the Middle East, in a memorandum which may have emanated from Lady Beecham, the pianist Betty Humby.[24] Distributed, at Storrs's request,

---

[22] 48.17/2 (21 Feb. and 12 May 1949).

[23] The manifesto was printed in the programme of Beecham's concert on 27 Apr. 1949, at which, uncharacteristically, he conducted Bach's Fourth 'Brandenburg' and Beethoven's 'Emperor' Concertos, the latter with Julius Katchen as soloist, and Vaughan Williams's *London Symphony*. It received further publicity at his birthday concert, sponsored by the *Daily Telegraph*, the proceeds of which were allotted to the Society's foundation fund.

[24] 48.2/16 (9 Sept. 1949). The Storrs Memorandum is undated: prob. July 1949.

to a dozen committee members and friends 'for favour of opinion and suggestion', its parade of obsolete attitudes and expectations was sufficient stimulus for a rambling and ultimately inconclusive debate. It proposed an appeal for new subscriptions at two levels of payment, the highest to be sought from unprosperous cadres: 5 shillings from members of the Incorporated Society of Musicians and students at the colleges of music—the latter being allowed to get up a concert, and invited to become associates upon graduation—and half that sum from members of the Musicians Union. Hesitant ISM recruits, such as those who could not get to London concerts, would be won over by the prospect of hearing them on the radio; serious musicians in the Union would be drawn by chances of additional employment; while 'dance band members also will like to think that this old Society counts them as musicians; pride or generosity, decency or sentiment is in all entertainers and they usually respond'. Additional half-crowns could also be extracted from players in 'every permanent orchestra', who should in any case become members or associates, for 'it is their duty to support this old Society if they are proud to be British'. Throughout the campaign it would be essential to stress the target of £100,000, in case the subscription required should seem 'insignificant' (one recipient scribbled at this point 'so, of course, it is!'). Concert agents, including 'ambitious newcomers', must be invited to tender for two extra concerts each season, at their own cost, but with artists and repertoire selected by the Society. There would be intense competition for this opportunity to acquire prestige. Further suggestions included rehearsal tickets for pupils at 'private London schools'; record recitals by the Gramophone Company, lectures and debates, all at half a crown a time; an annual Royal Albert Hall Ball, and a quarterly magazine.

Reactions to the proposals ranged from scepticism about likely recruits, particularly from the union's ranks, to outright rejection of the Ball—'please no' and three exclamations of 'NO' were typical comments. Student performances were similarly rejected out of hand, for they should 'not compete in the concert giving market'; as was the proposal to invite impresarios, which would be at best, 'undignified and unwelcome', at worst, an encouragement to 'mushroom managements . . . a mischievous suggestion'. A magazine might be welcome, but would 'make too much work', and lose money, as with similar publications by the Hallé and LPO. A lengthier response was contributed by Hugo Anson, associated with the RCM for more than thirty years, and its Registrar since 1939. His own views are mingled with gossip about 'criticism overheard', not, he stresses, by 'irresponsible critics', but by 'professional musicians who are keen to reaffirm the honourable status of the Society—a status which they feel is sinking'. Here are the obsessions of music's 'academe'—anxiety about institutional, personal,

and 'professional' status—along with some common sense, and a
sprinkle of malice. A groundswell of opinion, Anson claims, wants
the Society to be more independent, applying rules firmly so as to
limit appearances, for example, by individual conductors and soloists:
a reference to Lady Beecham. There should be more 'club feeling', and
concessions to members—a special part of the concert hall reserved to
them, an interval buffet, and opportunities to influence policy. The
question is, 'How does the Society differ from other concert giving
societies? If not, why must we belong?' Philharmonic concerts should
have a more distinctive character, a greater sense of direction and
purpose, 'even at the expense of offending some old faithfuls' (whose
tastes are not specified), or it 'may well fade out'. Since some of the
original reasons for founding the Society had disappeared 'we should
make some new reasons or lapse (God forbid)' because 'we are at
present merely floating without rudder or movement'.[25]

   Similar unease was expressed by a very different representative of
the old guard, a self-taught theatre conductor whose endearing traits
included a fondness for playing chess with his band to relieve the
tedium during performances. Ernest Irving (1878–1953) had raised himself
from pit drudgery to a position of influence in the Ealing film studios,
receiving dedications of work from Rawsthorne, Walton, and Vaughan
Williams, and eventually joining the Society's select list of honorary
members, to his understandable surprise and gratification.[26] A letter to
the critic Richard Capell, copy to the Society, is typically forthright:
'Thomas is our only conductor with the root of the matter in him.
He gained his experience in the ideal way as a wealthy and dictatorial amateur, and we are now reaping the benefit.' Nevertheless, it is
'becoming increasingly difficult for the RPS to find financial or artistic
justification for its "Methuselahsian" career'. It should seek closer links
'with the educational side of musical life', such as a Beecham Mozart
concert linked to the 'epoch making event' of the new Penguin Scores.[27]
That nicely contemporary idea was never taken up, but in his last
years Irving kept trying to persuade the Society to rethink its purpose
and prospects. Members, he believed, should remain 'an inner or select
body', and not be confused with associates and fellows. There would
have to be 'a clear restatement of objects', comparing the founders'
aims with present circumstances. Some traditional functions, such as
giving the first British performances of foreign works, had been taken
over by the far more prosperous BBC, which was obviously better
financed. But, he concluded, Beecham's long service should never be
forgotten, culminating in the provision of the 'best orchestra we ever
had, without cost to the Society'.[28]

---

[25] 48.17/2 (6 Oct. 1950).   [26] E. Irving, *Cue for Music* (1959), esp. chs. 34 and 35.
[27] 48.17/2 (20 July 1949). Penguin Books began to publish cheap miniature scores in
1949. The first was Mozart's Fortieth Symphony.   [28] 48.17/4 (26 Mar. 1952).

The treasurer's views were rather different, and set forth in advance of all other opinions. The Philharmonic, Baker complained, 'did not ask Sir Thomas Beecham' to launch a national appeal, and there was no 'moral right' to do so. Prepared to allow the value of his musical co-operation, he refused to accept 'his leadership in administration. We must remember that neither the Arts Council nor the BBC have ever attempted to dictate a policy' while Sir Thomas had 'never ceased from making attempts'.[29] Without any move towards an alternative policy, discussions were allowed to peter out, and the Society continued to drift, with occasional enlivenment or discomfort from Beecham's turbulence. Like the little boy in *Alice*, who only sneezes to annoy, because 'he knows it teases', he turned up in May 1950 with another grand scheme: to recruit 1,000 fresh subscribers, a committee of 'in-fluential amateurs', and, naughtily, 'a salaried organiser of the first class.' When Herbert Murrill, the BBC's head of music, commented that, in the face of such a scheme, the Society's own committee would become a 'mere appendage' to a 'vigorous orchestra, conductor, and organizing committee', Beecham insisted that he only wished to serve, and that his organization would remain subservient.[30] The next sneeze would earn a beating, and the opportunity came a few months later when Sir Thomas and his orchestra were embarked upon an American tour which drew ecstatic audiences and rapturous reviews everywhere, except for a sour letter to *The Times* from the composer Roy Harris which, registering lofty contempt for a 'steady barrage of hard-hitting advertising and months of very efficient sales organization', asked why English music was absent from the opening concert? One might expect the representative of an English institution to respond, if at all, with a modicum of tact to such a complaint; suggesting, for example, that the vigorous and successful promotion abroad of an exciting new orchestra, in hugely enjoyable programmes, was no bad thing, for Soci-ety or nation; and that English music could be left for another occasion. Instead Baker's letter explained that his organization was neither sponsor for the tour, nor responsible for its policy.[31] Returning home, Sir Thomas agreed to drop this 'unpleasant episode', but suggested that he might receive a letter assuring 'unabated loyalty', which was duly sent.[32]

A week later, home produce attracted few buyers when the BBCSO under Boult offered a symphony commissioned from Rawsthorne, Butterworth's *Shropshire Lad*, and Ireland's Piano Concerto, played by Eileen Joyce. Attendance was similarly poor in January 1951, when Raybould conducted the RPO in a Dvořák symphony, a suite by Gordon Jacob, and Walton's established masterpiece the Viola Con-certo, played superbly by Primrose. Sargent also did his bit with a Purcell Suite, the Fifth Symphony of Vaughan Williams, and *Hymnus*

[29] 48.17/2 (20 July 1949).   [30] 48.2/16 (5 May 1950).
[31] *The Times* (7 and 10 Nov. 1950).   [32] 48.17/4 (12 and 18 Jan. 1951).

Paradisi by Howells, a first London performance. The season had begun both patriotically and well, with Barbirolli bringing his Hallé Orchestra to play Rossini, Delius, the Sibelius Second and Vaughan Williams Sixth Symphonies, and the English composer there to present the Society's second 'Glorious John' with his gold medal. Costs were almost covered by that concert but, despite a common belief, expressed by the *Musical Times*, that not enough had been done in Festival of Britain year, the committee, gloomily looking at its season's accounts, concluded that 'people simply did not want to hear modern English music'.[33] Losses were approximately £2,250, and administrative costs added another £550. The Arts Council contributed £1,500, 'gramophone sales', thanks entirely to Beecham, a significant £1,000, and guarantors were called upon at 50 per cent to meet the balance.[34]

There had been some distancing from the 1951 celebrations because of Beecham's distaste for the Royal Festival Hall: shared by many experienced musicians in those first months of raw acoustic, but declared more vociferously. Nevertheless he was persuaded to open the next season there with a 'typically eclectic and insubstantial programme' which 'for connoisseurs of playing and conducting . . . was a constant delight'.[35] Thereafter responsibilities were shouldered with due seriousness. The next concert, conducted by Cameron and Kennedy Scott, consisted of a Haydn symphony, 'Here's a Health unto His Majesty', 'Ballets, Airs and Madrigals', *Eventyr* by Delius, a carol by Bax, and the first performance of Rubbra's Second Symphony in a revised edition. Succeeding concerts included the once-rejected Britten Violin Concerto (played by Gimpel and conducted by Beecham), John Gardner's First Symphony—the Hallé again with Barbirolli—Delius's *Brigg Fair*, and Iain Hamilton's Clarinet Concerto, which had been awarded a Philharmonic Prize. These efforts earned scant credit. It was necessary, for example, to remind the *News Chronicle* that five concerts had been reviewed without a single mention of the Society.[36] Because such concerts were expensive, an appeal for guarantees was sent out to 'influential firms connected with the world of music', who were assured that their support had been 'for many years a custom'. It was an ill-timed and poorly targeted scheme, unlikely to achieve much success by appealing haphazardly to an uncoordinated industry in process of realignment, where great fortunes would soon be made, but not in the disintegrating world of pianos and traditional publishing.[37]

[33] 48.2/16 (2 Feb. 1951). *MT* (Mar. and July 1951).

[34] 48.2/16 (10 May 1951). 48.17/4 (7 Oct. 1952).

[35] *MT* (Dec. 1951). The programme was: *Mastersingers* Overture, Haydn 'Drum Roll' Symphony, Debussy *Iberia*, Delius *In a Summer Garden*, and Rimsky-Korsakov *Coq d'or*.

[36] 48.17/4 (21 Feb. 1952).

[37] 48.17/4 (20 Sept. 1951). On the late-1950s transformation of the music industry, see Ehrlich, *Harmonious Alliance*, 126–39.

A more general appeal was met by a similarly limp response; even loyal supporters tending to be cordial, rather than munificent. For one it was a 'privilege to support the old Society in her hour of need', and the bust still worked its magic when, in the thrilling Scherzo movement of the Ninth Symphony she 'saw old Beethoven nod his head in approval', and contributed £5. Irving was also rich in sentiment about 'that lovely art which gives wings' and, leaping 'at the chance you give me to continue as a guarantor', enclosed 'my guinea for the 1954 call up'.[38] The flow of funds was quite inadequate for any grand policy, yet, as a letter to subscribers pointed out, the committee did not believe that it could 'justify acceptance' of outside support, when 'many members do not honour their obligations'.[39] Remaining members, in turn, were inclined to reiterate protests at the lack of incentives. When Stravinsky received his gold medal in 1954, a guarantor of 'many years', resigned in protest that it had been presented before 'a casual audience and not in the presence of a full compliment [sic] of our own distinguished members' who, he believed, had been excluded by high prices. In reply he was reminded that tickets for the concert, which was additional to the normal season and conducted by the composer, had been offered with pre-booking privilege for members, and had been priced from 5s to 30s, 'to prevent substantial loss'.[40] If such incidents suggested a distancing between committee and constituency, it may have been reinforced when friends of Albert Sammons reported, a few months later, that England's first great violinist was gravely ill, and suggested that a gold medal would be 'a very fine gesture'. They were told that there would be no more awards for some time.[41]

Finances continued to be grim throughout the 1950s, almost regardless of programmes or artists. A series of choral concerts celebrated the coronation, at huge cost; but even ventures which appeared profitable could mislead observers unacquainted with the economics of modern concert life. So when a prominent critic believed that a large audience for a 'venturesome' concert was evidence of profit, he had to be reminded that a full hall could still bring inadequate box-office receipts, and that adventurousness needed 'heavy subsidy'.[42] The cumulative

[38] 48.17/4 (21 June 1953). Irving's letter, in the same file, is not clearly dated: probably also June 1953. He died in October. His gift to the Society of the Vaughan Williams *Sinfonia antartica* score, earlier that year, after the first London performance, was a valuable bequest.
[39] 48.17/5 (1 Nov. 1954).   [40] 48.17/5 (20 May and 16 June. 1954).
[41] 48.17/5 (30 Oct. 1954). Sammons died in 1957. Subsequent reissues of his recordings, notably the Elgar Concerto, substantiated his claim to be regarded as a great virtuoso in the age of Kreisler and Heifetz: an unprecedented achievement among Englishmen. His colleague Lionel Tertis was more fortunate, receiving the gold medal in 1964, at the age of 88.
[42] 48.17/5 (20 and 21 Jan. 1954). The concert, by Barbirolli and the Hallé, included the first London performance of William Wordsworth's Third Symphony. The unworldly critic was the *Observer*'s Eric Blom.

effects of rising costs and diminishing support from the BBC contributed to a decline so precipitous that, despite such repeated acts of generosity as remission of fees by Barbirolli, Boult, and Myra Hess, to name only the most frequent of benefactors, a mere £6 was left in the bank by December 1957. £2,000 was needed immediately to meet current expenses and the next concert. It was, once again, 'the most serious financial crisis for years', and a committee, asked to contemplate the future, advised a reduction to six concerts a year. The season's deficit was more than £4,000, and life-saving measures included a 100 per cent call on guarantors.[43] In the following year losses were practically halved by the simple process of reducing activity; but concerts included premières of Gerhard's Violin Concerto, again by Gimpel, Vaughan Williams's Ninth Symphony, and Walton's Partita; and two conducted by Beecham. Since the first consisted of Schubert's Third Symphony and Mendelssohn's *Italian Symphony*, followed by Strauss's *Ein Heldenleben*, and the second was devoted to Berlioz's *Grande Messe des Morts*, they would have made an appropriate farewell. But what turned out to be his last concert for the Society, on 8 November 1959, was even more suitably eclectic: Mendelssohn's *The Fair Melusine*, a viola concerto by Ghedini, a ballet suite by Addison, and Beethoven's Seventh Symphony.

Orchestricide

Beecham died on 8 March 1961, and for the next few years the Royal Philharmonic Society's attempts to claw back the name which had been so lightly disposed earned it more intensive publicity, all bad, than at any period of its previous history. What appeared to be at stake by 1964, when the conflict excited wide interest, was not a private matter of an expiring contract, but a public issue of men's livelihood. Names, declared a respected critic, 'can't be given and taken away like telephone numbers: they are a symbol of identity, and should not be bestowed in the first place if liable years later to be revoked'. Disowning an orchestra as 'illegitimate', wrote another, could be regarded as 'tantamount to infanticide', or 'orchestricide'.[44] And the crime was all the more abhorrent because it would follow a similar outrage upon

[43] Declining BBC support: 48.17/4 (28 Nov., 9 and 22 Dec. 1952; 16 Feb. 1953). Financial crisis: 48.2/16 (13 Dec 1957; 7 Mar. 1958). Many e.g.s of artists' generosity are listed in the files, such as Piatigorsky returning his fee for playing the Walton Cello Concerto in Feb. 1957. A typical letter of thanks to Boult for conducting without fee is in 48.17/5 (20 Apr. 1956).
[44] 'Well, what's in a name?': Desmond Shawe-Taylor in *Sunday Times* (1 Nov. 1964). 'Orchestricide': *New Statesman* (23 Oct. 1964).

another orchestra. It is instructive to compare the Philharmonic Society's prolonged frustrations with Legge's abrupt dismissal of the Philharmonia in 1964, a deeper cut and separation than any mere change of name. With fateful symmetry the life-span of both orchestras seemed destined to coincide. Then within a few months, and after only short bursts of acrimony, the Philharmonia was born anew, to be called New Philharmonia until, with time's erosion, the prefix could be forgotten. The RPO separation, much less of an uprooting, degenerated into so lengthy and tortuous a controversy, that no account, even thirty years after the events, is likely to satisfy every reader: many of the participants are still alive and, at periodic intervals since 1964, questions of orchestral survival have become too much a cause for public concern to be relegated to history.

Legge later claimed to have been worrying about the Philharmonia's future since 1961, but his departure in 1964 was uncluttered by committee indecisions.[45] The Society, with much less of an orchestral involvement or responsibility, but lacking resolution, or ruthlessness, dithered and agonized over and beyond the same period of time—initially out of inertia and goodwill; later with intentions more muddled than malign—and even in the decisive months betrayed uncertainties about dispossession. So its undoubted right to declare a parting of the ways was battered by words, at every level of knowledge, sophistication, and benevolence, which sought to castigate, elucidate, and advise. Even the *Daily Mirror*'s celebrated columnist Cassandra had an opinion.[46] Although the RPO's original naming had been achieved in cloak and dagger style, and a lawyer's search in 1963 could find no written agreement for its launch in 1946, there was never any doubt that the Society's acquiescence—we have seen that it was rarely ever more than that—in the use of its name had always been completely dependent upon Beecham's presence; and a document to that effect was renewed each year. Thus, in July 1956 such a document was signed by Norman E. Millar, director of the Anglo-American Music Association, and by D. Ritson Smith, secretary of the Society, and contained the following clause:

The said Orchestra will perform only under the name of the Royal Philharmonic Orchestra otherwise than under the aegis of the Royal Philharmonic Society's Committee of Management in the following circumstances:—
(a) at concerts conducted by Sir Thomas Beecham, Bart.
(b) At any series of concerts or musical festivals or season of opera or ballet under the acknowledged artistic control of Sir Thomas Beecham, Bart., and organized by him.

---

[45] Legge's account of these events appears in Schwarzkopf, *Legge*, 103–6.
[46] Cassandra, 'By Royal Appointment', *Daily Mirror* (20 Aug. 1964).

(c) At such other musical performances of which the said Sir Thomas Beecham may be the organiser and/or acknowledged principal conductor.[47]

When Beecham died there was no hurry to disengage, but the link was 'discussed at length' at a committee meeting in May 1961, and it was resolved to seek a 'clearer picture' by asking Lady Beecham about the RPO's artistic direction and future policy. On 7 July Baker specifically said that there was no hurry to proceed, and on 22 September a colleague failed to persuade him to more resolute action. A year later, in November 1962, he informed the committee that he had resigned as a director of the orchestra, unhappy about its policy and debts to the Society, and had written to the Home Office about the impending break.[48] Even this was a weirdly indecisive letter, claiming that the title was an 'anomaly' for an orchestra which had 'lost its links, both artistic and sentimental' with the Society, yet going on to explain that the same orchestra had been booked for two 150th anniversary concerts, including one to commemorate the date of the Philharmonic's inauguration in 1813. Its lame conclusion was that the title should be retained until the end of the 1962/3 season, and then removed 'in the light of the completely changed conditions'.[49] Presumably the orchestra was expected to play along, in the interim, and then melt into oblivion, or adopt some other name. Certainly it was unhappy with its existing management, sending a round-robin letter of complaint to the Society on 27 November. Later it reported that there had been improvements, and asked for a further extension until the end of the 1964 Glyndebourne season, which the Society granted on 1 July 1963.

These comings and goings were no secret. The *Annual Register*, wearily summarizing a year of depression and half-filled concert halls, reported that initial 'dissension between the RPO and Lady Beecham', the resignation of Rudolf Kempe (Beecham's most respected colleague), and retirement of Lady Beecham, had been followed by the orchestra's reconstruction as a self-governing organization, Kempe's return, and a grant from the Musicians' Union.[50] In February 1964 the orchestra asked

---

[47] Subsequent agreements, with the identical clause, were signed in 1957 and 1958 by Millar and Leslie Regan.

[48] Committee of Management Minutes (2 Nov. 1962) (post-1960 records are held by the Society). This meeting also agreed to appoint a public relations consultant, part-time and honorary.

[49] Baker to Under-Secretary of State, Home Office (22 Oct. 1962). The concert on 8 Mar. 1963, in the presence of the Queen Mother, was conducted by Boult and consisted of Cherubini's *Anacréon* Overture, Sibelius's Seventh Symphony, Walton's Hindemith Variations (written in honour of the occasion), and Beethoven's Fifth Symphony. Other celebratory concerts were given by the Hallé (Barbirolli), Royal Liverpool Philharmonic (Monteux), New York Philharmonic (Bernstein), and Vienna Philharmonic (Karajan, with the great Philharmonia Chorus in Beethoven's Ninth Symphony).   [50] *Annual Register* (1963).

for further, possibly unlimited, extensions of time, with proposals for mutual benefit; and on 19 March sent its representatives to a meeting to discuss royalties. But it also launched a world-wide appeal which flooded the Society's modest office with pleas and protests, in letters and cables from orchestras, great and small, record companies, conservatories and universities, famous composers, conductors and instrumentalists, ordinary musicians, concert goers and members of the Society, in Britain, Australasia, Canada, and particularly in the United States, where Beecham's orchestra had made so many friends. The deluge was orchestrated, of course, with brilliance and dedication, by James Brown, an RPO player, campaigning from his 'kitchen table'. But among hundreds of communications there is no mistaking a pained sincerity of response, a stunned fear of 'immeasurable loss'—one writer thought it a final abdication of culture to Presley and the Beatles—a devotion to the memory of Sir Thomas and, in one American Anglophile's phrase, his 'Queen's Own' band.

The clamorous platform was now joined by a large and vociferous choir. In addition to those directly involved, and the usual musical commentators, there were two successive Home Secretaries—an election intervened in mid-chorus—and every kind of devotee, newfound enthusiast, columnist, and busybody. Among them was a politician and media personality of considerable self-importance, turned orchestral chairman, who had, 'one night . . . an inspiration', and wrote to the Queen Mother, who 'saved the orchestra' by becoming its patron.[51] Baker was still representing the Society in meetings at the Home Office, and talking darkly of action in the High Court, though a taste for litigation was fortunately not among his failings. Sir Thomas Armstrong took over later, with calmer effect. Extensive reports and commentary in the press were almost universally condemnatory, and not abated when the Society issued a statement of its case in March, which was ignored by the press, but sent out to members in May.[52] The *Annual Register* for 1964 again tried to freeze-frame a murky picture: a Conservative Home Secretary had ruled against continuance of title, but apparently without legal power 'to enforce protocol'; and at the

---

[51] R. J. Boothby, *Boothby: Recollections of a Rebel* (1978), 190–1. The same belief is expressed in R. Rhodes-James, *Bob Boothby* (1991), 404–5.

[52] See letter from Stravinsky (who had been recording with the orchestra) and a few other musicians in *The Times* (30 June) and Baker's pained reply (4 July); a dignified letter of remonstrance from Arrau in *The Times* (8 Aug. and others on 14 and 29 Aug.); 'Murder Plot Against Orchestra', and editorial comment in the *Daily Telegraph* (20 Aug.), and subsequent apology; a letter from Lord Somers in the *Sunday Times* (10 Oct). 'Title Fight', in *Music and Musicians*, (Oct. 1964), and an extensive autumn correspondence in *The Times* and *Daily Telegraph*. There were also several broadcasts, and a fierce pamphlet, printed and widely distributed.

end of the year his Labour successor had agreed to another six months' extension, pending further discussion. The press and general public eventually lost interest as the debate continued without resolution for many more months, sometimes in high places: Harold Wilson held brief consultation with the Musicians' Union. A battle-fatigued committee was, at one stage, even faced by the possibility, encouraged by the Home Office, of newly active participation in running the orchestra. Whatever the attractions of such conciliatory machinery in government circles, at a time when a 'beer and sandwiches' approach to industrial relations was fashionable, it could have been disastrous for the Society. Any formal association would have imposed burdens of cost and inflexibility, far in excess of existing levels of funding and administrative capacity. Amicably separate paths were a better compromise. The orchestra retained its title in its own right and in 1967 was happy to receive twenty-first birthday congratulations from the Society.

There were no further outbreaks of orchestricide, though the theory and practice of culling were expatiated at regular intervals. The only 'sensible way foward', declared a 1976 report, recalling an analysis by Peacock in 1970, was 'to phase out one or more of the orchestras' and give the remainder much higher subsidies.[53] It was never done and, as I write in December 1993, is again being contemplated, denounced, and abandoned.

Another Recovery

'Survival is not enough', proclaimed *The Times* in a 150th birthday message. 'Past, present and future' all required that the Society should 'rise above commercial competition, perhaps unite the competitors', and 'lead musical taste forward on the broadest level. That is its heritage and its only worthwhile destiny.'[54] With unlimited funding, an ominiscient committee, and Francesco Berger as secretary, the Philharmonic would still have been hard put to satisfy such requirements. Leading musical tastes ceased to be an acceptable pursuit. In an age of cultural relativism and unlimited access to all kinds of music, any attempt to provide determined leadership was only likely to arouse antagonism and polarize tastes, particularly if new music was espoused. By the late twentieth century, in stark contrast to its beginning, virtually nothing new had been assimilated into the repertoire of orchestral concerts for three decades.

[53] Lord Redcliffe-Maud, *Support for the Arts in England and Wales: A Report to the Calouste Gulbenkian Foundation* (1976), 124; A. Peacock, *Orchestral Resources in Great Britain* (Arts Council, 1970).

[54] 'Britain's Oldest and Most Exalted Musical Society', *The Times* (25 Jan. 1963).

The most determined attempt to lead taste was made by William Glock, who, as the BBC's Controller of Music between 1959 and 1973, tried to push 'British musical life out of the provincialism into which it had fallen'. He transformed the Proms, enlivened the BBCSO and attempted to reshape the repertoire, waging war against moribund tradition or, so enemies declared, against music which was tuneful, tonal, or simply British.[55] The Philharmonic was never in a position to embark upon such adventures; but, following the 1964 débâcle, as after every previous crisis in its history, it proved to be capable of doing rather more than survive. Progress required attention to administration, funding, and eventually to a reassessment of constituency and function. The committee was strengthened, first by such expert board room practitioners as Leslie Boosey and Wilfred Greenhouse Allt, and increasingly by men with practical experience of active music-making.[56] The latter were recruited both from within the Society, and as representatives of associated institutions. Thus John Denison, similar in background and experience to some of the Philharmonic's founders— he played the horn in various London orchestras during the 1930s— joined the committee in 1950 as an 'observer' from the Arts Council.[57] In the early 1960s George Baker was chairman and treasurer, with Myers Foggin as co-treasurer, and Leslie Regan honorary secretary, assisted by the long-serving administrative secretary Mrs Sylvia East. Established members included Sir Thomas Armstrong, Julian Herbage, and Dr William Cole; with Leslie Boosey and Mrs E. Tillett (the concert agent) as fellows' representatives. T. Ernest Bean, in charge of South Bank concert halls, represented the London County Council, John Cruft the British Council, John Denison the Arts Council, and Eric Warr the BBC. By 1970 Baker, Boosey, Cole, Foggin, and Herbage had been joined by such musicians as John Gardner, Anthony Lewis, Angus Morrison, and Peter Stadlen. Denison represented the Greater London Council, and other co-opted members included John Cruft, Barrie Iliffe, and for a while the avant-garde's most articulate advocate, Hans Keller. The full committee, numbering upwards of fifteen members, was no longer lacking in diversity of knowledge and opinion, though coherent policy may have been elusive.

Funding difficulties were enormously increased by steep rises in costs, and therefore in the risks attached to enterprising programmes. One example must suffice to illustrate a relentless trend. In 1967 the Society presented its gold medal to Kodály, and mounted a 'Tribute' consisting

---

[55] W. Glock, *Notes in Advance* (1991).

[56] The career of Leslie Boosey is extensively discussed in my *Harmonious Alliance*, esp. 108–9, 124–5, and 145–6. Dr Wilfred Greenhouse Allt (1889–1969), organist and examiner, listed in *Who's Who* some twenty organizations of which he was a member, usually as chairman or president.   [57] 48.2/16 (2 June 1950).

of the Te Deum, *Psalmus Hungaricus*, and *Háry János* Concert Suite, with
the RPO, four soloists, and various choirs, conducted by Dorati. A
major artistic undertaking and achievement, of precisely the kind expected from the Philharmonic, and applauded in the *Annual Register*, it
was also a financial disaster, losing more than £4,000. The rest of that
exemplary season included a Mozart–Stravinsky concert conducted by
Colin Davis; Boult and Brendel in Holst, Beethoven, and Mahler;
Boulez conducting Messiaen, Varèse, and Boulez; the Prague Symphony Orchestra; and Barbirolli's Hallé in Rawsthorne, Schoenberg
(*Pelleas and Melisande*) and Beethoven's Seventh Symphony. Total losses
exceeded £10,000, which had to be met by removing £2,500 from the
foundation fund and securing a large guarantee from the London
Orchestral Board, the organization through which Arts Council funds
were now distributed. During the following decade inflation was much
worse, one index for music estimating a threefold increase between
1970 and 1980.[58] The fees commanded by 'star' conductors were rising
absurdly fast, and becoming strategic to much concert planning.[59]
Since the Society's conductors had usually received less than its soloists,
and often gave their services free, this was a disturbing trend. And
mounting dissatisfaction with new music was now imposing insuperable
burdens upon those who aspired to lead tastes. 'Lack of communication between avant garde concerts and the public remained as great
as ever'; so, with ticket prices increasing, and music at home ever more
attractive, concert-goers simply avoided 'programmes of works which
they feared they would neither understand nor enjoy'.[60]

Yet the Philharmonic was still capable of marking its 175th anniversary with an ambitious series of concerts, linking past glories with
present achievements. There were visits by the Montreal, Paris, and
Leipzig Gewandhaus Orchestras, the latter, under Kurt Masur, reopen-
ing the revered Mendelssohn connection.[61] There were performances
of Beethoven's Ninth Symphony and Verdi's Requiem, and such Philharmonic standards as the Dvořák Cello Concerto, played by Ros-
tropovich, the Tchaikovsky Violin Concerto, by Perlman, and the Elgar
Concerto, in a reading by Nigel Kennedy which held even the *Musical
Times* critic 'spellbound'. Native capabilities of ensemble were demonstrated by the English Chamber Orchestra, joined by Evelyn Glennie
in a Milhaud concerto, and Felicity Lott in Britten's *Les Illuminations*;

[58] A. Peacock, E. Shoesmith, and G. Milner, *Inflation and the Performed Arts* (Arts Council,
1982), table 3.3.
[59] An e.g. which aroused wide comment was the cancellation of a Brighton Festival
concert because the conductor insisted on a fee of £2,000. Karajan, it was said, would have
required at least twice as much. *Annual Register* (1976).   [60] Ibid. (1975).
[61] In 1992 the Society became closely associated with Kurt Masur's campaign to save
Mendelssohn's house in Leipzig.

20. 175th anniversary: the Society's Patron examines the manuscript score
of Beethoven's Ninth Symphony, 8 March 1988

and by Simon Rattle's thoroughly rehearsed Birmingham Orchestra in Sibelius and Mahler. The first movement of Beethoven's 'Tenth Symphony', completed by Barry Cooper, received its world première. Lutoslawski, after a performance of his Third Symphony, was presented with the gold medal by Tippett. Special commissions included *Title Divine* by Geoffrey Burgon, and Panufnik's Ninth Symphony which, it was said, evoked 'no direct comparison' with a previously commissioned ninth, but was 'no divertimento either'.[62] Such activity was made possible by continuing public funding, and by access to newly fashionable business sponsorship. When the Arts Council abruptly withdrew its support in 1987, long after Beecham's sour prediction, the Society, in debt because of inescapable commitments, was left dependent upon continued access to such volatile sources of finance, and upon its own resources.

Among the latter nothing matched the importance of its artistic reputation and the attendant goodwill of musicians as, for the ump-teenth time, it proceeded to *reculer pour mieux sauter.* It was symbolic, perhaps, that the immediate financial crisis was met by selling to the British Library, for £600,000, a set of Haydn symphonies which had been purchased for rather less from Ayrton in 1847. The longer term would need organization—belated appointment of a professional ad-ministrator in 1990 was an essential step—and reappraisal of mem-bership and function. The Society could continue, without much expense, to exercise its right to bestow honours and awards, which would always be coveted so long as they were recognized as a profession's tributes to achievement and promise. In concert life the Society's most effective, and often quietest, patronage had always come from musicians: orches-tra and soloists giving their services below market rates, or free; such artists as Mendelssohn, Clara Schumann, Joachim, Kreisler, and Casals bestowing limitless musicianship, wise counsel, and prestige; great con-ductors taking no fee, even paying for rehearsals, as a matter of course; great composers burnishing the medal by receiving it. The first Phil-harmonic carried a name and reputation; and so long as the two were kept in harness it could, as ever, survive.

---

[62] Calum MacDonald in *Tempo*, 161/22 (Sept. 1987), 107.

Appendix 1

The Evolution of the Repertoire
Number of Works Performed Every Five Years

Note: Each figure gives the total number of performances for a period of five years, ending in the year stated. For most of the nineteenth century the season consisted of eight concerts within a calendar year; and the tables therefore fit precisely. Later seasons usually ran from winter to next spring, and the number of concerts sometimes varied. In order to make comparisons possible over a long period, the tables ignore such changes and continue to count performances by calendar years.

SYMPHONIES

5 years ending	Composer								Others
	Beeth.	Mozart	Haydn	Mendn.	Schub.	Spohr	Tchaik.	Brahms	
1817	14	16	27						16 (Ries 6, Clementi 3, Woelfl 2)
1822	19	23	23						16 (Ries 9, Clementi 4)
1827	33	17	22			3			5 (Romberg 2)
1832	30	18	20	2		2			4
1837	30	16	14	3		5			8 (Potter 4)
1842	32	16	14	1		7			5
1847	35	13	11	5		8			5
1852	34	14	9	9		5			3
1857	32	10	6	8		5			3
1862	32	12	9	8		5			7
1867	31	10	8	9		3			8
1872	32	9	7	9	4	3			12
1877	25	6	4	6	2			1	10 (Schum. 3)
1882	18	4	4	2	4			1	10 (Schum. 2)
1887	9	2	2	3	1	2		3	13 (Schum. 2)
1892	11	4	4	1	3			1	12 (Dvořák 2, Schum. 1, Cowen 1)
1897	10	2	2	3	1		3	3	9 (Schum. 3, Dvořák 1, Cowen 1)
1902	10	2	2		1		5	4	9 (Schum. 1)
1907	6	2	1		1		3	4	14 (Schum. 3, Dvořák 1)
1912	9	2			3		5		14 (Schum. 3, Franck 3, Dvořák 2)
1917	4	3					3		11 (Schum. 3, Elgar 2, Dvořák 1, Sib. 1)
1922	6	1	1				3	3	4 (Elgar 2)
1927	6	3	1					2	9 (Elgar 2, VW 2)
1932	4	3	3		4		3	3	8 (Dvořák 2, Bax 2)
1937	12	6	7		5		3	8	21 (Sib. 8, Schum. 3, Dvořák 3, Berlioz 2, Elgar 2, VW 2)
1942	8	12	6				3	5	23 (Sib. 6, Dvořák 4, Schum. 2, Moeran 2)
1947	7	6	4		3		4	5	13 (Sib. 4, Dvořák 2, VW 2)
1952	5	7	5		1		4	5	21 (Sib. 6, VW 5, Dvořák 2, Rubbra 2)
1957	10	5	3	2	4			5	23 (VW 3, Sib. 2, Elgar 2)
1962	4	4	5	2	3		1	2	19 (Mahler 3, Sib. 2, VW 2, Bruckner 2)
1967	5	3	4					5	18 (Sib. 5, Berlioz 2, Dvořák 2, Bruckner 2)
1972	3	2	4		1			1	19 (VW 3, Bruckner 2, Walton 2, Shostak. 2)
1977	3	5			2			2	14 (Bruckner 3, Shostak. 2, Tippett 2)

OVERTURES

5 years ending	Composer									Others
	Beeth.	Cherub.	Mozart	Weber	Spohr	Mendn.	Rossini	Stern. Benn.	Wagner	
1817	10	21	14							28
1822	19	19	10							24
1827	14	15	9	14						24
1832	11	12	5	18						18
1837	10	12	4	23			2			16
1842	8	9	5	21	9	4		3		21
1847	10	11	3	25	5	6		2		8
1852	9	10	5	22	5	8	2	1		14
1857	7	6	4	19	7	7	1	1	2	13
1862	8	7	3	23	6	8	2	2	1	5
1867	6	4	2	22	7	12	4	5	1	12
1872	8	6	4	16	5	11	2	4	3	13 (Schub. 2)
1877	7	3	4	17	1	6	2	5	6	15 (Berlioz 2)
1882	7	2	4	14	3	12	2	4	4	21 (Schum. 3, Sull. 3, Dvořák 3)
1887	6	1	2	5	5	13		2	10	20
1892	5	2	3	6	4	8	1		5	18 (Sull. 2)
1897	7	1		5	1	5		3	4	23 (Sull. 5)
1902	3	1		2		5			5	15 (Sull. 2)
1907	2	3				3			2	17 (Elgar 3, Sull. 2)
1912	3		1	2		5			6	14 (Tchaik. 2)
1917	1		5	1		2	1			14
1922	2			1		1	1		4	9
1927	4		2	4		2				9 (Berlioz 2)
1932	2		2			1	2		2	15
1937	3		1	4		1	7		5	11 (Berlioz 3)
1942	2			2		1			2	9
1947			1	3		3				16 (Berlioz 6)
1952	2		6	1		2	3		5	14 (Berlioz 5)
1957	3		2	1		3	1		1	10 (Berlioz 2, Walton 2)
1962	4		1	1		1	1		4	6 (Berlioz 4)
1967	2	1		1		1	1		1	7 (Berlioz 2)
1972	3					2			1	9 (Elgar 2, Holst 2)
1977	4			1		3			1	4

CONCERTOS

5 years ending	Composer						Others	
	Beeth.	Mozart	Schum.	Mendn.	Brahms	Tchaik.		
1817	2						6	
1822	2	1					17	
1827	1	4					22	(Mosch. 4, Hummel 3)
1832	7	2					21	(Mosch. 3, Hummel 2)
1837	4	2					31	(Mosch. 3, Hummel 3, Spohr 3, Weber 2)
1842	9	1		4			37	(Stern. Benn. 4, Hummel 3, Weber 3, Mosch. 2)
1847	7	1		4			40	(Spohr 9, Stern. Benn. 4, Vieuxtemps 3, Weber 2)
1852	9	4	2	5			27	(Spohr 4, Weber 2)
1857	8		5	7			22	(Spohr 4)
1862	9	1	4	7			28	(Spohr 7, Stern. Benn. 4, Hummel 2)
1867	6	4	5	6			22	(Spohr 7, Stern. Benn. 3, Weber 2)
1872	13	1	3	8			28	(Spohr 4, Stern. Benn. 3, Weber 2)
1877	9	1	3	6			22	(Spohr 2, Liszt 2, Rubin. 2)
1882	12		4	6	3		21	(Spohr 4, Bruch 2)
1887	9	2	1	5			15	(Bruch 2, Chopin 2, Dvořák 2)
1892	10	1	3	3	2		21	(Bruch 4, Rubin. 3, Chopin 2, Liszt 2, Grieg 2)
1897	8		3	3	1	4	30	(Bruch 3, St-Saëns 3, Weber 2, Dvořák 2, Grieg 2)
1902	7	1	2	2	2	3	24	(Liszt 5, Bruch 2, Chopin 2)
1907	6	2	1	2		4	29	(St-Saëns 6)
1912			2		3	2	25	(Liszt 4, Chopin 4, St-Saëns 3, Elgar 2)
1917	2		2		3	2	16	(Bach 2, Liszt 2, Franck 2, St-Saëns 2)
1922	3		1	1	2	1	20	(Bach 2, Delius 2)
1927	4	3	2		2		15	(Handel 2)
1932	5	7			2	2	23	(Bach 6, Elgar 2)
1937	5	7			3		28	(Bach 4, Dvořák 2)
1942	9	5	2		3		19	(Bach 3, Rachman. 2)
1947	2	5			2		16	(Prokofiev 2)
1952	1	1			4		16	
1957	4	2	1		1		10	(Walton 2)
1962	5	2			4		20	(Dvořák 2, Rachman. 2, Bartók 2, Berkeley 2)
1967	2	4	1		1	2	14	(Bartók 2)
1972	6	6	1		4	2	16	(Bartók 3, Shostak 2, Musgrave 2)
1977	6	6	1		3	1	16	(Bartók 3, Bach 3, Chopin 3, Vivaldi 2)

TONE-POEMS, RHAPSODIES, VARIATIONS, etc.

5 years ending	Composer										
	Liszt	Wagner	Tchaik.	Strauss	Rimsky.	Elgar	Sib.	Debussy	Delius	Strav.	Others
1902		4	3								16
1907		3	2	3	1						19 (Stanford 3)
1912	4	3	2	4	4	4	2	1	2		20
1917	2	1	1	4	3	2	1	1	7		32
1922	1	3		2	4	6		8	4	4	35 (Ravel 2)
1927		4		3	2	4	1	3	2	1	27 (Ravel 4)
1932		1		6		2	1	2	7	2	27 (Berlioz 3)
1937	1			4	1	2	4	4	12	2	30 (Berlioz 3, Dvořák 3, Ravel 2)
1942		1	2	3	1	4	5	8	6		30 (Brahms 2, Dvořák 2)

Appendix 2

Commissions, Dedications, and Probable First Performances

Notes: Entries refer to probable first performances in England, unless otherwise indicated. Information is drawn mainly from printed programmes, supplemented by the Society's archives, and contemporary critical comment. The programmes, particularly for early years, often fail to distinguish various categories: world première; first performance in England, London, or at the Philharmonic. Since individual works are sometimes imprecisely named, merely stating Symphony, Concerto, etc., this list is therefore tentative. Further research will doubtless reveal false attributions, and perhaps some additional first performances. Square brackets have been used to indicate claims which are known to be uncertain and identifications which are suggested, rather than probable.

Key: D = Commissioned by, or dedicated to, the Society
W = World première
L = First performance in London

1814

W	Ries: Symphony (14 Feb.)*
	L. G. Griffin: String Quartet (28 Feb.)
WD	L. Berger: Overture (18 Apr.)
W	Ries: Symphony
	Asioli: Symphony (2 May)
W	Crotch: Symphony [in F] (16 May)
[W]D	Cherubini: Overture (30 May)

1815

W	Kalkbrenner: Septet for piano, strings, and wind (13 Mar.)
WD	Cherubini: Overture in G (3 Apr.)
W	Ries: Piano Quintet in D, Op. 74 (17 Apr.)
WD	Cherubini: Symphony in D (1 May)
WD	Ries: Symphony (15 May)
W	Fiorillo: Overture

1816

WD	Ries: Bardic Overture (26 Feb.)
WD	Klengel: Piano Quintet
WD	Potter: Overture (11 Mar.)
WD	Ries: Symphony [No. 3 in E flat] (25 Mar.)
	Beethoven: Overture [Namensfeier]
	Beethoven: Symphony No. 5 (15 Apr.)
WD	Müller: Clarinet Quintet
WD	J. F. Burrowes: Overture
WD	Cherubini: Cantata *La Primavera* (29 Apr.)
WD	Clementi: Symphony
WD	Potter: Septet for piano, flute, and strings
WD	Fémy: Symphony [in E minor]

1817

	Beethoven: Overture *Fidelio* (24 Feb.)
W	Ries: Sextet in C for piano and strings, Op. 100 (28 Apr.)
D	Burghersh: Symphony (26 May)
	Beethoven: Symphony No. 7 (9 June)[+]

1818

	Hummel: Septet (23 Feb.)
	Spontini: Trio, 'E Ver—gli dissi' (9 Mar.)

* The printed programmes claim more first performances of symphonies by Ries than the list of his works allows. Some must have been repetitions. See C. Hill, *Ferdinand Ries, A Thematic Catalogue* (Armidale, NSW, 1977).

[+] The programme does not claim this as a first performance in England, but it is the first at which Beethoven's Seventh Symphony is identified by key. Unspecified Beethoven symphonies are listed in previous programmes, so there may have been an earlier première. See Ch. 1 n. 1.

W   Ries: Symphony (13 Apr.)
W   Sor: Aria (11 May)
       Mozart: Concert aria 'Ch'io mi scordi di te' (8 June)

1819

W   Clementi: Symphony (1 Mar.)
W   R. Lindley: Trio for violin and two cellos (19 Apr.)
WD   Ries: *Scena* 'Sia luminoso', WoO 79 (26 Apr.)
W   J. B. Cramer: Piano Concerto [No. 8 in D minor] (10 May)

1820

[W]   Spohr: Symphony [No. 2 in D minor] (10 Apr.)
       Beethoven: Piano Concerto [No. 1 in C] (8 May)
       Spohr: Symphony [No. 1 in E flat] (19 June)

1821

       Mozart: Piano Concerto in D, K.451 (12 Mar.)
WD   Spohr: Overture [in F]
WD   Bochsa: Septet for harp, wind, and double bass (28 May)
       [Moscheles: Piano Concerto (11 June)]

1822

       Hummel: Piano Concerto [in A minor] (25 Feb.)
                 Piano Concerto in B minor (29 Apr.)
       Kalkbrenner: Symphony
       A. Romberg: Overture Don Mendoza
       Mazas: Overture Corinne au Capitole (13 May)
W   Ries: Symphony
       Moscheles: Piano Concerto [No. 2 in E flat] (10 June)
L   Rossini: *Scena* 'Ogetto amabile'

1823

       Beethoven: Overture Die Weihe des Hauses (21 Apr.)
W   Clementi: Symphony

1824

       Beethoven: Piano Concerto No. 3 in C minor (8 Mar.)
W   Clementi: Overture (22 Mar.)
[W]   Kalkbrenner: Piano Concerto (7 June)

1825

       Weber: Overture *Euryanthe* (21 Feb.)
       Beethoven: Piano Concerto No. 4 in G (7 Mar.)
D   Symphony No. 9 (21 Mar.)
       Spontini: Overture *Olympia* (11 Apr.)
       Weber: Piano Concerto [No. 2 in E flat]
       Onslow: Overture *L'Alcalde de la Vega* (9 May)

1826

W Potter: Symphony [No. 1 in G minor] (29 May)

1827

    Maurer: Violin Concerto (5 Mar.)
W Schloesser: Overture (7 May)

1828

W Griesbach: Overture (28 Apr.)

1829

W Mendelssohn: Symphony No. 1 in C minor (with Scherzo from Octet orchestrated as movement 3 (25 May)

1830

    Rossini: Overture *William Tell* (15 Mar.)

1831

W Spohr: Overture *Der Alchymist* (6 June)

1832

WD Neukomm: Septet (Fantasia Concertante) for wind and double bass (12 Mar.)
    Mendelssohn: Overture Fingal's Cave (14 May)
            Piano Concerto No. 1 in G minor (28 May)
D Onslow: Symphony (18 June)

1833

WD J. B. Cramer: Piano Quintet in B flat (11 Mar.)
WD Moscheles: Grand Septet for piano, strings, clarinet, and horn (15 Apr.)
WD Mendelssohn: Symphony No. 4 in A, *Italian* (13 May)
WD Hummel: Piano Concerto in F (27 May)
WD Neukomm: *Fantasia drammatica on 'Paradise Lost'* (27 May)
WD Potter: Symphony in A minor
WD Mendelssohn: Trumpet Overture in C (10 June)

1834

WD H. R. Bishop: Cantata *The Seventh Day* (3 Mar.)
WD V. Novello: Dramatic Cantata *Rosalba* (17 Mar.)
WD Horsley: Motet Exultabo Te (7 Apr.)
    Mendelssohn: Overture Fair Melusine
W Moscheles: Piano Concerto No. 6 in B flat, 'Fantastique'
[WD Griesbach: Overture *Belshazzar's Feast*] (7 Apr.)
WD Mendelssohn: Concert aria 'Infelice', Op. 94 (19 May)

1835

W	Spohr: Symphony No. 4, *Die Weihe der Töne* (23 Feb.)
W	Maurer: Symphony (6 Apr.)
WD	Herz: Piano Concerto in D minor (8 June)

1836

	Mendelssohn: Overture Calm Sea and Prosperous Voyage (22 Feb.)
[W]	Lachner: Symphony in E flat (25 Apr.)
[W]	Bennett: Piano Concerto in C minor (25 Apr.)
WD	Bishop: Cantata *The Departure from Paradise* (6 June)

1837

L	Onslow: Symphony in A (27 Feb.)
	Ries: Overture L'Apparition (13 Mar.)
W	Potter: Overture *Cymbeline* (3 Apr.)
	Mozart (attrib.): Introduction and Fugue, KAnh.A52 (15 May)
[W	Bennett: Overture The Naiads (29 May)]

1838

L	Mendelssohn: Piano Concerto No. 2 in D minor (5 Mar.)
	Mayseder: Violin Concertino No. 2
W	Hausmann: *Concertino Dramatique* for cello and orchestra (23 Apr.)
	[Bennett: Piano Concerto No. 4 in F minor] (18 June)

1839

W	Moscheles: Piano Concerto No. 8 in D, 'Pastorale' (18 Mar.)
	[Bennett: Overture The Wood Nymphs] (22 Apr.)

1840

W	Reissiger: Overture *Yelva* (9 Mar.)
[W]	Spohr: Symphony No. 5 in C minor
	Symphony No. 6 in G, *Historical* (6 Apr.)
	[Joseph Strauss: Symphony in E flat] (8 June)

1841

L	Berlioz: Overture *Benvenuto Cellini* (15 Mar.)
L	Mendelssohn: Symphony No. 2, *Lobgesang* (15 Mar.)

1842

	Molique: Violin Concerto (18 Apr.)
	Alvars: Fantasia for harp
W	Molique: Symphony in D (16 May)
	Spohr: Symphony No. 7 in C, *Irdisches und Göttliches in Menschenleben* (30 May)
	Mendelssohn: Symphony No. 3 in A minor, *Scotch* (13 June)

1843

[Chopin: Piano Concerto No. 2 in F minor]
Nicolai: Song 'Ach Herr' (5 June)
Bennett: Konzertstück in A minor for piano and orchestra

1844

Beethoven: Overture Leonora No. 1 (13 May)
[Mendelssohn: Music from *A Midsummer Night's Dream* (27 May)
J. S. Bach: Overture and Suite [in D] (24 June)
Mendelssohn: Cantata *Die erste Walpurgisnacht* (8 July)
Beethoven: Music from *The Ruins of Athens*

1845

Vieuxtemps: Violin Concerto (14 Apr.)

1846

W   Spohr: Concertante for string quartet and orchestra (1 June)

1847

[Mendelssohn: *Scena*, 'On Lena's gloomy heath'] (15 Mar.)

1848

A. Hesse: Symphony No. 3 in B minor (13 Mar.)
Mendelssohn: 'Come ye sons of art' (10 Apr.)
Meyerbeer: Overture Struensee
[W]D   Spohr: Symphony No. 8 in G minor (1 May)
W   Griesbach: Overture *Titania* (15 May)

1850

W   Griesbach: Overture *Tempest* (6 May)
W   Thalberg: *Piano Variations on the Barcarolle from L'Elisir d'Amore* (20 May)
W   Benedict: Konzertstück in C minor for Piano and Orchestra (17 June)

1851

Mozart (attrib.): Violin Concerto in E flat (KAnh. C14.04) (7 Apr.)

1852

[Macfarren: Overture *Don Quixote*] (3 May)
[Hiller: Symphony 'In Freien'] (28 June)

1853

Schumann: Overture, Scherzo, and Finale (4 Apr.)
W   Molique: Cello Concerto (2 May)
Lindpaintner: Overture *Genueserin* (27 June)

1854

W   Rosenhain: Symphony (24 Apr.)
        Schumann: Symphony No. 1 in B flat (5 June)

1856

        Schumann: Cantata *Paradies und die Peri* (9 June)

1858

W   David: Violin Concerto No. 4 in E (12 Apr.)

1859

        [Joachim: Violin Concerto 'all'Ongarese'] (2 May)

1862

W   Piatti: Cello Concertino (16 June)
WD   Bennett: Overture Paradise and the Peri (14 July)

1863

W   Rietz: Fantasia Appassionata for cello (29 June)
        Tartini: Sonata Pastorale for cello and piano

1864

        Schumann: Symphony No. 2 in C (30 May)
WD   Bennett: Symphony in G minor (27 June)
W   Joachim: Violin Concerto
        Mozart: Concert aria 'Misero o sogno'

1865

        Molique: Flute Concerto (12 June)

1866

        [Gounod: Symphony No. 2 in E Flat] (28 May)

1867

        Gounod: Duet from *La Reine de Saba* (11 Mar.)
WD   Sullivan: Overture Marmion (3 June)

1868

        Schumann: *Introduction and Allegro Appassionato* for piano and orchestra
        (16 Mar.)
        Schubert: *Scena* 'Wo bin ich' from *Lazarus* (27 Apr.)
WD   Barnett: Overture symphonique (11 May)
W   Gounod: Overture *La Nonne sanglante* (25 May)
WD   Benedict: Overture *La selva incantata* (6 July)
        Bruch: Violin Concerto No. 1 in G minor

1869

W   Reinecke: Overture *König Manfred* (19 Apr.)
W   Graffigna: Canto Infernale *Lucifero* (31 May)

1870

_____

          Wagner: Prize Song from *Die Meistersinger* (25 Apr.)

1871

_____

[W]   Gounod: Symphony No. 1 in D, Saltarello, and 'There is a green hill
          far away' (8 Mar.)
L   Bottesini: Double bass Concerto in F sharp minor (8 May)

1872

_____

W   Gounod: Song 'The Worker' (29 Apr.)
          [J. S. Bach: 'Brandenburg' Concerto No. 3 in G] (24 June)
WD   Bennett: Prelude *Ajax* (8 July)

1873

_____

          Brahms: *Deutsches Requiem* (2 Apr.)
          Macfarren: Violin Concerto in G minor (12 May)
          Liszt: Symphonic poem *Tasso* (9 June)

1874

_____

          Lalo: Violin Concerto in F (18 May)
          Gounod: Bolero 'Ay, pobre curro mio' (15 June)
          Rheinberger: Overture The Taming of the Shrew

1875

_____

          Bennett: Funeral March from *Ajax* (18 Mar.)
WD   Macfarren: *Idyll in Memory of Sterndale Bennett* (5 July)
          Vieuxtemps: Violin Concerto No. 5 in A minor

1876

_____

          Rubinstein: Symphony No. 4 in D minor (29 May)

1877

_____

          Silas: Symphony in C (30 Apr.)

1878

_____

          Wieniawski: Violin Concerto No. 2 in D minor (12 June)

1880

_____

L   Macfarren: Overture *Hero and Leander* (5 Feb.)
W   H. Thomas: Overture Mountain, Lake and Moorland (19 Feb.)
L   Massenet: Overture *Phèdre* (4 Mar.)
L   Stephens: Overture A Recollection of the Past (28 Apr.)
          Benedict: Overture (30 June)

1881

_____

          Scharwenka: Piano Concerto No. 2 in C minor (24 Feb.)
          Berlioz: Dramatic Symphony *Roméo et Juliette* (10 Mar.)
WD   Cowen: Sinfonietta in A minor (12 May)

1882

	Liszt: Symphonic Poem *Hungaria* (23 Feb.)
W	Corder: Overture *Ossian* (9 Mar.)
L	Mendelssohn: *Scena* 'Che vuoi mio cor'
	Rubinstein: 'The Water Nymph' for solo and chorus
L	Stanford: Overture *The Veiled Prophet of Khorassan* (23 Mar.)
	Sgambati: Piano Concerto in G minor (11 May)
	Rubinstein: Oratorio *Paradise Lost* (9 June)

1883

	Bruch: *Scottish Fantasia* for violin and orchestra (15 Mar.)
	Sarasate: Danse Espagnole, and Romance
	Benedict: *Scena* 'Mary Stuart's Farewell' (25 Apr.)
WD	King: Prize Overture Among the Pines
	Liszt: *Hungarian Rhapsody*, No. 4
	Mackenzie: Ballad for orchestra *La Belle Dame sans Merci* (9 May)

1884

	Dvořák: Overture Husitzká (10 Mar.)
	Cowen: Symphony No. 4 in B flat minor (29 May)

1885

[WD	Ernst: Dramatic Overture (12 Mar.)]
WD	Wingham: Serenade for Orchestra—26 Mar.
W	Dvořák: Symphony No. 2 (7) in D minor (22 Apr.)
	Moszkowski: Symphonic poem *Jeanne d'Arc* (20 May)

1886

WD	Gadsby: Scene *The Forest of Arden* (4 Mar.)
	Moszkowski: Violin Concerto in C
	Dvořák: Violin Concerto in A minor (1 Apr.)
WD	Saint-Saëns: Symphony No. 3 in C (19 May)
WD	Moszkowski: Suite for orchestra (2 June)

1887

	Gounod: Concerto for Piano-Pedalier (21 Apr.)
WD	Corder: Suite *Roumanian* (19 May)
WD	Randegger: *Scena* 'Prayer of Nature' (9 June)
	Macfarren: Overture Kenilworth (15 June)

1888

L	Stanford: Prelude *Oedipus Rex* (15 Mar.)
L	Haydn: Symphony No. 54 in G (22 Mar.)
	Tchaikovsky: Serenade for Strings
	Theme and Variations from Third Suite
L	Prout: *Scena* 'The Song of Judith' (19 Apr.)
W	Widor: *Music to a Walpurgis Night*

Bizet: Suite *Jeux D'Enfants* (3 May)
Silas: Three Mythological Pieces for orchestra (17 May)
L   Barnett: *Pastoral Suite* (31 May)

1889

L   Stanford: Suite in D for violin and orchestra (28 Mar.)
Tchaikovsky: Suite No. 1 in D (11 Apr.)
L   Haydn: Symphony No. 51 in B flat (9 May)
W   Parry: Symphony in C 'English' (23 May)

1890

Grétry: Suite *Céphale et Procris* (13 Mar.)
L   Bach: Aria from Cantata *Phoebus and Pan* (13 Mar.)
Widor: Fantaisie for Piano and Orchestra
Benoit: Orchestral selection *Charlotte Corday* (27 Mar.)
Dvořák: Symphony No. 4 (8) in G (24 Apr.)
Mancinelli: Suite for Orchestra *Scène veneziane* (8 May)
W   Cliffe: Orchestral Picture *Cloud and Sunshine* (22 May)
Moszkowski: Suite for Orchestra in G minor (5 June)
Goring-Thomas: Duets 'Night Hymn at Sea' and 'Amours Villageois'
[Bach: Concerto for Strings in G ('Brandenburg' 6?)]

1891

Rubinstein: Overture *Antony and Cleopatra* (5 Mar.)
L   Stephens: Symphony in G (19 Mar.)
Sgambati: *Sinfonia epitalamio* (14 May)

1892

Grieg: *Scena* 'Der Einsame' (24 Mar.)
Bright: Fantasia No. 2 for piano and orchestra (11 May)

1893

W   Somervell: Ballad for orchestra *Helen of Kirkconnell* (23 Mar.)
L   Cliffe: Symphony No. 2 in E minor
Rheinberger: Overture *Demetrius* (18 May)
Tchaikovsky: Symphony No. 4 in F minor (1 June)

1894

Tchaikovsky: Symphony No. 6 in B minor (28 Feb.)
L   German: Symphony No. 2 in A minor
Grieg: Three Pieces *Sigurd Jorsalfar* (24 May)
Tchaikovsky: *Fantaisie de Concert* for piano and orchestra
S. Menter (orch. Tchaikovsky): Fantasia for piano and orchestra, *Ziegeunerweisen*

1895

Lamond: Overture Aus dem Schottischen Hochlände (7 Mar.)
W   Stanford: Symphony No. 5 in D, 'L'Allegro ed il Pensieroso' (20 Mar.)

W	Mackenzie: Two Pieces for orchestra, *From the North* (3 Apr.)
W	G. F. Bennett: Overture *Leonatus and Imogen* (16 May)
D	Parry: Symphony No. 3 in F (revised) (30 May)
	Chadwick: Overture Melpomene (13 June)

1896

	Borodin: Symphony No. 2 in B minor (27 Feb.)
W	Dvořák: Cello Concerto (19 Mar.)
WD	*Five Biblical Songs* with orchestra
W	Cowen: Suite de ballet *In Fairyland* (6 May)
L	German: Suite in Dm (20 May)

1897

W	Mackenzie: Scottish Piano Concerto (24 Mar.)
L	Cliffe: Violin Concerto in D minor (7 Apr.)
L	MacCunn: Suite *Highland Memories* (20 May)
W	Parry: Theme and Variations in E minor (3 June)
W	Cowen: *Scena* 'The Dream of Endymion' (17 June)
W	German: English Fantasia *In Commemoration*
	Tchaikovsky: *Variations for Cello and Orchestra on a Rococo Theme*
W	Bunning: Overture Spring and Youth (1 July)
	Glazunov: Symphony No. 4 in E flat
[W]	Humperdinck: Overture *Königskinder* (2 Dec.)
W	Mackenzie: Overture The Little Minister

1898

	Goldmark: Overture Im Frühling (10 Mar.)
WD	MacCunn: Ballet music from *Diarmid*
W	Corder: Dramatic scene 'Pippa Passes' (28 Apr.)

1899

	Borodin: Recit. and aria 'Lentement baisse le jour' from *Prince Igor* (19 Apr.)
W	Stanford: *Concert Variations on an English Theme* for piano and orchestra (4 May)

1900

W	Manns: Overture dramatique in D minor (8 Mar.)
W	Taylor: Suite *Scenes from an Everyday Romance* (24 May)
W	Cowen: Konzertstück in B flat for Piano and Orchestra (28 June)

1901

	Grädener: Violin Concerto in D (27 Feb.)
L	Parry: Orchestral song 'The Soldier's Tent'
L	Sauer: Piano Concerto in E minor (13 Mar.)
W	Wallace: Symphonic Poem No. 4 (27 Mar.)
W	Ronald: Song-Cycle *Summer-time* (23 May)
W	Elgar: Overture Cockaigne (20 June)

1902

W   Bell: Two movements from suite *Mother Carey* (27 Feb.)
L   Mozart: Music from *Les Petits Riens* (15 May)
W   Cowen: Coronation March (29 May)
    Rachmaninov: Piano Concerto No. 2 in C minor
W   Pitt: Five Poems for baritone and orchestra (2 July)
W   Randegger (the younger): Violin Concerto in D minor
L   Bedford: Nocturne 'Summer Down' for contralto and orchestra
L   Mackenzie: Overture The Cricket on the Hearth

1903

W   Cox: Overture *Pelleas and Melisande* (26 Feb.)
    D'Erlanger: Violin Concerto (12 Mar.)
L   Mackenzie: Orchestral suite *London day by day*
L   Hervey: Concert Overture Youth (26 Mar.)
    Sauer: Piano Concerto No. 2 in C minor
W   Somervell: *The Ballad of Thyra Lee* (28 May)
    Glazunov: Suite *Aus dem Mittelalter* (11 June)

1904

W   Carse: Symphonic Prelude to Byron's *Manfred* (2 Mar.)
    Charpentier: 'Depuis le jour' from *Louise*
    D'Indy: *Lied Maritime* (24 Mar.)
    Reyer: 'Reveil du Brunehilde' from *Sigurd* (28 Apr.)
    Venezia: Konzertstück for piano in A flat
L   German: *Rhapsody on March Themes* (30 June)

1905

W   Mackenzie: *Canadian Rhapsody* (29 Mar.)

1906

L   Weingartner: Symphony in G (27 Feb.)
L   Cowen: *Old English Dances*, set 2 (5 Apr.)
W   Bowen: Piano Concerto (31 May)
W   Holbrooke: Ballad *Annabel Lee* (14 June)
W   Taylor: *Variations on an African Theme*

1907

L   Enesco: Symphony in E flat (28 Feb.)
W   Hervey: Prelude to *Ione* (13 Mar.)
L   Nachez: Violin Concerto No. 2 in B minor (17 Apr.)
W   Bath: Song 'The Viking's War Song'
L   Chadwick: Symphonic Poem *Cleopatra* (16 May)

1908

    Hubay: Violin Concerto (29 Jan.)
W   Leoni: Vocal *scena* 'The Bells' (13 Feb.)

	Sibelius: Symphony No. 3 in C (27 Feb.)
W	Bowen: Viola Concerto (26 Mar.)
L	Berlioz: *Cléopâtre*
W	Delius: *In a Summer Garden* (11 Dec.)

1909

W	McEwen: Border Ballad *Grey Galloway* (2 Feb.)
L	Goldmark: Prelude Act II *Die Königin von Saba* (18 Feb.)
W	Hervey: Tone-poem *Summer*
W	Smyth: Overture The Wreckers (concert version) (3 Mar.)

1910

WD	Mancinelli: Romantic Overture (24 Feb.)
	Rachmaninov: Symphony No. 2 in E minor (19 May)
W	Elgar: Violin Concerto (10 Nov.)

1911

| | Liadov: *The Enchanted Lake, Baba-Yaga, Two Russian Popular Songs* (9 Feb.) |
| L | Rachmaninov: Piano Concerto No. 3 in D minor (7 Nov.) |

1912

W	Ronald: *Four Famous Lyrics* (22 Feb.)
W	Stanford: Symphony No. 7 in D minor
L	Hervey: Symphonic Variations *Life Moods* (21 Mar.)
W	Mackenzie: *Invocation*
W	Walford Davies: Suite in C (after Wordsworth) (21 Nov.)
W	Dunhill: Song Cycle *The Wind Among the Reeds*
	MacPherson: *Fantasy on Four Scots Tunes* (5 Dec.)
W	Parry: Symphonic Fantasia in B minor

1913

| W | O'Neill: Introduction, Mazurka, and Finale from ballet *A Forest Idyll* (30 Jan.) |
| | Skriabin: Symphony No. 1 in E (13 Mar.) |

1914

	Delius: *On Hearing the First Cuckoo in Spring* (20 Jan.)
	Summer Night on the River
W	Stanford: *Irish Rhapsody*, No. 4 (19 Feb.)
W	Bridge: *Dance Poem* (16 Mar.)
W	Scott: Two Passacaglias (3 Nov.)

1915

| L | Parry: *From Death to Life* (18 Mar.) |
| W | Gardiner: Fantasy (15 Nov.) |

1916

L	Debussy: *Iberia* (14 Feb.)
	Glinka: Selections from *A Life for the Tsar* (first concert performance) (11 Dec.)
W	Austin: *Palsgaard* (Four Danish Sketches)

1917

WD	German: Song 'Have you any news of my boy Jack?' (26 Feb.)
L	Debussy (orch. Goossens) *Clair de lune* (26 Nov.)

1918

L	Harrison: Tone-poem *Rapunzel* (11 Mar.)

1919

W	Delius: Violin Concerto (30 Jan.)
W	Holst: *The Planets* (excluding 'Venus' and 'Neptune') (27 Feb.)
W	German: *Theme and Six Diversions* (26 Mar.)
L	Stanford: Piano Concerto No. 2 (29 Apr.)
W	Debussy: Fantaisie for piano and orchestra (20 Nov.)
	Malipiero: *Pause del Silenzio* (4 Dec.)

1920

W	Delius: *Song of the High Hills* (26 Feb.)
W	Holst: *The Hymn of Jesus* (25 Mar.)
W	Stanford: Prelude to *The Travelling Companion* (4 Nov.)
L	Bax: *November Woods* (16 Dec.)

1921

	Bell: Symphonic Variations (24 Feb.)
W	Bax: Viola Concerto (17 Nov.)
W	Holst: Ballet music *The Perfect Fool* (1 Dec.)
	De Sabata: Symphonic-Poem *Juventus*

1922

W	Bainton: Concerto-Fantasia for piano and orchestra (26 Jan.)
W	V. Williams: *Pastoral Symphony*
W	Delius: Requiem (23 Mar.)
L	Strauss: Suite, *Le Bourgeois Gentilhomme* (23 Nov.)

1923

W	Hinton: *Scena* 'Semele' (25 Jan.)
L	McEwen: Symphony in C sharp minor, 'Solway' (22 Feb.)
	Honegger: *Chant de Joie* (22 Nov.)

1924

W	V. Williams: Song-cycle *On Wenlock Edge* (version for voice and orchestra (24 Jan.)

1925

L   Honegger: *Pacific 231* (29 Jan.)
      Prokofiev: Violin Concerto No. 1 in D (26 Feb.)
W   Howells: Piano Concerto in C (27 Apr.)
L   Holst: First Choral Symphony (29 Oct.)

1926

      Vuillemin: *En Kernéo*—28 Jan.
      Von Franckenstein: Rhapsody for orchestra (25 Feb.)

1927

      Bliss: Symphonic movement *Hymn to Apollo* (27 Jan.)
      Sibelius: Symphony No. 7 in C (8 Dec.)

1928

W   Walton: Sinfonia concertante for orchestra with piano (5 Jan.)
      Ravel: *Daphnis et Chloë* (complete concert version)
      Malipiero: Symphonic fragments from *St Francis of Assisi* (26 Jan.)
L   Holst: *Egdon Heath* (23 Feb.)
      Medtner: Piano Concerto No. 2 in C (1 Nov.)

1929

      Bartók: Rhapsody No. 1 for violin and orchestra (28 Nov.)
      Hauer: Orchestral Suite No. 7

1930

W   V. Williams: *Fantasia on Sussex Folk Songs* (13 Mar.)
W   Holst: Concerto for two violins and orchestra (3 Apr.)

1931

      Pizzetti: *Concerto dell' Estate* (19 Feb.)
      Bax: *A Northern Ballad* (3 Dec.)

1932

      Ravel: Piano Concerto (25 Feb.)

1933

W   Szymanowski: Symphony No. 4 in F, with piano solo (27 Jan.)
      Pizzetti: *Rondo veneziano* (7 Apr.)
W   Scott: *Disaster at Sea* (19 Oct.)

1934

L   Tailleferre: Overture to an Opéra Bouffe (15 Mar.)
W   Bax: *The Tale the Pine Trees Knew* (12 Apr.)
      Rossini–Resphigi: Suite *Rossiniana* (18 Oct.)
L   Sibelius: Incidental Music to *The Tempest*

1935

L   Rachmaninov: *Rhapsody on a Theme of Paganini*, for piano and orchestra (21 Mar.)
W   Schoenberg (after Monn): Cello Concerto (7 Nov.)
W   Bax: Symphony No. 6 (21 Nov.)

1936

L   Castelnuovo-Tedesco: Overture La Bisbetica Domata (19 Oct.)
L   Bruckner: Symphony No. 4 in E flat (original version) (12 Nov.)

1937

L   Pfitzner: Piano Concerto in E flat (25 Feb.)
W   Delius: Suite *Florida* (1 Apr.)
W   V. Williams: *Flourish for a Coronation*
     Rachmaninov: Symphony No. 3 in A minor (18 Nov.)

1938

W   Moeran: Symphony in G minor (13 Jan.)
[W] Boccherini: *Sinfonia funebre* in B flat (10 Mar.)
W   Benjamin: *Romantic Fantasy* for violin, viola, and orchestra (24 Mar.)
W   Bliss: Concert Suite from *Checkmate* (7 Apr.)
W   Brahms–Rubbra: *Variations on a Theme of Handel* (17 Nov.)

1939

     Weingartner: Sinfonietta for violin, viola, cello, and small orchestra (23 Feb.)
     Bloch: Violin Concerto (9 Mar.)

1940

W   Harty: *A John Field Suite* (1 Feb.)

1941

     Thompson: Symphony No. 2 in E (11 Jan.)
     Walton: Violin Concerto (1 Nov.)

1942

W   Bartók: Concerto for two pianos, percussion, and orchestra (first performance of revised version) (14 Nov.)

1944

     Barbirolli: *An Elizabethan Suite* (22 Jan.)
W   Medtner: Piano Concerto No. 3, 'Ballade' (29 Feb.)
W   Harris: Chorale for orchestra (first concert performance) (21 Oct.)

1946

W   Bax: *Northern Ballad*, No. 2 (16 Feb.)
     Barber: *Second Essay* for Orchestra (13 Apr.)

1948

W   V. Williams: Symphony No. 6 (21 Apr.)

1949

W   Rubbra: Symphony No. 5 (26 Jan.)

1950

WD   Rawsthorne: Symphony (15 Nov.)

1951

L   Jacob: Suite No. 3 (24 Jan.)
L   Howells: *Hymnus Paradisi* (18 Apr.)
W   Rubbra: Symphony No. 2 (revised version) (14 Nov.)

1952

L   Gardner: Symphony No. 1 in D minor (23 Jan.)
W   Hamilton: Clarinet Concerto, Op. 7 (23 Apr.)
W   Arnell: *Lord Byron—A Symphonic Portrait* (19 Nov.)

1953

L   V. Williams: *Sinfonia antartica* (21 Jan.)
W   Rubbra: Viola Concerto (15 Apr.)
         Debussy: François Villon Songs (orchestral version) (13 May)
L   Tippett: *Ritual Dances* (18 Nov.)
L   Martinů: Concerto Grosso

1954

L   Wordsworth: Symphony No. 3 (13 Jan.)
W   Rubbra: Symphony No. 6 (17 Nov.)

1955

W   Bliss: Act II of *The Olympians* (first concert performance) (26 Jan.)
W   Arnell: *Ode to the West Wind* (23 Feb.)
L   Fricker: Violin Concerto No. 2 (4 May)

1956

W   Bloch: Symphony (15 Feb.)
         Rubbra: *Improvisation* for violin and orchestra

1957

         Walton: Cello Concerto (13 Feb.)
L   Hindemith: *Sinfonia serena* (13 Mar.)
L   Zecchi: *Ricercare e Toccata*
         Martinů: *Frescoes of Piero Della Francesca* (10 Apr.)

1958

         Gerhard: Violin Concerto (12 Feb.)
WD   V. Williams: Symphony No. 9 (2 Apr.)
L   Walton: Partita for orchestra (2 May)

1959

W
Járdányi: Symphony *Vörösmarty* (14 Jan.)
Berkeley: Concerto for piano and double string orchestra (11 Feb.)
Blomdahl: Symphony No. 3, 'Facets' (2 Dec.)

1960

L
Badings: Concerto for two violins and orchestra (10 Feb.)
Walton: Symphony No. 2 (23 Nov.)

1961

Constant: Twenty-four Preludes (15 Feb.)
Henze: *Sonata per archi* (19 Apr.)

1962

Gerhard: Symphony No. 1 (14 Feb.)
Blacher: Piano Concerto No. 1 (14 Mar.)

1963

WD
Copland: Connotations for orchestra (13 Feb.)
Walton: *Variations on a Theme of Hindemith* (8 Mar.)

1966

W
Rawsthorne: Cello Concerto (6 Apr.)
Shostakovich: Cello Concerto No. 2 (5 Oct.)
WD
Hoddinott: *Variants for Orchestra* (2 Nov.)

1968

Gerhard: Symphony No. 4 (4 Dec.)

1969

WD
Musgrave: Clarinet Concerto (5 Feb.)
Walton: *Capriccio Burlesco* (5 Feb.)

1970

WD
Lutosławski: Cello Concerto (14 Oct.)

1971

WD
Joubert: Symphony No. 2 (24 Mar.)

1975

WD
Cooke: Symphony No. 4 (15 Jan.)
Messiaen: *Des canyons aux étoiles* (12 Nov.)

1978

L
Crosse: *Playground for Orchestra*, Op. 41 (17 May)
Lutoslawski: *Les Espaces du sommeil* (8 Nov.)

1979

W Wood: Chamber Concerto (revised version) (14 Nov.)
W Fricker: *Laudi Concertati*, Op. 80 (5 Dec.)

1980

   Alwyn: Symphony No. 5 (*Hydriotaphia*) (16 Apr.)

1982

   Bernstein: *Songfest* (14 Apr.)
WD Simpson: Symphony No. 8 (10 Nov.)

1984

L Britten: American Overture (22 Feb.)

1985

WD Musgrave and Bennett: *Moving into Aquarius* (23 Jan.)

1986

   Debussy: *Khamma* (*legende dansée*) (12 Mar.)
   Messiaen: Scenes from *Saint Francis* (26 Mar.)
   Chabrier: Prelude to *Marche joyeuse* (16 Apr.)
W Damase: Rhapsody for horn and orchestra
W Delius: American Rhapsody (10 Dec.)

1987

WD Panufnik: Symphony No. 9 (25 Feb.)
WD Burgon: Song-cycle *Title Divine* (22 Apr.)
L Morel: *Boreal* (11 Nov.)

1988

W Beethoven–Cooper: Symphony No. 10 (first movement) (18 Oct.)

1989

WD Arnold: Cello Concerto, Op. 136 (9 Mar.)
L Blake: *Nine Shakespeare Songs* (11 Apr.)

1990

L Woolrich: *Ghost in the Machine* (17 Oct.)

1991

L Simpson: Symphony No. 10 (31 Jan.)

1992

WD Saxton: *Paraphrase on Mozart's 'Idomeneo'*

Appendix 3

Philharmonic Orchestras 1860–1960

1860

First Violins
H. Blagrove (*Principal*)
M. Becker (*Principal*)
J. Banister
M. Bezeth
J. T. Carrodus
R. Clementi
G. A. Griesbach
H. Hill
L. Ries
J. W. Thirlwall
A. Tolbecque
I. B. Zerbini

Second Violins
W. Watson (*Principal*)
C. D. Betts
T. Browne
J. J. Calkin
H. Griesbach
J. Jay
J. M. Marshall
J. Newsham
E. Nickel
E. Payton
E. Perry
A. Streather

Violas
Webbe (*Principal*)

W. J. Glanville
R. Hann
W. Thomas
J. Thompson
H. J. Trust
J. Weslake
T. Westrop

Cellos
C. Lucas
W. H. Ayward
G. Calkin
T. Guest
T. W. Hancock
G. Paque
W. F. Reed
L. N. Schroeder

Double Basses
J. Howell (*Principal*)
W. J. Castell
T. Edgar
G. Flower
G. L. Mount
F. S. Pratten
J. Reynolds
C. Severn

Flutes
R. S. Pratten
E. Card

Oboes
A. Nicholson
H. Malsch

Clarinets
J. Williams
H. Lazarus

Bassoons
J. G. Waetzig
A. W. Chisholm

Horns
C. Harper
J. Catchpole
J. Kielbach
J. W. Standen

Trumpet
C. Zeiss
J. B. Irwin

Trombones
F. Cioffi
A. F. Germann
Webster

Drums
T. P. Chipp

1870

First Violins
L. Straus (*Principal*)
J. Banister
V. Buziau
R. Clementi

V. Collins
F. Crosa
G. W. Cubitt
J. Hennen
J. Ludwig

Max Vogell
J. Oppenheimer
J. W. Rendle
J. Rosenthal
T. Wells

Second Violins
E. Payton (*Principal*)
C. D. Betts
F. Carrodus
W. Easton
J. Earnshaw
W. H. Eayres
A. B. Fernandez
C. E. Frewin
J. W. Gunniss
O. Manns
N. Mori
F. Schoening
J. B. W. Thirlwall
H. Wheatley

Violas
R. Blagrove (*Principal*)
C. E. Asscher.
J. Brodelet
W. Egerton
M. Jacoby
A. J. Mapleson
T. Reynolds
H. Snyders
W. Thomas
T. Westrop

Cellos
W. Pettit (*Principal*)
W. H. Aylward
A. Van Biene
H. Daubert
T. Gough
H. Kleine

F. T. Quinton
L. Snyders
J. H. Trust
E. Vieuxtemps
H. Wohlers

Double Basses
G. Mount (*Principal*)
J. Beresford
W. Castell
T. Edgar
W. Griffiths
S. J. Jakeway
H. Progatzky
W. J. Strugnell
C. Wenkel
A. Winterbottom

Flutes
O. Svendsen
E. Card

Piccolo
Harrington Young

Oboes
W. Crozier
H. Malsch

Clarinets
H. Lazarus
G. Webb

Bassoons
J. G. Waetzig
A. W. Chisholm

Double Bassoon
H. Smith

Horns
V. Paquis
R. Keevill
W. Handley
R. D. Waterson

Trumpets
J. Wilmore
Paque

Trombones
W. Webster
H. Tull
Bartlett

Bass Tuba
W. F. Young

Drums
C. J. Thompson

Side Drums
J. A. Smith

Grosse Caisse
J. Orchard

Harps
J. Cheshire
W. Layland

1880

First Violins
L. Straus (*Principal*)
J. Berry
V. Buziau
T. Carrington
Cats Leon
W. H. Eayres
G. Erba
C. Ersfeld
A. Kummer
G. Palmer
C. Snewing
Van Heddgehem

T. Watson
W. Wiener

Second Violins
E. Payten (*Principal*)
G. W. Collins
A. B. Fernandes
J. W. Gunniss
A. J. Haynes
W. H. Levey
N. Mori
J. Phillipsborn
L. Szczepanowski

J. Spelmann
J. B. W. Thirlwall
L. Von der Finck

Violas
R. Blagrove (*Principal*)
E. E. Asscher
T. Barrett
Deane Ed.
W. Egerton
W. H. Hann
T. Reynolds
T. Westrop

Cellos
W. Pettit (*Principal*)
W. Buels
H. Daubert
H. P. Kleine
C. Ould
F. T. Quinton
J. F. Rudersdorff
Woolhouse
T. Serjeant

Double Basses
H. Progatzky (*Principal*)
B. Biehl
H. Burnett
W. Castell
F. Kendall
E. Ould
C. Wenkel
A. Winterbottom

Flutes
O. Svendsen
R. Samson

Piccolo
A. Jensen

Oboes
H. G. Lebon
A. Peisel

Cor Anglais
G. Horton

Clarinets
G. A. Clinton
G. J. Webb

Bass Clarinet
G. J. Augarde

Bassoons
G. W. Trout
T. Wotton

Double Bassoon
J. W. Hawes

Horns
C. Wendland
F. Garthwaite
S. Markland
A. Stock

Trumpets
W. Wilmore

P. J. Paque
R. Foghill
S. West

Trombones
W. B. Chattaway
Geard Chas
A. J. Phasey

Bombardon
J. Wilson

Drums
V. A. Chaine

Bass Drum & Cymbals
J. Smith

Side Drums
A. Smith

Triangle
A. Smith

Harp
E. R. Lockwood

Chorus Master
C. J. Beale

Organ
T. Pettit

1890

First Violins
J. T. Carrodus (*Principal*)
H. Bailey
G. H. Betjemann
J. W. Breeden
B. M. Carrodus
H. Gibson
H. Morley
E. W. Parfitt
A. W. Payne
J. W. Rendle
E. Roberts
C. Snewing
W. Sutton
A. Villin

Second Violins
W. H. Eayres (*Principal*)
E. Crooke
G. W. Cubitt
J. Earnshaw

F. A. Earnshaw
J. W. Gunniss
E. H. Hann
L. Jann
T. W. Lawrence
C. Newton
T. Oldaker
P. E. Ould
E. J. O'Brien
J. Spelman

Violas
R. Blagrove (*Principal*)
W. R. Bowie
H. Channell
C. W. Doyle
W. H. Hann
T. Lawrence
T. Reynolds
K. A. Stehling

W. W. Waud
W. T. Wood

Cellos
E. Howell (*Principal*)
J. Boatwright
G. T. Elliot
C. H. A. Gill
J. E. Hambleton
W. C. Hann
C. Ould
H. T. Trust
E. Woolhouse

Double Basses
A. C. White (*Principal*)
E. Carrodus
C. Harper
F. Kendall
E. F. Maney

E. Ould
W. Silvester
J. H. Waud
J. P. Waud

Piccolo
A. Jensen

Flutes
W. L. Barrett
R. Samson

Oboes
H. G. Lebon
H. Smith

Cor Anglais
E. V. Davies

Clarinets
G. A. Clinton
J. Clinton

Bass Clarinet
E. J. Augarde

Bassoons
W. B. Wotton
J. Anderson

Double Bassoon
R. Morton

Trumpets
W. Ellis
W. Morrow
F. A. Backwell
J. Solomon

Horns
T. E. Mann
R. Keevill
J. W. Standen
G. Lawrence Jun.

Trombones
C. Hadfield
C. Geard
J. Matt

Tuba
F. Blake

Timpani
V. A. Chaine

Side Drum
G. Baker

Bass Drum & Cymbals
W. G. Austin

Triangle
J. Baker

Harp
E. R. Lockwood

Organ
T. Pettit

Glockenspiel
J. Schroeder

Librarian
A. Mapleson

1900

First Violins
W. Parker Frye (*Principal*)
J. W. Breeden
A. Chadwick
W. A. Easton
R. Gray
H. Lewis
H. Morley
E. J. O'Brien
T. Oldaker
J. A. Orellana de.
J. W. Rendle
W. Richardson
A. E. Rowarth
C. Snewing
W. Sutton
A. Villin

Second Violins
W. H. Eayres (*Principal*)
R. Carrodus
E. Crooke
J. Earnshaw
C. E. Fairweather
J. W. Gunniss

E. H. Hann
Hann Walter
C. J. Hayes
E. Maney
C. Newton
W. H. Reed
J. Ricketts
F. Stewart
W. Sutcliffe
L. Szczepanowski

Violas
A. Hobday (*Principal*)
Ansell John
H. Channell
R. B. Creak
A. E. Dyson
W. H. Hann
Kearne Percy
H. R. Starr
K. A. Stehling
L. Tertis
H. J. Timothy
E. Tomlinson

Cellos
C. Ould (*Principal*)
P. Burnett
G. T. Elliot
J. T. Field
J. Geary
C. H. A. Gill
J. E. Hambleton
W. C. Hann
R. Melling
P. B. Parker
H. T. Trust
E. Woolhouse

Double Basses
A. C. White (*Principal*)
J. Bishop
W. A. Sutch
C. Hobday
F. Kendall
E. F. Maney
W. H. Stewart
W. R. Streather
J. P. Waud

C. Winterbottom
E. Whitmore

Piccolos
J. Wilcocke
G. Slight

Flutes
A. Fransella
A. Tootill

Oboes
W. M. Malsch
E. W. Davies
Horton Edgar

Cor Anglais
E. W. Davies

Clarinets
G. A. Clinton
P. Egerton

Bass Clarinets
E. Mills
E. Scoma

Bassoons
T. Wotton
E. F. James

Double Bassoon
W. Davis

Trumpets
W. Morrow
J. Solomon
F. A. Backwell
J. Simon Lloyd.

Horns
A. Borsdorf
J. Smith
H. Van der Meerschan
G. Wright

Trombones
C. Hadfield
A. E. Matt
J. Matt
W. A. Lettington

Tuba
R. W. Travis

Drums
C. Henderson

Side Drum
F. Merry

Bass Drum & Cymbals
J. Schroeder
R. W. Strachan

Triangle
J. Baker

Harps
Miss M. Timothy
Miss Molteno

Organ
Fountain Meen

Glockenspiel
J. Schroeder

Librarian
A. Mapleson

1905

First Violins
W. F. Parker (*Principal*)
J. W. Breeden
G. E. Cathie
R. Gray
E. Hopkinson
E. Lardner
H. Lewis
Lewis Philip
E. Maney
E. J. O'Brien
J. A. Orellana de.
W. H. Reed
W. Richardson
W. Sutton
W. Warner
G. H. Wilby

Second Violins
W. H. Eayres (*Principal*)
F. Bridge
R. Carrodus
A. C. Cazaubon

C. E. Fairweather
J. W. Gunniss
E. H. Hann
Hann Walter
C. J. Hayes
G. Leipold
G. Newton
J. Ricketts
W. Sutcliffe
L. Szczepanowski
H. P. Thomas
E. J. Underhill

Violas
Ansell John (*Principal*)
V. Addison
R. B. Creak
Cruft John
A. E. Dyson
Forsyth Cecil
H. K. Gardner
Kearne Percy
G. J. Penney

E. Shelton
H. R. Starr
E. Tomlinson

Cellos
C. Ould (*Principal*)
E. Woolhouse
G. T. Elliot
J. T. Field
J. E. Hambleton
W. G. Hann
A. Maney
R. Melling
M. Morgan
P. B. Parker
R. V. Tabb
H. T. Trust

Double Basses
C. Winterbottom (*Principal*)
P. E. Clayton
C. Hobday
E. F. Maney

W. Silvester
W. H. Stewart
W. R. Streather
W. A. Sutch
J. Waud Haydn.
E. Whitmore

Piccolos
J. Wilcocke
G. Slight

Flutes
A. Fransella
D. S. Wood

Oboes
W. M. Malsch
E. W. Davies
Horton Edgar

Cor Anglais
E. W. Davies

Clarinets
C. Draper
Gilmer Emile.

Bass Clarinet
F. Gomez

Bassoons
T. Wotton
E. F. James

Double Bassoon
W. Davis

Trumpets
W. Morrow
J. Solomon
J. Simon Lloyd

Horns
A. Borsdorf
J. Smith
H. Van der Meerschen
G. Wright

Trombones
C. Hadfield
A. E. Matt
R. Evans

Tuba
R. W. Travis

Drums
C. Henderson

Side Drum
F. Merry

Bass Drum & Cymbals
J. Schroeder
R. W. Strachan

Triangle
F. Merry

Harp
Miss M. Timothy

Glockenspiel
J. Schroeder

Librarian
A. Mapleson

1910–11

First Violins
J. Saunders (*Principal*)
J. W. Breeden
G. E. Cathie
R. Gray
E. Lardner
P. Lewis
G. S. Mackay
E. A. Maney
H. A. Newton
E. O'Brien
W. H. Reed
W. Richardson
E. J. Underhill
G. H. Wilby

Second Violins
T. F. Morris (*Principal*)
R. Carrodus
C. E. Fairweather
H. Gibson
E. E. Halfpenny
E. H. Hann
C. J. Hayes

C. Newton
H. W. Reeves
J. Ricketts
T. Sammons
F. Stewart
W. Sutcliffe
H. P. Thomas

Violas
H. W. Warner (*Principal*)
V. Addison
A. Ballin
F. H. Clark
J. B. Cox
Cruft John
A. E. Dyson
H. K. Gardner
T. Lawrence
G. Penney
A. Wright
H. Wyand

Cellos
B. P. Parker (*Principal*)

C. A. Crabbe
J. T. Field
C. Goodhead
W. Hobday
P. Jones
A. Maney
M. Morgan
J. E. Parr
R. V. Tabb

Double Basses
C. Winterbottom (*Principal*)
E. A. Carrodus
F. E. Clement
C. Hobday
W. Silvester
C. Stewart
W. R. Streather
W. A. Sutch
J. H. Waud
E. W. Whitmore

Piccolos
J. Wilcocke
G. Slight

Flutes
A. Fransella
D. S. Wood

Oboes
W. M. Malsch
E. W. Davies
E. Horton

Cor Anglais
E. W. Davies

Clarinets
C. Draper
O. Hill

Bass Clarinet
F. Gomez

Bassoons
E. F. James
E. W. Hinchliff

Double Bassoon
J. Groves

Trumpets
J. Solomon
F. G. James
J. L. Simon

Horns
A. Borsdorf
Borsdorf Oskar
H. Van der Meerschen
A. E. Brain

Trombones
Jesse Stamp
A. E. Matt
T. H. Guttridge

Contra-Bass Trombone
W. Reynolds

Tuba
R. Powis

Timpani
C. Henderson

Side Drum
F. Merry

Bass Drum & Cymbals
J. Schroeder
A. White

Triangle
F. Merry

Celesta
D. G. Gardner

Harp
Miss M. Timothy
Miss G. Mason

Glockenspiel
J. Schroeder

Organ
G. D. Gardner

Librarian
W. P. Rivers

1912–13

First Violins
J. Saunders (*Principal*)
W. H. Reed
A. Beckwith
G. E. Cathie
A. E. Crozier
H. Gibson
F. C. Grey
P. Lewis
G. S. Mackay
E. Meier
E. Messias
T. Petre
H. W. Reeves
C. B. Squire
F. Weist-Hill
C. Woodhouse

Second Violins
T. F. Morris (*Principal*)
G. H. Wilby
H. Cullerne
L. Falkman

J. Hainton
E. Hopkinson
H. Kinze
E. C. Laurence
T. Parker
F. S. Pearce
T. Peatfield
E. G. Pritchard
T. Sammons
W. Sear
E. J. Underhill
H. Webbe

Violas
H. W. Warner (*Principal*)
E. Tomlinson
V. Addison
N. Bath
A. Blackwood
E. Coates
R. Jeremy
H. Krause
J. Lockyer

W. J. Smith
H. Wyand
E. A. Yonge

Cellos
B. P. Parker (*Principal*)
C. Warwick-Evans
C. A. Crabbe
C. Goodhead
R. Grimson
E. Mason
J. Mundy
R. Purcell-Jones
C. Sharpe
R. V. Tabb
T. E. Weist-Hill
T. Werge

Double Basses
C. Winterbottom (*Principal*)
C. Hobday
E. A. Carrodus
F. E. Clement

E. Cruft
N. Morel
W. Silvester
W. A. Sutch
V. A. Watson
J. H. Waud

Piccolos
R. Murchie
G. S. Barton

Flutes
A. Fransella
D. S. Wood

Oboes
A. Foreman
W. S. Hinchliff
H. H. Stanislaus
W. H. Shepley

Cor Anglais
W. S. Hinchliff

Clarinets
C. Draper
H. Draper
R. Angus

Bass Clarinet
F. Gomez

Bassoons
E. F. James
W. James
E. W. Hinchliff
J. Groves

Double Bassoon
J. Groves

Horns
A. E. Brain, Jun.
A. H. Biran
O. Borsdorf
A. E. Brain, Sen.

Trumpets
J. Solomon
F. G. James
P. Anderson

Trombones
J. Stamp
A. Falkner
T. H. Guttridge

Tuba
F. Reynolds

Timpani
C. Henderson

Side Drum
F. Merry

Bass Drum & Cymbals
J. Schroeder
A. White

Triangle
F. Merry

Glockenspiel
J. Schroeder

Harps
Miss M. Timothy
Miss G. Mason

Organ
G. D. Gardner

Librarians
Goodwin and Tabb

1913–14

First Violins
J. Saunders (*Principal*)
 (Prin. New Sympb.
 Orch.)
A. E. Sammons
 (Prin. Beecham Symph.
 Orch.)
A. Beckwith
G. Cathie
A. E. Crozier
T. Fussell
H. Gibson
F. C. Grey
Lewis Philip
G. S. Mackay
E. Meier
W. H. Reed
H. W. Reeves
C. B. Squire

F. Weist-Hill
C. Woodhouse

Second Violins
T. Petre (*Principal*)
 (Prin. Beecham S.O.)
G. H. Wilby
H. Cullerne
J. Hainton
E. Hopkinson
H. Kinze
E. C. Laurence
E. Messias
T. Parker
F. S. Pearce
T. Peatfield
E. G. Pritchard
T. Sammons

W. Sear
E. J. Underhill
H. Webbe

Violas
H. W. Warner (*Principal*)
 (Prin. New S.O.)
E. Tomlinson
V. Addison
N. Bath
A. Blackwood
E. Coates
 (Prin. Queen's Hall O.)
R. Jeremy
H. Krause
J. Lockyer
 (Prin. Beecham S.O.)
W. J. Smith

H. Wyand
E. A. Yonge

Cellos
B. P. Parker (*Principal*)
C. Warwick-Evans
(Prin. Queen's Hall
Orch.)
C. A. Crabbe
C. Goodhead
R. Grimson
E. Mason
(Prin. New Symph.
Orch.)
J. Mundy
R. Purcell-Jones
(Prin. Royal Opera.)
C. Sharpe
R. V. Tabb
T. E. Weist-Hill
T. Werge

Double Basses
C. Winterbottom (*Principal*)
C. Hobday
(Prin. Beecham Symph.
Orch.)
E. A. Carrodus
(Prin. Royal Opera.)
F. E. Clement
E. Cruft
A. Lotter
(Prin. Queen's Hall
Orch.)
N. Morel
W. Silvester

V. A. Watson
F. Winterbottom

Piccolos
R. Murchie
G. S. Barton

Flutes
A. Fransella
D. S. Wood

Oboes
A. Foreman
W. S. Hinchliff

Cor Anglais
W. H. Shepley
H. G. Foreman

Clarinets
C. Draper
H. Draper

E flat Clarinet
R. Angus

Bass Clarinet
F. Gomez

Bassoons
E. F. James
W. James
E. W. Hiuchliff

Double Bassoon
J. Groves

Horns
A. E. Brain, Jun.
A. H. Brain
O. Borsdorf
A. E. Brain, Sen.

Trumpets
J. Solomon
F. G. James
P. Anderson

Trombones
Jesse Stamp
A. Falkner
T. H. Guttridge

Tuba
F. Reynolds

Timpani
C. Henderson

Side Drum
F. Merry

Bass Drum & Cymbals
J. Schroeder
A. White

Harps
Miss M. Timothy
G. Miss Mason

Organ
G. D. Gardner

Librarians
Goodwin and Tabb

1915–16

First Violins
J. Saunders (*Principal*)
W. H. Reed
W. A. Beckwith
G. S. Mackay
Lewis Philip
F. C. Grey
T. Fussell
E. Leggett
P. Levine
P. Brunet
J. Levy

E. Virgo
E. Carwardine
E. Maney

Second Violins
C. Woodhouse (*Principal*)
E. Hopkinson
F. S. Pearce
T. Sammons
H. Webbe
W. Sear
E. G. Pritchard

T. Parker
J. Hainton
E. J. Underhill
W. Mason
C. S. Greenhead
E. W. Simpson
V. Fawcett

Violas
H. W. Warner (*Principal*)
A. Hobday
V. Addison

W. Smith
N. Bath
R. Jeremy
A. Blackwood
H. Wyand
P. Sainton
C. Dorling

Cellos
B. P. Parker (*Principal*)
R. Purcell-Jones
T. Weist-Hill
C. A. Crabbe
R. V. Tabb
T. Werge
J. Mundy
C. Goodhead
H. Withers
F. Salmond

Double Basses
C. Winterbottom (*Principal*)
V. A. Watson
N. Morel
E. J. Cruft
W. Silvester
F. Winterbottom
E. A. Carrodus
F. E. Clement
N. Watson
S. Sterling

Flutes
A. Fransella
D. S. Wood
R. Murchie
G. S. Barton

Piccolo
R. Murchie

Oboes
A. Foreman
W. H. Hinchliff
W. H. Shepley

Cor Anglais
W. H. Hinchliff

Clarinets
H. W. Studely
J. Hughes
A. W. Augarde

Bass Clarinet
F. Moss

Bassoons
W. James
E. F. James
E. W. Hinchliff

Double Bassoon
P. Langdale

Horns
A. E. Brain, Jun.
A. H. Brain
O. Bradley
A. E. Brain, Sen.
H. F. Thornton
F. W. Salkeld

Trumpets
H. Barr
F. G. James
P. Anderson
F. Armitage

Trombones
J. Stamp
A. E. Faulkner
R. Evans

Tuba
F. Reynolds

Timpani
C. Turner

Percussion
J. Shroder
F. H. Wheelhouse
A. White
C. Hards
H. Locket

Glockenspiel
J. Shroder

Harps
Miss G. Mason
J. T. Cockerill

Celeste
T. Chapman

Pianoforte
Miss H. Cohen

Organ
H. Goss Custard

Orchestral Attendant
A. Newman

Librarians
Goodwin & Tabb, Ltd.

1920

First Violins
A. Beckwith (*Principal*)
C. B. Squire
G. S. Mackay
P. Lewis
F. C. Grey
H. Kinsey
E. Leggett
P. Levine
P. Brunet
H. Gibson

J. Meacham
H. Webbe
A. V. Fawcett
E. Carwardine
Essen Chas.
F. Stock

Second Violins
C. Woodhouse (*Principal*)
A. Hopkinson
P. W. Greenfield

W. Sear
A. Tibbetts
A. T. Mole
J. Hainton
E. J. Underhill
C. Kreshover
W. Mason
J. H. Pitt
J. Ricketts
T. Batty
H. Greenbaum

Violas
A. Hobday (*Principal*)
E. Tomlinson
E. Yonge
J. T. Lockyer
V. Addison
W. J. Smith
A. Blakemore
A. Blackwood
H. Wyand
P. Sainton

Cellos
B. P. Parker (*Principal*)
R. P. Jones
J. E. W. Hill
C. A. Crabbe
J. E. Parr
F. Casano
R. Grimson
C. Goodhead
G. B. Barbirolli
A. V. Tabb

Double Basses
C. Winterbottom (*Principal*)
C. Hobday
J. W. Merrett
V. A. Watson
E. Cruft
N. Morel
W. Silvester
H. S. Sterling

Flutes
A. Fransella
D. S. Wood
W. E. G. Walker

Piccolo
R. Murchie

Bass Flute
W. Carrodus

Oboes
A. Foreman
W. S. Hinchliffe
W. H. Shepley

Cor Anglais
W. S. Hinchliffe

Clarinets
C. Draper
H. P. Draper

Bass Clarinet
F. Gomez

Bassoons
W. James
E. F. James
E. W. Hinchliffe

Double Bassoon
J. Groves

Horns
A. E. Brain Jun.
F. W. Salkeld
A. H. Brain
A. E. Brain Sen.
H. F. Thornton
G. Manners

Trumpets
H. Barr

F. G. James
P. Anderson
F. Armitage

Trombones
J. Stamp
A. Faulkner
T. Guttridge

Tubas
F. Reynolds
W. Reynolds

Timpani
C. Turner
C. Bender

Percussion
J. Shroder
Hanrahan
H. Lockett
F. Deverall

Harp
J. T. Cockerill

Celeste
C. Woodhouse

Organist
E. S. Roper. Mus.Bac.
   F.R.C.O.

Orchestral Attendant
H. Hudson

*Librarians and Orchestral
   Managers*
Goodwin & Tabb, Ltd.

1930

First Violins
B. Reillie (*Principal*)
P. Frostick
P. Levine
V. Olof
W. Price
A. Mansell Edwards
M. Sanders
C. Oxley
A. Phillips
D. Taylor

T. Sammons
J. De Roode

Second Violins
A. Hopkinson (*Principal*)
S. Hall
J. Fry
A. Saens
H. Peros
D. Freedman

A. Balch
H. Ball
H. Chevreau
W. E. Coward

Violas
F. Howard (*Principal*)
J. Lockyer
W. Reynolds
C. Edwards

M. Stewart
E. Garinger
C. Dorling
J. Denman

Cellos
D. Cameron (*Principal*)
F. Casano
P. Talagrand
W. Bridge
C. Willoughby
J. Moore
G. Morgan
V. Marshall

Double Basses
H. Lodge (*Principal*)
G. Yates
G. Wilkes
F. Roberjot
J. Monch
*E. D. Chesterman

Flute
*R. Murchie

Oboes
L. Goossens (*Principal*)
J. McCarthy

Bassoons
P. Draper (*Principal*)
G. Alexandra

Horns
E. Chapman (*Principal*)
A. P. Barnes

Trumpets
*H. Barr (*Principal*)
A. Whitaker

Timpani
M. Flynn

* By Kind Permission of the BBC

1932 The London Philharmonic Orchestra

First Violins
P. Beard
B. Reillie
P. Frostick
B. H. Andrews
L. Levitus
E. Virgo
I. Losowsky
G. Whitaker
A. Amery-Nichols
D. Taylor
N. Comras
P. Morley
A. Balch
D. Freedman
A. G. Jones
F. R. Drake

Second Violins
G. Stratton
A. Hopkinson
H. Ball
W. Spratt
M. Sanders
L. Stein
R. Steel
A. Kirk
H. Collins
C. C. Draper
E. Morgan
W. Hulson
A. Filer
L. G. Richards

E. Roloff
H. Chevreau

Violas
F. Howard
J. Dyer
W. J. Smith
J. Cload
L. Birnbaum
I. Smith
W. Reynolds
G. M. Parker
B. Davis
J. Denman
W. Forbes
E. A. Christensen

Cellos
A. Pini
J. Moore
C. L. Willoughby
J. W. Francis
G. Marinari
G. Roth
B. Rickelman
T. G. Budd
F. W. Hodgkinson
D. F. Thomas

Double Basses
V. Watson
J. H. Silvester
S. Sterling

H. Green
J. Hatton
C. Gray
P. Stanley
G. Brookes
G. Hatton

Flutes
G. Jackson
P. Whitaker
J. Francis

Piccolo
L. Hopkinson

Oboes
L. Goossens
H. Lyons
W. Whitaker

Cor Anglais
H. S. Green

Clarinets
R. Kell
L. F. Collins

E flat Clarinet
E. J. Augarde

Bass Clarinet
A. G. Stuteley

Bassoons
J. Alexandra
G. Holbrooke
G. Vinter

Double Bassoon
A. Alexandra

Horns
F. Bradley
H. Burrows
T. Wood
F. Probyn
F. Hamilton
J. Phillips
J. Mason
G. Manners
R. West

Trumpets
J. H. Cozens
R. Dyson
R. Walton
H. Wild
F. L. Gyp

Trombones
E. T. Garvin
F. E. Stead
W. H. Coleman

Tenor Tuba
H. Smith

Tuba
W. Scannell

Timpani
J. P. Bradshaw

Percussion
M. E. Flynn
J. Hanrahan
S. Beckwith
H. C. Weston

Harps
M. Goossens
M. Cole
J. Wolfe

Secretary
F. Laurence

1935 The London Philharmonic Orchestra

First Violins
P. Beard
B. Andrews
D. Carl Taylor
L. Stone
R. Morley
E. Roloff
J. Boothroyd
P. Frostick
M. Clare
M. Quirk
H. Wright
H. Ball
A. Garth-Jones
A. Kirk

Second Violins
T. Jones
M. Beard
M. Sanders
A. Balch
T. Sammons
R. Steel
L. Connabeer
A. Amery-Nichols
W. Monro
C. Draper
R. Lauricello
F. Maybank

Violas
M. Ward

L. Birnbaum
W. J. Smith
J. Cload
T. Russell
H. Linden
E. Christensen
E. J. Foster

Cellos
L. Kennedy
D. Ffrangcon-Thomas
N. Attwell
E. Parker
M. Paxton
G. Roth
F. Leonard
F. Hodgkinson
T. Budd

Double Basses
V. Watson
J. H. Silvester
H. Green
C. Gray
J. Walton
G. Hatton

Flutes
G. Gilbert
P. Whitaker

Piccolo
A. Ackroyd

Oboes
L. Goossens
H. Halstead

Cor Anglais
H. S. Green

Clarinets
R. Kell
L. Collins

Bass Clarinet
R. Temple Savage

Bassoons
J. Alexandra
G. Alexandra

Double Bassoon
A. Bains

Horns
C. Gregory
A. Hyde
V. Burrows
J. Denison
F. Probyn

Trumpets
R. Walton
R. Dyson
H. Wild

Trombones	*Timpani*	*Celesta*
F. Stead	J. Bradshaw	F. White
E. Garvin		
W. Coleman	*Percussion*	*Organ*
	J. Hanrahan	A. Greir
	S. Beckwith	
Tenor Tuba	F. Bradshaw	*Orchestral Transport*
H. R. Smith		W. Knight
	Harps	
Tuba	M. Goossens	*Secretary*
W. Scannell	J. Wolfe	F. Laurence

1939–40 The London Philharmonic Orchestra

First Violins	B. Davis	*Bass Clarinet*
T. Matthews	L. Davis	R. Temple-Savage
R. Morley		
W. Reeves	*Cellos*	*Bassoons*
T. Carter	C. Sharpe	J. Alexandra
E. Roloff	N. Attwell	G. Alexandra
P. Frostick	B. Rickelman	
A. Garth-Jones	E. Parker	*Double Bassoons*
J. Wright	J. Long	A. Baines
H. Darnell	G. Walton	A. Penn
A. Chasey	S. Knussen	
W. Monro	P. Beavan	*Horns*
J. Buyers		C. Gregory
T. Jones	*Double Basses*	V. Burrows
H. Ball	J. Silvester	F. Bradley
	H. Green	F. Probyn
Second Violins	C. Gray	
R. Boothroyd	G. Brooks	*Trumpets*
H. Wright	H. Fawcett	R. Walton
M. Quirke	T. Alexander	R. Dyson
R. Whitaker		J. Cozens
T. Sammons	*Flutes*	
L. Connabeer	G. Gilbert	*Trombones*
C. Lake	P. Whitaker	F. Stead
A. Kirk		J. Mansfield
G. Whitaker	*Piccolo*	W. Coleman
H. Freeman	A. Ackroyd	
U. Tschaikowsky		*Tuba*
E. Simpson	*Oboes*	W. Scannell
	H. Halstead	
Violas	P. Newbury	*Timpani*
M. Ward	C. Crump	J. Bradshaw
A. McCordall		W. Bradshaw
J. Cload	*Cor Anglais*	
E. Christensen	P. Newbury	*Percussion*
W. Glasspool		F. Bradshaw
G. Patten	*Clarinets*	C. Kearney
A. Borsdorf	B. Walton	
V. Howard	E. Augarde	*Harp*
		W. Cockerill

Business Manager	*Librarian*	*Orchestra Attendant*
T. Russell	R. Temple-Savage	W. Knight

1950–1 The London Philharmonic Orchestra

First Violins
D. McCallum (*Leader*)
A. Leavins (*Principal*)
A. Hepton
A. Budagary
E. Roloff
J. Gorowski
M. Spivakowsky
W. Mony
J. Buyers
H. Wright
R. Good
H. Parfitt
P. Halling
D. Rael
I. Schlaen
K. Moore
N. Rouse
D. NacManson
J. Soutter
J. Ungerson

Second Violins
O. Rosen (*Principal*)
F. Maybank
A. Pievsky
A. Ross
M. Farren
E. Patston
A. Leech
A. Bryan
L. Salzedo
N. Lederman
N. Feiling
H. Greenwood
A. Howard
A. Parfrey

Violas
A. Cayzer (*Principal*)
J. B. Verity
A. Newnham
V. Howard
H. Legge
J. Fleetcroft
P. Vermont

J. B. James
L. Southworth
L. Birnbaum
M. Meek
L. Davis

Cellos
K. Horitz (*Principal*)
A. Ford
R. Briggs
J. Goe
S. Mant
R. Carr
G. Walton
F. Walker
F. Alexander
C. Prueveneers
J. Marchant
J. Holmes

Double Basses
J. Silvester (*Principal*)
E. Chesterman
C. Cheeseman
W. Colbourne
E. Ineson
D. E. Vaughan
A. Walton
G. Brooks

Flutes
G. Jackson (*Principal*)
C. Seville
R. Hanlon
L. Sanders

Oboes
T. MacDonagh (*Principal*)
L. Brain
J. Black
H. Baker

Clarinets
J. Brymer (*Principal*)
N. Tschaikov

Bassoons
G. Brooke (*Principal*)
E. Wilson
J. Shamlian
C. Walter Harding

Horns
D. Brain (*Principal*)
A. Thronger
I. Beers
A. Hyde
F. Probyn

Trumpets
R. Walton (*Principal*)
H. Barker
H. Dilley
F. Boyden

Trombones
S. Langston (*Principal*)
S. Brown
H. Nash
G. Kneller

Tuba
F. F. White (*Principal*)

Timpani
J. Bradshaw (*Principal*)

Percussion
L. Pocock (*Principal*)
F. Bradshaw
H. Kennings

Harps
T. Bonifacio

Orchestral Manager
B. Harris

Librarian
G. Brownfoot

1960 The Royal Philharmonic Orchestra

First Violins
R. Cohen (*Leader*)
A. Hepton
J. Hess
R. Ovens
P. Scherman
D. Francis
C. Thomas
M. Stolow
D. Bateman
A. Brown
R. Ingram
J. Davies
J. Fisher
M. Mayer
E. Giannicini
R. Whitehouse

Second Violins
G. Daines (*Principal*)
W. McInulty
A. Babynchuk
A. Pievsky
L. Salzedo
S. Wicebloom
N. Suggitt
M. Prescott
A. Ross
R. Larner
B. Newland
R. Robertson
I. Lester
L. Clay

Violas
F. Riddle (*Principal*)
M. Ward
L. Davis
J. Myers
T. Gray
D. Thompson
N. Bosworth
C. Kahn
M. Henderson
L. Lackland

J. Beavan
A. Smythe

Cellos
A. Pini (*Principal*)
H. Rogerson
H. Robinson
W. Simenauer
C. Sharpe
J. Whittaker
B. Vocadlo
J. Lowdell
M. Hayward
H. Dawson

Double Basses
E. Chesterman (*Principal*)
H. Fawcett
J. Upchurch
H. Green
F. Mackay
W. Sutcliffe
J. Steer
B. Scott

Flutes
G. Gilbert (*Principal*)
R. Raynes
G. Markham
C. Seville

Piccolos
G. Markham (*Principal*)
C. Seville

Oboes
T. MacDonagh (*Principal*)
L. Brain
R. Morgan

Cor Anglais
L. Brain

Clarinets
J. Brymer (*Principal*)

C. Chapman
W. Lear

E flat Clarinet
C. Chapman

Bass Clarinet
W. Lear

Bassoons
G. Brooke (*Principal*)
E. Wilson
V. Kennedy

Double Bassoon
V. Kennedy

Horns
J. Brown (*Principal*)
I. Beers
I. Harper
I. Keddie

Trumpets
P. Jones (*Principal*)
R. Copestake
D. Mason

Timpani
L. Pocock

Percussion
A. Fry (*Principal*)
H. Eastwood
D. Johnson
A. Dukes

Harp
T. Bonifacio

Librarian
G. Brownfoot

Orchestral Manager
J. Marchant

Appendix 4

Honorary Members

1826 Carl Maria von Weber	1885 Hans von Bülow
1829 Daniel François Auber	1886 Franz Rummel
1829 Jean François Lesueur	1887 Moritz Moszkowski
1829 Felix Mendelssohn	1887 Clara Schumann
1829 Jacob Meyerbeer	1888 Johann Svendsen
1829 George Onslow	1889 Edvard Grieg
1830 Johann Hummel	1889 Peter Ilyich Tchaikovsky
1836 Sigismund Thalberg	1889 Charles Marie Widor
1839 Gioacchino Rossini	1891 Franz Ondricek
1859 Hector Berlioz	1891 Eugene Ysaÿe
1859 Niels Gade	1893 Ignaz Paderewski
1859 Jacques François Halévy	1894 Max Bruch
1859 Moritz Hauptmann	1897 Emil Sauer
1859 Ferdinand Hiller	1897 Alexander Glazounov
1859 Franz Liszt	1899 Moritz Rosenthal
1859 Heinrich Marschner	1902 Sergei Rachmaninov
1859 Ignaz Moscheles	1902 Jules Emile Massenet
1859 Julius Rietz	1906 Raoul Pugno
1859 Anton Rubinstein	1906 Hans Richter
1859 Johannes Verhulst	1906 Richard Strauss
1860 Richard Wagner	1908 Jan Kubelik
1861 Euphrosyne Parepa-Rosa	1912 Wassily Safonoff
1869 Lucy Anderson	1913 Willem Mengelberg
1869 Otto Goldschmidt	1913 Arthur Nikisch
1869 Charles Gounod	1921 Alfred Cortot
1869 Stephen Heller	1921 Maurice Ravel
1869 Theresa Tietjens	1921 Igor Stravinsky
1870 Joseph Joachim	1921 Arturo Toscanini
1882 Johannes Brahms	1922 Harold Bauer
1882 Joachim Raff	1927 Leopold Stokowski
1882 Alberto Randegger	1929 Jean Sibelius
1882 Giuseppe Verdi	1930 Pablo Casals
1884 Antonin Dvořák	1948 Keith Douglas
1884 Sophie Menter	1948 John Mewburn Levien
1884 Wassily Sapellnikoff	1951 Frederic Austin
1884 Pablo Sarasate	1951 Ernest Irving
1885 Giovanni Bottesini	1953 Marion Scott

1953	Albert Schweitzer	1988	Claudio Arrau
1956	Paul Hindemith	1988	Julian Bream
1957	Gregor Piatigorsky	1988	Bernard Haitink
1959	Benno Moiseiwitsch	1989	John Denison
1960	George Baker	1989	Vernon Handley
1970	Aaron Copland	1990	Charles Groves
1971	William Glock	1990	Rafael Kubelik
1984	Eric Fenby	1991	Thomas Armstrong
1985	Lennox Berkeley	1991	Harrison Birtwistle
1985	Dietrich Fischer-Dieskau	1991	Pierre Boulez
1985	Yehudi Menuhin	1991	Elliott Carter
1985	Gerald Moore	1991	Joan Cross
1985	Peter Pears	1991	György Ligeti
1985	Solomon	1991	Paul Sacher
1986	Lorin Maazel	1993	HRH The Duchess of Kent
1987	Janet Baker	1994	Felix Aprahamian
1987	Peter Maxwell Davies	1994	Charles Mackerras
1987	Leon Goossens		

Appendix 5

Gold Medallists

1871	William Sterndale Bennett	1930	Ralph Vaughan Williams
1871	Christine Nilsson	1930	Gustav Holst
1871	Charles Gounod	1931	Arnold Bax
1871	Joseph Joachim	1934	Sergei Rachmaninov
1871	Helen Lemmens-Sherrington	1934	Edward German
1871	Arabella Goddard	1934	Hamilton Harty
1871	Charles Santley	1935	Jean Sibelius
1871	William G. Cusins	1936	Richard Strauss
1871	Theresa Tietjens	1937	Felix Weingartner
1871	Fanny Linzbauer	1937	Arturo Toscanini
1872	Euphrosyne Parepa-Rosa	1942	Myra Hess
1873	Hans von Bülow	1942	Serge Prokofiev
1876	Louisa Bodda-Pyne	1944	Adrian Boult
1876	Anton Rubinstein	1947	William Walton
1877	Johannes Brahms	1950	John Barbirolli
1880	Stanley Lucas	1953	Kathleen Ferrier
1895	Adelina Patti	1954	Igor Stravinsky
1897	Emma Albani	1957	Bruno Walter
1897	Ignacy Jan Paderewski	1959	Malcolm Sargent
1900	Edward Lloyd	1961	Artur Rubinstein
1901	Eugene Ysaÿe	1962	Yehudi Menuhin
1902	Jan Kubelik	1963	Arthur Bliss
1903	Clara Butt	1963	Pierre Monteux
1904	Fritz Kreisler	1964	Lionel Tertis
1909	Louise Kirkby Lunn	1964	Benjamin Britten
1910	Emil Sauer	1966	Dmitri Shostakovich
1912	Pablo Casals	1967	Zoltán Kodály
1912	Harold Bauer	1970	Mstislav Rostropovich
1912	Luisa Tetrazzini	1974	Vladimir Horowitz
1914	Muriel Foster	1975	Olivier Messiaen
1916	Vladimir de Pachmann	1976	Michael Tippett
1921	Henry Wood	1980	Clifford Curzon
1922	Alexander Mackenzie	1984	Herbert von Karajan
1923	Alfred Cortot	1986	Andres Segovia
1925	Frederick Delius	1986	Witold Lutoslawski
1925	Edward Elgar	1987	Leonard Bernstein
1928	Thomas Beecham	1988	Dietrich Fischer-Dieskau

1989	Georg Solti	1990	Sviatoslav Richter
1990	Claudio Arrau	1992	Isaac Stern
1990	Janet Baker	1993	Alfred Brendel
1990	Bernard Haitink	1994	Colin Davis

Index

COMPILED BY FREDERICK SMYTH

Page numbers in **bold type** indicate the more important entries and those in *italic* direct attention to illustrations or their captions; 'q' stands for 'quoted'. Abbreviations listed at page xi have been employed in this index; additionally, 'PS' and 'RPS' are used to denote the Philharmonic Society and the Royal Philharmonic Society respectively.

New Plastics Applications for the Automotive Industry

SP-1253

GLOBAL MOBILITY DATABASE

All SAE papers, standards, and selected books are abstracted and indexed in the Global Mobility Database.

Published by:
Society of Automotive Engineers, Inc.
400 Commonwealth Drive
Warrendale, PA 15096-0001
USA
Phone: (412) 776-4841
Fax: (412) 776-5760
February 1997

ISBN 1-56091-965-5
SAE/SP-97/1253
Library of Congress Catalog Card Number: 96-71861
Copyright 1997 Society of Automotive Engineers, Inc.

PREFACE

Today's automakers are embarking upon a new frontier that is continually growing and changing, and is filled with unchallenged areas of science and technology. OEMs have been forced by increasing government regulations and increased pressure from consumers to become pioneers on that frontier.

In order to be successful on that frontier, automakers must be imaginative, inventive, and innovative. Automotive designers and engineers are constantly using their imaginations and searching the uncharted pockets of science and technology in order to develop manufacturing materials and applications that enable them to meet government regulations and consumer demands, while minimizing costs and expanding their sales in the industry.

Every year SAE brings together engineers in the automotive industry to present their pioneering advances in automotive plastic components, processes, and technology, at the SAE International Congress and Exposition. The papers selected for this year's SAE special publication, New Plastics Applications for the Automotive Industry (SP-1253), are a cross-section of the technological advances in the plastics processing industry.

We hope that the papers presented in this SP will both inspire and remind you, the pioneers on that new frontier, that there are still unanswered questions in science, and unsolved technical challenges left to explore and conquer.

Peggy Malnati
Allison, Hull & Malnati

Session Organizer, Co-Chair

TABLE OF CONTENTS

Vibration, Dynamic Stress and Fatigue Life Analysis of Automotive Underhood Nylon Fans: Numerical and Experimental Investigation

Meda G. Lakshmikantha, Dennis Chiu, and Yoshiyuki Mita
USUI International Corp.

ABSTRACT

Vibration and fatigue study of glass-reinforced nylon, as an alternative material to steel for engine driven fans, is discussed. The use of nylon, which has a lower density than steel, offers a significant weight reduction and consequently less burden on the related underhood components and result in longer life for water pumps, fan clutches and drive belts. The temperature and humidity-dependent properties of nylon fan often works favorably from the view point of fatigue life, by shifting the fan's natural frequencies away from the occurrence of resonance. Nylon fans also offer more design flexibility without significantly affecting the cost.

Despite such apparent advantages very little literature in the automotive field has dealt with vibration and fatigue of nylon fans. In this paper, computer-based finite element method (FEA) is used as the analytical tool to determine the frequencies and stresses produced at different values of temperature, humidity, and vibration excitations. Comparisions were made against experimentally obtained data, and have seen good agreements. Fatigue analysis was also conducted in order to predict life-expectancy of the nylon fans.

I INTRODUCTION:

The most commonly used material for automotive engine driven fans is steel. However, use of such steel fan over a period of time may result in bearing and other problems for water pump. Further, spot welds and rivets which are weak structural points are commonly found in conventional assembled metal fans. Vibration and fatigue problems are also severe in steel fans. This adds additional warrantey problems for automotive manufacturer. The addition of more blades from cooling requirements or some other design changes may further aggravate this problem.

The use of plastic fans poses challenging structural problems. Plastic engine-driven fans usually have molded-in steel insert. The connection between plastic and steel portion is carried out by providing holes in the steel portion near the joining region and filling these holes by plastic. Hence such plastic fans are subjected to thermal stresses. These plastic fans are usually manufactured by injection molding process. This process of manufacturing results in weld lines which are weak compared to other portions of the fan. The finite element and experimental analysis procedures developed for the problems such as thermal stresses, weld lines, creep and other durability problems are described in our earlier paper[1].

Automotive underhood engine-driven fans are subjected to aerodynamic loading, centrifugal loading and thermal loading. In addition to these quasi-static loadings underhood fans are also subjected to dynamic/vibration loadings. Vibration loading results from unbalance of fan and misalignment between fan drive axis and water pump. The higher the unbalance or misalignment, the severer the vibration forces become. Time-varying loading on each blade due to complicated unevenly configured underhood packaging may also be accountable for vibration. The variarion of such areodynamic loading on each blade with time results in vibration loading. Mechanical properties of nylon such as yield strength and young's modulus vary with both temperature and humidity. Hence natural frequencies of plastic fans vary considerably with temperature and humidity. In practice unbalance and misalignment can be controlled to very low values. Hence structural analysis and subsequent fatigue analysis of nylon fan under only aerodynamic loading are discussed below.

II VIBRATION ANALYSIS:

FREQUENCIES AND VIBRATION MODES:

The first step in vibration analysis of any structure is the evaulation of normal modes and natural frequencies. The natural frequencies of fan depend on the mass and stiffness distribution. Since the shape and thickness of fan blades changes from hub to tip, only accurate representation by 3-D modeling will result in correct

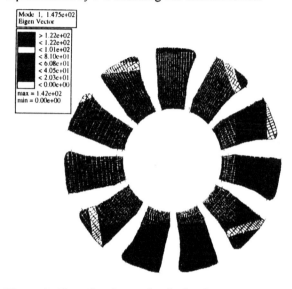

Figure 1. First vibration mode of nylon fan.

results. Further proper boundary conditions between plastic hub and steel insert should be given. The actual experiment for nylon fan is carried out by 'Shaker Test' in which a particular magnitude of loading is applied on fan with a slowly changing frequency. The resulting behaviour of fan under this type of loading is monitored by recording the response of strain gages located at critical positions. The positions of strain gages are obtained from the distribution of stress which are obtained from FEA. Since the stress distributions are different for different normal modes, several strain gages are needed to cover all the relevant natural frequencies. Mode shape for the first mode of fan and a typical strain gage response under a loading which is a function of frequency is shown in Figures 1 and 2. In Figure 2 the vertical axis gives strain values and horizontal axis gives frequencies. The frequencies at which strain peaks are the natural frequencies. For example Figure 2 shows that first natural frequency is given by 148.2 Hz. The natural frequencies of nylon fan changes with both temperature and moisture content. Figure 3 shows the FEA and experimental comparision of natural frequencies obtained for DAM (Dry As Molded) condition and at several temperatures. As can be seen from this figure, the results compare fairly well. The NASTRAN code[2] was used for FEA computations.

As can be seen from Figure 4 nylon fan experiences seven resonant vibration modes during in-vehicle

vibration experiment which is described in the next section. The vertical axis in Figure 4 is strain and horizontal axis gives time as the RPM of fan is increased. The natural frequencies of higher vibration modes of fan obtained by normal mode analysis by FEA (see Figure 5)

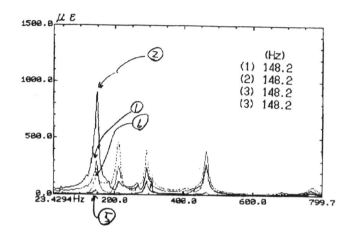

Figure 2. Experimentally determined response of strain gages in 'Shaker test'.

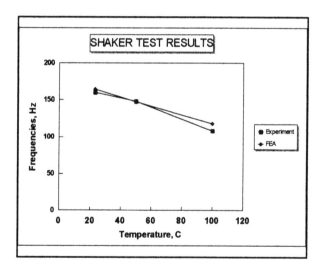

Figure 3. Comparision of natural frequencies of nylon fan at different temperatures.

are compared with those obtained from in-vehicle vibration test. The results of higher order modes are compared at 23 C, 50 C and 100 C. As shown in Figure 5 the results compare fairly well at all temperatures considered. Comparision of frequencies are made only for few modes.

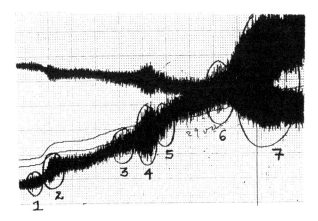

Figure 4. Response of strain gage mounted on nylon fan during in-vehicle vibration experiment.

III DYNAMIC STRESS ANALYSIS:

The vibration of fan in the underhood of a vehicle can be induced by various causes, such as angular misalignment between the fan and water pump, unbalance of fan, firing of engine, or aerodynamic interaction between the fan and sourrounding components. Some details regarding these vibratory sources are explained in the APPENDIX. Assuming that the major cause of vibration of fan is due to aeodynamic interaction between the fan and sourrounding components the following analysis is performed.

The magnitude of aerodynamic loading that is acting on a fan depends on the amount of air flowing through the fan, area of flow and the pressure difference across the blade. The resultant force on each blade can be decomposed into tangential and thrust forces. The tangential force per blade is obtained by dividing the torque obtained from experiments at a particular RPM with the mean radius of blade and number of blades. The thrust force is obtained using the following equation.

Total thrust at a particular PRM= (Volumetric air flow)^2, density of air/ (Acceleration due to gravity* airflow area) + Pressure difference * surface area of blades
.........................(1)

The volumetric airflow is obtained from experiments. The thrust force per blade is obtained by dividing total thrust force calculated using the above equation by the number of blades. The aerodynamic loading obtained from the combined experimental and analytical formula (at a particular RPM) is then used in the dynamic stress calculations by FEA. Since it is fairly involved to determine the amplitude of the fluctuating component of the loading as input to the vibtation, a simple assumption was made here to substitute it by the magnitude of steady loading. Averaged and uniform aerodynamic loading on each blade of fan is considered in the FEA calculations. The load is assumed to vary in a sinusoidal wave form in the time domain similar to the

one shown in the graph of Figure 7 which is an experimentally obtained curve. The mode acceleration method is used in dynamic stresss calculations. The dynamic stress calculations are performed at several temperatures.

The top portion of Figure 6 shows the normalized dynamic response (dynamic stress / input loading) of nylon fan at several natural frequencies of fan at 50 C. As can be seen from this Figure, it is clear that as the natural frequency is increased (higher order vibration modes) the dynamic response of nylon fan decreases. The bottom portion of Figure 6 shows dynamic response of the same fan at 100 C. It is clear from there that the normalized dynamic response of the same fan remains almost constant at all vibration modes considered in the analysis. Hence dynamic amplification of nylon fan is higher at higher temperatures as the natural frequencies are increased. This information should be kept in mind when designing a nylon fan for vibration.

IN-VEHICLE VIBRATION TEST:

In order to find out the actual vibration problems of the nylon fan, in-vehicle strain tests are carried out. Several strain gages are used on fan both in the steel and nylon portions. The strain gages are mounted at loctaions of high stress gradients (on both steel and nylon portions of fan) obtained from normal mode analysis using FEA. FEA dynamic stress calculations of fan using frequency response analysis at several vibration modes gives additional high stress positions. Further some more strain gages can be placed at positions of high mean stress as obtained by FEA. The mean stress on fan is obtained from combined centrifugal and aerodynamic loadings at a particular RPM. Slip ring assembley is used to transmit the strain signal from rotating fan to the processing equipment.

At UIC we have often observed that whenever the frequency corresponding to the fan speed falls into 1/4, 1/3 or 1/2 of the natural frequency of any of the vibration modes, resonance occurs. At lower RPM of fan this factor is 1/4, at higher RPM of fan this factor is 1/2 and at medium speed this factor is 1/3.

Once the fan speeds at which resonane may take place are known by the procedure as described above, the maginitude of aerodynamic loading to be used in frequency response analysis by FEA can be calculated using formula (1).

Frequency response analysis (FEA) is carried out to determine dynamic stress values. The value of aerodynamic loading used in FEA are obained from wind tunnel experiments. Due to unevenly packaged underhood compartment in vehicle, maginitude of areodynamic loading in vehicle can be different from those in wind tunnel experiment. Hence values of streses obtained from FEA can be approximate at best. From in-vehicle vibration experiments it is found that it

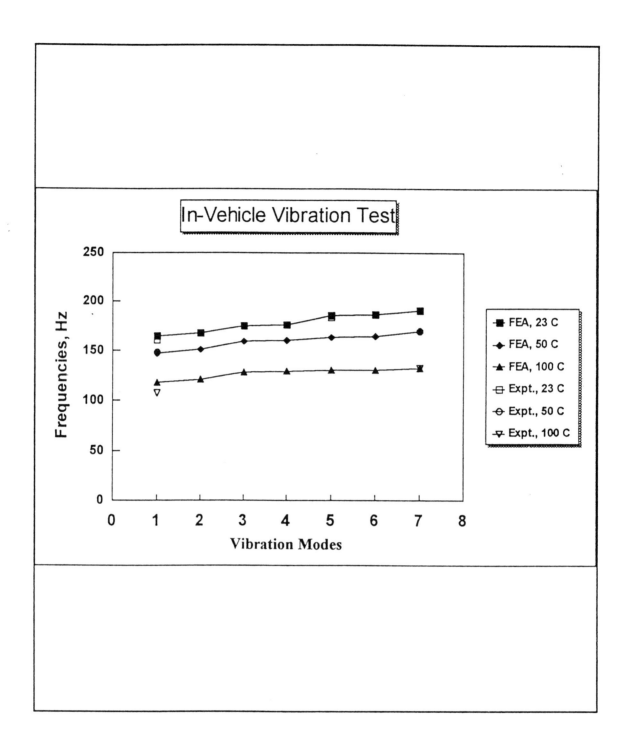

Figure 5. Comparision of natural frequencies of several vibration modes obtained from FEA with those obtained from experiments.

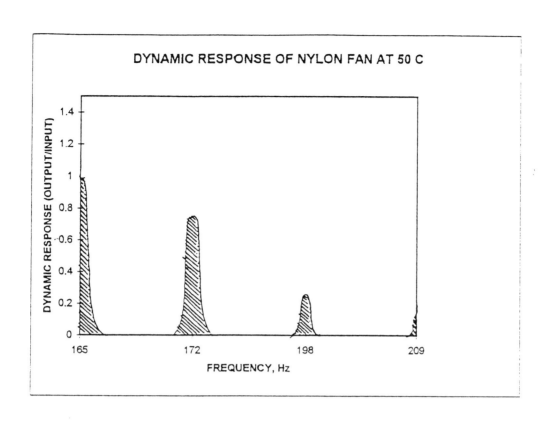

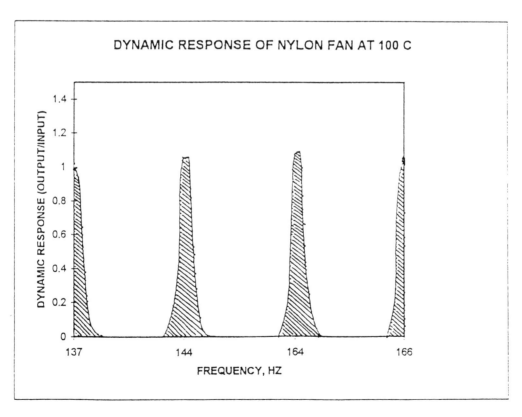

Figure 6. Normalized dynamic response of Nylon fan at 50 C and 100 C at several natutal frequencies of fan.

is locked condition (i.e., no slip between fan and fan drive) that gives the highest stresses.

Similar condition is used in FEA to determine the stresses in different vibration modes. In vibration stress analysis it is important to consider proper damping values; material properties are such that the plastic has significant amount of damping. A convenient way to determine the amount of damping present in a system is to measure the rate of decay of free oscillations. The larger the damping, the greater will be the rate of decay. The following equation was used to define the damping.

$$Ln(x(t)/x(t+T))=2\Pi\zeta/(\sqrt{1-\zeta^2}) \dots\dots\dots\dots(2)$$

In this case experiments on nylon material are carried out in DAM condition at 23C, 50 C and 100C. Based on experiments damping values are calculated and used as input to FEA.

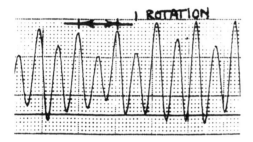

Figure 7. Strain gage response of higher mode in in-vehicle vibration test. In one rotation there are two 'humps'.

Figure 8 shows a graph of a typical strain gage output as the RPM of fan is increased. The top portion of figure (Y-axis) gives fan RPM. The engine speed was increased up to a value corresponding to 4600 fan RPM (clutch-fan locked condition is used in this case). As can be seen from this figure that there are atleast three resonances occuring at around 2000, 2800 and 4400 RPM's. Figure 9 shows FEA prediction for the same condition. It can be seen from these two figures that FEA can predict dynamic stress magnitudes consistent with the experimental results. Figure 10 shows maximum dynamic stress values obtained from in-vehicle strain test and FEA at temperatures of 23 C, 50 C and at 100 C. The top portion of figure shows results for Nylon and the bottom portion of figure shows results for steel insert of fan. The results shown in Figure 10 is for vehicle A and Fan A. As can be seen from this figure FEA gives slightly higher dynamic stress values compared to those obtained from in-vehicle strain test. Figure 11 shows similar results for vehicle B and fan B for both nylon and steel portions of the fan. Figure 12 shows dynamic stress values for a single fan and three different vehicles. The dynamic stress values obtained from in-vehicle strain test and the method we have described in this paper (using FEA) are shown in this figure. It is clear from all these comparisions that method we have described in this paper using FEA can

predict the dynamic stress amplitudes at different speeds of fan (at different natural frequencies of fan) and at different temperatures fairly well at least in the fans and vehicles considered in the present study.

From the above analysis it is clear that numerical simulation gives maximum dynamic stress values in both steel and nylon and compare fairly well with those obtained from experiments.

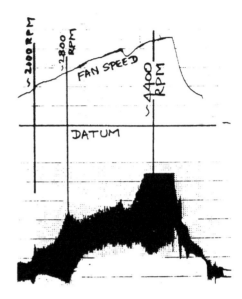

Figure 8. Strain gage response at underhood temperature of 100 C during in-vehicle vibration test. The horizontal axis is time and vertical axis is strain. The top portion of Figure shows RPM of fan.

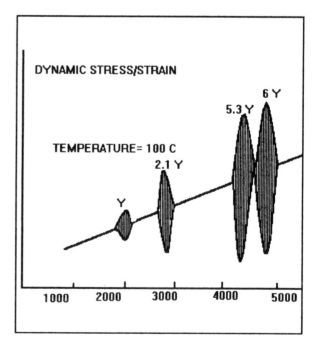

Figure 9. FEA prediction of amplitude of dynamic stresses/strains at underhood temperature of 100 C at different RPM of fan.

6

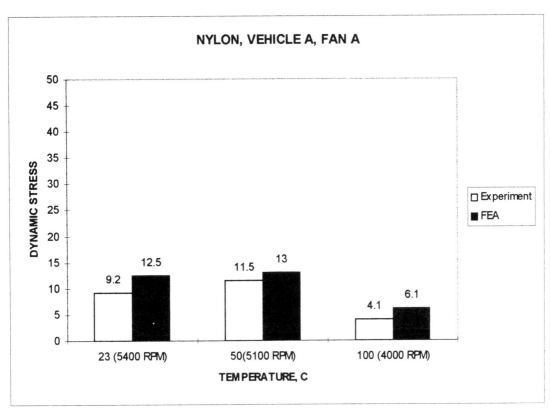

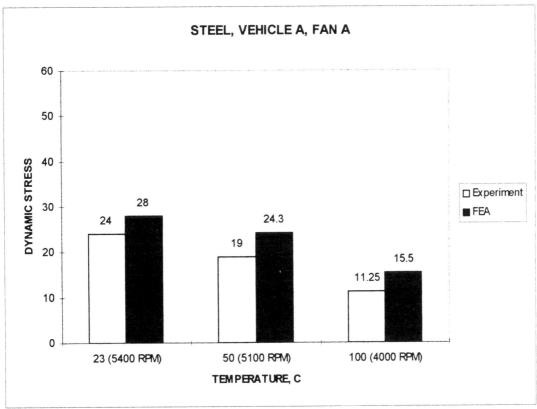

Figure 10. Comparision of dynamic stresses obtained using FEA and In-Vehicle strain test for both nylon and steel portions of nylon fan A. Fan A: 510 mm diameter, 11 blades.

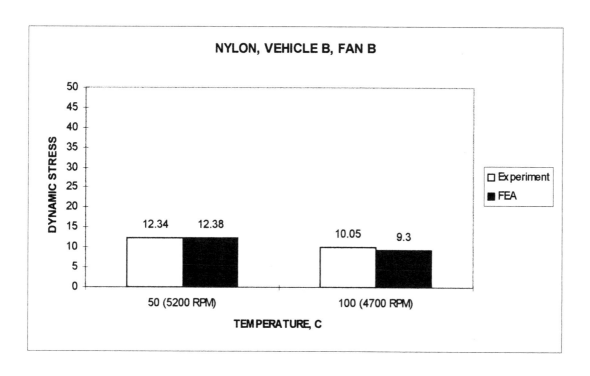

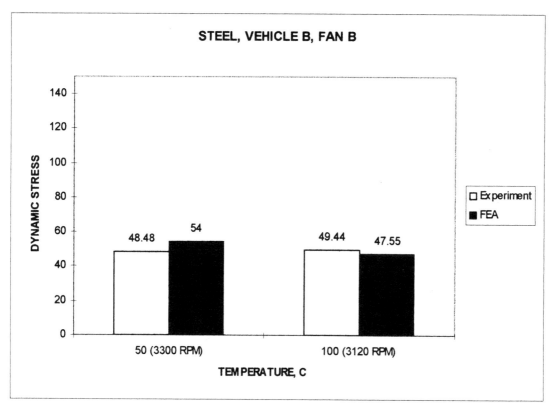

Figure 11. Comparision of dynamic stresses obtained using FEA and In-Vehicle strain test for both nylon and steel portions of nylon fan. Fan B: 490 mm diameter, 10 blades.

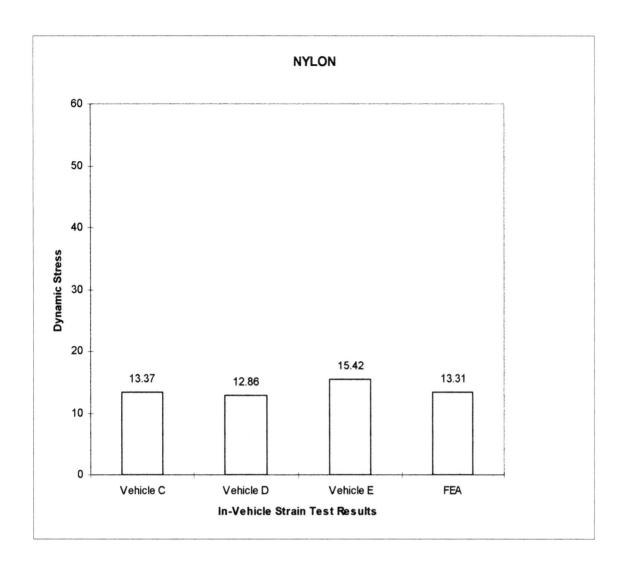

Figure 12. Comparision of dynamic stresses at a point obtained from in-vehicle strain test and FEA.

IV FATIGUE ANALYSIS:

RESONANCE BENCH LIFE TEST:

Fatigue tests are designed to measure the relative ability of plastics materials to withstand repeated stresses or other cyclic phenomena. In the case of plastic fans vibration loading caused by airflow produces alternate compression and tension of fan blades due to aerodynamic loading along with mean stress due to combined centrifugal and aerodynamic loadings. Such alternate cyclic loading cause mechanical deterioration and progressive fracture, leading to failure in service. Typical fatigue tests are carried out on machines designed to subject a cantilever test piece to reversal flexural loading cycles at different stress/strain levels. Number of cycles before failure are recorded for each stress level. Data are normally presented in plots of log stress versus log cycles called S-N curves for specific cycle rates and environmental temperatures. With thermoplastics there is an added complication that heat build up by the frequency of the cyclic stress may contribute to failure. Hence in thermoplastics different S-N curves can be produced for the same material by testing at different temperatures, humidity, mean stresses, frequencies, and methods such as testing in tension rather than in bending.

Most published data on the fatigue properties are for completely reversed alternating stresses, that is, the mean stress of the cycle is equal to zero. Since in the case of fan, vibration occurs while the fan is under rotation, mean stress is non-zero. Under such circumstances when the fatigue data for a specified mean stress and design life are not avaliable for plastic, the influence of nonzero mean stress can be estimated from empirical relationships that relate failure at a given life, under zero mean stress, to failure at the same life under zero mean cyclic stress. One widely used formula is Goodman's linear relationship, which is

$$S_a = S(1 - S_m/S_u) \qquad \ldots\ldots\ldots\ldots\ldots\ldots(3)$$

Where S_a is the alternating stress associated with some nonzero mean stress, S_m. S is the alternating fatigue strength at zero mean stress. S_u is the ultimate tensile strength.

Most data are determined from tests at a constant stress amplitude. In the case of fan as shown in Figure 7, aerodynamic loading under resonance induces alternating stress amplitude. Such changes, referred to as "Spectrum loading", make the direct use of standard fatigue S-N curves inappropriate. Hence it is difficult to determine the fatigue life using the conventional constant stress/strain amplitude S-N fatigue curves.

Hence a way to get around this problem is obtained by assuming a certain amount of permanent damage at a given stress amplitude and number of cycles. Further

the operation of fan subsequently at different stress amplitude and number of cycles will produce additional fatigue damage and a sequential accumulation of total damage, which at a critical value will cause fatigue failure. Although there are several 'Cumulative damage theories' one of the simplest of these is called 'Miner's law' or the linear damage rule. The Miner's rule is given by

$$\text{Total damage} = (n_1/N_1)s_1 + (n_2/N_2)s_2 + (n_3/N_3)s_3 + \ldots\ldots + \ldots\ldots + \ldots\ldots \qquad \ldots\ldots\ldots (4)$$

where n_1 is number of cycles of loading of constant stress amplitude s_1 and N average number of cycles to failure. The second term in the above equation gives the damage fraction from cycles of different constant stress amplitude s_2. Fatigue failure will occur when the total damage is unity.

In plastic fans the most important factor to be determined before starting resonance bench fatigue life test is to establish critical resonance condition in in-vehicle vibration strain test i.e., determing temperature, rpm, position and maginitude of highest stress. It is not always the highest stress or temperature condition which gives critical situation. The stress values obtained from in-vehicle vibration test at different temperatures (23 C, 50 C & 100 C) have to be compared to fatigue strengths (different at different temperature) at 10^7 cycles to obtain critical condition. Where 10^7 cycles can be considered to be the maximum number of cycles which a nylon fan be subjected to during its life time. Saftey factors at different temperatures can be calculated . Saftey factor is defined as the ratio of fatigue strength at 10^7 cycles to average dynamic stress at a particular temperature. The condition which gives the lowest saftey factor is the critical condition. This procedure of averaging the maximum and minimum stress and comparing the averaged stress with the fatigue strength works well only if the differences in maximum dynamic stress and minimum dynamic stress is very small. If not, cumulative damage at all three different temperatures using equation (4) should be calculated. The condition corresponding to maximum value of cumulative damage is the critical condition.

THE INFLUENCE OF NON-ZERO MEAN STRESS ON FATIGUE (CORRECTED SAFTEY FACTORS/CUMULATIVE DAMAGE):

The saftey factors calculated above are based on the yield strength at 10^7 cycles with zero mean stress. But in practice mean stress exists since fan is subjected to combined centrifugal and aerodynamic loading inaddition to vibration loading. Hence maximum strength at 10^7 cycles should be lower. Using the equation given by Goodman (equation 3) strengths should be corrected. This changes the saftey factors and cumulative damage. The saftey factors in the presence of mean stress are calculated again if the differences in maximum dynamic stress and minimum stress is very less. If not, cumulative damage at all three different temperatures using equation (4) should be calculated. The reciprocal of cumulative damage given by equation (4) gives fatigue life in number of blocks. In case of fan considered in the present paper the condition corresponding to maximum value of cumulative damage corresponds to 50 C. The cumulative damage calculated using equation (4) corresponding to different stress maginities obtained from the in-vehicle vibration test happened to be considerably less than unity and the fatigue life predicted by this procedure exceeds 10^7 cycles in this case. From 'Resonance bench life test' it is found that the experimental nylon fan considered passed 10^7 cycles without showing any cracks.

V SPIN BURST TEST

Another item in typical durability tests is "Spin-burst" test. The fan is subjected to high rotational speeds in a "vacuum" chamber until failure occurs. The speed at failure of fan is recorded. The results obtained in the foregoing sections (by experimental in-vehicle strain tests) can also be used to predict the speed of failure.

The position of strain gages used in in-vehicle strain test is based on information (high stress positions)obtained from FEA. Normal mode analysis, which is one part of the dynamic analysis, was used to determine the locations of high stresses where the strain gages would be attached. Both of steady and fluctuating components of the fan loading were used in FEA analysis.

In some cases of blade shapes of automotive fans [1] FEA gives a maximum mean stress value, under only centrifugal loading, which is close to maximum mean stress obtained under combined aerodynamic and centrifugal loadings. Hence maximum mean stress obtained during in-vehicle vibration test by combined centrifugal and aerodynamic loading can be considered almost equal to maximum stress obtained only by centrifugal loading. Considering this fact we can use the mean stress result obtained during in-vehicle strain test to extrapolate to predict the 'Burst' RPM of fan. The stresses produced under centrifugal loading is proportional to square of the speed of fan. The maximum mean stress obtained in in-vehicle strain test at room temperature is 49.7 MPa at 5400 RPM. This gives a linearly extrapolated 'Burst' speed of 10,800 RPM. The same fan gave a 'Burst' speed of 11,000 RPM from actual 'BURST TEST' experiment. It should be noted here that the stress value is linearly extrapolated. If the material behaviour under stress is non-linear then we can not perform this type of linear extrapolation. Since the strain gage locations in our experiments are obtained from FEA, the comparision made here is a good indication of the accuracy of the FEA prediction on the high stress regions.

VI SUMMARY AND CONCLUSIONS:

Modeling and vibration analysis of glass filled nylon fan using linear finite element method is carried out and Shaker test and In-vehicle vibration experiments in controlled conditions are carried out to verify the accuracy of results obtained from FEA. The natural frequencies of nylon fan are calculated from FEA and are also obtained using Shaker test at several different temperatures. Natural frequencies obtained at several temperatures using FEA compares fairly well with those obtained from experiments.

The dynamic stresses on both nylon and steel portions of the fan are also obtained from In-vehicle strain test at several different temperatures. Assuming that the main source of vibration is due to aerodynamic interaction between the fan and sourrounding components and assuming that the amplitude of the vibration excitation is the same as the static fan loading, frequency response analysis of fan using FEA is carried out. Comparision of dynamic stresses obtained from In-vehicle vibration strain test and experiments is made at several different temperatures and vibration modes. This comparision shows that the method described in this paper using FEA gives fairly good results for the fans and vehicles considered in this paper. Further, the methodology to obtain fatigue life of nylon fan under vibration loading is described.

ACKNOWLEDGEMENT:

The authors would like to express their appreciation to M. Hatori of USUI Kokusai Sangyo Kaisha, Ltd, Japan and David Esio of UIC for carrying out some of our experiments and to Dr. Sukeyuki Kobayashi of UIC for his suggestions and discussions.

REFERENCES:

1. Meda G. Lakshmikantha and H. Ito: ' Method of Research Approach for Structural Analysis Automotive Plastic Fans: Analytical and Experimental Investigation', SAE paper no. 960143. 1996 SAE International Congress and Exposition, Detroit, Michigan.

2. CSA/NASTRAN user's manual, Volume I, CSAR, California, 1994.

3. Theory of Vibration with applications by William T. Thomson, Prentice-Hall of India Private Limited, New Delhi,1975.

4. An Introduction to the Theory of Aeroelasticity, Y. C. Fung, Dover Publications, Inc., New York, 1993.

APPENDIX

SOURCE OF VIBRATION:

The vibration of fan in the underhood envirnoment can be caused due to following reasons.

1) unbalance of fan and misalignment between the fan and water pump:

The unbalance of fan usually results due to physical imperfection in the fan. The dynamic response x(t) of fan under unbalance is given by

$$x(t) = \frac{(m/k)a\omega^2 \sin(\omega t - \Theta_1)}{\sqrt{(1-(\omega/\omega_n)^2)^2 + (2\zeta\omega/\omega_n)^2}} + X e^{-\zeta\omega_n t} \sin((\sqrt{1-\zeta^2})\omega_n t + \Theta)$$

Where 'm' is the unbalanced mass, ω is the rotational velocity, 'a' is the eccentricity of unbalanced mass and ζ is the damping ratio.

The resonance of fan due to unbalance is obtained whenever the frequency of unbalanced mass in a rotating fan is equal to the natural frequency of nylon fan. In the fan A considered in this paper the lowest natural frequency of fan at 100 C is 108 Hz. The maximum limit on the RPM of fan considered in this case is 5500 i.e.,91.6 Hz. Hence forcing frequency due to unbalance of fan is lower than the lowest natural frequency of fan. In a typical Engineering Specification the maximum allowable unbalance in a engine driven plastic fan is 30 gm-cm. An equation similar to the one above can be derived for resonance caused due to misalignment of fan. In a typical Engineering Specification the maximum allowable misalignment angle between the fan and water pump is 0.005 radians. In this case also the forcing frequency doesn't match with the lowest natural frequency of fan. Hence neither unbalance nor misalignment may result in resonance of fan considered in this paper.

2) Firing of engine:

The engine used in the present case is a four stroke 10 cylinder engine. Hence there are five firings for every revolution which gives a firing frequency of 425 Hz at 5100 RPM. The strain gage output of nylon fan (at 50 C and at 5100 RPM of fan) at resonance condition gives a frequency of 169.5Hz which is the natural frequency of fan. Also at 2900 RPM the firing frequency is 241.6 Hz where as the strain gage output at the resonance condition of fan (at 50 C and at 2900 RPM of fan) gives a frequency of 148 Hz which also is the natural

frequency of fan. Hence engine firing may not be the major contributing factor for fan vibrations in the case of fan considered in this paper.

3) unevenly distributed aerodynamic forces:

The fan in the underhood compartment is subjected to unevenly distributed aerodynamic forces due to unevenly and tightly packaged underhood compartment.

In order to isolate the source of vibration, a simple experiment was carried out. The fan was rotated in open air to see whether resonance of fan can be observed either due to unbalance of the fan or due to misalignment. In order to perform this test, strain gages were mounted on the fan at relevant positions as obtained from FEA. No noticeable dynamic strains on the fan were observed during this experiment. Further, a backboard with blocks facing the back of fan was used to represent the engine block with pulleys. When the experiment was repeated with this backboard appreciable dynamic strains on the fan were observed whenever resonance conditions were reached. Hence it can be concluded that the main cause of vibration of fan in our case is due to interaction of air between the fan, pulleys and engine block. Similar explanation can be given for other fans considered in this paper.

970073

Thermoset Polyester Composites (BMC) vs ETP (Engineering Thermoplastics) in Under the Hood Applications

Larry E. Nunnery, Jr.
Bulk Molding Compounds, Inc.

Impossible as it may be to imagine a world without frisbees and hula hoops, Ban-Lon, Dacron, Leatherette and Pink Flamingos - much less, kitchen cabinets fashioned from polyester panels - there was a time when plastic had not achieved its iconic status. When the hulk of the Titanic was discovered, the French government gave would be claimants the salvaged lost property. What most impressed Charles Josselin, Secretary of the French Merchant Marine, was that the long list of everyday objects found (buttons, bracelets, leather goods, ivory combs, mirror cases, hair brushes, etc.), not one was made out of plastic. "That, if nothing else, " he quipped at a press conference, "shows how much times have changed." Yes, changed indeed! In 1979, the global volume of plastic production outstripped that of steel. We formally entered the Plastic Age from Astro Turf to foam cups to automotive under-the-hood applications.

The applications for high performance plastic (HPP) under-the-hood are boundless. BCC (Business Communications Co.) of Norwalk, CT reports that total plastic used in automobiles by the year 2000 will exceed 3.5 billion pounds representing a three percent (3%) annual growth. Under-the-hood parts will exceed 1.5 billion pounds by the year 2000. Lighting, engine covers, fuel systems, timing chain covers, brake systems and many more offer significant growth for high performance plastics (HPP).

So what are we looking for in this COST/PERFORMANCE RATIO?

What do we mean by cost?

(1) Cost per cubic inch.
(2) Cost of processing.
(3) Cost of tooling.
(4) Cost of assembly.
(5) Cost of recycling.
(6) Cost of packaging.
(7) Cost of handling.
(8) Cost based on functionality.

All of these factors play a major role in what materials you, the automotive engineer, will select for a given under-the-hood application. Cost is the overall driving force because traditional materials have worked in the past and we most probably could make them work in the future. We are here to talk about the fastest material explosion in the history of mankind. From polyetherrether-ketone to high heat polycarbonate to PBT to reinforced nylon to new thermoset composites, the list of alternatives keeps right on growing.

We have already determined that Cost is the "beginning and the end". Maybe, just maybe, we should try to determine what is needed for the application and not take the input of some plastic marketing person on what is the most perfect under-the-hood material development since the Titanic.

So what are the properties we need to develop a successful application?

Look at the alternator cap in Ferrari Motor Corp's. Formula One race car. They needed a material that could maintain its "strength, integrity and electrical resistance" in continuous service at temperatures as high as 300° F (150° C). The nod went to 30% glass fiber reinforced PEEK molding compound. PEEK also provides excellent resistance to oils, greases, and to the vibration experienced in service. Two connector supports were also molded from 30% glass PEEK. This information comes from the 1988 February issue of Machine Design. What properties did Ferrari need. What properties did Machine Design think Ferrari needed?

Strength and integrity? We're not sure what that means. Electrical resistance? Most plastics do well; PVC does a good job at appreciably less cost. Do not forget, Cost, "The Beginning and The End."

"Continuous Service" at temperatures as high as 300° F...... A good one, if we know what "Continuous Service" means. Resistance to oil and greases; yes, that means chemical resistance. Resistance to vibration in the service environment, does that relate to Tg (Glass Transition

Temperature)?

If we turn to a vinyl ester BMC application, the 4.0 liter V-8 valve covers, the major reason given for the switch from metal was a weight savings. BMC covers weigh approximately 40% less than steel covers and 25% less than covers that are die cast . In this case, Ford also got lower noise, vibration and harshness levels. Molded-in grooves that hold a silicone gasket improved sealability. The molded cover also reduced assembly costs because of the molded-in integral retainers for spark plug wires.

Next let's turn to radiator tanks traditionally made of metal. Nylon 6/6 is the material of choice for Blackstone cooling systems made for BMW, Volvo and Fiat. The reason given was weight savings, reduced assembly costs, and resistance to oil, grease and glycol. Nylon 6/6 can withstand high temperatures and pressures as well.

How about headlamp reflectors? Heat resistance, dimensional stability at elevated temperatures, chemical resistance and low creep list a few of the material requirements.

So what can we learn from each of these successful applications of HPP?

Load bearing at temperature.

Chemical resistance at temperature.

Electrical properties.

Mechanical properties.

FR or flammability characteristics.

Processability.

Recyclability.

Compounding considerations/ Customization.

And, Oh Yes, Cost!

If we try to rank these needs, we must take a general approach, but this is the task at hand.

    (1) Thermal
    (2) Mechanical
    (3) Chemical
    (4) Electrical
    (5) Flammability
    (6) Processability
    (7) Customization
    (8) Recyclability

We all know that COST is No. 1, but for this discussion we are looking at performance properties.

THERMAL/MECHANICAL

"History has proven time after time that heat deflection temperature (HDT) is an absolutely useless number."

The glass transition (Tg) of a material is the thermal/mechanical characteristic that must be studied and understood to make an intelligent engineering selection. The long term performance of a part being designed depends directly on the long term integrity of the material chosen.

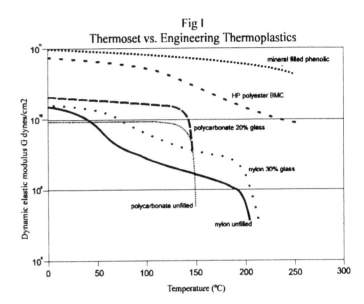

Fig I
Thermoset vs. Engineering Thermoplastics

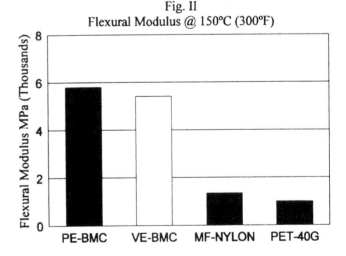

Fig. II
Flexural Modulus @ 150°C (300°F)

Historically, the long term integrity of a plastic has been one of the most difficult aspects of an application to evaluate. Dynamic Mechanical Analysis (DMA) measures modulus and energy dissipation properties under stress. Such measurements provide quantitative and qualitative information about the long term performance of the material. This method of analysis can help identify and predict a plastic's behavior and resistance to creep at changing temperatures. DMA, TGA and Instrumented Impact technology are all key tools to help better select the proper material.

CHEMICAL RESISTANCE

This area is a tough one to get a handle on. Let us compare mineral filled nylon, glass PET and polyester based high performance composites (BMC) and study the effect of long term exposure to hot motor oil and anti-freeze/coolant. Below you will see that flexural properties, impact properties and barcol hardness all change with exposure.

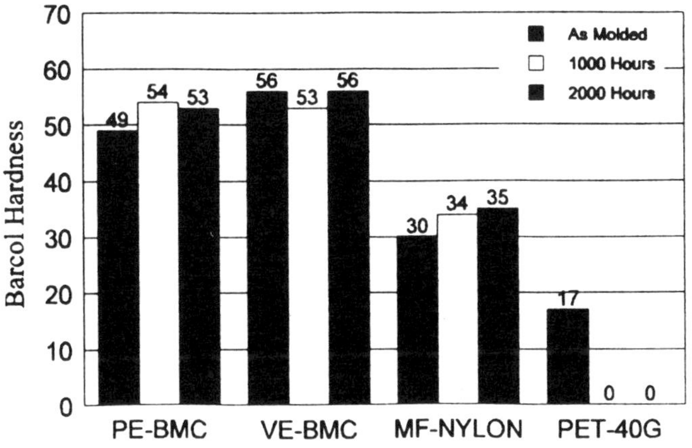

All of the samples were affected by exposure to the automotive engine fluids. In every case, the cross linked materials (PE BMC & VE BMC) held up better.

Don't forget that H2O is a chemical. If we look back at our radiator application, Nylon 6/6 was the material selected by Blackstone Cooling Systems. A good material for this application? If we look at Figures VI and VII that

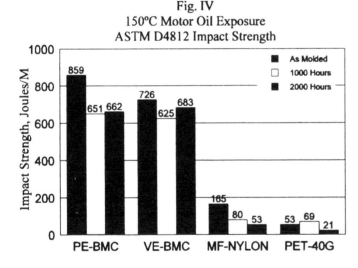

Fig. III
150°C Motor Oil Exposure
Flexural Strength - 1/8" Specimens

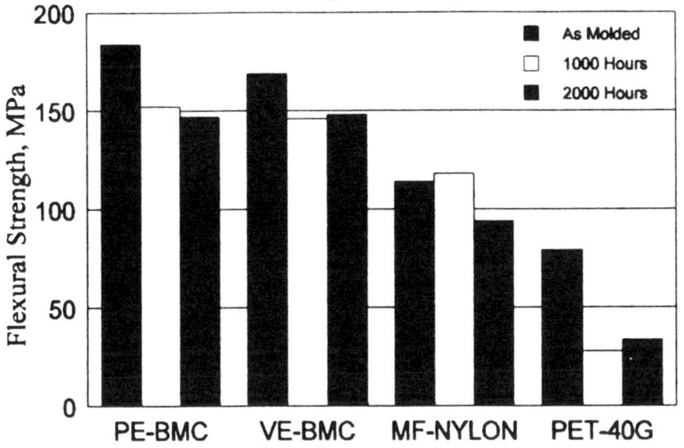

Fig. IV
150°C Motor Oil Exposure
ASTM D4812 Impact Strength

Fig. V
150°C Motor Oil Exposure
Barcol Hardness

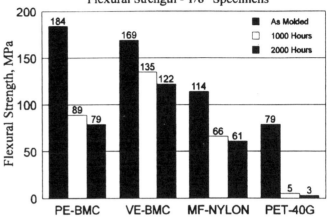

Fig. VI
102°C (215°F) Antifreeze/Coolant Exposure
Flexural Strength - 1/8" Specimens

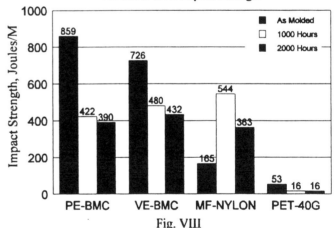

Fig. VII
102°C (215°F) Antifreeze/Coolant Exposure
ASTM D4812 Impact Strength

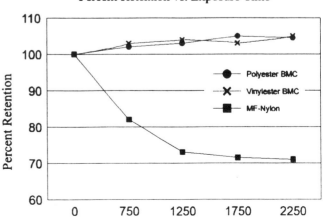

Fig. VIII
Flexural Modulus at 50% Relative Humidity
Percent Retention vs. Exposure Time

illustrate coolant exposure and Figure VIII which shows a relative humidy exposure comparison of PE BMC, VE BMC and MF Nylon 6/6, we may think twice about our material selection.

ELECTRICAL PROPERTIES/FR

Most types of HPP (High Performance Plastics) offer grades that can meet or exceed the electrical and flame resistant requirements of under-the-hood applications; PBT, Nylons, PE BMC, VE BMC can all do the job.

PROCESSABILITY

In this area, engineering thermoplastic materials (ETP) have a clear advantage. The development of equipment to injection mold with automation and the reduced need for secondary operations make the cost of processing less with the ETP's. Based on the growth of automotive lighting and valve covers, the processing technologies for PE BMC and VE BMC have shown great advancement in the last five (5) years. With advancements in tooling like cold runner manifolds, gate cutters, vacuum, in mold cure sensors and pressure sensors, the gap is continuously being narrowed.

CUSTOMIZATION

Clearly the domain of the thermoset composites. These materials are cold blended, not cooked, and small batch compounding is possible. These materials offer a vast choice of properties. "Customization" means the ability to develop a property performance profile to meet the real needs of the application at the lowest possible cost.

RECYCLING

Clearly an advantage of ETP. "You Can Recycle Thermosets" but you don't get the same impact on cost. ETP can normally be mixed back into the process creating a zero waste situation. Thermoset scrap must be reduced to a fine particle size filler. Thermoset composites have been produced using several different loadings of recycled fillers. Thermal properties show no change while there is little or no effect on impact, flexural or tensile strength.

COST

If we look at cost per cubic inch, thermoset PE BMC and VE BMC win hands down (See Figure IX). As we said when we started this discussion, you have to look at all the cost factors and the need to rank them.

HPP (High Performance Plastics) - Lets give each technology a report card.

REPORT CARD
THE LOWER THE BETTER

	RATING FACTOR 1-10	ETP	THERMOSET POLYESTER BASE COMPOSITES
Cost/Cubic Inch	9	X 7 (63)	4 (36)
Cost of Processing	4	X 2 (8)	3 (12)
Cost of Tooling	3	X 2 (6)	2 (6)
Cost of Assembly	3	X 2 (6)	3 (9)
Cost of Recycling	1	X 1 (1)	3 (3)
Cost of Packaging	1	X 1 (1)	2 (2)
Cost of Handling	1	X 1 (1)	2 (2)
Cost Based on Functionality	4	X 4 (16)	5 (20)
Total		102	90

LONG TERM COST

When looking at the use of a limited petrochemical feedstock, the far gone conclusion is that global "per barrel" pricing will continue to escalate. Thermoset materials have a market advantage in that only 20-30% of these products are petroleum based while thermoplastics are 60-100%.

CONCLUSION

Don't forget Leatherette and Ping Flamingos. What we have said here is there are good offerings on both ends of the material selection spectrum. When you are looking at semi-crystalline, amorphous or alloys, don't forget that other family, called thermoset composites. The "Beginning and the End" may not be cost, but <u>Value</u>!

ACKNOWLEDGEMENTS

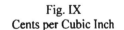
Fig. IX
Cents per Cubic Inch

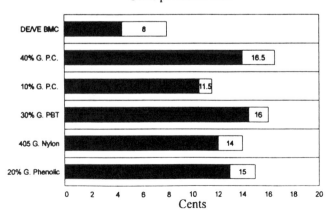

	Cents
DE/VE BMC	8
40% G. P.C.	16.5
10% G. P.C.	11.5
30% G. PBT	16
405 G. Nylon	14
20% G. Phenolic	15

(1) Plastic: The Making of a Synthetic Century by Stephen Fenichell
    1996, Pub. Harper Collins

(2) Advantage of Thermoset Composites In Automotive Engine Applications
    1993, R.S. Krigbaum, SAE Technical Paper

(3) Thermoplastics/Thermosets
    Plastic Engineering, Aug. 1996, Victor Wigojsky

(4) Performance Resins Target Low Cost, High Volume
    June '96, Modern Plastics, Peter Mapleston

(5) Tooling Innovations For Thermoset Molding
    Plastic Engineering, Aug. '96, Larry E. Nunnery, III

(6) SMC: A Third Generation
    June '95, Composites Technology, Joe McDermott

Compatibility of External Life Coolant Systems with Plastic Components

Amy S. Lapain
The Dow Chemical Co.

Edward A. Luibrand
Chrysler Corp.

ABSTRACT

The ethylene glycols which the OEM's are using today in the engine cooling systems have been under review by the federal government as proposed restricted substances, meaning that in the near future coolants must be screened by the OEM and reformulated or redesigned. In order to minimize handling of the coolant systems, ethylene glycol based systems containing organic acids as the primary corrosion inhibitors (vs. the conventional inorganic inhibitors widely utilized today) are being introduced to the market. The primary advantage of these systems is non-depletion of the inhibitors, allowing extended service intervals, where the coolant is changed between 100,000 - 200,000 miles versus 30,000 - 50,000 miles with the current systems utilizing inorganic inhibitors. This benefits the consumer and the environment

Plastic components are widely used in coolant systems where radiator end tanks, water pump impellers, inlets, outlets, and thermostat housings can be polymeric. A study was conducted in which a number of engineering plastics were exposed to long life coolants at elevated temperatures and pressures to determine the effect of the coolant. The intent of the study was to provide insight into plastics which can withstand the hot acid environment of extended life coolants during usage. Several extended life coolant systems were investigated, including one containing 100% remanufactured glycol, furthering a more environmental friendly system.

INTRODUCTION

North American OEMs are changing engine coolant inhibitor technology used in cooling systems to allow extended service intervals and because of new proposed federal government regulations. Most systems will continue to be ethylene glycol based; however, the main change will come in the inhibitor packages. Conventional inhibitor technology is silicate - phosphate based which can form a scale on the metal and plastic surfaces within the coolant system. Silicate based inhibitors are effective but they are depleted quickly and as such, new coolant must be added to insure sufficient inhibitor is in solution to allow a new silicate layer to be formed. Organic acid based systems used in long life coolants are buffered at a lower pH and minimize production of degradation products that are aggressive to aluminum; however the solvent effects of these new inhibitors may have adverse effects on the plastics currently used within typical cooling water systems.

The purpose of this paper is to discuss the performance of plastic components that may be affected by these new coolants. Several coolant formulations were used including propylene glycol, standard ethylene glycol, 100% virgin and 100% remanufactured long life ethylene glycol. The term remanufactured coolant refers to post consumer glycol that has been received through a central collection agency, distilled, filtered and replenished. Plastics tested in the coolants include nylon 66 (PA66), polyphthalamide (PPA), syndiotactic polystyrene (SPS), polyphenylene sulfide (PPS) and aliphatic aromatic polyamid (6TMPMDT). The nylon 66 and polyphthalamide materials were specifically compounded for increased hydrolytic stability. The Polyphenylene Sulfide grades tested included both hydrolytically stabilized and standard linear grades. Various temperatures were also investigated in a high pressure environment.

MATERIALS

COOLANTS - Several coolant systems were tested at various temperatures. These are shown in Table 1. The standard ethylene glycol was tested at 116°C, 127°C and 138°C. A propylene glycol system and two other long life ethylene glycol systems (100% remanufactured and 100% virgin) were run at 127°C. This temperature was chosen because it is commonly used as a maximum use temperature without system overheat. It was also a standard glycol resistance test temperature used in OEM material standards prior to the release of SAE J1639 which uses a 125°C testing temperature. Systems have also been seen to run as high as 138°C so this was chosen as a worse case scenario.

PLASTICS - The plastic materials used for this testing are summarized in Table 2. These were chosen because they are current or potential materials for use in coolant applications. Syndiotactic polystyrene has been proposed for use in these applications and will be compared to those materials traditionally used. A previous SAE paper by Bank, Wessel and Kolb (930088) describes the attributes of syndiotactic polystyrene. SPS is a semi-crystalline polymer synthesized from styrene monomer via metallocene catalysis. Because of it's semi-crystalline nature, the products exhibit attributes that are significantly different from atactic polystyrene. These include a high melting point, excellent hydrocarbon resistance, a high degree of dimensional stability and excellent electrical performance. Glass reinforcement is added at various levels to produce a range of products with higher temperature resistance, increased modulus and superior creep resistance. The glass reinforcement also acts to bridge the crystalline regions effectively tying them together. This model is illustrated in Figure 1. This process allows the crystalline regions to control the dimensional integrity of the system at elevated temperatures resulting in HDTUL performance in the range of 248°C. Figure 2 shows the relative thermal performance of SPS versus the other materials used in coolant applications. In addition, SPS is more hydrolytically stable than nearly all other competitive engineering thermoplastics as indicated in Figure 3. Moisture is not a concern during processing or post processing conditions.

EXPERIMENTAL METHOD

Chemical resistance testing was completed using the test apparatus shown in Figure 4. As the figure indicates, tensile bars were submerged in a reactor which is equipped with three heater bands, two thermocouples, two pressure sensing transducers and a frangible pressure device set to release pressures above 700 kPa (100 psi). Temperature control and monitoring of both temperature and operating pressure was accomplished through the use of a Camile® process control/ data acquisition unit running on a personal computer. The actual exposure was conducted by charging the reactor with the fluid of interests and then submerging a rack loaded with tensile bars in the fluid. The reactor is then sealed and ramped to temperature. Since the system is sealed, pressure builds within the reactor due to the expansion of fluid as the temperature is increased. Pressure was normalized at 172 kPa (25 psi) for each experiment by addition of a nitrogen pressure boost to the head space of the reactor for sample tested at 116°C and 127°C while the internal

pressure of the system tested at 138°C was sufficient to not warrant the N2 boost. Temperatures and pressures were chosen using SAEJ1639 as a minimum requirement which states 125°C and 110 kPa (16psi) as the preferred testing conditions. ASTM type I tensile specimens were immersed in a mixture of 50% coolant and 50% water. At various intervals, samples were pulled from the chambers and tested against the controls. SAEJ1639 also states a 1000 hour (41 day) test period. Materials were tested for this length of time or longer if the coolants were considered long life. Coolant was also removed at each interval and tested for chemical degradation.

Tensile, Flexural and Weight loss properties were taken at various intervals. Tensile and elongation testing was done according to ASTM D638. Flexural modulus was evaluated using ASTM D790. Changes in weight were also studied in each system to determine susceptibility to hydrolysis after the indicated exposure.

Comparisons were made between the materials at various temperatures in the ethylene glycol coolant. These were then compared to the propylene glycol coolant. The effects of the 100% virgin ethylene glycol coolant were then compared to the 100% remanufactured coolant as well as to the other fluids. Figure 5 is a legend for figures 6-9.

RESULTS AND DISCUSSION

TENSILE STRENGTH - Tensile strength results are shown in figures 6A-6F. As the figures indicate SPS exhibits a gradual decline in tensile strength at 116°C in the ethylene glycol coolant while at 127°C and 138°C it shows the most significant drop during the first 7 days, becomes saturated, and then remains steady throughout the remainder of the testing. The strength of the PPA resin also falls is the first 7 days for all three temperatures as it absorbs moisture. It then levels off for nearly 40 days at 116°C and 127°C but shows a large tensile loss if exposed at 138°C for the same period. The aliphatic aromatic polyamid is similar to the PPA but is affected at a slower rate. It falls slightly at 127°C and drops off significantly at the end of 40 days at 138°C. PPS remains constant at 116°C. At 127°C and 138°C it falls slightly and levels off for the remainder of the test. Nylon 66 looses half of its strength in the first 7 days. It levels off at 116°C but drops to nearly 0% retention after 40 days at 138°C.

The SPS materials behaved the same in the propylene glycol coolant when compared to the ethylene glycol coolant with respect to tensile strength. The aliphatic aromatic polyamid had a more noticeable drop in the propylene glycol. The nylon 6,6, which was not tested at 127°C in the ethylene glycol had a large decrease during the first 7 days of testing in the propylene glycol and then leveled off similar to that seen in the ethylene glycol at 116°C. The PPS materials maintained their properties in the propylene glycol.

There were no appreciable difference in the tensile strength behavior when comparing how the resins performed in the 100% remanufactured ethylene glycol versus 100% virgin ethylene glycol coolant for 40 days; however longer exposure periods show that PPA is sensitive to remanufactured long life coolants.

TENSILE ELONGATION - Tensile Elongation is shown in figures 7A-7F. The SPS materials remained fairly constant in tensile elongation at all three temperatures in the ethylene glycol coolant. The PPS remained fairly constant but exhibited a very slight increase over the first 7 days as temperature increased. The PA66 demonstrated a significant increase at 7 days and then dropped off consistently through the remainder of the test at 116°C and drastically at 127°C. The aliphatic aromatic polyamid and PPA increased in elongation similarly at all three temperatures after 7 days. They generally saw a drop for the remainder of the testing period. It is interesting to note that both aliphatic aromatic polyamid and PPA dropped dramatically in elongation after 40 days at 137°C indicating a fundamental change in the material.

The PPA, aliphatic aromatic polyamid, and PA 66 materials did better in the propylene glycol than ethylene glycol. PA 66 in propylene glycol at 126°C had similar results of that in the ethylene glycol at 116°C. PPA and aliphatic aromatic polyamid in propylene glycol increased similarly as in ethylene glycol but after 40 days maintained more than 2% elongation versus 0.4% in ethylene glycol. The other materials behaved similar in the propylene glycol and the ethylene glycol.

There were no significant changes in the behavior of the tensile elongation when comparing all polymers in 100% remanufactured versus 100% virgin coolants. The only difference is that the PPA material dropped slightly more in the remanufactured coolant at 111 days.

FLEXURAL MODULUS - Figures 8A-8F illustrate flexural modulus behavior. SPS maintained a constant flexural modulus at 116°C in the ethylene glycol coolant. The 40% glass reinforced SPS dropped off as the temperature increased approaching the value of the 30% glass reinforced SPS. The nylon 66 had an initial drop at 7 days for 116°C and 138°C and then leveled off at 116°C while continuing to drop at 138°C. PPA lost modulus quickly at all three temperatures. It leveled off at 116°C but showed significant temperature sensitivity by decreasing more noticeably as the temperature increased. The aliphatic aromatic polyamid maintained its stiffness better than PPA during the first 7 days of the test and though it follows the PPA curve thereafter, it shows an ability to maintain stiffness over a longer period

of time. The PPS maintained flexural properties throughout the testing period.

There were no distinct differences when comparing the flexural modulus results of any of the tested materials in either the standard ethylene glycol or propylene glycol. Similarly, there was no difference in flexural modulus when comparing how the resins performed in the 100% remanufactured ethylene glycol versus 100% virgin ethylene glycol coolant at 40 days. Results were slightly worse in all the resins for remanufactured coolant when tested to 111 days.

WEIGHT GAIN - Weight gain is illustrated in figures 9A-9F. PPS and SPS had no significant weight changes at any of the three temperatures (less than 1%). PPA and aliphatic aromatic polyamid showed a larger weight gain of about 3% at 116°C, increasing to 5% at 138°C in the standard ethylene glycol coolant. At 138°C the nylon 66 had a huge initial weight gain of 14% and then dropped off dramatically such that it had a negative weight gain of 8%. This indicates that hydrolysis is occurring causing a breakdown of the nylon 66 polymer.

The materials behaved nearly the same with respect to weight gain in the propylene and ethylene glycol. Propylene glycol had a slightly worse effect causing an increase in weight of an additional 1% in SPS, aliphatic aromatic polyamid and PPA while having no effect on PPS. There were no appreciable difference in percent weight gain when comparing how the resins performed in the 100% remanufactured ethylene glycol versus 100% virgin ethylene glycol coolant.

SUMMARY OBSERVATIONS-Chemical resistance of PPS and SPS remain nearly equivalent in all types of coolants and temperatures tested. Nylon 66, aliphatic aromatic polyamid and PPA show some variations depending on coolant and dramatic changes with temperature. At 127°C or below, however, any of the tested materials could function acceptably in most coolant applications.

Aliphatic aromatic polyamid and PPA increased slightly in weight and elongation over time. This was due mostly to moisture absorption/saturation. One significant difference between the two is that aliphatic aromatic polyamid generally absorbed the coolant more slowly resulting in a more gradual loss of tensile and flexural properties rather than a quick drop in the first 7 days as seen in PPA. SPS showed most if its property changes during the first 7 days; however this is not due to moisture absorption.

At 40 days and 126°C, neither the long life virgin, remanufactured, nor the propylene glycol coolants showed any significant chemical effects on any of the tested materials. In general, propylene glycol was slightly less harmful than ethylene glycol in all but weight gain. Remanufactured coolant was equivalent to long life coolant at 40 days but had a worse effect on several materials when extended to 111 days of testing. It is not known whether or not this change over time is due to decomposition of the coolant or coolant additives. The long life coolants tested up to 40 days indicate that decomposition has not occurred. Coolants aged up to 111 days will be evaluated at a later time.

CONCLUSION

Coolant applications represent a new and challenging arena for the use of engineering thermoplastics. Syndiotactic polystyrene, a new engineering polymer, exhibits the performance characteristics necessary for success in this application area. After long term testing in ethylene and propylene glycol and reformulated coolants, it was verified that SPS behaves better than most other materials currently being used in coolant applications. It maintains strength, elongation, flexural properties and dimension with improved hydrolytic stability. Though the initial strength of SPS is below that of PPA, aliphatic aromatic polyamid, and nylon 66, its chemical resistance to coolants are superior, being less affected by changes in glycol composition and increased temperature. Also SPS appears to be the only polymer besides PPS which can be used in glycol at temperatures of 137 °C for prolonged periods in ethylene glycols. PPS is undoubtedly the superior material for initial and maintained strength, stiffness, and dimensional stability, yet it is more expensive than other resins tested. As a result, SPS may be a cost effective alternative to many existing plastics applications that exist within the automotive coolant system today.

ACKNOWLEDGEMENTS

The authors gratefully acknowledge Dave Bank, Mike Young, Kevin Connor and James Steele.

Table 1: Summary of Coolant Systems

Coolant	Cooling System	Inhibitor	Recycle Content	Temperatures Tested
A	Ethylene Glycol	Standard		240°F, 260°F, 280°F
B	Propylene Glycol	Low Silicate		260°F
C	Ethylene Glycol	Low Silicate / Organic Acid	100% Virgin	260°F
D	Ethylene Glycol	Low Silicate Organic Acid	100% Recycle	260°F

Table 2: Summary of Resins Tested.

Material Type	Abbreviation	Filler Content	Hydrolytically Stabilized?
Aliphatic Aromatic Polyamid	6TMPMDT	45	N/A
Nylon 6/6	PA66	33	Yes
Polyphenylene Sulfide	PPS	40	N/A
Polyphenylene Sulfide	PPS (2)	40	Yes
Polyphthalamide	PPA	45	Yes
Syndiotactic Polystyrene	SPS	30	N/A
Syndiotactic Polystyrene	SPS	40	N/A

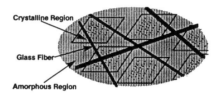

Figure 1: Schematic illustration of the effect of glass reinforcement

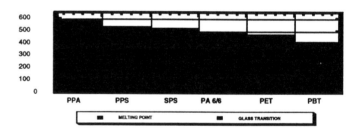

Figure 2: Heat Performance of Resins used in Coolant Applications in °F

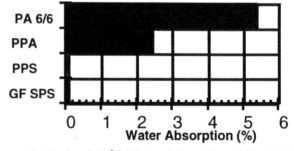

Figure 3: 28 day / 23 °C Water Adsorption of Materials used in Coolant Applications

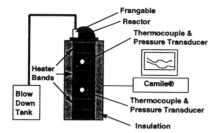

Figure 4: Schematic illustration of coolant testing apparatus

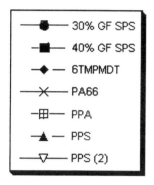

Figure 5: Legend for Figures 6-9.

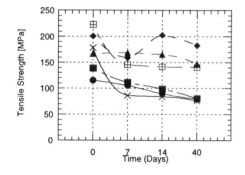

Figure 6A: Tensile Strength vs. Time for Resins in Standard Ethylene Glycol at 116°C

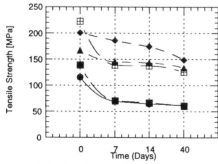

Figure 6B: Tensile Strength vs. Time for Resins

in Standard Ethylene Glycol at 127°C

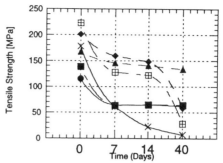

Figure 6C: Tensile Strength vs. Time for Resins in Standard Ethylene Glycol at 138°C

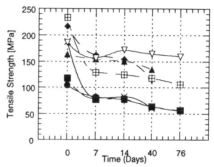

Figure 6D: Tensile Strength vs. Time for Resins in Propylene Glycol at 128°C

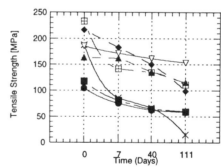

Figure 6E: Tensile Strength vs. Time for Resins in 100 % Virgin Ethylene Glycol at 128°C (Long Life)

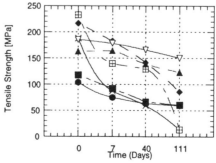

Figure 6F: Tensile Strength vs. Time for Resins in 100 % Reformulated Ethylene Glycol at 127°C (Long Life)

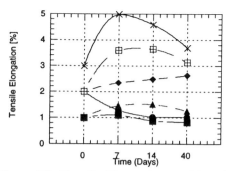

Figure 7A: Tensile Elongation vs. Time for Resins in Standard Ethylene Glycol at 116°C

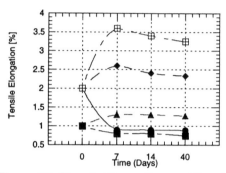

Figure 7B: Tensile Elongation vs. Time for Resins in Standard Ethylene Glycol at 127°C

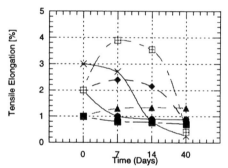

Figure 7C: Tensile Elongation vs. Time for Resins in Standard Ethylene Glycol at 138°C

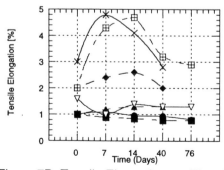

Figure 7D: Tensile Elongation vs. Time for Resins in Propylene Glycol at 127°C

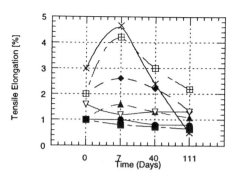

Figure 7E: Tensile Elongation vs. Time for Resins in 100% Virgin Ethylene Glycol at 127°C (Long Life)

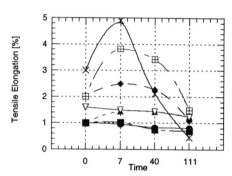

Figure 7F: Tensile Elongation vs. Time for Resins in 100% Reformulated Ethylene Glycol at 127°C (Long Life)

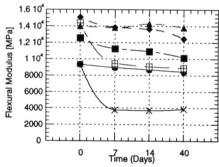

Figure 8A: Flexural Modulus vs. Time for Resins in Standard Ethylene Glycol at 116°C

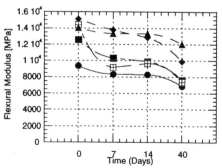

Figure 8B: Flexural Modulus vs. Time for Resins in Standard Ethylene Glycol at 127°C

24

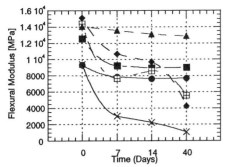

Figure 8C: Flexural Modulus vs. Time for Resins in Standard Ethylene Glycol at 138°C

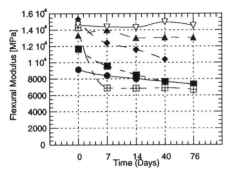

Figure 8D: Flexural Modulus vs. Time for Resins in Propylene Glycol at 127°C

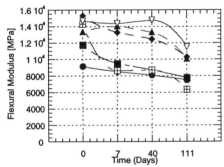

Figure 8E: Flexural Modulus vs. Time for Resins in 100% Virgin Ethylene Glycol at 127°C (Long Life)

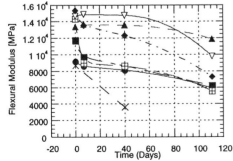

Figure 8F: Flexural Modulus vs. Time for Resins in 100% Reformulated Ethylene Glycol at 127°C (Long Life)

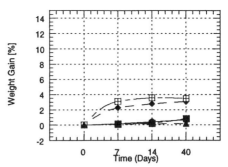

Figure 9A Weight Gain vs. Time for Resins in Standard Ethylene Glycol at 116°C

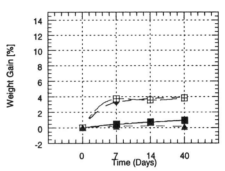

Figure 9B Weight Gain vs. Time for Resins in Standard Ethylene Glycol at 127°C

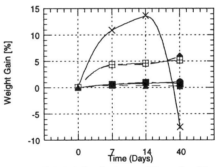

Figure 9C:Weight Gain vs. Time for Resins in Standard Ethylene Glycol at 138°C

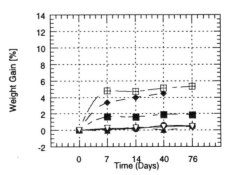

Figure 9D Weight Gain vs. Time for Resins in Propylene Glycol at 127°C

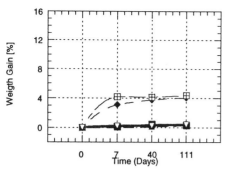

Figure 9E: Weight Gain vs. Time for Resins
in 100% Virgin Ethylene Glycol at 127°C (Long Life)

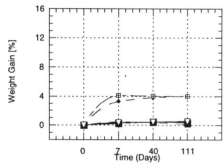

Figure 9F: Weight Gain vs. Time for Resins
in 100% Reformulated Ethylene Glycol at 127°C (Long
Life)

970076

Vibration Welded Composite Intake Manifolds - Design Considerations and Material Selection Criteria

Jordan Lee
General Motors Powertrain

Lisa Roessler
E.I. du Pont de Nemours & Co. Inc.

ABSTRACT

Successful design, development and production of composite intake manifolds require detailed knowledge of the interactions between the manifold's design, functional requirements, manufacturing method, and the composite material used for its construction. This paper provides the background necessary to understand these interactions, and reviews important criteria on selecting the best composite material for a given application. The following outlines the topics reviewed in this paper.

A. **INTRODUCTION**
B. **BENEFITS OF COMPOSITE INTAKE MANIFOLDS**
   1. Cost
   2. Mass
   3. Air Flow
C. **MANUFACTURING METHODS BY REGION**
   1. North America
   2. Europe
D. **COMPOSITE INTAKE MANIFOLD DESIGN CONSIDERATIONS**
   1. Stress
   2. Radiated Noise
   3. Burst Strength
   4. Temperature
E. **COMPOSITE INTAKE MANIFOLD MANUFACTURING METHODS.**
   1. Lost Core Molding
   2. Vibration Welding
   3. Other Methods
F. **VIBRATION WELDING PROCESS CONSIDERATIONS**
   1. Design Constraints
   2. Material Compatibility
   3. Glass Loading
   4. Molded-In Stresses
G. **COMPOSITE MATERIAL CONSIDERATIONS FOR WELDED INTAKE MANIFOLDS**
   1. Base Material
   2. Glass Loading
   3. Additives
H. **COMPOSITE MATERIAL SELECTION CRITERIA**
I. **SUMMARY**

A. INTRODUCTION

As the number of composite air intake manifold applications grow worldwide, the manufacturing industry has developed several proven methods for their construction. In this paper, we will review the benefits of composite intake manifolds, discuss important design considerations and requirements of composite intake manifolds, and review the various methods of manufacturing. We will then focus on the vibration welding process, which promises to be an effective low cost method of manufacture. With regard to vibration welding, we will discuss the various composite material choices available, and offer guidelines to ensure the composite material selected provides robust manufacturing and allows the manifold to achieve its design requirements.

B. BENEFITS OF COMPOSITE INTAKE MANIFOLDS

Glass reinforced polyamide (GR PA), also referred to as glass reinforced nylon or composite material, is rapidly gaining favor as the material of choice for intake manifold construction. Compared to sand cast aluminum, it offers three distinct advantages: lower cost, lower mass, and a smoother interior surface finish.

1. Cost

Compared to conventional sand cast aluminum intake manifolds, composite intake manifolds are typically less expensive in terms of piece cost and capital investment. Lower cost results from reduced material cost, on a pound per manifold basis, as well as the reduction in the number of operations, thus equipment, needed to manufacture a finished part. Typical manufacturing operations as a function of method are shown in Table 1.

Table 1

Typical Manufacturing Operations vs. Manufacturing Method

Sand Cast Aluminum	Lost Core Composite	Vibration Welded Composite
Mold Core	Mold Core	Mold Pieces
Form Cope & Drag (Mold)	Overmold Core	Weld Pieces
Cast Manifold	Core Removal	De-Flash
Core Removal	Wash Out	Insert Installation
De-Gate & De-Flash	De-Flash	
Wash Out	Insert Installation	
Machine Flanges		
Machine Holes & Threads		
Wash Out		

Note that the vibration welding process requires the least amount of operations to produce an intake manifold. With regard to piece cost, Figure 1 illustrates the difference for a future production intake manifold application which was quoted using the three different manufacturing methods shown in Table 1.

Figure 1

Cost Comparison of a Future Intake Manifold Application

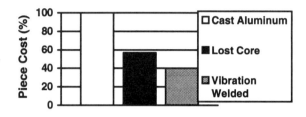

2. Mass

Automotive manufacturers strive to reduce vehicle mass in order to improve performance and fuel economy. Compared to sand cast aluminum intake manifolds, composite manifolds offer a significant reduction in mass.

Figure 2 shows a comparison of density between the two materials. Note that density alone contributes to a 50% reduction in mass. Mass is reduced further by virtue of wall section thickness. With conventional sand cast aluminum, wall section thickness is approximately 4 mm. With composite intake manifold manufacturing techniques this can be reduced to 3 mm.

Figure 2

Comparison of Density

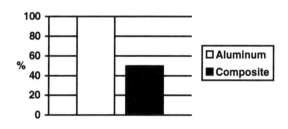

3. Air Flow

The air flow efficiency of an intake manifold is affected by the roughness of the interior surfaces that form the air flow path. Rough surfaces contribute to increased drag which lowers air flow efficiency and thus air flow capacity. The interior surfaces of a composite intake manifold are significantly smoother than those of a sand cast manifold. As a result, when an intake manifold's air flow path design is held constant, a composite intake manifold exhibits an increase in air flow capacity of approximately 3%. A 3% increase in air flow capacity can result in up to a 3% increase in peak power.[1] Composite intake manifolds offer an additional air flow benefit due to the process's precision in forming the air flow path. This precision, which is typical with most injection molding processes, allows the configuration of the air flow path to be optimized, thus yielding improvements in air flow efficiency. This level of manufacturing precision is not possible with conventional sand casting methods.

As discussed, composite intake manifolds offer several distinct advantages when compared to their sand cast aluminum counterparts. Lower cost, lower mass, and increased air flow performance can be expected.

C. MANUFACTURING METHODS BY REGION

The preferred method used for composite intake manifold manufacturing appears to differ from region to region throughout the world. These preferences also appear to change over time. For example, in North America today, the preferred manufacturing method is lost core molding, but current trends indicate that is changing. In fact, forecasts predict that the majority of composite intake manifolds will be manufactured using the vibration welding technique by the year 1997 (worldwide). By the year 2000, over six million composite intake manifolds will be manufactured by the vibration welding process.[2]

In Europe, the vibration welding method is already used extensively for composite intake manifold manufacturing. In fact, vibration welded composite intake manifolds began in the European market 25 years ago. The knowledge and experience gained in Europe, coupled with a significant cost advantage over lost core molding, appear to be responsible for establishing the trend within the North American market to adopt this manufacturing technology. Table 2[3] shows the percentage of composite intake manifolds that will be vibration welded.

Table 2

Market Penetration of Vibration Welded Composite Intake Manifolds through the Year 2000

North American Intake Manifold Production		European Intake Manifold Production	
Year	% of Total Intake Manifold Production	Year	% of Total Intake Manifold Production
1996	0%	1996	45%
1997	7%	1997	59%
1998	5%	1998	62%
1999	16%	1999	62%
2000	18%	2000	62%

D. COMPOSITE INTAKE MANIFOLD DESIGN CONSIDERATIONS

An intake manifold must meet certain functional and dependability requirements regardless of the material it is manufactured from. The requirements, which are predominately affected by the material and manufacturing method, are discussed in this section.

1. Stress

The intake manifold must be able to withstand stress levels incurred under both normal and extreme operating conditions. The predominate variables that affect stress include the structural design of the intake manifold, the vibration levels produced by the engine, and the temperature of the intake manifold's operating environment.

Operating temperature is an important consideration when using composite materials because temperature has a significant affect on the material's modulus. Underhood temperature extremes can range from -40 °C to + 130 °C. At extremely low temperatures, fatigue failure is a concern. At extremely high temperatures excessive material creep is a concern.

In order to assure structural integrity of a composite intake manifold, maximum stress should not exceed 13.78 MPa, inclusive of all extreme operating conditions. This guideline is applicable for the two most common composite materials used today for intake manifolds, PA 6 and PA 66.

Finite Element Analysis should be performed at -40 °C, +25 °C, and +130 °C, using expected engine vibration input profiles, to assess stress. If the resultant levels do not exceed 13.78 MPa, stress related failures should not be a concern.

2. Radiated Noise

Automotive manufacturers continually strive to produce vehicles that emit low noise levels. As a result, all components, including the intake manifold, are scrutinized in order to minimize their contribution to noise. In this regard, intake manifold radiated noise, which is noise that results from vibration of the intake manifold's surfaces, is of particular concern.

Radiated noise is a function of the vibration energy (frequency and magnitude) being transmitted into the intake manifold, as well as the intake manifold's response to this energy. Generally, to reduce radiated noise, it is desirable to reduce the energy being transmitted into the intake manifold as well as ensure the intake manifold's surfaces are very stiff.

Significant surface stiffness is an attempt to raise the natural frequency of the surfaces, also referred to as panels, to a level which will not become excited by engine operation. Since stiffness is a function of design configuration as well as material modulus, it is very important to emphasize design configuration stiffness when using composite materials, which have a relatively low modulus compared to aluminum. Figure 3 compares the modulus of 33% glass reinforced PA 66 and PA 6 to that of aluminum.

Figure 3

**Modulus Comparison
for Manifold Materials**

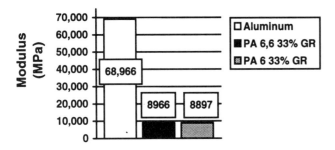

Vibration welded intake manifolds offer opportunities to improve surface stiffness compared to lost core composite intake manifolds. For instance, the weld flange can be used to strategically provide structural stiffness to reduce radiated noise. It is also possible to provide additional structural elements, such as posts between panels, which are welded together during the assembly operation. Proper placement of these posts can act to significantly improve structural stiffness without adversely affecting air flow.

Reducing the energy being transmitted into the intake manifold can be accomplished by isolating the intake manifold from the cylinder head via a compliant gasket and rubber isolated fasteners. A promising alternative is to rely on the beneficial characteristics of the composite material itself, such as its modulus and damping characteristics. In this instance, the intake manifold runners are designed to act as compliant members between the cylinder head and the intake manifold plenum. The vibration energy is dissipated by the compliance of the runners before it reaches the plenum. As a result, the plenum surfaces, which are most prone to radiate noise due to their relatively large surface areas, do not become excited into resonance thus radiated noise is reduced.

With the use of predictive noise analysis and structural finite element analysis, it is possible to design and manufacture a composite intake manifold that is both structurally sound, and exhibit low radiated noise.

3. Burst Strength

The burst strength of an intake manifold refers to the maximum internal pressure the manifold can withstand before it breaks. The intent of this requirement is to ensure the

manifold can withstand a severe engine backfire without failing.

The peak pressure during a severe engine backfire is dependent on many variables. These variables include the air/fuel ratio inside the manifold during the event, the throttled volume of the intake manifold, and possible leakage paths. Leakage can occur through the Exhaust Gas Recirculation system (EGR), the throttle body, the Positive Crankcase Ventilation system (PCV), and even past the intake and exhaust valves. In order to determine the peak pressure for a particular application, a thorough, detailed analysis is needed that accounts for the combustion event and all potential sources of leakage.[4]

Backfire analysis must be performed in order to establish the actual burst strength requirements for a particular intake manifold design. Though a general guideline, based on the assessment of various engine backfire test conditions, suggests that most severe engine backfire events will not exceed 8.0 bar of peak pressure. The pressure rise of the event is typically 20 to 40 milliseconds in duration.[5] When evaluating the burst strength of a composite intake manifold, it is important to perform testing near the expected pressure rise rate since the behavior of the composite material is highly dependent on the rate at which stress is applied.

Many factors need to be understood to predict the burst strength performance of a composite intake manifold. These factors include material properties such as tensile strength, modulus and impact strength. It is also important to know how these material properties change as a function of temperature, humidity, and most importantly, long term aging conditions. Long term aging conditions refer to the operating and environmental conditions an intake manifold may be exposed to over a vehicle's life, which may be 10+ years and or 100,000+ miles.

In general, physical properties of any composite material will degrade as a function of heat and time. For example, laboratory tests which simulate heat aging have shown that the tensile strength of a heat stabilized 33% glass reinforced PA 66 can degrade by up to 25%.[6] As a result, degradation of properties will effect the burst strength of an intake manifold, but the magnitude of the effect is difficult to predict since burst strength is also highly dependent on many other variables such as other material properties, their interactions, as well as the intake manifold's design.

In one particular example, the burst strength of a lost core PA 66 intake manifold degraded by 18% after being lab aged.[7] It is highly probable that this 18% reduction in burst strength is unique to this manifold only, due to the reasons discussed above. Therefore, it is wise to perform burst testing on actual heat aged intake manifolds rather than rely on a degradation target. This is the only way to ensure adequate burst strength of the intake manifold over the life of the vehicle.

Other factors that may influence the burst strength of a composite intake manifold include the manufacturing method (lost core molding as opposed to vibration welding) and the material selection (PA 66 as opposed to PA 6). Experimental testing has shown that components made with PA 6 have exhibited higher burst strength than the same component made with PA 66. This is because PA 6 is inherently tougher than conventional PA 66. This increase in toughness allows the material to "stretch" in response to a sudden load (severe engine backfire) as opposed to fracturing which may occur with a less tough material.

Recently, a new grade of PA 66 has become commercially available which yields similar, if not better, burst strength characteristics as PA 6. This new material, referred to as "Weld Enhanced" PA 66, provides improved burst strength while still maintaining the other desirable characteristics of conventional PA 66. The data given in Table 3 shows the results of an experiment which evaluated the burst strength of a vibration welded composite box that was molded using the three different composite materials discussed.

Table 3

Burst Strength for Various Nylons

Material	Burst Pressure (MPa)
PA 6 30% GR	9.9
PA 66 30% GR	8.5
Weld Enhanced PA 66 30% GR	11.6

With regard to the manufacturing process's effect on burst strength, vibration welded composite intake manifolds suffer an inherent disadvantage because the tensile strength is weaker along the weld since reinforcing glass fiber does not cross the weld boundary. Instead, the glass fibers tend to become oriented parallel to the weld flange during the welding operation. This causes the weld joint itself to be only as strong as the base material without glass reinforcement. This disadvantage can easily be compensated for by increasing the area of the weld. Additionally, the inclusion of posts between surfaces, as discussed previously with regard to radiated noise, can be used to significantly increase burst strength.

By understanding and accounting for all of the factors that affect the burst strength of a composite intake manifold, in particular a vibration welded composite intake manifold, burst strength should not be an issue.

4. Temperature

Temperature is an important design consideration for composite intake manifolds. Generally, in North America, underhood temperature extremes can be as low as -40 °C and as high as +130 °C. As mentioned previously, these

temperature extremes have a significant effect on the modulus of composite material. Figure 4 shows the effect temperature has on the modulus of unreinforced PA 66.

Figure 4

Modulus of PA 6,6 vs. Temperature

Design considerations for a composite intake manifold operating in these environmental extremes include stress related failures during low temperature operation, and excessive creep and increased radiated noise during high temperature operation. Adherence to the maximum stress level guideline given earlier (13.78 MPa) should eliminate concern for stress and creep failures. With regard to radiated noise, predictive noise analysis should be performed at elevated temperatures to uncover any potential problems.

Internal intake manifold temperatures with engines incorporating Exhaust Gas Recirculation systems (EGR) are usually not an issue if good design practice for introducing EGR into a composite intake manifold is followed (there are many good examples in production today). Problems can occur when a malfunctioning EGR valve results in abnormally high temperatures. Experiments have shown that on one particular L4 engine application, maximum internal surface temperature, measured on the interior surface of the intake manifold near EGR introduction, reached a peak of 77 °C when the EGR valve functioned properly. With a malfunctioning EGR valve, maximum internal surface temperature reached 225 °C in one local area (Figure 5). Note that the melt temperatures of PA 6 and PA 66 are 222° C and 255° C, respectively. Though EGR valve malfunctions are rare, the intake manifold should be able to withstand this type of failure, without incident, regardless of its material or design.

Figure 5

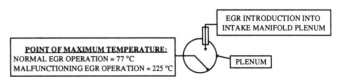

E. COMPOSITE INTAKE MANIFOLD MANUFACTURING METHODS

The two most popular manufacturing methods for producing composite intake manifolds today are lost core molding and vibration welding. This section will briefly review each process, as well as discuss other alternatives.

1. Lost Core Molding

This process has been successfully used for many years in Europe and North America to produce intake manifolds. The first step (see Figure 6) involves casting a core using a low melt temperature metal alloy, tin bismuth, which typically has a melt temperature of approximately 138 °C. The solidified core is then placed in another mold and composite material is injected into this mold and surrounds the core. Upon solidification of the composite material, the overmolded core is removed from the mold and placed in a core melt-out station. The core material is then melted out (molten core material is transported back to the core casting equipment for re-use) thus resulting in a molded intake manifold. The final steps involve washing the intake manifold, and performing secondary operations such as flash removal and installation of inserts.

Figure 6

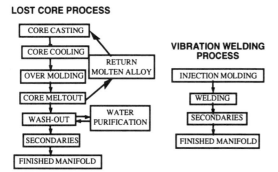

Lost core manifolds are produced almost exclusively from PA 66 in order to provide a greater melt temperature differential between the composite material and the metal alloy core. This difference in melt temperature is important during the melt out process since it requires temperatures of approximately 190 °C to ensure thorough, and quick removal of the core. Recall that the melt temperature of PA 66 and PA 6 is 255 °C and 223 °C respectively. If the intake manifold's temperature during melt out approaches the melt temperature of the composite material it is made from, dimensional stability could suffer.

Lost core molding involves many steps which must be precisely controlled in order to produce good quality parts. In particular, core molding, core melt out, and manifold wash out require specialized equipment which can be very expensive to obtain and operate. As a result, the vibration welding manufacturing process appears to be gaining favor.

2. Vibration Welding

Vibration welded composite intake manifolds are manufactured by joining molded pieces to form a finished part. Unlike the lost core process, a core is not required (see Figure 6), thus core molding, core handling, core melt out, and manifold washout equipment are not needed.

The intake manifold is literally assembled from multiple pieces, as few as two in some instances, and as the name implies the pieces are joined by vibrating them relative to one another until they are welded together.

The vibration welding equipment functions by fixturing one piece of the intake manifold to a moveable platen, and the other piece is fixtured to a stationary platen. A crankshaft mechanism drives the moveable platen, at a specific amplitude and frequency, relative to the stationary platen while pressure is applied. The amplitude, frequency, pressure, and welding time can be varied in order to optimize the weld joint. Typical frequencies of operation are 100 to 240 Hz. Alignment of the parts is not a concern because once the joint is melted, the equipment realigns the parts and they are held in position until the weld solidifies.

Vibration welded intake manifolds are produced predominately from PA 6 and PA 66. In fact throughout the world today, 62% of vibration welded intake manifolds are produced with glass reinforced PA 66, and 35% are produced from glass reinforced PA 6. [8]. As previously mentioned, PA 6 offers an advantage regarding burst strength compared to conventional PA 66. But with the recent availability of a weld enhanced grade of PA 66, this advantage is no longer apparent.

Compared to lost core molding, the vibration welding process is proving to be a simple, robust, low cost method to manufacture composite intake manifolds.

3. Other Methods

Though this section focuses on the two most popular methods for manufacturing composite intake manifolds, lost core and vibration welding, there are other methods in use today as well as under study.

One alternative approach involves attaching multiple pieces together with screws to form an assembly. In this example, a simple injection molded part is attached to a cast aluminum part to form an intake manifold. The "bolted" joint incorporates a gasket to provide sealing between the pieces. The advantage of this method is the elimination of the more complex processes associated with lost core and vibration welding. The disadvantage is increased cost since each intake manifold now incorporates a composite component as well as a cast aluminum component. Increased assembly complexity as well as increased part count is also a disadvantage.

Alternatives to vibration welding as a method to join composite components are also being pursued. One approach is referred to as "hot plate" welding. In this instance, a component's weld flange is literally heated on a hot plate until the joint melts, and then the components are quickly pressed and held together until the joint solidifies. Though this process has been used successfully with other components, there are no production intake manifold applications available today.

F. VIBRATION WELDING PROCESS CONSIDERATIONS

Several factors must be considered in order to successfully use the vibration welding process to manufacture an intake manifold. These factors include constraints placed on the intake manifold's design to facilitate welding, material compatibility with the process, the amount of reinforcing glass fiber (glass loading) used in the material, and induced stress which result from the molding operation.

1. Design Constraints

Although many different geometry's can be vibration welded, not every intake manifold's design can be split into separate shells while still maintaining functional and structural integrity. The manifold must have a design that can sensibly be split along one or more weld joints. If one weld joint is not possible, the intake manifold can be manufactured using more weld joints, and shells, as appropriate.

The "perfect" weld joint would lie in a single horizontal plane, so that the pressure applied to the joint during the welding operation is uniform at all locations along the joint, thus yielding an optimum, uniform, "perfect" weld. With modern intake manifold designs and packaging constraints, it is usually not possibly to achieve a horizontal weld joint. As a result, the pressure will vary along the joint and melting during the welding process can be inconsistent. Potentially, the weld could be weak in certain areas. Careful testing of the weld joint is the only guarantee that a given geometry is acceptable. In most instances, the weld joint will need to be "developed" until adequate strength is obtained.

Another consideration is to allow for adequate space to perform the welding operation. Adequate space must be designed into the manifold to allow for relative movement of the shells during the welding process. At lower welding frequencies, there must be at least 2 mm of clearance so that one shell can move past the other to generate friction which melts the material. Higher welding frequencies may require up to 5 mm of clearance between the shells.

Placement of the weld joint is also important in order to ensure optimum air flow efficiency. It is desirable to configure the joint so it is parallel to the direction of air flow, rather than perpendicular, in order to reduce the possibility of weld flash or shell misalignment obstructing air flow. This is most critical inside the intake manifold runners.

For additional details on weld flange design considerations, review SAE paper 950230 (Vibration Welding: A Low Cost Assembly Process for Thermoplastic Intake Manifolds)[9].

2. Material Compatibility

Although all known thermoplastics are weldable using the vibration welding technique, the strongest welds are formed if the manifold shells are made from the same material, where melt point and viscosity are the same. The most common thermoplastics used for vibration welded intake manifolds are PA 66 and PA 6 (62% and 35% respectively as discussed previously).

PA 6 is often considered more "weldable" than PA 66 because it melts at a lower temperature, takes less energy to melt, and less of the composite actually liquefies at the melt point. Melting is actually the phase change from solid to liquid for only the crystalline region of PA. The amorphous region does not change to a liquid. Since PA 6 is approximately 5 to 10% less crystalline than PA 66 (and 5 to 10% more amorphous) less of the material liquefies during melting, therefore less energy is required to melt PA 6 during welding. This also results in shorter weld cycle times for PA 6.

The viscosity of PA 6 is also slightly higher than PA 66 when molten, since the amorphous region stays intact as discussed above. This results in a slight advantage for PA 6 during the welding operation because the molten material will remain at the joint as opposed to a less viscous material which may migrate away from the joint. This disadvantage with PA 66 can be overcome by intelligent design of the joint as described in SAE paper 950230 referenced earlier.

Even with these differences, PA 66 is the material of choice for many other vibration welded components used in the automotive industry. In fact, automotive applications of vibration welded components using PA 66 date back to the early 1970's. Applications include evaporative emission canisters, air cleaners, brake fluid reservoirs, power steering reservoirs, and engine air intake ducts.

3. Glass Loading

The glass loading, or percent by weight of glass in the composite material, should be determined by the strength and stiffness needed for a particular application. Though generally, glass loading is kept below 45% to ensure a generous outer layer of resin (base polymer) at the surface of the molded part which is essential for optimum weld integrity.

With more than 45% glass is it nearly impossible to obtain a resin rich surface. If adequate resin is not available at the surfaces being welded, the elongation properties of the welded joint are unfavorably affected.[10] Note that with welded components, the reinforcing glass fiber does not cross the weld line. As a result, component strength must be addressed by balancing both material strength and weld strength. For reference, it appears that the optimum glass loading which yields the best balance of material strength and weld strength is between 25 and 35%, well below the stated 45% maximum.

4. Molded-In Stresses

It is important during the molding operation to minimize molded-in stress within the part. If molded-in stresses exist, the part will eventually relax to its unstressed state, as a function of time and temperature, possibly changing the shape of the part (warping).

Typically, welding is performed directly after molding while the part is still warm, compliant, and dry. Dry parts ensure strong welds. In some cases, exposure to air at 23° C and 50% RH is sufficient to degrade weld strength by one half.[11] A warm and compliant part helps ensure the part is fixed in the proper orientation during welding making the welded joint more consistent in strength. Though if molded-in stresses exist, and are large enough, warping may still occur upon relaxation. Therefore it is important to minimize molded-in stresses.

Molded-in stresses can be minimized by following general recommendations for molding composites. For example, it is desirable to achieve consistent, uniform cooling of the composite material as it solidifies within the mold. This is accomplished by incorporating adequate and evenly spaced cooling lines within the mold tooling. Following component design recommendations such as maintaining consistent wall thickness and rounding sharp corners are also beneficial.

Ultimately, the objective is to ensure the polymer chains freeze (solidify) after they reach their ideal orientation. If freezing occurs before the ideal orientation is reached, part deformation will occur as the polymer chains continue realign (stress relaxation).

Although PA 6 and high temperature nylons have a tendency to warp less than PA 66, the design of the part has the most significant influence on warpage. The material may be significant when molding large, flat parts like wheel rims, but on parts with more complex geometries, like intake manifolds, the design and molding parameters have significantly more influence on warp.

As previously mentioned, adherence to good design and manufacturing guidelines should reduce concerns with warpage. In some instances though, it may be necessary to incorporate warp allowances within the mold tooling known as windage. This involves measuring the actual warpage on a molded part, correcting the mold so that it produces a part that warps in the opposite direction, thus after relaxation the part reaches the desired shape.

G. COMPOSITE MATERIAL CONSIDERATIONS FOR WELDED INTAKE MANIFOLDS

Different grades of composite materials are used to address specific application needs. The grade of composite is dependent on the base polymer, glass content, as well as other additives. The resultant composite material can vary significantly in properties and performance. Therefore, it is important to understand these differences in order to select the best material for the application.

1. Base Material

The base material refers to the polymer type used in the composite. PA 66 and PA 6 are two polyamides produced using different monomer chemicals. These chemicals affect the thermal properties, chemical resistance, and physical properties of the base material. Some of the properties most critical to intake manifolds are included in Table 4.

Table 4

Physical Properties of PA 6 and PA 66

Physical Property	33% GR PA 6 (Zytel® 73G33L)	33% GR PA 66 (Zytel® 70G33L)
Melting Point (°C)	223	255
HDT (@ 18.2 MPa) (°C)	200	253
Tensile Strength (MPa)	175	186
Elongation (%) 50% RH	5	4
Creep Modulus @ 23°C 20 MPa; 1000 hrs;50% rh	3100*	7700*
Impact after 3000 hrs at 140° C (GPa) Unnotched Charpy	29 (28% retention)*	38 (75% retention)*
Flexural Modulus(MPa)	8900	9000

* Measured on 30% GR material instead of 33%

Melt point and heat deflection temperature (HDT) give an indication of thermal integrity. At the melt point, the crystalline portion of the composite transforms from solid to liquid, thus the properties reported for the composite are no longer valid. HDT is the temperature at which an arbitrary amount of deflection occurs with a given stress (18.2 MPa is shown above). The higher the temperature, the more thermal resistance the composite material is. Note that PA 66 has a higher melt point and higher HDT than PA 6.

Tensile strength is the most important single indication of material strength. It indicates the highest level of stress the material can withstand before failure. Elongation refers to the amount the material can stretch before failure occurs. Moderate elongation, values of approximately 3 to 5%, indicate the material's ability to absorb rapid impact and shock. A material exhibiting high tensile strength and low elongation would be brittle and fracture easily upon impact. The most desirable combination for intake manifolds is high tensile strength and high elongation, although the two properties usually are mutually exclusive. In general, PA 66 has higher tensile strength and slightly lower elongation than PA 6.

Creep is the measure of the total long-term deformation of the composite material caused by an applied stress. Note that the applied stress is significantly below the tensile strength value. Creep increases with time, temperature, and moisture. It is obvious from Table 5 that PA 66 deforms significantly less than PA 6 under the same stress.

Minimizing creep is important in order to retain desired dimensions. Areas of concern regarding intake manifolds include the dimensional stability of the gasket sealing surfaces as well as maintaining bolt clamping. In this instance, excessive creep at bolted joints may allow the bolt to loosen.

Impact testing measures the energy required to break the material. The Charpy impact test is one method of assessing a material's impact strength by measuring the energy required to break a standard size molded test bar. Note that the creep modulus and impact values shown in Table 4 were performed on samples that have been heat aged (see Table 4 for specific conditions). As mentioned previously, physical properties degrade with heat aging, therefore it is more important to consider the performance of the composite material after it is heat aged. This is particularly important regarding the failure modes of a composite intake manifold, especially burst strength. The data indicates that after heat aging, PA 66 has better retention of impact properties, also referred to as toughness, than PA 6 after aging.

Flexural modulus is a measure of how stiff the composite material is. This modulus is influenced more with glass loading (described in the following section) than it is with the base polymer.

Chemical resistance is also affected by the base polymer. PA 66 exhibits better chemical resistance than PA 6 due to its higher crystallinity. As a result, it fares better in polar solvents, like glycol or water. Many North American intake manifolds have coolant (ethylene glycol) channels molded into the manifolds and resistance becomes important. Table 5 compares the tensile strength of PA 66 to PA 6 after exposure to ethylene glycol.

Table 5

Resistance to Ethylene Glycol (Automotive Coolant)

Tensile Strength after 28 days Exposure to a 50/50 Mixture of Ethylene Glycol & Water at 130 °C	
Material	Tensile Strength (MPa)
PA 66 33% Glass Reinforced	59.3
PA 6 35% Glass Reinforced	44.1

It is important to note that the physical properties shown in Table 4 will change as a function of moisture content of the material. PA materials are naturally hydroscopic and they will absorb moisture over time, typically as much a 1 to 2% by weight after long term exposure. As a result, material properties may be reported at "dry as molded" or "conditioned" with moisture test conditions. Tensile strength usually degrades with moisture content while toughness usually increases. Note that PA 6 is more hydroscopic than PA 66. Understanding the actual material properties which result from the environment the material is being used in is essential.

In summary, with regard to the base polymer, a comparison of PA 66 to PA 6 allows the following conclusions to be made:

- PA 66 has higher thermal resistance
- PA 66 has better chemical resistance
- PA 66 has higher tensile strength
- PA 66 exhibits better dimensional stability
- PA 6 exhibits better weldability
- PA 6 has slightly higher elongation

Though the focus of this section was on PA 66 and PA 6, due to their predominant use for intake manifold manufacturing today, other base polymers can be used when these two are not feasible. For instance, turbocharged engine applications may require materials with higher temperature resistance than PA 66. To address these needs, there is a family of high temperature nylons that are available, such as PA 46. In fact, there is a current European production application of a vibration welded PA 46 intake manifold which is used on a passenger car turbocharged diesel engine.

Higher temperature resistance is generally attributed to increased crystallinity. PA 46 material is approximately 70% crystalline compared to PA 66 which is approximately 50% crystalline. The melt point for these two materials are 295 °C and 255 °C respectively. An additional choice is PA 6T/MPMD,P, also referred to as high temperature nylon (HTN), which has a melt point of 305 °C. HTN also exhibits considerably less warp, because of its semi aromatic polymer structure, than either PA 66 or PA 6 which have linear chain polymer structures.

High temperature nylons also offer a few disadvantages. In particular, in order to process (mold) these materials, it is necessary to elevate the mold temperature significantly above 100 °C. This usually requires that hot oil, rather than water, be used to maintain mold temperature. Increased mold cycle times may also be an issue. The other disadvantage is cost compared to standard PA.

2. Glass Loading

Most intake manifold applications use glass reinforcement loading between 25% and 35%, with 30%, 33% and 35% being the most common. These levels of glass seem to give the best balance of strength, stiffness, and elongation properties for intake manifold applications. As the glass loading is increased, stiffness (defined as tensile modulus) and tensile strength increases. Table 6 shows the relationship of glass loading to stiffness and tensile strength using PA 6 as an example.

Table 6

**Glass Loading Effects on Material Properties of PA 6
Test Conditions: Measured Dry As Molded at 23 ° C**

PA 6	Tensile Strength (MPa)	Tensile Modulus (Stiffness) (MPa)
15% GR PA 6	135	6000
30% GR PA 6	180	9600
45% GR PA 6	210	15300

However, as discussed earlier, it is important to balance material strength and weld strength when designing vibration welded components. Increased glass reinforcement does not influence weld strength since glass does not cross the weld boundary. In fact, glass reinforcement above 45% has proven detrimental to weld strength, as previously discussed.

3. Additives

An additive is a generic name given to any low level chemical, less than 1% by mass, which is added to the base material to improve processing and or stabilize the material's properties. Typically, additives do not affect the initial physical properties of the material.

Heat stabilizers are very common additives which are used to improve the long term heat aging characteristics of the polymer. This is probably the most important additive relative to long term performance of a composite intake manifold. As an example, without a heat stabilizer PA 66 has a tensile strength of approximately 20 MPa after 2000 hours of laboratory heat aging at 132 °C. With the addition of a copper heat stabilizer, much of the tensile strength is retained yielding a value of 90 MPa.

It should be noted that additives do add cost, and may discolor the material slightly. However, the benefits of heat stabilizers obviously outweigh these issues with regard to long term performance of composite intake manifolds.

H. COMPOSITE MATERIAL SELECTION CRITERIA

When choosing the appropriate material for a composite intake manifold, the manifold's functional requirements as well as its manufacturing process requirements deserve significant consideration and understanding. The result of these considerations, which were discussed in detail within this paper, lead to a logical material selection process.

Figure 7 flowcharts the path for selecting the appropriate composite material based on the intake manifold's design and manufacturing requirements.

Figure 7

Material Selection Criteria for Composite Intake Manifolds

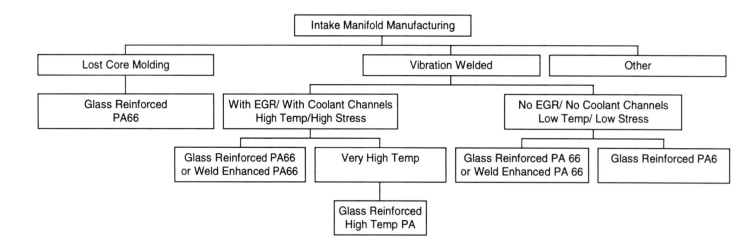

With regard to material selection the following conclusions can be made:

- PA 66 is the natural choice for composite intake manifolds produced using the lost core manufacturing method. Its melt point is significantly higher than this manufacturing method's core melt out process which ensures dimensional stability of the intake manifold. PA 66 also exhibits better physical properties, temperature resistance, and chemical resistance when compared to PA 6.

- Weld enhanced PA 66 is the best choice for vibration welded intake manifolds. It offers superior material properties when compared to PA 6, the same material properties as conventional PA 66, and incorporates additives which improve the toughness, hence burst strength, of the welded joint.

- PA 66 is a good choice for vibration welded intake manifolds that operate in a high stress / high temperature environment. Due to its better chemical resistance than PA 6, it is also suitable for manifold applications that incorporate coolant channels within the intake manifold.

- PA 6 is a good choice for vibration welded intake manifolds due to its excellent weldability and burst strength characteristics. Though the material properties of PA 6 necessitate that the intake manifold operate in a low stress / low temperature environment (usually no EGR) and not incorporate coolant channels within the intake manifold.

- High temperature resistant nylons, such as PA 46 and PA 6T/MPMD,P, are suitable when the temperature environment excludes PA 66. Turbocharged engine applications are an example where very high temperature resistance may be required.

I. SUMMARY

Designing a composite intake manifold is a complicated process that involves many design, manufacturing, and material considerations. This paper provides the necessary background to understand the benefits of using composite materials, as well as understand the intricacies of all the ensuing interactions. These interactions include the intake manifold's design, function, manufacturing method, and the material used for its construction. This paper further simplifies the material choice decision by providing a flowchart, based on data provided in the paper, to aid in the decision making process.

Specific details reviewed in this paper include:

- **Benefits of Composite Intake Manifolds**

- **Composite Intake Manifold Design Consideration**

- **Composite Intake Manifold Manufacturing Methods**

- **Vibration Welding Process Considerations**

- **Composite Material Considerations for Welded Intake Manifolds**

- **Composite Material Selection Criteria**

[1] Host, Ray (GM Powertrain Analysis Group), personal communication, March 19, 1996.

[2] Branson Automotive "Intake Manifold Production Forecasts", 1996.

[3] DuPont Global Air Intake Manifold Database

[4] McCandlish, Peter (DELPHI Energy & Engine Management Systems), personal communication, July 25, 1996.

[5] Bekirov, Aksel, Jerry Fly (DELPHI Energy & Engine Management Systems), personal communication, February 23, 1993.

[6] Design Handbook for DuPont Engineering Plastics, Module II. Figure 144/ Effect of Oven Aging at Different Temperatures on Tensile Strength of Heat Stabilized, Glass Reinforced Zytel® 70G33HS1L.

[7] Douglas, Ken (GM Powertrain), personal communication, July 25, 1996.

[8] DuPont Global Air Intake Manifold Database.

[9] Nelson, Kenneth W., "Vibration Welding: A Low Cost Assembly Process for Thermoplastic Intake Manifolds", SAE Technical Paper Series #950230, International Congress and Exposition, 1996.

[10] Kohan, Melvin I.,ed., "Nylon Plastics Handbook,"; Hanser Publishers: New York, 1995 ; p. 464.

[11] Webber, T. G. In "Encyclopedia of Polymers Science and Engineering"; John Wiley and Sons: New York, 1985; 2nd Edition, Vol. 3, pp. 746-758.

Correlation of Warpage Predicted with Computer Simulation to Actual Warpage for a Glass-Reinforced Nylon Powertrain Part

Dennis R. Que
LDM Technologies

Copyright 1997 Society of Automotive Engineers, Inc.

ABSTRACT

The warpage of an injection molded 50% long glass (by wt.), nylon (PA66) composite part was studied experimentally and correlated to simulation. The simulation was performed using the Moldflow Fiber module, and Moldflow with empirical shrinkage coefficients. The results consisted of out-of-plane deflection on the mating surface and shrinkage between locations on the perimeter of the part. The results compared favorably to experimental results for the direction of warp. The effect of different packing phase parameters on warp was not predicted correctly. The predicted magnitude of warp varied greatly between the two computer programs.

INTRODUCTION

The use of injection molded thermoplastic composite components is made more difficult by their tendency to warp. The ability to accurately predict warp can help to determine the best material and develop a part design, tool design, and molding process which minimizes warp. Several commercial software programs are available to predict warp. The accuracy of these programs has only been demonstrated in the literature for a few cases such as a radiator end tank (Zheng) and a plaque with several holes (Glozer). To understand the usefulness of warpage analysis it is necessary to understand which phenomena it models correctly and that which it fails to predict. Some of the questions this study helps to address are: what process parameters affect warpage, if the predictions are accurate enough to build warpage compensation into the tool from the start, if the simulation can be used to optimize the process conditions with respect to warp, and what is the best Moldflow simulation program to use.

PART DESCRIPTION

This correlation study was performed on an asymmetric box or cover-like geometry. The wall thickness varies nominally between 4.0 mm and 5.5 mm with locally thinner and thicker regions. The component has a single gate in the center of the part. There are eleven holes around the flange, at which measurements were taken. The part geometry is shown below in Fig. 1.

MOLDING TRIAL

The correlation study consisted of an instrumented mold trial conducted as part of design of experiments (DOE), followed by modeling and computer

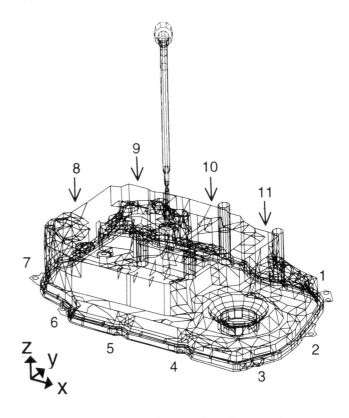

Figure 1: Flange Hole Numbering Convention Shown On Surface Mesh Used to Create Finite Element Mesh

simulation.

The molding trial was performed on a Toshiba ISE950 press instrumented to record the hydraulic pressure, melt pressure, and the screw position throughout the cycle, for every cycle. All process settings were held constant except packing pressure, packing time, and hold pressure. These were varied in a full factorial DOE design. The specific settings and run order are given in Table 1. These parameters were

Table 1: Full Factorial DOE Layout for Mold Trial

	Factors		
DOE Row #	Pack Time (sec)	Pack Pressure (MPa)	Hold Pressure (MPa)
1	10	4.14	5.52
2	3	4.14	5.52
3	10	4.14	2.07
4	3	4.14	2.07
5	3	5.52	5.52
6	10	5.52	5.52
7	3	5.52	2.07
8	10	5.52	2.07

found from earlier Taguchi DOE's to be the most significant factors, other than cooling time, affecting the warpage of this part. For each row in the DOE or each unique set of process conditions five parts were molded. The last three parts were retained for warpage measurements on a coordinate measuring machine (CMM).

The screw position data was recorded and used to establish the precise fill time and fill profile for input into the computer simulation. The nominal fill time was 4.25 sec. The melt pressure was taken at the base of the nozzle to find the precise time and pressure that the polymer solidified under. The nominal pack time, pack pressure and hold pressure is given in Table 1 above. The nominal hold time was 20 sec. The cooling conditions were maintained constant. The cooling time was 42 sec., measured from the end of the hold time. The cavity temperature was set to 102°C and the core to 118°C. At the end of the trial, the melt temperature was measured to be 313°C by an open air purge with a pre-heated thermocouple.

EXPERIMENTAL WARPAGE MEASUREMENT

The molded parts cooled with air freely circulating on all sides. The parts were measured on a CMM 24-48 hours after molding. They were minimally constrained at three points. The center of each hole around the flange was measured to determine the x-y

position and the z-deflection was measured at a point 2-3 mm outside the O.D. of the metal insert. The numbering convention established is to start at the right-most hole in Fig. 1 and call that hole 1. Holes 2 through 11 follow by proceeding clockwise around the perimeter of the part.

The experimental warpage in the x-y plane was found by comparing the x-y position of each hole in the part to the position of the core pins in the mold. The z-deflection due to warpage was determined by comparing the measured z-deflection to the z-coordinate from the CAD data at the same location.

MOLDING RESULTS

The magnitude of the z-deflection was greatest at hole 3, see Fig. 1. The average z-deflection at this hole for each of the eight sets of process conditions is shown in Table 2. The largest main effect, at hole 3, is

Table 2: Average Measured Z-deflection

DOE Row #	Z-defl. Hole 3 (mm)
1	6.01
2	7.39
3	7.16
4	6.36
5	7.01
6	7.48
7	7.51
8	6.96

seen for pack pressure. The average effect is 0.51 mm, favoring the lower pack pressure. This is only shown to be statistically significant when run-order restrictions are considered negligible. In that case the p-value is 0.036. No other main effects at hole 3 were statistically significant. The effect of pack pressure was also found to be significant at holes 4 and 5, assuming run-order restrictions are negligible. The p-values are 0.009 for both cases. The three-way interaction between pack pressure, pack time and hold pressure was also found to be significant for holes 2, 3, 4, and 5, again neglecting the run-order restrictions.

SOLUTION METHODS

The computer simulation was performed using material data generated at Moldflow's lab specifically for the grade of material used, LNP PDX-R-92238. The data consisted of viscosity, pvT (pressure, volume, Temp.), Moldflow shrinkage coefficients and various other material constants such as: specific heat and no-flow temperature. The mechanical properties were supplied by the resin manufacturer.

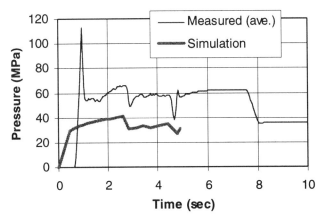

Figure 2: Fill Pressure Correlation for Process Conditions from Row 7.

Flow simulation was performed without cooling. Cooling simulation was performed and flow simulation was run a second time with the non-isothermal conditions calculated in cooling. Five of the eight sets of process conditions were run with the simulation. The specific row numbers are: 2, 4, 5, 7, and 8.

Prior to predicting warpage, the shrinkage strains were obtained using Moldflow with experimentally obtained shrinkage coefficients and with the fiber module from Moldflow.

MOLDFLOW EMPIRICAL METHOD - In the first solution method, the shrinkage coefficients are obtained from measurements on plaques molded at various conditions of: hold pressure, hold time, melt temperature, mold temperature, injection rate, and wall thickness. These measurements are entered into a mathematical model which produces coefficients for Eq. 1, the shrinkage parallel ($SH_\parallel$), and Eq. 2, the shrinkage perpendicular ($SH_\perp$).

$$SH_\parallel = a_1 f(SH_{PVT}) + a_2 f(crystallization) +$$
$$a_3 f(mold\ restraint) + a_4 f(orientation) \quad (1)$$
$$+ a_5$$

$$SH_\perp = b_1 f(SH_{PVT}) + b_2 f(crystallization) +$$
$$b_3 f(mold\ restraint) + b_4 f(orientation) \quad (2)$$
$$+ b_5$$

MOLDFLOW FIBER METHOD - The warpage was also calculated with the MF/Fiber module. This method calculates parallel and perpendicular coefficients of thermal expansion from the individual properties of the matrix and fiber. The micromechanics model from Chamberlain is used (Bowles and Tompkins). The coefficients of thermal expansion are combined into a

shrinkage function which is in agreement with the pvT data.

The shrinkage strains were transferred to a non-linear structural finite element code, MF/Warp, where the warped shape was predicted.

RESULTS CORRELATION

PRESSURE - The pressure from the simulation under-predicted the actual injection pressure. This can be seen in Fig. 2. The large peak in the measured pressure is due to the nozzle freezing off between shots. The trend in the pressure from simulation follows the measured trend well.

MOLD TEMPERATURE - On the core half, the cycle average mold temperature correlated within 0 to +29°C with the measured temperature at the end of the cycle. On the cavity, the correlation was within +14 to +28°C. The location of hot and cold areas on the surface was generally correct.

WARPAGE - The magnitude of the warpage was predicted best by the empirical method. The predicted trend with respect to process conditions was nearly identical for either method. The simulation failed to predict the decrease in warpage when going from row 2 to row 4, see Figure 3 and 4. This shows a possible weakness in the ability of the simulation to predict the effect of hold pressure on warp.

The z-deflection around the perimeter of the part is predicted well except at holes 7 and 8. Figure 5 compares the measured values to the simulation for the process conditions from row 7. For the same process conditions, the x-y deflection is plotted in Figure 6. Only at hole 10 was the prediction in the complete opposite direction.

The fiber method under predicted the magnitude of the warp. The actual results are shown as well as results scaled by a factor of 4. This allows a more direct comparison between the predicted trends.

DISCUSSION

EXPERIMENT DESIGN - The validity of the effects of processing conditions on warpage is left to question because of the inability to find statistical significance, except when neglecting run-order restrictions. The experiment could have been designed differently to more easily prove the significance of the effects. Three aspects could have been changed. 1) The experiment could have been run without run-order restrictions. This would entail changing process conditions at random for each sample retained. The process parameters under investigation must rapidly stabilize for this approach to be economical.

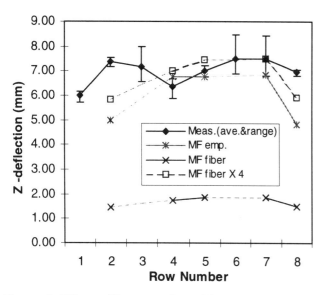

Figure 3: Effect of Process Condition on Warpage at Hole 3

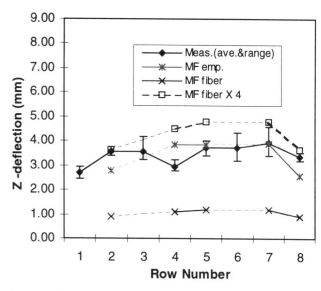

Figure 4: Effect of Process Conditions on Warpage at Hole 4

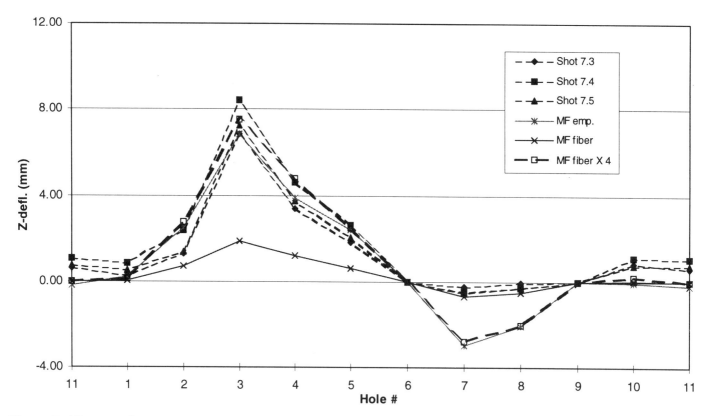

Figure 5: Warpage Around Perimeter For Process Conditions From Row 7

2) The difference between the high and low levels of the factors could have been greater. From table 1, the difference for the high and low pack pressure is quite little, yet it was the most significant effect. Before starting the experiment it is beneficial to probe the boundary of the process window by producing a few parts at the extremes. 3) More parts at each set of process conditions could have been produced.

PACKING CORRELATION - The process experimentation indicates that the packing parameters have the greatest effect on warpage, with the exception of cycle time. This suggests that the fiber orientation and shrinkage which occurs at this point is key to accurately predicting the warp. At this point in the process the polymer is undergoing a transition from liquid to solid. This transition is modeled as a step function in the simulation. Empirical data on when this critical transition occurs leads to a more accurate prediction of the magnitude of the warpage (Shay).

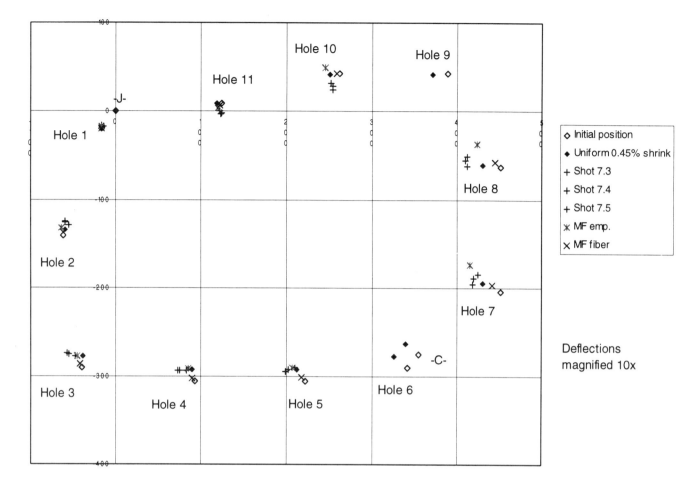

Figure 6: Warpage In X-Y Plane For Process Conditions From Row 7 --View From Bottom

THREE-WAY INTERACTION - The significance of the three-way interaction indicates that the individual levels of the packing pressure stages do not have an independent effect on warpage. To reach the lowest warp, the inter-relatedness of the factors must be considered. This suggests that there may be an optimum integral under the pressure-time curve to reach the lowest warp. After some investigation this relationship was not apparent.

CONCLUSION

The warpage simulation is fairly accurate when supplemented by experimental data. Without the extra empirical data the simulation can be useful for predicting the general direction of the warp. The ability of the simulation to the critical effect that packing parameters have on warp is poor. Therefore it cannot be used for virtual DOE's to reduce warp. The warpage of this type of part and material is mostly a function of part design and gating. Since warpage of the part is not very sensitive to process conditions, a fixed part design (including warpage correction) and gating should produce dimensionally consistent parts.

ACKNOWLEDGMENTS

John Ulicny at GMR & D, for his assistance in setting up and performing the DOE as well as statistically testing for the significance of the factors.

LNP Engineering Plastics, for providing the material and Moldflow material testing used in this study.

REFERENCES

Bowles and Tompkins. Journal of Composite Materials, vol. 23, 1989, pp. 370-388.

Shay, Robert, Peter Foss and Charles Mentzer. "Comparison of C-mold Predictions and Experimental Shrinkages: Fiber-filled Materials". ANTEC '96 Proceedings.

Glozer, G. "You Can Accurately Predict Warpage". Plastics Technology, vol. 41, no. 5, May 1995, pp. 60-62.

Zheng, R., *et al.* "Predicting Warpage of Injection Molded Fiber-reinforced Plastics". ANTEC '95 Proceedings, pp. 478-483.

Composite Covers for Noise Attenuation

Eric R. Sattler
BASF Corp.

ABSTRACT

Plastic parts have been proliferating the underhood environment for mass and cost savings. Noise control can become an issue with these parts. A noise cover can solve these problems. Data in this paper demonstrate the acoustical absorption capabilities of a nylon 6 / foam composite cover. Using these data, it becomes possible to predict the amount of attenuation using various thickness' of open-cell foam and nylon 6. The three most important factors to use when designing a new cover are acoustical absorption, transmission loss, and percentage of acoustical leakage around the cover or barrier.

INTRODUCTION

Due to the inherent weight and cost savings, plastic parts are becoming more commonplace in automobiles, especially under the hood. Due to the lower mass and stiffness of plastic materials, however, it is becoming more difficult to meet the stringent noise requirements as put forth by the OEMs. This is especially true for higher frequency sounds. If noise control is an issue, a solution in the form of a noise cover can be successfully used to manage this offending sound. This paper will review the results of acoustical testing on a series of nylon plaques in combination with two different types of open-cell foams. The purpose of the test was to determine which combination would prove to be optimum for attenuating underhood sounds of various frequencies.

BACKGROUND

Two opposing problems concern today's automotive engineer. The first is the ever-tightening federal noise emission requirements and the second is the increasing popularity of thermoplastic underhood components. Acoustical attenuation of a part is based on four factors: part stiffness, part mass, material damping characteristics, and the part's transfer function. In the conversion of a component from metal to plastic, one material is generally preferred. The material damping characteristics are, therefore, fixed. Once an adequate design is settled upon, the part stiffness is also fixed. Although it would be advantageous from an acoustical point of view to increase the mass of the part, overall it is an undesirable action to take. This leaves the part's transfer function as the sole means to attenuate noise. In the past, structurally treating the individual surfaces of the part was sufficient to control the offending noises. These noises had a frequency below 1500 Hertz. As we have become more educated in our preferences and more sophisticated in our technology, this methodology is becoming insufficient. Noise problems today typically occur in the 3,000 to 10,000 Hertz range, are not structural in nature, and cannot be easily handled using historical structural solutions. For cases in which the offending sounds cannot be adequately attenuated, noise (or engine) covers have witnessed increased usage. A noise cover complements the low mass and cost of the plastic part while reducing noise levels to those of (or lower than) the replaced metal parts.

A series of laboratory tests was conducted in order to determine what optimum combination of nylon plaque and open-cell foam can be used to attenuate the offending noise. The tests conducted were Acoustical Absorption and Transmission Loss. Acoustical absorption was not measured for these plaques as it was felt that whatever absorption there might be would be insignificant compared to the open-cell foam. These data, allied with a factor reflecting acoustical leakage, can be combined to determine a curve known as Insertion Loss. Insertion loss is an approximation of the difference in emitted sound energy between an environment with and without a noise covers as a function of frequency. These tests were conducted from 100 Hertz to a maximum frequency of 10,000 Hertz.

METHODOLOGY

One material was used for the thermoplastic cover portion of the noise cover assembly. A typical material currently in use is a heat-stabilized grade of nylon 6 with 35% glass reinforcement. Plaques of this material in 2 mm, 3 mm, and 4 mm thickness' (110 mm x 110 mm) were tested. Two open-cell foams were tested. The first is a commercially available grade of an MDI-based urethane foam specially formulated for acoustical absorption characteristics. The advantage of this foam is that it is fairly inexpensive and can be foamed in location to fit any parts unusual geometry. The second foam is an open-celled version of foamed melamine. This material is also currently in use for underhood noise control. The advantage of this material is that it is inherently flame-proof and can withstand a long-term temperature exposure of 150° C. Pads of these materials measuring either 370 mm x 370 mm or 1100 mm x 1100 mm were used in three thicknesses. The thicknesses used for both foams were 10 mm, 20 mm, and 30 mm.

Acoustical absorption properties were measured using a Rieter Globe-brand Alpha Cabin and measurements were taken using their standard recommendations. This cabin is essentially an acoustically reflective chamber in which no two opposing walls are parallel. A sample measuring 1.21 m^2 is placed on the floor of the cabin. Loudspeakers located in the corners of the cabin establish a uniform sound field of a known frequency and sound pressure level. A microphone located on a centrally located rotating boom circulates in the cabin to record the sound pressure level drop-off after switching off the loudspeakers. A more absorptive material will attenuate more sound pressure than a reflective material. The foam pads were pieced together to form the required area for the test. An absorption coefficient of 1.0 would indicate that the incident sound is completely absorbed into the foam. This technique was derived from a series of equations that were established long ago, when acoustical absorption was in its infancy. Due to some errors in these equations, it is possible to record an absorption coefficient of up to 1.2. This should in no way reflect on the validity of the data. This simply points out the errors of those equations that were laid out long ago.

Transmission loss was measured on the nylon/foam composite structures using a typical two-chamber apparatus with the sample located between the two chambers. One of the chambers is used as a sound source, the other as a receiver. Located in the "source" side are a loudspeaker and three microphones. The sound pressure level, as measured by the three microphones, is averaged and considered to be the sound input. The "receiver" side has one microphone and measures the system response. The level of the receiver side is subtracted from the average input of the source side to obtain transmission loss data. This was performed over the frequency range of 100 to 10,000 Hertz. A correction factor as specified by the SAE J1400 standard procedure was employed. A sample size of 440 mm x 440 mm is typically used in these tests. Since the plaques were smaller than this, a series of sixteen plaques were arranged in a 4 x 4 pattern and glued together using a hot melt adhesive. This technique was effective except for a few anomalies in the upper frequency ranges.

RESULTS

ACOUSTICAL ABSORPTION - Figures 1 through 5 show the results of acoustical absorption testing on the two foam samples.

Figure 1 is the resultant curves obtained from urethane samples 10 mm, 20 mm, and 30 mm thick. In this figure, one can see that the 30 mm sample dominates in the 400 - 1600 Hertz range. The 20 mm sample has approximately the same absorption characteristics as the 30 mm sample from 1600 Hz. and up. The 10 mm thick sample absorption performance joins up with the other two samples at about 3500 Hz. Figure 2 repeats these tests for the foamed melamine material. In this case, the 30 mm thick sample dominates across the entire frequency range tested.

Figure 3 compares the performance of the two 10 mm thick samples. It can be seen that the melamine material slightly outperforms the urethane in the 400 - 1600 Hz. range. In the range above 1600 Hz, the urethane material is the performance champion. Figure 4 compares the performance of the two 20 mm thick samples. The materials perform similarly, with the urethane material slightly outperforming the melamine below 3200 Hz. Figure 5 compares the performance of the two 30 mm thick samples. Here, the melamine exhibits a slightly superior performance above 1000 Hz.

Figures 1 - 5 each has at least one sample that shows a significant drop at the 6300 Hz. 1/3 octave band. This was primarily due to calibration difficulties. A standard sample of material with known absorption properties was tested and the measured value was approximately 15% lower than the known actual value.

TRANSMISSION LOSS - Figures 6 - 16 display results of acoustical transmission loss testing on samples using both urethane foam and melamine foam adhered to nylon plaques 2, 3, and 4 mm thick.

Figure 6 presents the transmission loss data for various combinations of the polyurethane foam, 10 mm and 30 mm thick, with plaques, 2, 3 and 4 mm thick. The 30 mm thick foam combined with the 4 mm plaque had the highest transmission loss for frequencies above 1000 Hz. The 4 mm plaque/10 mm foam combination performed superior to other combinations below 1000 Hz. Figure 7 displays the results of 30 mm thick melamine foam adhered to nylon plaques 2 and 4 mm thick. Again, the 4 mm thick plaque samples outperform the 2 mm thick plaque samples.

Figure 8 carries the melamine foam testing further by displaying the results for 10 mm samples adhered to 2, 3, and 4 mm thick plaques. While the 4 mm thick sample outperformed the others, it is interesting to note that it performed only *slightly* better than the 3 mm thick sample. Figure 9 compares the transmission loss properties of a 2 mm thick plaque without foam and with 10, 20, and 30 mm thick melamine foam samples. Not surprisingly, the 30 mm thick foam sample had the highest transmission loss of these four samples. Again, though, it was not significantly higher than the 20 mm thick sample. Figure 10 is a comparison of the transmission loss of a 3 mm thick plaque with no foam and with a 10 mm thick sample of melamine foam. The sample with foam outperforms the no-foam sample above 1500 Hz. Figure 11 shows the results of testing 4 mm thick plaques with no foam, with 10 mm melamine foam, and with 30 mm melamine foam samples. Again, the 30 mm thick foam sample dominated this test series.

Figures 12 - 16 are direct comparisons of urethane foam to melamine foam, using the same combinations of plaque and sample thickness. Figure 12 shows the results for a 2 mm thick plaque and 10 mm thick foam sample. Except for a band around 4000 to 5000 Hz, the urethane foam displays a superior transmission loss performance over the melamine foam. This unexpected drop-off band anomaly can be attributed to "acoustical leaks" of the plaque assembly. They may also be due to "coincidence," an acoustical phenomenon in which the wavelength in the panel matches the wavelength of sound at certain angles of incidence allowing more sound to easily pass through the panel. This was witnessed in other tests as well.

Figure 13 shows the test results for 2 mm thick plaques and 30 mm thick foam samples. Again, the urethane foam displayed better transmission loss performance than the melamine foam. Figure 14 shows the results of 3 mm thick plaques with 10 mm thick foam samples. The urethane sample performed fairly similarly to the melamine sample above about 2000 Hz. Figure 15 has the results of 4 mm thick plaques with 10 mm thick foam samples. The urethane foam sample outperforms the melamine foam sample from 400 to about 3000 Hz. In this test, one can witness a sharp roll-off of properties for the melamine plaque and plain plaque at 1000 Hz. This is, again, an anomaly as described previously. This occurs again at 7000 Hz. and should be considered an anomaly of the testing method, not of the materials tested. In Figure 16, 4 mm thick plaques were tested with 30 mm thick samples of foams. The urethane foam sample dominated the test from about 1000 to 6000 Hz.

INSERTION LOSS - Insertion loss is a combination of source-side absorption and barrier transmission loss. The insertion loss for any barrier combination may be approximated by the following equation:

$$IL(dB) = 10 \, Log\{[\alpha / (A_L + \tau)] + 1\} \qquad \text{(Eq. 1)}$$

where,

α is the absorption coefficient of the barrier combination, $(I_{absorbed} / I_{incident})$

A_L is the percentage "leakage" of the barrier combination, (< 1.00)

τ is the transmission coefficient calculated from the transmission loss, $(I_{transmitted} / I_{incident})$, or, more simply,

$$\tau = log^{-1}(-\text{Trans. Loss} / 10) \qquad \text{(Eq. 2)}$$

Note that at high frequencies, α will approach a plateau value and that τ will be very small as compared to A_L. Thus, at high frequencies, the Insertion Loss approximation is:

$$IL(dB) = 10 \, Log\{[\alpha / A_L] +1\} \qquad \text{(Eq. 3)}$$

If the acoustical absorption coefficient, α, has a maximum value of 1.0, and the acoustical leakage, A_L, has a value of 0.03 (3% of the area is not covered by the barrier), the maximum insertion loss available is approximately 15 dB. This is consistent with the fact that a barrier with a hole in it will have some maximum insertion loss determined by the size of the hole and the strength of the acoustic field inside the barrier.

Figures 17 and 18 show the calculated insertion loss for barriers using melamine foam and urethane foam, respectively. On figure 17, one can see that the nylon plaque thickness has very little influence on the insertion loss characteristic of a barrier. The three foam thicknesses, 10, 20, and 30 mm are all grouped together. Below about 3000 Hz, there is a substantial difference in the insertion loss characteristic of a barrier depending upon foam thickness. Above that frequency, however, there is only a 1 - 2 dB difference between a 10 mm foam combination and a 30 mm foam combination. These results are repeated on figure 18 using urethane foam. This can be attributed to the absorption property of each material reaching a plateau after a certain frequency. Once this maximum plateau is reached, the insertion loss peak is also attained and remains constant. Therefore, materials that reach the same maximum absorption peak will ultimately (at higher frequencies) also have the same insertion loss.

In order to increase our knowledge of acoustical absorptive systems, other experiments were conducted using two plaques separated by gaps. These gapped plaques contained several acoustic damping media including air, a partial vacuum, sand, talc, and other materials. Although this work is not yet complete, a table of the results to date is included in Table 1 attached.

Plaques of 2 and 4 mm thicknesses were chosen since they most closely replicate those thicknesses that can be practically molded and are currently used in an underhood environment. It is interesting to note that, following the mass law, doubling the mass of a plaque (by doubling its thickness) will increase the transmission loss by 6 dBA. Some of these absorptive media can be considered as potential fillers for an engine noise cover. Of these fillers, sand and oil seem to offer the best absorption characteristics.

CONCLUSION

These two foams, urethane and melamine, will attenuate noises up to about 15 dBA (Insertion Loss). There seems to be a very slight edge given to the urethane at frequencies below 1000 Hz. Above 1000 Hz, these two foam systems seem to perform similarly. Noises below 1000 Hz can normally be attenuated using structural means. Above 1000 Hz, a cover might be required to attain required noise levels. When using a cover, the thickness of the nylon portion of the cover system seems to have no effect on noise attenuation. A foam thickness of 20 mm seems to be adequate for all frequencies above 1000 Hz. Above 3000 Hz, the

difference between a 30 mm foam thickness and a 10 mm foam thickness is only about 1 dBA (Insertion Loss).

Where foam cannot be used, it might be possible to create a double-layer noise cover, using an alternative absorbing media, to attenuate these offending noises. While these parts will certainly be heavier than the foam/nylon systems, they offer an excellent means of noise reduction for specific circumstances.

FUTURE WORK - Currently, the urethane foam used in this test is twenty times denser than the melamine foam. The melamine foam has a long-term temperature exposure capability of 150° C, 30° C higher than the capability of the urethane. Efforts are underway to reduce the density of the urethane and increase its maximum temperature capability without affecting its acoustical properties. Since both materials are effectively open-cell sponges, more testing should be conducted using a relatively impermeable film on one side of the foam to determine its effect. This film would decrease the amount of underhood fluids that can potentially be absorbed by the foam, reducing the possibility of having an oil-soaked acoustical absorber and all of the problems associated with that.

More work will have to be performed on the "filled" dual-plaque systems in order to better compare these data. In special cases where a foam might not be feasible, these systems might be an excellent alternative to consider.

ACKNOWLEDGMENTS

My thanks to Dr. Edward Green of Roush Anatrol without whom this paper would surely not be possible.

Table 1
Alternative Absorber Materials

System	Each Plaque Thickness (mm)	Gap Size and Filling Media	Transmission Loss (dBA)	System Mass (g)
1	2	2 mm air	39.2	193
2	4	2 mm air	46.9	383
3	2	3 mm air	42.4	198
4	2+4	2 mm air	49.3	285
5	2	2 mm air at 200 mbar	40.7	190
6	4	2 mm air at 200 mbar	44.7	394
7	2	3 mm talc	44.7	245
8	2	3 mm sand	50.6	321
9	2	3 mm oil	46.1	242
10	2	3 mm walnut shells	43.5	211
11	2	3 mm Cellasto®	44.6	222
12	2 (single)	- - -	36.4	88
13	4 (single)	- - -	41.1	171

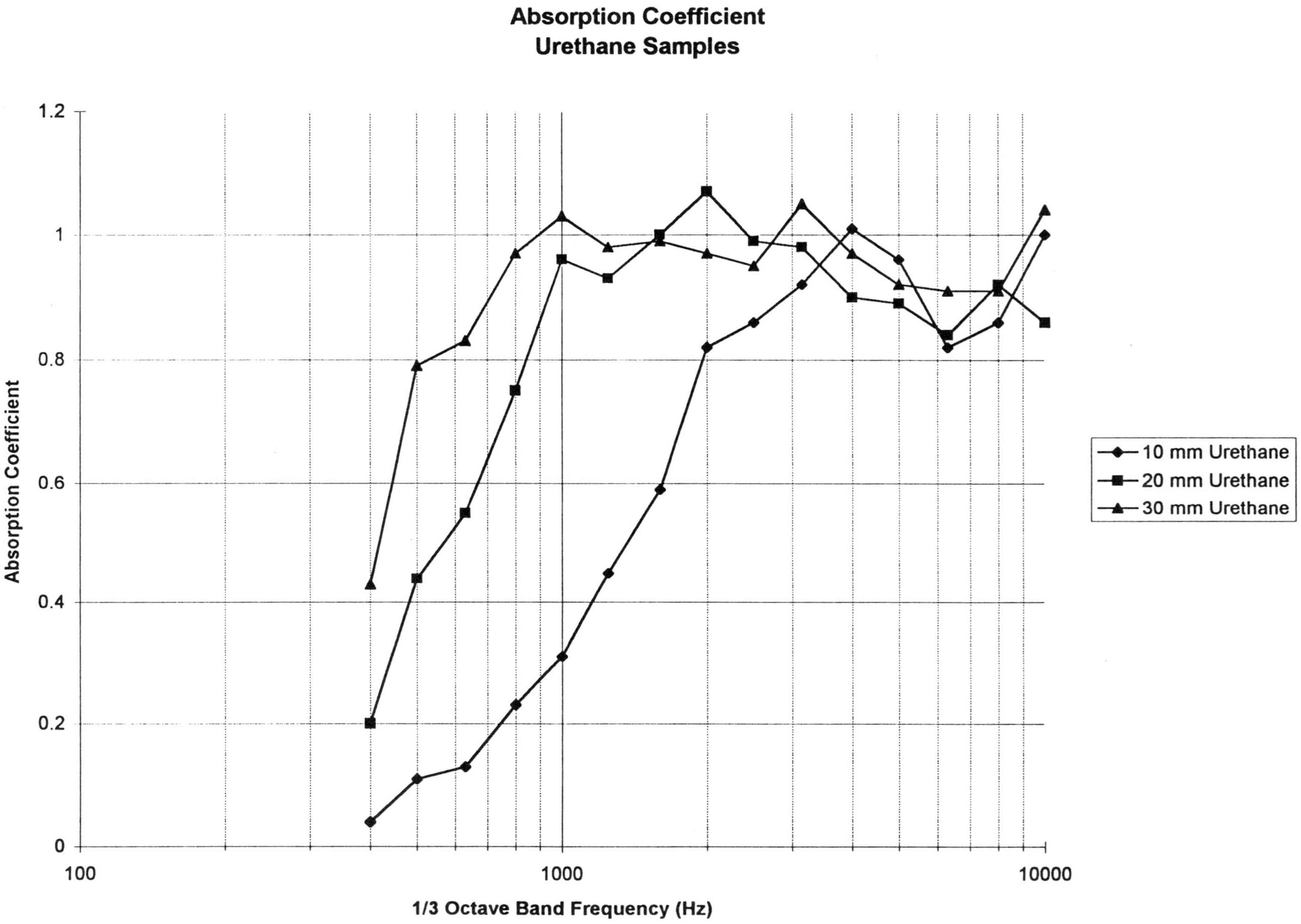
Absorption Coefficient
Urethane Samples
Absorption Coefficient
1.2
1
0.8
0.6
0.4
0.2
0
100
1000
10000
1/3 Octave Band Frequency (Hz)
10 mm Urethane
20 mm Urethane
30 mm Urethane

Figure 1

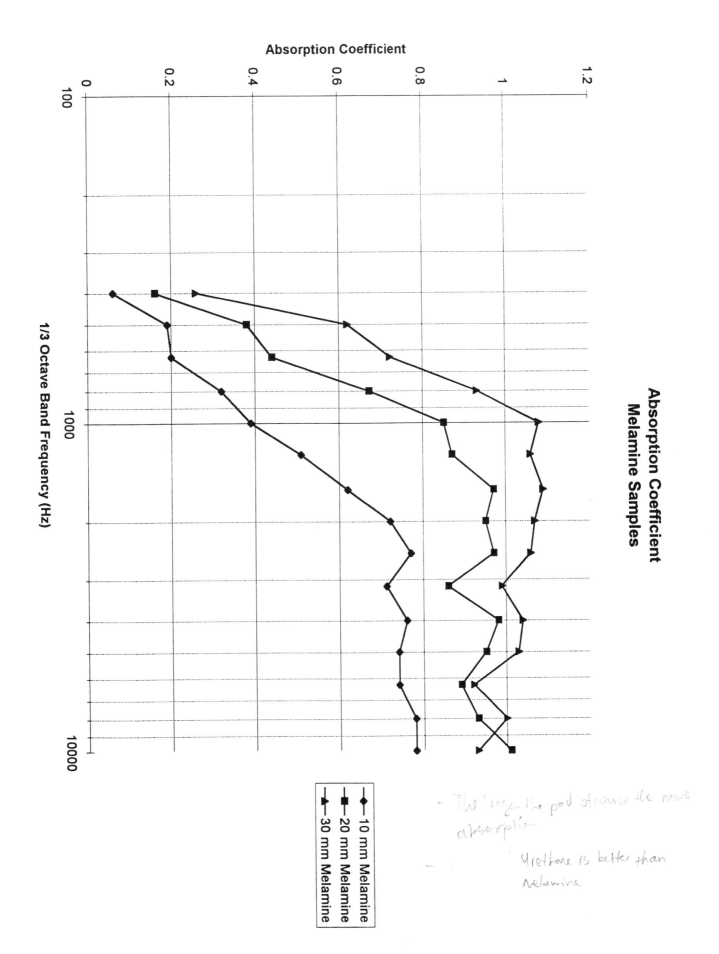

Figure 2

Absorption Coefficient
Melamine Samples

Absorption Coefficient

1/3 Octave Band Frequency (Hz)

— 10 mm Melamine
— 20 mm Melamine
— 30 mm Melamine

- The larger the pad ofcourse the more absorption

- Urethane is better than Melamine

51

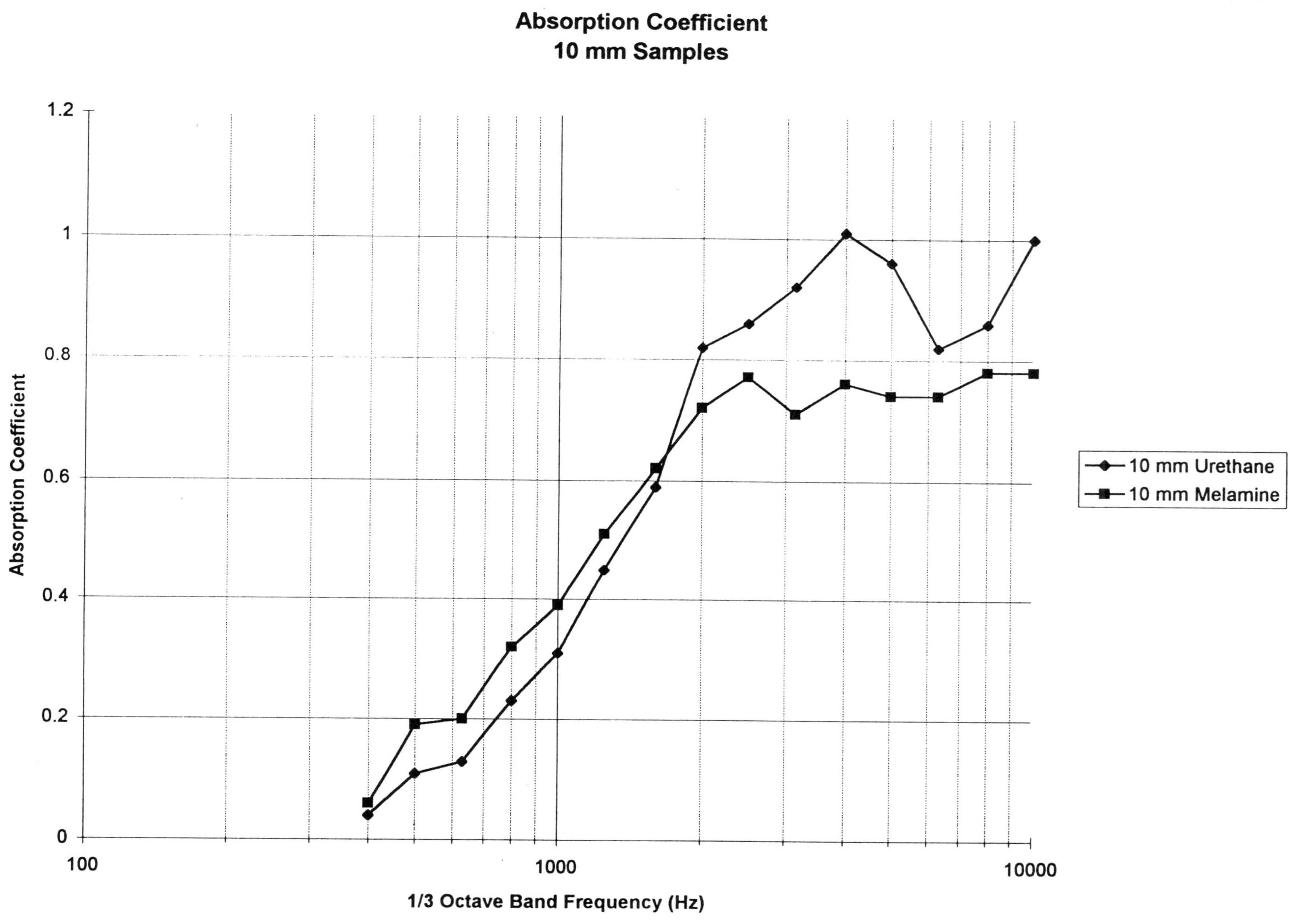

Absorption Coefficient
10 mm Samples
1.2
1
0.8
0.6
0.4
0.2
0
Absorption Coefficient
100
1000
10000
1/3 Octave Band Frequency (Hz)
10 mm Urethane
10 mm Melamine

Figure 3

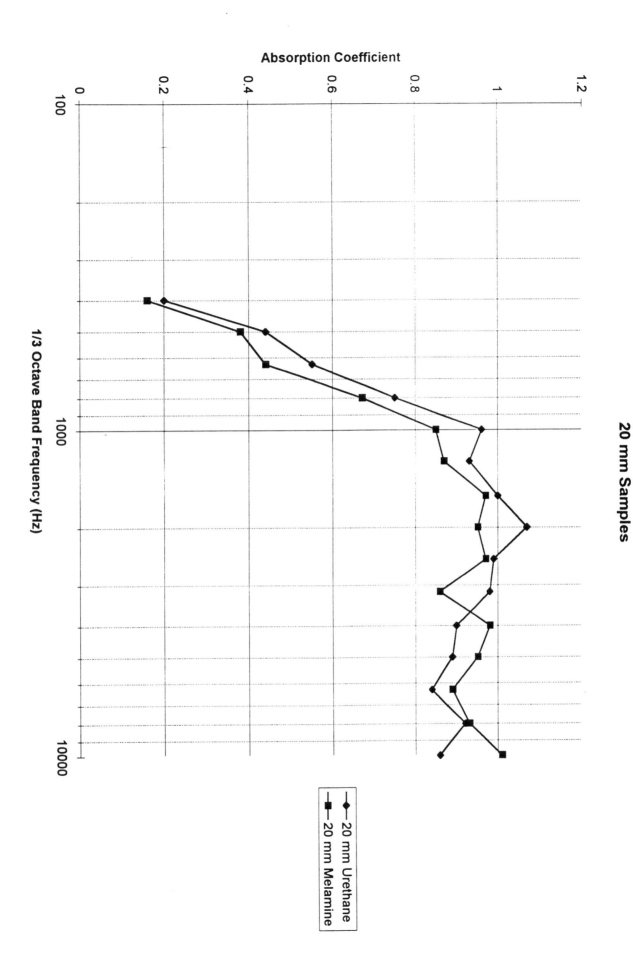

Absorption Coefficient
20 mm Samples

Absorption Coefficient

1/3 Octave Band Frequency (Hz)

◆ 20 mm Urethane
■ 20 mm Melamine

Figure 4

53

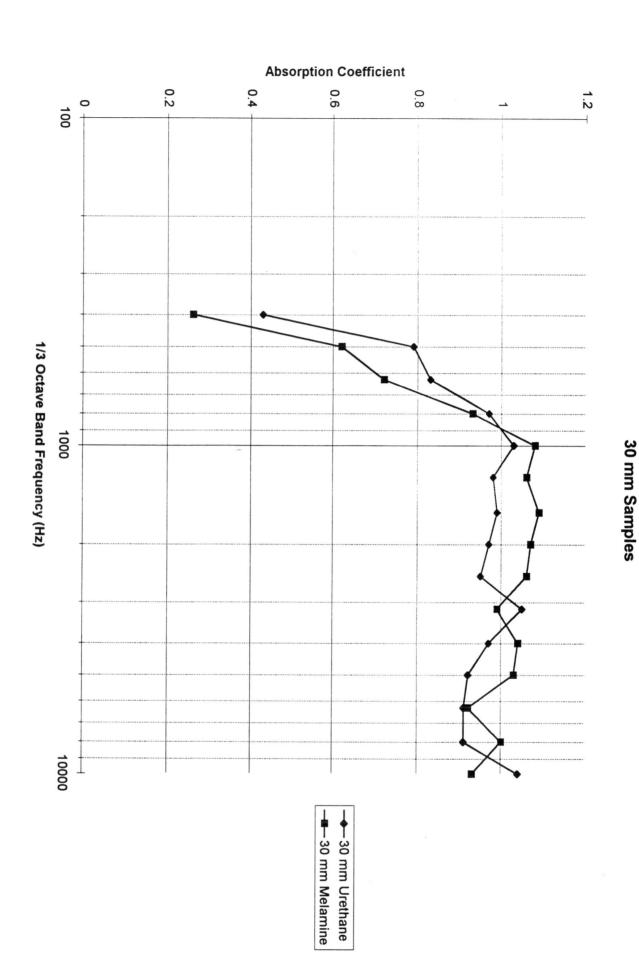

**Absorption Coefficient
30 mm Samples**

Figure 5

30 mm Urethane
30 mm Melamine

54

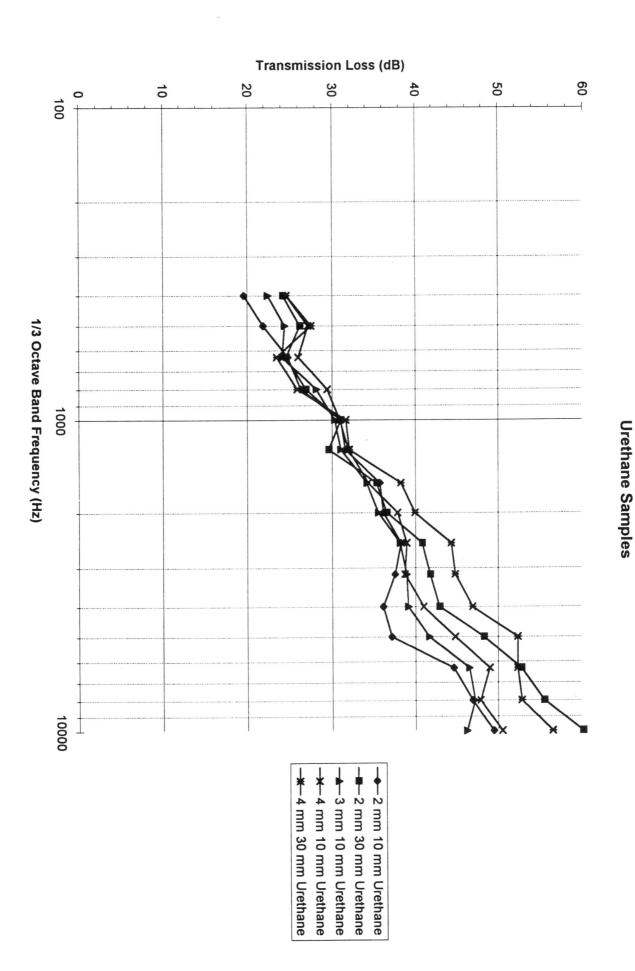

Transmission Loss
Urethane Samples

Transmission Loss (dB)

1/3 Octave Band Frequency (Hz)

Figure 6

◆— 2 mm 10 mm Urethane
■— 2 mm 30 mm Urethane
▲— 3 mm 10 mm Urethane
✕— 4 mm 10 mm Urethane
✳— 4 mm 30 mm Urethane

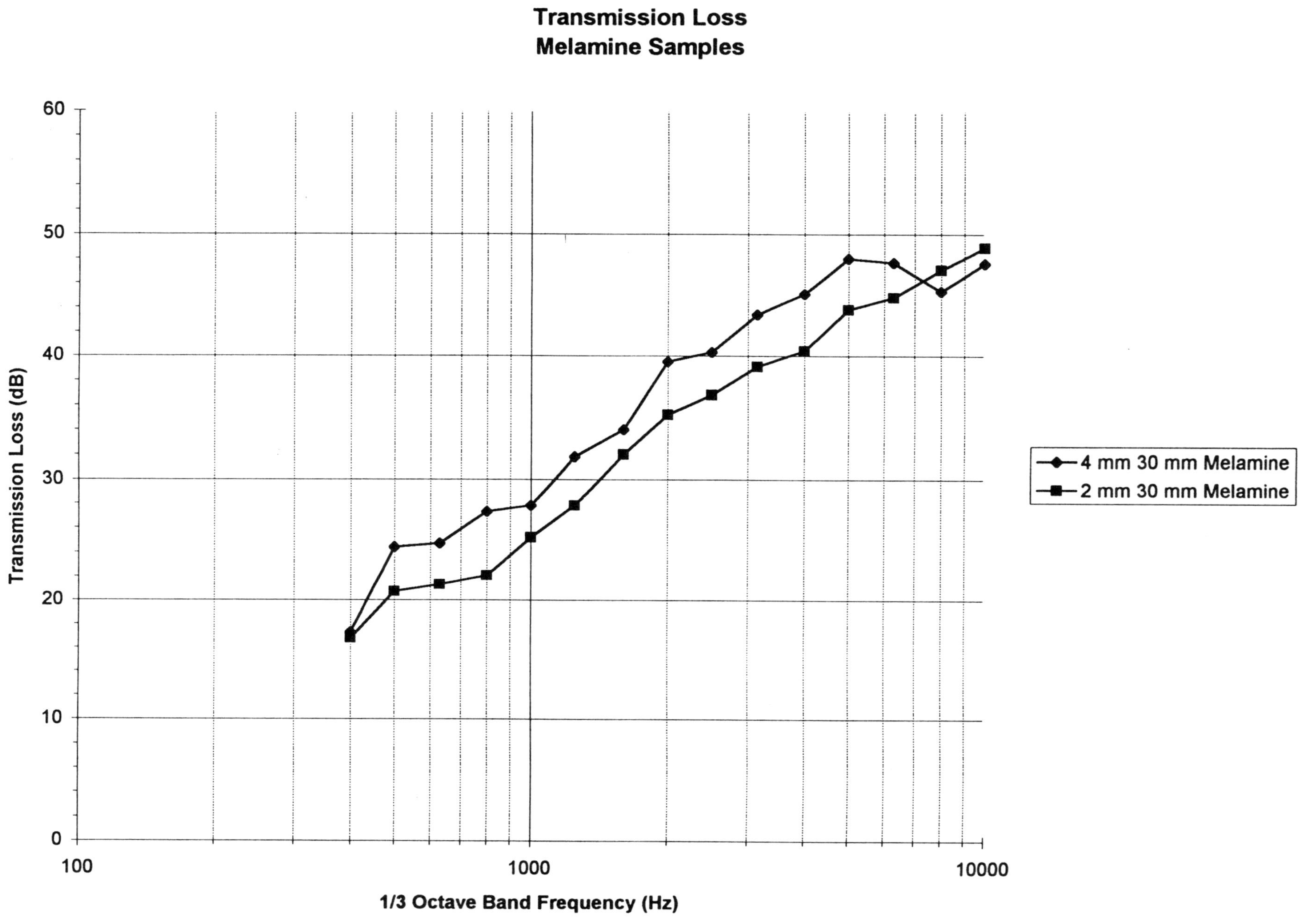

Transmission Loss
Melamine Samples
Transmission Loss (dB)
0
10
20
30
40
50
60
100
1000
10000
1/3 Octave Band Frequency (Hz)
4 mm 30 mm Melamine
2 mm 30 mm Melamine

Figure 7

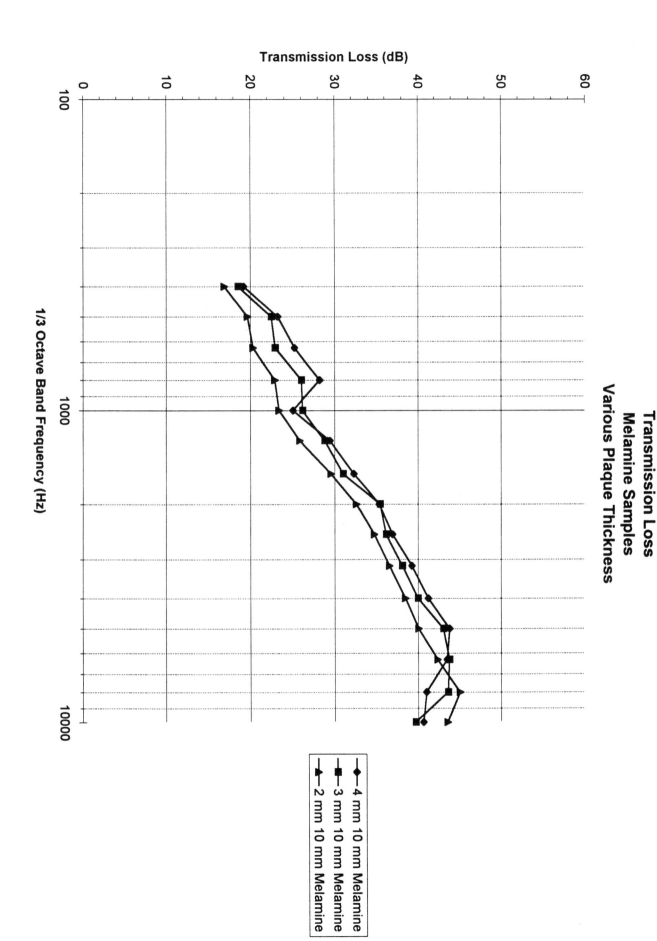

Figure 8

57

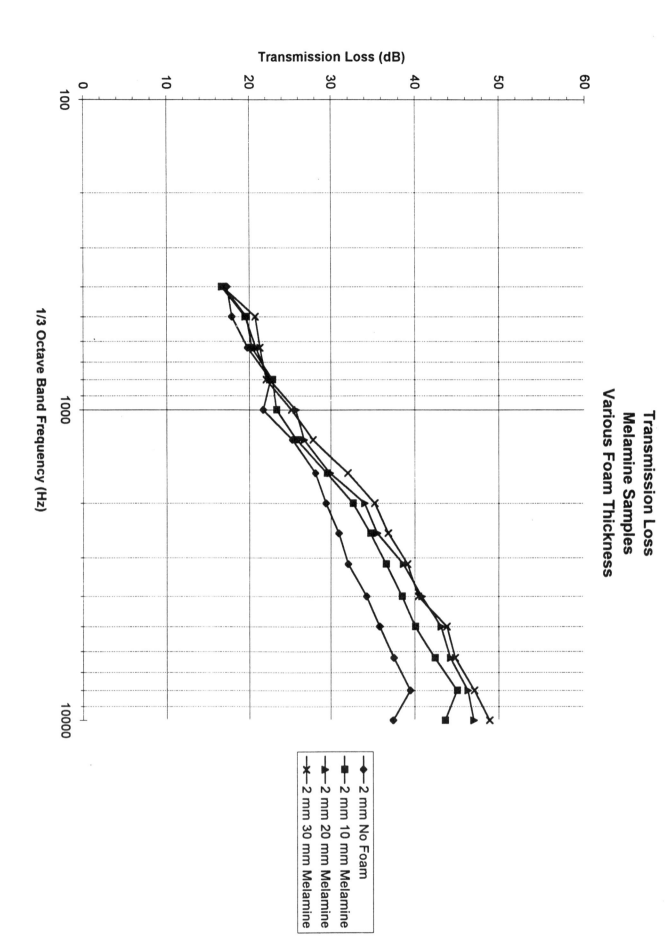

Figure 9

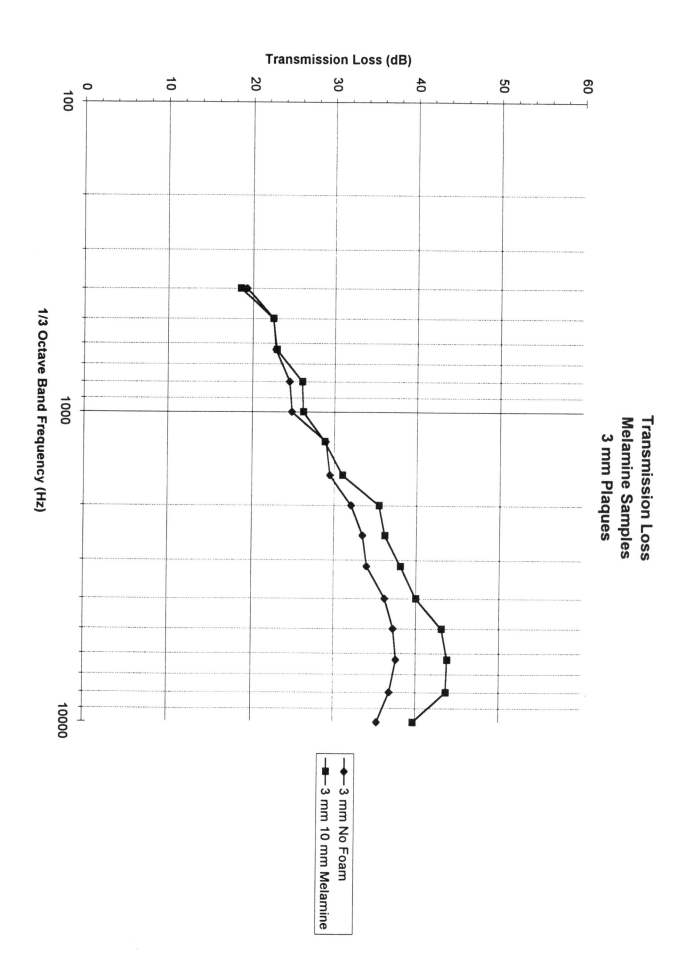

Transmission Loss
Melamine Samples
3 mm Plaques

Transmission Loss (dB)

1/3 Octave Band Frequency (Hz)

—♦— 3 mm No Foam
—■— 3 mm 10 mm Melamine

Figure 10

59

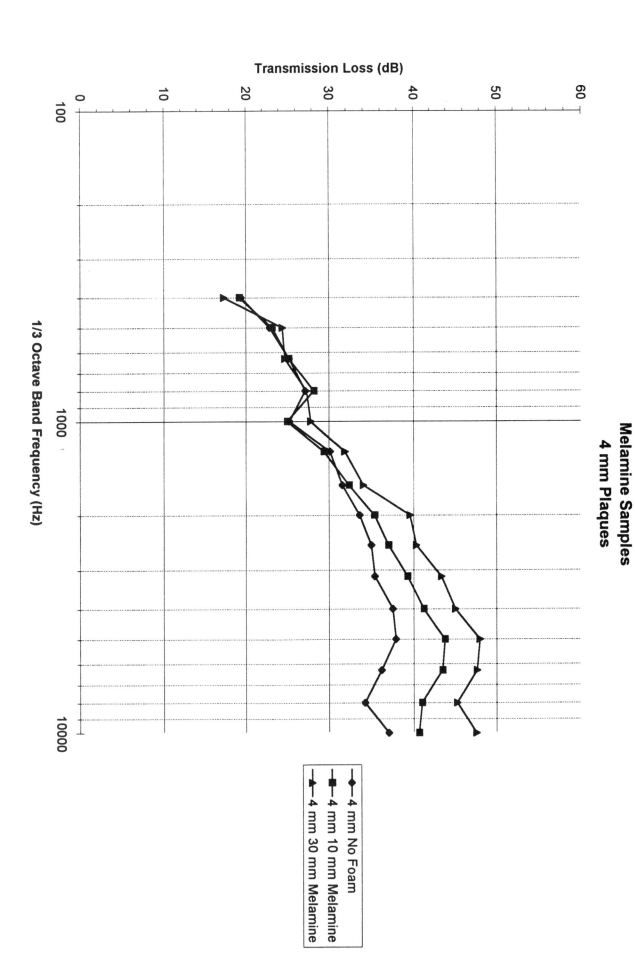

Transmission Loss
Melamine Samples
4 mm Plaques

Transmission Loss (dB)

1/3 Octave Band Frequency (Hz)

Figure 11

- ◆ 4 mm No Foam
- ■ 4 mm 10 mm Melamine
- ▲ 4 mm 30 mm Melamine

60

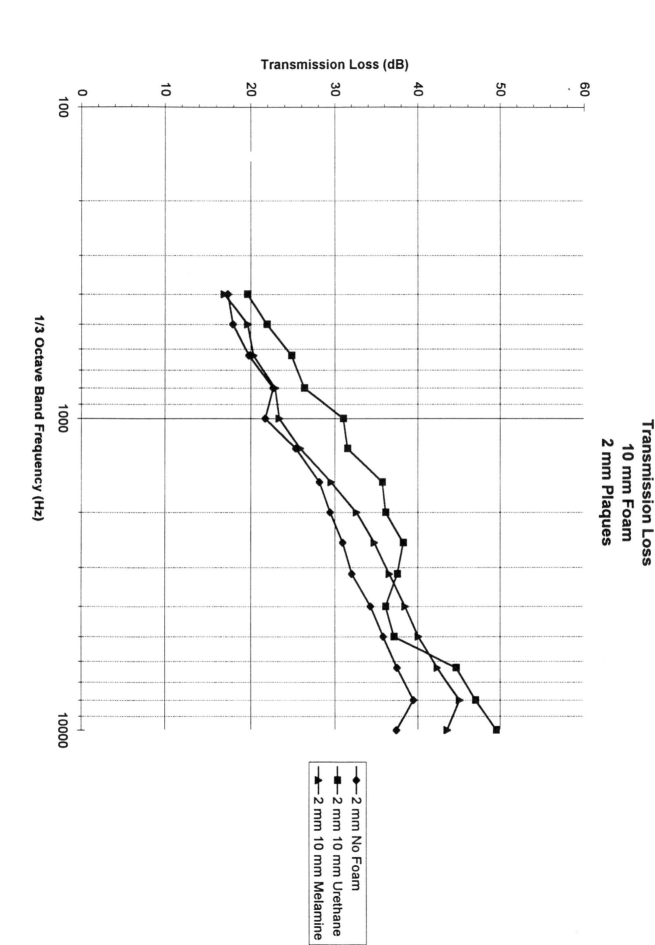

Transmission Loss
10 mm Foam
2 mm Plaques

Transmission Loss (dB)

1/3 Octave Band Frequency (Hz)

Figure 12

Legend:
- 2 mm No Foam
- 2 mm 10 mm Urethane
- 2 mm 10 mm Melamine

61

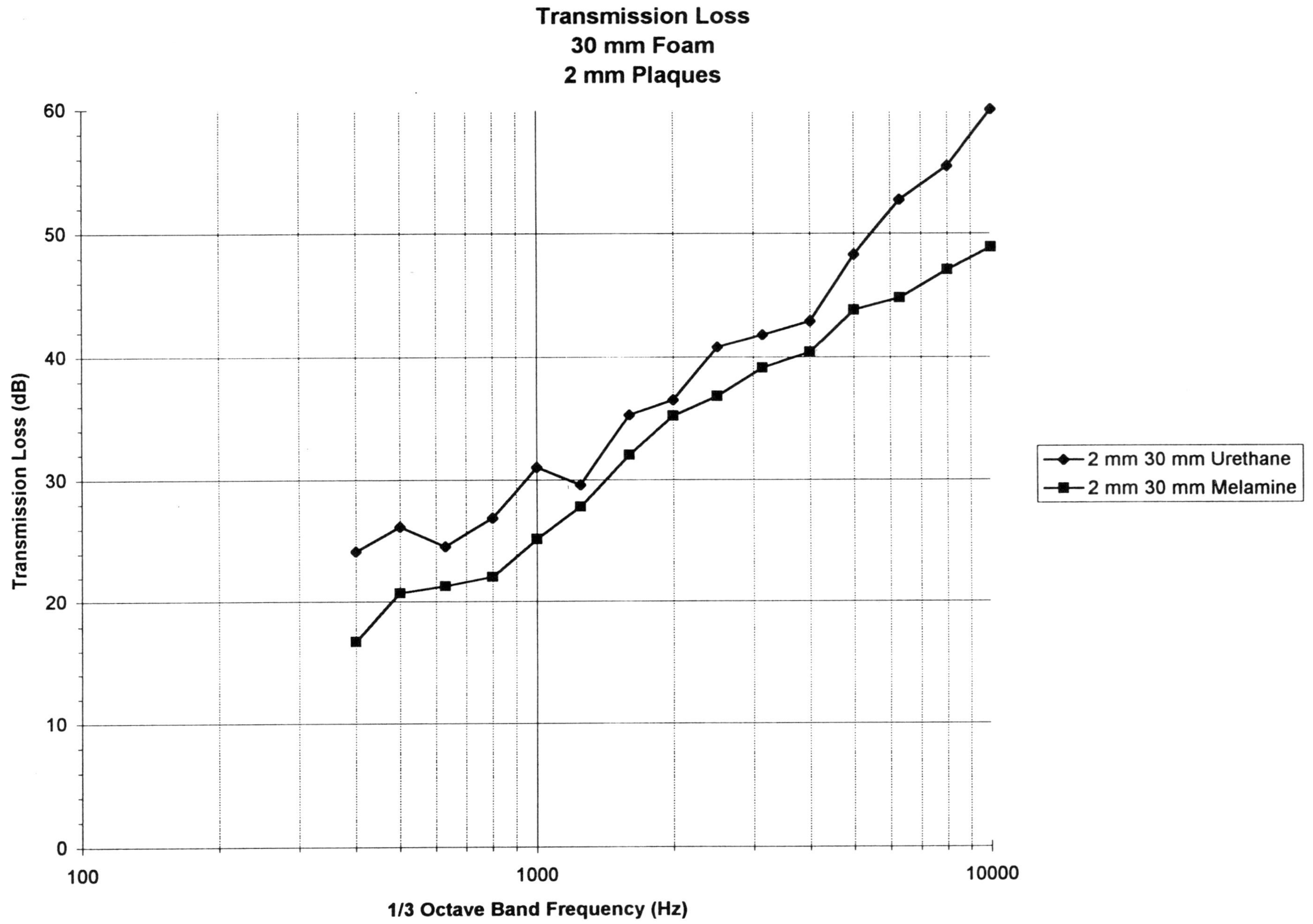

Transmission Loss
30 mm Foam
2 mm Plaques
Transmission Loss (dB)
60
50
40
30
20
10
0
100
1000
10000
1/3 Octave Band Frequency (Hz)
2 mm 30 mm Urethane
2 mm 30 mm Melamine

Figure 13

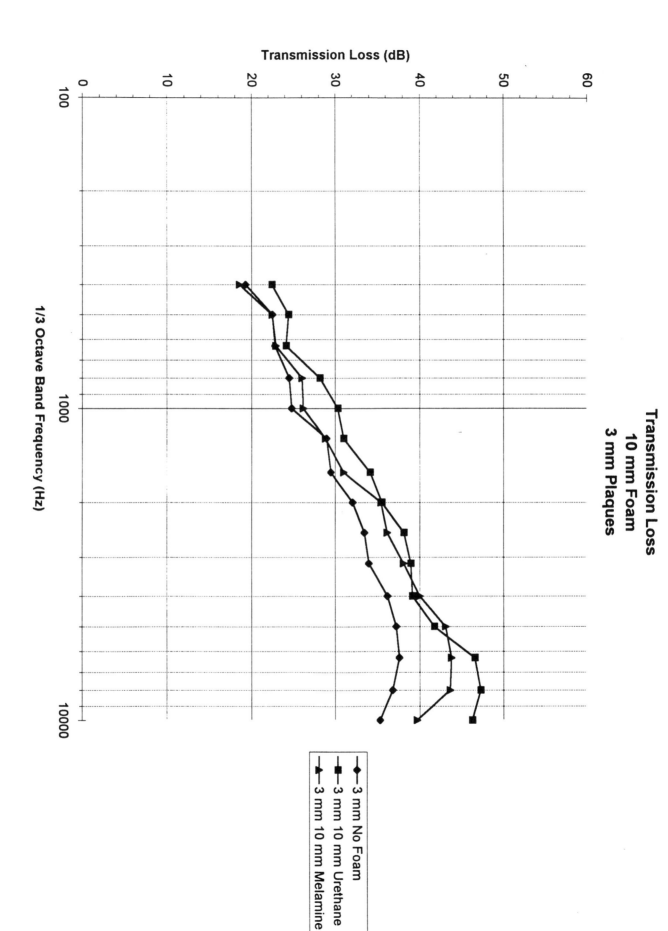

**Transmission Loss
10 mm Foam
3 mm Plaques**

Transmission Loss (dB)

1/3 Octave Band Frequency (Hz)

Figure 14

♦ 3 mm No Foam
■ 3 mm 10 mm Urethane
▲ 3 mm 10 mm Melamine

63

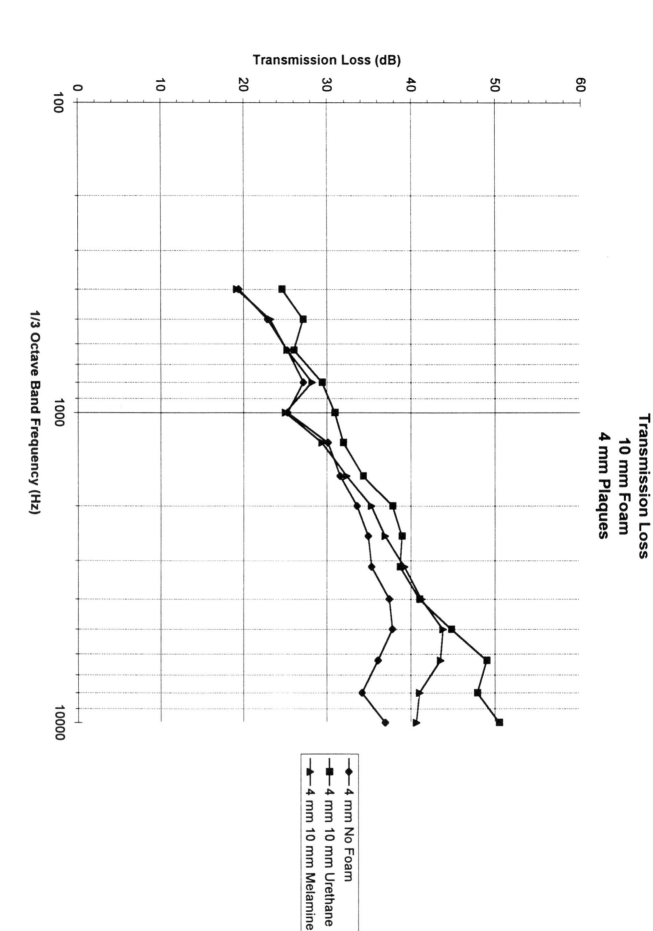

Figure 15

Transmission Loss
10 mm Foam
4 mm Plaques

Transmission Loss (dB)

1/3 Octave Band Frequency (Hz)

Legend:
- 4 mm No Foam
- 4 mm 10 mm Urethane
- 4 mm 10 mm Melamine

64

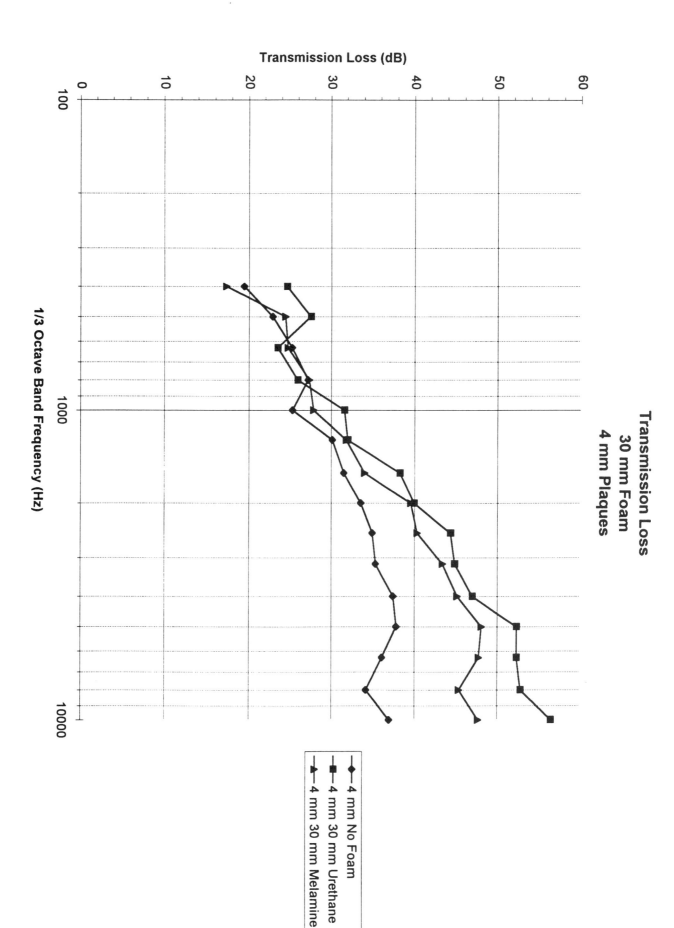

Transmission Loss
30 mm Foam
4 mm Plaques

Transmission Loss (dB)

1/3 Octave Band Frequency (Hz)

- 4 mm No Foam
- 4 mm 30 mm Urethane
- 4 mm 30 mm Melamine

Figure 16

65

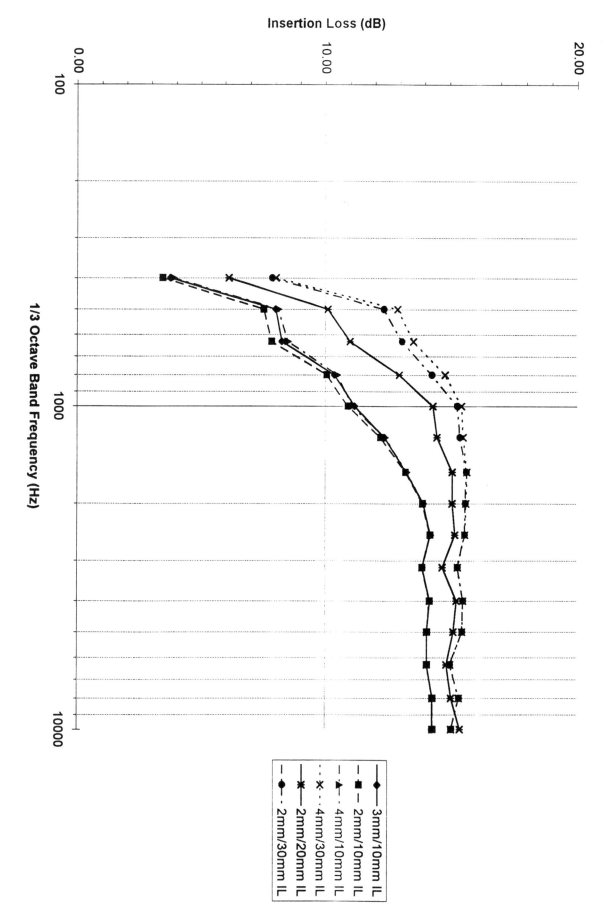

Insertion Loss
Melamine Foam Samples

Insertion Loss (dB)

1/3 Octave Band Frequency (Hz)

Figure 17

Legend:
- 3mm/10mm IL
- 2mm/10mm IL
- 4mm/10mm IL
- 4mm/30mm IL
- 2mm/20mm IL
- 2mm/30mm IL

66

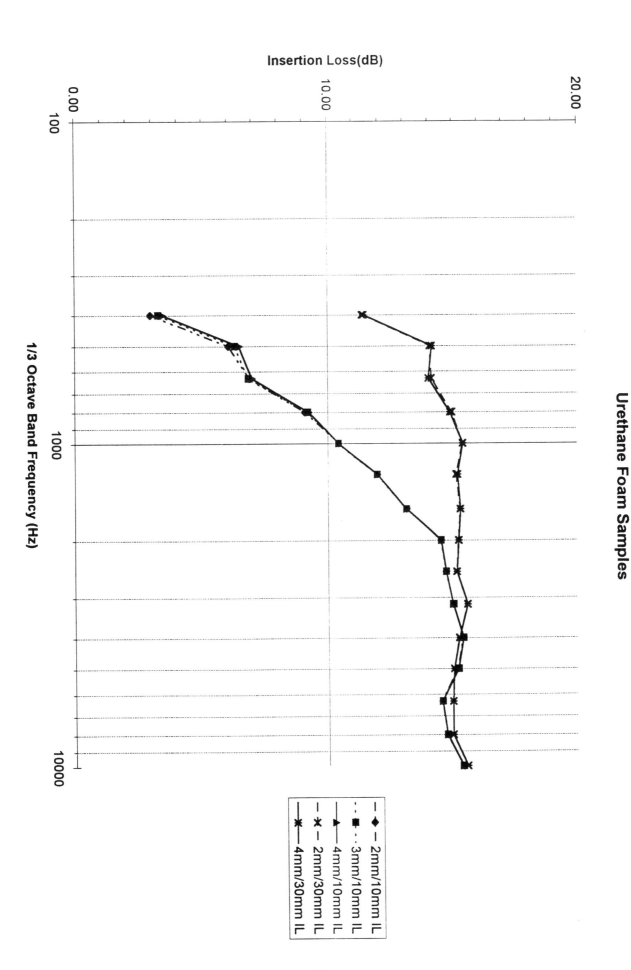

Figure 18

970079

A Concise History of Thermoplastic Sealing Engine Cover Systems

James D. Francis and Mark Schuchardt
E.I. du Pont de Nemours & Co.

ABSTRACT:

The technology to manufacture thermoplastic rocker covers has evolved significantly since early applications in the US launched in 1980. New sealing methods and the widespread use of aluminum in cylinder heads make it easier to take advantage of the cost, weight and part integration opportunities that thermoplastics and the injection molding process have to offer.

By understanding these developments, a functional, lightweight, low-cost, full-featured cover can be designed and manufactured.

INTRODUCTION

{Note: There are many covers on today's engines. This paper deals with those that must provide structure and sealing as well as allow for periodic removal. Valve covers, rocker covers, timing chain covers, etc all fit this criteria. This paper will refer to all of these as "engine covers," but the reader should not consider this terminology to include styling covers or non-sealing timing belt covers, which have different requirements.}

Engineering thermoplastics, and the injection molding process, represent a means for engine designers to integrate parts, facilitate assembly, reduce weight and lower the costs of their engine covers. Recent advances in technology and the use of computer-aided techniques to increase understanding of the interplay between flange geometry, bolt spacing and seal design, have spurred increased usage of thermoplastic sealing covers in other regions. It is interesting to see this trend, considering that the first commercial examples of these components came out of North America, and have subsequently been abandoned in this region.

The first attempts to capitalize on the advantages of thermoplastic covers did not always meet with complete success. This resulted in the development of a negative perception of this technology, particularly in the North American engineering community. This misunderstanding has propagated even while the technology was being developed in other regions.

Although the impression of the early covers is not generally positive, for the most part, these components served their function adequately and provided valuable experience. However, the seals used were not entirely sufficient for the task and, in some cases, cover failures occurred. It's important to keep in mind that stamped steel covers, the standard technology of the day, were better understood but still exhibited the same "failures." Steel covers, particularly with the cork/rubber and die-cut synthetic gaskets popular for the time, could leak if the bolts weren't properly tightened, if the cover was bent or compression wasn't controlled. Finally, while steel covers would not fracture, they were prone to rust and corrosion. It is difficult to see how these systems would have provided consistent sealing for today's extended warranty periods.

All materials and manufacturing processes have their advantages and disadvantages. The designer's role is to select the technology that maximizes the advantages and apply it in such a way as to minimize the disadvantages.

This paper will analyze early experiences with thermoplastic covers and will discuss failure modes. Each key detail or feature will be expanded upon to describe the current thinking on materials and designs. Where possible, "rules of thumb" will be provided to assist the designer.

HISTORY:

In the mid 1970s most North American automakers were working to improve gas mileage by reducing vehicle weight. One area that promised a significant savings (50%-80% reduction) was the replacement of steel rocker covers with plastic. These programs went commercial in the early '80s and, quickly, four engines debuted with thermoplastic rocker covers. These engines were:

Table 1: US Thermoplastic Engine Covers

Engine	Cover Material
Cadillac V8	Glass Reinforced 6/6 Nylon
Cadillac V4-6-8	Glass Reinforced 6/6 Nylon
Jeep 4 Cylinder	Glass Reinforced Polyester
Jeep 6 Cylinder	Glass Reinforced Polyester

Each of these covers used a room temperature vulcanized (RTV) silicone as a seal.

The V8s used a form in place RTV, which was applied to one of the components immediately preceding assembly. The idea was to adhere the cover to the cylinder head. This type of silicone had very little compressibility and was prone to leak if the adhesion between the mating parts was compromised. This adhesion was effected by variation in materials, differential thermal growth (of the plastic cover and the cast iron head), surface finish/cleanliness of mating parts, and the bolt spacing.

The 4 and 6 cylinder engines used a cure in place RTV. This material was applied to the sealing flange of the cover and allowed to cure prior to assembly. This material acted more as a compression gasket than an adhesive and was, as such, not susceptible to variables that affected the form in place seals. However, the process to "manufacture" the gasket was not sufficiently robust to eliminate failures. These systems were affected by the contact of the wet adhesive with any contaminant, control of the bead height, and lap joints at the start/stop of the application.

While the parts were adequate overall, there were higher incidents of oil leakage and/or repair for each of these programs. Because of this, engineering teams were assembled to correct the situation. Unfortunately, sophisticated silicone gaskets, either press in place or carrier mounted, were not yet production ready, so these teams focused on attempting to either:

- Increase the amount or quality of the adhesion, or:
- Decrease the forces that would "pry" the adhesive joint apart.

Several ingenious proposals were developed as "stopgap" measures to correct real and perceived problems with these covers. They included modifying the surface finish on the cover and the cast iron head to enhance adhesion, metal inserts and back-up plates to allow increased bolt loads, and complicated manufacturing processes that attempted to control the adhesive application and curing. While these measures met with some success, the "elegant" solution required to validate thermoplastic engine covers and bring them into widespread use, did not occur, at least not in this time frame. Thus, many in the North American engineering community were left with the conclusion:

"Thermoplastic engine covers leak."

That may have been a valid then, but it certainly isn't valid now. Several significant changes have, once again, made this technology attractive:

- The wide-spread manufacture of compressible silicone and acrylic gaskets which seal with variations in sealing forces.
- The replacement of cast iron heads with aluminum. The coefficient of linear thermal expansion of aluminum can be matched with several types of thermoplastics.
- The redesign of various bolt patterns, which are friendlier to low modulus materials.

FAILURE MODE - OIL LEAKAGE:

Several factors effect the leak integrity of a thermoplastic cover system. These factors are:

- Cover material and geometry
- Sectional properties of the seal flange
- Bolt design, spacing and location
- Seal material and manufacturing process
- Seal cross section

COVER MATERIAL: Simply put, oil leakage will occur if a thermoplastic cover is designed to mimic a traditional steel one. As engineering materials, thermoplastics have several unique properties, and each of these, if not properly addressed, can be a direct cause to cover leakage. Compared to metal, thermoplastics are:

- Much less stiff
- Non-linear
- Dependent on temperature and moisture
- Susceptible to stress relaxation
- Anisotropic

Compared to steel, engineering thermoplastics have a Young's modulus (stress/strain) significantly lower than steel (see Table 2), which will vary as a function of strain (see Figure 1). The modulus will also vary according to the environment (see Figure 2). The technique for working with these types of materials in critical applications is to use design tools to develop an understanding of the environment and stress on the component for the various criteria and geometry, and then select a material capable of performing as required.

Table 2: Young's Modulus for Various Materials

Material	Young's Modulus	
	ksi	GPa
Steel	30,000	207
Aluminum	10,300	71
Magnesium	6,500	45
6/6 Nylon* (23° C)	400 - 1,600	3 - 11
PET Polyester* (23° C)	1,300 - 2,600	9 - 18

* Indicates nominal 33% glass reinforcement

Figure 1: Typical Stress Strain Curves for Nylon and Steel

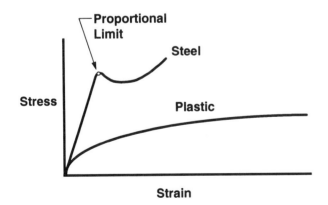

Thermoplastics are prone to stress relaxation when they are subjected to high loads over long periods of time. This phenomenon is accelerated at higher temperatures. In order to assure that bolts do not lose their preload and begin to de-energize the seal, it is necessary to account for this stress relaxation. This topic will be fully covered later; however, it is essential that

some design consideration be given to ensure this situation does not happen.

Figure 2: Effect Of Temperature and Moisture On Glass Reinforced Nylon

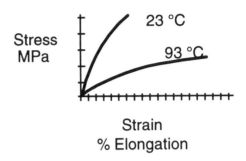

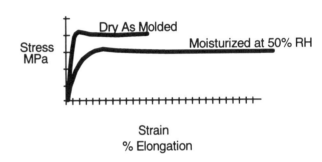

Anisotropic materials have properties dependent on the direction of loading. Since all thermoplastic materials suitable for structural underhood applications use glass to provide sufficient stiffness, etc and since glass is a unidirectional product, it follows that these products will be anisotropic. In general, these products will be stiffer and stronger in the direction in which the glass orients. It is very important to realize that glass orientation will also effect how the part shrinks during manufacturing, and, hence, how much the part will warp. This effect can be reduced by replacing some of the glass reinforcement with mineral.

Again, all these issues can be handled with the judicious use of design tools and material properties. What is most important is that the design team understands that part function is affected by material properties and by how the part is manufactured.

With the development of modern computer-aided engineering tools, contending with these issues is, relatively speaking, straightforward. But the key to success still seems to be one of awareness.

SECTIONAL PROPERTIES OF THE SEAL FLANGE: The section modulus of the seal flange, in many respects, may be more significant to the success of a design than the material's Young's Modulus. This variable is limited only by the imagination of the designer and the available "real estate" for an application. Ribbing, design of the seal groove, and attachment geometry to the cover wall all effect the theoretical "stiffness" of the section itself. Anything that will increase this value will help minimize the potential for oil leakage.

One of the most critical aspects of the seal flange is how well it conforms to the mating surface on the head. If there is too much variation, the overall thickness of the gasket will have to be increased to make up for it. Naturally, this will increase the stress in areas where the variation is less. The goal should be to reduce this variation by (1)using a minimum and uniform part thickness, (2) understanding part warpage by carefully prototyping the design, (3) factoring in the shrinkage that does occur in the final tool design, and finally (4) bearing in mind that it's more important to conform to the head flange when bolted into position, than it is to have a perfectly flat part.

For some part designs, the actual shrinkage/warpage of prototype components has been used to cut the production tooling. Done correctly, this method can produce extremely flat components in an easily controlled process. (Note: if using this method, remember that gate design and location, tooling design and materials, as well as other factors will influence shrinkage).

Since the differential shrinkage always occurs where two walls join together, particular attention must be given to the corners of any cover. Additional stiffening may be required to insure that this warpage and/or creep does not de-energize the seals. The safest tack would be to locate a bolt at all corners.

BOLT DESIGN, SPACING AND LOCATION:
Various bolts can be used to retain the cover; however, the type of bolt used has a pronounced impact on the effectiveness of the system. Bolting systems used for steel covers are almost always inappropriate for thermoplastic covers. This phenomena occurs because the preload, necessary to retain the bolts, puts the plastic under constant compression that will eventually result in creep. When the material creeps, the bolt could loosen and provide a leak path.

An alternative is to eliminate the need for preload by using a thread adhesive to assure bolt retention. In some of the early cover system designs, the silicone adhesive seemed to serve this function, therefore, so there were no reports of cover bolts loosening.

Other, somewhat more elegant alternatives include: (1) the use of shoulder bolts. In these types of systems, the preload is generated by the stretching of the bolt threads against the bolts shank, which bottoms out against the head rather than the plastic. (2) the use of metal inserts which transmit the bolt torque to the head without stressing the plastic (see Figure 3).

Figure 3: Various Bolting Schemes

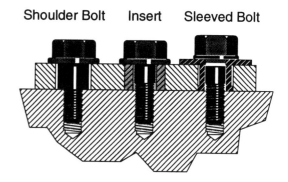

Shoulder Bolt   Insert   Sleeved Bolt

Perhaps the most interesting solution to this issue is the use of a rubber isolated sleeve fastener (see Figure 4). This fastener is a bolt which has a metal sleeve within which is captured a grommet. The force is supported by this grommet, which acts as a spring between the bolt head and the plastic. This type of fastener has the added benefit of helping to isolate the cover from vibration and reducing noise. Note that the durometer of the grommet must be tailored to the durometer of the gasket in order to assure proper sealing.

The use of inserts or sleeved fasteners has the significant advantage of allowing the deflection of bolt preload over a longer grip length over a longer grip length. This results in a lower spring rate than a shoulder bolt and will allow the bolt to absorb changes in the stiffness and dimensions of the flange/gasket system as a function of the environment.

Figure 4: Rubber Isolated Sleeve Fasteners

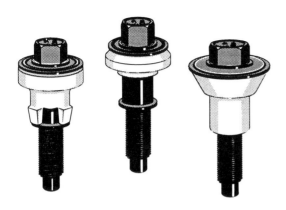

In addition to the type of bolt used, the location and the spacing of the bolts are critical. If the bolts are too far apart (see Figure 5, Method "A")., then the sealing pressure generated by the flange pushing down on the gasket will place excessive stress in the plastic and cause creep which may allow cover to leak. That is assuming the cover can be sealed in the first place. Naturally, bolts placed too close together result in costs of manufacture issues.

**Figure 5: Bolting Schemes
(Method "B" is Preferred)**

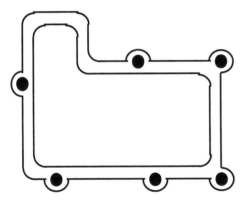

(A)

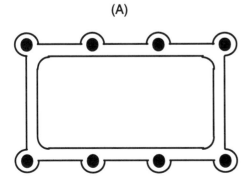

(B)

Experience has indicated that a bolt spacing of approximately 100 mm to be a good rule of thumb. Wider spacing is possible but will require tighter tolerances on the flatness of the sealing flange. For instance, a cover with a 150 mm spacing between bolts should function if the flatness variation is held to less than 0.8 mm.

As noted earlier, our experience shows that most successful thermoplastic covers have bolts located at, or very near, the corners of the cover. The maximum cantilever (distance from bolt to corner of cover) which would be possible is sensitive to the actual geometry of the cover. While it is theoretically possible to stiffen the corners of the cover, to maintain required sealing force, great care must be exercised. Since thermal expansion of any structure will cause additional stresses at the joints, unrestrained corners may have a tendency to "bow upwards" during thermal cycling. Particularly at cold temperature, when the stiffness of the material is significantly increased. Experience indicates that a cantilever of about 20 mm is possible with very simple cover geometry.

Even with these guidelines, it is wise to analyze a specific design using CAE tools and to thoroughly test prototypes.

SEAL MATERIAL (CONFORMABILITY): Die cut gaskets require high compressive forces which can caused the seal flange to deform and leak - even on a steel cover. Cork/rubber gaskets were very compressible, but would take a permanent set with time and temperature. As noted earlier, form in place RTV systems were susceptible to differential thermal expansion breaking the adhesive bond and allowing oil leakage. The cure in place systems relied on compression to seal, but were easily damaged by a difficult manufacturing process.

These reasons resulted in seal materials and manufacturing processes undergoing tremendous changes in the last 15 years. Molded gaskets made from silicone, flourosilicones, ethylene acrylics and poly acrylics, in conjunction with new design features and fastening systems, have replaced the old RTVs and die cut gaskets.

As noted the first seals for thermoplastic covers were RTV silicones which have no compression properties. In use, they acted as an adhesive which bonded the flange of the cover to the head and, therefore, stress relaxation didn't occur between the bolt locations because there was no stress present. However, since the head was cast iron, differential thermal expansion would put the adhesive into shear and weaken the integrity of the joint. Thus, the potential for leaks increased with the age of the engine.

HOW TO SUCCEED:

A successful development is not the result of a specific material selection. Nor is it the result of a certain manufacturing technique. The successful development occurs when the time is taken to understand the requirements of components as individual pieces and as parts of an integrated system.

Be realistic: It is not always necessary to meet all of the criteria for a metal cover in order to produce a functional thermoplastic one. Take advantage of the differences in materials.

Be patient: This is a little different and there is always a learning curve. Every design is different and extra time may be needed to work it out, the first time.

Finally, use thermoplastics properties and processes to their best advantage. They allow the designer the flexibility to:

- Use thin walls
- Provide intricate features
- Eliminate corrosion protection
- Weld on other components
- Integrate other functions

There are already examples of an integrated cover and air cleaner, the future will probably hold designs where the entire air induction system is combined.

Thermoplastic rocker covers are being used in all regions of the world. They have been selected because they provide functionality, weight benefits, corrosion resistance, integration opportunities and recyclability. What's more, with today's technologies, they don't leak.

970659

Scratch and Mar Resistance of Mineral-Filled Polypropylene Materials

J. Chu and L. Rumao
Ford Motor Co.

B. Coleman
ATC, Inc.

ABSTRACT

Pigmented & mineral-filled PP (PF-PP) is marketed as a potential alternative to ABS for automotive interior applications. However, PF-PP is easily damaged by scratching its surface, thus limiting its acceptance for interior applications. This study investigates the test methods to quantify the extent of scratch & mar damage, and the effect of different mineral fillers towards improving the scratch & mar resistance of PF-PP.

INTRODUCTION

Significant cost savings would be found in replacing ABS with PF-PP for interior automotive components. However, PF-PP's susceptibility to scratch & mar damage hinders its use for these applications. Although scratch & mar prevention during shipping/handling/assembly can be managed by the OEM, there can be no such control once the parts enter customer service. The scratchability of PF-PP is not only a warranty issue, but also a customer satisfaction concern. As a result, the PF-PP parts are usually top-coated, thus eliminating the cost savings when considered as a substitute for ABS. The intention of this study is to evaluate the effect of different mineral fillers on the scratch & mar resistance of PF-PP and to find an appropriate test method to quantify such data.

Many factors, such as filler type, additives, lubricant, impact modifier, polymer type, etc., affect tribological properties of plastic materials. Typically, three methods are used to improve the tribological properties of plastic materials 1) modifying the polymer molecular structure such as its crystallinity, 2) blending polymers, 3) producing polymer composite with various fillers and additives. However, without an appropriate test method to quantitatively evaluate the degree of scratch and mar, it is difficult to conduct material development work and to gauge its efficiency to improve its performance.

Generally, scratch & mar resistance is related to wear resistance of a given surface [1]. Therefore, factors affecting wear resistance should have an effect on the scratch & mar resistance as well. Since surface hardness is associated the wear resistance of a material, a strong correlation between hardness and scratch resistance has been reported [2,3]. In standard indentation hardness tests (such as Rockwell), the direction of the load is normal to the surface. Likewise, a tangential force is applied in the presence of normal load for the scratch test.

EXPERIMENTAL

MATERIALS-Samples of PF-PP copolymers with different mineral fillers were obtained from ATC, Inc. The minerals used were talc and wollastonite. The median particle sizes is 3 µm for talc and 8 µm for wollastonite. The Mohs hardness of fillers are 1.0 for talc and 4.5 for wollastonite. The plaques (101.6 X 127.0 X 3.2 mm) used for scratch test were injection molded using side gating. The surfaces of the plaques were smooth on one side and grained on the other. Medium dark graphite color concentrate (obtained from Ferro Corp.) was added at 4 wt.%.

For comparison between PP and ABS, two grades of ABS materials (obtained from Dow Chemicals) were used in this study. The ABS plaques were smooth on both sides and were the same color as the PP plaques. Detailed descriptions of these materials are listed in Table I.

Table I. Materials used in this study.

Code	Materials
A1	Unfilled PP
A2	PP with 13% Talc, 5% impact modifier
A3	PP with 6.5% Talc, 5% impact modifier and 6.5% Wollastonite
A4	PP with 13% Wollastonite, 5% impact modifier
A5	PP with 13% Wollastonite, 5% impact modifier and 0.5% lubricant
D1	ABS, Dow Magnum 541 resin
D2	ABS, Dow Magnum 344 HP resin

SCRATCH TEST-This test is based on Ford Lab Test Method (FLTM) BN108-13. A simple machine was used to create scratches that simulate customer usage. This apparatus consisted of a movable platform connected to five beams (250 mm long). A scratch pin is attached to the opposite end of each beam. On the tip of each pin is a highly polished steel ball (1 mm +/- 0.1 mm in diameter). Each pin is loaded with a different weight exerting different forces on the surface of the test plaques. The forces were 7N, 6N, 3N, 1N and 0.6 N. The beams were driven by compressed air to draw the pins across the polymer surface to generate scratches on the surface of the specimen. Sliding velocity was approximately 100 mm/s. All tests were done at room temperature and samples were conditioned at 25°C for more than 24 h prior to testing. Although the FLTM requires that only grained surface are to be evaluated, both the grained and the smooth surfaces were tested for PP in this study.

After the plaques were scratched, the plaques were evaluated by an image analyzer with a Sony XC-77CE monochrome camera, Seescan Custom II Lighting Unit with ND8 filter and "Scratch Assessment System, Version 1v00." The camera objective was positioned at an angle of 90° and a distance of 225 mm from the scratch. The objective should be able to register a portion of the scratch about 60 mm long. 250 views were taken perpendicular to each individual scratch line at predetermined intervals. An electronic signal for each scratch line was integrated and recorded. Finally, the percentage of visible marking of the scratch was produced and reported.

The width and depth of the scratch were measured with a laser profilometer (UBM Microfocus Measurement, MRB Research Corp.). The software used was the UBSOFT System X2020-2A Optical Interface. Resolution was set at 400 p/mm. All the measurements were done on the smooth surfaces of the plaques.

RESULTS

The scratch visibility of various materials was measured by the image analyzer. Results from the various loads are shown in Figs. 1 and 2 for both grained and smooth surfaces respectively. Unfilled PP (A1) showed the least scratch visibility on both surfaces at all loads. Due to the sensitivity limit of the image analyzer or the software used, results were indistinguishable on the smooth surfaces for loads of 6N and under. PP filled with 13% talc (A2) showed the most scratch visibility. Scratch visibility decreased as the content of wollastonite in the PP increased (A3, A4). Scratch visibility decreased even more with the addition of 0.5 % lubricant (A5). This trend was more evident on the grained surfaces. For ABS specimens, scratch visibility was measured on the smooth surfaces only. The scratch visibility of both ABS materials fell between that of the talc-filled PP (A2) and the wollastonite-filled PP (A3).

The depth and width of the scratch were measured by the laser profilometer; a typical surface profile is shown in Fig. 3. Ridges of plastically deformed materials were produced on both sides of the scratch

(groove). Extensive ripples running transverse to the length of the scratch were observed at the bottom of scratches. Two types of measurements were made for both scratch depth and width. The "apparent depth" is the distance between the peak of the ridge and the bottom of the groove. The "true depth" is the distance between the plaque surface and the bottom of the groove. Similarly, the "apparent width" is the distance between the peaks of the ridges and the "true width" is the width of the scratch on the plaque surface.

Scratch dimensions for each material are plotted for the 6 and 7 N loads (Figs. 4 and 5). As shown in Fig. 4, the unfilled PP (A1) had the most shallow scratch (both apparent and true depth) for both loads plotted. On the other hand, talc-filled PP (A2) had the deepest scratch for both loads. The addition of wollastonite (A3, A4) reduced the scratch depth significantly. No distinctive improvement was observed for scratch depth with the addition of lubricant (A5). One of the ABS specimens (D1) had comparable scratch depth to the wollastonite-filled PP. The scratch depth of the other ABS specimen (D2) fell between the talc-filled (A2) and wollastonite-filled (A3) PP. As expected, the apparent scratch depth was more sensitive to material variation than the true depth.

A different trend was observed for the scratch width, as shown in Fig. 5. Random differences were observed between the scratch width (both apparent and true width) of the various materials. This is due to the geometry of the indentor. The scratch width is approximately 1/4 of the indentor diameter. The resulting indentation depth/ width ratio was 1:16. As a result, the narrow sides of the scratch are more likely to experience elastic recovery and obscure the scratch-width measurement. Therefore, the scratch depth can give a higher sensitivity for scratch dimension measurement than the scratch width. Besides the scratches from 6 N and 7 N loads, the laser profilometer was only able to detect the scratch of 3N load for the talc-filled PP (A2). The scratches that resulted from the 1 N and 0.6 N loads could not be detected for any of the specimens. These results correlated with the data obtained by the image analyzer, as shown in Fig. 2.

In addition, the apparent scratch depth was plotted against the scratch visibility for the scratches made by 7 N load, as shown in Figure 6. Good correlation was found between the visibility and depth of the scratch for all PP samples. The scratch visibility increased as the scratch depth increased. One of the ABS specimens was an exception to this trend for unknown reasons.

DISCUSSION

This study attempts to quantify the extent of scratches by both the image analyzer, as specified by the FLTM, and by the laser profilometer. Laser profilometer seems to be a suitable method to evaluate the scratch performance of materials on a relatively smooth surface. A predominant issue regarding the visibility evaluation of scratch and mar is that it can be affected by a number of factors. The color, gloss and grain of the test specimen can directly affect the evaluation result. Additionally, the molding and curing parameters that are implemented in manufacturing the test specimens can significantly alter the surface morphology and properties. Currently, the image analyzer is a popular technique in quantifying the scratch and mar performance of materials. However, as shown in Figs. 1 and 2, the visibility of the scratch is dependent on the surface texture of the specimen. The image analyzer seems to have less sensitivity on the smooth surface than on the grained surface. This is due to the indentors "bouncing" on and off of the grained surface and "gliding" across the smooth surface. This "bouncing" creates a greater force between the indentor and the specimen on the "landing points." As a result, more contrast was observed by the image analyzer for the grained surface. In this study, the scratch depth measured by the laser profilometer seems to be consistent with image analyzer results (see Figure 6) for the higher loads on the smooth surface. Therefore, the laser profilometer seems to be an effective technique to evaluate various materials without being affected by the surface texture.

Studies have been done to investigate the mechanisms for whitening due to stress induced by scratching [4]. In addition to the craze or crack in the matrix, voids are also generated in the matrix/filler interface [5]. It is also possible that the macromolecules were aligned and created a difference refractive index and mechanisms of whitening that resulted. Consequently, a deep scratch will cause more damage and whitening than a shallow scratch. Replacing talc with wollastonite in conventional FP-PP seems to be effective in reducing the scratch depth and the amount of damage (and whitening) to the surface of the specimen. This may be due to the wollastonite having a higher Mohs hardness than the talc.

CONCLUSION

- Good correlation was found between scratch visibility as measured by the image analyzer and scratch depth by the laser profilometer. The deeper scratch in PP materials relates to the increased scratch visibility. The laser profilometer seems to be a better method to measure the scratch depth, regardless of the texture of the surface.

- The wollastonite-filled PP showed better scratch performance than the more common talc-filled PP. The lubricant used in this study only slightly reduced scratch depth and visibility.

REFERENCE

1. "*Tribology of Plastic Materials*", Ed. Y. Yamaguchi, 1990, Elsevier, New York.
2. B. J. Briscoe, P. D. Evans, S. K. Biswas and S. K. Sinha, *Tribology Inter.*, 1996, Vol. 29, No. 2, p 93.
3. E. K. L. Lau, K. Swain, S. Srinivasan, *Proc. TPO Conference*, Oct. 1996, Novi, MI.
4. R. Kody, D. Martin, *Polym. Eng. Sci.*, Jan. 1996, Vol. 36, No. 2, p 298.
5. S. Xavier, J. M. Schultz, K. Friedrich, *J. Mater. Sci.*, 1990, Vol. 25, p 2411.

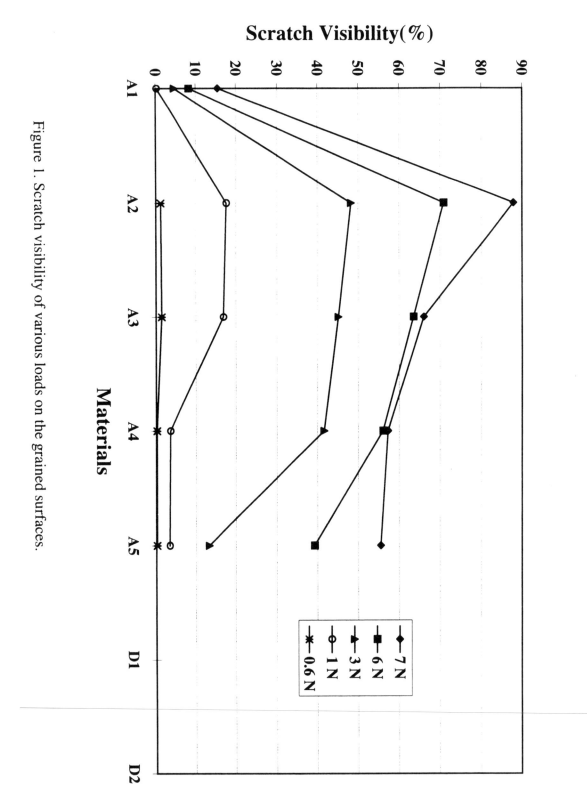

Figure 1. Scratch visibility of various loads on the grained surfaces.

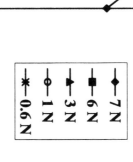

Figure 2. Scratch visibility of various loads on the smooth surface.

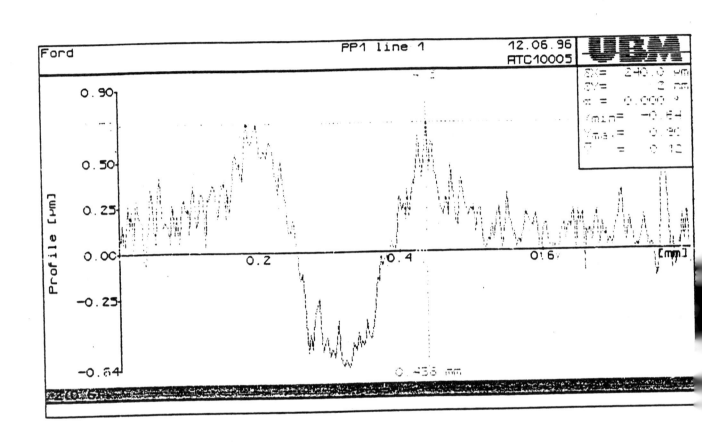

Figure 3. A typical surface profile measured by laser profilometer.

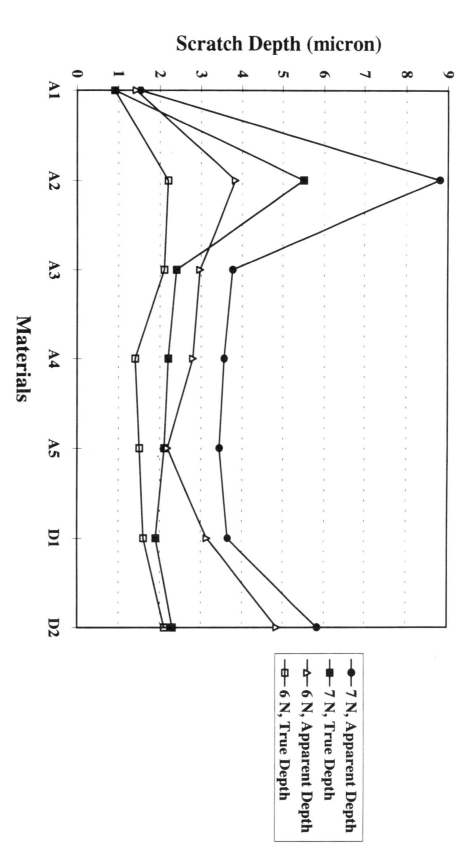

Figure 4. Scratch depth for various materials.

81

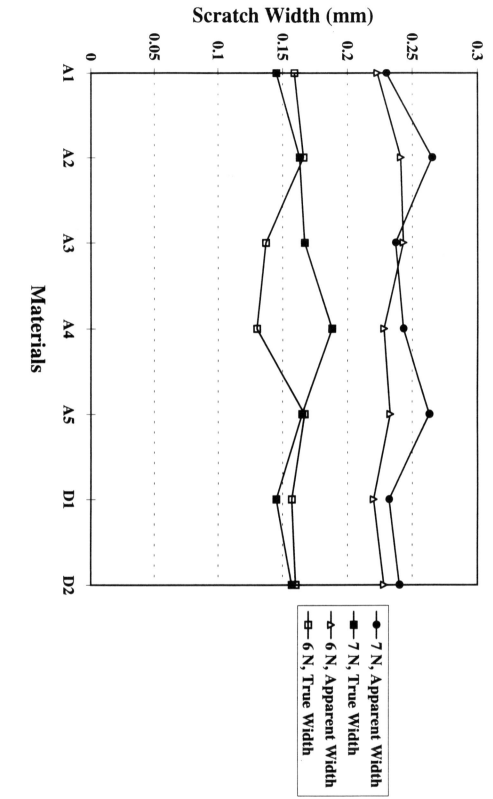

Figure 5. Scratch width for various materials.

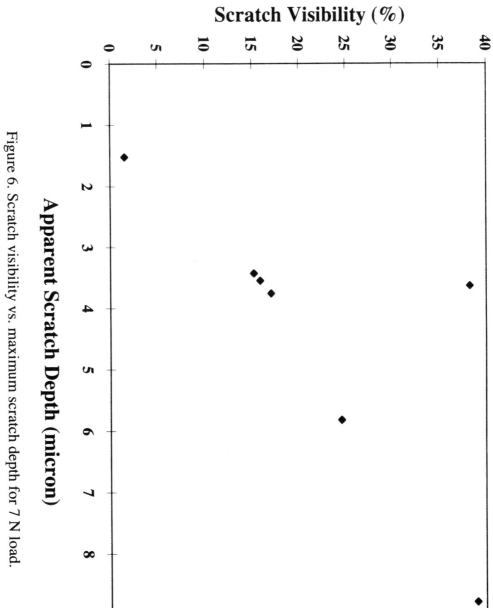

Figure 6. Scratch visibility vs. maximum scratch depth for 7 N load.

970660

High Temperature Dimensionally Stable Polyester Engineering Resin

George Collins, Mengshi Lu, Paul DeStio, Robert Imes, and Suzanne Nelsen

Hoechst Celanese Corp.

ABSTRACT

Glass reinforced poly(ethylene terephthalate) polyester molding resins are currently used in various applications for automobiles. These include assemblies such as windshield wiper plenums. Expanding its use into new applications requires that the molded polyester part be able to withstand additional automotive fabrication steps and be tough and dimensionally stable in use. While PET based material is currently used for applications that are affixed to the car body after oven treatment, customers have specifically expressed the need to simplify the automobile assembly sequence by using materials that can withstand the 200°C ovens used to cure car body coatings. Existing commercial grades do not meet all of the additional specific dimensional requirements, although the heat deflection temperature at 1.8 MPa of these types of materials can be well above 200 °C. A laboratory sag test using tensile bars also indicated dimensional changes occurred at 200°C but failed to reveal the causes for this instability. A three point bending creep recovery test was developed to investigate this issue. It was found that cold crystallization of the polymer matrix took place during the heating to 200°C within the first 5 minutes and corresponding dimensional movements occurred. Use of this technique also predicted that some specific additives would improve the resistance to deformation in the end use. A new Impet® [1] grade, EKX-163, is developed that has higher deformation resistance. The preliminary results from a customer trial confirmed the superior dimensional stability of EKX-163 in the end use, and the validity of the test.

INTRODUCTION

Impet® resins are injection moldable thermoplastics polyesters made with up to 100% post-consumer recycled PET. They are reinforced with 10 - 45% glass fibers or with combinations of mineral/glass fibers. Typical applications for automobiles include distributor housings, electrical system components, and windshield wiper components. Expanding its use into parts such as grille opening retainers (GOR) and external panels requires that the molded polyester part be able to withstand the automotive fabrication steps and be dimensionally stable in use. Specifically, the parts must be able to survive the thermal program of the electrodeposition coating (E-coat) protocol without sagging or warping at condition of 200°C for 30 minutes.

A typical GOR structure is schematically illustrated in Figure 1. As a design criterion, the nominal dimensional movement for a GOR should be no more than 1 mm under E-coating condition. A current material (Material A) which is PET reinforced with both glass and mineral does not meet this requirement as shown in Figure 2. The measurement shown in Figure 2 was done by a highly precise automated apparatus at 19 different positions of a typical GOR. It is apparent that the dimensional change is random and some changes are close to or even surpass the 1 mm criteria. Thus the GOR made from this material could only be mounted to a vehicle after coating protocol and this does not satisfy the customer need. It is more desirable to have an injection moldable resin that can survive the E-coating protocol, so that the GOR could be mounted before oven treatment.

The objective of this research project is to develop a new material based on PET that gives better dimensional stability and can survive the E-coating condition. In order to achieve this goal, we felt that it was very important to find a good lab test method in the first place. After a review of various test methods, a Dynamic Mechanical Analysis (DMA) creep recovery protocol was found to be fairly simple to simulate E-coating condition and yet it could trace the dimensional change precisely over time. This test method eventually led us to identify a formulation, designated as EKX-163, that gives significantly better performance than the current material (Material A) as demonstrated by this newly developed lab test program that simulates the E-coating condition. The superior dimensional stability of EKX-163 was also confirmed by the measurements using the above mentioned automated instrument on GORs molded from EKX-163. The mechanism for

---

[1] Impet® is a Registered Trademark of Hoechst Celanese Corp.

dimensional change at E-coating condition will also be discussed.

TEST METHODS

HEAT DISTORTION TEMPERATURE Although Figure 2 clearly indicates the unsatisfactory dimensional movement of a GOR made of Material A, it does not reveal any physical cause contributing to this movement. Common knowledge suggests that the dimensional stability may relate to heat distortion temperature (HDT). If the HDT of a material is not high enough, it may get soft at 200°C and start to sag. However, Material A and Material B (a glass filled grade PET) both have a HDT higher than 200°C (206°C and 229°C respectively). This indicates that an HDT over 200°C is a necessary but not sufficient factor for dimensional stability at E-coating condition. The dimensional change at 200°C is not because the materials get soft, but other mechanisms.

SAG MEASUREMENT A sag-like test has been used for evaluating the dimensional movement under E-coating condition using tensile bars. This test is schematically illustrated in Figure 3. Although this test seems to be easy and a reasonable simulation of real conditions, it is quite crude and results from this test can only give an overall approximate estimate without much insight knowledge. Also, the accuracy of this test may not be good enough to distinguish the subtle differences in formulation we were going to develop. However, during the course of this work, this test was still used as a primary screening tool since it could easily single out the less effective materials. Table I summarizes the HDT and sag properties of Materials A and B in conjunction with an SMC material. From the sag value and HDT, Material B seems to be a better candidate than Material A. However, parts made of Material B had severe warpage problem because it has only fiberglass as reinforcement. The SMC material met the dimensional requirement at E-coating condition, although the sag value of this material is only marginally better than Material A.

DYNAMIC MECHANICAL THERMAL ANALYSIS (DMTA) Figure 4 shows the dynamic mechanical properties of Materials A and B as a function of temperature. The storage modulus drop at around 80°C is attributed to the glass transition of the PET matrix. The moduli of both materials after the glass transition temperature, however, remain more or less constant up to 230°C and then drop abruptly due to melting. There is no evidence that these materials get soft or lose modulus at 200°C. Figure 5 shows the storage moduli of Materials A and B at 200°C as a function of time. The temperature was increased rapidly to 200°C and held at that temperature while measuring the modulus. It is interesting to note that the storage modulus actually increases slightly over time after the original drop as the ambient temperature passes the

glass transition temperature to 200°C. PET is well known for its slow crystallization kinetics. It is highly possible that the PET matrix was not fully crystallized after molding although some crystallization nucleant was added to both materials. The PET matrix may have experienced a cold crystallization process as the temperature rises above its Tg and this process continued at 200°C. Cold crystallization can increase crystallinity, leading to higher modulus and stiffness, which may be considered beneficial for dimensional stability. However, cold crystallization can also cause shrinkage. Because of the complex geometry of GOR (see Fig. 1), this shrinkage can be very uneven, thus causing all kinds of random movement as observed in Figure 2.

DMA CREEP RECOVERY TEST The DMTA test certainly gives more information about the material behavior at E-coating conditions. However, this test measures the change in modulus over time and temperature, which has indirect connection with the dimensional changes. A direct test method that uses flexural or tensile bars is more desirable.

Figure 6 illustrates a Perkin-Elmer DMA 7e fixture that can measure the dimensional change precisely under three-point bending mode through various thermal programs. A test specimen cut from a flexural bar or tensile bar is rested on the fixture at either end. The programmable probe is lowered and brought into contact with the top side of the specimen at a position midway between the two ends. The approximate dimensions of the test specimen is 20 mm long x 12.5 mm wide x 3.2 mm thick. The sample rests on knife-edged supports across its width at the two ends producing a supported span of exactly 20 mm. The knife-edged probe across the width is lowered onto the topside of the specimen. Using this test fixture and specimen configuration, the temperature and probe could be programmed independently. The temperature could be programmed to heat, cool or hold isothermally at a specified temperature. The probe could be controlled by programming force or position. This provided the opportunity to evaluate test pieces in thermal mechanical analysis (TMA), creep recovery, and dynamic mechanical analysis (DMA) modes.

Using the creep recovery protocol can allow us to trace the dimensional movement of a test specimen precisely over different time and temperature program. In order to simulate the actual E-coating condition, the oven is pre-heated to 200°C before the start of this program. After that temperature is reached, the test specimen is mounted into position and the run is started. The measured oven temperature at that point is about 120 - 150°C. 7000 mN force is immediately applied to the test piece at the start of the program as the temperature increases from the starting temperature to 200°C. At the end of the initial 30 min at 200°C, the sample is cooled at 15°C/min to 30°C and held at this final temperature for 10 minutes. The 7000 mN probe force was held until the sample reached 30°C, then it was released. This was taken to be the physical simulation of a piece being placed in a 200°C oven under stress, and the stress being removed when the piece was removed from the oven and cooled to ambient temperature.

RESULTS AND DISCUSSION

Figure 7 illustrates the response of the current Material A sample to this program. It is apparent that the test specimen experienced some dimensional movement and this movement occurred in the first 5 minutes after the test began. This observation is consistent with our earlier observation that the sample had a density change due to cold crystallization. In addition, there is the possibility that there are internal stresses that arises from the non-equilibrium nature of the molding process. When the part is heated, the molecular mobility present at high temperature allows the internal structure to respond to these stresses and local deformation can result.

At this point, it becomes rather clear that the direction for improving the dimensional stability of the current Material A should be those that can accelerate the crystallization process and/or reduce the effect of this process. Experiments with different types and levels of nucleants did not solve the entire issue. After investigating various formulations, we eventually identified a new PET-based material, EKX-163, that performed better in this DMA creep recovery test protocol, as shown in Figure 8. It is apparent that EKX-163 has a better deformation resistance compared to Material A.

In a customer trial, some GORs were molded using the newly developed EKX-163. Selected pieces were subjected to an oven set at 200°C. Some parts were placed in different positions and one GOR was mounted on a measurement fixture that allows position to be determined before and after oven treatment. Each GOR is about 1575 mm long. The overall shrinkage for EKX-163 is 1.6 mm vs. 3.2 mm for Material A, a 50% reduction. The movements at 8 indexed positions at three directions (x, y, z) after oven protocol for a GOR made of EKX-163 is plotted in comparison to that for Material A, shown in Figure 9. For most measurements, the change in position is less for the EKX-163 GOR than for the Material A GOR. The overall average of the absolute value of the position change is 12 mm for Material A and 8.4 mm for EKX-163, a reduction in position movement of about 33%. This performance had a positive impact on the customer.

Table II summarizes the physical properties of EKX-163.

CONCLUSION

The cause of dimensional movement for a GOR made from Material A has been identified as shrinkage due to cold crystallization of incompletely crystallized PET matrix during the heating to 200°C as well as mold stress relaxation, based on the newly developed DMA and TMA test program. The DMA creep recovery test has the advantage of monitoring the real-time dimensional movement very precisely over various temperature program. The results from this test method are certainly more accurate and informative than the old sag-like test and HDT measurement, and they seem to correlate with tests on real GORs very well. Certainly, HDT is still relevant, but it is a necessary, not a sufficient factor. The ways to improve the dimensional stability of this type of material were proposed to be those that can increase the crystallinity of PET during molding. A new PET-based material, Impet® EKX-163, was developed using the DMA creep recovery test as a screening tool. The crystallinity study by DSC shows that Material A has a heat of fusion of 24.3 J/g while it is 29.1 J/g for EKX-163. This certainly supports our hypothesis. From both our lab DMA creep recovery test and the actual test on molded GORs, Impet® EKX-163 proved to be more dimensionally stable than Material A at E-coating conditions.

ACKNOWLEDGMENTS

The authors would like to thank Allen Towne for his assistance in heat sag measurement. Dr. Joe Menczel did the crystallinity study. His help is greatly appreciated.

ADDITIONAL SOURCES

Here are any additional sources. This is an optional section.

DEFINITIONS, ACRONYMS, ABBREVIATIONS

Here is the Definitions section. This is an optional section.

Table I: Heat Sag and HDT for current materials

	Heat Sag after 30 min at 200 °C (mm)	HDT at 1.8 Mpa (°C)
Material A		
as molded	2.01	206
annealed	1.50	
Material B		
as molded	0.51	229
SMC material	1.27	304

Table II: Physical Properties of Impet® EKX-163

Impet® EKX-163 is a mineral/fiberglass reinforced product developed for use in elevated temperature applications. The product has an excellent balance of processing and mechanical proerties

PROPERTIES	Test Method	UNITS	VALUE
Specific Gravity	ISO 1183		1.725
MECHANICAL PROPERTIES			
Tensile Strength @ Break	ISO 527	MPa	128.2
Elongation @ Break	ISO 527	%	1.3
Tensile Modulus	ISO 527	GPa	15.6
Flexural Strength	ISO 178	MPa	203
Flexural Modulus	ISO 178	GPa	13.9
Notched Izod Impact Strength	ISO 180	KJ/m^2	7.2
Unnotched Izod Impact Strength	ISO 180	KJ/m^2	34
THERMAL PROPERTIES			
DTUL @ 0.45 MPa	ISO 75	°C	244
DTUL @ 1.8 MPa	ISO 75	°C	218

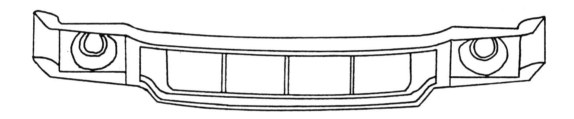

Fig.1

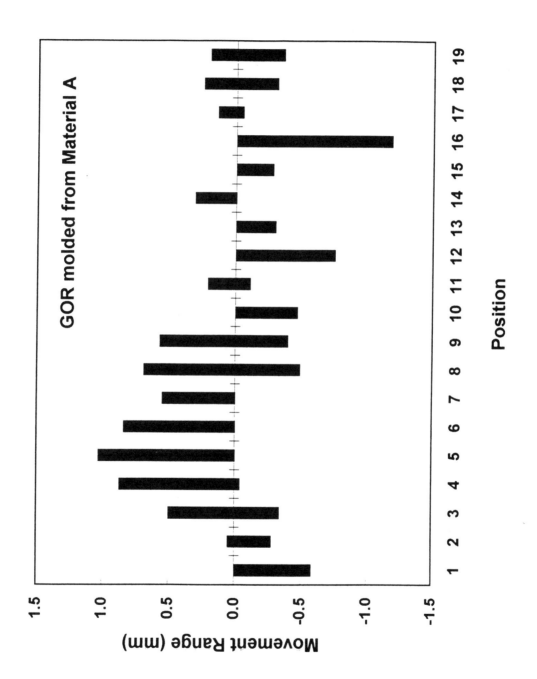

Fig. 2

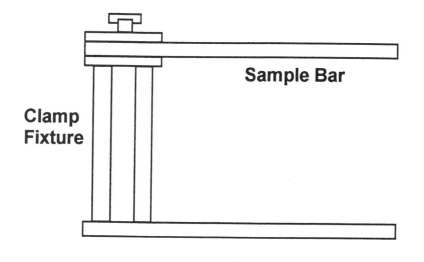

Sample Bar

Clamp
Fixture

200 C for 30 min

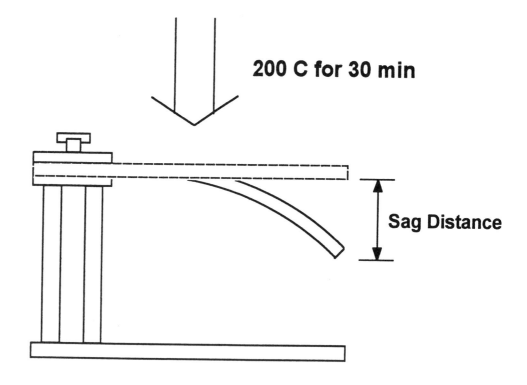

Sag Distance

Fig. 3

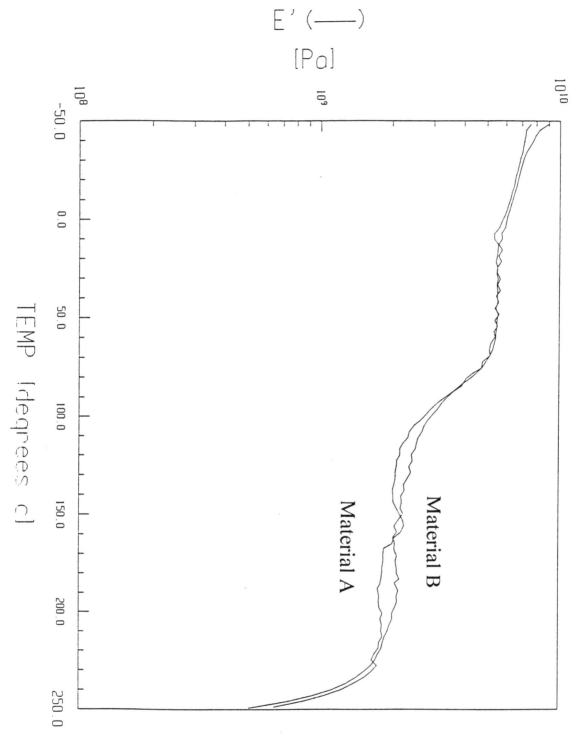

Dynamic Mechanical Thermal Analysis

E' (———)

[Pa]

10^{10}

10^9

10^8

TEMP [degrees c]

-50.0   0.0   50.0   100.0   150.0   200.0   250.0

Material A

Material B

93

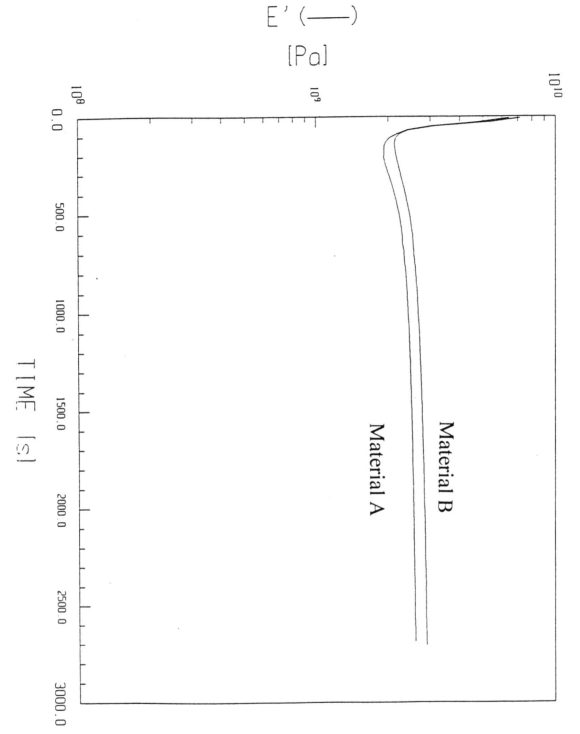

Dynamic Mechanical Thermal Analysis

E' (——) [Pa]

Material B

Material A

TIME [s]

Fig 5

94

Three-Point Bending

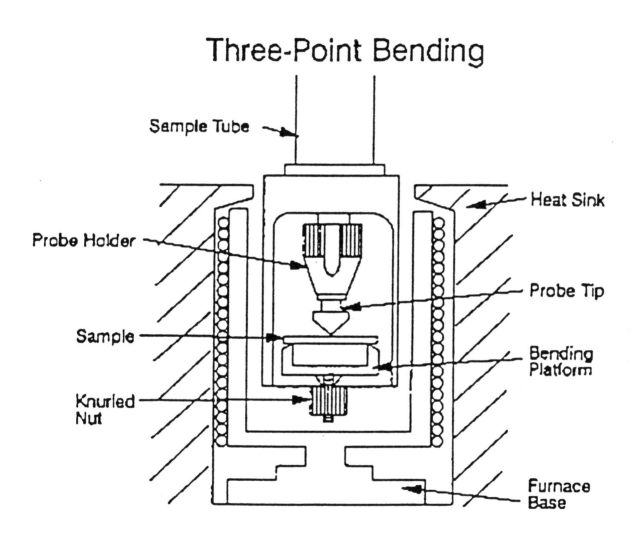

Sample Tube

Heat Sink

Probe Holder

Probe Tip

Sample

Bending Platform

Knurled Nut

Furnace Base

Fig. 6

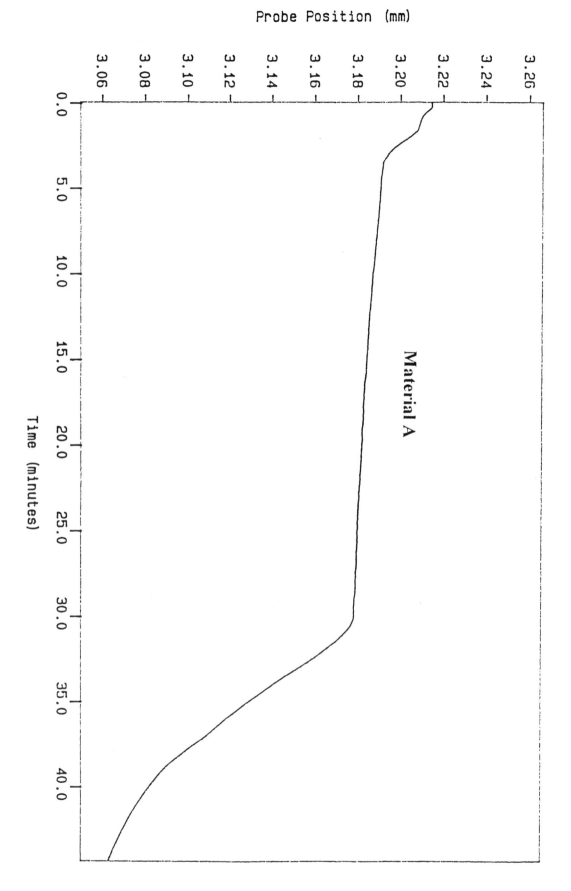

DMA Creep Recovery in 3 Point Bending

Material A

Probe Position (mm)

Time (minutes)

96

Fig 7

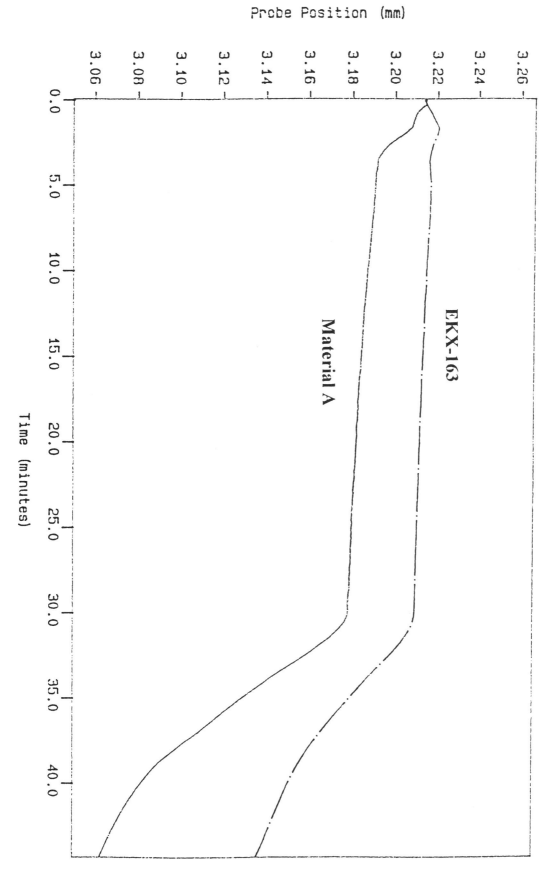

DMA Creep Recovery in 3 Point Bending

Probe Position (mm)

Time (minutes)

EKX-163

Material A

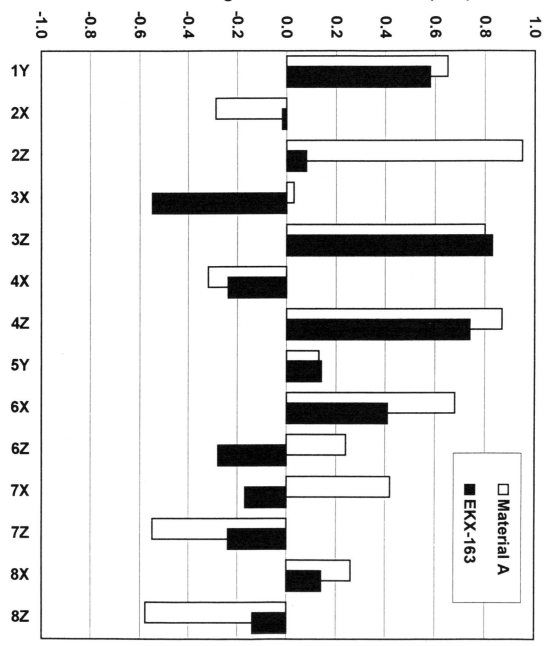

Fig. 9

98

Effects of Temperature and Crack Tip Opening Rate on Fracture Behavior of CNBR Modified Epoxy Adhesives Under Mode I Loading

Kazuo Kimura, Kimiyoshi Naito, and Toru Fujii
Doshisha Univ.

ABSTRACT

The effects of temperature, crack tip opening rate and rubber content on static fracture characteristics of CNBR (Cross-linked acryloNitrile Butadiene Rubber) modified epoxy adhesives were investigated under mode I loading. Loading-unloading tests were statically performed by using DCB (Double Cantilever Beam) specimens.

The fracture toughness increased with increasing the rubber content. The fracture toughness of CNBR modified and unmodified epoxy adhesives was much influenced by temperature and crack tip opening rate. The surface topology of fractured surface was changed by temperature and type of adhesive.

INTRODUCTION

Epoxy based adhesives are often used as structural adhesives to bond main and sub-elements due to their superior mechanical properties. However, conventional epoxy adhesives have a poor resistance to crack initiation and its growth.

Rubber modification is one of the effective methods for toughening epoxy resins. Liquid rubber modifications such as CTBN(Carboxyl-Terminated Butadiene-acryloNitrile) have ever been major methods[1,2]. Cross-linked acryloNitrile Butadiene Rubber (CNBR) modification is one of the new methods for toughening epoxy resins[3]. In the case of CNBR modified epoxy, sub-micro rubber particles are admixed with epoxy resin before curing and epoxy resin can contain the rubber particles whose diameters are almost constant after curing. Therefore, it is expected that rubber modification using CNBR brings major improvements in toughness without significant losses in other important properties and can be used at a wide range of environments. However the environmental effects on the fracture behaviour of CNBR modified epoxy adhesives have not been well known. In this study, we investigated the effects of temperature and crack tip opening rate on static fracture of CNBR modified epoxy adhesives under mode I loading.

EXPERIMENTAL PROCEDURE

SPECIMEN-Epikote 828 (Shell) is the epoxy used in this investigation. Four types of adhesives were tested: unmodified epoxy and CNBR modified epoxy(whose rubber contents are 2.8%, 5.5% and 8.9% in weight). Three point bending test was carried out to investigate characteristics of epoxy adhesives in bulk. DCB specimens were used to evaluate the static crack growth properties of epoxy adhesives under mode I loading. **Figure 1, 2** show dimensions of coupon specimen for three point bending and DCB specimen. Coupon specimens were cut out of cured epoxy resin sheets. A carbon steel, S55C, was used as adherends for DCB specimen. The bonding surface was ground with sandpaper and cleaned. Teflon (polytetrafluoroethylene) films were inserted between adherends to control thickness of adhesive layer(=0.3mm) and make pre-crack.
All specimens were kept at 23±3°C and 65±5% humidity in chamber for three days prior to curing at 80°C for an hour in an electronic furnace. Fillets of adhesives bonding on surface of adherend were removed with a knife and sandpaper.

THREE POINTS BENDING TEST-Static loads were applied to specimens. Two types of epoxy adhesive were tested: unmodified and 5.5 wt% CNBR adhesives. Four different cross-head speeds (= 0.1, 1, 10, 100 mm/min) were applied to the specimens at room temperature to examine the effect of loading rate on the failure characteristics in bulk. At five different temperature(= -20, 0, 23, 50, 80 °C) failure characteristics were examined at constant cross-head speed(= 1.0 mm/min). An Instron test machine and a servo hydraulic testing machine were used for these tests.

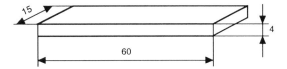

Figure 1. Dimensions of coupon specimens

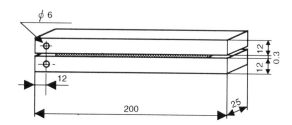

Figure 2. Dimensions of DCB specimens

FRACTURE TEST-Loading-Unloading tests were statically performed by using DCB specimens. Four types of epoxy adhesives were tested: unmodified and CNBR modified(Rubber content = 2.8, 5.5 and 8.9 wt%) adhesives. We measured the distance between loading points with an extensometer and the applied load to estimate the compliance of specimen. We observed the crack propagation in the adhesive layer with a microscope to measure the crack length. The compliance method was used to evaluate mode I strain energy release rate. The tensile load was applied at various cross-head speeds(= 0.01, 0.1, 1, 10 mm/min) at room temperature and at various temperatures(= -20, 0, 23, 50, 80 °C) at constant cross-head speed(= 1.0 mm/min). The experimental set up is shown in **Figure 3**. An Instron test machine and a servo hydraulic testing machine were used for the tests.

The crack extension resistance at several stages during failure was evaluated by means of strain energy release rate. Mall and Ramamurthy showed that the relation between compliance "λ" and crack length "a" can be expressed by the following equation[4]:

$$\lambda = Ca^3 \quad (1)$$

Where, C is experimental constant. In this study, we approached this relation to a three dimensional polynomial expression as follow.

$$\lambda = C_1 a^3 + C_2 a^2 + C_3 a + C_4 \quad (2)$$

Where C_1, C_2, C_3 and C_4 are experimental constants.

Strain energy release rate, G, can be calculated with following expression[5]:

$$G = \frac{P^2}{2B}\frac{d\lambda}{da} \quad (3)$$

Where B is the width of specimen and P is applied load.

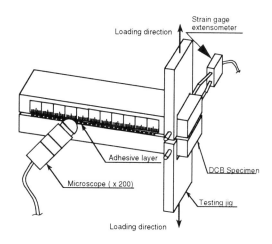

Figure 3. Testing system

Figure 4 shows the schematical relation between the crack extension resistance and the crack extension length called as R-curve and strain energy release rate curve(G-curve) in which the load is constant. The point of contact of R-curve and G-curve indicate initiation of unstable crack growth[6]. We defined the strain energy release rate of this point the fracture toughness.

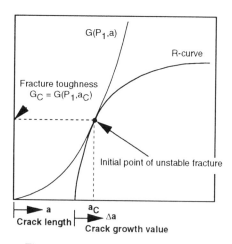

Figure 4. The method to estimate a fracture toughness

The crack tip opening rate was defined by Smiley [7] for DCB specimen in **Figure 5**. The crack opening displacement rate is given as following equation:

$$Y(X) = \dot{U}\left(3aX^2 - X^3\right)/2a^3 \quad (4)$$

Therefore, the crack tip opening rate is defined as the crack opening displacement rate, $\dot{U}$, at some arbitrarily small distance from the crack tip , $X=\varepsilon$.

Thus for $\varepsilon<<a$:

$$\dot{Y}_{ct} = \frac{3\dot{U}\varepsilon^2}{2a^2} \quad (5)$$

For the data presented in this paper, ε was chosen $\varepsilon=1$.

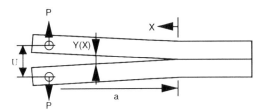

Figure 5. DCB specimen geometry

OBSERVATION OF FRACTURED SURFACE-We observed aspects of fractured surface of DCB specimen with a scanning electronic microscope(SEM) to explain the effects of rubber content and test temperature on fracture behaviour. The roughness of fracture surface of DCB specimen was traced with a laser microscope to explain the effects.

RESULTS AND DISCUSSION

THREE POINTS BENDING TEST FOR BULK SPECIMEN-**Figure 6 and 7** show the relation between Young's modulus and cross-head speed, and the relation between Young's moduli and temperature respectively for unmodified and 5.5 wt% CNBR modified adhesives. **In figure 6**, the Young's modulus of unmodified epoxy were always higher than those of CNBR modified adhesive. The Young's moduli of unmodified adhesive gradually increased around 1 mm/min and abruptly increased from 10 to 100 mm/min with increasing the cross-head speed. The Young's modulus of CNBR modified adhesive gradually increased with increasing the cross-head speed in this range. **In figure 7**, the Young's modulus of unmodified epoxy were always higher than those of CNBR modified adhesive. The Young's moduli of both adhesives decreased as the temperature was increased. Especially, around 23°C the Young's modulus of both adhesives abruptly decreased. At 50 and 80°C, both adhesives had very small Young's moduli.

Admixing rubber particles caused a decrease in the Young's modulus of adhesive because the Young's moduli of rubber particles are much smaller than those of epoxy resin. The

visco-elastoplastic nature of the materials caused a decrease in the Young's modulus due to decreasing the cross-head speed and increasing temperature.

In high cross-head speed or at low temperature , both adhesives brittly fractured after small deformation. In low cross-head speed and at high temperature , both adhesives showed ductile failure. CNBR modified adhesive was more ductile than unmodified adhesive over the examined cross-head speed and temperature range.

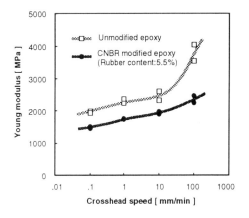

Figure 6. Young's modulus of epoxy adhesives in bulk as a function of crosshead speed

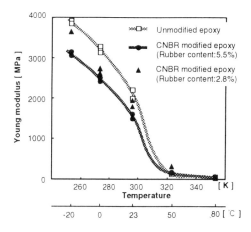

Figure 7. Young's modulus of epoxy adhesives in bulk as a function of temperature

STATIC FRACTURE TEST-**Figure 8** shows R-curves at various cross-head speeds(=0.1, 1, 10). (a) and (b) show unmodified and 5.5 wt% CNBR modified adhesives respectively. The maximum strain energy release rate, Gmax, of 5.5 wt% CNBR modified adhesive was higher than that of unmodified adhesive in the examined range. The features of R-curves of both adhesives were sensitive to the cross-head speed. At low cross-head speed (=0.1mm/min), the crack extension resistance increased with increasing the crack extension length. On the other hand, at high cross-head speeds(1,10 mm/min), at first, the crack extension resistance increased with increasing the crack extension length, and then decreased to the stable value after maximized.

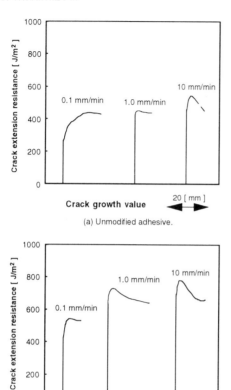

Figure 8. Crack extension resistance curve at various cross-head speed.

Figure 9 shows R-curves at various temperature(=-20, 0, 23 and 50°C). (a) and (b) show unmodified and 5.5 wt% CNBR modified adhesives respectively. In this temperature range, the Gmax of 5.5wt%CNBR modified adhesive was higher than that of unmodified adhesive. The Gmax of both adhesives increased with increasing temperature. Temperature much influenced the behaviour of R-curves for both adhesives. Especially, the features of R-curves were divided into two types. In high temperature range, the crack extension resistance increased with increasing the crack extension length. In low and middle temperature, at first the crack extension resistance increased with increasing the crack extension length, and then decreased to the stable value after maximised.

The features of R-curves in high temperature correspond to those at low cross-head speed and those in low temperature range correspond to those at high cross-head speed. However, the value of crack extension resistance did not correspond.

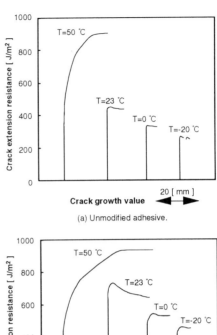

Figure 9. Crack extension resistance curve at various temparature

Figure 10 shows the relation between fracture toughness and the crack tip opening rate for unmodified and CNBR modified (rubber content: 5.5, 8.9 wt%) adhesives. The fracture toughness of both adhesives increased with increasing the crack tip opening rate. The increment of CNBR modified adhesive was larger than that of unmodified adhesive. It was found the visco-elastoplastic nature of CNBR modified adhesive more affected the fracture toughness than that of unmodified adhesive.

Figure 11 shows the fracture toughness with respect to test temperature for unmodified and CNBR modified adhesives. At the range from -20°C to 40°C the fracture toughness increases with increasing the rubber content. The fracture toughness of all adhesives shows a gradual increase and then abrupt increase as the temperature is increased. However, at 80°C, the fracture toughness has begun to decrease and the crack has begun to propagate at interface. The fracture toughnesses were maximized at each value. The maximum fracture toughness shifted to lower temperature with increasing the rubber content. The fracture toughness of the high content epoxy adhesive began to decrease at relatively low temperature. For instance, the fracture toughness of 8.9 wt% CNBR modified adhesive abruptly increased at 0 to 23°C, and has begun to decrease at 50°C. The fracture toughness of unmodified adhesive abruptly increased at 40 to 50°C, and has begun to decrease at 80°C.

The large plastic deformation ahead of crack tip due to temperature rise or rubber content causes the increase of the fracture toughness. The stress concentration around the rubber particles act as the initiation sites for the plastic deformation. At high temperature, the reduction of the interfacial strength between adhesive and adherend caused interfacial failure. As a result, the fracture toughness decreased at high temperature.

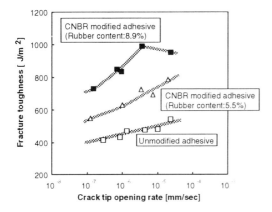

Figure 10. Fracture toughnesses of epoxy adhesives plotted against crack tip opening rate

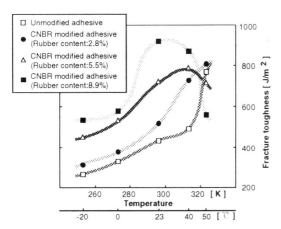

Figure 11. Fracture toughnesses of epoxy adhesives plotted against temperature

FRACTURED SURFACE-Previously, we had investigated that significant change on the fracture surface is not found even if the fracture toughness increased with increasing the crack tip opening displacement rate[8]. In this section, we investigate the effect of temperature on fractured surface.

Figure 12 shows SEM photographs of fractured surfaces for unmodified and 5.5 wt% CNBR modified adhesives at various temperatures. **Figure 13** shows the traces of the fractured surfaces. All adhesives failed in a cohesive failure manner. The topology of these surfaces is variable with respect to temperature and sort of adhesive. At -20°C, the glassy region was scattering over the fractured surfaces of both adhesives (other region gave the fine dimples), and both surfaces were relatively even based on tracing with the laser microscope. The fractured surface of unmodified adhesive was occupied more with the glassy region than that of 5.5 wt % CNBR modified adhesive. At 0°C, the fine dimples occupied all over the fractured surface of both adhesives. At 23°C both adhesives gave larger unevenness comparing with at 0°C. The most uneven surface was given at 50°C for unmodified adhesives, and at 23°C for 5.5 wt% CNBR modified adhesive. The more complex surface, the higher fracture toughness was given for both adhesives. We think large plastic deformation, until the fractures, causes the uneven fractured surface and dissipation of large energy .

TYPES OF CRACK PROPAGATION-In our study, three distinct types of crack propagation based on the feature of R-curves with respect to temperature, crack tip opening displacement rate and sort of adhesive could be observed for unmodified and CNBR modified adhesives as follow.
(1) Stable ductile failure
(2) Unstable brittle failure
(3) Combined failure
In the case of (1), the crack extension resistance increases with crack extension. This manner can be observed for both adhesives at high temperature and at low crack tip opening displacement rate. In the case of (2), the crack propagates in a stick slip manner. This manner was observed for unmodified adhesive at low temperature and high crack tip opening displacement rate.
The manner (3) takes a middle position of (1) and (2). The crack extension resistance increases with the crack extension and then decreases after maximized.

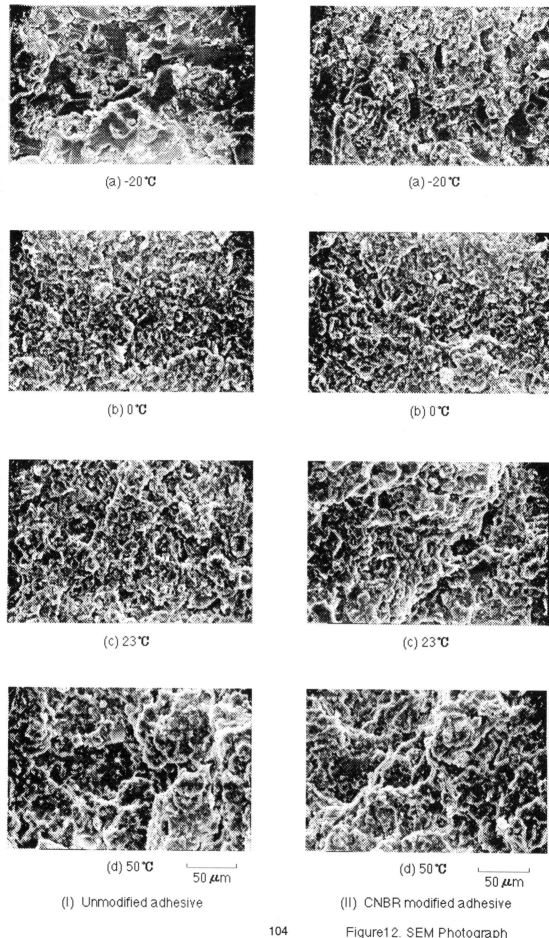

(a) -20℃   (a) -20℃

(b) 0℃   (b) 0℃

(c) 23℃   (c) 23℃

(d) 50℃   50 μm   (d) 50℃   50 μm

(I) Unmodified adhesive   (II) CNBR modified adhesive

Figure12. SEM Photograph

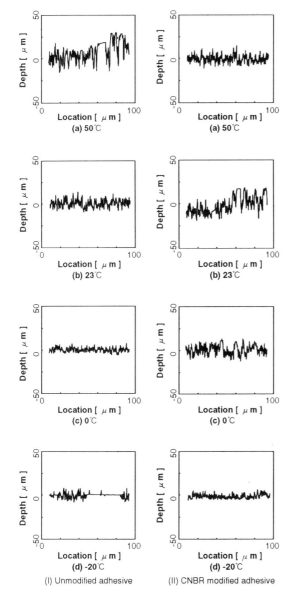

Depth [μm]
Location [μm]
(a) 50℃

Depth [μm]
Location [μm]
(b) 23℃

Depth [μm]
Location [μm]
(c) 0℃

Depth [μm]
Location [μm]
(d) -20℃

(I) Unmodified adhesive

(II) CNBR modified adhesive

Figure 13. Fractured surface traces

(3) At low temperature, the fracture toughness of all adhesives was relatively low and the smooth fractured surface indicated that failure occurred in a brittle fashion. The fracture toughness increased with increasing temperature at the range of each individual adhesive. At high temperature, the topology of the fracture surface is relatively complex, which indicates ductile failure. At higher temperature, the fracture toughness decreased and the cracks propagate at the interface.

(4) From -20°C to 40°C, the fracture toughness increased with the increase of rubber content.

(5) The fracture toughness increased with increasing the crack tip opening rate. The fracture toughness of the rubber modified epoxy adhesive is more sensitive to crack tip opening rate than unmodified adhesive.

(6) Temperature, crack tip opening displacement rate and type of adhesive affected fracture manner. Stable ductile failure, Unstable brittle failure and Combined failure were observed for unmodified and CNBR modified adhesives.

REFERENCES

[1]A.J.Kinloch , Structural Adhesives , Elsevier Applied Science Publishers (1986) , pp.127-200.

[2]A.F.Yee and R.A.Pearson , " Fractgraphy and Failure Mechanisms of Rubber Modified Epoxide Resins " Fractography and Failure Mechanisms of Polymers and Composites , Ann Arbor , Department of Materials Science and Engineering , University of Michigan , Michigan , USA , pp.292-350.

[3]T.Ueno , " Toughening of Epoxy Resins by Modification with Cross linked Rubber , " Nippon Settyaku Gakkaishi , Vol.31 , No.11 (1995) , pp.471-478.

[4]S.Mall and G.Ramamurthy , " Effect of Bond Thickness on Fracture and Fatigue Strength of Adhesive Bonded Composite Joints , " International journal of adhesion and adhesives , Vol.9 , No.1(1989) , pp.33-37.

[5]H.Kobayashi , Hakairikigaku , Kyouritu Syuppan Inc.(1993) , pp.46.

[6]H.Okamura , Senkei Hakai Rikigaku Nyuumon, Baifuukann (1976) , pp.154.

[7]A.J.Smiley and R.B.Pipes , " Rate Effects on Mode I Interlaminar Fracture Toughness in Composite Materials , " Journal of Composite Materials , Vol.21-July (1986) pp.670-687.

[8]Masahiro Tsuchida , Kimiyoshi NAITO , Toru FUJII , "Effects of CNBR Modification on Mode I Fracture of Epoxy Adhesives for Automotive Application" , SAE Technical Paper Series(1995).

CONCLUSIONS

The effect of rubber content, temperature and crack tip opening rate on the static fracture characteristics of epoxy adhesive under mode I loading were investigated. The following conclusions were obtained from our experiment.

(1) The Young's moduli of unmodified and CNBR modified adhesives increased with increasing the cross-head speed and decreasing temperature.

(2) The feature of R-curves of both adhesives in high temperature corresponds to those at low cross-head speed and those in low temperature corresponds to those at high temperature.

970662

Options in Mechanical Characterization of Engineering Thermoplastics for More Effective Material Modeling Practices

Dan Woodman
GE Plastics

ABSTRACT

Despite their high volume of usage, polymers are barely a century old and as such are still a relatively new class of engineering materials. However, plastics are increasingly being used for load-bearing components in demanding thermal, mechanical, and chemical environments. Therefore, the engineering community has a high need to be able to analyze and predict the performance of these materials in order to design parts faster and more accurately. But proper engineering design requires both accurate mechanical properties to define material behavior and effective analysis techniques to predict part performance based on those data.

The purpose of this paper is to assess the current effectiveness of materials characterization technology to account for various loading conditions and processing/materials considerations as they relate to material modeling for use in structural analysis. Relatively simple techniques will be presented to interpret performance and compare material data obtained via standard industry testing procedures and then convert these data into a form that can be used directly in engineering analysis.

INTRODUCTION

Engineering thermoplastics are being used more frequently in load-bearing applications. At the same time, companies are striving to increase product quality and reduce time-to-market cycles for new product introductions. As a result, part designers have an increasing need to be able to analyze and predict performance better.

Structural analysis requires three key components in order to model real life:

1. Geometry,
2. Environment, and
3. Material characterization.

Most analysts spend a great deal of time properly constructing the geometry of a part and properly loading and constraining it, yet they then input material data without much thought. However, materials characterization affects the results of the analysis as much as geometry and environment.

The need for better materials characterization is very important when dealing with engineering thermoplastics. These materials are challenging to design with because they are sensitive to a number of environmental factors (see below) and they are typically designed much closer to their engineering limits than other engineering materials. The purpose of this paper is to discuss some of the issues that must be considered when modeling engineering thermoplastics, and some potential ways to address these issues. Key issues include:

- Temperature effects,
- Differentials between compressive and tensile properties,
- Non-linear material properties and geometry,
- Creep and stress relaxation,
- Strain-rate sensitivity,
- Fiber orientation,
- Knit-line strength, and
- Various other processing effects.

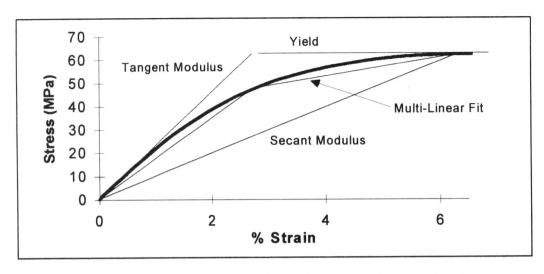

Figure 1: Engineering Stress/Strain for Impact-Modified, High-Flow Polycarbonate

BASIC MATERIAL PROPERTIES

There are a number of basic engineering material properties that are used in most types of analysis. Some of these – e.g. elastic modulus, Poisson's ratio, yield stress, and density – are typically found on a data sheet in the form of a single (monotonic) datapoint. However, it is not advisable to use the monotonic elastic modulus or yield stress values without consulting a stress/strain curve to better interpret how these values were obtained.

One of the best known material properties is elastic modulus, a value that is obtained from the linear portion of the stress/strain curve. Often the flexural modulus is substituted for the elastic modulus because the desirable data are not available. But these data are not always interchangeable, and use of the incorrect information can lead to a great deal of error when analyzing the performance of engineering thermoplastics or other polymers. This is because the test for flexural modulus assumes a linear-elastic stress distribution through the thickness of a homogeneous sample. But material non-linearity, the contribution of transverse shear stiffness, and non-uniform fiber distribution in glass-filled systems can lead to a significant difference between a material's elastic and flexural modulus values.

Engineering thermoplastics typically have a non-linear elastic region due to time-dependent, viscoelastic effects, which makes it difficult to identify a precise yield point for the material (see Figure 1). As a result, there are many ways that the elastic region can be handled. A tangent, secant, or multilinear fit can be used in this region. If the application being designed is not to exceed yield, and if unloading response is not a concern, then the material can be modeled as hyperelastic. Depending on the rate of loading used during material testing to obtain the datasheet values, and how greatly that rate differs from the rate of loading experienced by the actual application, viscoelastic effects could be different in the application. Both the tangent and secant modului introduce error, and the multilinear fit causes difficulty in interpreting variables

such as plastic strain. When evaluating a given application, the approach that introduces the most acceptable error should be selected, depending on the type of analysis being performed.

Most material models used in finite-element analysis (FEA) codes require the definition of true stress vs. true strain (see Figure 2). The true stress and true strain are defined as the *instantaneous* load/unit area and the change in length with respect to the *current* length of the sample. In contrast, engineering stress is defined as load/original area, and engineering strain is change in length/original length of the sample. If an engineering stress vs. engineering strain curve is the only data available, formulae are readily available to convert the engineering stress and strain values to true stress and strain:

$$\varepsilon = \ln(1 + e) \qquad (1)$$

$$\sigma = S * \exp(\varepsilon) \qquad (2)$$

where: S and e are engineering stress and strain

and: σ and ε are true stress and strain

However, these formulae assume uniform necking along the gauge section (see Figure 3). If the necking characteristics of the test specimen cannot be verified, these equations should not be used. Many engineering thermoplastics that fail in a ductile fashion will exhibit stable necking. As a result, they can sometimes be modeled as elastic-perfectly plastic within the range of stress the application will experience.

There are 2 variables that affect the mechanical characterization of engineering thermoplastics more than others: temperature and strain rate. As temperature rises, the elastic modulus and yield stress of a material decrease, and the elongation and viscoelastic effects increase. As the strain rate increases, the secant modulus and yield stress increase, and the engineering strain to failure decreases due

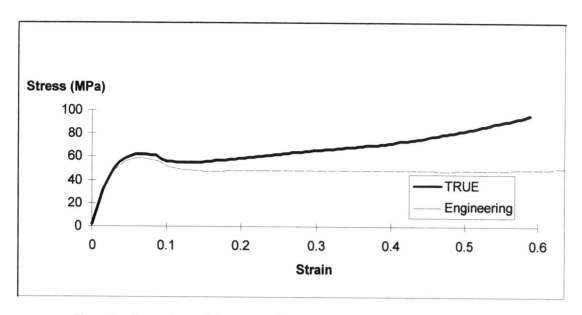

Figure 2: Comparison of True vs. Engineering Stress and Strain for Polycarbonate

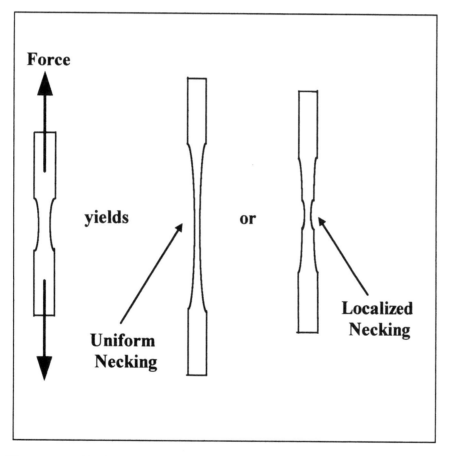

Figure 3: Typical Uniform vs. Localized Necking for ASTM Type I Tensile Bars Molded from an Engineering Thermoplastic

in part to more localized necking. As a result, the material in question needs to be tested at a temperature and strain rate close to that of the application being analyzed, or the material model needs to be adjusted.

One final note about interpreting sample test data. Geometries that exhibit high levels of triaxial stress cannot easily undergo plasticity. Therefore, resins that exhibit ductile behavior in uniaxial and biaxial stress may fail in a brittle manner during triaxial loading, since plasticity is not present, thereby allowing the stress to rise to level where brittle cracking may begin. For example, a tensile test specimen in uniaxial tension could fail at a much higher strain than that seen in a notched Izod impact test, where stress exists in a triaxial state. Therefore, the stress state of the sample used to generate material data must be compared to the stress state of the application. The results must be interpreted correctly, and in some cases additional testing will need to be performed on samples with similar stress states.

Most engineering thermoplastics also exhibit different properties in tension than they do in compression. Typically the yield stress in compression is 10% to 20% higher than it is in tension. However, glass- or rubber-filled materials can have significantly different yield stress values in compression and tension. Therefore, care should be taken to understand how the stress state in an application compares to that of the sample used to generate the material data. A preliminary analysis can be conducted in order to examine the stress state.

NON-LINEAR MODELING

Thermoplastics can typically undergo a large amount of deformation prior to yielding or failure. In many cases, an application can be designed to yield and take advantage of thermoplastics' ability to recover strain over time, returning to nearly the same shape they held prior to application of the load.

Many applications will require that static analysis using an implicit code be performed with software that can handle non-linear geometry. In this type of analysis, the geometrical stiffness matrix will be updated throughout the deformation. If the deformations become larger than the wall thickness of the part, then a non-linear geometry option should be used.

CREEP AND STRESS RELAXATION

One characteristic of thermoplastics is viscoelasticity. Some designers think that this makes these materials unsuitable for use in structural applications. However, this behavior can be designed around by using the proper analytical tools.

To be successful at this, a designer must first determine if the stress level, temperature, and time for the material in question results in a linear-elastic, linear-viscoelastic, or non-linear-viscoelastic material response. These terms refer to the relationship of the response of the material to an excitation. An approach using creep deformation maps to answer this question has been proposed by Hasan [1]. In this approach, a graph of temperature vs. time is constructed for various stress levels that bound the linear and non-linear-viscoelastic range.

A creep curve of strain vs. time can be used to determine the material's response to a constant load. The test must be conducted at the same temperature and stress level that the application will be subjected to in its end-use environment, and it should be conducted for the same time of interest. In order to determine the stress level, an analysis will have to be conducted on the application assuming no viscoelasticity. From such an analysis, a representative stress level is derived in the areas that will most affect the results of interest. In some cases, the stress level will be affected by the viscoelastic response; so the stress level will have to be verified after a viscoelastic material model has been introduced.

If the response shown is linear elastic, then there will be no increase in strain during the time of interest. In this case, viscoelastic effects are not incorporated into the material model, and only the elastic modulus is used.

A linear viscoelastic response will result in a proportional increase in steady-state response with an input. If the interface between the boundary of applied traction and the boundary on which displacements are prescribed does not change with time, then the correspondence principle applies. An apparent modulus can be calculated and substituted for the elastic modulus in a static analysis. However, when the contact surface between 2 parts varies, this condition is violated. In cases such as this, a creep compliance curve can be calculated using strain vs. time data. A Prony series can be determined and implemented in some codes, as the process shown in Figure 4 outlines. A steady-state compliance must be known and implemented if the analysis is going to be extrapolated to a time greater than that measured in the test data used to develop the Prony series.

In order to extrapolate to a different stress level, there must be 2 creep curves available for the material of interest derived at the same temperature. An interpolation/extrapolation routine can then be performed to generate a compliance curve at the new stress level. Some codes have implemented a Williams-Landell-Ferry (WLF) shift to scale the time variable in order to account for a change in temperature. However, to do this, the material must be thermo-rheologically simple. Graphically this means that a change in temperature results in a constant shift of the relaxation or creep response time on a log-log scale (see Figure 5). For engineering thermoplastics at temperatures below their glass transition temperature (T_g), both the compliance and time axes typically need to be shifted. And since the WLF shift function only impacts the time axis, there is no way to accurately adjust for a different temperature. This is an area where further research needs to be performed. In order to check whether or not a material is thermo-rheologically simple, the material needs to be tested at 2 or more temperatures with the same stress

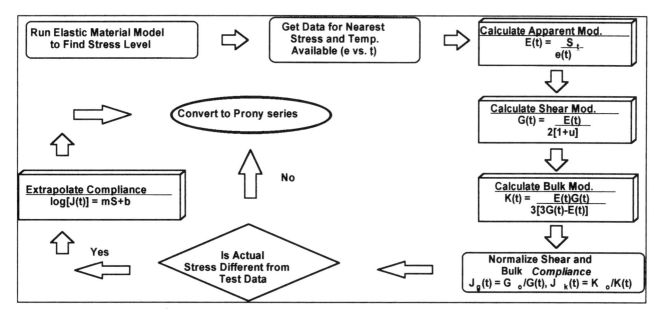

Figure 4: Process to Implement Prony Series in Some Codes

level. These creep curves are then plotted on a log-log scale to graphically determine if there is a shift. The Prony process shown in Figure 4 has been performed on a standard ASTM D-2990 tensile creep test specimen using the ABAQUS® Standard structural analysis code. The stress values were extrapolated from test data gathered at 3.45 to 6.90 MPa for a polycarbonate/acrylonitrile butadiene styrene (PC/ABS) resin at 80C. The extrapolated predictions were very close to the test results, as shown in Figure 6.

A non-linear viscoelastic response will yield a steady-state response that is not proportional to any excitations such as creep stress level. There are many proposed methods that can be used to handle this, such as with activation energies as proposed by Hasan [1]. This is another area where further research is needed.

Stress relaxation behavior is governed by the same mechanisms as creep. Therefore, the same principles apply as those for creep.

HIGH STRAIN-RATE IMPACT

During impact, material in the application is subjected to a variety of loading rates throughout the duration of the event. The resulting material strain, therefore, varies as a function of time. And the manner in which the material responds depends on the strain rate. Therefore, the material must be characterized for the range of strain rates to which the application will be subjected. Unfortunately, the strain rate in the application will change from location to location in the part and it will vary at any one location over time. Furthermore, there is no way to predict – based on velocity, energy, mass, geometry, or any other variables – what the strain rates will be in most applications prior to running a preliminary analysis.

The truly linear-elastic portion of the stress/strain curve does not vary with strain rate. If a tangential elastic modulus is used, it will not change with strain rate. Therefore, a tangential elastic modulus will not need to vary with strain rate. As the strain rate increases, the viscoelastic effect in the elastic region will decrease and the response will approach the tangential modulus. The secant modulus will vary with strain rate and will tend to increase as the strain rate increases [2].

The yield stress will increase as the strain rate increases. The relationship for many engineering thermoplastics tends to be a constant percentage increase for each decade of strain-rate increase. If a material is tested at 2 different strain rates, the % increase/decade can be calculated and applied in the material model. In the LS-DYNA3D® code, this can be implemented as a load curve.

The failure criteria are dependent upon the strain rate. Therefore, tests need to be conducted on a sample of the material to determine if it will fail in a brittle or ductile manner. An analysis of the same case needs to be conducted in order to determine the stress or strain at which failure occurs for the appropriate strain rate. The strain rate must first be determined in the area of the highest strain, near the level that failure is expected, unless a function can be implemented in the analysis code. Picking a single failure criteria is an iterative process. However, for many engineering thermoplastics, failure criteria are not very strain-rate sensitive.

Third-stage strain hardening is relatively insensitive to the strain rate. Therefore, a uniaxial compression test can be conducted to characterize that portion of the curve. The curve is shifted on the stress axes until the yield stress is appropriate. The material response can then be constructed from all the above features. Figure 7 summarizes how strain rate affects most engineering thermoplastics. Only the initial part of the curve is shown.

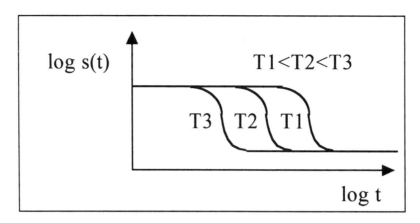

Figure 5: Stress Relaxation Response of a Material Plotted on a Log-Log Scale to Determine if the Material is Thermo-Rheologically Simple

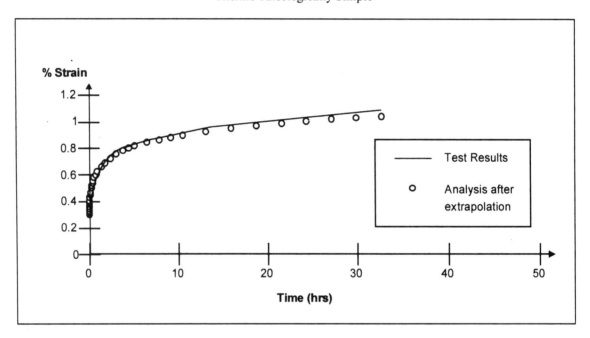

Figure 6: Test vs. Actual Strain for Extrapolated Stress

PROCESSING ISSUES

During the injection molding process, short-glass-fiber-filled engineering thermoplastics will develop orthotropic material properties due to fiber alignment predominantly in the direction of flow (near the surface of the part), and fiber orientation predominantly in the cross-flow direction (on the part's mid-plane). Creators of the C-Mold® filling and ABAQUS® structural analysis codes have jointly developed the ability to transfer fiber-orientation data for accurate orthotropic characterization of fiber-filled materials. Many times the gating and processing conditions are unknown, or the analyst does not have access to both codes. In such situations, an alternative approach would be to group elements where the direction of the melt-front advancement is similar and roughly known.

An orthotropic material model is given and the tensile test modulus, which is measured in the flow direction, is used to represent material properties in the flow direction. Frequently the cross-flow modulus value can be estimated from a rule of mixtures, as seen in Eq. (3), below. For example, if the material has 30% glass, the cross-flow direction modulus is 70% of the flow direction.

$$E_c = (1 - f_g) E_f \qquad (3)$$

Where:
E_c	=	Cross-Flow-Direction Modulus
f_g	=	Fraction of Glass Filler (100 % Glass Filler)
E_f	=	Flow-Direction Modulus

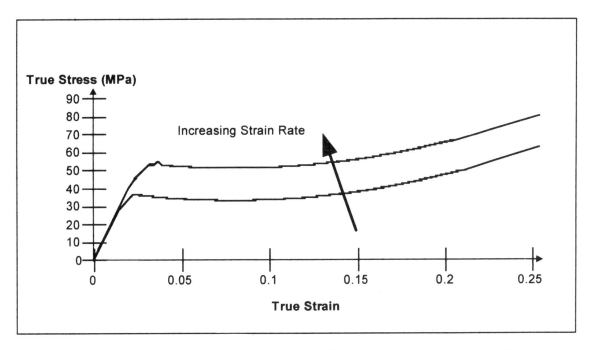

Figure 7: Stress/Strain Curve for Impact-Modified Polyphenylene Ether at 2 Strain Rates

Yet another area that is not well researched is knitline strength. A knitline is a weaker section in a part formed where 2 melt fronts come together during the injection molding process. The strength of this joint is dependent upon the strength of the material, as well as the temperature of the fronts at the time of formation, cavity pressure, and other processing conditions. It is possible that failure could occur along the knitline, which would be missed if no knitline were modeled. The number and location of knitlines are dependent upon the processing conditions and gating scenario of a given part. A filling analysis is the best way to determine the locations of knitlines, as well as the processing variables mentioned above. A double-ended tensile bar can be tested to determine the strength of the knitline at similar processing conditions. However, the relationship between these variables and the knitline strength for various materials is not readily available. In the absence of other options, being aware of the locations of knitlines and designing to reduce stress in these areas is the best approach.

Other variables that can affect material properties are the material's processing conditions in the mold. Predominant among these variables are the shear and temperature history experienced by the polymer. If, for example, the material is injected at a high rate and with an excessive temperature, the polymer chains may break, resulting in a weaker, poor-performing part. It is particularly important to verify that the material was processed correctly if a correlation effort is underway.

SUMMARY

Engineering thermoplastics are being used in more challenging applications in order to bring innovative solutions to market faster and with less expense. But in order to ensure success, it is very important to be able to accurately model these applications. An integral part of the accuracy of the final solution is the characterization of the material. Since engineering thermoplastics are a very challenging class of materials to model, extra attention must be paid to the topics covered in this paper.

Different techniques to handle the elastic portion of the stress/strain curve have been discussed, as well as methods to handle yielding. The effects of temperature, strain rate, and stress state on the mechanical properties have also been discussed and should be considered when using material data in an analysis. For many applications it is important to use non-linear geometric and material modeling.

In addition, the viscoelastic creep condition has been discussed, including determination for the type of behavior present and suggestions on how to address linear elastic, linear viscoelastic, and non-linear viscoelastic applications. Since thermoplastics are being used increasingly for energy management applications in impact events, and because they are sensitive to the strain rate, the behavior of engineering thermoplastics at varying strain rates was discussed. Finally, processing conditions such as fiber orientation, knitline strength, and processing variables need to be considered closely, particularly during a correlation effort.

# # # # #

® ABAQUS is a Registered Trademark of Hibbit, Karlsson, Sorensen, Inc.
® LS-DYNA3D is a Registered Trademark of Livermore Software Technology Corp.
® C-MOLD is a Registered Trademark of Advanced CAE Technology, Inc. (ACTech).

REFERENCES

1. Hasan, Omar, "Use of Deformation Maps in Predicting Time Dependent Deformation of Thermoplastics," ANTEC '96, pp. 3223-3228. Clark, C. "High Strain-Rate Characterization of Thermoplastics Used for Energy Management Applications," SAE International Congress & Exposition, Feb. 28-Mar. 3, 1994, Paper No. 940882.

2. Clark, C., Locke, D., "High Strain Rate Testing of Engineering Thermoplastics for Head Impact Applications," SAE International Congress & Exposition, Feb. 26-29, 1996, Paper # 960153.

Studies on Optimizing the Cryogenic Process for Recycling Plated Plastic to Achieve Improved Quality of Remolded Parts

Richard Dom and Gary Shawhan
American Society of Electroplated Plastics

Jackie Kuzio, Angela Spell, and Matt Warren
Air Products and Chemicals, Inc.

ABSTRACT

Electroplated plastic from hubcaps was cryogenically ground and magnetically separated into a metallic and a recyclable plastic stream. A high purity plastic was achieved using a magnetic, multi-pass separation process. The ground plastic was pelletized and molded. The recycled samples revealed properties very similar to a pure, unprocessed resin and a unplated, control plastic which had been cryogenically ground and remolded. Only elongation properties of the plated and unplated, processed material degraded as compared to the pure resin. The favorable recycled resin performance warrants additional testing of electroplated plastics and investigating the benefits of incorporating varying percentages of this recycled material with virgin resin.

INTRODUCTION

Today the automotive industry is expanding its use of decoratively plated plastics for new applications in both interior and exterior trim. Plated plastics are also being considered for the shielding of various automotive electronics components, computer control systems, displays, entertainment/navigation systems, and connector assemblies. An increasing stimulus propelling the acceptance of plated plastics in the automotive industry is the availability of cost-effective, high-quality recycling strategies that allow reuse of the base resin material at the end of initial part life.

The major automotive companies have adopted strategies for plastic parts manufacture that require minimum percentages of recycled material be incorporated into newly molded components. As an example, 25% or more recycled plastic content may be incorporated with virgin material into a newly manufactured part in order to meet this requirement. Predicting the performance and quality of these remolded parts is dependent on having a clean recycled resin stream that closely mirrors the properties of virgin material. It is also important to understand the history of the resin, which can affect the recovered resin's properties.

Pure resin streams are difficult to obtain in commercial recycling. In most cases, streams are contaminated due to the incorporation of foreign materials including paints, adhesives, and/or metal coatings that were part of prior manufacturing processes.

Recognizing these issues, the American Society of Electroplated Plastics and Air Products and Chemicals, Inc. have undertaken studies concerning plated plastics recycling using cryogenic process technology. Initial studies focused on general characterization of the cryogenic process and its capability to achieve metal-free resin streams. Additionally, the performance of remolded and replated plastics was investigated. In general these studies indicated that further work would be required to refine the various metal/plastic separation methods, with the ultimate objective of achieving a high-purity/high-value resin stream that could be beneficially incorporated into commercial recycle/reuse strategies.

This paper updates the capabilities of cryogenic plated plastics recycling processes, including the impact of cryogenics on different magnetic separation procedures and the properties of the resultant recovered resins. The studies reported in the paper are all related to decoratively plated plastics. Specifically, data is presented on the physical and dynamic properties of remolded parts. These properties include flexural strength, flexural modulus, and heat distortion temperature (HDT). Fracture properties, including elongation-at-break and Izod impact strength are also reported for the various separation methods tested.

Additionally, data has been collected documenting recycled resin purity based on the various separation techniques. Plating studies on remolded plaques at 100% regrind are reported. This includes plating adhesion data as well as adhesion after thermal cycling.

American Society of Electroplated Plastics - This is a joint study undertaken by members of the American Society of Electroplated Plastics and by Air Products and Chemicals, Inc. The American Society of Electroplated Plastics is a trade organization comprised of electroplating companies, material suppliers to the electroplating industry and users of electroplated parts.

The society's goals are:

1. The advancement of electroplating technology
2. The development of standards and guidelines for the electroplated plastic industry
3. The education of all those interested in electroplated plastic parts

Air Products and Chemicals, Inc. is a major industrial gas and chemical company. Since their founding in 1940, Air Products has strived to enhance customers' manufacturing processes using innovative techniques that employ industrial gases.

Recognizing the importance of recycling to the future of electroplated parts, the American Society of Electroplated Plastics has taken the initiative to work with industry to advance the state-of-the-art of recycling plated plastics. Special contributions to this study by member companies are acknowledged at the end of this paper.

Program Background - The first applications of electroplated plastics occurred in the automotive industry, where electroplated copper and nickel, followed by a chrome finish, were plated onto acrylonitrile butadiene styrene (ABS) plastic. Current design trends in the automotive industry favor increased use of decorative trim for both interior and exterior applications. Decoratively plated plastics use has also continued to expand into a broad range of industries including plumbing, hardware, appliances, consumer electronics, and jewelry. The automotive industry however, remains plastic plating technology's largest single application.

The emphasis on recycling and reuse in the automotive industry has increased significantly over the last 5 to 7 years. OEM requirements for the incorporation of minimum levels of recycled plastic in new part manufacture have helped drive the need for improved recycling technology. An additional impetus to recycling is the use of new, high performance resins by the automotive market. Since these higher performance resins also tend to be higher value materials, they can command higher prices in the recycled resin market. Continued commercial acceptance and growth in the use of these recycled materials, however, are very dependent upon the following:

1. Cost of the recycled resin
2. Properties of the recycled resin
3. Appearance of recycled resin as a remolded part

Thermoplastics Recycling - The primary objective of the thermoplastics recycling process is to obtain pure, clean resin at a competitive market price. Plastics that are intended to be recycled can be categorized in one of several ways to define the process strategies that need to be considered. The optimum situation for recycling thermoplastics is one in which the recycle stream is homogeneous with no foreign materials (e.g., paint finishes, metal coatings, inserts, adhesives, or other polymers). More commonly, the recycle streams are not homogeneous and contain one or more of these foreign materials based on their manufacturing history. When residual materials remain within the recovered resin, they will compromise the quality of the resin. Clearly, to reuse resins from a non-homogeneous stream, foreign materials must be removed. Electroplated plastics are not homogeneous. An electroplated part consists of the base plastic, typically ABS, and metallic plating. The total metal thickness is typically 0.0381 to 0.0508 mm.

The decorative plastics plating process employs an operations sequence that is practiced with reasonable consistency worldwide. This sequence is summarized in Table I (minus the rinsing that is incorporated between each process step). Incorporated into this scheme is a significant amount of nickel. Nickel is ferromagnetic and can facilitate the separation of the metal coating from the base resin through low-cost, magnetic means. The principal commercial coating compositions for plating plastics are summarized in Table II.

Table I.   Overview of Decorative Plating on Plastics Process Cycle

Pre-Etch	Acid Copper Strike
Etch	Copper Electroplate
Promoter	Semi-Bright Nickel
Catalyst	Bright Nickel
Accelerator	Micro-Discontinuous Nickel
Electroless Plate	Chromium

Table II.   Typical Thickness of Metal Layers for Plated Plastics

Decorative Plate Layers	Thickness (micron)
Electroless Copper/or Nickel	0.381-0.635
Electroplated Copper	10.2-50.8
Electroplated Nickel	5.08-30.5
Electroplated Chrome	0.254-0.381

CRYOGENIC RECYCLING TECHNOLOGY

Cryogenics can generally be defined as processes that employ liquefied gases (or cryogens), which boil below 38°C. However, since most of the atmospheric gases (oxygen, argon, nitrogen) boil below -157°C, the definition that will be used for the purpose of this paper will be that of a liquefied gas that boils below -157°C. Liquid nitrogen boils at -196°C and is the cryogen used in the process discussed in this paper.

Figure 1 provides an illustration of the basic process scheme for recycling plated plastics using cryogenics. This scheme consists of coarse and fine-size reduction steps, followed by separation. Of course, this scheme is intended to separate the metallic coating from the base resin. It is not intended to separate base resins, such as ABS and PC.

To begin the recycling process, plated plastic parts, in their original form, are placed into a granulator for coarse size reduction. The granulator functions to densify the material to be processed and to increase the functional surface area before exposure to the cryogenic steps. The granulator chops the material with high-speed rotating cutting knives.

Granulated material is fed to a fine-size reduction step. The fine-size reduction step uses a cryogenic cooling conveyor followed by a hammermill. The cooling conveyor is basically a back-mixed, co-current heat exchanger that uses a screw-type design to both meter the polymer into the hammermill and to facilitate contact between the polymer and the liquid nitrogen.

The purpose of this process step is to ensure complete cooling of the material before it enters the hammermill. Complete cooling assists debonding by taking advantage of the differential thermal coefficients of expansion of the base resin and metallic plating, allowing selective separation methods to be employed. Cryogenics helps minimize both the work and heat associated with the grinding processes and avoids exposing the resin to excessive heat and possible deterioration of the resin's physical properties. Particle sizes of 8 to 80 mesh are typically produced by the fine-size reduction step.

The final processing step can make use of a variety of separation techniques. Magnetic separation, electrostatic separation, density separation, and particle screening are just some of the methods that can be used to affect removal of plating contaminants from the resin. In this study, the presence of nickel in the metallic coating makes magnetic separation attractive.

The basic processing scheme used during this study can be summarized as follows:

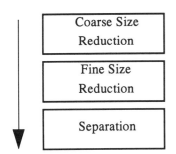

Schmiemann, et. al. [1] compared the physical properties of decoratively electroplated ABS from Bayer that had been processed by a cryogenic grinding process to those of virgin material. The impact strength and tensile modulus of elasticity of the recycled ABS was essentially the same as those for virgin material. However, the elongation at break of the recycled material was almost a factor of ten less than that of the virgin material (refer to Table III). Taschler and Shawhan [2] achieved similar results using a Polycarbonate (PC)/ABS blend from GE Plastics, (refer to Table IV). The flexural yield stress, the flexural modulus, and the heat deflection temperature of the recycled PC/ABS were essentially the same as those for virgin material. But the impact strength of the recycled resin was approximately one-half that of the virgin material. The melt index of the recycled material increased to 10.1 versus the 3.9 of the virgin material (refer to Table V).

Table III. **Decoratively Electroplated ABS Results of Schmiemann, et. al.**

Property	Pure Bay Blend	100% Recyclate
Impact Strength ISO 180/1A 23C (kJm^2)	46	38
Elongation @ Break (%)	138	12
Modulus of Elasticity in Tension (N/mm^2)	1890	1860
Residual metal content (weight %)	0	0.3

Table IV. **Decoratively Plated PC/ABS Results of Taschler and Shawhan**

Property	PC/ABS Control	100% Recyclate
Tensile Strength (MPa)	NA	NA
Tensile Elongation @ break (%)	139	12
Tensile Modulus (GPa)	1.89	1.86
Flexural Strength (MPa)	86.3	81.3
Flexural Modulus (GPa)	1.90	2.03

NA - not available

Table V. **Decoratively Plated PC/ABS Results of Taschler and Shawhan**

Property	PC/ABS Control	100% Recyclate
Izod Impact (23°C) (kJ/m^2)	20.8	11.3
Instrumented Impact Total Energy (23°C) (J)	NA	NA
Heat Distortion Temperature (1,820kPa) (°C)	113	103
Melt Flow Index 10kg/220°C (ISO)	3.9	10.1
Specific Gravity, solid	NA	NA

The data from these two studies indicates that the physical properties of the recycled materials are close to, but not exactly equal to the properties of virgin polymers. This difference could be due to residual metallic particles in the recycled resin. The difference could also be due to the difference in thermal histories between the recycled and the virgin material. The main objective of this study is to understand the cause for the difference in physical properties. The study will also examine the optimization of the recycling process.

STUDY OF CRYOGENICALLY RECYCLED PLASTICS

Overview of Cryogenic Processing - Decoratively plated hubcap centers (Figure 2) molded from General Electric Resin PC/ABS resin were processed using the cryogenic grinding methods outlined previously. Two controls were used to provide baseline data for comparison to the recycled and remolded material properties. These include a supply of virgin PC/ABS resin and unplated hubcaps (Figure 2) molded from this resin.

Cryogenic grinding was performed on both the plated and unplated hubcaps. Separation of metal from the cryogenically processed plated material was performed using different magnetic separation procedures. These variations in processing were intended to determine the conditions required to achieve optimum resin purity and to assess the impact of the process on the physical properties of the remolded material.

In this study the material was granulated at ambient conditions to a 6.35mm to 12.7mm size (Figure 3). Following granulation, the material was cryogenically ground using a Pulva 2DH hammermill with a 6.35mm round hole screen. Figure 4 shows a sample of the cryogenically ground material before magnetic separation.

Metal Separation and Removal Methodology - A principal objective of this study was the evaluation of various techniques for metal separation and removal. The previous study by Taschler and Shawhan used only a single pass over a permanent drum magnet. This study showed a high level of metal in the recovered resin. The separation technique employed in this study included a baseline evaluation of the drum magnet used in the previous study and use of an induced-roll magnetic separator. A series of varying amperage settings on the induced-roll magnet were evaluated to determine the optimum metal separation conditions. In all cases, a first pass, or scalper pass, was employed at a consistent 0.1 amp condition to achieve an initial bulk removal of metal from the sample. The second and third passes were then conducted at varying amperage to determine the effect on final resin purity. Table VI presents the results of these tests. There were no significant differences in the results of applying 1, 2, or 3 amps during the second and third passes.

Table VI. Magnetic Separation Results Using the Induced-Roll Magnet with Varying Amperage

Material	Pass Number	Weight Non-Magnetic (g)	Weight Magnetic (g)	Removed* (%)	Overall Non-Magnetic Yield** (%)
1.0 amps	1st	1404	267	16	
	2nd	1251	105	6	
	3rd	1135	76	5	68
2.0 amps	1st	1370	255	16	
	2nd	1215	106	7	
	3rd	1132	67	4	70
3.0 amps	1st	1575	296	16	
	2nd	1454	117	6	
	3rd	1353	78	4	72

* weight of the magnetic fraction divided by the initial sample weight X 100

** weight of non-magnetic fraction after 3rd pass divided by initial sample weight X 100

One important aspect of cryogenic grinding is the resulting particle size distribution. Table VII provides a summary of the distribution of the particle sizes achieved for cryogenic grinding prior to the application of various separation methods. Figure 5 shows samples of the 10, 20, 30 and 40 mesh sizes at the bottom of the photo versus the unsized material at the top of the photo.

Table VII. Distribution of Particle Sizes After Cryogenic Grinding

Screen Size	% Passing
80	6
60	12
40	31
30	50
20	71
10	97

In a second series of induced-roll magnetic separation trials, a constant current of 3.0 amps was utilized during the second and third passes. This setting applied to material that had been screened to 10, 20, 30, and 40 mesh size respectively. Table VIII presents the magnetic separation results for each pass. The 10 mesh material resulted in a significantly greater amount of material being removed in the scalper pass. This may be attributed to the magnet's ability to attract larger particles during separation. It should be noted that particles were occasionally found to have resin still attached to the metal.

Table VIII. Magnetic Separation Results Using the Induced-Roll Magnet with Varying Particle Size

Material	Pass Number	Weight Non-Magnetic (g)	Weight Magnetic (g)	Removed* (%)	Overall Non-Magnetic Yield** (%)
10 mesh	1st	1325	970	42	
	2nd	1129	167	7	
	3rd	1074	48	2	47
20 mesh	1st	1645	343	17	
	2nd	1547	92	5	
	3rd	1519	23	1	76
30 mesh	1st	1503	147	9	
	2nd	1435	59	4	
	3rd	1411	27	2	86
40 mesh	1st	1495	150	9	
	2nd	1402	54	3	
	3rd	1334	29	2	81

* weight of the magnetic fraction divided by the initial sample weight X100

** weight of non-magnetic fraction after 3rd pass divided by initial sample weight X 100

As indicated in the above table, a total nonmagnetic yield of about 80-85% can be expected when an induced-roll magnet is used at a 3.0 amp setting for smaller particle resins of the 30-40 mesh range.

Tests were conducted on a higher volumes of material to verify the above results. The 10 and 40 mesh samples were selected based on the variation noted above. These results are shown in Table IX.

Table IX. Magnetic Separation Results From Induced-Roll Magnetic Separation with High Volume of Material

Material	Pass Number	Weight Non-Magnetic (g)	Weight Magnetic (g)	Removed* (%)	Overall Non-Magnetic Yield** (%)
10 mesh	1st	10,578	7,688	42	
	2nd	9,384	909	9	
	3rd	8,527	327	4	47
40 mesh	1st	11,803	1,142	9	
	2nd	11,260	368	3	
	3rd	10,906	100	1	84

* weight of magnetic fraction divided by initial sample weight X 100

** weight of non-magnetic fraction after 3rd pass divided by initial sample weight X 100

The verification of the purity achievable through this process was an essential element in this study. As shown in Table X the consistency of the resin purity was excellent. There was also a clear contrast in purity between the unseparated material and the processed material. Most importantly, the ash value of the samples that were not plated closely resembled those obtained from the cryogenically recycled material. Thus, it can be concluded that there was very little metallic contamination following induced-roll magnetic separation.

Table X. Ash Content Analysis-Purity of Separation

Analytical Analysis	Weight %*	Standard Deviation
unseparated/unsized	18.47	1.074
drum magnet	1.50	0.095
molded unplated	0.883	0.007
10 mesh @3.0 amps	1.09	0.023
20 mesh @3.0 amps	1.12	0.055
30 mesh @3.0 amps	1.10	0.076
40 mesh @3.0 amps	1.19	0.046
unsized @1.0 amps	1.17	0.029
unsized @2.0 amps	1.14	0.060
unsized @3.0 amps	1.15	0.052

*Average of three readings per sample

PERFORMANCE DATA FOR RECYCLED AND REMOLDED PLASTICS

The ultimate value of any recycling technology is in the quality of the recovered resin and the performance achievable when this resin is used to make a new part. The 10 and 40 mesh samples separated at 3.0 amps in the induced-roll magnet were used for performance testing. Virgin PC/ABS resin was used as a control for this study. It should be noted that this control sample was a virgin resin with no heat history and no pigments or additional fillers. The virgin resin was tested in its pellet form. An unplated sample was used as a second control sample to elucidate the effect of heat history and pigment addition. The unplated sample was processed identically to the metal plated samples.

Mechanical properties of the injection molded recycled material are shown in Table XI. The tensile strength, tensile modulus, flexural strength, and flexural modulus results indicate minimal changes from the virgin material. In general, the mechanical properties of the recovered resin show excellent retention of the performance characteristics associated with the virgin material.

Significant deterioration of the elongation properties was evident. This finding was consistent with the previous study. Elongation performance is a property that could be sensitive to the either the heat history of the resin or to the presence of impurities in the resin. Polymer heat deterioration is an irreversible property, whether derived from the original molding process, heat exposure during service, or during the recycling process (e.g. the heat of grinding). Importantly, with cryogenic processing, the heat of grinding is tightly controlled through cryogenic cooling. The poor elongation results of both the plated and unplated plastic indicate that the degradation of the elongation performance is a result of the heat history of the resin rather than the presence of metal impurities.

Table XI. **Mechanical Properties of Re-molded Parts - Injection Molds Control vs. 100% Recyclates**

Property	PC/ABS Control	no plating	10 mesh	40 mesh
Tensile Strength (MPa)	52.8	49.6	49.8	49.3
Tensile Elongation @ break (%)	104	27	11	11
Tensile Modulus (GPa)	1.48	1.46	1.52	1.53
Flexural Strength (MPa)	79.8	75.2	75.8	75.2
Flexural Modulus (GPa)	1.94	1.94	1.93	1.92

Compression molding is a convenient process for preparing test samples. Since there are expected differences in the resin's directional flow during compression molding, when compared to injection molding, the mechanical properties of compression molded samples were also evaluated. This is presented in Table XII.

The elongation at break results for the compression molding tests exhibited high variability. In particular, the average of four test results for the 10 mesh sample was 35%. Three of the values were 51.1%, 41.1% and 35.5% while one value was 11.1%. Visual examination of the sample with a low value result revealed local particle contamination.

Table XII. **Mechanical Properties of Remolded Parts Using Compression Molding* Samples Control vs. 100% Recyclates**

Property	PC/ABS Control	no plating	10 mesh	40 mesh	Drum Plastic
Tensile Strength (MPa)	42.8	44.9	43.3	44.8	44.5
Tensile Elongation @ break (%)	90	44	35	24	12
Tensile Modulus (GPa)	1.62	1.64	1.66	1.66	1.70

* Data supplied by APCI's analytical laboratory

** Material was not extruded and pelletized, tested in the cryogenic powdered form.

Table XIII presents impact thermal and physical properties of injection molded parts. These results were obtained for the 10 and 40 mesh samples with direct comparisons to the virgin PC/ABS control and the recycled but unplated material. The Izod impact strength values are somewhat lower for the recycled material, but are still very respectable. Since the Izod impact strength is a fracture property it would be expected to show the greatest influence from prior heat history. A similar effect is observed from the measured total impact energy results shown in Table XIII. The heat distortion temperature (HDT) results showed very little difference between the control and the recycled material. In general, these data support a high value added for the recovered material.

Table XIII. **Impact, Thermal, and Physical Properties of Injection Molded Parts Control vs. 100% Recyclates**

Property	PC/ABS Control	no plating	10 mesh	40 mesh
Izod Impact (23°C) (kJ/m^2)	25.0	20.4	17.9	18.3
Instrumented Impact Total Energy (23°C) (J)	49.2	40.8	35.0	32.9
Heat Distortion Temperature (1.82 MPa) (°C)	101	98	96	95
Specific Gravity, Solid	1.096	1.108	1.104	1.109

ADHESION RESULTS FOR REPLATED SAMPLES

Plaques were remolded with 100% recycled material and replated. A comparison was then made to the virgin control and the previously molded but unplated regrind. The results, presented in Table XIV, indicate that there is a slight deterioration in the adhesion of the metal to the base resin for the unplated and plated recycled material. The deterioration in the adhesion results of both the plated and unplated plastic indicate that the degradation of the adhesion performance is a result of the heat history of the resin rather than the presence of metal impurities.

Table XIV. Adhesion Results for Replated Material Control vs. 100% Recyclates

Condition	Test #1	Test#2	Test #3
PC/ABS Control (kPa)	41.4	27.6	34.5
Unplated (kPa)	24.1	24.1	24.1
10 Mesh (kPa)	22.4	19.0	20.7
40 Mesh (kPa)	20.7	27.6	24.1

In addition to the above adhesion results for the as-plated condition, thermal cycle testing was performed on the same samples. Two different methods were employed to evaluate the performance of the replated material. This included ASTM testing for 3 cycles from +85°C to -40°C and the ASEP TP201 procedure which operates from +93°C to -40°C. In both testing procedures there was only minor cracking visible after the first cycle and no additional deterioration was noted after further thermal cycling as shown in Table XV.

Table XV. Thermal Cycling of Replated Material

Recycled Material	ASTM Test +85°C to -40°C	ASEP Test +93°C to -40°C
10 mesh	Slight Cracking 1st Cycle	Slight Cracking 1st Cycle
	No Additional Cracking Cycle 2 and 3	No Additional Cracking Cycle 2 and 3
40 mesh	Slight Cracking 1st Cycle	Slight Cracking 1st Cycle
	No Additional Cracking Cycle 2 and 3	No Additional Cracking Cycle 2 and 3

PROCESSING COSTS

The cryogenic size reduction costs are presented in Table XVI. The nitrogen consumption and power costs associated with cryogenic grinding are provided. These are based on the production rate achieved during this study. Overall, the cryogenic size reduction processing produced a low processing cost of $US 0.103 per kilogram of recycled material.

Table XVI. Cryogenic Size Reduction Processing Costs

		Cost/kg Input ($US)
Throughput Rate, kg/hr of material	617 kg/hr	
Nitrogen Consumption, kg/kg of material	0.77 kg/kg	$0.101
Energy Consumption, (56 hp Connected Load)*	~20KW/hr	$0.002
Total: Power & Liquid N_2, Power Calculated @ $0.05/KWH Nitrogen Calculated @ $0.13/kg		$0.103

* 56 hp connected load based on 30 hp for the granulator, 25 hp for the grinding mill, and 1 hp for the cooling conveyor

The above costs are reflective of expected commercial costs since the cryogenic grinding demonstration facility uses commercial scale equipment. Facility amortization costs can also be expected to be modest since the equipment capital requirement to establish such a facility is approximately $260,000 ($US). A breakdown of the capital costs is presented in Table XVII.

Table XVII. Capital Equipment Cost Requirements for the Cryogenic Grinding Process

Equipment	Cost
Knife-blade Granulator	$70,000
Liquid Nitrogen Grinding System (Cooling conveyor, liquid nitrogen flow controls, hammer mill)	$100,000
Magnetic Separation Equipment (Scalping plus two high intensity magnets)	$90,000
Total Capital (excluding installation)	$260,000

* Cooling conveyor capable of processing 1000+ kg/hr plated scrap. Granulator, mill and magnetic separators designed for ~680-820 kg/hr. All values in $US.

SUMMARY/CONCLUSIONS

Recycling of plated plastics using standard cyrogenic grinding and separation procedures resulted in very favorable reclaimed resin properties as compared to both virgin and unplated recycled resins.

Elongation of the recycled material was significantly less than that of the virgin resin. The poor elongation results of both the plated and unplated plastic indicate that the degradation of the elongation performance is a result of the thermal history of the resin rather than the presence of metal impurities.

121

Improved separation was verified using a multi-pass method with induced-roll magnets. This was supported by both the ash analysis results and the close similarity of the unplated and plated recycled resin properties.

Grinding the resin to a smaller particle size improved recycled resin yield during induced-roll magnetic separation.

Adhesion characteristics of replated, recycled material showed only a slight difference from virgin resin, producing very favorable results. Thermal cycling tests also showed only small differences between the behavior of virgin material and the recycled samples.

The testing in this study was conducted with 100% recycled material. Since this is not a commercially realistic situation, additional studies on remolded and replated production parts should be conducted incorporating varying percentages of recycled material with virgin resin.

ACKNOWLEDGMENTS

The authors would like to give special recognition to the efforts and contributions of certain individuals who supported this study. The efforts of various members of the American Society of Electroplated Plastics played an important role in the organization and execution of this study. Likewise, the efforts of individuals at GE Plastics and Air Products and Chemicals, Inc. deserve special recognition.

- Ted Solarz: GE Plastics - Analytical Testing: Mechanical, Impact, Flexural, Physical Properties

- Jim Wilson: GE Plastics - Coordination and Support for the Project

- Bob Myers: Plastic Platers - Replating and Adhesion/Thermal Cycle Testing

- Ed Durkin: Plastic Platers - Support and Coordination of Company Activities

- Joe Stockunas and Tim Boland: Air Products and Chemicals, Inc. - Support for the Project

- Scott Schraden: Air Products and Chemicals, Inc.- Cryogenic Size Reduction

- Air Products and Chemicals Analytical Laboratories: Ash Testing, Compression Molding Testing

REFERENCES

1. Schmiemann et. al. Kunstoffe Plast Europe, March 1994.

2. Taschler and Shawhan, Recyclability of Plated Plastic using Cryogenic Technology, published for the American Society of Electroplated Plastics, 1994.

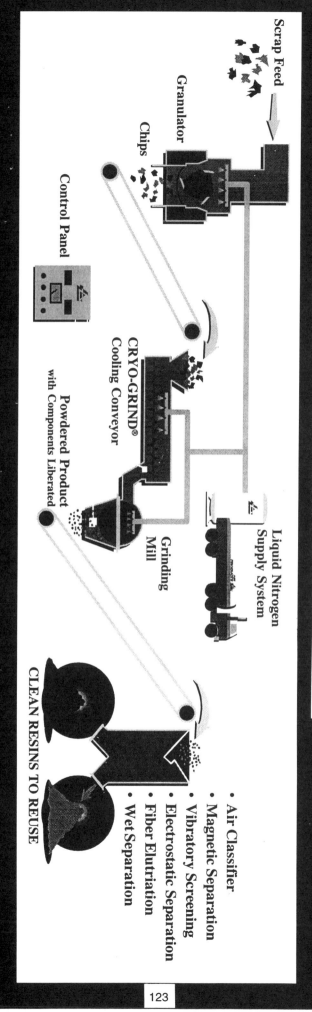

Figure 1 Overview of Cryogenic Recycling Process

Scrap Feed

Granulator

Chips

Control Panel

CRYO-GRIND®
Cooling Conveyor

Liquid Nitrogen
Supply System

Grinding
Mill

Powdered Product
with Components Liberated

- Air Classifier
- Magnetic Separation
- Vibratory Screening
- Electrostatic Separation
- Fiber Elutriation
- Wet Separation

CLEAN RESINS TO REUSE

**Figure 2 Unplated hub caps and plated hub cap
centers used for the study**

Figure 3 Sample of plated hub cap centers after
granulation

Figure 4 Sample of cryogenically ground, plated plastic

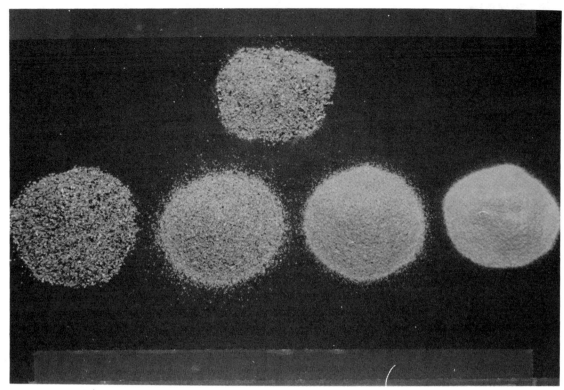

Figure 5 Samples of screened material. Top of photo
is the cryogenically ground material. Bottom of
photo, from right to left is the 40, 30, 20 and
10 mesh screened material.

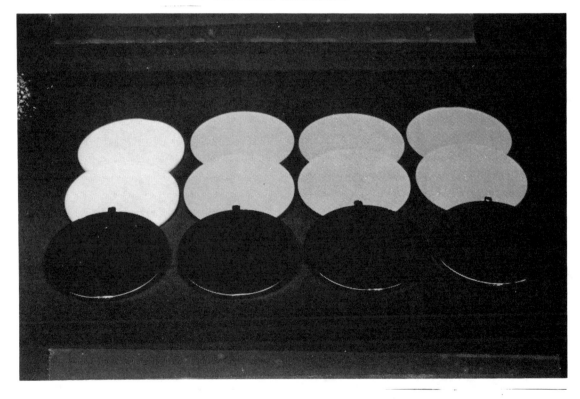

Figure 6 Re-molded disks. Lower front is the control
followed, by 40 and the 10 mesh materials
respectively

970665

Robotic Extrusion for Complex Profiles using a Thermoplastic Vulcanizate

D. E. Peterson
Advanced Elastomer Systems, L.P. USA

A. Van Meesche, B. Böwe, and W. J. Cantillon
Advanced Elastomer Systems NV/SA

ABSTRACT

An innovative robotic extrusion technology has been developed by Advanced Elastomer Systems NV/SA (AES) and Gepoc Verfahrenstechnik GmbH in Germany. This technology has proven ideal for producing a soft sealing member on a rigid substrate with a thermoplastic vulcanizate as the soft sealing member.

This new robotic extrusion technology will open up a wide range of engineered applications for bonding a soft sealing member to a hard substrate in automotive, construction, appliance and other markets. Potential automotive applications include cowl seals, lighting lens gaskets, and belly pan seals.

PROCESS DESCRIPTION - The difference between conventional extrusion processes and the process for robotic extrusion, using a polypropylene/EPDM thermoplastic vulcanizate (TPV) include the following:
- A specially formulated grade of Santoprene® rubber (121-60 E500)
- an extruder capable of generating very high shear
- a flexible, high pressure, heated hose to convey the melt from the extruder to the die
- an innovative extrusion die
- a 6-axis robot to guide the die
- a support system

The combination of these attributes results in an innovative robotic technology system able to produce high-tech parts in hard/soft combinations. This means that complex profiles in TPV can be produced very economically both in solid or multi-cavity designs. (Figure 1.)

TPV Material Selection - Advanced Elastomer Systems (AES) polymer chemists have been successful in developing a unique grade of TPV which demonstrates excellent processing while maintaining good physical property performance. This grade exhibits a very low viscosity after if has been plastified in the extruder. This is particularly important because the plastified TPV must pass through the heated hose from the extruder exit to the extrusion die with a minimum pressure drop. Once the material is extruded onto the substrate, the low viscosity melt has to remain stable to maintain the extruded profile shape and dimensions. This is especially important when hollow profiles are extruded around the bends/corners of the substrates. The support molds, or simply gravitation will shape the profiles as well.

The molten TPV must be delivered under a constant pressure. Therefore, the robotic extrusion process functions best if the extruder is running continuously. A two-way valve is used to divert the polymer stream intermittently. This allows direct recycling of the material within a closed-loop system.

This special grade of TPV has been heat stabilized. This allows it to be submitted to numerous recyclings without detrimental effects on the physical properties of the material. The mechanical properties for this grade are designed for a majority of applications where tensile and tear strength, combined with very good sealing performance, are critical. This is extremely important for the automotive industry. The product has only a 6 % loss per decade at 70°C, when submitted to extended stress relaxation testing, as per the ISO 3384A standard.

Other Shore A durometer hardness grades are being developed for the robotic extrusion system.

EXTRUDER DESIGN - The extruder used in the robotic extrusion system should be a minimum of 30:1 L/D. A grooved feed section (4 L/D) is also highly recommended in combination with a high shear screw with a minimum of 3:1 compression ratio. A high shear barrier screw from Battenfeld Extrusionstechnik - Germany is highly suited for proper plastification. Such an extruder, with low-end temperature settings and equipped with a proper drive, will provide the very low melt viscosity required of the TPV at a low melt temperature.

FLEXIBLE HOSE - A flexible, high pressure heated hose is fixed to the extruder head at one end by a special

127

adapter. This hose can withstand a maximum pressure of 35000 KPa at a maximum temperature of 210°C. The process with TPV runs at medium pressure with a temperature of between 195°C and 200°C. The other end of the hose is linked to the extrusion die. The die is manipulated in the X-Y-Z directions by the end of the robotic arm. Support of the constantly moving heated hose is extremely important to ensure that it does not twist and/or kink during the movement of the robotic arm.

INNOVATIVE EXTRUSION DIE - The extrusion die has to perform two major tasks in the robotic extrusion system. First, it must give the exact shape to the profile; and second, it must apply pressure to laminate the profile to the substrate. The shape of the profile die, and consequently the TPV profile, is obtained by using the standard principles for TPV extrusion dies. The land length of the die plays an important role in producing a smooth profile surface.

The melt stability of the profile of the TPV is important depending on how the profile is fixed to the substrate. When using large diameter bulb seals or multi-cavity seals at the edge of the substrate, it is recommended that an aluminum or silicone rubber support mold be used. This helps to retain the shape of the profile. There is an option to apply air support through the extrusion die to the bulb seal, which is similar to conventional bulb seal extrusion. (Figure 2 - A Variety of Profiles Can be Extruded by the Robotic Extrusion System).

THE ROBOT - The robotic extrusion system must be a 6-axis robot to allow the production of profiles in the X-Y-Z direction. This will make the process more economically advantageous. The robot head needs a minimum working space of 1.5 meter from the 0-center and should have a minimum effective capacity of 30 kg. This will allow the production of high tolerance extruded profiles onto the substrate.

RANGE OF SUBSTRATES - Any type of substrate can be used with this process providing it can withstand the thermal and mechanical constraints of the robotic extrusion system (210°C). Reinforced polypropylene or specifically modified polyamides are the materials of choice, since these materials will easily bond to the TPV melt by heat welding.

Metal substrates are also well suited due to their rigidity. Bonding of the TPV profiles can be achieved by mechanical locking when the metal has been punched or perforated .

Preheating is recommended for solid metallic or non-polyolefinic surfaces, as well as the application of an adhesive, to achieve a strong bond between the substrate and the TPV profile.

Robotic extrusion onto glass has been well developed with this process. Prototypes using clip-in and pop-out glazing systems have been achieved [1]. The proprietary technology for robotic glazing systems will be handled by Sekurit Saint-Gobain Deutschland GmbH & Co. K.G. and Gepoc Verfahrenstechnik GmbH.

A VARIETY OF APPLICATIONS - The robotic extrusion system is very versatile. Only the extrusion die, and occasionally the support mold, have to be changed when changing parts. This provides a significant economic advantage over dual-injection molding, as the investment for an extrusion die and support mold is only a fraction of that needed for a two-component injection molded system. The time to change over is also significantly reduced.

Hollow or multi-cavity profiles can be produced by the robotic extrusion technology. This is very difficult or impossible via 2-component injection molding. The hollow complex profiles provide a superior performance and improved long-term sealability versus flat sealing strips produced by the injection molding process, even though both use TPV as the sealing member.

The first commercial application produced by the robotic extrusion system processing method was a belly-pan seal. This belly pan is used on a luxury German car and was commercialized by POLYNORM Roosendaal B.V., Automotive Division, in the Netherlands. Other potential applications include:
- engine encapsulation parts
- sunroof profiles
- gaskets in hard/soft combinations
- edge protection for metal parts
- seals in complex lighting systems
- seals in glazing systems.

SUMMARY

Robotic extrusion of TPV is an innovative technology for complex parts development in hard/soft combinations with the unique possibility to produce three-dimensional hollow sealing profiles.

Sekurit Saint-Gobain Group is the sole global producer of robotic extrusion. Advanced Elastomer Systems NV/SA has a license for the development of robotic extrusion of TPV onto non-glass substrates. Gepoc Verfahrenstechnik GmbH designs and develops turnkey projects and equipment for fully integrated robotic extrusion systems. Gepoc is a part of Sekurit Saint-Gobain.

Many other new applications using this unique and highly performing sealing technology are presently under development in automotive, construction, applicances and other markets. Potential non-automotive applications include appliance door seals and construction gaskets.

REFERENCE

R. Kötte and D. Witt, "Neue Möglichkeiten für einbaufertige Scheibenmodule-Fahrzeugverglasung," Expert Verlag, Rennigen 1995.

Santoprene® is a Registered Trademark of Monsanto Company, licensed to Advanced Elastomer Systems, L.P.

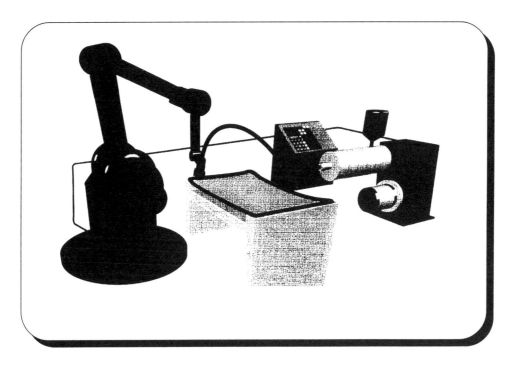

Fig. 1: Schematic of robotic extrusion system.

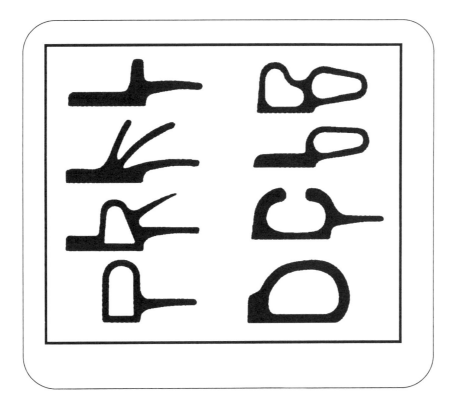

Fig. 2: A variety of profiles can be extruded by the robotic extrusion system.

970666

What's New in Plastics Injection Molding Processes for Automotive Applications: An Update

Peter F. Grelle and Kenneth A. Kerouac
Dow Plastics

ABSTRACT

Over the last ten years, the plastics industry has been under pressure by many industries, such as automotive, to resolve issues from an application point of view, such as value engineering, part quality, and time to market.

Value engineering programs have been a major thrust for the last several years in many industries. These programs have taken the form of low cost materials, systems integration, part weight reduction, and lower fabrication costs. The automotive industry, forced by foreign competition during the 1980s, has also led the way in providing an emphasis toward improved part quality resulting in longer part life cycles. In addition, automotive producers are shortening their design engineering phase which has caused the plastics industry to find methods to more rapidly move technology from research and development to end-use applications.

This paper will review some new process techniques that are answering the demand of the automotive plastics industry for lower cost and faster time to market. This paper will review Pulsed Cooling and Induction Heating for Mold Temperature Control, Multi-Live Feed Molding, Lamellar Injection Molding, Injection-Compression Molding, Lost Core Molding, the Maus-Galic Process, and Pressurized Sealed Cavity Injection Molding.

PULSED COOLING AND INDUCTION HEATING FOR MOLD TEMPERATURE CONTROL

In a conventional injection molding process with a continuous flow of coolant through the mold, injection of the polymer takes place at what is, from a thermal standpoint, the worst moment in the cycle for injection. The mold is at its coldest point in the cycle after cooling and ejecting the part and having remained open to the air momentarily before closing the next shot.

With pulsed cooling temperature control, coolant flow does not occur until the end of the injection stage, when a signal is sent to a series of solenoids that open the valves to flush cold water through the mold. The valves are closed when probes in the mold steel or in the water line itself send a signal to the controller that the desired set point has been reached. Coolant flow is then halted until the end of injection of the next shot.

For higher temperature conditions, particularly those requiring hot oil mold heating, induction coils may be employed to provide background heating prior to polymer injection. The coils are inserted into the slots in each half of the mold and, rather than heating the mold steel directly, turn the mold itself into a heater via the induction effect. The efficiency of induction heating depends on the thermal resistivity of the steel.

These modes of temperature control have a number of potential benefits. Molds can be filled under lower stress conditions, resulting in parts with

131

better dimensional stability and lower birefringence in clear parts. A more uniform temperature gradient across the mold can contribute to more uniform shrinkage and crystallinity formation, leading to reduced warpage and distortion and in some cases reduced cycle time as well. More uniform temperature gradients also promote improved aesthetics, including reduced gloss gradients. The use of induction coils may provide a cleaner, more energy efficient alternative to hot oil temperature control.

Potential applications may include transparent parts such as cluster lenses, or unpainted parts such as interior trim components targeted for non-painted, molded-in color aesthetics. Center gated parts that are usually prone to being hotter in the center can be molded under more uniform temperature conditions with a possible reduction in cycle time. Large panels, which may tend to vary more in shrinkage or crystallinity as a function of flow length can now be molded to more uniform conditions across the cavity.

MULTI-LIVE FEED MOLDING

In 1992, a process was introduced in the United States that was developed in the United Kingdom for the elimination of weld lines found in many plastic injected molded parts. Later. other advantages were found utilizing this process, referred to as Multi-Live Feed Molding. With the use of equipment attached to the machine at the nozzle/mold interface, the process creates an action that moves the melt inside a cavity which increases the melt temperature at the end of fill. Figure# 1 illustrates the three steps involved in the multi-live feed molding process.

Advantages of multi-live feed molding include:

1. Elimination of weld or knit lines.

2. Elimination of sink marks and warpage due to improved part packing.

3. Improved part dimensional stability.

4. Reduction of internal part stresses.

5. Improved molding window, and increased tool design flexibility.

6. Controlled fiber reinforcement orientation for reinforced materials.

A disadvantage of the multi-live feed molding process is that a license needs to be bought to use the process, which include equipment and installation. Equipment, however, is not complicated.

The equipment used involves three components: a processing head, a hydraulic pump, and a controller. This equipment is attached at the end of the barrel and consists of two cylinders that are controlled hydraulically, and split up the melt stream.

The process functions as follows:,

1. The mold cavity is filled to about 95% of fill.

2. When transition occurs at the holding phase of the injection cycle, the hydraulic cylinders begin to move out of phase causing the melt in the cavity to move back and forth creating heat, which eliminates weld lines, and packs out the parts eliminating sink marks.

3. In the next step, the cylinders move together in phase to pack out the part.

Studies performed by Grossman, Malloy, and Gardner in 1993 show how multi-live feed molding has improved weldline strength in polypropylene, liquid crystal polymer (LCP), polycarbonate, and improved properties in glass-filled nylon due to fiber orientation. Also, this study shows an example of how multi-live feed molding reduced reject rates and reduced finishing costs for eyeglass frames. Another application where multi-live feed molding showed major improvements was in television and video cassette recorder remote controls, where due to elimination of weld lines, secondary finishing costs were reduced dramatically.

LAMELLAR INJECTION MOLDING

Lamellar Injection Molding, a process developed by the Dow Chemical Company, combines coextrusion and injection molding to create a micron scale layered blend morphology in complex parts. As shown in Figure #2, two to three layers of plastic material are extruded separately, and later are combined with a 3-5 layer feedblock with multipliers to form a melt stream with hundreds of layers. Property enhancements as a result of lamellar morphology can equal those of multi-layer coextrusion and coinjection technology. The following describes how lamellar injection molding works.

First, two injection cylinders are used to generate individual melt streams with two components. The individual melt streams are then combined in a feedblock to arrange a three layer structure. The combined stream passes through a series of layer multipliers which repeatedly subdivide and stack the layers to increase the number and reduce the thickness. The melt stream passes through a standard injection nozzle to fill a mold cavity. Figure # shows a diagram of the lamellar injection molding process.

Adhesive materials and resin compatibilizing agents can be used to bond non-adhering polymers. Possible applications of this process in automotive applications include injection molding of interior trim and instrument panels where more than one material is used.

INJECTION-COMPRESSION MOLDING

Injection-compression molding is a process that combines the fast cycles of injection molding with the low pressure, low stress conditions of compression molding. The polymer is injected into an expanded cavity that eventually closes to the actual dimensions of the part. The compression action allows a more even pressure distribution across the surface of the part rather than relying on pressure transfer from the screw to the cavity. Figure #3 shows the sequence in which injection-compression molding operates.

The injection-compression process is characterized by three major variants:

1. *Method* (Clamp motion vs in-mold actuation)

2. *Sequencing* (Simultaneous, where compression takes place as the polymer is injected) vs

sequential, where compression follows the injection)

3. *Mold Gap* which dictates the amount of cavity expansion and is driven primarily by the application (small for optical lenses vs large for in-mold decorating).

Benefits of the technique include the following;

1. Reductions in molding pressures and clamp tonnage.

2. Reduced molded -in stresses leading to reduced birefringence and better dimensional stability.

3. Ability to pack the part after gate freeze-off.

Limitations of injection-compression molding include:

1. Restriction of geometry to relatively flat and simple shapes.

2. Potential for halo formation depending on the method used.

3. Possibility of expensive tooling and machine modification considerations.

Ideal characteristics for injection-compression parts include center-gating, few 3-D details such as deep bosses and ribs, and a fairly symmetrical fill pattern. The process can lend itself well to interior trim panels, cluster lenses, wheelcovers, glove box doors, and other potential applications including thin-wall parts, and in-mold decorated components.

LOST CORE MOLDING TECHNOLOGY

Lost core molding technology has started being looked at by a several manufacturers of automotive parts in the United States in recent years. One of the first uses of this technology was in the United Kingdom in the manufacture of intake manifolds for Ford Europe, where a thermoset polymer was used.

Advantages of this process include:

1. Reduction in part weight.

2. Parts consolidation.

3. Increased ability to make parts ready to assemble.

4. Reduction in overall manufacturing costs.

5. Elimination of machining of parts.

6. Capability to make some very complex parts.

7. Improved smooth surfaces causing a decrease in gas flow resistance.

8. Reduced noise.

9. Ability to make deep holes with little or no tapers.

Lost core molding technology involves six different steps, as shown in Figure #4:

1. First, a metal is fabricated or cast from an alloy, specifically Tin-Bismuth, in a tool at a melt temperature of 138 C.

2. The core is then removed from the mold onto a cooling conveyer which cools the system without breaking the surface.

3. The core is then placed into an injection molding machine with a vertical clamp and rotary table, either manually or via robotics.

4. The core is then melted out using inductive or thermal melt out techniques.

5. After plastic parts are removed from the mold, parts are cleaned with water at 60 C.

6. Parts then go into final assembly.

A number of applications currently use lost core molding technology. These include air intake manifolds, pump impellers and housings, tennis racquets, and hot water heating pumps.

MAUS-GALIC PROCESS

A U.S. patent by Steven Maus and George Galic granted in 1994 describes a technique for fabricating optical disks and lenses. Mold surfaces are heated using circulating heat transfer fluids supplied by a hot side reservoir to a very high temperature to prevent the plastic material in the mold from skinning or solidifying. Next, this mold surface is rapidly cooled using circulating heat transfer fluids supplied from a cold side reservoir. Thus, the molding cycle consists of a heating phase, where the mold surface is raised by the hot reservoir fluid to a point above the melt or glass transition temperature of the plastic material, and a cooling phase where the mold surface temperature is lowered to a point below the melt or glass transition temperature of the plastic material. The larger the difference in the hot and cool temperatures, the faster the molding cycle. Figure #5 illustrates a schematic drawing of the Maus-Galic Process.

This process provides parts with low internal stresses and low birefringence. Possible applications for this process are in automotive headlamps, tail-lights, and transparent instrument cluster enclosures.

PRESSURIZED SEALED CAVITY INJECTION MOLDING

Milko Guergov of M&C Advanced Processes patented a process in 1995 that converts an injection molding machine into a pneumatic system in communication with a sealed mold cavity. This process is found to reduce cycle time and part weight, improve surface quality, reduce warpage, surface stresses and sinks, and enhance part design capability. The following describes how the pressurized sealed cavity injection molding process operates.

The mold cavity and melt are pressurized, with single loop programmable controller establishing and maintaining a substantially constant pressure differential between the air pressure in the cavity and the melt pressure throughout injection.

Electronic signals are provided by pressure transducers in the mold cavity and barrel to pressure controllers, which derive a single process variable sent to the programmable logic controller. These signals adjust the injection pressure. Pressure development is scanned every 2 msec. with a single process variable. This variable represents the static pressure of the melt in the cavity, based on several factors. The increased static pressure of the melt front causes earlier contact between the melt, and the walls of the mold, drastically improving cooling. Figure #6 shows the method and process control for performing injection molding in a pressurized cavity.

Benefits found from this process include:

1. Reduced cycle time of 20%.

2. Reduced rejects due to less scrap due to improved control of shrink and warp.

3. Reduced clamp tonnages of 20-30%.

4. Reduced injection pressures of up to 40%.

Also, for structural foamed parts, weight reductions of up to 25-30% are achievable in comparison to 5% found in gas counterpressure structural foam parts. Improved surface aesthetics over conventional low pressure structural foam processes are found.

Applications for the pressurized sealed cavity injection molding technology include structural instrument panel components, interior trim, and exterior trim parts.

SUMMARY

The new processes discussed in this paper show potential in answering the needs of the automotive industry for lower cost solutions, improved quality, and faster time to market.

Work done thus far in lost core molding has begun to provide part integration in under hood applications. Lamellar Injection Molding offers the same potential to achieve lower part and assembly costs via part integration. Multi-Live Feed Injection Molding, Pulsed Cooling and Induction Heating for Mold Temperature Control, Injection-Compression Molding, the Maus-Galic Process, and Pressurized Sealed Cavity Molding technologies offer opportunities in part quality improvement and reduced costs from cycle time reduction.

Challenges in making plastic automotive components over the next few years will prove out

how viable these technologies are, and how new technology will continue to answer the questions of how to reduce costs, improve quality, and how to get new plastic automotive products rapidly to market.

ACKNOWLEDGMENTS

The authors would like to acknowledge the following people and companies for their contributions in the preparation of this paper;
Donn Seres, Injection Molding Industries
Elliot Grossman, Scortec, British Technology Group
Milko Guergov, M&C Advanced Processes

NOTICE: The information herein is provided in good faith, but no warranty, expressed or implied, is given. Nor freedom from any patent owned by the Dow Chemical Company, or any party to be inferred

REFERENCES

1. *"SCORIM Goes Commercial,"* Injection Molding Magazine, June 1995, pp. 74.

2. Malloy, R., *"Improving Weld Line Strengths Using a Multi-Live Feed Injection Molding Process,"* Proceedings from the 1993 SPE RETEC , Rochester, N.Y., pp. w-1.

3. Grossman, E., *"SCORIM Principles, Capabilities, and Applications,"* Proceedings from the 23rd Annual SPI Structural Plastics Conference, Boston, Ma., April, 1995, pp. 153.

4. Barger, M.A., et al, *"Lamellar Injection Molding Process for Multiphase Polymer Systems,"* Proceedings from the 51st Annual SPE Annual Technical Conference (ANTEC), New Orleans, La., April, 1993, pp. 544

5. Moore, S., *"Injection-Compression Molding Possible on Standard Machines,"* Modern Plastics , December, 1995, pp. 23.

6. Ogando, J., *"In-Mold Textile Laminating Give Boost to Injection-Compression,"* Plastics Technology, April, 1996, pp. 17-19

7. Smock, D., *"Want to Reduce Material Costs? Take a Look at ICM,"* Plastics World, September, 1995, pp. 31-39.

8. Tajima, H., *"The Application of Automotive Parts Having Skin Substrate Structure with Injection-Compression Molding Process,"* SAE Paper #950563, Presented at the 1994 SAE Conference, Detroit, Mi., February, 1994

9. Stevenson,James F., et al, *Innovation in Polymer Processing-Molding*, Hanser Publishers, New York, 1996, Pg. 358

10. *"The Latest Wrinkles in Lost-Core Molding,,"* Injection Molding Magazine, Nov. 1995, pg. 90.

11. Maus, S.M., et al, *U.S. Patent No. 5,376,317.*

12. Guergov, M., *U.S. Patent No. 5,441,680.*

13. Galli. E., *"Pressurized Sealed-Cavity Molding,"* Injection Molding Magazine, July, 1996, pp.45.

BIOGRAPHY

Peter F. Grelle is a Development Leader in the Automotive Product and Technical Development Group of the Dow Chemical Company, Detroit, Michigan. He joined Dow in 1989 after working with the Monsanto Company, the Winchester Group of Olin Corporation, and Wellman Inc., Plastics Division. Peter received his BS in Plastics Technology from Lowell Technological Institute in 1974, and MS in Plastics Engineering from the University of Massachusetts at Lowell in 1980. He holds four U.S. and international patents in plastics product design, and has authored over 20 publications in the areas of structural foam plastics, recycling, plastics materials, part design, and plastics process technology. Peter is Vice-Chairman of the Society of Plastics Engineers Injection Molding Division Board of Directors, and Program Chairman of the 1997 SPI Structural Plastics Conference.

Kenneth A. Kerouac is a Senior Development Engineer with the Applied Fabrication Technology (AFT) Group in the Technical Service and Development Group of the Dow Chemical Company, Midland, Michigan. Ken joined Dow in 1987 after receiving his BS in Plastics Engineering from the University of Massachusetts at Lowell. He worked in the Automotive TS&D Group servicing customers at OEM and Tier 1 levels before assuming his current position in 1994. In his role with the AFT Group, he is responsible for injection molding process development and customer support with special emphasis on gas assisted molding. He is currently an officer on the Mid-Michigan section of the SPE, and a member of the Injection Molding Division.

Out-of Phase Oscillation
(Fill)

In-Phase Oscillation
(Pack)

Holding Phase

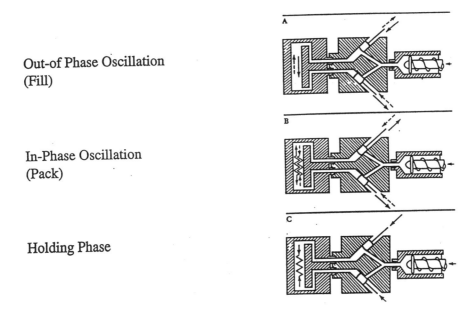

Figure 1. Sequence of Operations- Multi-Live Feed Molding (Ref.#3)

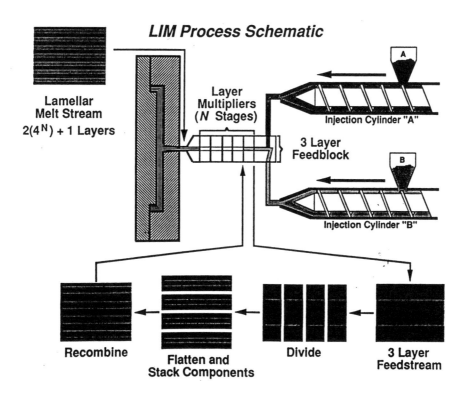

Figure 2. Schematic Drawing of the Lamellar Injection Molding Process

The Injection - Compression Process

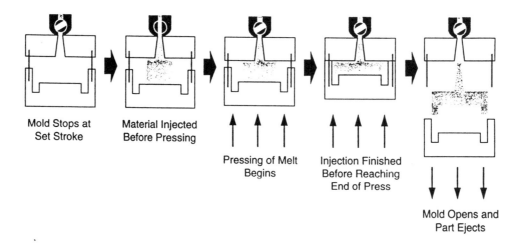

Mold Stops at Set Stroke

Material Injected Before Pressing

Pressing of Melt Begins

Injection Finished Before Reaching End of Press

Mold Opens and Part Ejects

Figure 3. The Injection-Compression Molding Process (Ref.# 9)

The Lost Core Molding Process

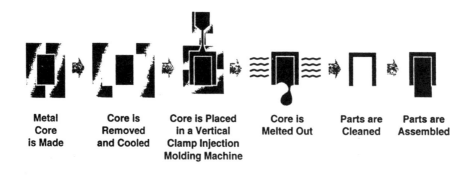

Metal Core is Made

Core is Removed and Cooled

Core is Placed in a Vertical Clamp Injection Molding Machine

Core is Melted Out

Parts are Cleaned

Parts are Assembled

Figure 4. The Lost Core Molding Process

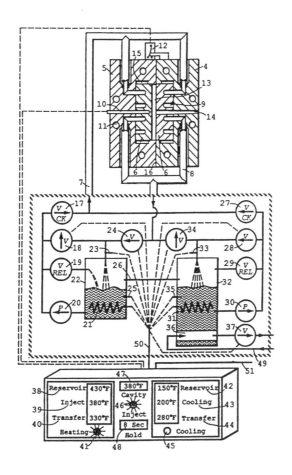

Figure 5. Schematic Drawing of the Maus-Galic Process (Ref.# 11)

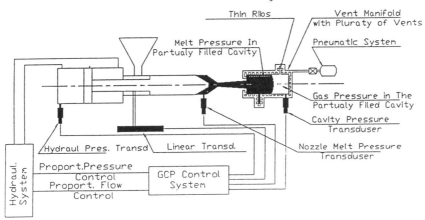

Figure 6. Method and Process Control for Injection Molding in a Pre-Pressurized Cavity.

Filling a Specific Shaped Cavity with a Thermoplastic Polymer by Injection Molding: Relations with Mechanical Properties

Geraldine Benoit-Cervantes
VALEO Wiper Systems

[handwritten margin notes:]
↑ strength to weight ratio
· stiffness to weight ratio
creep resistance
– use chopped fiber as reinforcement

ABSTRACT

During injection molding of thermoplastics the filling depends on the material's rheological properties, on the characteristics of the mold and also on the process parameters. Thanks to the elaboration of short shots, it is possible to reconstruct the main successive steps of the filling and to know the advancing melt flow. The choice of specific cavities and particular injection gates allow for filling to be studied in many different cases. The disposition of barriers inside the cavities gives opportunity to orient the flow.

Experimental studies consider the injection of polyester and polyamide unfilled and reinforced with short glass fibres. Original results in terms of filling are shown on images. We compare experimental fillings with theoretical fillings obtained with a rheological simulation software. Good agreement is proved for unfilled materials. For reinforced materials results diverge because jetting observed on the short shots can not be taken into account during simulation.

The regime of melt flow entering the cavity has an important influence on the structure, properties and appearance of injection molded parts. That is why correlation between filling and mechanical properties are examined thanks to ultrasonic measurements of modulus. A study in terms of anisotropic properties is investigated.

INTRODUCTION

There is nowadays a growing use of reinforced composites with thermoplastics polymers in demanding applications because higher properties are obtained while keeping the advantages of mass production through injection molding.

The importance of fiber-filled thermoplastics has experienced a major growth in recent years. This is understandable because of the superior mechanical and thermal properties of the composites. The advantage of fiber-filled materials arises from the fact that these are anisotropic, and hence their mechanical and physical properties are also anisotropic; the composite is stronger along the direction of the orientation of fibers, and weaker along the transverse direction. Several reviews have appeared on this subject [1,2,3].

Injection molding is probably the most widespread and economical of plastic processing operations. There have only been few experimental studies of the way in which molds fill. The pioneering study by Spencer and Gilmore [4] visualized the filling of an end-gated disk mold by polystyrene melts. Later flow visualization studies of injection molding have been reported by Oda et al. [5], Chan et al. [6] and White and Dietz [7].

One of the most important problem in injection molding short-fiber-reinforced materials is the eventual orientation of the fibers in the part. The use of glass fibers could lead to a particular filling of the cavity during injection molding. It is usual to observe the jetting phenomena for example.

In this work, we put the focus on the strong relation existing between molding process and mechanical properties of a plastic part. Our purpose is to carry out an experimental study of flow patterns during injection molding. We will consider different kind of materials, cavities and injection gate sections. Filling is studied thanks to the use of short shots. The influence of flow on fiber orientation is observed with a Scanning Electron Microscope. Finally we compare our experimental observations with results coming from a filling simulation software.

MATERIALS

The materials used for this work were in a pellet form 2 mm in diameter and 3 mm long. The materials studied were polyamide (PA) and polybutylene terephtalate (PBT) with and without short-glass-fiber-reinforcement, which were kindly supplied by a huge chemical group. All of the materials are commercial grades of thermoplastics. The nominal weight fraction of fibers is Mf = 0.30. The measure of Mf is obtained after burning off the resin. The fiber diameter is about 10μm and a fiber length distribution analysis leads to a nominal value of 300 μm. The various materials and their designations are summarized in Table I. PA and PBT have a glass transition temperature of about 50~60°C. These polymers exhibit respectively a crystalline melting transition of about 260°C and 220°C.

Table I: *Thermoplastic Materials Investigated*

Sample	Polymer Type	Polymer .designation	Glass fiber amount in weight %	Young Modulus (MPa)	Density
1	Polybutylène Terephtalate	PBT	0	2600	1.30
2		G.F PBT	30	8500	1.53
3	Polyamide	PA 66	0	3000	1.14
4		G.F PA 66	30	8500	1.37

Only the PBT that contains fibers is rheologically characterized. The extrusion of polymer melts was made using a Göttfert 2002 capillary rheometer. A series of dies of diameter 1 mm and L/Ds of 10, 20 and 30 were used. All experiments were carried out at 260°C.

The total pressure drop may be expressed as the sum of a capillary and an «ends» (entrance plus exit) pressure loss. The «ends» pressure losses were determined from the intercept of a Bagley plot using Equations 1a and 1b. The apparent shear rate at the capillary die wall $\dot{\gamma}_w$ is given by equation 2.

$$P_{total} = \Delta P_{cap} + \Delta P_{ends} \qquad \text{Eq.1a}$$

$$P_{total} = 4.\sigma_w.L/D + \Delta P_{ends} \qquad \text{Eq.1b}$$

$$\dot{\gamma}_w = \frac{32 \times Q}{\prod \times D^3} \qquad \text{Eq. 2}$$

The viscosity function of the polymer melt is shown in Figure 1. More details concerning the experiments are given in the mechanical thesis [8].

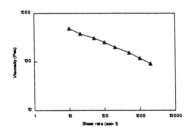

Figure 1: *Viscosity-Shear rate data for G.F PBT. T = 260 °C, D=1 mm, L=10mm.*

THE SAMPLES

TENSILE SPECIMEN- The geometry of the tensile specimen is specified on Figure 2. Three molds containing different cavities allow us to study tensile specimens with different gates. We study pinpoint and large section gates. All the specimen are summarized in Figure 3.

Figure 2: *Flat Tensile specimen (NF-T 51001).*

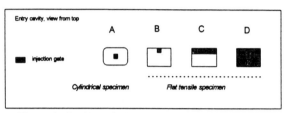

Figure 3: *Position of injection gate on tensile specimen.*

FATIGUE SPECIMEN- This kind of specimen presents characteristics that are very interesting for the study of flow. The thickness is constant, the injection gate is very small compared to section S and the width is changing along the x direction. The specimen is shown on Figure 4.

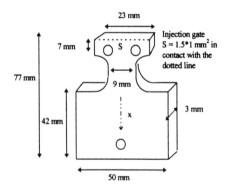

Figure 4: *Fatigue specimen (ASTM n° D-1708).*

One of the molds is designed to give the opportunity to include barriers inside the cavity of the fatigue specimen. The barriers we studied are shown on Figure 5. Barrier n° 1a, 1b and 4 exist on all the fatigue specimen as summarized on Table II. Barriers placed on line with the injection gate can greatly modify the flow patterns.

Oda *et al.* [2] studied several type of mold including barriers. They observed weld lines or flow marks in the final molded part, which correspond to the region where jetting occurs. They only considered plastics without fibers.

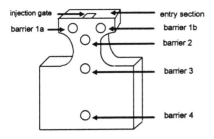

Figure 5: *Position of barriers in the fatigue specimen.*

All the specimens were molded on a Demag and a Boy injection molding machine (respectively, models D60-182 and 50M) in an ASTM test mold. The screw diameter is 32 mm. The mold heating or cooling was done by water circulation through the mold cavity. The mold temperature was monitored by a digital temperature indicator. It is maintained at 80°C for both materials. The melt plastic is maintained at 270°C for the PBT and 300°C for the PA.

The polymers were dried in a vacuum oven before molding per the manufacturers' recommendations. The predrying of pellets is particularly important for PBT and PA, to prevent hydrolytic degradation in melt processing. A drying cycle of 120°C/4h was used.

All the specimens were molded only after the machine had attained steady state with respect to the preset melt and temperature. Specimens with and without barriers were molded under identical machine conditions.

Table II: *Characteristics of molded specimens.*

Sample	Specimen type	Gate section (mm²)	Barrier	Material	Entry section (mm²)
A	Tensile	Pinpoint 2*1	No	G.F PBT	6*5
B		Pinpoint 3*1.5	No		18*3
C		Large 20*1.5	No		20*3.5
D		Large 20*4	No		20*4
E	Fatigue	Pinpoint 1.5*1	No	G.F PBT, PA, G.F PA	23*3
F			n*2,	G.F PBT	
G			n*3		

OBSERVATION OF FILLING

SHORT SHOTS- When the part is ejected from the mold it is very difficult to know how the cavity filled during the plastic melt injection. We hence created some short shots by decreasing the melt volume necessary for a complete part.

We start injecting a low volume of melt material. We increase the volume step by step until the cavity is full. For each value of melt volume, 5 experiments are made in exactly the same conditions to see if the process

is reproducible. We observe a good repeat of the filling phenomena in all cases of volume, whether the material is filled or not.

After each shot corresponding to a certain amount of material, we cool the mold before ejecting the part. We observe the "short shots" directly after the ejection. It is a simple way to rebuild the different steps of filling that occurs inside the mold. The technique is quite easy to investigate because the variation of volume is made by modifying the displacement of the piston thanks to a ruler on the injection molding machine.

SCANNING ELECTRON MICROSCOPE- Electron micrographs are made using a scanning electron microscope type JSM 5800 low vacuum from Jeol. It allows us to study the orientation of fibers on a surface whether the fiber shape appears through the observation like figure 6 shows. If fibers are oriented along the flow direction, they appear like rod on the part surface while they appear like circles in a transversal section of the part.

This kind of microscopy gives a good contrast between matrix and glass fibers without any preliminary treatment. Also the metallographic polishing is not necessary, fibers appear in white while the matrix is black. Because fibers are submerged in the matrix, we can know the position of flows during the filling by studying the position and the orientation of fibers in specific location of the part after molding.

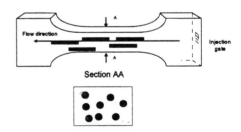

Figure 6: *Appearance of fiber through microscope. (Fibers appear in dark)*

MECHANICAL MEASUREMENTS

Two methods were used to measure the Young modulus. A tensometer with extensometer grips was used for tensile testing on large specimens.

A linear behavior was observed in the initial part of the strain/stress curve and the Young modulus was consequently derived in the standard manner. The geometry of the specimen cut in an injected fatigue specimen is given on Figure 7.

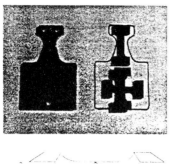

Figure 7: *Tensile specimen for classical characterization.*

Modulus can also be measured using an ultrasonic technique. The method is based on the fact that ultrasonic wave velocity depends on the material in which it goes through. The more the material is rigid, the more the velocity wave is high.

Two ultrasonic transducers are fixed on opposite faces of the test sample, one being the emitter while the other is the receptor. A quartz oscillator is used to emit the longitudinal wave. Principle of the technique is summarized on Figure 8 and detailed elsewhere [9]. By measuring the longitudinal and transverse wave velocity and knowing the specific gravity ρ, we obtained the E modulus thanks to equations 3, 4a and 4b.

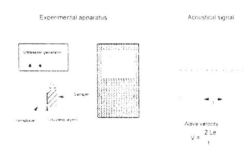

Figure 8: *Principle of Young modulus measurement with ultrasonic waves.*

The advantages of the technique are first the rapidity of experiment and second the opportunity to study small specimens to determine located modulus for the study of anisotropy. Small geometry is shown on Figure 9: the dimension of the specimen is 2*5 mm in plane xy while the thickness is 3 mm.

Figure 9: *Tensile specimen for ultrasonic characterization. (Specimen are delimited in white lines)*

$$\mu = \frac{v_L^2 - 2v_T^2}{2 \times \left(v_L^2 - v_T^2\right)} \qquad \text{Eq. 3}$$

$$v_L^2 = \frac{E}{\rho} \times \frac{1-\mu}{(1+\mu) \times (1-2\mu)} \qquad \text{E q. 4 a}$$

$$v_T^2 = \frac{E}{2\rho \times (1+\mu)} \qquad \text{E q. 4 b}$$

STUDY OF FILLING

RESULTS- The fillings obtained with the tensile tests A, B C and D are shown on figure 10, 11, 12 and 13. The cavities fill step by step as the short shots proved. Velocity injection is the same in all cases.

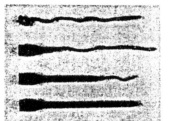

Figure 10: *Polymer melt filling specimen A.*

Figure 11: *Polymer melt filling specimen B.*

Figure 12: *Polymer melt filling specimen C*

Figure 13: *Polymer melt filling specimen D.*

Thanks to the short shorts we study the filling of the cavity included barriers. The pictures called (a) represent the specimen without barrier, considered as the reference specimen. The pictures called (b) and (c) contain respectively a barrier close and far from the injection gate. The 6 figures following show 5 steps of filling before complete filling (see Fig.19).

Figure 14: *Filling for 21% of the total weigths of the part.*

Figure 15: *Filling for 38% of the total weight of the part.*

Figure 16: *Filling for 49% of the total weight of the part.*

Figure 17: *Filling for 66% of the total weight of the part*

Figure 18: *Filling for 79% of the total weight of the part.*

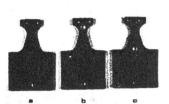

Figure 19: *Filling for 100% of the total weight of the part*

Whether the matrix contains glass fibers or not, the flow patterns during the cavity filling is not the same. Figure 20 shows 3 steps of filling obtained with these two kind of materials.

Figure 20: *Influence of fibers on 3 steps of filling.*

DISCUSSION

FLOW DURING FILLINGS- The first parameter we studied is the injection gate section. Whatever the position of the small injection gate is, the jetting phenomena is observed (see Figures 14 and 15). The melt enters in the cavity like a jet with a high kinetic energy. The filling starts with jetting and follows with a simple filling as soon as the jet strikes through an obstacle, which is here the bottom wall of the cavity. When the material gets through the injection gate it undergoes a strong shear. The temperature of the mold is very low compared to that of the material. Consequently the jet freezes as soon as it enters in the cavity. After the first step of filling as the melt material enters in the cavity the jet is swallowed by the simple filling.

In the case of a larger section injection gate (see sample C), we observe some kind of melt waves due to the limiting advance of the melt front because there is only one free wall (see Figure 16). When the section is decreasing in the middle of the sample the material is piling up and generates the presence of a simple filling. When the section of the injection gate is as large as the entering section of the sample, only the simple filling is present. The material is in contact with 4 walls as soon as it goes through the gate (see Fig.17).

Results we obtained during our experiments show that the section of the injection gate is an important parameter to predict the flow shape. Spencer and

Gilmore [4] observed two types of flow: one involving a uniformly expanding front and a second involving jetting, which they associated with small diameter gates. Some authors [5,6] who studied the jetting made some die swelling measurement after cooling. Melt elasticity would seem to play an important role in determining which type of mold filling exists. It is elastic memory and normal stresses that give rise to the high values of extrudate swell exhibited by polymer melts [10,11].

Chan *et al.* [6] show that extrudate swell decreases with addition of glass fibers (see figure 21). That reduction is due to the addition of particulate solids, it seems a general reason as similar effects have been observed in other systems, e.g., carbon black [12]. The mechanism of this is not well understood. It is in part attributable to the lower proportion of polymer in filled extrudates, but this is insufficient to understand. The mechanism of reduced swell involves the reasons for a general reduction in elastic recovery due to the addition of particulate solids. A reasonable hypothesis is that oriented fibers have little tendency on their own to disorient on exiting from the die. They are too bulky to be influenced by Brownian motion. Their failure to disorient prevents any significant swell. The fibers play an opposite role relative to melt elasticity as they do in steady shear flow.

It is clear that the jetting of the fiber-filled melts is due to the decreased extrudate swell. The presence of barriers along the flow allow us to eliminate the jetting, whether the barrier is far or close to the injection gate. To avoid jetting in injection molding, one must be sure to carefully design the gating so that melt is injected in such a manner as to directly contact an obstacle.

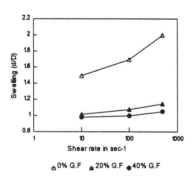

Figure 21: *Influence of glass fiber content on the swelling. PS melt at 180°C, L/D = 40. [3]*

RIGIDITY MEASUREMENT- When we tested the specimens sketched on Figure 7 we measured a stiffness parameter that gives information on the Young modulus of the material resulting from the molding of the part. Results are given in Table 3. The rigidity is quite the same for samples A and C. As the fiber quantity is the same for both materials the difference can only come from a difference of orientation. If the flow pattern have been conventional (see Figure 22), we should have

found the same results for samples A and B. Results proved that the flow can present a jetting phenomena as shown on Figure 20.

Table III: *Effect of fibre orientation on rigidity.*

Specimen G.F PBT	Rigidity parameter $(N/m^3)*10^9$	Breaking load (MPa)
A	195	76
B	162	69
C	182	78

 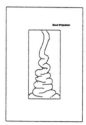

Figure 22: *Filling of a rectangular mold by vertically downward injection; (a) simple uniform molding filling; (b) jetting.*

ULTRASONIC MEASUREMENT- The advantage of this technique is the opportunity to measure local modulus. Also the size of test specimens is very small. That is why we were able to measure Young modulus in different locations of the fatigue test specimen as shown on Figure 23. Results in terms of longitudinal wave velocity in x-direction is given on Figure 24. Modulus value are given in Table IV.

In case of random orientation of fibers we should have found the same modulus for all the samples. As we already have seen with the classical technique Young modulus is higher on Position 1 rather than Positions 6 and 7. From this we can conclude that fibers are oriented in specific directions according to their positions in the molded part.

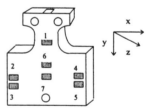

Figure 23: *Location of microspecimen for ultrasonic measurements.*

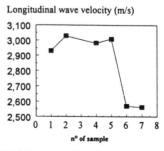

Figure 24: *Influence of location on the wave velocity measured with ultrasonic technique.*

Table IV: *Located modulus measurement in fatigue test specimen.*

Sample	Modulus (MPa)
1	6600
2	6650
3	6500
4	6750
5	6450
6	6300
7	6300

MICROSCOPIC OBSERVATIONS- To confirm our previous conclusions we observe the surface in plane xz of the samples called position 1 and 6. Micrographs are shown on Figure 25 and 26. On Figure 25, fibers appear like uneven circle while on Figure 26 we see mainly rods. These observations mean that fibers are oriented in z direction for all the positions except Positions 6 and 7, where they are oriented in the x direction.

Figure 25: *Scanning electron micrograph of surface xz in location 4 of fatigue specimen.*

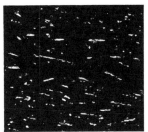

Figure 26: *Scanning electron micrograph of surface xz in location 6 of fatigue specimen.*

SIMULATION OF FILLING

Commercial software are able to simulate filling during the injection molding process. It is very interesting to see if the software can reproduce the particulate filling that occurs with the presence of fibers. We must be aware that the presence of fibers changes the flow patterns and modifies the filling and the orientation of fibers included in the matrix.

Figures 27 and 28 shows 3 steps of filling corresponding to experiments from Figure 20. Correlation between experience and simulation is made in terms of time. Dark areas represent the advancing front. The meshing represent the cavity.

No difference appears when the simulation is made with the reinforced or non-reinforced system although there is a real difference as the experience

testifies. The shapes of the advancing front is the same between calculation and simulation concerning the unfilled material. The jetting we observe during the experience of filling with reinforced material is not reproducible. Calculation considers fountain flow [13] so it is obvious that it cannot show the jetting phenomenon.

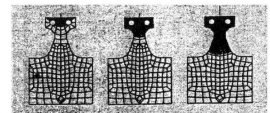

Figure 27: *Theoretical filling of fatigue specimen with PA 66*

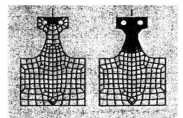

Figure 28: *Theoretical filling of fatigue specimen with PA 66 containig glass fibers*

CONCLUSION

Short shots are a good experimental technique to know the shape of the advancing front during the filling of a cavity. Flow depends on the cavity, the injection gate, the material and molding conditions. The presence of fibres could bring complex flows by influencing fibre orientation inside matrix. Obviously the more intricate the shape, the more complex the flow pattern during the molding process, and hence the more difficult the control of the orientation. Reinforced materials generate specific flow usually called jetting that can be eliminated by the presence of barriers inside the cavity on line with an injection gate.

In an industrial environment, it is necessary to know the real mechanical properties of a part to optimize the design using structural calculation. The difference of properties we can observe between two part geometries molded with the same material could come from a difference of fiber orientation resulting from the molding process. Development cost are high and simulation is a good solution to decrease development time. In the rheology field, filling simulation gives satisfying result for unfilled material. Jetting cannot be observed through simulation.

Molding process requires a good knowledge of material rheology to optimize design and to obtain best properties on the part. Simulation is a good help, but results must be taken cautiously.

REFERENCES

[1] J.C Halpin, J.L Kardos, J. Appl. Phys., Vol.**43**, 5 (1972).

[2] I. Arvanitoyannis and E. Psomiadou, J. Appl .Polym. Sci, **51**, 1883 (1994).

[3] C. Bert and R. A. Kline, Polym. Composites, **6**, 133 (1985).

[4] R. S Spencer, G.D. Gilmore, J. Colloid. Sci, **6**, 118 (1951).

[5] K. Oda, J.L. White, E.S. Clark, Polym. Eng. Sci., **16**, 585 (1976).

[6] Y. Chan, J.L. White, Y. Oyanagi, Polym. Eng. Sci., **18**, 268 (1978).

[7] J.L White, W.Dietz, Polym. Eng. Sci., **19**, 1081 (1979).

[8] G.Benoit-Cervantes, Thesis, University P et M Curie, 1997, France. Rheology of injection molding process applied to a technical part in glass fibre reinforced thermoplastic.

[9] Gilles DeSa, technical work during a training for l'Université de Versailles, 1996.

[10] J.L. White and J.F. Roman, J. Appl. Polym. Sci,**20**, 1005 (1976).

[11] R.S. Spencer, R.E. Dillon, J. Colloid. Sci., **3**, 180 (1948).

[12] J.L. White, J.W. Crowder, J. Appl. Polym. Sci., **18**, 1013 (1974).

[13] Z.Tadmor, J. Appl. Polym.Sci.,**18**, 1753 (1974).

ABBREVIATIONS

M_f = weight fraction of fibre

PA = Polyamide

PBT = Polybutylene Terephtalate

L = round hole die length

D = die diameter

L/D = aspect ratio of die

ΔP_{cap} = pressure in the capillary

ΔP_{ends} = pressure at the end of the die

τW = shear stress at the channel wall

Q = volumetric flow rate

V_L = longitudinal wave velocity

V_T = transversal wave velocity

ρ = specific gravity

E = Young modulus

$\dot{\gamma}_w$ = apparent (or Newtonian-based) shear rate at the wall.

Calibration Procedure for Standardization of SAE J175 Shock Absorbers

Carolyn Wilson and Ed Rosa
American Racing Equipment of Kentucky, Inc.

ABSTRACT

In the design phase of aluminum wheels for passenger cars, the wheel's ability to withstand low speed side impacts with minimal damage inflicted to the wheel is of major concern. There are two side impact test standards available today. The one that appears to better simulate an actual wheel-curb impact situation is the SAE J175-88. Part of the test setup includes a deflection check of elastomeric shock absorbers under specified load. The authors have devised a technique to obtain the data for this calibration from a monotonic load/displacement curve. Curve fitting is followed by intercept calculation and a check against specifications.The specified elastomer deflection range under load dictates the expected dynamic response in the actual test. Therefore, in addition to the SAE recommended natural rubber, the authors also investigated the deflection characteristics of alternative polymeric materials, such as EPDM, neoprene and urethane. The technique used to obtain the data yielded repeatable results, based on replication trials. Polymeric materials of different chemistry but similar Shore A durometer hardness values did not yield the same deflection at intercept.

INTRODUCTION

Passenger car wheels equipped with small tires show an offset of about 25.4 mm between the top of a regular sidewalk curb and the lowest point of the wheel outboard flange. Therefore, wheel-curb impact--side impact-- is an important factor to be taken into consideration during design, qualification, manufacturing process planning and actual production. Even at low speeds the energy involved in side impacts can lead to loss of use due to wheel breakage. So, specialized tests for quality/reliability evaluation of wheel strength under side impact conditions are required in both developmental and production phases . One standardized impact test to assess side impact wheel reliability was published by SAE (SAE J175, issued 1970)[1]. Later a more realistic version was published by ISO (ISO 7141-1981)[2] and was later adopted by SAE (SAE J175, June 1988)[3]. In the original SAE J175 test standard the wheel is mounted on a pedestal at 30° angle with the horizon. A constant weight of 908 kg is connected to a set of load/displacement controlled springs, simulating a typical vehicle suspension system. The springs are supported by a 100 kg striker that contacts the wheel's outboard face first as the weight-springs-striker, suitably guided, is allowed to fall freely from a specified height. After the striker contacts the wheel, the spring system (now under compression) absorbs part of the initial potential energy while decelerating the main weight until load reversal occurs .

In the ISO test, the striker system mass is obtained from an equation based on the wheel design load .The wheel inclination relative to the curb simulating striking mass is a more realistic 13°. The striker edge and wheel flange are offset by 25.4mm, therefore a 170 to 250 mm chordal contact is obtained which well simulates a typical curb impact. The striker-mass system contacts the wheel directly as it is dropped onto the wheel-tire mount from a height of 230mm above the rim. Elastomeric shock absorbers suitably positioned under the pedestal supporting the wheel, dissipate the remaining kinetic energy through dampened oscillatory motion simulating a regular suspension system .

The authors have found that the ISO test is a quick, yet effective tool to assess the quality of hub-spoke junction strength. The dampening characteristics of the elastomeric shock aborbers might affect the resulting behavior of the wheel being impacted. So a program has been initiated to study these shock absorbers in more detail.

In this paper the authors present the following:

1) Propose a new approach to check shock absorbers deflection calibration.

2) Use the new approach to assess the performance of five different elastomeric materials.

MAIN BODY

CALIBRATION TECHNIQUE- Per SAE J175 the 4 shock absorbers supporting the wheel-tire assembly shall deflect in the 6.75-8.25 mm range, when a 1000 kg load is applied to the center of the wheel mounting pedestal. To the best of the authors knowledge, there is no procedure or technique to easily accomplish this task due to time dependent relaxation of the elastomeric shock absorbers.

The authors use a simple 3.6 ton hydraulic jack, centered on the 13° adaptor, to lift the 1000 kg mass, as seen in Figure 1.

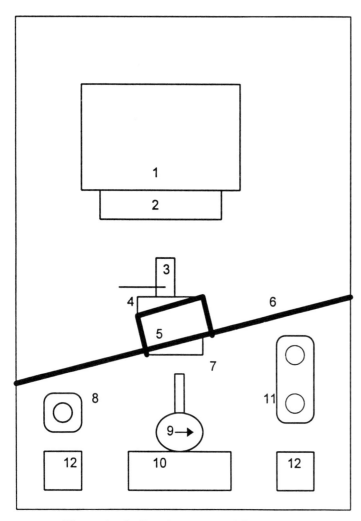

Figure 1 - Calibration set up of SAE-J175 shock absorbers: (1) 1000 kg mass, (2) striker, (3) 3.6

ton hydraulic jack, (4) 13° insert to level jack base, (5) tire-wheel assembly mounting pedestal, (6) 13° base supporting the pedestal, (7) leveling pad for dial indicator plunger contact, (8) hinged bracket supporting the 13° base, (9) dial indicator, (10) dial indicator base, (11) rear hinged bracket, (12) shock absorbers (4 places).

First, the dial indicator is zeroed with the 13° adapter only sitting on the pedestal. Next, the 3.2 kg hydraulic jack is placed and centered on top of the pedestal and the deflection due to its weight, is recorded for future deflection correction, if this deflection is significant. The dial indicator is zeroed again and the 1000 Kg mass-striker is slowly lowered until it is barely touching the top of the hydraulic lifter. The control switch is set to load-cell readout and the initial load-cell value (1000 kg) is recorded. The hydraulic actuator is then manually operated to steadily raise the ram against the striker. One operator does the cranking and the other reads the load. Due to time dependent relaxation, it is important that the load be recorded as soon as a specified deflection is reached. Therefore both operators need to keep constant communication throughout the measuring range. The authors use .508 mm displacement steps. As the elastic potential of the shock absorbers is depleted, the dial indicator displacement reaches a plateau and the measurement is stopped.

The dimensional measurements and ASTM D2240[4], Shore A durometer hardness are obtained for each set of elastomeric materials before the calibration test. The authors do one replication test for each batch of shock absorbers received from the supplier. To obtain the calibration curves, the following operations are performed:

1) Calibration load = Initial load - Load obtained at each dial indicator displacement recorded:

$$CL = 1000 - L_{(x\ displacement\ recorded)} \qquad (1)$$

where   CL = calibration load

L = load recorded when x displacement is reached.

2) Plot Calibration Load- Dial Indicator Displacement pairs and obtain best fit correlation equation. The initial deflection due to jack weight in the authors lab is only .025 mm and is not taken into consideration.

$$CL = A_0 + A_1(x) + A_2(x)^2 + A.... \qquad (2)$$

where:

A_0, A_1, A_2 = Coefficients obtained from best fit correlation equation.

x = recorded displacement under given load before the onset of any time dependent relaxation.

3) Eliminate tail end points in the elastic depletion range to yield $R^2 = .97$ or better.

4) Compare initial and replicate data sets. Statistical techniques can be used if equation coefficients show significant differences.

5) Use numerical methods of root finding to obtain the deflection under 1000 Kg from the equations obtained.

6) Compare intercept obtained with SAE J175 specification (6.75 - 8.25 mm).

MATERIALS AND CHARACTERISTICS - Table 1 shows the materials used in each set of shock absorbers. With the exception of the natural rubber, which was machined from sheet stock, all other materials were molded.

TABLE 1 - Shock Absorber Characteristics

Identification	Material	Shore A Durom.	Diameter mm	Height mm
A1	Neoprene	45	50.7	27.2
A2	Neoprene	45	50.7	27.2
B1	Urethane	42	50.3	26.9
B2	Urethane	42	50.3	26.9
C1	EPDM	40	50.2	26.7
C2	EPDM	40	50.2	26.7
D1	Natural R.	39	50.0	24.9
D2	Natural R.	39	50.0	24.9
E1	Neoprene	50	50.5	* 27.4

*Only one sample of 4 available.

RESULTS-

The data obtained for the Neoprene samples, A1 and A2, resulted in the following equations:

$$\text{Neoprene A1, } CL = 3.76 \, x^2 + 70.84 \, x \quad (3)$$

$$\text{Neoprene A2, } CL = 3.67 \, x^2 + 70.54 \, x \quad (4)$$

Both equations exhibited $R^2 = .991$.

The data obtained for the Urethane samples, B1 and B2, resulted in the following equations:

$$\text{Urethane B1, } CL = 7.96 \, x^2 + 65.48 \, x \quad (5)$$

$$\text{Urethane B2, } CL = 8.37 \, x^2 + 61.60 \, x \quad (6)$$

Both equations exhibited $R^2 = .996$.

The data obtained for the EPDM samples, C1 and C2, yielded the following equations:

$$\text{EPDM C1, } CL = 4.54 \, x^2 + 62.34 \, x \quad (7)$$

$$\text{EPDM C2, } CL = 4.25 \, x^2 + 67.21 \, x \quad (8)$$

Both equations exhibited $R^2 = .995$.

The data obtained for the natural rubber samples, D1 and D2, yielded the following equations:

Natural Rubber D1,

$$CL = 7.34 \, x^2 + 71.88 \, x \quad (9)$$

Natural Rubber D2,

$$CL = 7.87 \, x^2 + 66.50 \, x \quad (10)$$

Both equations exhibited $R^2 = .999$.

The data obtained for the Shore A 50 durometer hardness Neoprene, sample E1, yielded the following equation:

$$CL = 2.61 \, x^2 + 86.7 \, x \quad (11)$$

The correlation coefficient was $R^2 = .998$.

Table 2 shows the equation coefficients and the calculated intercepts at 1000 Kg.

Table 2 - Calibration load equation coefficients and calculated displacement

Material	A2	A1	Calc. Displ-mm	Load kg
Neopr(A1)	3.76	70.84	9.49	1000.1
Neopr(A2)	3.67	70.54	9.41	1000.1
Ureth(B1)	7.96	65.48	7.82	1000.1
Ureth(B2)	8.37	61.60	7.86	1000.1
EPDM(C1)	4.54	62.34	9.49	1000.1
EPDM(C2)	4.25	67.21	9.35	1000.1
Natur(D1)	7.34	71.88	7.76	1000.1
Natur(D2)	7.87	66.50	7.81	1000.1
Neop(E1)	2.61	86.70	9.06	1000.1

The intercepts at 1000 kg obtained from Table 2 were tested against the SAE - J175 specification limits, 6.75 mm -- 8.25 mm. As seen in Table 2, only the Urethane samples and the natural rubber met the specs. Note that the repeatability of the intercepts obtained was good.

An attempt to correlate the Shore A durometer hardness of the samples with the compressive bulk behavior yielded poor results. In fact only the EPDM and the Neoprenes were negatively correlated to their Shore A hardness values.

The first derivatives of the equations obtained:

$$d(CL)/dx = 2 A_2 x + A_1 \qquad (12)$$

where: $d(CL)/dx$ = derivative (kg/mm)

A2, A1 = equation coefficients

were used to obtain the "rate of compression" that takes place at the 7.5 mm displacement.. Urethane and natural rubber both showed $d(CL)/dx$ values in the range 181 to 187 (kg/mm) , whereas the neoprenes, and the EPDM samples exhibited values in the 125 to 130 (kg/mm).

DISCUSSION:

The authors have shown that the technique to obtain the curves and the intercepts yielded fairly repeatable results. It also eliminates the guesswork involved in just applying the 1000 Kg mass on the 13° adapter and quickly trying to read the initial deflection--a method that is probably being used in every test lab performing wheel side impact tests. As seen in Figure 8, materials such as natural rubber and urethane meet the SAE J175 specifications.

Correlation studies to check effects of material hardness, as measured by the Shore A durometer, with the compressive displacement have shown a poor least squares fit, in the hardness range tested. It appears that a change of more than 10 Shore A durometer hardness points is needed to cause a statistically significant change in the bulk compressive behavior.

It was thought that the first derivative dCL/dx of the curves obtained at a given deflection would be a better indicator of the elastomer compressibility . The results apparently show that the composition, and may be the additives added to the materials, control the compression rate. In these preliminary trials the authors could not obtain the expected correlation between material hardness and rate of compression.

CONCLUSIONS:

The following conclusions can be drawn from this work:

1) The technique to obtain the shock absorbers deflection under specified load yielded repeatable results. These appear to be dependent on the polymeric material makeup.

2) Attempts to equate the Shore A durometer hardness of the various materials used to the bulk compressive behavior, as expected, resulted in a negative slope. However from a statistical viewpoint, as measured by R^2 , this correlation was not very strong, perhaps because the hardness range of the samples tested was too narrow.

3) The natural rubber , which is the material of choice in the SAE J175 specifications, met the required deflection. Urethane also met the SAE J175 specified deflection under 1000 kg.

REFERENCES

1) SAE J175, issued 1970, SAE Handbook, Society of Automotive Engineers, Inc., Warrendale, PA, 1990, pp. 31.08-09.

2) ISO 7141 - 1981, International Standard ISO 7141, First Edition- 1981-10-01, UDC 629.113.012.3: 620.178.7.

3) SAE J175, June 1988, SAE Handbook, Society of Automotive Engineers, Inc., Warrendale, PA, 1990, pp. 31.08-09.

4) ASTM D2240 - Test Method for Rubber Properties - Durometer Hardness - ASTM, Philadelphia, PA 19103.

New Thermoplastic Polyesters Designed for Aggressive USCAR Specifications

Suzanne R. Redding and James M. Finan
GE Plastics

ABSTRACT

Thermoplastic polyesters are the materials of choice in a wide variety of applications, including automotive electronics, due to their excellent balance of cost versus performance and their ease of use in complicated designs. As with any material, thermoplastic polyesters do have limitations. Typical polyesters are susceptible to hydrolysis – the breaking of bonds within the polymer chain by water molecules, under certain environmental conditions such as a combination of high temperature and humidity. Upon hydrolysis, the mechanical properties of a typical polyester suffer significant deterioration due to a decrease in molecular weight.

Recent standardization efforts within the automotive industry, under the USCAR banner, have highlighted the need for thermoplastic polyesters that can withstand aggressive temperature and humidity cycling. One company has recently developed a new technology that controls hydrolysis and significantly extends the performance of thermoplastic polyesters. The new hydrolysis-resistant polyesters are cost-effective materials for those applications which must survive the Class III and IV USCAR exposures. This paper will detail the performance and chemistry of the new hydrolysis-resistant polyesters and review their applications within the connector industry.

INTRODUCTION

Polybutylene terephthalate (PBT) is a semi-crystalline thermoplastic polymer formed by a condensation process. Standard PBT is widely available in the marketplace. Each supplier offers a range of grades and blends designed to ensure the most cost-effective, tailored performance. If desired, PBT can easily be modified during the manufacturing process by the addition of impact modifiers, fiberglass and/or minerals. PBT has many advantages over other polymers within the same relative price range, including:

- Outstanding chemical resistance,
- Excellent dimensional stability,
- Low moisture absorption,
- High heat resistance,
- Superior dielectric strength,
- High strength/weight ratio,
- Inherent lubricity, and
- Good surface finish.

This combination of properties and ease of use have effectively made PBT the material of choice in a wide variety of applications.

Thermoplastic polyesters, however, do have limitations. As part of the polyester family, PBT is subject to hydrolysis. The hydrolysis of polyesters has been widely studied and is well documented. Hydrolysis results in chain cleavage, which, with sufficient loss in molecular weight, leads to a loss of mechanical properties. A variety of factors can affect the hydrolytic stability of polyesters, including:

- Molecular weight,
- The presence of end groups,
- Residual polymerization catalyst, and
- Additives (i.e. glass, mineral fillers, flame retardants, etc., which can be a source of instability due to pH changes and contamination).

In general, thermoplastic polyesters have good retention of properties when exposed to water below their glass transition temperature (T_g). For PBT, this is about 50 to 60C. However, at temperatures above the T_g, accelerated hydrolysis may occur.

Recent standardization efforts within the automotive industry and in particular USCAR, have emphasized the need for polyesters that can maintain properties even under very aggressive conditions of high humidity at elevated temperatures – conditions at which hydrolysis would typically occur. The hydrolysis reaction can be either acid or base catalyzed; however, under humid aging conditions, the acid-catalyzed pathway is dominant. The mechanism for acid hydrolysis is represented by the equilibrium below:

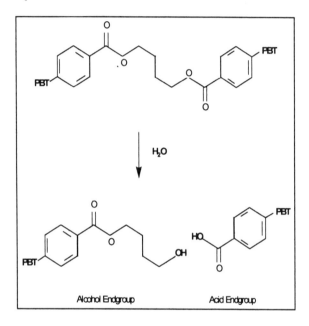

Figure 1: Hydrolysis Reaction

Hydrolysis of PBT by this mechanism is dependent upon the carboxylic acid end-group (CEG) concentration present in the material. CEG concentration is typically measured in milliequivalents per kilogram (meq/kg). In general, the lower the carboxylic acid end-group concentration in a PBT resin, the better its resistance to hydrolytic degradation. Because the hydrolysis mechanism is autocatalytic, increases in acid content can give rise to accelerated degradation. There are several sources for residual CEGs in polyester resins:

- As a direct result of the polymerization process;
- As a by-product of thermal degradation during melt processing; and
- As a consequence of chain cleavage during the hydrolysis reaction.

Understanding and controlling these reactions are critical in stabilizing PBT.

THE DEVELOPMENT OF USCAR

The United States Council for Automotive Research, better known as USCAR, was legally founded as a partnership in 1992 to address concerns regarding the competitiveness of the domestic automotive industry in a global market. The council was chartered to facilitate a cooperative edge to the normally competitive relationship between the Big 3 – Ford, General Motors, and Chrysler – via basic research and development programs in a variety of technological areas or consortium. The consortium are currently focused on areas such as computer modeling and prediction (CAD/CAM), vehicle recycling, electric vehicle development, automotive materials, and electrical wiring components. The individual consortia are comprised of members from each of the Big 3 partners as well as from the general automotive sector including finished parts and materials suppliers.

The Electric Wiring Components Applications Partnership, (EWCAP), was established as one of the consortia in 1994 with a mission similar to that of the parent council, USCAR. EWCAP encourages cooperative research and development including the joint sharing of technologies and resources to develop common electrical connection systems among the Big 3. The goals of EWCAP can be summarized as follows:

- To ensure the competitiveness of the domestic automotive industry in a global market;
- To establish common families of "best-in-class" connection systems; and
- To establish a standard "footprint" for electrical components common to the major partners.

EWCAP develops specifications that can easily be applied to both current and future component designs. The specifications include general requirements such as record retention and reporting procedures, performance requirements for specific components, and standardized test conditions and procedures to cover both the mechanical and electrical functions of the system.

The first EWCAP specification, PF-1, focuses on validating connector and terminal performance. Within the PF-1 specification, terminal types are split into four categories: 1 mm, 1.5 mm, 2.8 mm, and 0.25 in. (6.4 mm).

Four environmental exposures denoted as USCAR classifications I through IV are also called out in the PF-1 specification. In general, the automotive industry recognizes that the underhood environment is very tough on the individual components within the engine compartment due to the presence of a variety of chemicals as well as heat and humidity levels. The classifications were developed in part as an acknowledgment of this fact, as well as to address the growing concern regarding true component functionality and actual lifetime, as well as the potential effects on warranty and/or service issues. The environmental exposures, designed to simulate accelerated end-use aging, include multiple cycles of extreme temperatures from -40 to 155C, with relative humidity levels ranging from 10 to 95%. The environmental conditions of the most aggressive classifications of USCAR – Classes III and IV – are clarified by illustrations shown in Figure 2.

While the EWCAP efforts have driven the standardization of component testing, Ford has also developed a less stringent test, sometimes referred to as the Post Radiator test (also shown in Figure 2) to more closely simulate real-life vehicle conditions. Based on actual test results, Ford's test dictates that the worst-case ambient conditions possible under-the-hood are 49C with 100% relative humidity (RH). As this ambient air passes through the engine compartment, however, the air heats to 93C and then falls to 30% RH. The choice of specifications that a component must meet will effectively drive the final component design as well as the material(s) selection.

HYDROLYSIS-RESISTANT POLYESTERS

The approach to controlling hydrolysis within polyesters used by one company (GE Plastics) is based on modification of the resin with a proprietary stabilization technology during manufacturing. This technology reduces the concentration of carboxylic acid end groups and also offers control of CEG formation during processing and hydrolysis. A new family of hydrolysis (hydro)-resistant polyesters has been produced and commercialized. These materials are able to maintain low carboxyl end-group concentrations for long periods of time under extremely harsh testing conditions as well as in real-life environments for each application.

Initially, commercial development of this technology focused on a high viscosity material for an extrusion application in the wire and cable market. In 1993, the company introduced an unreinforced hydro-resistant PBT for use in loose tube fiber-optic cables. This material validated the stabilization technology by providing excellent hydrolytic resistance, as well as enhanced product capability after processing and during the lifetime of the cable.

The unreinforced hydro-resistant PBT is unsuitable for use in injection molding applications due to its inherently high viscosity, which is required to maintain melt strength during the extrusion process. To address this need, a new lower viscosity, unfilled hydro-resistant polyester has now been developed for use in injection molding. It is interesting to note that the improved hydrolysis

resistance of the polymer is not dependent on the product's initial molecular weight.

Figure 3 illustrates the effects of the new stabilization technology on unreinforced polyesters. The graphs show the generation of acid end groups under accelerated test conditions of 120C and 100% RH. The measurement of CEGs provides a chemical understanding of the material's performance under hydrolytic aging. The decrease in the CEG level for the hydro-resistant PBT demonstrates the effectiveness of the new stabilization technology in controlling acid end-group generation. Results for the new material contrast with those for standard PBT, which exhibits an increase in CEG immediately upon aging – behavior that is true of any unmodified PBT irrespective of initial CEG content. Material performance will begin to deteriorate at CEG levels over 70 meq/kg.

As the data in Table I indicate, the physical properties of standard PBTs are maintained and even enhanced by use of the new stabilization technology. Values listed in the table were measured prior to heat/humidity testing or conditioning.

The hydro-resistant materials have been designed to perform with similar rheological behavior to standard polyesters, as illustrated by the following graphs in Figures 4. The new hydro-resistant product line has also recently been expanded to include a hydro-resistant 30%-fiberglass-filled polyester. Comparisons of physical properties, rheology, and spiral flow performance are shown in Table II and Figure 4, respectively. Development efforts are ongoing within the company. A number of reinforced, hydro-resistant polyesters with lower glass levels and mixtures of glass and mineral for enhanced dimensional capability are currently in the process of being commercialized. The new stabilization technology will next be applied to products that are blends or alloys of the basic PBT polyester with other polymers. Values listed in the table were measured prior to heat/humidity testing or conditioning.

MATERIALS IN USCAR TODAY

Environmental exposure and mechanical and chemical testing have been performed on both actual components and standard ASTM test specimens for a variety of the company's materials to define which grades meet the required performance for each of the USCAR classifications, as well as Ford's Post Radiator test. Both standard and hydro-resistant polyesters have been fully tested. The results indicate that standard polyesters meet USCAR Class I and II exposure requirements. In addition, standard glass-and/or mineral-reinforced polyesters are also able to withstand USCAR Class III conditions, but fail to meet Class IV requirements. Standard unfilled PBT grades are not able to maintain their physical properties following exposure to either USCAR Class

III or IV conditions. In fact, only the new hydro-resistant PBTs can withstand the conditions called forth in USCAR Class IV, satisfactorily maintaining their physical properties. Included below in Figures 5 and 6 are actual test results for a variety of polyesters as measured on standard ASTM specimens after Post Radiator, Class III, and Class IV exposures.

Testing on application specimens such as connectors has also been conducted following the Post-Radiator, Class III and Class IV exposure protocols. Results for 4-way submersible connectors molded of both a standard and a hydro-resistant, 30%-glass-reinforced PBT are shown in Figure 7. As these graphs show, the new stabilization technology resulted in definitive performance improvements in the areas of lock fatigue, housing and terminal retention, as well as pull strength. Further testing is ongoing.

CONCLUSIONS

The connector industry – especially that segment selling into automotive underhood applications – continues to be increasingly challenged. New performance requirements of automotive connectors under the USCAR standardization efforts are an excellent example of just one of these challenges. While design improvements on the connector and wiring assemblies are possible, they are generally not enough to overcome the inherent limitations of the base material – standard thermoplastic polyester – under the severe underhood environmental conditions. In order to most effectively meet the demands of the Big 3, alternative materials or improved thermoplastic polyesters are mandatory. The new stabilization technology developed by GE Plastics controls the hydrolysis reaction of thermoplastic polyester both during processing of individual components, as well as throughout the lifetime of the final product assembly. Performance is dramatically extended and the excellent balance of properties, processability, and cost that has historically favored the use of polyesters in these applications is maintained.

# # # # #

Table I: Property Comparison of Unfilled PBTs

Property	Hydro-Resistant PBT	Standard PBT
Melt Viscosity (poise)	4,000	4,000
Tensile Strength (MPa)	55.2	51.7
Tensile Elongation (%)	200	200
Flexural Modulus (MPa)	2413	2344
Flexural Strength (MPa)	82.7	82.7

Table II: Property Comparison of 30%-Fiberglass-Filled PBTs

Property	Hydro Resistant PBT	Standard PBT
Melt Viscosity (poise)	11,000	11,000
Tensile Strength (MPa)	117	119
Flexural Modulus (MPa)	6895	7585
Flexural Strength (MPa)	193	190
Heat Distortion @ 1.8 MPa (°C)	207	207

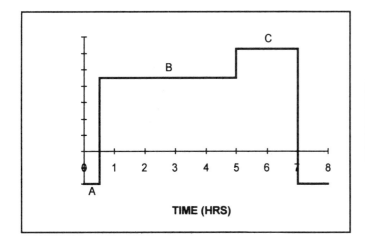

EXPOSURE	TEMPERATURE (C)		
	A	B	C
USCAR - Class III	-40	90	125
USCAR - Class IV	-40	90	155
Post Radiator	-40	90	125

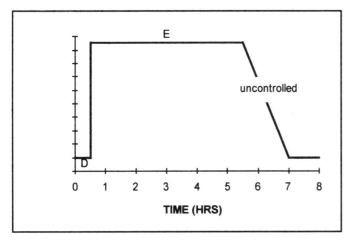

EXPOSURE	RELATIVE HUMIDITY (%	
	D	E
USCAR - Class III	10	95
USCAR - Class IV	10	95
Post Radiator	10	30

Figure 2: Time vs. Temperature (°C) and Humidity (%RH) Exposure Comparisons for USCAR Classes III & IV & Ford Post Radiator Tests

■ VALOX 325E Unreinforced PBT

□ VALOX HR326 Unreinforced, Hydro-Resistant PBT

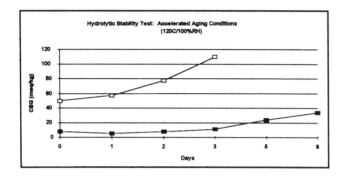

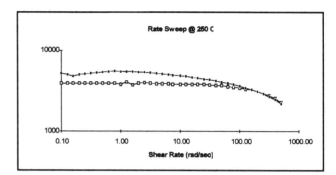

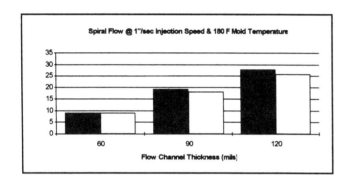

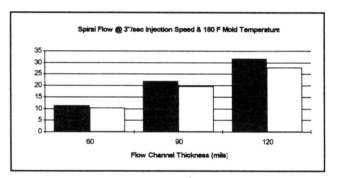

Figure 3: Stability & Flow Comparison for Unreinforced PBT

158

Stability & Flow Comparison: Fiberglass Reinforced PBT

■ **VALOX 420:**
   30% GR PBT

□ **VALOX HR426: 30%**
   GR PBT, Hydro-
   Resistant

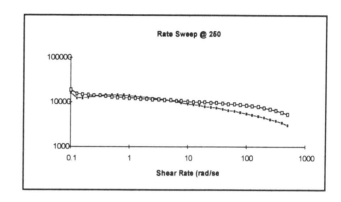

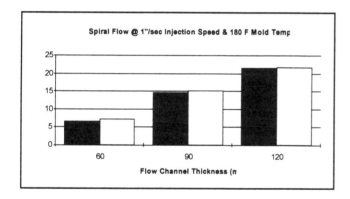

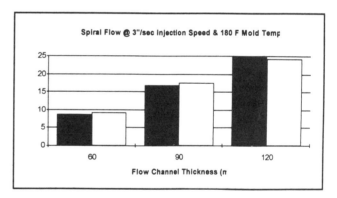

Figure 4: Stability & Flow Comparisons for Hydro-Resistant Fiberglass-Reinforced PBT and Standard Reinforced PBT

VALOX VAC3001: Unreinforced PBT

VALOX HR326: Unreinforced PBT, Hydro-Resistant

■ Post Radiator   ▯ USCAR - Class 3   ♦ USCAR - Class 4

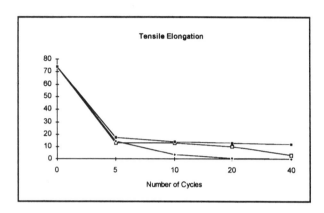

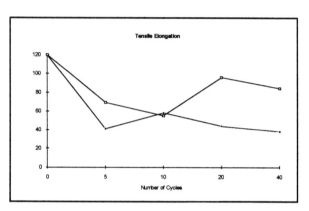

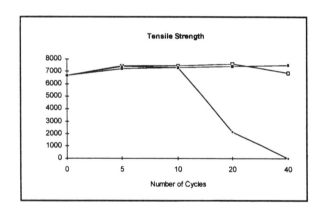

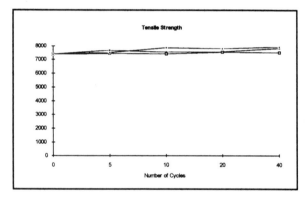

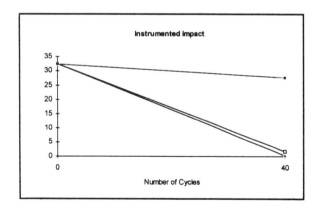

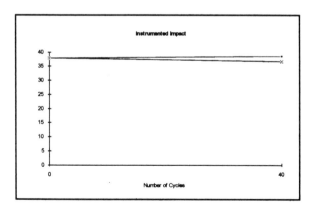

Figure 5: Results for a Variety of PBT Resins as Tested on Post Radiator, and USCAR Class III & IV Exposures

VALOX 430: 30 % GR PBT, Impact Modified

VALOX HR426: 30 % GR PBT, Hydro-Resistant

■ Post Radiator ☐ USCAR - Class 3 ◆ USCAR - Class 4

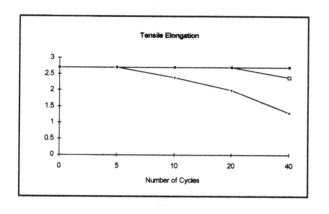
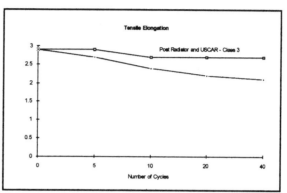
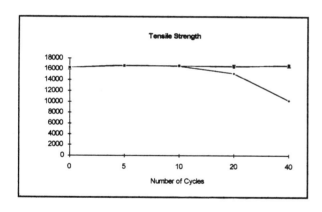
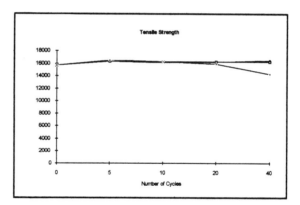
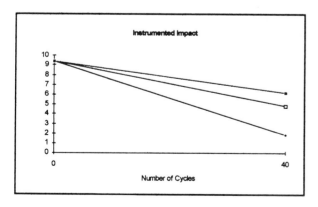
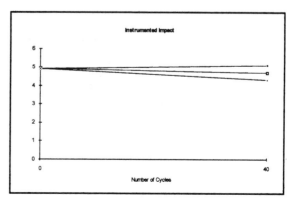

Figure 6: Results for a Variety of PBT Resins as Tested on Post Radiator, and USCAR Class III & IV Exposures

VALOX 420R
30% GR PBT w/
Mold Release

VALOX HR426 30%
GR PBT, Hydro-
Resistant

■ Control   ◻ Post Radiator   ▨ USCAR - Class 3   ■ USCAR - Class 4

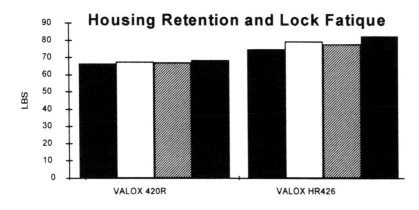

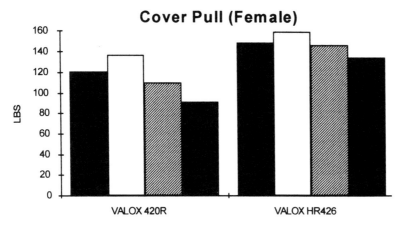

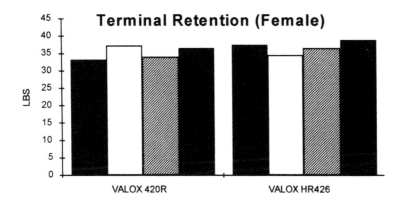

Figure 7: Results for 4-Way Submersible Connectors Molded of Standard & Hydro-Resistant, 30% GR PBT Resin

Recent Developments in Shredder Downstream Separation Processes and Recycling Options for Automotive Shredder Residue

V. Sendijarevic, B. Pokorski, D. Klempner, and K. C. Frisch
University of Detroit Mercy

ABSTRACT

Between 10- and 11-million scrap vehicles are being recycled each year in the United States by the automotive shredder industry. Presently, they are able to recover 95% of the ferrous and non-ferrous metals in an automobile, which translates to roughly 75% of the total car weight. However, up to 3-million tons of waste, commonly known as fluff or automotive shredder residue (ASR), are generated and landfilled by automotive shredders every year. In order to increase the efficiency of recovery of both ferrous and non-ferrous metals from the shredded vehicles, many new developments have been made in separation technology in the last few years. This paper describes recent developments in shredder downstream separation processes and recycling options for automotive shredder residue.

INTRODUCTION

Between 10- and 11-million scrap vehicles (cars, trucks and vans) are recycled each year in the United States [1]. Scrap vehicles are first transferred to dismantlers where used parts that are in serviceable condition are removed, as well as tires, fuel tanks, batteries, catalytic converters, lubricants and other fluids. The remaining hulks are generally crushed for easier transportation to one of 211 (in North America) heavy-duty shredders [2], where they are mechanically fragmented by hammer mills into 25-50 mm diameter pieces for more efficient separation of ferrous and non-ferrous metals. Up to 95% of the total automobile's ferrous and nonferrous metals are recycled [3], which amounts up to about 75% of the total vehicle weight [3-6]. This translates

into recovering of 10-11 million tons of ferrous metals [5,7-9] and 0.8 million tons of non-ferrous metals [3,9,10] each year. In addition to automobiles, shredders are also recycling several million discarded household appliances and other industrial, commercial and household scrap (durable goods) [11,12].

Unfortunately, up to 3-million tons of waste (automotive shredder residue or fluff) is generated every year by the shredding of automobiles in the United States [5,8,11-15]. Presently, (ASR), which contains urethane foams, fabrics, vinyl upholstery, padding, rubber, plastics, polymer composites, glass, sand, dirt, and even gravel and wood, is directly landfilled. In some states ASR can be used as a day cover at the landfills [3].

As a result of the decreasing total weight of average automobiles and increasing content of plastics and polymer composites, the weight ratio of metal to ASR has been decreasing steadily, resulting in smaller amounts of recovered metals and larger amounts of ASR per car. The overall amount of plastics and polymer composites in U.S. automobiles increased from 5.0% in 1978 to 7.7% in 1992. In the same time period, the total weight of the average passenger car decreased from 1,572 to 1,411 Kg [5,16]. In addition to this, the cost to landfill ASR is increasing as landfill space is decreasing [7]. The disposal of ASR contributes almost 50% to the operating costs of some shredders [8]. However, the disposal of ASR is more an environmental than an economic necessity. In Europe, for example, ASR may be prohibited from being landfilled in the near future (as it already is in Switzerland). The shipping of wastes, including ASR, from country to country is currently prohibited in Europe. In fact, the European governments are making the recycling of automobiles and household appliances the responsibility of the manufacturers. In some U.S. states, ASR has already been classified as a regulatory waste [17] and most probably other states will follow a similar environmental policy in the future.

Dismantling of automobiles has been an important consideration in addition to recycling and landfilling of ASR. The idea is to design and manufacture cars for closed-loop recycling - easy dismantling and recycling of the individual components into new vehicle components. Results of recent studies carried out for the Vehicle Recycling Partnership of the United States Council for Automotive Research have revealed two major problems with this approach. Dismantling is labor intensive and thus expensive, even with a proper design for disassembly. An even larger problem is the recycling of dismantled components. Almost every single component (system) is a complex composite, which must be shredded in order to carry out any recycling. In some cases shredded components such as headliners, car doors, and instrument panels look very similar to some types of ASR with almost the same degree of recycling difficulty. Recognizing these challenges, it has been proposed that a combination of dismantling of reusable parts and parts which can economically be recycled be used in combination with shredding of the remaining scrap as a future approach to the recycling of the car [1]. It thus seems that shredding may be a very important part of the recycling solution for cars for the foreseeable future and recycling of ASR the only alternative to landfilling.

A major problem in utilization of ASR is the presence of polychlorinated bisphenols (PCBs) and residual heavy metals, especially lead [18]. In addition to this, most ASR can potentially be utilized only as a construction material, which is a relatively low-value application (competing with very inexpensive materials) or as fuel, which is already relatively inexpensive in the United States. This means that for at least a portion of ASR, a value-added application should be developed in order to cover expenses for additional grinding and separation of ASR components, and removal of residual heavy metals. Most probably, an integral recycling solution for ASR will require recovering energy from at least one portion of ASR. Energy recovery as a part of the solution for utilization of ASR has been proposed in a recent update on the activities of the Vehicle Recycling Development Center [1]. The energy can be utilized for secondary grinding and separation processes as well as for chemical recycling. The chemical recycling process is a potentially value-added application for ASR.

DEVELOPMENT OF AUTOMOTIVE SHREDDING OPERATIONS

In the past, a junked car was usually brought to a junk yard where reusable parts were removed and sold. The auto hulk was then burned to aid in recovery of ferrous metals. This contributed as much as 5% to the air pollution in major cities. At this point the car was "hand shredded" with sledge hammers, chisels, wrenches and axes. This process was slow and extremely labor intensive [19].

At that time, only tin cans were being shredded for reuse. However, this technology was slowly adapted to shred automobile parts, and eventually the entire automobile. In 1963 Leonard Fritz, founder and current chairman of Huron Valley Steel, modified a Hammermill rock crusher to process metal [10]. As the need for cleaner steel grew, separation technologies were adapted from the mining industry to separate the ferrous metals from the shredded materials. The recovered steel was the main income for the automotive scrap shredding industry for many years. Any non-ferrous metals recovered contributed directly to the profits. However, the automobile manufacturers began to lower the amount of metal in their cars and the sale of non-ferrous metals became a very important source of income for shredders. This induced the shredding industry to invest heavily in new separation technologies in order to recover more non-ferrous metals. With the ferrous and non-ferrous metal streams generating money, there is only one stream left which needs to be addressed: the non-metal stream or automotive shredder residue. However, the key to understanding what to do with ASR is to understand the process by which it is generated.

A typical, early shredding process was primarily designed for recovery of ferrous metals (Figure 1). As can be seen, there are three main streams: the ferrous metal, the non-ferrous shredder residue and automotive shredder fluff. The non-ferrous shredder residue contains non-ferrous metals and heavy materials that could not be separated by cyclone or other separation techniques (for example, flotation). The automotive shredder fluff contains polyurethane foam and other light non-metallic materials. It may also contain some small aluminum particles due to their low density.

The ferrous metals are sold to the steel industry. The non-ferrous shredder residue, which contains roughly 50% non-metals [10], is sold to companies that specialize in non-ferrous metal recovery, and finally the automotive shredder residue is landfilled.

In order to increase the efficiency of recovering both ferrous and non-ferrous metals, many improvements have been made in separation technology in the last several years. A typical, generic shredding facility flow diagram is shown in Figure 2. After the initial shredding of an automobile, most of the ferrous metals are immediately removed and collected. Next, the non-ferrous shredder residue enters the downstream separation. The first piece of equipment encountered is usually a rising current separator for wet shredding, or a cyclone or Z-Box for dry shredding. The purpose of this equipment is to make a first separation or cut of non-ferrous metals from the non-ferrous shredder residue. Sometimes, this step is not part of the process.

The resulting non-ferrous metal shredder residue is then screened into three or four fractions, depending on the process. The smallest particles, or fines, which are smaller than approximately 10-15 mm, are usually recombined with the other reject streams without further separation. The streams with particles smaller than approximately 40 mm and streams with particles smaller than approximately 100 mm usually go through another magnetic separation to remove any ferrous metals left and then enter the eddy current separators. The eddy current separators usually separate the last of the non-ferrous metals from the non-ferrous metal shredder residue. Finally, the greater-than 100 mm stream, if applicable, usually contains large pieces of aluminum, rubber hoses, large plastic pieces, brass and other non-ferrous materials that are hand sorted. Sometimes, the recovered non-ferrous metals may be reprocessed on another shift to upgrade the nonferrous metals even further. The non-metals are usually recombined into the final form of ASR.

The screening processes utilize either a multiple-level vibratory separating screen, commercially known as a Bivi-tec screen, or a rotating trommel. The Bivi-tec screen generally produces three streams, while the rotating trommel produces four streams. The fourth stream is produced when the largest pieces that are unable to fall through the holes, fall out of the rotating tube.

As can be seen, some processes have as many as four reject streams that may be termed ASR. However, there are subtleties that distinguish each stream that the unfamiliar outsider must become aware of before analyzing samples. Flotation fluff, for example, exhibit different properties from cyclone fluff or wastes generated from the non-ferrous shredder residue after separation of the non-ferrous metals. Fines are different from all other automotive shredder wastes. These streams contain less than 20% of combustibles (organic fraction). Some ASR streams with larger particle sizes contain 60%or more combustibles. The overall concentration of combustibles increases with increase in particle size of the ASR stream [18].

Another variation on the downstream separation is decoupling of the shredding and separation processes. This means that after the separation of the ferrous metals (directly after shredding), the non-ferrous shredder residue is stockpiled and fed to the downstream separation system as a separate material. This allows the operators to shred the automobiles at the most efficient rate possible without concern as to whether the downstream separation processes can keep up.

Similarly, this allows the downstream separation processes to operate at their most efficient speed.

This theme of separating and recombining streams with certain properties such as size or density, to make the separation of non-ferrous metals more efficient, is occurring throughout the industry. In fact, this is the major factor that has contributed to the confusion surrounding the term ASR. Many researchers have claimed that ASR is a very heterogenous material, changing from facility to facility and even from day to day at a single facility. On the contrary, samples taken from one of the ASR streams are relatively consistent. Therefore, when analyzing an ASR sample, care must be taken when specifying which stream is to be sampled. It is also imperative to know what type of downstream process was used to obtain that stream. Different separation processes yield widely different streams [18].

The non-ferrous metal stream, which may contain as much as 50% non-metals, is usually shipped to an outside company for separation. One such company is Huron Valley Steel Corporation which recycles over 50% of the total non-ferrous metals from ASR generated in the United States. Huron Valley Steel Corporation uses a unique combination of heavy media separation, eddy current and imaging technology to separate non-ferrous metals. Metal distillation of zinc, to 99.995% purity, is also carried out as well as aluminum smelting [10].

RECYCLING OPTIONS FOR AUTOMOTIVE SHREDDER RESIDUE

A number of alternatives to disposal of ASR have been investigated. Several studies described incineration as the way to recover the heating value of the ASR [20-24]. The heating value of the ASR is over a broad range, with an average of 12,560 KJ/Kg [9,21]. A number of incineration units for combustion of ASR were built in the past, but none of these units is in operation today [8]. The problems are both economical and environmental. One problem is the fact that less than 50% of ASR is combustible [8,17,21], resulting in a huge amount of ash [21], which may be considered a hazardous regulatory waste because of the potentially large content of heavy metals (concentrated in the ash), requiring solidification and stabilization before disposal.

Pyrolysis, the thermal decomposition of organic materials in an oxygen-deficient environment, has also been considered as a potential method for recycling of ASR [3,15,17,25-31]. Pyrolysis may be a way to reclaim 100% of the organic content of ASR. However, the resulting oils and gases might require pretreatment (decontamination) prior to utilization as fuels. An additional problem is the huge amount of solid residue (up to 70%) [3,17], contaminated with heavy metals, and 4 to 12 wt.% pyrolytic water [17], which must be treated as a hazardous waste before disposal.

Recently, a multistage technology for separation and upgrading of three potentially marketable materials from ASR was reported [9,32]. In the first stage, ASR was separated into three streams: flexible polyurethane foams, fines, and "plastics-rich streams". However, the foam separated from the ASR contained about 30% dirt. The foam was cleaned utilizing organic solvents in order to meet the quality requirements for recycled foam scrap. In order to meet the requirements of the cement industry, the fines had to be separated into two fractions: magnetic and nonmagnetic [9]. Solvent extraction was also utilized in separating ABS from the "plastics-rich stream," but the ABS contained about 2% of methacrylate derivatives and polyvinylchloride (PVC) [9]. The costs of such multiple separation and upgrading processes required for foams, fines and ABS are probably prohibitive.

Separation of ASR plastic components was also carried out utilizing a heavy-medium separation technique. A series of brine cells was employed to separate plastics according to their specific gravities. Although 100% separation was not achieved, it was demonstrated that certain plastics could be concentrated in the various fractions [20,33]. Regardless of the separation expenses, the question is if such separated plastic streams, most probably containing a small amount of plastics different from the main stream, contaminated with hard particles (such as metal, gravel, sand and dirt) and other ASR components such as hydraulic oils, lubricants, and battery fluids, may be utilized in value-added applications.

In some studies, glycolysis and hydrolysis were utilized for recycling of the flexible foam recovered from the ASR [33-36]. Hydrolysis and glycolysis of polyurethane foams resulted in two main products, polyols and polyamines, which were successfully utilized in the preparation of flexible foam formulations for automotive applications [35,36]. The question is if a multiple separation process followed by hydroglycolysis of the foam can be economically competitive with hydroglycolysis of industrial foam scrap which does not require separation and cleaning. Recently, BASF Corporation's Polymer Division and Philip Environmental formed a joint venture to recycle polyurethane products. The technology is based on glycolysis [37]. Initially, post-industrial scrap such as polyurethane bumpers will be recycled, and in the future, post-consumer polyurethane scrap will also be recycled at the same facilities.

A feasibility study on converting ASR into composite materials utilizing thermoplastic processing was also carried out [3,38-43]. The presence of hard objects in the waste and its poor flowability were the major limitations of this recycling method. In addition, poor surface adhesion occurred, which may result in leaching of hazardous metals and other contaminants (oils, lubricants, PCBs, and other organics).

Recently, at the Polymer Institute and the Environmental Center of the University of Detroit Mercy, isocyanate-based binders were successfully utilized to recycle ASR by binding the ASR to yield various ASR composites [44-46]. Potential applications of these composites are dunnage for packaging and transportation, and sound and vibration damping materials for automotive and other industries. Composites were prepared with various types of isocyanate-based binders and ASR.

The feasibility of utilizing ASR in concrete [47] and asphalt for road applications [48] has also being studied with some promising results.

CONCLUSION

In order to increase the efficiency of recovering both ferrous and non-ferrous metals from shredded vehicles, much progress has been made in separation technology in the last few years. A typical automotive shredder generates four ASR streams with different particle sizes and compositions. However, various ASR streams are usually recombined into one stream and disposed of in landfills. For both technical and economical purposes, it would be important to consider recycling options for individual ASR streams rather than for the recombined waste.

Major problems in utilization of ASR are the presence of residual heavy metals and PCBs, as well as a relatively high concentration of inorganic, non-combustible materials (about 50%).

A number of recycling options for ASR has been investigated including energy recovery (combustion), recovery of organic components for fuel and feed stock applications (pyrolysis), chemical recycling such as glycolysis and hydrolysis, separation of individual plastics, recycling ASR into composite materials utilizing thermoplastic processing or isocyanate-based binders, and utilization of ASR in concrete and asphalt for road applications. So far, these approaches are not sufficiently cost-effective to compete with disposal.

In order to eliminate landfilling of ASR, an integral car recycling approach is needed that requires a close collaboration between the automotive shredding industry and automotive manufacturers. The shredding industry must provide expertise and technology for shredding, sizing and separation of ASR components for recycling according to their densities and particle sizes. The car manufacturers must design cars for easy dismantling of reusable components and components that can be easily recycled, and for recycling of automotive shredder residue.

ACKNOWLEDGMENTS

The authors would like to acknowledge the financial support of the Michigan Materials and Processing Institute, the Vehicle Recycling Partnership and the U.S. Environmental Protection

Agency (Assistance ID No. CR 820478-01-5). In addition, the authors would also like to thank the shredding industry for their input and assistance.

REFERENCES

1. Poston, E.I., "An Update on the Vehicle Recycling Development Center," *MMPI News & Views*, Vol 7, No. 2, 1996, p.1

2. "U.S. Shredder Installations Increase," *Recycling Today*, July 1995, p. 60.

3. Day, M., "Recycling Options for Automotive Shredder Residue," *Automotive Materials Recycling*, SAE/SP-1034, Paper 941022, February, 1994, p. 41.

4. Lang, N.A., "Auto Industry Targets Fluff for Recycling," *Waste Age*, January 1995, p. 77.

5. Jody, B.J., Daniels, E.J., Bonsignore, P.V., and Brockmeier, N.F., "Recovering Recyclable Materials from Shredder Residue," *JOM*, February 1994, p. 40.

6. Berry, B., "Automakers Want to Recycle All of the Car," *Iron Age*, February 1992, p. 28.

7. "Recycling and the Automobile," *Automotive Engineering*, October 1992, p. 41.

8. Jody, B.J., and Daniels, E.J., "Automobile Shredder Residue:Treatment Options," *Hazardous Waste & Hazardous Materials*, Vol. 3, No. 3, 1991, p. 219, Mary Ann Liebert, Inc., Publishers.

9. Jody, B.J., Daniels, E.J., and Pomykala Jr., J.A., "Progress in Recycling of Automobile Shredder Residue," Proceedings of Sessions and Symposia sponsored by Extraction and Processing Division, TMS Annual Meeting in Anaheim, California, February 4-9 1996, p. 585.

10. Kiser, K., "Sorting Savvy," *Scrap*, Vol 53 (4), 1996, 84.

11. U.S. Environmental Protection Agency, "PCB, Lead, and Cadmium Levels in Shredder Waste Materials: A Pilot Study," Final Report, Contract No. 68-02-4293 (Westat), 68-02-4252 (MRI), and 68-02-4294 (BCL), U.S. Environmental Protection Agency, Washington, DC, April 1991.

12. Bhakta, P.N.H., "Recent Technology and Trends in Automotive Recycling," *JOM*, February 1994, p. 36.

13. Bigness, J., "ENVIRONMENT: As Auto Companies Put More Plastics in Their Cars, Recyclers Can Recycle Less," *The Wall Street Journal*, July 10, 1995.

14. Braslaw, J., Labana, S.S. and Killgoar Jr., P.C., "Recycling Plastics from the Automobile of the Future," *Plastics and Rubber Processing and Applications*, 13, 1990, 229.

15. Braslaw, J., Melotic, D.J., Gealer, R.L. and Wingfield Jr., R.C., "Hydrocarbon Generation During the Inert Gas Pyrolysis of Automobile Shredder Waste," *Thermochimica*, 186, 1991, 1.

16. Motor Vehicle Manufacturers Association, *"MVMA Motor Vehicle Facts & Figures, 92,"* Detroit, MI, 1993.

17. Shen, Z., Day, M., Cooney, J.D., Lu, G., Briens, C.L., and Bergougnou, M.A., "Ultrapyrolysis of Automobile Shredder Residue," *The Canadian Journal of Chemical Engineering*, 73, 1995, 357.

18. Sendijarevic, V., Sendijarevic, A., Ullah, H., Ghazi, S., Pokorski, B., Klempner, D. and Frisch, K.C., "Recycle of Automotive Shredder Residue," Proceedings of the Third Annual Automotive & Transportation Interiors Conference, Detroit, May 7-9, 1996, pp. 70-80.

19. "The Newell Shredder," The American Society of Mechanical Engineers, September, 1994.

20. Dean K.C., Sterner J.W., Shirts M.B., and Froisland L.J., "Bureau of Mines Research on Recycling Scrapped Automobiles," Bulletin 684, U.S. Bureau of Mines, Washington, DC, 1985.

21. Hubble W.S., Most I.G., and Wolman M.R., "Investigation of the Energy Value of Automobile Shredder Residue," U.S. Department of Energy Report DOE/ID-12551, 1987.

22. Bilbrey Jr. J.H., Sterner J.H., and Valdez E.G., "Resource Recovery from Automobile Shredder Residue," *Conservation and Recycling Journal*, 1979.

23. Ellsworth R.D., Ballinger E.D., and Engdahl R.B.,"Preliminary Survey of Development of an Incineratorfor Removal of Combustibles from Scrapped Automobile Bodies," Final Report Prepared for Institute of Scrap Iron and Steel, Battelle Memorial Institute, August 1957.

24. Bilbrey J.H., Dean K.C., Sterner J.W., "Design and Operation of an Automobile and Railroad Car Incinerator," *Metal Soc.* American Institute of Mechanical Engineers Reprint A 74-88, 1974.

25. Roy C., de Caumia B., and Mallette P., "Vacuum Pyrolysis of Automobile Shredder Residue," paper presented at IGTConference: Energy from Biomass and Wastes XVI, Orlando, FL, Mar. 2-6, 1992.

26. Jones F.L., "Industrial Applications of AutomotiveShredder Fluff," in Advanced Composite Materials: NewDevelopments and Applications Conference Proceedings, Detroit, MI, Sept. 30 - Oct. 3, 1991, pp. 601-609

27. Poston I. E., "Recycling of Auto Shredder Residue,"Proceedings of the 11th Annual ESD Advanced CompositesConference & Exposition, Dearborn, Michigan, November 6-9, 1995, p. 629.

28. Van Stolk A.G., Lewis A.C., and Snavely C.A., "A NewGasification Process for Auto Fluff Depolymerization of Auto Shredder Residues into Hydrogen and Carbon Monoxide," Antec 91, 1991, p. 2142.

29. Arrington S.C., "Pyrolysis Conversion of Commingled Solid Waste Including Auto Shredder Residue," Presented at Auto Recycle 92, November 1992.

30. Pierce A., "Gasification of Heterogenous Polymers via Catalytic Extraction Processing: Auto ShredderResidue-Case Study," presented at Auto Recycle 92, November 1992.

31. Kaminsky W., "Possibilities and Limits of Pyrolysis,"Macromol. Chem., Macromol. Symp. 57, 145-160, 1992.

32. Bonsignore P.V., Jody B.J., and Daniels E., "Separation Techniques for Auto Shredder Residue," SAE Paper 910854, p. 59

33. Valdez E.G., Dean K.C., Bilbrey Jr. J.H., and Mahony L.R., "Recovering Polyurethane Foam and Other Plastics from Auto-Shredder Reject," U.S. Bureau ofMines, Report of Investigations 8091, 1975.

34. Gerlock J., Braslaw J., and Zinbo M., "Polyurethane Waste Recycling. 1. Glycolysis and Hydroglycolysis of Water-Blown Foams," *Ind. Eng. Chem. Process Des. Dev.*,23, No. 3, 1984, 545.

35. Braslaw J., and Gerlock J.L., "Polyurethane Waste Recycling. 2. Polyol Recovery and Purification," *Ind. Eng. Chem. Process Des. Dev.*, 23, No. 3, 1984, 552.

36. Mahoney L.R., Weiner S.A., and Farris F.C., "Hydrolysis of Polyurethane Foam Waste," *Environmental Science and Technology*, 8(2) 1974.

37. "BASF, Philip Team up to Recycle PU Parts," *Plastics News*, October 28, 1996.

38. Crawford W.J., and Manson J.A., "Use of AutomobileScrap as Filler in Polymeric Composites," ACS PolymerPreprints 24, 432-433, 1983.

39. DeAngelis G.J., Porter B., and Deanin R.D., "The Effect of Hydrogen Bonding Additives on the Clean Light Fluff Plastics Fraction from Automobile Shredders," Antec 85, April 29-May 2, 1985, pp.1316-1317.

40. Deanin R.D., and Nadkarni C.S., "Recycling of theMixed Plastics Fraction from Junked Autos. I. Low Pressure Molding," *Adv. Polym. Technol.* 4, 1984, 173.

41. Deanin R.D., and Yniguez A.R., "Recycling of Mixed Plastics Fraction from Junked Autos. II. High-Pressure Molding," *Adv. Polym. Technol.* 4, 1984, 277.

42. Deanin R.D., Busby D.M., DeAngelis G.J., Kharod A.M., Margosiak J.S., and Porter B.G., "Recycling of Mixed Plastics Fraction from Junked Autos. III. Melt Flow Improvers," Proceedings of the American ChemicalSociety Division of Polymeric Materials, Science andEngineering, 53, Washington DC, 1985, pp. 826-829.

43. Spaak A., "Use of Secondary Recycled Plastics," in Plastics Institute of America's Proceedings of Plastics Recycling as a Future Business Opportunity, Technomic Publ. Co., Lancaster, PA, 1986, pp. 26-51.

44. Frisch K.C., Sendijarevic A., Sendijarevic, V., and Klempner D., "Utilization of Polymeric Isocyanate-Based Binders in Recycling of Automotive Shredder Fluff," Proceedings of Cellular Polymers III, 3rd International Conference, RAPRA Technology LTD., Conventry, England, April 27-28, 1995.

45. Sendijarevic V., Sendijarevic A., Chen Z., Ullah H., Klempner D., and Frisch K.C., "Recycling of Automotive Shredder Residue Using isocyanate-Based Binders,"Proceedings of

the SPI Polyurethane 1995, September 26-29, 1995, p. 397.

46.   Sendijarevic V., Sendijarevic A., Ullah H.M., Frisch,K.C. and Klempner D., "Utilization of Automotive Shredder Residue in Composite Applications,"Proceedings of the 11th Annual ESD Advanced Composites Conference & Exposition, Dearborn, Michigan, November 6-9, 1995, p. 617.

47.   Soroushian P., Drzal L.T., Ravanbakhsh S., Bhurke A.S., and Shin E.E., "Reycling of Automobile Plastics in Concrete Construction: A Research and Demonstration Project," Report for The Michigan Materials andProcessing Institute (MMPI) and the American PlasticsCouncil, January 1996.

48.   Dutta U., Ibadat I., Bhowmik P., Han H., Kavanaugh and Klempner D., "Feasibility of Using ASR in Asphalt Pavement Mix," Report for the EPA (CR 820478-01-4),University of Detroit Mercy, Detroit, Michigan, September 1995.

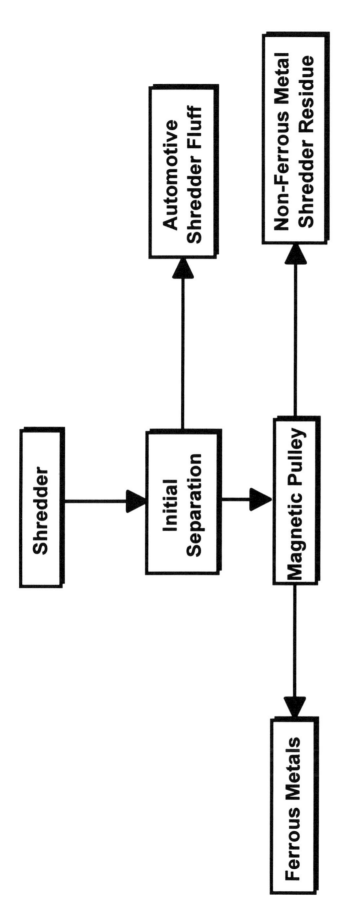

Figure 1: Early shredding facility layout.

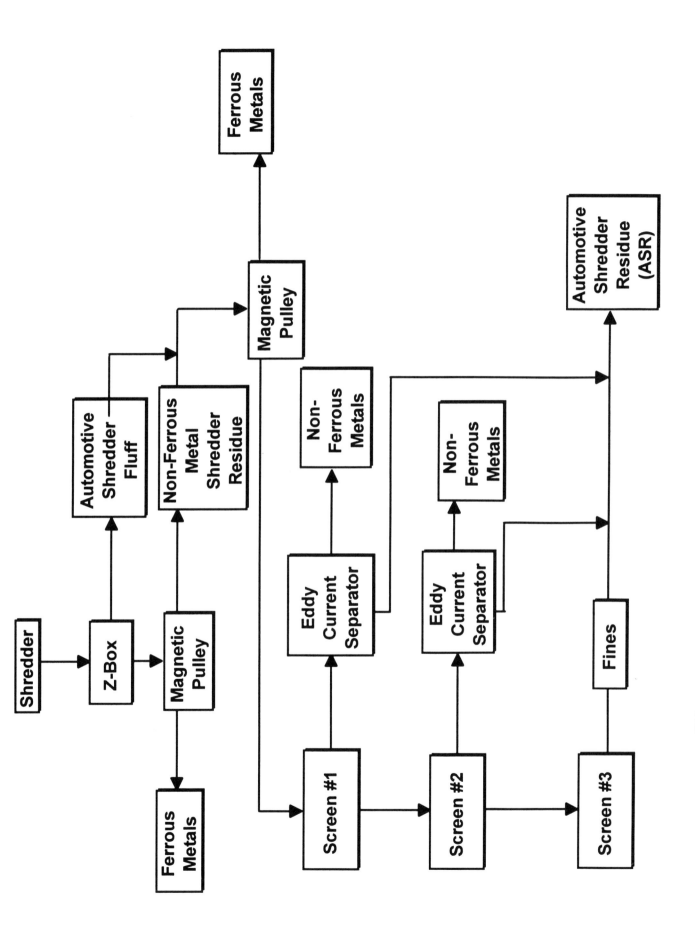

Figure 2: Upgraded shredding facility layout